INVITATION TO THE THEATRE

 INVITATION

GEORGE R. KERNODLE
University of Arkansas

TO THE THEATRE

Harcourt, Brace & World, Inc.
New York / Chicago / San Francisco / Atlanta

FRONT ENDPAPER: Première of the New York City Ballet production of
George Balanchine's *Don Quixote,* May 28, 1965. Balanchine himself danced
the title role in this performance. Photo Mel Finkelstein.

BACK ENDPAPER: Lobby of the Metropolitan Opera House on opening night,
September 16, 1966, photographed with a fisheye lens. Photo Wide World.

Library of Congress Catalog Card Number: 67-12523

PRINTED IN THE UNITED STATES OF AMERICA

ACKNOWLEDGMENTS *The author wishes to thank the following for permission to reprint material used in this book.*

ACTAC (Theatrical & Cinematic) Ltd. for material from THE LADY'S NOT FOR BURNING
   by Christopher Fry.
George Allen & Unwin Ltd. for material from RIDERS TO THE SEA by John M. Synge.
Brandt & Brandt for material from THE SECOND MAN by S. N. Behrman.

ACKNOWLEDGMENTS *continue on p. 655.*

CONTENTS

PREFACE   *vii*

PART ONE

KINDS OF PLAYS   3

v

vi

Contents

PREFACE

This introductory textbook invites the student to take a broad view of the theatre arts. It considers all major forms of theatre, whether spoken, sung, or danced; whether performed behind a proscenium or on an open stage, on Broadway or in a community or college art theatre, on stage or on the movie or television screen. It shows how playwrights both past and present have shaped their plays in different ways to express different aspects of their times and their own diverse attitudes toward life. Finally, it describes the ways in which the director, the actor, and the designer work together to create a production that is a unique work of art.

Part One presents the main classifications of drama: the theatre of reality (from naturalism to epic realism), the theatre of romance (including the musical, the opera, and the dance), the theatre of exaltation (tragedy), the theatre of comedy, and the theatre of disruption (from expressionism to the theatre of the absurd). Part Two, which follows the director, the actor, and the designer as they analyze the play and give it form, color, and movement, deals with the large creative processes rather than with such technical matters as the building of sets. Part Three, on the mass media, treats not only styles and techniques in the movies and in radio and television drama but also problems of public policy and standards of taste for the popular arts. Part Four is a single chapter on evaluating the play and writing a review.

Each dramatic form is presented in historical perspective in order to show how present forms have developed out of those of the past and how the various forms are related to styles of acting, setting, and building as well as to their times. Thus the student can see, for example, how intimate theatres and "method" acting grew naturally out of a realistic age; how musicals, ballets, and operas have changed from romantic spectacles to the sharper forms of recent years; and how film and broadcast dramas have been shaped by technical processes and the mass audience.

In the exercises that follow each chapter the student is invited to participate in the creative process—in some by analyzing a particular aspect of a play or production, in others by trying a bit of his own writing, directing, acting, or designing. Some of the exercises suggest individual or group demonstrations that the instructor may present for the class, and more than a dozen scenes from a variety of kinds of plays are included as examples and practice exercises. Extensive annotated lists of plays and critical works at the end of each chapter will aid the student in following up a particular interest or writing a special report or paper. At the end of the last chapter is a list of useful general books on the theatre.

ACKNOWLEDGMENTS   My colleagues and students in the Basic Course in the Arts at the University of Arkansas who have struggled with the various revisions of that course will find many of their comments and suggestions in this book.

A large number of people have helped find and prepare the pictures. I am proud to include so many examples from college productions, as they show the high achievement possible when students work seriously under trained instructors. I am especially grateful to Professor Ethelyn Pauley of Humboldt State College, to the late Bobbie Okerbloom, and to Martha Sutherland of the University of Arkansas, who have prepared many drawings under my direction, and to the following for one or more very useful drawings: Professors Donald Creason and Mary Davis of the University of Florida, Professor Paul Reinhardt of the University of Texas, Professor Robert C. Burroughs of the University of Arizona, and Mr. Claude Marks.

For reading the manuscript or some parts of it I am indebted to Professor Paul Kozelka of Columbia University, Professor Luther S. Mansfield of Williams College, Professors Harold Barrows and Beaumont Bruestle of the University of Tulsa, and Professor Eleanor King and Professor and Mrs. Blair Hart of the University of Arkansas. The design chapter has benefited by suggestions from Professor John Ashby Conway of the University of Washington, Professor Mordecai Gorelik of Southern Illinois University, Professor Orville K. Larson of the University of Bridgeport, Professor Preston Magruder of the University of Arkansas, Mr. James Hull Miller, Professor Paul Reinhardt of the University of Texas, and Professor Richard L. Scammon of Indiana University. The chapter on broadcast drama has been read and criticized by Professor A. William Bluem of Syracuse University, editor of *Television Quarterly,* Professor Hector Currie of the University of Cincinnati, and Professor Stuart Hyde of San Francisco State College. At every step I have had the assistance of Portia Kernodle, my wife, who has taken special responsibility for the chapters on the movies.

INVITATION TO THE THEATRE

 PART ONE

KINDS OF PLAYS

An invitation to the theatre is an invitation to see life lived at a
higher intensity, not frittered away but concentrated and filled with
meaning. Each kind of play presents a different attitude toward
life, shaped by the intent of the playwright and the production.
The realistic play invites us to take a serious, scientific attitude
as we watch man, this creature with animal drives, trying to make
something of himself and his environment. The musical, opera,
or ballet invites us to forget the drab world of every day and
follow the paths of romance, where sensuous beauty, fine feelings,
and lofty ideals are more important than dull facts. A great
tragedy or a religious or historical festival play exalts our spirits
with pride as a man dares to pursue his spiritual destiny in the
face of a challenging universe. Some plays present the
miscalculations and frantic schemes of human beings in such a
farcical way that we get a hearty laugh and see what fools we are
to take life too seriously. Another kind of comedy gives us more
thoughtful laughter as we see sophisticated characters making a
game of their disagreements, trying to impose logic and philosophy
on the changing patterns of human relations. Many recent plays

OPPOSITE   Brecht's *The Good Woman of Setzuan*. University of Texas
production, directed by Francis Hodge and designed by John Rothgeb.

ask us to look at the disruption of the modern world and at the same time to laugh and to shudder at the cruelty and terror lurking behind its meaningless chatter.

As each kind of play develops a different attitude toward life, it makes a different demand on the theatre, the designer, the actor, and the audience. The size and shape of the theatre building and the form of the setting help to determine the expectation of the audience. For realistic plays, we have built small, intimate theatres and developed a low-voiced, realistic style of acting. For operas, ballets, and musical comedies, we expect a large stage filled with painted scenery—a romantic picture world set at a distance behind a proscenium frame. For historical plays at national shrines, we borrow from the sacred Greek festivals the hillside amphitheatre and some of the patterns of exalted action, reinforced by music and dance. For elevated moods, we study the Greek and Elizabethan plays and reshape theatres, settings, and acting to catch something of their tragic grandeur.

Some plays can be described as comedy, tragedy, melodrama, or farce, to use the favorite classification of nineteenth-century critics and scholars, but most of the new kinds of plays developed in the last century and a half do not fit into any of these old categories. Instead of trying to define romanticism, realism, expressionism, existentialism, and the theatre of the absurd as historical movements (which they are) or treating them as modes of playwriting and production (which they are), it seems much simpler to consider the plays of realism, romance, and disruption in the way audiences consider them—as additional kinds of plays, parallel to the old categories of comedy and tragedy.

Although for the audience every good play is in a category by itself, expressing a particular attitude in its own manner, we do make comparisons among similar plays and we like to have some classifications, imperfect and tentative as any system of classification is bound to be. The first part of this book will distinguish six kinds of plays according to six different purposes for which a person might go to the theatre at different times—for a sense of reality, for color and romance, for exaltation, for a hearty laugh, for thoughtful laughter, or for an understanding of the disruption of the modern world. But a play often appeals to several interests, and a playwright in his lifetime may explore many different attitudes toward life. Each generation of playwrights creates its own kinds of plays as it redefines the attitudes inherited from the past. Out of many partial views and passing attitudes, each playgoer and reader must create his own broad vision of life.

CHAPTER ONE

THE THEATRE OF REALISM

Realism set out nearly a hundred years ago to create an "illusion of reality" on the stage. The theatre was to show nothing but the unadorned truth; all artifice, all formulas, styles, and interpretations were to be eliminated. Settings, properties, costumes, speech, and movement were to correspond so exactly to the world outside that the audience would forget it was in a theatre, supposing instead that it was looking into a real room with one wall removed, the "convention of the fourth wall." Thus the realists were determined to deal directly with life itself. A play was to represent a slice of life. In time, the terms "representational" and "representationalism" came to be applied to realism, and "presentational" and "presentationalism" to all techniques, historical or new, that require the actor to speak directly to the audience or in any way to remind the audience that it is in a theatre rather than watching a bit of actual life.

The early realists were sure that they had found the one valid approach to the theatre and that it would only be a matter of time and enlightenment before all other kinds of plays would be driven out: romantic plays would eventually seem foolish or dangerously deceptive, and both comedy and tragedy would be absorbed into realism. Instead, it has been the concept of realism that has undergone a process of evolution. On the one hand, it was soon found that actual life could never be put on the stage, that the most dedicated realist had to select his material and interpret it, if unconsciously, from some point of view. And, on the other hand, it became clear that the central intent of realism—to show man in relation to his environment—could effectively be accomplished in a number of ways, not all of them new to the theatre. During the century of its existence, the realistic tradition has been modified and redefined, and in recent decades it has absorbed many of the techniques that were once considered presentational.

This chapter will describe six closely related ways of creating the "illusion of reality" in the theatre—realism as established by the beginning of the twentieth century, two early modifications of realism called "selected realism" and "stylized realism" that appeared in the 1920s, and three ways of dealing with reality that have had a growing importance in the last three decades: abstract realism, the Oriental realism of make-believe, and epic realism.

Realism and Naturalism

The terms *realism* and *naturalism* are often used interchangeably. When a distinction is made, *realism* is the more general term, including the early, rather cheerful developments in the middle of the nineteenth century and all the variants of realism in the twentieth century, while *naturalism* is applied to a particular development in the wide movement of realism. Beginning in the 1880s and continuing into the early twentieth century as an active force, naturalism was based on an explicit philosophy of determinism—the belief that man has no freedom of will or choice but is "determined" by heredity and environment—and an interest in exposing the more brutal aspects of man's animal nature. When scene designers make a distinction in the two terms, they consider that a realistic setting has real details, at least in the foreground, and a casual effect without too obvious a sense of design, while a naturalistic setting has so many details and so little order that the setting obviously dominates the characters. When a distinction is made, many

FIGURE *1.1* Realism in setting, directing, and acting. The actors, seen in a box set, are absorbed in the detail of the environment, making a clear, balanced picture, but one without obvious design. Odets' *Awake and Sing*. New York, 1935. Photo Vandamm.

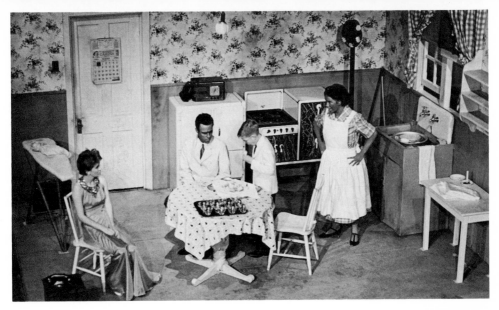

FIGURE *1.2* Naturalism. Real details are put on the stage with no apparent design or arrangement. McCullers' *The Member of the Wedding*. Baylor University production.

plays could be described as either realistic or naturalistic. In this book the term "naturalism" will be used only when the uncompromising aspects are emphasized—that is, when the deterministic philosophy is very apparent and when basic animal drives, like sex, hunger, and greed, are important in the play.

Realism began in the nineteenth century as a turning away from the far-away and long ago of the romantics to a concern with the here and now, from imaginary fantasies of adventure to a journalistic study of how people live, from idealistic speculation to pragmatic concern with actual problems, from the glamour of princes and heroes to the struggles of ordinary people. The delight of the realistic writer in ordinary life and people has been well expressed by W. Somerset Maugham, the twentieth-century English novelist and playwright, in his autobiographical book, *The Summing Up:* "The ordinary is the writer's richer field. Its unexpectedness, its singularity, its infinite variety afford unending material. The great man is too often all of a piece: it is the little man that is a bundle of contradictory elements. He is inexhaustible: you never come to the end of the surprises he has in store for you."

Before the middle of the nineteenth century, many novels dealt in a realistic way with ordinary people and their surroundings, but the theatre lagged far behind. A few plays in the 1850s and 60s made tentative explorations in a cheerful, shallow realism, but the main theatre fare continued to be artificial comedies, romantic spectacles, and melodramas. In 1873 Émile Zola, who became a leader in the naturalistic movement, wrote a preface to his play *Thérèse Raquin* in which he heaped scorn on the current theatre, on its "pomposity, unreality, platitudes." In heroic dramas he found nothing but "medieval scrap-iron, secret doors, poisoned wine," and he was even more contemptuous of melodrama, "that middle-class offspring of the romantic

7

movement . . . even more passé and lifeless," with its "false sentimentality . . . kidnapped children, recovered documents, immodest boastings." Zola believed that the decaying theatre would be replaced by a new realistic theatre based on the scientific study of the actual world. "I have the profound conviction," he wrote, "that the experimental and scientific spirit of the century is going to reach the theatre, and in this lies the only possible regeneration for our stage."

The scientific spirit of the century, which affected all realists whether or not they espoused a naturalistic philosophy, indeed transformed the theatre. It taught writers to be objective observers, carefully studying real people living in real places. Where the romantics had liked local color as a picturesque decoration, the scientific realists studied the impact of the environment on character. Where the romantics conceived of characters as embodiments of large, clear passions, the realists watched for the influence of the environment on the basic drives. As Zola wrote, "There are no more wrathful men, avaricious men, deceitful, gluttonous, slothful, envious or proud men, there are only men whose inner forces, whose untamed energies, whose desire for activity, for battle, and for triumph have been misdirected."

From the beginning of the nineteenth century, increasing interest was shown in biology, the study of how creatures live and grow and especially how they react to their environment. The climax of biological study came in 1859 with the publication of Charles Darwin's *Origin of Species,* which offered the theory that animals evolve from lower forms and that man is no different from other animals in this respect. The principles of "natural selection" and "survival of the fittest" accounted for the survival of animals that made the best adaptation to the environment. The new science of sociology, which emphasized the power of the social environment, was also developed toward the middle of the century.

Scientific developments, while casting doubt on divine purpose and freedom of the will, seemed to sanction the acquisition of wealth by the new industrialists and to promise great material progress through technology. This growing materialism alarmed idealistic philosophers. Emerson cried out, "Things are in the saddle and ride mankind," and Thoreau declared, "Our life is frittered away by details. . . . Simplify, simplify." But Walt Whitman had a deep respect for the facts discovered by science, for common lives and real things which the poet and artist must endow with "glows and glories and final illustriousness."

Ultimately, science and materialism affected all concepts of the nature and destiny of man, but their immediate, quite visible effect in the theatre was the absorbing interest in properties and little pantomime business on the stage. Things became as important as actors. André Antoine, who revolutionized directing in his Paris productions before the turn of the century, loved to have an abundance of objects as small props on his stage. "Nothing," he said, "makes an interior look more lived in. These are the imponderables which give a sense of intimacy and lend authentic character to the environment the director seeks to recreate. Among so many objects . . . the per-

Kinds of Plays

FIGURE *1.3* Realism in painting. The variety of detail recreates an environment. The diagonal composition, leading the eye into depth, gives the viewer a sense of being in the midst of the action. *Cotton Market in New Orleans,* a painting by Degas. Musée de Pau, France.

formers' acting becomes, without their realizing it and almost in spite of themselves, more human, more intense, and more alive in attitudes and gestures." Anton Chekhov, who is to many people the greatest Russian writer, created his characters out of their little daily actions. One of the directors who worked with him wrote, "He represented human beings only as he had observed them in life, and he could not dissociate them from their surroundings: from the rosy morning or the blue twilight, from sounds, odours, rain, trembling shutters, the lamp, the stove, the samovar, the piano, the harmonica, tobacco, the sisters, the in-laws, neighbors, song, drink, from everyday existence, from the million trifles that give warmth to life." That last phrase—"the million trifles that give warmth to life"—might be the motto of the whole movement.

In the 1880s the deeper wave of realism, called "naturalism," went much further than the exploration of daily life by probing into the violent forces that lie under the surface. The watchword of this new phase was "science." Science demanded that Victorian ladies forget their delicacy and cut open frogs in the laboratory to find out the biological facts of life, that they forget their modesty and expose their "limbs" to sunshine on the beach. The more the delicate ladies were scandalized, the more the naturalistic realists were determined to make them face the basic facts of hunger, greed, sex—drives too danger-

9

ous to ignore. A Viennese physician named Sigmund Freud insisted that if the basic drives are not given normal outlet they may emerge indirectly in distorted and destructive ways, and that the only chance for health is to make the conscious mind aware of those hatreds and drives regularly suppressed because they are not pretty or respectable.

The cities of the time were a mass of slums which a hundred years of industrial exploitation had filled with poverty, depravity, and misery. But science promised that careful observation of actual conditions would enable man to change his world. Idealistic young people volunteered to work in settlement houses and to fight for labor unions, better working conditions, better housing. Artists determined to make the world see, to break through the cheerful surface realism, with its conventional pictures of the humble poor, and to show the hatred, drunkenness, and debauchery of the victims of poverty, who survived through forlorn delusions and dreams of escape. Zola compared the novelist to a doctor demonstrating a scientific experiment as he wrote his "experimental" novels to show how people actually lived—as butchers, drunkards, or prostitutes. Maxim Gorki wrote one of the most powerful naturalistic plays, *The Lower Depths* (1902), to show the suffering and the dreams, as well as the depravity, of the human dregs in one cellar room.

Conventional people were outraged, and a quarrel began that has gone on for more than eighty years. One side accuses the other of reveling in sensational, ugly subjects. The same derogatory terms that were thrown at Henrik Ibsen and Zola in the 1880s have been used again for Tennessee Williams and Edward Albee. The defenders, still ardent crusaders, insist that disease can touch anyone and that the careful study of disease is indispensable for preventing and curing it. They maintain that nowhere does Zola or Gorki or Williams or any other major naturalistic writer show suffering without throwing some light of understanding on it. They believe that the writer must be as objective and as ruthless as a doctor cutting a cancer out of the body to restore the patient to health.

One of the greatest objections to nineteenth-century melodramas and farces was that they never really faced a problem. After several acts of suspense, the missing papers were recovered, the accused hero was proved innocent, the long-lost child was found, the uncle returned with a fortune, or lightning struck the wicked. The problem faded away completely. No one had to face a major loss or adjust to people who were mixtures of good and bad. Naturalistic plays shocked late Victorian and early twentieth-century audiences by actually facing problems. When the Victorian idealist said, "Keep your eyes on the stars," the scientific naturalist said, "Do that and you'll fall in a ditch!"

In Ibsen's *A Doll's House* (1879), the husband, Torvald, is just such a cheerful idealist, sure that nothing ugly will ever disturb his home. When he discovers that his charming little wife, Nora, has innocently forged her father's name and that he might be disgraced by the exposure, he turns on her in anger, but when he finds that someone is willing to cover up for her, he

Kinds of Plays

forgives her. It is she who cannot forgive him for his selfishness and hypocrisy. Only a child could pretend that nothing has happened in their relationship. She realizes that he has never treated her as an adult, and she walks out of the house to try to find herself, with a slam of the door that was heard all over the world.

With *A Doll's House* Ibsen became the European champion of truth versus conventional hypocrisy. In this battle he perfected the "well-made play" with which the French dramatist Eugène Scribe had had such success a half-century before—a very compact play of few characters with careful exposition, logical progression, great suspense, and strong conflict, all leading up to surprising climaxes and effective curtains. Alexandre Dumas *fils* and several others had used the well-made play for such social problems as the fallen woman, divorce, and financial and family crises, without really questioning the basic attitudes of nineteenth-century society. Ibsen used the compactness and power of the form to show a series of men and women who rebelled against the popular assumptions of the time.

Ibsen's next play, *Ghosts* (1881), made an even more shocking attack on convention, disclosing that a respectable man had brought venereal disease into his family and thus treating openly a subject that had been absolutely taboo on the stage. The leading character, Mrs. Alving, should have left her deceitful husband, but her conventional pastor persuaded her to stay and do her "duty." After the husband is dead she thinks she will be free from the influences of the past, but her son has inherited his father's syphilis, and his mind breaks. She has to choose between giving him poison, as he has begged her to do, and caring for him as an idiot. Naturalistic characters face painful dilemmas, not the picturesque problems of romantic heroes.

Ibsen showed in later plays the difficulties created by exposing the truth. In *An Enemy of the People* (1882), society appears as an enemy of truth: the townspeople, hoping to make money from their new municipal baths, almost destroy the doctor who discovers that the water is dangerously impure. *The Wild Duck* (1884), on the other hand, shows that not all people have the strength to face the truth: a misguided young truth seeker destroys a family by forcing them to face the false illusions by which they had been living for many years.

Such plays found, and still find, an audience of people who do not like to be duped. If life can be ugly, it is better to know it. If people are complex, drama should show their weaknesses, cruelties, and even crimes as well as the front they present in public. The theatre is better than a keyhole for revealing private lives, even of heroes. Victorian sentimentality had built up such an idealized picture of mankind that it was a great satisfaction to find that in reality people are not always what they seem. After the Little Evas, sweet grandmothers, and other conventional characters in novels and plays, it was a shock, but a satisfying shock, to see in Zona Gale's play *Miss Lulu Bett* (1920) a horrid brat of a child and a grandmother full of hate. Stephen Crane's *The Red Badge of Courage* was the first popular novel to show a soldier frankly afraid in battle. Bernard Shaw in *Arms and the Man* (1894)

FIGURE *1.4* Realism. Variety and subtle detail give convincing reality to a group of girls in a boarding school. Hellman's *The Children's Hour*. New York, 1934. Photo Vandamm.

depicted a heroine who rejects the conventional hero and chooses the practical man, who is more concerned with food than battles. Shaw's *Man and Superman* (1903) shows a modest heroine relentlessly pursuing her reluctant man. Lillian Hellman has written some of the strongest exposés of the damage that quite plausible people can do. In *The Children's Hour* (1934), a neurotic, spoiled schoolgirl and a gentle, well-meaning grandmother destroy the lives of two schoolteachers. Her most famous play, *The Little Foxes* (1939), shows an apparently loving, close-knit southern family ready to tear each other apart in their greed and ambition. In another of Miss Hellman's southern plays, *Toys in the Attic* (1960), a loving sister realizes suddenly that her feeling for her brother is incestuous and that she loves him only when he is a failure and needs her.

Thus a burning zeal informed much naturalistic literature, a zeal to tear off the mask of respectability and show man in his real nature, a determination to face facts, to explore, to learn, to teach, to expose corruption and hypocrisy. If something stank, it had to be brought into the open. Chekhov said, "To make a man better, you must first show him what he is." To make society better, Shaw showed respectable people some of the unpleasant facts of economic life; for instance, he showed churchgoing landlords that the slum properties from which they collected their rents bred disease and crime and that people would do better to build a decent world for the workers than to depend on such charities as the Salvation Army to keep the workers from rebelling. The radicals looked for a revolution, a war between labor and capital. The liberals put their hopes in new laws, labor unions, schools, settlement houses, and slum clearance. Both liberals and radicals welcomed the new realistic art, whether in the simpler form of realism or the

12

Kinds of Plays

grimmer form of naturalism. They believed that only by seeing actual conditions and particular cases—in paintings, in novels, in plays—would the general public ever realize what the conditions were or even recognize that slum dwellers had human feelings. Since that first enthusiasm, the transformation of man's environment has been so vast in all the industrialized nations of the world that it is no wonder that emerging nations, from Russia to Africa, look to "social realism" as the most important form of art. Realistic art has helped create that transformation.

In America, where the impact of industrial and urban development on literature came later than in Europe, there was some interest in realism from the 1880s on, but the greatest interest came after the First World War, in 1918, and especially with the decade of the depression, 1929 to 1939. *The Grapes of Wrath,* the most impressive novel of the depression years, portrayed the growing anger of the Joads, a family who left their drought-and-mortgage-ridden farm in Oklahoma to make an epic trek across the desert and join the more industrialized slums of California. John Steinbeck, when he wrote it, was vaguely expecting some great revolutionary holocaust: bad environments must be changed. Even more shocking were the plays *Tobacco Road* (dramatized in 1933 from Erskine Caldwell's novel) and Sidney Kingsley's *Dead End*

FIGURE *1.5* Realism or naturalism showing the influence of environment on character. The grouping is complex and varied, clear but not obviously designed. Kingsley's *Dead End.* New York, 1935. Directed and designed by Norman Bel Geddes. Hoblitzelle Theatre Arts Library, The University of Texas.

(1935), which reinforced the hopes of the New Deal of the Franklin D. Roosevelt era. Both exploded the myth that the poor can help themselves. *Tobacco Road* made even its grossly comic hillbillies seem human and touching. The old Georgia farmer, Jeeter Lester, trying to keep going after he had exhausted the economic and moral resources of his environment, demonstrated the collapse of laissez-faire economics and the need for outside help. *Dead End,* though equally violent and shocking, was more hopeful. Bringing together on the stage a slum alley and the courtyard of a luxury apartment house, and the people who lived in them, it studied the effects of these entirely different environments on each other. The play shows in detail how alley boys learn to be gangsters. An alumnus of the slums, now a famous killer returning home for the last time, teaches the boys how to follow in his footsteps and thereby spurs a young architecture student to work toward improving the housing of his slum neighbors instead of dreaming of escape with the rich. Ironically, it is the killer who is full of conventional sentiments. He expects a tearful scene of forgiveness with his mother and hopes to recapture the fresh innocence of his first love affair and take the girl with him in his flight from justice. The young actor who wants to sample the irony, the half-suppressed surging emotions, the bitter resentments of the naturalism of the 1930s could do no better than to act out Baby-face Martin's scenes with his mother and with his former sweetheart, Francey (see Exercises 1 and 2, pp. 55–58). The mother is no sentimental stereotype, and the girl has become a prostitute. The dialogue is harsh but poignant, and violent emotions smolder under the surface.

IMPRESSIONISM—THE AESTHETICS OF REALISM

The ending of *Dead End* is unusually hopeful. With the New Deal slum clearance and rehousing program under way, audiences could believe that the young architect in the play might be capable of decisive action, of turning the gangster over to the police and taking the reward money to rescue one particular boy, and of dedicating himself to building new housing to replace the crowded, corrupting alleys. For a moment the play bursts into melodramatic action: the villain is killed and the hero chooses the right path. But for all the other characters there is no such gesture of decision. The mother, sick at heart, curses her murderer son in a tense monotone, scarcely raising her voice. She sees clearly that his life is evil, that he will be destroyed, and that her younger children will also become prostitutes and criminals. She is caught, helpless, one strand in a complex web of people and alleys and poverty. Most of the characters in the play drift, not even seeing moral values clearly but suffering, struggling, and dreaming of impossible escapes. Except for the one decisive action, there is little plot, but there are many vivid bits of characterization. The main progression of the play is not the story of the architect that emerges from the background at some moments, nor the story of the life and death of a gangster, but a succession of moods, like a piece of impressionist music, blending together many little conflicts and discords. And a similar structural pattern can be found in many

Kinds of Plays

FIGURE *1.6* Impressionism. The special mood of local color and time of day is created by the suggestive power of a few details. The environment controls the characters. Andrade's *Time of the Harvest*. Western Reserve University production, directed by Nadine Miles and designed by Henry Kurth.

other plays. Most realistic and naturalistic plays, in fact, are organized, directed, and acted by techniques that correspond very closely to the techniques of impressionism in painting and music. While we have not been in the habit of applying the term impressionism to realism, we can understand realism far better if we notice that painting, music, and drama responded in much the same way to the same historical developments of the late nineteenth century and that all three make use of much the same patterns and create the same moods. The aesthetics of impressionism in painting and music and of realism and naturalism in the theatre are much the same. Hence we may speak of the many plays of realism and naturalism in which strong conflicts are kept muted as impressionist plays. Even those plays in which violence breaks out at some point may employ impressionist techniques.

Impressionism was developed in the latter half of the nineteenth century in reaction to the strident intensities of romanticism. In Europe and America people had grown weary of the large gestures of assertion, of the crashing thunder of Brahms and Wagner, of the noble canvases depicting Washington crossing the Delaware or Custer's Last Stand, of scenic spectacle and exaggerated "ham" style of acting in the melodramas, of heroic dramas about Indian chieftains, ancient Roman rebels, medieval knights, or leaders of robber bands. Painters became interested in the passing moods of the local landscape, the atmosphere of various times of day, and the special qualities of jugs, tables, and fabrics. Claude Monet wanted to catch in his paintings the impression of a cathedral half lost in the haze of early morning or a bridge in a foggy London twilight. Weather, time of day, and local color were extremely important to the impressionists. The French composer Claude Debussy was fascinated by sea, clouds, mist, and rain, by the thought of a cathedral with its chimes deep under the sea, by the local color of a Spanish

15

FIGURE *1.7* Impressionism. The tragedy of two characters who are defeated by their environment is relieved by picturesque beauty and the hypnotic moods of changing time of day. Davis' *Ethan Frome,* from the novel of Edith Wharton. Western Reserve University production, directed by Nadine Miles and designed by Henry Kurth.

town at festival time. In the 1890s he was working out a music of new harmonies, weaving many little themes into rich textures of mood and avoiding most of the conventional harmonies and expected progressions. In both his melodic scales and orchestral effects he took hints from Oriental music, after hearing a gamelan orchestra from Indo-China at the Paris Exposition of 1889. He muted his trumpets and violins, divided his strings into many voices, used cymbals and drums lightly, and through and over that complex web he made sparkle the dewdrops of harp, celesta, and triangle, with contrasting thuds of sacks of beans and Oriental blocks. No strong, clear-cut melody stood out, but the many voices of many instruments wove a thick texture of many slight discords.

Realistic playwrights and actors from the 1860s and 70s had begun to present contemporary characters in ordinary houses, busy at ordinary tasks, surrounded by real things, and to make surface detail suggest subtleties of character and feeling. By the 1890s, in Moscow, Constantin Stanislavsky was working out a new kind of acting that drew on the genuine reactions of real people and, avoiding conventional gestures and large oratorical effects, portrayed the complex interplay of quiet characters through subtle indications of changing emotions beneath the surface. In both form and philosophy most realism in the theatre corresponds to impressionism in the other arts.

Now, more than a half-century after impressionism reached its first flowering, the basic attitude toward life that produced it is clearer. The techniques of impressionism—in painting, the tiny dots of color, the bold brush strokes, the blurred lines that blend gardens, bridges, trees, and people into soft-focus images; in music, the overlapping sequences, the massed chords, the exotic harmonies that blend the fragments of melodies into muted discords; in the theatre, the details of setting and properties, the overlapping bits of

16

Kinds of Plays

dialogue and background sounds, the tentative gestures and movements that blend the characters and the locality into rich moods—express the belief, conscious in the plays and implicit in the painting and music, that man has no freedom from the environment of which he is a product and helpless victim, a belief basic, as we have seen, to realism and especially to naturalism. Foreground disappears into background, melody into accompaniment, and individual decisions into unconscious natural and social forces. Man may struggle to escape his environment, he may be in conflict with it in many ways, but he is himself one of the threads in the complex web. In impressionist plays, as in impressionist music, there is never a decisive beginning or end, never a clear-cut climax or turn, because man is not expected to make a major decision. The chromatic and whole-tone scales of Debussy, unlike the regular major and minor scales, have no home or resting place but allow a melody to drift on and on, never arriving. In some of Renoir's paintings of the eighties and nineties, the faces, clothing, hair, cats, plants, and background are all blended together with the same soft brush strokes; man does not take on a distinct character of his own to make him stand out from the background. In the muted naturalistic plays, violence may smolder beneath the surface and even erupt offstage, but the main characters are bewildered victims who do not understand their own feelings.

For characters without free will there is no moral praise or blame. Eugene O'Neill had Anna in *Anna Christie* (1921) give up trying to measure blame since no one is responsible for his actions. She says, "It aint your fault, and it aint mine, and it aint his neither. We're all poor nuts, and things happen, and we get mixed in wrong, that's all." Characters are defined and motivated not by moral principles or clear ethical choices, but by the rhythm, color, feel, taste, and smell of their environment, by the gradual impact of the thousand slightly discordant trifles that make up their lives. To present such passive people, the playwright does not use strong decision or clear-cut change. But the complex texture that he weaves into the rich background, using suggestions of mood, hints of half-formed desires and impulses, and fragments of abortive action, can be more expressive than the strong plots of typical nineteenth-century plays.

Chekhov's plays show how impressionistic patterns were worked out in the theatre. They are all mood studies of groups of people caught in situations they can do nothing about. Uncle Vanya, in the 1899 play of that name, gets so angry about his frustrations that he shoots at his brother-in-law, but he misses, and only feels a fool for trying to change what he knows will not be changed. In *The Three Sisters* (1901), the sisters fret through four acts at the dullness and oppression of the provincial town they live in and plan constantly to escape to Moscow, but they never do. They are caught by family ties and by habits they cannot change. A thousand and one conflicts arise and stir people deeply, showing slightly on the surface and sometimes catching the attention of other characters, sometimes going unnoticed in the continuous flow of little actions. At times all the characters on stage are caught by

17

the same mood of joy or sadness, but often several characters carry on their own separate sequences. While the Moscow Art Theatre made its greatest impression with the deep melancholy moods of its Chekhov productions, the author insisted that his plays were comedies, and some actors have achieved excellent performances by playing up the many points of comedy that make a character ridiculous, without losing one bit of Chekhov's deep sympathy for suffering. That combination of comic and tragic is usually the greatest appeal of impressionist plays. Once the idea is accepted that life goes on no matter how many hearts are broken, there can be all the deeper sympathy for failure and suffering, even with laughter at the absurd context of the suffering.

Perhaps the favorite Chekhov of most people is *The Cherry Orchard* (1904), a very touching, sad, yet funny study of a group of people trying to hold on to the moods and meanings of an old aristocratic estate. Madame Ranevsky, the owner, returns to the estate after spending all her money on a worthless man in Paris. If only she will subdivide the estate and lease the lots for summer villas, she can have a good income. Her business adviser, the son of one of her father's serfs, is ready to help. But she and her brother cannot make up their minds. The actual plot is very simple. In Act I, at her arrival at daybreak, she cannot make up her mind to do anything. In Act II, in a twilight walk, listening to distant music, she still cannot do anything. In Act III, at a big party, she is waiting for news that the estate has been sold. In Act IV, she departs for Paris again. Around her are her brother, daughter, and foster daughter, the governess, old friends of the family, the business

FIGURE *1.8* Realism or impressionism. A mood of reminiscence and indecision is suggested in this twilight setting. Chekhov's *The Cherry Orchard*. Carnegie Tech Theatre production, directed by Lawrence Carra. Photo Daniel P. Franks.

friend who buys the estate, the former tutor of her drowned boy, the upstart valet who is glad to be going back to Paris, all laughing, teasing, dreaming of the past and dreading the future, doing anything to avoid adjusting to a changing world. They are hopeless, helpless people, but the author looks at them with great warmth and affection (see Exercise 3, p. 58).

After the Bolshevik Revolution in 1917, the Russians could justify performances of Chekhov because he so obviously showed the unhappiness and uselessness of the old aristocrats and because many of his characters look forward to a future when a man can work and give his life fulfillment. But Chekhov's great popularity has been in the West, where the complexity of modern life has made confusion and frustration increasingly frequent.

One of the earliest American plays to use the techniques of impressionism was Susan Glaspell's one-act, *Trifles* (1916). Everything is done by indirection and suggestion. The two main characters never come on stage; the man is dead and his wife is in jail, suspected of his murder. On stage we see the sheriff looking for a sensational motive, while his wife and a neighbor look over the little things about the house—the "trifles." In casual talk they gradually reconstruct the lonely life the woman must have led and the feeling of desperation that smoldered for years beneath the surface and finally drove her to killing her husband. But moods of frustration were not common dramatic material in the 1920s because the go-getters did not admit frustration and unhappy Americans could escape to Greenwich Village or to the Left Bank in Paris. With the depression of the 1930s and the darkening clouds of impending war, however, large numbers of Americans, in the land of perennial optimism, could understand and respond to such moods. One play that catches beautifully the feeling of weary helplessness of the depression decade is Tennessee Williams' *The Glass Menagerie* (1944). Like the plays of Chekhov, it is a rich mood-study of a group of helpless victims, loving and torturing one another but unable to change or break away. Already uprooted from the security of the plantation in the Mississippi Delta and deserted by the father, the Wingfields—mother, son, and crippled daughter—seethe and quarrel in a dreary apartment in St. Louis. The mother dreams of departed glory and of a rich gentleman caller who will marry her daughter. But the daughter is too fragile to cope with the modern world and escapes into the world of small glass animals that she collects. The son, trapped in a dreary job and tortured by his family problems, dreams of following the example of his father and running away. The darkening international situation gives encouragement to his hope of exploding out of his frustrations, and he has already taken out papers in the merchant marine. But this is no final solution of the family problems. Unlike most naturalists, however, Williams does not show to the last detail the suffering and defeat of his characters but softens the effect of the play by presenting it as a nostalgic review of the past. The son tells the audience that he has wandered restlessly over the wartime world but has been unable to escape his memories. The audience sees only as much as he allows himself to remember.

The Theatre of Realism

Thus impressionism accepted the idea of man's helplessness in a baffling world but sought for understanding and for compassion. If it could not trace any clear purpose or large meaning in the absurd contradictions of life, it could at least discover a rich, vibrant texture in man's relation to his environment.

INTIMATE THEATRES FOR REALISM

Impressionist plays in particular, but indeed all the new plays of realism and naturalism, demanded not only a new kind of playwriting and acting but a new kind of theatre. No form of realism had a chance in the large nineteenth-century theatres, which were built to accommodate from two to four thousand people and included from three to six balconies. In such a theatre the large stage, on which were sometimes presented spectacular scenes with horses and hundreds of people, was a vast open space with scenery consisting of painted flats and backdrops. For interiors, pieces of furniture from the property rooms were spread around the bare stage floor in conventional arrangements—a sofa here, a table and two chairs there—supplemented at times by furniture painted on the wings and backdrop. The actors expected to act close to the footlights, where their large gestures could be seen and their loud oratorical voices could be heard clearly throughout the house. André Antoine, the pioneer of new realistic production in Paris, expressed his disgust when he saw a simple play called *Grand'mère* presented at the Odeon Theatre in a vast, paneled, cream-and-gold salon. He wrote: "The characters . . . of *Grand'mère* are people like ourselves. They live, not in vast halls having the dimensions of cathedrals, but in interiors like ours, around their fireplaces, under the lamp, around the table—and not at all, as in the classic repertory, in front of the prompter's box."

The new movement started with a few bold enterprising groups late in the nineteenth century, but it was so successful that by the 1920s practically all the new theatres in Western Europe and America were small, with about 1,000 to 1,500 seats, and the newer college theatres of America now usually seat three or four hundred. The idea of the intimate theatre has won out, and in spite of a hundred experiments in new directions the realistic approach still dominates the theatre.

The first great step was taken in London in 1865 when a Mr. and Mrs. Bancroft refurbished a small neglected theatre, gathered a group of young actors, and found a new director and playwright, T. W. Robertson. Robertson put his actors in the midst of real furniture and properties, real doors, ceilings, and windows, using the upstage as well as the downstage areas. He achieved a subtle ensemble acting more realistic than had been known before, making his sentimental scenes with everyday people very convincing by "new school" acting. His critics made fun of his "teacup and saucer" realism, however, and soon it came to seem mild and superficial.

A stronger impetus was given by the Norwegian rebel Henrik Ibsen, who in 1879 turned from romantic plays of history to write realistic plays that shook all Europe. Although he himself founded no theatre, he furnished the

Kinds of Plays

FIGURE *1.9* Early realism. Real details are used to suggest sentimental emotions. Robertson's *Ours*. London, 1866.

inspiration for the new theatres throughout the world. The first of the new "free" theatres—the Théâtre Libre in Paris—was founded in 1887 by André Antoine, who made his living working for the gas company. In a tiny hall, using real furniture, some of which he carted through the streets from his mother's dining room, he and a group of amateur actors made a strong impression and in a short while attracted a sizable audience. In 1889 a similar Free Theatre opened in Berlin with Ibsen's *Ghosts,* and soon was presenting Gerhart Hauptmann, a realistic German playwright of major importance. In 1890 London followed with the Independent Theatre, and it, too, found a native playwright, Bernard Shaw, to follow Ibsen. The intimate noncommercial theatre in Dublin, the Abbey Theatre, was at first devoted to the poetic mythical plays of William Butler Yeats, but John Millington Synge soon gave the rich poetic language of Ireland a realistic turn. Then in the 1920s Sean O'Casey wrote some of the most powerful, and beautiful, realistic plays the twentieth century has seen.

Most important of the new theatres was the Moscow Art Theatre, founded in 1897 by Constantin Stanislavsky and his partner. Anton Chekhov was the new playwright who ensured its success. The only one of the pioneer theatres that was able to establish a lasting institution, it is still the principal theatre in Moscow.

In New York the intimate theatre came a little later, in 1920, when the Provincetown Playhouse produced Eugene O'Neill's first three-act play, *Beyond the Horizon.* A converted stable on MacDougal Street, the Provincetown Playhouse was even smaller than the realistic theatres of Europe, but it made a tremendous impression. As an acting institution it did not last long, but soon the Theatre Guild, a more successful organization, and even the commercial producers adopted its ideals of honesty and realistic acting. This was the

FIGURE *1.10* Realism. Diagonal lines and dynamic variations of level weave the individuals into the web of environment. Inge's *Bus Stop*. Mankato State College production, directed by Ted Paul and designed by Burton E. Meisel.

pattern of most of the pioneers—a brave new start that pointed the way for others and proved that a new audience was ready.

The new intimate theatres presented no such painted stage pictures as the nineteenth century had seen. The proscenium arch was simplified or, in many cases, eliminated as a decorative element, leaving only a functional opening to view the "slice of life." Footlights, whose associations with glaring romantic spectacle and "ham" acting close to the "foots" made them especially distasteful, were eliminated or hidden under removable sections of the floor for the few times when some artificial effect might be needed. The Cleveland Playhouse, a beautiful example of the intimate theatre, has no decorative proscenium and no footlights but only two or three plain dark steps leading the audience, in their minds, right onto the stage.

The box setting, the basic setting for realism, gives three complete walls and a ceiling, as though the fourth wall has been removed. Occasionally actors have supposed a fireplace and even windows in the missing wall, but it was soon found better to ignore that wall and keep the actors looking not toward the audience but at the properties and action on the stage.

Ibsen and Chekhov liked glimpses of other rooms in the setting, to carry out the impression that space was continuous and that life flowed on without bounds. August Strindberg, the most important Swedish playwright of the new movement, soon found the square box set too conventional and liked to place the back walls and a table on the diagonal, both to allow the actors to face toward each other more casually and to suggest space going into the distance. New playwrights and directors likewise thought that there should be no sharp boundaries in time, that scenes of a slice of life should end on

22

Kinds of Plays

quiet, unemphatic moments. Of course there should be no orchestra to build up to the opening scene with a romantic overture and no line-up of actors in a curtain call at the end. T. W. Robertson originated the tableau curtain call, freezing all the actors in character as if they were ready to continue the last scene, but most realistic directors eliminated even that.

With the changes in theatres and plays came new ideals of directing: keep the actors focused on some center of interest on the stage; make full use of many different playing areas; enrich the action with frequent use of properties and body reactions. The visit of the Moscow Art Theatre company to New York in 1923 left a lasting impression as the ultimate in an art that hid all art. In their staging, nothing was obviously arranged, yet everything was meticulously clear. The actors seemed to have their backs to the audience constantly and to be absorbed in something behind the furniture or the other actors; no one ever moved out into a clear open space; no one ever seemed to turn toward the audience. Yet the casualness was so carefully planned that for every important line the speaker just happened to have his face visible. Despite what appeared to be informal composition and random movement, the attention of the audience was always carried straight to the important person or action. Though each character seemed to carry on a life completely independent of the others, so strong was the basic rhythm that they all became part of one compelling action. There was no star, no predominant character, but rather a perfect ensemble. The foreground and background were one, and properties, costumes, doors, lamps, window curtains, lights— no less than the actors—performed their parts.

THE STANISLAVSKY METHOD OF ACTING

The impressive triumphs achieved by the Moscow Art Theatre company were made possible by a new approach to realistic acting which stimulated the inner life of the actor so that the drama might be revealed in voice tone and body tensions—beyond, between, and sometimes in contradiction to the lines. As director of the company, Stanislavsky developed the principles of the "method," which has become the basis of most acting schools in the United States as well as in Russia. Assuming that his students were familiar with traditional techniques and were working many hours a week in courses in movement, dance, fencing, voice placement, singing, and diction, he concentrated on the inner preparation of the actor, which has described fully in *An Actor Prepares,* the most admired book on acting in modern times.

Stanislavsky wanted to free the actor from distractions and false actions, to teach him to relax each part of the body from unnecessary tensions, but even more to free him from conventional techniques of projection inherited from the nineteenth century. Stanislavsky hated the standard arrangement of the stage, the stock furniture that pushed the actor down to the footlights to repeat the conventional postures and gestures of the old school of actors. He turned the actor away from the audience and related him to the real objects on the stage, to the other characters, and to the thoughts and objectives inherent in the play. By concentrating on properties and the sequence of

23

realistic business, the actor would forget the audience and his own tensions and would have no excuse for stately tread, loud declamation, or resounding intonation. With long practice and concentration, he could transform himself and make a completely new creation of each role. But serious treatment of a role required the actor to spend days in thinking, feeling, acting, and speaking as the character would, and to visit the kinds of houses, streets, and neighborhoods associated with the character in order to get the feel of the environment. It required him to come into the theatre hours before the performance and put himself into the right mood by virtually becoming the character. Success depended on creating the right atmosphere for such actors. It was for them, more than for the audience, that properties had to be just right. Completely dedicated to the serious purposes of the theatre, Stanislavsky and his followers hoped to discover and reveal to the public the real meaning of human existence. The theatre was in essence to be life itself.

In preparing a play, Stanislavsky set an objective or purpose for each small scene and a "super-objective" or overall guiding purpose for the play as a whole. In *An Actor Prepares,* he tells of his work on Molière's *The Imaginary Invalid.* At first he took as the objective for the main character "I wish to be sick," but he found that the play was becoming a dreary psychological tragedy. Only when he realized that a truer objective was "I wish to be thought sick" did the play take life as a jolly comedy. Playing the part of the disdainful aristocrat in Goldoni's *Mistress of the Inn,* he at first took the objective "I wish to hate women." But when he realized that the character really loved women and that a better objective would be "I wish to do my courting on the sly," the comedy became lighter and gayer. After months of performance, the company found a still richer way of acting when they realized that the mistress of the inn, courted by all men, was the Mistress of Our Lives, Woman.

The carrying of the objective into the various scenes of the play Stanislavsky called the "adaptation." At first the adaptations must be spontaneous, from the subconscious. Then, with the help of the director, the actor must select the convincing adaptations, make them conscious, and learn to keep a sustained "motor adjustment." Thus Stanislavsky wanted a planned control, but only after a free period of improvisation and rehearsal, and he wanted some fresh element, some new bit of reality, in every performance to stimulate the subconscious and bring about the fusion of acting and real life.

Stanislavsky's method is a precise way of expressing the vision of man implied in naturalistic literature—that is, man caught by heredity and environment, victim of his lower drives, never fully expressing his thoughts in words even when he is deeply stirred. Stark Young, a drama critic who admired naturalistic acting, described it in one of his *Letters from Dead Actors,* a letter that he imagined the French classic actress Rachel might have written to Pauline Lord, creator of the role of Anna Christie in O'Neill's play in 1921:

> . . . And so now I can grant the theory of your school of acting. It is to represent in terms of repressed emotion all that is terrible in one's life. To concentrate in your body a bitter, mute violence. To get the effect by the

Kinds of Plays

negative; to speak by keeping silent; to move us terribly by what you do *not* do. . . . What you do best so far is the backwash of violent passion, the after-mood, the parching tongue, the gray despair of that which is past but remains as a darker, inverted, inarticulate tragedy.

Young realized that although the style was totally different from Rachel's own classic method, a good actress would recognize merit in another style.

The fact that modern acting has been very effective for naturalistic plays suggests that there can be many other styles of acting to express other basic attitudes toward life. Even for the abstract realism of Thornton Wilder's *Our Town* (1938), the acting will be different from acting that expresses the heavy hopelessness and defeat of the people in Gorki's *The Lower Depths*. For the romantic moods of musical comedy, dance, and opera, the idealized concept of character calls for a still different approach. In the more exalted plays, such as Greek or Elizabethan tragedy, while the acting must be honest and convincing, its scale will be quite different from that of the subtle movement appropriate to the frustrated indoor characters of Chekhov.

The increasing revival of old plays, both in schools and in repertory companies, has brought with it the realization that Stanislavsky's method put too much emphasis on creating completely new characters and avoiding any techniques that had been used before. This cult of originality now seems excessive. Only the genius, and perhaps not even he, can depend on creativity alone. The average competent artist needs to know a large number of techniques that can be developed only through many generations. The "method" itself has become a tradition, with a corpus of techniques. Used by good actors these techniques can be extremely effective. Used by shallow actors, they seem as empty as the larger techniques of the stock-company actors of nineteenth-century melodrama. The good actors, Henry Irving and Tommaso Salvini, for example, made nineteenth-century acting convincing. We are realizing again that a good actor, with proper study and care, can make the sweeping gestures of the Shakespearean tradition as honest as the repressed tensions of naturalism, and far more expressive of Shakespearean nobility.

Selected Realism and Stylized Realism

In almost all the realistic or naturalistic plays we have examined so far, man is seen as the victim of an environment that thwarts his wishes. His angers and hopes may smolder in frustration, but all he can do is face destruction or fret as his life wastes away, eroded by time. If the early naturalistic writer looked to what the future would do in changing the environment, he saw no hope of escape for the characters in his own novel or play. His immediate picture was pessimistic; his ending, as we shall see, was one of the patterns of modern tragedy, asking the audience rather than the gods to take responsibility and do something about the environment. But there are other ways of showing man's relation to the environment, other kinds of realism in which the victim does not so docilely accept defeat. Even as modern man has recognized the importance of environment, he has felt a determina-

FIGURE *1.11*　Selected realism. The details of a middle-class Norwegian home are simplified and organized into a design of dignity. Alla Nazimova and Harry Ellerbe in Ibsen's *Ghosts*. New York, 1935. Photo Vandamm.

tion either to control or to destroy it, and rapid development of science and technology has given him confidence in his ability to do so. Two variants of realistic theatre, similar in some ways, express this confidence. One is based on man's strife with his environment and his partial victory—a variant that may be called *selected realism,* in which things no longer overwhelm the individual and in which the local color, though it may be rich in mood, is not so stifling as in naturalistic plays. The other variant, which may be called *stylized realism,* shows an explosive attack on the environment. Although they followed rather different lines of development, selected realism leading to a comedy of social problems and stylized realism to expressionism, they can be bracketed together as two modifications of realism that no longer treated man as a passive victim. In both, man asserts himself and either brings his environment into a working partnership or splits it into fragments.

Actually, it is selected realism that is seen in most of the plays and productions of the twentieth century. Even if audiences are willing to see an occasional extreme example of naturalism, and to admit that many people are limited by their heredity and defeated by their environment, their normal view has been far from desperate.

Escape has not always seemed a futile dream, as it does in Chekhov's plays. Many people have escaped from slums and small towns. Many people have become rich and moved away from their cramping environment or have asserted themselves and improved it. Many popular novels and plays have presented a serious struggle with environment leading to at least partial triumph. If the main character has been defeated, there is often hope that the next generation will succeed. That was the pattern of the most talked-about novel of the 1920s, *Main Street,* by Sinclair Lewis, in which small-town conformity won a temporary victory but stirred the victim to the secret determination that her young son would some day win where she had failed. In Sidney Howard's play *The Silver Cord* (1926), the conflict between a possessive

Kinds of Plays

mother and her sons builds to violent scenes which end in the defeat of one son but the successful escape of the other. Escape is gloriously successful in *The Barretts of Wimpole Street* (1930) by Rudolf Besier, in which Robert Browning, like a medieval knight, rescues his love, Elizabeth Barrett, from the father, who has tried to keep her an invalid under his own morbid control.

On the other hand, some plays suggest that the environment may not be so bad as it has seemed, that escape may not be necessary. Perhaps nature is not always the enemy of man. Perhaps it does not really matter that the hero, wishing to escape, is held back by the unconscious forces of nature and that his conscious wish is defeated. In Shaw's *Man and Superman,* though the tone is that of a vigorous high-comedy quarrel between a man and woman, the theme is the same naturalistic one of an attempt to escape. Jack Tanner, feeling that marriage would be the end of his intellectual independence, struggles to escape the wiles and powerful appeal of Ann Whitefield, who seems the essence of blind nature, determined to use him and destroy him just to get the race continued, without regard for his human, intelligent purposes. Yet when he does capitulate there is no defeat. He has had a dream of a great debate that his predecessor, Don Juan, holds in hell, a dream that ends with Don Juan and Donna Anna leaving the comfortable world of hell to tackle the difficult job of creating a higher, more intellectual man—a superman. When Jack realizes that woman, the blind force of nature, may also will the intelligent, as Donna Anna did, he no longer objects to giving in to nature through marriage.

In two vigorous American comedies of the 1920s, a comic hero suffers an exasperating defeat that pleases the audience. The actress mother in *The*

FIGURE *1.12* Selected realism. A few details of Greek architecture are used in a strong, simple design for a comic fantasy. Alfred Lunt and Lynn Fontanne in Giraudoux's *Amphytrion 38.* New York, 1938. Designed by Lee Simonson. Photo Vandamm.

Royal Family (1928), a play suggested by the Barrymore family of actors, becomes so outraged at the conflict between her private life and her career that she swears she will never go on the stage again. But when the maid announces that it is time for the first act, her old loyalties and habits reassert themselves and she rushes off to her duty. A similar struggle extends throughout *The Front Page* (1928), a fast-moving play about newspapers, court trials, and politics. A young reporter is trying to finish the scoop on a case so that he can be free to marry and can escape from his hectic career. When he finally gets on the train with the girl, however, his boss calls the police' to bring him back, and the audience knows he will never get away. But why should he escape such an exciting environment?

In plays like these the human personality is not absorbed in the background. A few bold characters assert their will with sharp comic acting more positive than "method" acting. The stage setting does not present the full, overwhelming detail of naturalism but only enough detail for the action or for local color. If the play indicates that the characters have some control over their destiny, it is fitting that the setting show the artistic control of the designer. It can have elements of good composition—good line, form, proportion, rhythm, color, and even a fair amount of symmetry—elements that would be neglected or hidden in a naturalistic, slice-of-life play.

Most realists have not been willing to go as far in selection as the very abstract designs of Adolphe Appia and Gordon Craig, which we will examine in the chapter on design. Craig, especially, was an insinuating propagandist: his designs were constant reminders of the excitement of sheer line, bold contrasts of masses, and the joy of clean empty spaces between simple forms. Twentieth-century realists still wanted a convincing indication of the actual

FIGURE *1.13* Abstract masses and spaces. Two suggestive scene designs by Gordon Craig from his magazine *The Mask*.

world, but they could see human character as having a degree of independence and nature as having a degree of order. In their view, man could come to terms with his environment. He could face his kitchen or his back yard and learn to understand it. Perhaps this is the domestic, rural, or small-town vision of realism—a preindustrial, pre-Freudian view not yet involved in the fragmenting complexity of the modern city or the psychological terrors of the split personality. The stage picture—background people and background material world—was still intact.

Both naturalism, in which the individual is overwhelmed by details, and selected realism, in which the individual has some control, still kept an objective view of one real place at a time. But that objective view did not suffice when the naturalistic character felt menaced by the machine age and when his irrational fears burst into his conscious mind. It was not so much the immediate surroundings that terrified him as isolated images: rhythmic mechanized sounds, dehumanized groups of people, fragments of many past experiences. This explosive conflict called not for selected realism but for stylized realism, which kept the central character intact but, in order to present the violence of the conflict, used abstraction and distortion to break up the environment into fantastic fragments.

Eugene O'Neill's *The Hairy Ape* (1922) is an excellent example of stylized realism. Yank, a ship's stoker, is a typical naturalistic character who makes a blind attack on the environment, ignorant of how that environment might be improved but acutely aware of the spiritual anguish of not belonging to it. He has tried to identify himself with the steel, the coal, the power and speed of his time, but he finds that the machine age needs only his muscle; he has become a dehumanized brute, a "hairy ape." At first the ship's crew are presented in the rich variety of types and nationalities that O'Neill had handled so brilliantly in his naturalistic short plays of the sea. But life had been different on a sailing vessel. As old Paddy says, " 'Twas them days men belonged to the ships, not now. 'Twas them days a ship was part of the sea, and a man was part of a ship, and the sea joined all together and made it one." He has nothing but contempt for the new ship of the industrial age: "black smoke from the funnels smudging the sea, smudging the decks—the bloody engines pounding and throbbing and shaking—wid divil a sight of sun or a breath of clean air—choking our lungs wid coal dust—breaking our backs and hearts in the hell of the stokehole—feeding the bloody furnace—feeding our lives along with the coal, I'm thinking—caged in by steel from a sight of the sky like bloody apes in the zoo." The alienation of the crew in this mechanized environment is indicated by a stylized laughter, a barking laughter with a brazen quality, "as if their throats were phonograph horns."

The provocation for Yank's explosion is the appearance in the furnace room of the daughter of a steel magnate, herself as alienated as Yank. Her contempt and horror show him what a degraded brute he has become. But before he will accept his dehumanization, he makes a frantic attack on the world, escaping from the ship and throwing himself with anger against the rich people coming out of a church on Fifth Avenue. Here O'Neill shows a

FIGURE *1.14* Stylized realism. Jones in his fantasy sees the crocodile god. O'Neill's *The Emperor Jones*. Design by Donald Oenslager for Yale University production. Photo Peter A. Juley and Son.

mechanized world through stylization of movement and business. The people pay no attention to Yank but walk along in rows repeating their inane chatter (see Exercise 5, p. 60). In some productions they wear masks. This scene of stylized realism indicates the twisted life of Yank's mind as well. The street and the people are shown not objectively but subjectively, distorted, as they would appear to a bewildered mind. It is only the environment that is unreal, however; Yank remains the typical naturalistic victim, but one who refuses to accept his fate and explodes in violence. Deep in his puzzled mind he realizes that his alienation cannot be cured by any slight improvement in the environment. He has been thrown out of the office of a labor union, where he offered to help blow up the city; violence does not "belong." In the end he tries the zoo, with the apes. But the real ape hugs him and crushes him to death—not even with the animals can he "belong." The play offers interesting possibilities for an actor's interpretation of one kind of realism (see Exercise 6, p. 61).

The expressionistic distortion in *The Hairy Ape* is only incidental, intended to show the mental state of the main character. The more extended and systematic stylization of the environment in O'Neill's earlier play *The Emperor Jones* (1920) is usually considered expressionistic. Yet in this play as well the main character is a naturalistic victim in explosive conflict with his environment. A clever Negro pullman porter, Brutus Jones, exploiting the ignorant natives of an island in the Caribbean, had himself made Emperor. When the natives become restless under his rule, he tries to escape, but in the terrors of the jungle night, he loses the veneer of civilization and is destroyed, not so much by the natives as by his own fears. As in "The Congo"

Kinds of Plays

by Vachel Lindsay, the primitive jungle repossesses modern man. The environment is stylized in the regular drumbeat—one of the most famous theatrical devices of early twentieth-century theatre—which starts early in the play and continues without interruption, through the brief intermissions, right to the end. The environment, as much subjective as local, is stylized also in the phantoms that appear to Jones each time he pauses in his flight. Each hallucination goes further into his past, peeling off another level of his consciousness. First there are just vague shapes, then crap games, fights, trials, and chain gangs of his own past, and finally the crocodile gods of his primitive ancestors, all stylized in mechanical, terrifying, rhythmic movement. By using an abstract and symbolic form, O'Neill makes his play suggest the primitive violence that lurks beneath the surface of modern man and the violence of colonial peoples, ready to turn on their exploiters and destroy them. Here both exploiter and exploited are black.

Both plays are so dominated by single characters that they can be called *monodramas*. As we shall see, they have much in common with the plays of full expressionism, in which both the main characters and the background are stylized, and they anticipate several of the developments of the middle of the century. We shall find a similar conflict between a few fully developed characters and a fragmented environment in the epic plays of Bertolt Brecht. As the existentialists in the 1950s and 60s emphasized the subjective life of the lone individual and cast doubt on the meaningful continuity of the outside world, the monodrama became important again in the work of Eugène Ionesco and some of John Osborne's plays, where one character is real but all other characters are seen as stylized pieces of his experience.

Stylization is one kind of abstraction, but the theatre before the middle of this century had developed other kinds of abstraction which were more

FIGURE *1.15* Stylized realism. Environment is treated as primitive fantasy. Obey's *Noah*. New York, 1935. Designed by Cleon Throckmorton. Photo Vandamm.

thoroughgoing than selected realism and more flexible and subtle than stylized realism. It remains to look at three other ways of presenting reality, ways that are usually classified as nonrealistic but that are being absorbed into the main tradition of realism: abstract realism, Oriental realism of make-believe, and epic realism.

Abstract Realism

Thornton Wilder in 1938 called on the New York audience to take a new view of reality, to see the daily details of American life abstracted from the usual box setting of realistic environment. His *Our Town* used no front curtain, no scenery, and no properties except a few chairs, a couple of ladders, and trellises pushed out at one moment "for those who think they have to have scenery." A Stage Manager came out to chat with the audience and point out what they were to imagine on the stage—two kitchens, a back yard, or a drugstore counter, with the rest of the town imagined in the background. He moved chairs as they were needed, and occasionally he became a minor character—the soda fountain clerk or the minister for the wedding. The play was equally free in time as the Stage Manager introduced scenes or stopped them, mentioning what was going to happen to different characters or what had happened in the past. Since there is no strong plot, Wilder freely arranged his series of scenes to demonstrate in three separate acts three aspects of one theme.

The theme of the first act is the daily life of the town, from the first preparations for breakfast and the arrival of the newsboy and milkman to the return from choir practice in the moonlight and the settling down for the night. In the second act, the daily kitchen and breakfast activity is concentrated on getting ready for the wedding of Emily and George, but before the wedding scene itself there is a flashback to a drugstore scene showing the first time

FIGURE *1.16* Abstract realism. The everyday characters of a small town are seen not in a realistic setting but against a wide view of time and eternity. A scene of young love in a drugstore is presented without realistic details. Wilder's *Our Town*. New York, 1938. Photo Vandamm.

FIGURE *1.17* Abstract realism. Death and eternity are suggested by simple theatrical means. The living characters stand with umbrellas around Emily's grave, while she joins the rows of the sitting dead. Wilder's *Our Town*. New York, 1938. Photo Vandamm.

the couple knew they were made for each other. With the method of make-believe well established in two acts, it is easy to move on to the cemetery in the third act, the chairs now set in rows to represent graves where the dead sit and speak. Emily, a new arrival, realizes that she can revisit the living and decides to look at her own twelfth birthday. A few feet in front of the sitting dead, she watches her mother start the day, until the pain of seeing her youthful self in the light of later time becomes too strong, and she gladly returns to take her place on the hilltop.

Free from the limitations of a realistic setting and actual breakfast dishes, Wilder can show each individual moment against a wide panorama of time and place. In the imagination are conjured up the streets, stores, churches, trains, and milk wagons of the town, the twins born over in Polish town, the grandparents in the cemetery on the hill, the early settlers, the Indians, the rocks of the mountains, millions of years old. The Stage Manager sends the mind back to the daily life of Babylon and Rome, and forward to the future of these small-town American people and to people who may look back at them thousands of years from now. Each action of Emily and George and their parents and neighbors in Grover's Corners, New Hampshire, is the center of circles of waves that extend out in time and space as far as the mind can conceive. The first act ends with the younger sister's awestruck recital of the address on a letter her friend has received: "It said: Jane Crofut; the Crofut Farm; Grover's Corners; Sutton County; New Hampshire; United States of America; Continent of North America; Western Hemisphere; the Earth; the Solar System; the Universe; the Mind of God—that's what it said on the envelope—and the postman brought it just the same." The last act ends with the dead quietly talking about the stars and the millions of years it takes their light to reach the earth. Everyday life, seen by so many naturalistic writers as restrictive, petty, and degrading, takes on a glow of importance when thus abstracted from realistic scenery and set in a wide perspective of time and place.

The Theatre of Realism

Wilder derived the device of looking at a moment from two points in time from the novels of Marcel Proust. For Proust, time was destructive and experience meaningless except as isolated moments of the past might be recaptured and enjoyed in memory through the recollection of how senses, feelings, and moods had been aroused in the original experience. In Wilder's wide perspective of time, however, the little events of daily life are not meaningless or disconnected. In *Our Town,* the sentimental recognition that time passes is painful to Emily, but it makes her see human life more clearly in a wider philosophical framework. Wilder does not accept a grubby materialistic view. "It ain't houses and it ain't names, and it ain't earth, and it ain't even the stars—everybody knows in their bones that something is eternal, and that something has to do with human beings." Even the people in the cemetery are waiting "for the eternal part in them to come out clear." By his abstract staging, Wilder makes the timeless human quality of his characters come out clear.

There has been no other play just like *Our Town* and the several one-acts that Wilder wrote in exploring the new form, but their influence has been enormous. The success of *Our Town* all over the world has greatly encouraged other playwrights and producers to use more flexible, imaginative staging, with open platforms and no scenery or only suggestive pieces, using narrators or masters of ceremony who interrupt the actors or bring them on stage as the theme requires, in any plan of time or space the audience can be persuaded to imagine.

The Oriental Realism of Make-Believe

It was the Chinese theatre that suggested to Wilder his new approach in *Our Town.* He had grown up in China, where his father was an American consul, and he was fascinated by the free, highly imaginative methods of the Oriental theatre. Instead of copying the spectacular aspects

FIGURE *1.18*   Oriental make-believe. Masks of the Japanese Noh theatre. Drawn by Bobbie Okerbloom.

FIGURE *1.19*   An Oriental platform for actor, chorus, and musicians. A traditional Japanese Noh theatre on the estate of a feudal lord. Drawn by Bobbie Okerbloom.

FIGURE *1.20*   For the popular Japanese audience scenic spectacle is combined with make-believe. Eighteenth-century Japanese Kabuki theatre. Drawn by Bobbie Okerbloom.

FIGURE *1.21* Conventionalized Oriental movement and grouping in the midst of elaborate scenery. Some entrances are made along the *hanamichi* or runway. *Benten the Thief,* a traditional Japanese Kabuki play. University of Hawaii production, directed by Earle Ernst.

that appeal to the romantic taste for the exotic—the fantastic legendary plots, the bright-colored costumes, the painted faces—Wilder learned from the Chinese theatre that even the important events of everyday life can be presented by actors on an open platform, reacting not to a realistic setting but to the private thoughts and personal relations of the characters.

A few Chinese plays had been known in the West before *Our Town,* but they were considered the opposite of realism and had been presented in such a way that audiences might laugh at the property man and other unfamiliar stage conventions or might be entranced by the exotic stories of long ago. After *Our Town* was produced in 1938, the West began to take a new look at the Orient and to see Oriental theatre not just as romantic escape from reality, not just as ceremonial and playful treatment of human relations, but as a fundamental way of treating reality. The Chinese theatre in particular has had such an impact on the tradition of realism that it can be treated in this chapter rather than with the Western theatre of color and romance.

Still a living art, the Chinese theatre uses plays that are three hundred to seven hundred years old and traditions that were well established by the Tang dynasty, more than a thousand years ago. The Chinese stage has no front curtain, scenery, or realistic properties. A temple-canopy, sometimes held up by two lacquer columns, decorates the acting area, and the back of the stage is a decorated screen or beautiful embroidered cloth that carries the imagination into romantic realms of fancy but tells nothing about each particular scene. Both the orchestra and the property man are on stage in sight all the time.

The Oriental method of presentation is children's make-believe raised to a high art. In the first place, it recognizes that reality in the theatre is entirely a matter of the mind and imagination of the audience, of what they want and expect to believe. Adults are not basically different from children, who in their imaginations freely turn any chairs, rocks, sticks, tools, or boards, any old

Kinds of Plays

FIGURE *1.22*   The traditional Chinese platform theatre, showing property men and orchestra on stage. The play shows a general arriving in a chariot before the gate of a city. Drawn by Claude Marks.

FIGURE *1.23*   A decorative conventionalized panel set against a chair to indicate mountains. In this scene from a traditional Chinese play a general in colorful costume is pursuing bandits through mountain paths. Drawn by Martha Sutherland.

clothes or pieces of cloth into the palaces, weapons, jewels, and costumes needed for their stories. On the Chinese stage, the actor, entering by one of the conventional doorways in the back cloth, comes down to address the audience and tells exactly who he is and what his motives and plans are (see Exercises 9 and 10, pp. 62–63). If he is to enter a house, he indicates by an elaborate pantomime that he is sliding the two doors apart, stepping over the threshold, and then closing the doors after him. If he is to sit, the property man brings a chair to put under him, and neither the actor nor the audience pays any attention. The same standard chairs and tables serve for all kinds of levels—hills, walls, river banks, platforms. If the property man sets the chairs on the table, the actor climbs a high mountain pass. To indicate a journey by chariot, the actor trots with crouched steps between two flags on which wheels are painted (FIGURE 1.22). It matters little if he has only a whip to suggest that he is riding a horse. It matters much what skill he shows, with the aid of the whip, in suggesting the essence of a man getting on or off a horse.

The few scenic effects are highly conventionalized. To indicate mountain country, small panels painted with the traditional mountain and stream pattern are brought out and leaned against a chair or table (FIGURE 1.23). To show an attack on a gate, attendants hold up a long pole from which is hung a cloth painted to represent a section of wall with a gate, and behind it the defending general climbs on a chair and table to speak from above the wall (FIGURE 1.24). But such scenic devices are subterfuge; it is the actor who

FIGURE 1.24 Actors climbing a mountain in traditional Chinese theatre style. Conventional chairs and tables serve to indicate differences in level. *The Yellow Jacket.* University of Tulsa production, directed by Beaumont Bruestle and designed and costumed by Harold Barrows.

FIGURE *1.25* Mei Lan Fang, a Chinese actor who won worldwide fame, in a traditional female role. The long sleeves become part of the dance and gesture as the hand is either hidden or free. Photographed on his visit to America in 1930 by Vandamm.

creates the reality—marching, riding, shouting, brandishing his weapons, whirling, fighting furious duels with all the rage of battle but rarely coming close enough to even touch weapons with his opponent, shivering to create the illusion of a storm while a demon of winter dances and the property man shakes paper snow from a box.

The characters also sing many songs so that the drama seems almost an opera, and there are some formal dances and many stylized movements. The orchestra accompanies everything, reinforcing the melody and rhythm of the songs, giving shape and rhythm to the action by marking each step, gesture, and movement, using a dozen instruments—flutes, violins, gongs, drums, bells, cymbals, and blocks of wood.

In many of the Hong Kong theatres, as in the Chinese theatres that existed in New York and San Francisco until recently, the popular fare is military plays, with music that sounds very noisy to Western ears. But the famous Peking actor Mei Lan Fang, on his tour of America in 1930, showed that the method could serve even better with the more delicate music of the Ming dramas, with their tender scenes of love and domestic sorrows and joys. One of the finest actors this country had ever seen, Mei Lan Fang demonstrated that the conventional method of the Oriental theatre can create an illusion of reality just as convincing as our theatre of realistic detail, and perhaps more compelling. In spite of the conventional means—men acting girls' parts, song instead of colloquial speech, sustained dance movements instead of fumbling starts and stops, traditional gestures with hands, sleeves, and head—or, rather, through the use of these indirect means, he created his own world of heightened reality.

Best known of the plays close to actual Chinese texts is *The Circle of Chalk,* 39

FIGURE *1.26* A colorful imitation of the Chinese stage, with the property man at one side and the orchestra at the other. *The Circle of Chalk*. University of Iowa production, directed by Harold Crain, designed by A. S. Gillette, and costumed by Berneice Prisk.

which exists in English in several translations and has been performed many times, especially by college groups. It is the Oriental version of the wisdom of Solomon. To determine which of two claimants is the mother of the child, the Emperor uses the test of the circle of chalk. The child is placed within it, and the women are told that only the mother can remove him. Actually the Emperor knows that the true mother will not hurt his arm by jerking him away from the other woman; therefore, he correctly declares that the woman who removes him from the circle is a false claimant. There is more conventional romance in *Lady Precious Stream,* which made a great impression in both London and New York in the 1930s in an adaptation by S. I. Hsiung. The young heroine chooses to marry the gardener and, when he goes away, waits faithfully in poverty in spite of the machinations of her wicked brother-in-law. But when her husband returns, pursued by the loving Princess of the Western Regions, she makes him play some high-comedy games before she will take him back, and the Princess has to agree to be only a second wife. In the English adaptation, the Princess wears Russian costume and has helped make him her King but has not yet married him, and she agrees to remain his friend, paying full deference to the position of the little wife.

Song, dance, and masks or painted faces, so important in the Eastern theatres, are usually omitted or merely suggested in adaptations for the West. Some translations of Chinese plays try to keep the poetic language, at least for the speeches that were operatic arias in the original, and most producers set such lyric passages off by some kind of instrumental accompaniment in imitation of Chinese style. *Lute Song,* which had a very successful Broadway production in 1946 with Mary Martin playing the forsaken wife, had simple prose dialogue and some songs, in a style rather like musical comedy but vaguely Chinese. The production was magnificent, with costumes, mobile screens, and hanging cloths designed by Robert Edmond Jones. American audiences are fascinated by the elaborate painted faces for character roles that add to the exotic charm of both the Chinese theatre and the Japanese

Kinds of Plays

Kabuki (FIGURE *1.20*). It has not been so easy to find Western equivalents for the ceremonial austerity of the Japanese Noh theatre (FIGURE *1.19*) or the exquisite Noh masks (FIGURE *1.18*), though several poets and musicians have tried, notably the poet William Butler Yeats. Ignorant of Oriental music and dance, most Western performers have not tried to do more than suggest an exotic exaltation in speech or gesture. But now many people are seriously studying Oriental music and even more are studying Oriental dance, and a few directors are attempting to produce the classic plays of India, Siam, China, and Japan with song, chant, and dance movement (FIGURE *12.6*).

More and more, the Western theatre in the twentieth century has moved toward the freedom and imagination of the Oriental theatre. Not only in such deliberate imitations as *Our Town* and John Patrick's *The Teahouse of the August Moon* (1953) but in many purely Western plays the audience is let in on the process of performance. As recently as the 1920s an audience would have been shocked and embarrassed to see the stagehands in action, but now audiences are delighted to see the settings changed as part of the flow of the story. Writers on play production used to level their scorn at any stray tendency of the actor to recognize that the audience was present, but today many plays contain speeches addressed to the audience, actors turn some of their acting to the front, and television actors often face into the camera with recognition of the audience. Designers and directors now often bring actors onto a more open playing area with only suggestive fragments of settings. In Ionesco's *The Chairs,* two actors make hundreds of invisible people arrive to hear a world-shaking announcement. Samuel Beckett's characters face their lonely destinies with little help from real backgrounds. In Friedrich Duerren-

FIGURE *1.27* Theatre of make-believe in the West. Actors are costumed as lion and oxen, and stylized units of scenery serve to indicate the city of Rome. Shaw's *Androcles and the Lion.* New York, 1946. Photo Vandamm.

matt's *The Visit,* the crowd, train, town councils, and events of many days are compacted and suggested by the actors as freely as in an Oriental play. Even animals may now be brought on the stage in an Oriental fashion, though, to be sure, in 1913 Bernard Shaw used an actor for his lion in *Androcles and the Lion.* The real lion used in the movie version in the 1950s only proved how much less convincing a real beast can be than an actor acting as one. In the 1960–61 season alone, three popular plays in New York introduced stage horses, not live ones, into the action. In the musical *Tenderloin,* an attempt was made to create a realistic illusion by half hiding the supposed horses behind a wall and using elaborate machinery to show realistic heads and rumps moving up and down, but both the musical *Camelot* and the serious drama *Becket* frankly brought on the actors prancing on raised stilt-shoes, wearing the frames of hobbyhorses around their waists. Clearly, mid-twentieth-century audiences are becoming accustomed to make-believe and consider it an acceptable way of dealing with reality.

Epic Realism

The Western synthesis of all the forms of realism and all the techniques that have broken up the early conventions of realism is to be found in epic realism, sometimes called *narrative realism.* Epic theatre differs so much from the realism of 1880 to 1920 that many people consider it one of the revolts against realism, yet it differs from expressionism and the theatre of the absurd in attempting to piece all its fragments together into one meaningful picture of the real world. If it breaks up the solid box set of the naturalists, it still relates the individual to the wider aspects of environment. Audiences have expanded their concept of realism, and instead of thinking of one realism and many artificial devices that violate reality they now accept almost any device that seems pertinent to the subject. Cut-down or symbolic settings, masks, songs, addresses to the audience, asides, narratives, announcements, projected slides, charts, posters, movies, tableaux, formal Elizabethan backgrounds or simple curtains on wires, multiple settings similar to the row of "mansions" used on the medieval stage—devices which used to appear only in fantasies and dream plays—may be combined, alternated, or used in some parts of a play to give a strong sense that this is not romantic escape but scientific fact.

Whereas traditional realism concentrates on a few individuals in relation to their immediate environment, the epic uses its more theatrical devices to show a wider social, historical, political, and economic background. Gerhart Hauptmann attempted to portray such an expanded environment in *The Weavers* (1892), a very impressive play that explores, in five acts and five very real settings, as many different views of the violent revolt of a group of workers. But five scenes were not enough, and many other episodes that gave provocation for the rising anger of the workers had to be left offstage and were merely mentioned in the dialogue. Since that time, ways have been found to transcend the strict limits of early naturalism. Instead of having a hero

Kinds of Plays

explain to his wife how he has been wiped out in the stock market, we can bring on a brief scene of buyers and sellers at the stock market or flash stock quotations, announcements, and headlines on a screen. Not only does this create more exciting theatre but it takes quite a different perspective on man, a perspective that makes use of the studies of sociology, politics, and economics. In the industrial, urban world of today, one's immediate environment may affect one's life less than a political speech, a market report, or a strike on the other side of the earth. The left-wing German director Erwin Piscator put this realization in extreme terms: "Not man's relation to himself, not his relation to God, but his relation to society is the main issue. . . . No longer the individual with his private, personal destiny, but the age itself, the destiny of the masses is the heroic factor of the new dramaturgy."

The movies learned very early to cut in brief scenes of public events as background for the story, and soon a further technique called *montage* was developed, in which images were piled up, one after the other or several on a divided screen at the same time. The method was useful not only for indicating the passing of time but for showing the changes wrought by time. A similar method was developed in the novel, the most famous example being John Dos Passos' trilogy, *U.S.A.* The main episodes are conveyed in swift, vivid close-ups of a few characters, with little indication of background events. Between episodes Dos Passos uses three special devices to add background to the main stories: a "newsreel" containing snatches of popular songs, slogans, headlines, and lists of news items; a "camera eye," in stream-of-consciousness form, giving memories of the important characters; and an occasional brief biography of a public figure. Together these devices make up a chronicle or epic history of two decades in American life.

This combination of realistic main plot with sketchy between-scenes for social background also worked well in the theatre. A full realistic setting could be used for the main plot while actors of the background scenes addressed the audience directly, moving across the front of the stage or appearing at the sides, either with no setting at all or with a few properties brought on stage in sight of the audience. But this combination of box-set story with forestage or side-stage choral figures still left the principal emphasis on a few individuals and their immediate surroundings. Why not do without the box set and give the main stage the same free treatment that worked so well for the forestage or side-stage group? Epic theatre thus developed a number of combinations of simplified settings, movable properties, conventionalized curtains, screens, platforms, and projection screens.

THE RANGE OF EPIC THEATRE
In the 1920s, Piscator made a tremendous impression in Berlin with a dramatization of a satiric novel about a stupid Czech soldier, *The Good Soldier Schweik*. A long sequence showed the journey to the war, with people, furniture, and miniature settings moving by on a treadmill, backed by a screen on which were projected by turns movies of the towns and war camps the soldiers passed, satiric cartoon sketches by George Grosz, and

43

FIGURE *1.28*   Lyric theatre in epic form. The chorus of cows serve as witnesses at the trial of Joan of Arc. Claudel and Honegger's *Joan of Arc at the Stake,* with Vera Zorina as Joan. University of Kansas production, directed by Jack Brooking. Masks by Don Ferguson.

slogans, ironic facts, and other bits of information. To the bitter, defeated, inflation-ridden Germans of the 1920s, this objective panorama seemed the epitome of the idiocy of war.

A French poet, Paul Claudel, was also at this time experimenting with techniques which we now see were moving in the direction of epic theatre. While he was French ambassador to Japan, he became interested in Japanese theatre. His experiments, partly inspired by this influence, took him outside the regular theatre into opera and dramatic oratorio. Not until they were revived in mid-century, however, did they have an impact on theatre audiences. *Joan of Arc at the Stake,* with music by Arthur Honegger, presents a trial or hearing to which Joan and other witnesses return. The actors sometimes sing their lines and sometimes speak them against the musical background provided by the chorus and orchestra. By reenacting the main events and yet commenting on them from outside, they give a sense of the wide sweep and significance of the events that no series of separate realistic scenes could give. The performance of Vera Zorina with the Philadelphia Orchestra, beautifully recorded, is a model for both playwrights and actors to study, even if they know little French.

Another epic play of Claudel, *The Book of Christopher Columbus,* had a few performances when it was first set by Darius Milhaud as a full opera. But after the Second World War, when Jean-Louis Barrault produced it with new, incidental music by Milhaud, it proved to be a very effective piece of epic theatre for both French and American audiences. It, too, is a hearing, a judgment, with an expositor who calls the forlorn old Columbus out of a lowly inn in Valladolid to come on to the forestage and watch as another actor, playing Columbus, presents the story. The techniques employed include moving pictures, symbolic images, and vague shadows projected on a screen; ballads and narratives; and dialogue that both occurs within the event and describes its significance from a later time. The play reviews Columbus' long career, showing the boy's departure from home in Genoa, the appeal to the King of Spain, the mutiny of the sailors, the curses of the gods of the New

World, and finally an apotheosis as Queen Isabella leads Columbus toward the gates of glory. It is like a trial, with accusation and defense spoken directly to the audience, then illustrated by the dramatic scenes and made theatrical through music, movement, mobile scenery, and projections.

During the 1930s America saw its own forms of epic theatre developed, partly by aggressive labor groups and partly by scientists and journalists interested in the wider implications of human events. Sidney Howard's *Yellow Jack,* produced in 1934, was a landmark. It set on the stage a series of moments in the long fight to control yellow fever, from laboratories in London, West Africa, and Cuba to tents where soldiers died from yellow fever or served as guinea pigs for the long experiments. The few characters who linked the different scenes were united by involvement in a very important human endeavor. There was neither direct address to the audience nor projection of pictures as in other epic plays, but the play was a story of medicine and not a story of individuals.

An even more striking integration of individual stories and social background was seen the following year in Clifford Odets' *Waiting for Lefty* (1935). The central problem of the play was one of primary importance in America in the 1930s: that of organizing workers for direct action to raise wages. The unifying situation is a meeting of taxi drivers considering whether or not to strike. In flashbacks each driver acts out his own desperate problem—the boy unable to get married on his wages, the young husband about to lose his family—each scene in a pool of light against the background of the shadowy figures of the other drivers.

American problems on a nationwide scale were staged in the Living Newspaper, which was developed by the Federal Theatre, a part of Works Progress Administration, the New Deal project to give jobs to large numbers of unemployed. Theatre people and journalists together worked out a new kind of documentary theatre, dramatizing one subject at a time, somewhat as in the "March of Time," a radio and movie feature for many years. The first impressive edition of the Living Newspaper was *Triple-A Plowed Under,* the story of the farm problem and the first attempt of the New Deal agency to solve it. In twenty-six rapid scenes, farmers and city customers were shown buying and selling, burning wheat, dumping milk trucks, and rioting at farm foreclosures, while congressmen, Secretary of Agriculture Henry Wallace, wheat-exchange bidders, and Supreme Court members acted, spoke, or exhorted. An expositor's voice came over the loud-speaker, and statistics, news items, faces, and scenes were flashed on a screen. Not a single human figure held the focus for more than a moment, but the swift mounting of interrelated events proved that a demonstration lesson in civics could be exciting entertainment. There was more human appeal in a later issue called *One-Third of a Nation,* a Living Newspaper about housing. In a large setting of a four-story tenement, a fire and a family tragedy started the little man, Mr. Buttonkooper, inquiring of police, politicians, and inspectors as to how conditions had gotten so bad, why property owners did so little to improve them, and what might be done by government-supported rehousing. Onto the forestage were brought many demonstration scenes. One of the most vivid showed the history of the city in miniature, as land dealers set up a little plot of grass, with street signs a few feet apart, and sold off one lot after another to the crowds of immigrants who arrived and sat close together on the stage, each filling his plot of land. Far more than the first Living Newspaper plays, this one gave glimpses of individuals with whom the audience could sympathize and identify. While some Europeans, following Bertolt Brecht, seem to feel that too much emotional identification and illusion keep the audience from seeing the wider meaning of the play, Americans like to have a few individuals they can know and care about, even when the issue is a general one.

One of the best examples of epic theatre is Wilder's *The Skin of Our Teeth* (1942). It is not always categorized as epic theatre, because instead of social, economic, and political problems it deals with historic and mythical events and philosophical, religious, and metaphysical ideas. But its purpose is the same as that of other epic dramas—to break through the shell of the particular in order to reveal wider implications. We shall examine the play in more detail later, in relation to the theatre of the absurd, but the epic techniques used are worth noting here. The play dramatizes man's perennial need to pick up some threads of civilization and start over again after a catastrophe—here, the ice age, the flood, and war. The epic method includes the use of an expositor speaking over the loud-speaker, slides, allegorical figures, myths and parables, and finally a parade of actors quoting passages from Plato, Spinoza, and the Book of Genesis.

When we examine Arthur Miller's *Death of a Salesman* (1949) as a modern tragedy, we will find that it too is a play in which techniques of the epic theatre are used to show the wide implications of the problems of sympathetic central characters. The techniques are very different from the realism of the first two decades of this century—the settings are flexible and mobile and the scenes flow from present to past, from objective to subjective, interrupting each other with brilliant ironic effect. Yet audiences accept the play as completely realistic. Some critics try to distinguish between early realism and these "theatricalist" techniques, but audiences no longer think of the techniques as nonrealistic. As long as a play deals convincingly with a real current problem, epic drama is completely acceptable as a form of realism. As its most ardent advocate, Bertolt Brecht, kept insisting, epic theatre aims not to charm or entertain an audience but to bring it to see the truth.

BRECHT AND EPIC THEATRE

Most discussion of epic theatre is concerned with the plays and theories of Bertolt Brecht, as though he had invented the whole movement. But, as we have seen, many other people have contributed to it. Today Brecht's techniques are no longer novel, and we like him for his characters and—ironically, since he was forever preaching against illusion or too much sympathy—for his poetry and for the anguished plight of his main figures.

Brecht started writing in the chaotic, disillusioned Germany of the 1920s, when in both politics and theatre old ideas were being questioned and new

Kinds of Plays

forms were being tried. During the war, he had been a medical orderly helping to chop off limbs and patch men up quickly so that they could go back
into the trenches and be shot at again. After the war, he saw the lines of unemployed, the abortive attempts of labor groups to gain control, the terrible
inflation that wiped out all savings, the corruption, venality, and exploitation
in the cities. He enjoyed the satiric songs of the cabaret, the rowdy give-and-
take in the sports arena. He saw Max Reinhardt's productions of *The Circle
of Chalk* in Chinese style and of the eighteenth-century comedy *A Servant of
Two Masters* in the improvised-platform style of a *commedia dell' arte* troupe.
The dadaists in France were showing their contempt for established order.
The popular image of America was vivid—a land of great enthusiasm for
sports and great attainment in science and technology but of shocking contrasts between corrupt millionaires and exploited laborers—and Brecht looked
on it with both fascination and horror.

Brecht's most sensational success came in 1928 with *The Threepenny
Opera,* a bitter-sad musical satire based on John Gay's *Beggar's Opera,* which
had been the sensation of London in the 1720s and had a spectacular revival
there in the 1920s. Brecht created his own grotesque picture of the world of
beggars, thieves, and corrupt officials, of love, exploitation, and betrayal, with
many bitter comments on human depravity and with forebodings of destruction. The young composer Kurt Weill, creating a German version of American popular music, wrote songs for it that still haunt the mind. In the 1950s
the show was revived in a small off-Broadway theatre, with Lotte Lenya,
Weill's widow, playing the same leading role she had created in Germany in

FIGURE *1.29* The ironies of war.
The individual woman in her
peddler's wagon tries to survive in
the chaos of the Thirty Years'
War. Brecht's *Mother Courage,*
with Lotte Lenya in the title role.
Ruhrfestspiele Recklinghausen,
1965. Photo German Information
Center.

1928. Here, for the first time, the play caught the American audience and had a run of more than seven years.

Whereas this early play showed a cynical, demonic individual, Macheath, or "Mack the Knife," triumphing in a ruthless world, *Mother Courage and Her Children* (1941), like most of Brecht's later plays, shows a more sympathetic character trying to survive in a world that outrages all sense of what is human. Dragging her peddler's wagon across central Europe through the Thirty Years' War, Mother Courage loses her sons to the corruption of war and sees her daughter scarred and maimed and finally shot for trying to save victims of the war. After each blow, she hides her feelings and bravely takes to the road. The many songs, instead of giving charm to the piece, increase the ironic sense of the futility of war.

Two of Brecht's later plays that have been widely produced in America take the form of parables, and both borrow in method from the Chinese theatre. In *The Good Woman of Setzuan* (1943), a kind-hearted girl, set up in a shop by three roaming gods, finds that her kind heart has no place in the world of business. To save herself from complete ruin, she disguises herself as a male cousin so that she can deal ruthlessly with her kinsmen and her trading associates. She finds no way to reconcile the two ways of life. The gods only smile and tell her to go on being good, leaving the audience to conclude that perhaps they themselves should change the world of starving dependents and ruthless trade and not ask one young woman to try to lift the universe. The other parable, *The Caucasian Chalk Circle* (1948), gives an entirely new ending to the old Chinese play. Another tender-hearted girl, running away from the palace during a revolution, rescues the young prince abandoned by the heartless mother. Although the child repeatedly gets her into trouble, she loves him and takes care of him. Later the mother demands to have the child back, needing him in order to claim large estates. But a picturesque judge, the village rogue Azdak, sets up the old test of the circle of

48

FIGURE *1.30* Epic realism. Steps provide for changing relationships among characters, and simple settings in the background suggest place. Brecht's *The Good Woman of Setzuan.* University of Illinois production, directed by Charles H. Shattuck and designed by Joseph W. Scott.

FIGURES *1.31 and 1.32* Two quite different textures achieved in different productions of the same play. Brecht's *The Caucasian Chalk Circle*. University of Illinois production, directed by Charles H. Shattuck, designed by George McKinney, and costumed by Genevieve Richardson, and Carnegie Tech Theatre production, directed by Lawrence Carra, designed by Don Beaman, lighted by Bob Wolff, and costumed by Alan Kinnel.

chalk. The real mother easily pulls the child out, because the one who really loves him refuses to jerk his tender arm. The judge gives the child to the loving foster mother, repudiating old ideas of legitimacy and showing that things should go to those who are good for them, "the children to the motherly, the carts to the good drivers." In presenting the play, Brecht wanted only simple indications of setting. The Berliner Ensemble used a revolving stage and a series of small light-colored cloths on which line drawings were sketched; for instance, for the scene of the girl and her soldier sweetheart on two sides of the river, the cloths carried sketches of trees and the revolving stage brought around two rows of small reeds.

Much of Brecht's theory was developed in negative form as an attack on the established conventions of the realistic stage. He despised the conventional audience looking for emotional thrills and identifying themselves with helpless heroes on the stage. Such an audience, he felt, did not think or judge, but only drifted in pity and empathy. The play showed them man as a known thing, his fate settled and finished. Their emotions were stirred, then exhausted, and at the end they were reconciled to their imperfect world. But Brecht wanted to wake up his audience, to make them think, compare, question, and see the implication of the play for their own world, not just lose themselves in the psychological problems of the leisure class. Hence he theorized a great deal about breaking the illusion, about interrupting devices, about keeping the emotions in check. His favorite term, the *Verfremdungs-Effekt*, has usually been translated as "alienation" or "A-effect," but perhaps a better English word is "objectivity." He wanted on the stage the objectivity of a lecture by a scientist, with important demonstrations, to be watched thoughtfully. He disliked the naturalistic or Stanislavsky approach to acting in which the actor lost himself in complete identification with the character. The actor, for Brecht, could indicate a character and his social implication far better by standing at a distance. Often Brecht would tell an actor, "Say to yourself, 'He said,' in order to show the character to the audience." It is an audience-oriented kind of acting, whereas the Stanislavsky actor tries to forget the audience. Brecht was especially fascinated by Chinese acting, which presented the character with objectivity.

The term "alienation" used in connection with Brecht has caused much confusion: many people suppose that Brecht wanted to give only a cold, dull lecture. He invented the term when actors thought that talking directly toward the audience or changing scenery before the audience would break the illusion. Brecht was perfectly willing to break that kind of illusion; he was sure that the theatre would be better without it. Today, when we so easily accept the methods of epic theatre, we realize that an actor can create a new kind of illusion, even with interruptions and the fast epic pace. Certainly the central characters of Brecht, when they are well played, carry a high degree of sympathy and identification. It is not cold acting but the interruption by the narrator or by the contrasting scenes, in *Our Town* as well as in Brecht, that sets the characters at a greater aesthetic distance.

It is not coldness we want for the A-effect, but rather a more indirect way

Kinds of Plays

of showing emotions and a more broken rhythm. We have no time to indulge in expressing our surprise or grief; instead we see our emotions interrupted and superseded by the noisy movement of events. In the nineteenth century, actors used slow, sustained sobs and tears to express the emotion of Little Eva and Uncle Tom. Our rhythm is better expressed by the drum, the shot, the crash, the blare of a trumpet, or the jazz band. In *Mother Courage,* there is no time for the mother to grieve over her dead daughter. War is beginning again, she starts out on her trek, and loud military music expresses far better than she can both the intensity of her feeling and the irony of her situation. Archibald MacLeish in *J. B.* (1958) uses a similar alienation for ironic contrast in the scenes where J. B. and Sarah learn of the deaths of their children. In the first of these scenes, the drunken soldiers do not realize that the parents had not heard of their son's death. In the second, a crass photographer and a prostitute take a flash picture in the parents' faces, driving J. B. to furious anger. Audiences today are very self-conscious in the presence of a direct expression of strong emotion. The loose form of epic theatre makes it easy to superimpose an indirect intensity.

Above all, epic theatre is flexible and mobile—in setting, in acting, in its use of all aspects of theatre. Not all the fantastic stage equipment which nineteenth-century German engineers devised to lift or turn or roll realistic settings could move fast enough. Only the moving picture can show full backgrounds with speed. So epic theatre omits heavy scenery and focuses attention on the action. Audiences do not expect the kind of illusion that comes in watching a curtain open and pretending to look into a complete picture of a real place. Simple, mobile settings that change before the eyes seemed at first an entertaining novelty, but they have become a natural and convincing aspect of theatre. Some epic productions have used a complex façade, like an Eliza-

FIGURE *1.33* Epic realism. A number of cells in a prison are united in one simplified scenic structure. The individual stories add up to an indictment of the police state. Kingsley's *Darkness at Noon.* Cleveland Playhouse production, directed and designed by Frederic McConnell.

bethan stage, with upper and lower stages, either separate or connected by ramps and steps. With modern spotlighting and area lighting, it is easy to black out one area and bring a light up on another where action is already under way or to open small curtains and change simple decorative elements. Sidney Kingsley's *Darkness at Noon* (1951), a drama about Russian political trials during Stalin's time, calls for a number of prison cells equally visible to the audience. Some productions have placed several small settings side by side, as in the medieval simultaneous stage, and some, like the Cleveland Playhouse production, have used a façade like an Elizabethan stage (FIGURE *1.33*). But many epic productions have been even simpler, with properties, symbolic settings, miniature settings, or simple screens and curtains brought on as the action requires and moved by whatever means is easiest, whether let down from above, rolled in on wagons or turntables, or brought in by actors. The details are usually realistic and may be rich in texture, such as rough wood, old cloth, leather. There seems no need to hide lighting equipment, and spotlights are often placed and moved in sight of the audience. If a moon is needed, why paint it on the backdrop in nineteenth-century style or use the early twentieth-century illusion of an actor standing in moonlight from a hidden source? With the frankness of the Oriental theatre, epic style accepts a disk hung by a conspicuous chain or supported by a visible framework.

Most interesting of all these mobilities is the demonstration group or the choric mass, a device that had already been explored by Strindberg, as we shall see in Chapter 9. Simple propaganda plays and public affairs skits use a compact group of actors who can suddenly step into different roles for each episode. In *The Caucasian Chalk Circle,* Brecht has only three figures who are complete individuals, and in his production with the Berliner Ensemble he used a choric mass who part of the time sat listening to the Story Teller, then put on half-masks as they entered the story as the many other characters in the long sequence of events. The theatre thus approaches the casual forms of the oratorio, the *commedia dell' arte,* and the night club show in which the master of ceremonies has multiple roles.

What emerges in a Brecht play is a heightened sense of the individual struggling heroically in a chaotic world. In the back of his mind, Brecht looked to a Marxist revolution and the coming of Communism, but his plays do not celebrate any Communist order: they show the failure to maintain humane values in a corrupt bourgeois world. It is not surprising that they have great appeal in Western countries and, except in the special showcase of the Berliner Ensemble in East Berlin, have had little approval by the Communists, for though they make a telling diagnosis, they allow for solutions other than Communism. Brecht's epic realism may therefore be compared to the stylized realism of O'Neill's monodramas, *The Hairy Ape* and *The Emperor Jones,* although Brecht's main characters adapt themselves and maintain their integrity, yielding to pressures, like a Victorian heroine, only in appearance, not with the heart. The opposing characters may be as simple as the villains of Victorian melodrama. But the dilemma of the main character is not just a problem of personal relations or of good or bad motives. Many of

Kinds of Plays

Brecht's principal characters have no motivation at all; they are mere symptoms of a fragmented society. Hence the central portrait is built up by a large number of confrontations with the fragments of that society—symbolic characters, who are often more functional than individual, and the facts, statistics, and localities that belong to society. No one fragment is all-determining; hence there is no need for a full, enclosing, naturalistic setting. Yet each fragment must be convincing, with the right feel, smell, texture, dialect. The audience itself has to put all the fragments together and, while concerned over the plight of the individual, ask how a better social order could be built. Hence epic drama belongs to the main tradition of realism with its insistence on fact. The goal in epic theatre is the better understanding of the actual world, with the hope of improving it.

Brecht went further than the other epic playwrights in bringing back some of the theatrical intensities that had been discarded by the early realists. Realism is in one sense an impoverished form of theatre, neglecting dance, song, poetry, rhetoric, gesture, and all rhythms except those of local color. Brecht, who is himself considered one of the greatest of German poets, used song constantly and in addition often employed dance, masks, and any other intensity he could think of or borrow from other theatre traditions. The significant thing, he insisted, is that these devices must be used not to make an artificial, formalized theatre but to bring to the audience an awareness of the world today. Epic theatre is theatrical, but it is realism.

THE PERVASIVE SHADOW OF EPIC THEATRE

To dramatize the struggle between the individual and the social forces, Brecht did not hesitate to use both fanciful and historical backgrounds: an imaginary provincial country in *The Caucasian Chalk Circle*, a far-from-real China in *The Good Woman of Setzuan*, the Thirty Years' War in *Mother Courage*, and Renaissance Florence in *Galileo* (1943). But two British epic productions brought to New York in 1965—*Marat/Sade*, an English adaptation of Peter Weiss's German play, and Peter Shaffer's *The Royal Hunt of the Sun*—went much further than Brecht in mixing fantasy with history and in using all the intensities of music, dance, and poetry. These plays, like Brecht's, are concerned with violence and revolution, but they also deal much more with the spiritual dilemma of the individual than Brecht did. In *The Royal Hunt of the Sun*, the cynical, greedy Spanish conqueror Pizarro finds new understanding of faith and trust as he sees his men kill the Sun-Emperor of Peru, Atahuallpa. The play will be considered again as an example of modern tragedy, but it is also an excellent example of epic theatre. The many scenes are played continuously on a bare sloping platform, with the emperor standing majestically on an upper stage framed by a twelve-foot medallion of gold, the symbol of the sun. The choral group of soldiers and Indians mime the climb up the Andes, the battles, and the processions and chant songs of worship or lament. Visual elements are used not as background but as symbol. The curtain that ends the first act, for instance, is not the standard curtain of the theatre but a vast blood-stained cloth dragged from

53

The Theatre of Realism

FIGURE *1.34* Political leadership in a mad world. History, politics, and psychology are treated in epic form with theatrical intensity. Peter Weiss's *Marat/Sade*. Royal Shakespeare Company production, directed by Peter Brook and designed by Sally Jacobs. Photo Morris Newcombe.

the middle of the sun-medallion by howling Indians to billow out over the stage and mark the completion of the mime of the great massacre.

Even more striking use is made of a choral group in the second British import, which was directed by Peter Brook: *Marat/Sade,* or, to use the full title, *The Persecution and Assassination of Marat as Performed by the Inmates of the Asylum of Charenton under the Direction of the Marquis de Sade.* Since the characters are supposedly played by the inmates of an insane asylum, a great range of bizarre intensities, macabre tones, and group rhythms is possible. The play outdoes Brecht in making the audience take an objective and distant view as the contradictory and ironic political debates are spoken in the midst of the distorted sounds and movements of the insane. We shall study the play further in the section on the theatre of the absurd, with which it has much in common. Yet it is an epic play, relating personal philosophies to the wider political scene. It is more bitter and disillusioned than that early epic play on the French Revolution, Georg Büchner's *Danton's Death* (1835), and yet it challenges the audience to try to achieve the objectives of social revolution without the madness of revolutions of the past. As the author himself said in an interview in the *New York Times,* "We have to find solutions . . . , understand the political questions, even if we often get tired of them and they seem to us just absurd and mad."

Epic theatre seems in some ways the most characteristic and effective

Kinds of Plays

theatre form of the twentieth century. It borrows some of the best features from theatres of the past—primitive, Oriental, Greek, and Elizabethan—and absorbs many of the modern attitudes of the other arts—expressionism, abstraction, surrealism, and symbolism. As we have seen, it can handle both history and fantasy. It can deal with religious and metaphysical ideas and wide social, economic, and political forces while keeping a vivid concern with the immediate. It can relate the inner life to the outer experience. Where naturalism and early realism found no place for most of the intensities of art, epic realism has brought back into the main stream of the theatre exciting words, colors, movements, and rhythms—elements that early in the century could be found only in revivals of old plays or in the escapist theatre of romance. And, as we shall see later, epic theatre has greatly changed our approach to directing, acting, and design. At its best epic theatre is far more than a flexible device for propaganda or for demonstration of diverse facts and ideas on the stage. It can be a very rich and exciting theatrical experience, tracing the development of human character in relation to many events, subjective and objective. It is one of our mid-century approaches to what we sometimes speak of as "total theatre," a theatre that draws on all the appeals to the eye, the ear, the mind, and the soul.

In its many forms, realism has been the most vital and serious approach to theatre in the twentieth century. Even as it has transcended a naive interest in surface details to show people in their deeper psychological and philosophical aspects through selected and abstract realism and to study people in wider perspective through epic realism, it has kept the strong scientific purpose of understanding the world as it is in the hope of improving it. The simple excitement of discovery has not yet been exhausted, and the early forms of realism and naturalism have persisted alongside the modified or more complex varieties. As we shall see in Part III, several of the new developments in moviemaking since the Second World War—the Italian realism of the forties, the French "New Wave" of the fifties, and the realism of the English "Angry Young Men" in the fifties and sixties—have gained their vitality from the same interest in man's environment that motivated Zola and Antoine at the end of the last century. The realistic approach has made a strong impact on the old traditions of tragedy and comedy and has even at times imbued the theatre of color and romance, apparently so different from realism, with some of its serious concerns.

EXERCISES AND DEMONSTRATIONS

1. NATURALISM. In Sidney Kingsley's *Dead End,* Baby-face Martin, a gangster murderer, back in the slums where he grew up, hopes for a sentimental farewell with his mother before running away from New York. Violent, confused emotions smolder beneath the surface, occasionally erupting but mostly held down to a weary monotone. The rhythm is broken into spurts because no words can relieve the tight inner tensions.

55

MARTIN Hello, Mom! How are yuh? (*Pause.*) It's me. (*No recognition.*) I had my face fixed.

(*There is a moment of silence. She finally speaks in an almost inaudible monotone.*)

MRS. MARTIN Yuh no good tramp!

MARTIN Mom!

MRS. MARTIN What're yuh doin' here?

MARTIN Aintcha glad tuh see me? (*She suddenly smacks him a sharp crack across the cheek.*)

MRS. MARTIN That's how glad I am.

MARTIN (*rubs his cheek. He stammers*) 'At's a great hello.

MRS. MARTIN Yuh dog! Yuh stinkin' yellow dog yuh!

MARTIN Mom! What kin' a talk is 'at? Gese, Mom . . .

MRS. MARTIN Don't call me Mom! Yuh ain't no son a mine. What do yuh want from me now?

MARTIN Nuttin'. I just . . .

MRS. MARTIN (*Her voice rises, shrill, hysterical*) Then git out a here! Before I crack yuh goddam face again. Git out a here!

MARTIN (*flaring*) Why, yuh ole tramp, I killed a guy fer lookin' at me da way yew are!

MRS. MARTIN (*stares at him and nods slowly. Then, quietly*) Yeah . . . You're a killer all right. . . . You're a murderer . . . you're a butcher, sure! Why don't yuh leave me ferget yuh? Ain' I got troubles enough with the cops and newspapers botherin' me? An' Johnny and Martha . . .

MARTIN What's a mattuh wid 'em?

MRS. MARTIN None a yer business! Just leave us alone! Yuh never brought nothin' but trouble. Don't come back like a bad penny! . . . Just stay away and leave us alone . . . an' die . . . but leave us alone! (*She turns her back on him, and starts to go.*)

MARTIN Hey, wait!

MRS. MARTIN (*pauses*) What?

MARTIN Need any dough?

MRS. MARTIN Keep yer blood money.

MARTIN Yuh gonna rat on me . . . gonna tell a cops?

MRS. MARTIN No. They'll get yuh soon enough.

MARTIN Not me! Not Martin! Huh, not Baby-face Martin!

MRS. MARTIN (*mutters*) Baby-face! Baby-face! I remember . . . (*She begins to sob, clutching her stomach.*) In here . . . in here! Kickin'! That's where yuh come from. God! I ought to be cut open here fer givin' yuh life . . . murderer!!! (*She shuffles away, up the street, weeping quietly. His hand goes to his cheek.*)

2. NATURALISM. This scene from *Dead End* illustrates the dream of escape confronting the appalling facts. Baby-face Martin, dreaming of regaining his boyhood innocence, hunts up his former sweetheart to get her to run away with him. She has been told someone is waiting for her in the old alley by the river.

FRANCEY Fuh th' love a God! Marty! (*Eagerly*) How are yuh, Marty?

MARTIN Read duh papers!

FRANCEY Yuh did somethin' to yuh face.

56

MARTIN   Yeah. Plastic, dey call it.

FRANCEY   They said yuh wuz out aroun' Coloradah—th' noospapuhs! Gee, I'm glad to see yuh! (MARTIN *slips his arm around her waist and draws her tight to his body. As his lips grope for hers,* FRANCEY *turns her face away.* MARTIN *tries to pull her face around. She cries furiously*) No . . . don' kiss me on a lips!

MARTIN   (*releasing her, puzzled*)   What? What's a matter? (*He can't believe this. He frowns.*) I ain't good enough for yuh?

FRANCEY   (*quickly*)   No. It ain't dat. It ain't yew. It's me. I got a sore on my mouth. Fuh yuhr own good, I don't want yuh to kiss me, dat's why.

MARTIN   I ain't nevuh fuhgot da way yew kiss.

FRANCEY   (*wistfully*)   I ain't neithuh. (*She laughs.*) Go on! You wit all yer fancy dames. Where do I come off?

MARTIN   Dey don't mean nuttin'.

FRANCEY   Dat chorus goil . . . what's 'er name?

MARTIN   Nuttin'. She ain't got nuttin' . . . no guts, no fire. . . . But yew been boinin' in my blood . . . evuh since . . .

FRANCEY   An' yew been in mine . . . if yuh wanna know.

MARTIN   Remembuh dat foist night . . . on a roof?

FRANCEY   Yeah, I remembuh . . . da sky was full a stars, an' I was full a dreamy ideas. Dat was me foist time. I was fourteen, goin' on fifteen.

MARTIN   Yeah. It wuz mine too. It wuz terrific. Hit me right wheah I live . . . like my back wuz meltin'. An' I wuz so sca'd when yuh started laffin' an' cryin', crazy like . . . (*They both laugh, enjoying the memory, a little embarrassed by it.*)

.   .   .

FRANCEY   A couple a crazy kids we were! We wuz gonna git married. I bought a ring at da five an' dime staw.

MARTIN   Yeah. Ony we didn' have money enough fuh de license. Gee, it seems like yestiddy. We wuz talkin' about it right heah.

FRANCEY   Yestiddy! It seems like a million yeahs!

MARTIN   (*as voices are heard coming from the East River Terrace*)   Wait! (*They separate. Someone goes by.*)

FRANCEY   Marty, listen! Yuh got ta take care a yuhself. Yuh gotta go way an' hide. I don' want 'em to git yuh!

.   .   .

MARTIN   I'll tell yuh what . . . I'll scram out a heah. I'll scram . . . if yew come wit me.

FRANCEY   Ah, what do yuh want me fer? A broken-down hoor.

MARTIN   Shut up!

FRANCEY   I wouldn' be good fuh yuh.

MARTIN   I know what I want.

FRANCEY   (*laughs, crazily*)   Yeah. Dis is a swell pipe-dream I'm havin'! I'm Minnie de Moocher kickin' a gong aroun'!

MARTIN   Listen! I got de dough now, kid. We kin do it now.

FRANCEY   But I'm sick, Marty! Don't yuh see? I'm sick!

MARTIN   What's a matter wid yuh?

FRANCEY   (*almost inaudibly*)   What do yuh think?

(MARTIN *looks at her for a long time. He sees her. The nostalgic dream is finished. His lips begin to curl in disgust.*)

MARTIN   Why didncha git a job?

FRANCEY   Dey don' grow on trees!
MARTIN   Why didncha starve foist?
FRANCEY   Why didnchou?
(MARTIN *makes no effort to conceal his growing disgust. Turns away.*
FRANCEY *suddenly shouts, fiercely, at the top of her lungs*)
FRANCEY   Well what ta hell did yuh expect?
MARTIN   I don' know.

3. IMPRESSIONISM.   The scene is not so brutal as those from *Dead End.*
The inner action is not shown in the words, but the actor must express the
confused feelings by a suppressed tone and hesitant rhythm. The scene is
near the end of Chekhov's *Cherry Orchard.* Everyone expects Lopahin to
propose to Varya, but he fails to do it. He is a very successful rising businessman, but he has been too busy to learn much about human relations, and
Varya, though only a foster daughter of the aristocrats, has somehow frightened him. Still, he has assured Madame Ranevsky that he will propose to her
and settle the matter. Varya comes in and pretends to be looking for something she packed in the luggage.

VARYA (*looking a long while over the things*)   It is strange, I can't find it
    anywhere.
LOPAHIN   What are you looking for?
VARYA   I packed it myself, and I can't remember. (*A pause.*)
LOPAHIN   Where are you going now, Varvara Mihailovna?
VARYA   I? To the Ragulins. I have arranged to go to them to look after the
    house—as a housekeeper.
LOPAHIN   That's in Yashnevo? It'll be seventy miles away. (*A pause.*) So
    this is the end of life in this house!
VARYA (*looking among the things*)   Where is it? Perhaps I put it in the
    trunk. Yes, life in this house is over—there will be no more of it.
LOPAHIN   And I'm just off to Kharkov—by this next train. I've a lot of
    business there. I'm leaving Epihodov here, and I've taken him on.
VARYA   Really!
LOPAHIN   This time last year we had snow already, if you remember; but
    now it's so fine and sunny. Though it's cold, to be sure—three degrees
    of frost.
VARYA   I haven't looked. (*A pause.*) And besides, our thermometer's
    broken. (*A pause.*)
(*Voice at the door from the yard: "Yermolay Alexeyevitch!"*)
LOPAHIN (*as though he had long been expecting this summons*)   This
    minute!
(LOPAHIN *goes out quickly.* VARYA, *sitting on the floor and laying her head
on a bag full of clothes, sobs quietly.*)

4. IMPLICIT ACTING IN REALISM.   Contrast the explicit acting of both the
classic tradition and nineteenth-century melodrama with the implicit acting
used in all the early varieties of realism and often in epic realism. For explicit
acting, the character consciously describes his feeling in words while the actor
illustrates the words by appropriate tones and gestures. For implicit acting,

EXERCISES AND DEMONSTRATIONS

the actor must develop the deeper feelings that the character is scarcely conscious of or is trying to hide.

The following passages from three plays show emotional exits of women, two with explicit description of feelings and one with the complex deeper feelings implied. The first passage is from Aeschylus' *Prometheus Bound* (fifth century B.C.) in Edith Hamilton's translation. The second is from *Uncle Tom's Cabin* (1852), George L. Aiken's dramatization of the novel by Harriet Beecher Stowe. The third is from Lillian Hellman's *The Little Foxes* (1939).

a. The girl Io, fleeing from Zeus's attentions and tormented by the gadfly sent by Hera, the Queen of Heaven, describes in words her maddening torture and despair as she again takes up her long flight.

> Io   Oh, misery. Oh, misery.
> A frenzy tears me.
> Madness strikes my mind.
> I burn. A frantic sting—
> an arrow never forged with fire.
> My heart is beating at its walls in terror.
> My eyes are whirling wheels.
> Away. Away. A raging wind of fury
> sweeps through me.
> My tongue has lost its power.
> My words are like a turbid stream,
> wild waves that dash against a surging sea,
> the black sea of madness. (*Exit* Io.)

b. Eliza, running away with her child who has been sold, overhears three men who have traced her to a house near the river, greedy to capture her and sell her. She expresses her fears and decisions very explicitly.

ELIZA   Powers of mercy, protect me! How shall I escape these human blood-hounds? Ah! the window—the river of ice! That dark stream lies between me and liberty! Surely the ice will bear my trifling weight. It is my only chance of escape—better sink beneath the cold waters, with my child locked in my arms, than have him torn from me and sold into bondage. He sleeps upon my breast.—Heaven, I put my trust in thee! (*Gets out of window.*)

MARKS   Well, Tom Loker, what do you say?

LOKER   It'll do! (*Strikes his hand violently on the table.*—ELIZA *screams.*— *They both start to their feet.*—ELIZA *disappears.*—*Music, chord.*)

HALEY   By the land, there she is now! (*They all rush to the window.*)

MARKS   She's making for the river!

LOKER   Let's after her!

Scene V. Snow Landscape—Music.

(*Enter* ELIZA *with* HARRY [*her child*], *hurriedly.*)

ELIZA   They press upon my footsteps—the river is my only hope. Heaven grant me strength to reach it, ere they overtake me! Courage, my child! —we will be free—or perish! (*Rushes off. Music continues.*)

c. Aunt Birdie, the fragile aristocrat in *The Little Foxes,* frightened and ordered about by her husband and his brother, works up her nerve to try to rescue her niece from the plans of the scheming family. When her husband slaps her, she has to hide her feelings. She is fragile and delicate but suggests strong contradictory emotions underneath.

> BIRDIE (*whispering frantically, holding* ALEXANDRA's *hands*) He's my son. My own son. But you are more to me—more to me than my own child. I love you more than anybody else—
>
> ALEXANDRA Don't worry about the horses. I'm sorry I told you.
>
> BIRDIE (*her voice rising*) *I am not worrying about the horses.* I am worrying about *you.* You are *not* going to marry Leo. I am not going to let them do that to you—
>
> ALEXANDRA Marry? to Leo? (*Laughs*) I wouldn't marry, Aunt Birdie. I've never even thought about it—
>
> BIRDIE But they have thought about it. (*Wildly*) Zan, I couldn't stand to think about such a thing. You and—
>
> (OSCAR *has come into the doorway on* ALEXANDRA's *speech. He is standing quietly, listening.*)
>
> ALEXANDRA (*laughs*) But I'm not going to marry. And I'm certainly not going to marry Leo.
>
> BIRDIE Don't you understand? They'll make you. They'll make you—
>
> ALEXANDRA (*takes* BIRDIE's *hands, quietly, firmly*) That's foolish, Aunt Birdie. I'm grown now. Nobody can make me do anything.
>
> BIRDIE I just couldn't stand—
>
> OSCAR (*sharply*) Birdie. (BIRDIE *looks up, draws quickly away from* ALEXANDRA. *She stands rigid, frightened. Quietly*) Birdie, get your hat and coat.
>
> ADDIE (*calls from upstairs*) Come on, baby. Your mama's waiting for you, and she ain't nobody to keep waiting.
>
> ALEXANDRA All right. (*Then softly, embracing* BIRDIE) Good night, Aunt Birdie. (*As she passes* OSCAR) Good night, Uncle Oscar. (BIRDIE *begins to move slowly toward the door as* ALEXANDRA *climbs the stairs.* ALEXANDRA *is almost out of view when* BIRDIE *reaches* OSCAR *in the doorway. As* BIRDIE *quickly attempts to pass him, he slaps her hard, across the face.* BIRDIE *cries out, puts her hand to her face. On the cry,* ALEXANDRA *turns, begins to run down the stairs.*)
>
> ALEXANDRA Aunt Birdie! What happened? What happened? I—
>
> BIRDIE (*softly, without turning*) Nothing, darling. Nothing happened. I only—I only twisted my ankle. (*She goes out.* ALEXANDRA *stands on the stairs looking after her as if she were puzzled and frightened.*)

5. STYLIZED ENVIRONMENT. In *The Hairy Ape,* O'Neill faces Yank with a stylized group of rich people coming out of a Fifth Avenue church and repeating a few trite phrases in unison and in a mechanical, exaggerated rhythm. Write and perform a similar stylized chatter for other groups who would be equally preoccupied and indifferent to Yank's need to communicate—at a sports event, a dance, a discussion of a favorite television actor, etc. Each director will elaborate the tone and movement. Here is O'Neill's suggestion of what he wanted:

EXERCISES AND DEMONSTRATIONS

The crowd from church enter from the right, sauntering slowly and affect-
edly, their heads held stiffly up, looking neither to right nor left, talking in
toneless, simpering voices. The women are rouged, calcimined, dyed, over-
dressed to the nth degree. The men are in Prince Alberts, high hats, spats,
canes, etc. A procession of gaudy marionettes, yet with something of the
relentless horror of Frankensteins in their detached, mechanical unawareness.

VOICES Dear Doctor Caiphas! He is so sincere!
What was the sermon? I dozed off.
About the radicals, my dear—and the false doctrines that are being
preached.
We must organize a hundred per cent American bazaar.
And let everyone contribute one one-hundredth per cent of their
income tax.
What an original idea!
We can devote the proceeds to rehabilitating the veil of the temple.
But that has been done so many times.

YANK (*glaring from one to the other of them—with an insulting snort of*
scorn) Huh! Huh! (*Without seeming to see him, they make wide*
detours to avoid the spot where he stands in the middle of the sidewalk.)

6. NATURALISTIC CHARACTER IN A STYLIZED ENVIRONMENT. In this
scene of O'Neill's *The Hairy Ape,* Yank has just been thrown out of a labor
union office. O'Neill pictures him as brooding disconsolately like Rodin's
"The Thinker," but an actor might also explore his thwarted violence on
foot, shadowboxing, ready to punch back at the people who have rejected
him, then half relaxing but realizing that hostility faces him on every side.

YANK (*bitterly*) So dem boids don't tink I belong neider. Aw, to hell wit
'em! Dey're in de wrong pew—de same old bull—soap-boxes and Salvation Army—no guts! Cut out an hour offen de job a day and make
me happy! Gimme a dollar more a day and make me happy! Tree
square a day, and cauliflowers in de front yard—ekal rights—a woman
and kids—a lousy vote—and I'm all fixed for Jesus, huh? Aw, hell!
What does dat get yuh? Dis ting's in your inside, but it ain't your
belly. Feedin' your face—sinkers and coffee—dat don't touch it. It's
way down—at de bottom. Yuh can't grab it, and yuh can't stop it. It
moves, and everything moves. It stops and de whole woild stops. Dat's
me now—I don't tick, see?—I'm a busted Ingersoll, dat's what. Steel
was me, and I owned de woild. Now I ain't steel, and de woild owns
me. Aw, hell! I can't see—it's all dark, get me? It's all wrong! (*He*
turns a bitter mocking face up like an ape gibbering at the moon.)
Say, youse up dere, Man in de Moon, yuh look so wise, gimme de
answer, huh? Slip me de inside dope, de information right from de
stable—where do I get off at, huh?

7. FRUSTRATED NATURALISTIC CHARACTER IN STYLIZED ENVIRONMENT.
Write a composite group of scenes about a young man either in college or beginning to make his way in a city as he comes into contact with different
people and institutions and finds that nobody is interested in his private feel-

ings, that he is treated as just another number. Arrange the speeches and scenes in climactic order, with some phrases repeated over and over in growing intensity until the young man bursts out in violent protest or angry attack.

8. ACTING IN ABSTRACT REALISM. Select characters and scenes from Thornton Wilder's *Our Town* for practice in suggesting meaning beyond the immediate action. Many scenes are solos or are almost completely abstracted from the other characters and the place. The Stage Manager, who is himself a resident of the town and a folksy, old-fashioned New England character, makes an interesting subject for interpretation. He talks directly to the audience and often points out the places on the stage where the audience is to imagine certain things. One of his best acting scenes is his introduction for the last act, starting with relaxed chatter about changes in Grover's Corners and the family tombstones, moving on to the historical tombstones and then to that "something way down deep that's eternal about every human being." None of the other characters speaks directly to the audience, but several have their enraptured moments when they see the far-reaching implications of what they are saying. Try the drugstore scene of the second act when George and Emily first realize that they are meant for each other. In the midst of imagined everyday surroundings and with short phrases of dialogue, the characters must convey a hushed sense of the importance of the moment in their lives. Good solos are Rebecca's awestruck recital at the end of the first act of the address on the letter received by her friend and Emily's farewell to Grover's Corners near the end of the play, in which the lines carry her feeling of loving enchantment.

9. ACTING IN ORIENTAL MAKE-BELIEVE. This scene is the self-introduction of Mrs. Ma, the first wife of the rich Lord Ma, in *The Circle of Chalk* (Ethel Van der Veer's version). The gong rings out as the actress enters. The orchestra accompanies her walk downstage with a melody that emphasizes her voluptuous, ruthless character. Putting her hands together in front of her, she makes circles in the air toward the audience as she bows. She points and makes the audience aware of where the clerk is expected to appear. The opening song should have some lyric intensity, with a change to a more direct manner yet very insinuating and knowing, the lady confiding her feelings almost with a wink at the audience. She might carry a fan, closing it vigorously when thinking of murdering her husband but flirting and insinuating with it.

MRS. MA   The men do not cease
To eulogize my charms,
And because I desire their pleasure
There is vermilion upon my lips
And bright colors glorify my cheeks.
The rouge and white paint may disappear;
It takes only a basin
Of pure water.

EXERCISES AND DEMONSTRATIONS

I occupy the important position of First Wife to Ma Chun-shing. He has a Second Wife by the name of Hai-t'ang, a daughter of some person named Ch'ang. She has given our husband a son who is already five years of age. . . . For me, I have succeeded in imposing upon the confidence of my lord Ma. Near here dwells a clerk named Ch'ao, who is as handsome as a spring morning and passionately adores the gentler sex. I maintain with him certain relations and appreciate his rare qualities. Also, my particular wish, my most ardent desire, is to undo this Ma Chun-shing, in order to live always with Ch'ao as a wife with her husband. Today, seeing that the excellent lord Ma is from home, I have sent someone to Ch'ao with a request that he pass by here. I hope that any moment he may arrive.

10. ACTING IN ORIENTAL MAKE-BELIEVE. Try the self-introduction of Ch'ao in *The Circle of Chalk*. The clerk Ch'ao, obviously a dashing, wicked schemer, struts on with high, exaggerated steps and bows elaborately to three sections of the audience. At "I shall enter," he carefully opens the imaginary sliding doors and steps over the six-inch threshold.

CH'AO   My station in life
Is that of a clerk.
But privately
There are two things I love
Surpassingly:
Good wine
And the women
Of other men.

What is the present object of my affections? A lady whose cheeks rival the most beautiful flowers. . . . My name is Ch'ao. I hold the position of clerk at the court of Ch'ing-ch'iu. Near here lives the First Wife of the Yuan-wei, Ma Chun-shing. One day when he invited me to dine with him, I saw by chance this Wife who is endowed with a most seductive face, the equal of which it may be doubted if heaven or earth has ever produced. The sight of this charming beauty struck deep into my heart. Night and day she is present in my thoughts, before the eyes of my mind. I imagine that she also had fixed her regard upon me because, imposing upon the confidence of her husband, she would hold with me certain relations not entirely in accord with morality. She has begged me to come to see her today. Let us go and see her. We do not yet know what is the motive of the message. I now have arrived at the house where she lives. I shall enter without being announced. . . . Madam, you have commanded my presence. May I learn what you desire of me?

11. DEMONSTRATION OF SOCIAL CHANGE IN EPIC THEATRE. Write a scenario list of topics and scenes that could be staged with simple properties and few actors to show the various attitudes, personal and institutional, involved in a social change—for example, a new tax, a new regulation, a new custom, a new way of getting around an old regulation.

63

12. USE OF DEBATE AND DEMONSTRATION IN EPIC THEATRE.   Plan an animated, dramatized debate, creating for each side of the question a character with personal reasons for defending it and inventing several short scenes showing the particular people who are affected and the important people who state the principles involved or the conclusions to be drawn.

13. ANIMATED REPORT IN EPIC THEATRE.   Write and stage an animated report, for example, a report of an investigation or a treasurer's report, using several actors as characterized participants or witnesses or as persons who bring in facts. What visual aids, including devices used in television commercials, can be brought in or adapted for an open stage?

14. DRAMATIZATION OF A NEWS EVENT IN EPIC THEATRE.   Write a composite scene for the Living Newspaper, dramatizing moments of a news event to show how it affects or involves a variety of people. Plan dramatic scenes, announcements or proclamations, and visual elaboration such as still photographs to be projected on a wall or screen and statements and headlines to be shown on placards let down from above the stage or brought on by actors.

SUGGESTED READING

PLAYS: REALISM AND NATURALISM

A cheerful, sentimental realism appeared in T. W. Robertson, *Caste* (1867), but the naturalistic struggle of the individual against his environment was established by Henrik Ibsen's plays of the eighties, starting with *A Doll's House* (1879), followed by *Ghosts* (1881), *An Enemy of the People* (1882), *The Wild Duck* (1884), and *Hedda Gabler* (1890). Even more drastic in their naturalism are August Strindberg's *The Father* (1887) and the shorter *Miss Julie* (1888). In Russia, Anton Chekhov showed the helpless struggle of middle- and upper-class people in *The Three Sisters* (1901) and *The Cherry Orchard* (1904), while Maxim Gorki presented the suffering dregs in *The Lower Depths* (1902). In Ireland, Sean O'Casey made naturalism comic and poetic, especially in *Juno and the Paycock* (1924). Eugene O'Neill established naturalism in America, and his one-acts of the sea, called *Moon of the Caribbees* or *The Long Voyage Home* (1916–18), are among the best examples of impressionist technique. His best full-length naturalistic plays are *Beyond the Horizon* (1920), *Anna Christie* (1921), *Desire Under the Elms* (1924), and *Long Day's Journey into Night* (1956). A city block is dramatized in Elmer Rice, *Street Scene* (1929). Naturalism is comic and racy in Jack Kirkland and Erskine Caldwell, *Tobacco Road* (1933). Frustration leads to some hope of social reform in Clifford Odets, *Awake and Sing!* (1935), and to a strong hope in Sidney Kingsley, *Dead End* (1935). Tennessee Williams created a tender naturalism in *The Glass Menagerie* (1944) and *Night of the Iguana* (1961) and a much more relentless struggle with difficult facts in *A Streetcar Named Desire* (1947) and *Cat on a Hot Tin Roof* (1955). In *All My Sons* (1947) Arthur Miller continued the compact play form initiated by Ibsen, as did William Inge in *Come Back, Little Sheba* (1950), *Picnic* (1952), and *Bus Stop* (1955). The most vivid English play of the new realism of the 1950s is Shelagh Delaney, *A Taste of Honey* (1958).

64

Most strong modern plays can be called selected realism or comedy melo-dramas, from Arthur W. Pinero, *The Second Mrs. Tanqueray* (1887), on. Bernard Shaw's plays usually add some elements of high comedy, as in *Candida* (1895), *The Devil's Disciple* (1897), and *Man and Superman* (1903). Many twentieth-century plays of this kind are studies of a particular environment: war, in Max-well Anderson and Laurence Stallings, *What Price Glory* (1924); night clubs and gangsters, in George Abbott and Philip Dunning, *Broadway* (1926); young wage earners, in Maxwell Anderson, *Saturday's Children* (1927); a newspaper staff, in Ben Hecht and Charles MacArthur, *The Front Page* (1928); stage actors, in George S. Kaufman and Edna Ferber, *The Royal Family* (1928) and *Stage Door* (1936); conniving congressmen, in Anderson, *Both Your Houses* (1933).

A possessive mother is defeated in Sidney Howard, *The Silver Cord* (1926), and a possessive father is defeated by the poet Robert Browning in Rudolf Besier, *The Barretts of Wimpole Street* (1930). Economic evil is defeated in Lillian Hellman, *The Little Foxes* (1939), and Fascist evil in her *The Watch on the Rhine* (1941). Men alienated by war rejoin the human race in Robert Ardrey, *Thunder Rock* (1939), and John Patrick, *The Hasty Heart* (1945). Triumph over physical handicap is the theme of Dore Schary, *Sunrise at Campobello* (1959), about Franklin Delano Roosevelt, and William Gibson, *The Miracle Worker* (1959), about Helen Keller. The struggle of a rising Negro family in the city is the theme of Lorraine Hansberry, *A Raisin in the Sun* (1959).

PLAYS: ABSTRACT REALISM

Before Thornton Wilder wrote *Our Town* (1938), he experimented with the form in several one-act plays, notably *The Pullman Car Hiawatha, The Happy Journey from Camden to Trenton,* and *The Long Christmas Dinner,* published together in 1931.

PLAYS: MONODRAMAS OF STYLIZED REALISM

The monodramas of Eugene O'Neill, *The Emperor Jones* (1920) and *The Hairy Ape* (1922), were followed not only by fully expressionist plays but by a number of monodramas that present rather fully one or two characters against a baffling fragmented environment, notably Eugène Ionesco, *The Chairs* (1952) and *The Killer* (1959), John Osborne, *Luther* (1961) and *Inadmissible Evidence* (1964), and Arthur Miller, *After the Fall* (1963).

PLAYS: EPIC REALISM

In presenting larger aspects of the French Revolution, Georg Büchner antici-pated the epic drama in *Danton's Death* (1835). Paul Claudel's *The Book of Christopher Columbus* and *The Satin Slipper* were published in 1930. Sidney Howard told the story of the fight against yellow fever in *Yellow Jack* (1934), and Moss Hart told the story of Air Force training in *Winged Victory* (1943). Bertolt Brecht's most noteworthy plays are *The Threepenny Opera* (1928), *Mother Courage* (1941), *Galileo* (1943), *The Good Woman of Setzuan* (1943), and *The Caucasian Chalk Circle* (1948). Thornton Wilder used epic techniques in *Our Town* and *The Skin of Our Teeth* (1942). The historical American festival plays,

65

as we shall see, use many epic techniques. Especially interesting is the play about the Alamo by Ramsey Yelvington, *A Cloud of Witnesses* (1959). Three plays of the sixties use epic techniques to present strong historical figures against a wide background: Thomas More in Robert Bolt, *A Man for All Seasons* (1960), Pizarro and the Inca Emperor Atahuallpa in Peter Shaffer, *The Royal Hunt of the Sun* (1964), and the revolutionary leader Marat in Peter Weiss, *The Persecution and Assassination of Marat as Performed by the Inmates of the Asylum of Charenton Under the Direction of the Marquis de Sade* (English version by Geoffrey Skelton, verse adaptation by Adrian Mitchell, 1964).

CRITICAL WORKS: REALISM AND NATURALISM

The best full discussion of realism and the ways in which it has been modified in the twentieth century is John Gassner, *Form and Idea in Modern Theatre* (1956), expanded as *Directions in Modern Theatre and Drama* (1965). A vivid account of the naturalist revolution and the new "free theatre" of the 1880s and 90s is John Mason Brown, *The Modern Theatre in Revolt* (1929), reprinted in his *Dramatis Personae** (1963). A full account of the social purposes of realism and several of the revolts against realism is found in Mordecai Gorelik, *New Theatres for Old** (1940). Two books on Zola present the early ideals of realism and naturalism: Bess G. Sondel, *Zola's Naturalistic Theory with Particular Reference to the Drama* (1939), and Lawson A. Carter, *Zola and the Theatre* (1963).

Completely opposed views are expressed in Sheldon Cheney, *The Theatre: Three Thousand Years of Drama, Acting, and Stagecraft* (1929), which shows a strong prejudice against realism, and Lee Simonson, *The Stage Is Set** (1932), which shows how much theatres of the past made use of realistic detail and illusion. A vivid comment on realism is Henry Adler's short article, "To Hell with Society," reprinted from the *Tulane Drama Review* in R. W. Corrigan, *The Theatre in the Twentieth Century** (1963). Jean-Paul Sartre dismisses local color and environment as unimportant in "Forgers of Myths," *Theatre Arts* (1946), reprinted in Rosamond Gilder, *Theatre Arts Anthology* (1950), and Corrigan, *The Modern Theatre* (1964).

Constantin Stanislavsky's lively autobiography, *My Life in Art** (1923), also published in English in Moscow in a different arrangement, can be supplemented by the autobiography of his partner, V. Nemirovitch-Dantchenko, *My Life in the Russian Theatre* (1936; repr., 1966).

Stanislavsky's three books on acting—*An Actor Prepares* (1936) on inner techniques, *Building a Character* (1949) and *Creating a Role* (1961) on outer techniques—can be supplemented by his analytical notes on particular plays, *Stanislavsky Produces Othello* (1948) and *The Sea Gull as Produced by Stanislavsky* (1952). Two pupils and associates of Stanislavsky have written elementary textbooks for Americans: Richard Boleslavsky, *Acting: The First Six Lessons* (1933), and Michael Chekhov, *To the Actor: On the Technique of Acting* (1953). The experience of the Group Theatre in the thirties, the first American group to use the Stanislavsky method, is told by one of the founders, Harold Clurman, in *The Fervent Years** (1945). Two issues of the *Tulane Drama Review* (T25 and T26, Autumn and Winter, 1964), devoted to "Stanislavski and America," give reminiscences and analyses by a number of people.

66   * Available in paperback edition.

Thornton Wilder's great following of readers and audiences around the world and his hopeful view of man have provoked many attacks and some ardent defense. Rex Burbank, *Thornton Wilder* (1961), gives a good general view of Wilder and calls attention to such good articles on Wilder as that by Malcolm Cowley in the *Saturday Review of Literature,* now *Saturday Review,* (Oct. 6, 1956), and one by Edmund Fuller in *The American Scholar,* XXVIII (Spring, 1959).

CRITICAL WORKS: ORIENTAL THEATRE

The best short book on the Chinese theatre, Jack Chen, *The Chinese Theatre* (1922), has long been out of print. A. C. Scott, *The Classical Theatre of China* (1957), and Cecilia Zung, *Secrets of the Chinese Theatre* (1937; repr., 1964), are very useful. Good color photographs and a good text in English appear in Kalvodová-Sís-Vaniš, *The Chinese Theatre* (1959). L. C. Arlington's full account, *The Chinese Theatre,* with splendid color illustrations, was published in several languages in Shanghai in 1930, and the English version was reprinted in New York by Blom in 1965. For a survey of translations and adaptations, see Henry W. Wells, "Chinese Drama in English," in *Yearbook of Comparative Literature* (1965). An anthology of the stories and best scenes of a large number of plays, *Famous Chinese Plays,* edited by Arlington and Harold Acton, was reprinted by Russell and Russell in 1964.

The two early twentieth-century books on the Japanese Noh theatre have recently been reprinted in paperback: Ernest F. Fenellosa and Ezra Pound, *"Noh" or Accomplishment** (1917), and Arthur Waley, *The Nō Plays of Japan** (1922). Both contain good introductions and translations. Shio Sakanishi presents several of the Noh farcical interludes in *The Ink-Smeared Lady and Other Kyogen** (1960).

The Japanese Travel Bureau has issued in several revisions a good short booklet on Japanese Noh plays. Z. Toki is the author of one version (1954). There are several de luxe books on Noh stage, costumes, and masks. The booklet by Seiroku Noma, *Masks* (1957), is excellent. *Theatre in Japan,* compiled by the Japanese National Commission for UNESCO and published in 1963 by the Ministry of Finance in Tokyo, is a good summary and introduction to the more popular plays the tourist is likely to see on the Noh, Kabuki, and puppet stages. *The Noh Drama,* a collection of thirty plays in new translations, is published in three volumes, beginning in 1955.

Zoe Kincaid, *Kabuki: The Popular Stage of Japan* (1925), is still useful, but more up-to-date are Earle Ernst, *The Kabuki Theatre* (1957) and *Three Japanese Plays from the Traditional Theatre* (1959). *Four Major Plays of Chikamatsu,* translated by Donald Keene* (1961), is a selection from Keene's translations of eleven plays, *Major Plays of Chikamatsu* (1961). Faubian Bowers has a lively sketch of the popular Kabuki in *Japanese Theatre** (1959), and in *Theatre in the East: A Survey of Asian Dance and Drama* (1951) he includes China, India, and South Asia as well as Japan.

* Available in paperback edition.

67

Mordecai Gorelik has written on epic theatre in "Theatre as a Tribunal," Ch. 9 of *New Theatres for Old** (1940), and in "An Epic Catechism," *Tulane Drama Review* (T5, Autumn, 1959). The Living Newspaper is described by Hallie Flanagan in her account of the Federal Theatre, *Arena* (1940).

The most active American promoter and expositor of Bertolt Brecht has been Eric Bentley, who wrote about him in *The Playwright as Thinker** (1946), translated two plays in *Parables for the Theatre** (1948; rev. ed., 1965), and edited *Seven Plays by Bertolt Brecht* (1961).

Three lively books on Brecht are Jack Willett, *The Theatre of Bertolt Brecht* (1959), Martin Esslin, *Brecht: His Life and Work* (1960), and Ronald Gray, *Brecht** (1961). Eric Bentley wrote a full review of the Willett and Esslin books in the *Tulane Drama Review* (T8, Summer, 1960). The *Tulane Drama Review* for Autumn, 1961 (T13), was devoted to Brecht, with an especially good article by Werner Hecht, "The Development of Brecht's Theory of the Epic, 1918–1933." Martin Esslin added another article, "Brecht, the Absurd, and the Future," in the *Tulane Drama Review* for Summer, 1963 (T20).

68   * Available in paperback edition.

SUGGESTED READING

CHAPTER TWO

THE THEATRE OF ROMANCE: ROMANTIC DRAMA AND THE MUSICAL

The Romantic Play

Some people go to the theatre not for a realistic picture of the world they live in but for color and romance. They want exotic scenery, music and dance, and a sad-sweet story of long ago or faraway. They want to escape from the petty, the dull, the usual, to find release from daily frustration. They want to identify with the romantic hero, who does big things, makes exciting journeys, takes great risks. Where ordinary life is frittered away in deflated impulses, tentative efforts, irrelevancies, and delays, the romantic hero lives life to its fullest intensity. He makes no compromises, appeases no one in power. Every issue is clear to him and of the utmost importance. Chance brings great opportunities, and he takes full advantage of them. If he is defeated, he goes down fighting, sure that his cause is just and that some day the evil will be overcome.

It is an axiom of the romantic stage that nobody is tongue-tied or clumsy. Romeo pours forth his soul to Juliet in the inspired verse of Shakespeare or in gorgeous operatic song. Gravity and other laws of the universe are ignored as skaters swing around curves and leap over obstacles with complete power over space. Ballet dancers rise into the air and land again without a suggestion of weight or muscle. In the movie of *South Pacific,* Lieutenant Cable, a perfect swimmer, pursues his lovely native girl into the water and under the water, with a freedom known only in dreams. To listen to a romantic play or watch a romantic spectacle is to forget the limitations of the material world and move into a world with laws and ideals of its own.

DEVELOPMENT OF THE ROMANTIC IDEALS

The two greatest ideals of romance, developed in the Middle Ages and still of first importance in our concepts of what man should be, are the ideals of the knight-champion and the knight-lover. Feudalism created an ideal of a knight loyal to his lord and ready at all times to fight to protect the castle. The Crusades developed that champion into the knight-errant, ready to recover the Holy Land from the Infidel or to go about rescuing innocent maidens and the poor or persecuted. In a sacred ceremony, he dedicated his sword and himself to the protection of the weak and the endless fight against evil. His obstacles were fantastic dragons, evil magicians, and cruel tyrants.

The troubadour poets gathered around the famous Eleanor of Aquitaine, who was for a time Queen of France, then for many years Queen of England. Under her guidance, they created another version of the knight that has had even more influence on the modern world, the knight in love. It is no exag-

FIGURE *2.1* The large nineteenth-century theatre for romantic spectacle, with a heavy setting for the first act of Shakespeare's *Romeo and Juliet*. The Booth Theatre, New York, opened by Edwin Booth in 1869. Museum of the City of New York.

FIGURE *2.2* Romantic setting in a large nineteenth-century theatre. Sheridan's *Pizarro* at Covent Garden Theatre, London, 1804. Radio Times Hulton.

geration to say that the modern concept of passionate, dedicated, transforming love is an invention of the poets of the twelfth and thirteenth centuries. Before that time, love had been a youthful adventure or a family partnership. Now the worship of woman became a new religion, with the woman on a pedestal and the man an abject slave at her feet. This "Court of Love" game, which gives us the words "courting" and "courtship" as well as "courtesy," puts love at the center of a man's life. It is one of the major attempts that have been made to shift the emphasis in the relations between the sexes from the physical to the spiritual. It calls on the woman to be very difficult and distant. The young man gets one glimpse of her beauty and is transformed forever. He shows a long list of medical symptoms—he can't eat or sleep, he grows pale, he wanders in melancholy groves by moonlight. He may write poems for his lady or sing a serenade at her window, but he actually sees little of her. She sets him difficult tasks that may take years to perform. Sometimes he pictures her as so far removed from the real world that it would be a sacrilege to win her and touch her. It may be better to yearn unhappily for the ideal than to desecrate it by turning it into reality. That dilemma has greatly complicated the psychology of love ever since, but it has been a great stimulation to romantic art; yearning, absence, and longing make excellent songs.

Romantic love was invented outside of marriage. It was assumed that the lady was already married to someone else; hence the attachment must be secret. There seemed no chance for real love in marriage. By the strict doc-

The Theatre of Romance

trine of the medieval church, all passion, even in marriage, was a sin. Besides, feudal marriages were alliances of convenience, not of choice, and true love must be free and spontaneous—a gift, not a bond or duty. It was not until three hundred years later, in Shakespeare's time, when the rising middle class was developing new ideals, that it became possible to think of romantic love in marriage. *Romeo and Juliet,* written about 1594, was the first great poetic drama to celebrate the union of love with marriage. Romeo uses the medieval imagery of worship: Juliet is a saint, her hand a shrine—"If I profane with my unworthiest hand this holy shrine . . . ." Romeo also sees her in terms of stars and skies and as the rare distant goods of which a merchant dreams. He says,

> I am no pilot; yet wert thou as far
> As that vast shore washed with the farthest sea,
> I should adventure for such merchandise.

That dedication to love and adventure made Shakespeare's plays the first great romantic dramas. The history plays, too, have romantic elements. They are full of wars and rebellions, the storming of castles, challenges and duels, threats and denunciations. There are songs and clowns, and intimate scenes alternate with splendid processions and coronations. The whole range of human experience is shown with magnificent costumes and pageantry. Shakespeare's Richard III is a scheming villain, wicked enough to adorn a child's tale of adventure, and a young champion kills him in the end. The poetic young King Richard II is defeated and killed, but the idealistic Prince Hal, leaving his tavern revelry, comes to the rescue of his father and becomes the successful warrior-king, Henry V, who conquers France and brings back the

FIGURE *2.3* Romantic play in a college theatre. While the setting is austere, spectacle is achieved in costumes and shields. Schiller's *Mary Stuart.* University of Illinois production, directed by Clara Behringer and costumed by Genevieve Richardson.

FIGURE *2.4* Melodramatic action in the nineteenth-century theatre. The heroine escapes from the villain by leaping into the water of a cave. Poster for Boucicault's *Colleen Bawn*.

French princess as his bride. Shakespeare adds characterization and ironies that transcend the basic plots, but one finds in his plays the eternal themes of romance.

Shakespeare's comedies are set in the faraway, never-never land of romance: the enchanted moonlit woods of *A Midsummer Night's Dream,* where the Fairy King and Queen hold their revels and the mischievous Puck helps delude foolish mortals; the Forest of Arden; the seacoast of Illyria or Bohemia; the fabulous orchards, gardens, and courts of an Italy Shakespeare had never seen. There are handsome princes and charming ladies, wicked usurpers and envious villains spreading terrible lies, powerful magicians and magic herbs, long-lost brothers found again, and statues that come to life. It is a bitter-sweet world where "journeys end in lovers meeting," where "parting is such sweet sorrow," where "the course of true love never did run smooth," where "present mirth hath present laughter" because "youth's a thing will not endure." It is a world of accident, chance, evil, and delusion, where everything is transitory and beauty and virtue pass away too quickly. But it is also a world of faith and love and hope, of noble purpose and high adventure.

After the French Revolution, a new "romantic" movement gave fresh impetus to the old formulas and introduced new themes and characters. Following Rousseau's exaltation of the free man, the hero became a rebel against a corrupt society, either stirring up wars of liberation or seeking out high mountains or deep caves where he could question the universe. Goethe's *Faust* most fully expressed the rebellious spirit of the time—the release of irrepressible yearning, the rejection of old rules, and the angry attack on all the institutions of society. Faust is torn between God and the Devil, between day and night, between creation and destruction. He wants all experience, but when he gains the love of Marguerite he destroys her and feels more lonely than ever in his guilt. In poetry, fiction, and drama, the rebel dominated the imagination. Lord Byron, most daring and turbulent of the English poets, created heroes in his own image, proud and rebellious, maimed and tortured by some secret guilt.

73

The Theatre of Romance

FIGURE *2.5* Melodrama spoofed in a college revival. Daly's *Under the Gaslight* at the Show Boat, University of Minnesota.

The melodrama was the poor man's romantic play. It simplified the complex hero by dividing him into two characters—a spotless hero and a deep-dyed villain. It kept the guilty hero but made the guilt false, a lie invented by the villain. Sometimes the hero himself thought he was guilty, but always at the end he was cleared by the proper papers or confession. As the name implies, the melodrama used music, not only songs and dances but background music, to accompany the emotional scenes and sometimes to set off each movement, gesture, or speech. Often long sequences were performed in pantomime, and when a group action led to a climax, the tableau would be held still for several seconds. As the heroine fled from danger and the villain pursued her, the greatest excitement was the chase—out windows, over roofs, off bridges into the water, through fires, floods, earthquakes, explosions, train wrecks. The old wing-and-backdrop scenery inherited from the Renaissance and the seventeenth century had to keep moving and make room for all kinds of platforms, steps, towers, trap doors, and trick effects, to thrill the spectators. Burlesque revivals of old-fashioned melodramas amuse sophisticated audiences today by exaggerating the trite sentiments and expressing all emotions in a few patterned gestures. Nineteenth-century actors had a far greater range of gesture and were completely convincing to their devoted fans. They built one of the widest popular audiences in history and took them directly into the movie and television drama of the twentieth century.

The appeal of melodrama has remained the same on the movie or television screen as it was on the nineteenth-century stage. By setting a good hero against a wicked villain, it captures the most elemental sympathies. Whether the villain is a feudal lord mistreating his peasants, a banker threatening to

Kinds of Plays

FIGURE *2.6* Romantic melodrama in Russia. The nobleman abducts a girl from the poor man's house. The State Dramatic Theatre production, Leningrad, 1832. From Derjavine's *A Century of the State Theatre.*

foreclose the mortgage in order to get the heroine in his power, a heartless father driving his daughter and her innocent babe out into the storm, a Western cattle rustler, a city gangster, or a Nazi or Communist spy plotting to blow up the capital, we know that the hero must come to the rescue and come fast. When the villain in the movie *One-Eyed Jacks* ties Marlon Brando to a hitching post and horsewhips him until he can no longer stand and then crushes his fingers with a blow of a rifle butt, we are ready for the most direct

FIGURE *2.7* Melodramatic acting in the nineteenth-century theatre. The strong situations are made clear and obvious. A newspaper illustration of *The Favorite of Fortune.* London, 1866. Radio Times Hulton.

kind of revenge. Anybody who would torture a dog, a child, or a helpless man is a monster and should get his deserts.

On the positive side, the romantic hero is often a pioneer in a new land, an inventor of a great boon to mankind, or a savior bringing rescue from fire, starvation, or massacre. On the page these heroes seem very much alike, with little character of their own; but put a good-looking actor in the role, who can speak, sing, or dance well, and he becomes the incarnation of our romantic dreams.

TWO ROMANTIC PLAYS

Let us examine two romantic dramas of first rank: a late nineteenth-century play—*Cyrano de Bergerac* (1897), by the French dramatist, Edmond Rostand—which uses poetry, historical costume, duels, serenades, battles, and crowds; and a motion picture of 1948—*The Red Shoes*—which uses a contemporary setting, ballet dances, music, beautiful scenery, and a symbolic play-within-a-play. If we cannot easily find a twentieth-century romantic play of the stature of *Cyrano,* it is because recent poets have followed the more austere patterns of tragedy. Maxwell Anderson roused great hopes in the 1930s with his heroic dramas in the Shakespearean tradition, *Elizabeth the Queen, Mary of Scotland,* and *Valley Forge,* but his poetry has faded and we are now more interested in his plays that are concerned with modern problems. Modern comedies that use romantic stories of love and adventure attempt neither the wide sweep nor the poetic intensity of romance. A few of the prose plays of the French playwright Jean Anouilh, most notably *Becket* (1959), have achieved considerable romantic sweep, but even *Becket* was better as a movie. Romance must have high intensity of some kind—if not poetry and song, at least the technicolor of the screen. On the stage, romance today is found either in a revival of Shakespeare or some other poetic play of the past or in the theatre of music and dance.

Cyrano is a brave and dashing French soldier of the time of Richelieu and the Three Musketeers. He is endowed with unlimited strength, ability, and wit, but he has one great defect, an enormous nose. His soul is full of love for his cousin, Roxane, but he dares not speak to her of love because he is mortally afraid of being laughed at for his grotesque face. In the first act Cyrano, at a theatrical performance, indulges in a dozen reckless whims. He drives off the stage a fat actor he does not like, then tosses his month's income to the puzzled manager; he overwhelms a young upstart who had tried to insult his nose with the famous speech in which he demonstrates a dozen witty ways of pointing at a nose, then kills him while making a poem to match his strokes; and, finally, hearing that Roxane wants to see him, he goes out alone to fight a hundred ruffians waiting in the alley. What a fool! But what a gesture!

When Cyrano finds that Roxane is enamored of Christian, a handsome new cadet in his company, he hides his own feeling and tells Christian the words that will win her, even whispering romance under her balcony until Christian can climb up and take the kiss. When Christian is killed in battle,

Kinds of Plays

FIGURE 2.8 The romantic hero wins his battle. José Ferrer in Rostand's *Cyrano de Bergerac*. New York, 1946. Photo Culver Pictures.

Cyrano still sustains Roxane's delusion, and only years later, as he is dying, does she learn that it was Cyrano's mind and soul she loved. The real world finally stops Cyrano—he is almost starving and is gravely wounded but still he bravely defies his enemies to the last, pays his daily visit to Roxane in the convent where she lives, and dies on his feet facing death with "What's that you say? Hopeless?—Why, very well!/ But a man does not fight merely to win!/ No—no—better to know one fights in vain!" In triumph over all man's limitations, the romantic hero carries his white plume high in the air to the end.

The hero and heroine of the romantic movie *The Red Shoes* are a musician and a ballet dancer. Through ability and courage they attain the highest success, but their two careers then conflict and the girl kills herself. After the movie is over, the realistic mind can reflect that it is quite possible for a girl to have both a husband and a career, and that if one ballet manager is obdurate, there are other managers in the world. But no one thinks of this during the movie; romance has no place for compromise—the mood of high dedication demands all or nothing.

The hero, Julian Kraster, a poor music student in London, and the heroine, Victoria Page, a rich girl who finally gets the impresario to see her dance, are hired in subordinate places in a ballet company, but their genius is soon recognized. The impresario needs a new score to replace the poor one, and lo! Julian produces it from his pocket, already completed. He needs a new dancer for the *Ballet of the Red Shoes* and offers Vicky the leading role. Love is fully expressed in music and dance as Julian conducts the orchestra and Vicky dances. Glorious days of rehearsal build to a triumphant opening in Monte Carlo. After the performance, the lovers ride on and on in an old-fashioned carriage by Mediterranean moonlight, knowing that this is the perfect moment.

77

But the demonic impresario is determined to make Vicky the greatest dancer in the world, and he will not permit divided loyalty. She leaves the company and marries Julian, but the dance draws her back. In the *Ballet of the Red Shoes,* based on the story of Hans Christian Andersen, the shoes are magic—never tiring, carrying the dancer into the streets, the forests and fields, through dreams and nightmares, stopping only with death. Just before the next opening, at Monte Carlo again, Julian comes to Vicky's dressing room, having left the London opening of his opera, and she realizes that she cannot have both her career and her love but that she cannot stop dancing. She runs out of the theatre, across the terrace, and leaps down to be run over by the train below. In a broken voice the impresario announces her death to the audience, and the other dancers sadly but bravely dance out the ballet, leaving an empty space for her. Dedication is more important than love or life.

STRUCTURE OF THE ROMANTIC PLAY

The essence of romance is freedom. Where realism is bound by fact and classicism by logic, the romantic play is bound by neither. The romantic hero, as we have seen, gains freedom by triumphing over the everyday world of fact. The romantic play gains freedom in structure by disregarding the strict logical organization of the classical form. The compact classic play, whether ancient Greek tragedy, neoclassic tragedy, or the "well-made" problem drama of the last hundred years, is tightly organized by logic, each development linked to the preceding with the strongest chains of causality. The three unities of one time, one place, and one action are observed by the omission of subplots and the limitation to the final climactic episode. Colorful public events and violent acts are left offstage, and only private decisions and reactions are shown. In the classic view, the individual is summed up in the one great decision he makes.

The romantic structure stands in sharp contrast to the classic. The two romances just described are typical. Most romantic plays have a very loose structure, with many different characters involved in many different episodes and treated in a variety of comic and serious moods. The three unities are disregarded. On first impression, a romantic play seems to have no unity at all but only a chaotic indulgence in irresponsible freedom. The story is told from the beginning with the kind of wandering narrative loved by children. Spectacle is lavishly exploited, seemingly for the sheer love of color and movement. The romantic hero goes from one big scene to another, taking part in impressive social, religious, or political ceremonies that have no apparent connection with one another. Classic-minded critics object to comic scenes in serious plays, suggesting that comic relief would be better achieved by bringing on the clowns as a separate intermission act. But writers of romances believe that the structure is meaningful, and they go to a great deal of trouble to integrate its many elements into one large plan.

The free structure of the romantic play expresses the romantic view of the universe as complex, infinitely varied, paradoxical, and mysterious. Since it is an open universe, unfinished and unmeasured, no one act or crisis is all-

Kinds of Plays

important. Each character must try many things, his individuality developing gradually as a result of wide experience. He must be seen not merely in his private life but also on colorful public occasions. Not one conscious decision—analyzed and debated, then final and overwhelming—but many decisions, made in the heat of action over a long period of time, are what shape the romantic character, who in turn gives unity to the play.

The structure is explicable on aesthetic as well as philosophical grounds. Where classic art emphasizes unity, romantic art revels in variety, risking the loss of a strong sense of unity in order to represent the broad scope of human experience. The romantic artist feels such zest for experience that he wants to include everything in the story, especially what is picturesque and intense. But the variety he presents is not without order and meaning. Comedy is set next to tragedy so that each may enhance the other by contrast. In combining prose and poetry, clowns and kings, crowd revelry and individual distress, the grotesque and the charming, the playwright increases the intensity of each experience. In the preface to his play *Cromwell* (1827), Victor Hugo wrote an ardent defense of the grotesque in art, emphasizing its value for contrast. Nothing, it seemed to him, could be more insipid than the monotony of the classic play with its one even, noble tone.

In later chapters we shall see the development of the romantic structure in the sprawling cycles of the medieval mystery plays. We shall analyze the romantic elements in Shakespeare's tragedies and note how the hero's individual problem is given a wider political significance in a series of spectacular ceremonies. We have already studied the epic play, whose structure also differs radically from that of the compact play of the classic tradition. Yet there is actually more difference than similarity between the loose epic structure and the loose romantic structure, for epic theatre uses spectacle only sparingly and subordinates the characters to a strong theme. In Part III we shall examine the structure of the screen play and find that it has much in common with both epic theatre and romance, particularly with romance. As we have seen in *The Red Shoes,* a film can indulge to the fullest the taste for narrative episodes, for variety of characters, for contrasting moods, and for color and spectacle. The film play outdoes the stage play in romantic variety, but it too has its principles of structural unity.

ROMANCE AS ESCAPE

Romance has been under strong attack from several sides in the twentieth century. Literal minds are impatient with fantasy and dismiss romance as a child's daydream of old fairy tales and legends. Overserious reformers, especially the revolutionary Marxists, have attacked it as bourgeois, as another opiate of the people that, like conventional religion, distracts workers from their duty to the state and wastes their time and emotions. Realists are skeptical of romance because they think that its impossible ideals make people unwilling to face the world as it is. Naturalists treat it as a pipe dream which beguiles man while nature destroys him. The *avant-garde* makes fun of it because it is old-fashioned. Some psychologists are disturbed because the romantic lover seems to prefer his unsatisfied longing to real love or because he associates his love with death, like the neurotic Tristan of Wagner's opera. If Christian, the stupid, good-looking lover in *Cyrano,* had lived, Roxane would have married him, to find out too late that she really loved Cyrano. Only a romantic death saved the day.

Yet in spite of all objections, romance is here to stay. Calling it escape does not convince its devotees, who claim that the traditional romantic stories touch on age-old concepts of human destiny. In art, as in science and philosophy, it is necessary to achieve a distance, a degree of abstraction, in order to see the immediate object in its wider relationships. The workman lays down his tools—he "escapes" from his work—when he stops to take a look at the blueprint. When he comes back to the job he knows more about it; he understands what can be done. The person seeing a romantic play may momentarily forget the immediate problems of his life, but he wakes from the dream with a new perspective on the patterns of human aspiration and desire.

In recent years the followers of the depth psychology of Freud and Jung find great significance not only in sleeping dreams but in daydreams, especially the traditional daydreams handed down for thousands of years in myth and romance. Such daydreams not only trace the patterns of fear and hope that lie deep in the subconscious but are maps of the roads in search of the self.

One of the most basic patterns of ancient myth, adopted in the romances of later times, is the obligatory journey or quest. In many different story forms we see the hero receiving his call, leaving his home, passing through gates and over obstacles, getting advice and instruction from mysterious monks,

FIGURE *2.9* The enchanted forest of romance. Free from the corrupt demands of the court, characters test each other in search of true identity. The Theatre Guild production of Shakespeare's *As You Like It,* with Katharine Hepburn, 1950. Photo Vandamm.

pilgrims, wise men, and kind ladies, talking with animals—cousins from his zoological past—and prophets—mentors from his religious past. He must penetrate the enchanted castle, the sacred grove, the bottom of the sea, or the underground cave, be baptized under water, retreat to the wilderness, pass three days in the tomb, experience the dark night of the soul. He must come face to face with the ultimate, test himself, and find the great secret of power and health. Students of mythology notice that all the great heroes of legend and most of the divine founders of religions had similar temptations and trials and undertook such symbolic journeys or pilgrimages.

The journey or quest, which has been the basic pattern of initiation into the tribe or the fraternity and all the great religions, may be understood today as a symbol of psychiatric reconstruction. The high point of many Western melodramas is the trek into the hills to hunt out the hidden camp of evil and rescue the love and treasure or the agonizing test in the desert of extreme heat or cold. In its shallow, conventional way, the Western carries the audience into the depths of the subconscious, to return to surface reality with new strength and vitality. The psychoanalyst might say that a particular patient must make a secret journey into a canyon unexplored on the traditional romantic journey, but not for a second would he consider that the symbolic journeys of romance had no relation to the realities of everyday life.

A similar quest may underlie even a modern play like Arthur Miller's *Death of a Salesman,* which includes the story of a son leaving home in search of identity and going west to lands of enchantment, the ranches of Wyoming and Texas. Finding all doors closed, he must get the key by returning to his lost father. To find his father, he must fight his way past obstacles in a journey back to his own hidden self.

For centuries Shakespeare's romantic comedies have given audiences and readers not only the dramatic pleasure of a happy ending after anxious trials and sad distress but a sense of spiritual renewal. Many critics have commented on the fact that the characters seem to take part in the deep seasonal rhythms of nature and in the religious processes of salvation. Shakespeare surrounds them with visual and verbal images drawn from popular folklore and Christian doctrine. As his hero wanders through enchanted forests, endures cosmic tempests, or encounters the baffling magic of moonlight, he finds his long-lost father, brother, or sister. He reestablishes his identity and finds his true love. As he takes part in the rites of winter sacrifice and the festivals of the rebirth of spring, he sees the chaos of the storm replaced by the harmony of music and poetry and the cruelty of nature redeemed by divine forgiveness, grace, and love. Audiences follow the old romantic journey into the soul, but the playwright has illuminated and spiritualized it. Such an experience cannot be dismissed as romantic escape.

A PICTURE STAGE FOR ROMANCE

Romance calls for a colorful stage. For a romantic play, for musicals, opera, or ballet, the stage presents a series of beautiful pictures that change rapidly, often in sight of the audience, the whole framed by the per-

FIGURE *2.10* Early perspective setting of solid two-faced or angle wings. Two rows of wings on a sloping floor lead up to a painted cloth drop to give the illusion of a long street. The Tragic Scene from Sebastiano Serlio's *Architecture,* Book II, Paris, 1545.

manent proscenium and sometimes also by a brightly painted inner frame hung especially for the show. Modern design and lighting have, of course, brought changes, but in most of its elements the romantic picture stage is a traditional theatre form that has served for four centuries—a theatre of illusion.

This picture stage was invented as a solid, three-dimensional architectural setting for the courts of Renaissance Italy. Since there was at first no thought of changing the setting, it was substantial, and in one Renaissance theatre, the Teatro Olimpico at Vicenza, Italy, the scenery is still standing. At the beginning of the sixteenth century, when Italian princes started to revive classic plays and produce new plays in imitation of the classics, they had their architects build this kind of stage at the end of their ballrooms. It was a simple thing to put two rows of small houses on the stage, building only the two sides of each house that would be seen. But the ballroom stage was not large enough to extend the houses to an ideal depth, and the architects realized that a forced perspective would look better anyway. So they devised frames at the back holding a two-dimensional canvas on which was painted a suitable background in perspective, with a boxlike shaping of the four sides of the picture. The stage floor was sloped, and the houses at the sides diminished in size, for the right perspective effect. The first completely illusionistic theatre in the world had come into existence. Contemporary reports were ecstatic about the splendor and reality of the picture. In 1545, Sebastiano Serlio, an Italian architect working in Paris, published a book on architectural design with three engravings of scenes and directions for building them, and the stately perspective settings, sparkling with bright-colored lights, were soon known in the court productions all over Europe (FIGURE *2.10*).

In the next century, however, as the masque and the opera replaced the

82

Kinds of Plays

classic play for the entertainment of the aristocrats and as opera won a wide popular following, the Serlian perspective setting, so solid and dignified, was replaced by lightweight, flat, painted wings and backdrops, and scenery that could be changed became the rage. Some operas showed a dozen or more changes of setting. Instead of Serlio's solid wings, the Baroque designer used a nest of flat wings. His scene might show first a woodland grove of six flat, painted "wood wings" at each side leading to a cloth at the back painted with more woods. Then, at a signal from the prompter, a stagehand out of sight at each nest of wings slid back the front wing, which moved in a groove in the floor and another groove above, to reveal the next wing, perhaps painted as a rocky cave. At the same time, the back cloth was slid out to reveal the next cloth. For the large court productions, architects devised an elaborate system for pulling out all the wings and back shutters of each setting with ropes controlled by a capstan under the stage. As higher lofts were built above the stage in the eighteenth century, it became possible to "fly" the back cloth instead of pulling it in grooves; since then the system has been called a "wing-and-backdrop stage." Baroque audiences delighted in seeing the settings change in a few seconds before their eyes. The system was excellent for repertory companies, furnishing colorful painted settings at low cost and making possible quick set changes.

It was the elaboration of the painted setting that caused difficulty. For the changing of steps, platforms, and three-dimensional effects, the curtain had to be lowered, and the continuity of the play was broken. Nineteenth- and

FIGURE *2.11*   Early seventeenth-century perspective setting of flat wings, backdrop, and cloud machines. Opera design by Lodovico Burnacini. Metropolitan Museum of Art.

FIGURE *2.12* Late seventeenth-century perspective setting. Four flat wings on each side and four flat borders above lead to an elaborate painted backdrop. Opera design by one of the Bibiena family.

twentieth-century engineers devised elaborate machinery—pulleys and ropes for flying heavy scenery, wagon stages, jackknife stages, turntables, and even elevator stages—that makes a well-equipped modern theatre extremely expensive. Still it took so much time to get a beautiful painted picture ready to disclose to the audience that an opera composer sometimes wrote an intermezzo to fill the time.

During the nineteenth century, the picture stage reached a peak of painted illusion. There was a rage for tableau effects, especially in the popular melodramas, and as many as thirty might be used in a single play. *Ben Hur* started its great stage career in 1899 with as much emphasis on pictorial effect as there has been in later movie productions. The first act alone had fourteen changes, each setting designed by a different painter—A Lonely Desert, Joppa Gate, Damascus Gate, Herod's Palace, Imperial Gardens, House Top, Street in Jerusalem, House Top, Imperial Gardens, Roman Galley, Grove of Daphne, Lake by Moonlight, House of Simonides, and Salon in the Palace on the Island. The chariot race was run on a treadmill by real horses and chariots, as a panorama painted on cloth attached to huge rollers moved across the back of the stage. The galley scenes filled the stage with rows of oarsmen and faded into a scene of the tempestuous sea with a boat that sank out of sight through the stage floor, leaving Ben Hur and his captain tossing on a raft. Such effects became obsolete only after the motion picture had proved its superiority in spectacle.

Kinds of Plays

FIGURE *2.13* Climax of a seventeenth-century opera. Jupiter and his celestial court are let down in a cloud machine. Flat wings on perspective lines lead to the backdrop. Drawn from several Italian sources by Martha Sutherland.

FIGURE *2.14* An elaborate nineteenth-century setting for Shakespeare. Solid steps and downstage structures are combined with painted wings and backdrop. Charles Kean's production of *The Merchant of Venice,* London, 1858. Radio Times Hulton.

FIGURE *2.15*   Wings and backdrop in a college revival. Dumas's *Camille*. At the Show Boat, University of Minnesota.

Similar painted settings were expected for Shakespeare, giving Shylock a very real-looking Venice (FIGURE *2–14*) and Juliet a beautiful balcony, even if the audience had to wait for long changes and Shakespeare's cinematic rhythm of many short scenes had to be broken up. It is no wonder that more and more twentieth-century producers turn back to medieval or Elizabethan stage forms that used little or no change of scenery, and let the splendor of Shakespeare appear in the costumes, the processions, and the sound of the words.

But for such romantic plays as *Cyrano* and *Becket* and for opera, the musical, and ballet, even if lighter forms are used and changes and transitions are made in sight of the audience, we still expect a colorful painted picture.

The Musical

Romantic plays are still written and produced, but to America for the last four decades romance has meant a musical. Indeed, although it has gone almost unnoticed by theatre historians and serious critics, the American musical has been one of the most impressive forms of theatre in this century. Most people have called it "musical comedy." But in recent years it often carries such deep emotion, such rich characterization, and even so much serious thought, that it is not just comedy. It is, of course, the chief theatre attraction for tourists in New York. By December, 1958, a little over two years after its opening, Lerner and Loewe's *My Fair Lady* had taken in ten million dollars at the box office, and when it was announced that Mary Martin would appear in a new musical by Rodgers and Hammerstein, *The Sound of Music* (1959), more than three million dollars came in

Kinds of Plays

for the advance ticket sale. Only a very popular movie attraction, playing many theatres all over the world, can match such records.

For London and Paris audiences, American musicals surpass those of all other countries and seem the most distinctive theatrical contribution of America. Borrowing from the sentimental Viennese operetta, from the satirical Parisian comic opera and revue, even from the English Christmas pantomime, and using ideas from vaudeville, music halls, and burlesque, Americans have created a form that catches the energy and dash, the combination of skepticism and faith, the naive heart on the sophisticated sleeve that is the active image of America.

Until recently critics and highbrows looked down on the musical. Historically it is not the "legitimate stage," a term used since Charles II issued licenses to two London theatres, giving them a monopoly on the production of drama and leaving musical entertainment to street mountebanks who clowned and sang songs and sold snake oil. Grand opera found a wide audience in Italy, as we shall see, and became the favorite display of the kings of France, the Hapsburg emperors in Vienna, and the social barons of New York, Chicago, and Dallas. But the promotion of the lowbrow musical has been left to actor-singers, composers, and managers.

When the Pulitzer prize for drama went to a musical in 1931, the world began to wake up. *Of Thee I Sing* was read widely and printed in the important anthologies. But although the Pulitzer prize judges honored George S. Kaufman and Morris Ryskind for the book and Ira Gershwin for the lyrics, they showed lingering prejudice against the popular musical by refusing to include the name of the composer, George Gershwin. Finally, however, serious critics have come to respect the musical, recognizing that when story, characters, music, dance, and spectacle are all integrated, it is one of the higher dramatic achievements of the modern age.

FIGURE *2.16* Costumes for a musical comedy that needs both farcical exaggeration and glamour. Jimmy Savo plays a clownish servant. Rodgers and Hart's *The Boys from Syracuse,* adapted from Shakespeare's *The Comedy of Errors.* Photo Vandamm.

In the past, of course, a musical show was often a hodgepodge. For thousands of years audiences have gathered to see entertainers who danced, sang, walked a tightrope, gave character sketches, or stood on their heads. London still has its music halls, and vaudeville lasted in this country until the 1920s and 30s, presenting, sometimes five times a day, a series of "acts" that varied from acrobats and jugglers to top prize fighters or opera stars doing "bits." Some performers were very skillful, and managers took great care to arrange the varied pieces in a sequence of contrast and climax. Many popular television shows follow the same tradition, alternating solo songs, choruses of singers and dancers, and whatever famous personality may be available. The master of ceremonies may take great care in how he arranges his sequence and how he introduces his trained seals, but the audience expects a miscellany of small bits that have no connection with one another and leave no overall impression. Yet even the "revue," a variety show of many parts, whether an elaborate production like the famous Folies Bergères of Paris and the Ziegfeld Follies of the twenties in New York or a more modest production like many of the occasional revues of the last three decades, ties the material together in some scheme or order. The fans of Elvis Presley were delighted when his virtuoso performances were incorporated in movies with a framework of story, setting, and character. A song and a singer take on a larger dimension in a musical.

Even more than the actor in the legitimate play, the skilled performer in the musical is the center of the piece, and libretto, lyrics, songs, and dances must all be planned to set him off at his best. Hence there is always the temptation to put in something specially for him, whether it harmonizes with the rest of the show or not. It used to be expected that, whatever the plot or locale of the musical, the noted comedian W. C. Fields would stop the show at some point to do one of the juggling acts he had made famous in his vaudeville days. Another old timer, DeWolf Hopper, was expected to give "Casey at the Bat" as part of a curtain speech. It is not too surprising that a lady who knew Paul Robeson's reputation for his superb singing of "Old Man River" left his performance of *Othello* lamenting that this song had not been included.

Dance numbers in a show have often been loosely connected with the main events. Some of the outdoor pageants of American history use Indian dances and square dances, both appropriate to the background but not always to the play. Before Captain John Smith or Daniel Boone is brought before the Chief or the Council of Feathered Braves, it is effective enough to present an Indian war dance. For a wedding or a farewell party for the soldiers, a swinging square dance shows the warmth of the community, but sometimes a folk dance is brought in even if there is no better tie than to have someone say, "Yonder comes a bunch of people; looks like they're going to do a square dance."

Far too often, not only in musicals but in opera and ballet, variety is achieved with a flimsy excuse, as in the musical *The Girl from Utah* (1914). The setting was a London "arts ball," where there was already a

Kinds of Plays

FIGURE 2.17 Romance and comedy in spectacular surroundings. A story of daring women of the 1860s is dramatized by large painted settings, colorful costumes, song, and dance. Arlen and Harburg's *Bloomer Girl*. New York, 1944. Photo Vandamm.

mixture of costumes, but when the heroine started to sing "I'd Like to Wander with Alice in Wonderland" it shifted to an elaborate Moorish scene with the chorus in Oriental costumes. Some very famous songs have had only a tenuous motivation. Victor Herbert's popular "Kiss Me Again" was part of an intrusive specialty number in *Mlle. Modiste* (1905) that would not have been missed if, as the producers urged, it had been omitted. The heroine was a stage-struck employee of a Paris hat shop daydreaming of the parts she might do for her debut in the theatre. Picturing herself as a country maid, she performed a gavotte; then, as a lady of the court, a polonaise; finally, as a soulful heroine, she began the slow melody that has become the most loved of the American versions of the Viennese waltz. The haunting melody "Vilia" in *The Merry Widow* (1905) serves vaguely to remind the audience of the sylvan background of the heroine, a lady in disguise, but it is really an intrusive song, pleasing in itself but not necessary for the play. "Wunderbar" is a delight in *Kiss Me, Kate* (1948), but the show could go on just as well without it. At the party in *The Boy Friend* (1954), the Spanish dance is a satire on just such intrusive night club acts.

A contrast to these divertissements is "The Rain in Spain" in *My Fair Lady* (1956), which does not interrupt the drama at all. The tango is danced with gusto, but the song celebrates a triumph for the three characters when Eliza at last has pronounced the words correctly. It is one of the high points of the play and a thrilling moment in modern theatre. It belongs.

A good musical must be more than a play with songs and dances added. A good show song does not interrupt the drama or weaken its force but carries the drama further, expressing feelings and ideas the characters are compelled to utter but could not express in any other way. The play and the songs must together make something greater than either could be alone. We enjoy listen-

89

The Theatre of Romance

FIGURE *2.18* Romance with a take-off on the costumes and gestures of the twenties. The English musical *The Boy Friend*. University of Kansas production, directed by Sidney Berger and designed and costumed by Jim Gohl.

ing to a good song from a musical at a concert, in a night club, or on television, but it has a much greater impact in its original context.

Besides following the turns and moods of the story, the songs must have a sequence that helps give form to the show. There are good opening ensembles, good finales, good lively songs for the eccentric characters, good patter songs for the comedians. The love song is a happy thing when the lovers first sing it, but very different when they are separated and the lonely girl (or sometimes the boy) starts to sing it again. Such a love song can often provide a more effective ending for the first act than a large ensemble. At the end of the show, the whole company must be brought on to give public endorsement and celebration of the reunion of the lovers. The strongest pattern for a musical plot is still boy meets girl, boy loses girl, boy gets girl.

SONGS IN THE MUSICAL

What makes a good show song? Nobody has the final answer. A fresh song may be effective without fitting any of the old formulas, and the old formulas do not guarantee a good song, though they can indicate some effective ways in which a song can belong.

For one thing, a song can tell the audience directly who the character is and what his philosophy of life is. It is amazing that the same audiences that want a drama to be indirect and implicit—to be "natural"—are delighted when a character comes right out and tells in song who he is and what he thinks. In a musical, the old device of a soliloquy or self-introduction, common to both the Oriental and the European theatre until less than a hundred years ago, is still accepted as reality.

90

Kinds of Plays

The "heavy," who is often comic, is especially apt to tell, fairly early in the play, what makes him tick. The father in *Mlle. Modiste,* when asked why he behaves as he does, bursts into a lively song, "I Want What I Want When I Want It." Most famous of all self-explanations are the autobiographical songs of the old men of Gilbert and Sullivan, beginning with the Judge in their first success, *Trial by Jury* (1875). As everyone in the courtroom rises to hail his entrance and announces that he will tell how he became a judge ("and a good judge too"), he sings the earliest of a long line of genially cynical songs about calculated success. After he married a rich man's "elderly ugly daughter," his rise was easy. The best tongue-twisting introduction is the song of the Major General in *The Pirates of Penzance,* which begins

> I am the very pattern of a modern Major General,
> I've information vegetable, animal, and mineral

and includes such tongue twisters as

> I'm very well acquainted, too, with matters mathematical,
> I understand equations, both the simple and quadratical.

But the most famous Gilbert and Sullivan self-introduction is the first entrance of Sir Joseph Porter as "ruler of the Queen's Navee" in *H.M.S. Pinafore.* His gay, disillusioned self-avowal begins

> I am the monarch of the sea,
> The ruler of the Queen's Navee
> Whose praise Great Britain loudly chants,

followed by the chorus "and so do his sisters, and his cousins, and his aunts," and a frank recital of his indoor training for a naval career:

> When I was a lad I served a term
> As office boy to an attorney's firm.
> I cleaned the windows and I swept the floor
> And I polished up the handle of the big front door.
> I polished up that handle so carefulee
> That now I am the ruler of the Queen's Navee.

In *My Fair Lady,* the obvious heavy is Eliza's father, Doolittle, who has the top comic song of the show, in which he expresses his determination to get by all the rules and precautions in this world "with a little bit of luck." But Henry Higgins, who serves the functions of both a heavy and a romantic lead, has a good song of self-analysis, "I'm an ordinary man . . . who desires to live his life free of strife." That quiet mood is interrupted by the alternate stanzas, at a furious speed, deploring the wreckage if you "let a woman in your life." The song is delightfully ironic, for the audience knows that Higgins is by no means the mild person he claims to be and, without realizing what it will mean, has just let a woman in his life. Whether by irony, as in Higgins' song, or by the earnest directness of Kate's "I Hate Men" in *Kiss Me, Kate,* a good show song must characterize; it must let us know more about the people in the story.

Love songs, as one might expect, are indispensable to a musical. Since the time of the troubadours, a romantic hero has been inspired by love. Even when the plot is concerned with other things—politics, art, revenge, or making a living—there is a love story and at least one love song. The love waltz was at the center of the Viennese operetta, as we know from *The Merry Widow, The Chocolate Soldier* ("My Hero"), and several Johann Strauss operettas. Victor Herbert naturalized the Viennese pattern in this country with many charming love songs. Nearer our own day, Sigmund Romberg started several generations singing "You Are My Song of Love" from *Blossom Time,* the romantic musical set in Vienna that was trouped to even the small cities all over America in the 1920s, and "Deep in My Heart" from *The Student Prince.* The waltz is more energetic and the lyric is nearer to everyday diction as the nurse from Little Rock sings "I'm in Love with a Wonderful Guy" in *South Pacific* (1949), but the passion is still there. Not all the slow love songs are waltzes. When Higgins is at last pleased with her, Eliza sings her delight in a two-step, "I Could Have Danced All Night."

Love lyrics are often as simple as "My Darling, My Darling" of *Where's Charley?* (1948) or as direct as "O, Rose Marie, I love you, I'm always thinking of you" from *Rose Marie* (1924) or as declarative as "Bess, You Is My Woman Now" from George Gershwin's famous folk opera, *Porgy and Bess* (1935). More interesting lyrics have appeared when the love song celebrates some gift, flower, place, or season associated with the love. Among the liveliest are "Tea for Two" from *No, No, Nanette* (1924), which has been hummed and danced to for some four decades, and "Surrey with the Fringe on Top" from *Oklahoma!* (1943), which tells the audience how much Laurey and Curly are in love before they have admitted it to each other.

Playful love songs can express complex nuances in relationship. In Gilbert and Sullivan's *The Mikado,* Nanki-Poo and Yum-Yum must not admit their love because she is betrothed to Ko-Ko. Their subterfuge is to show what they would do if it were not for the law:

> Were you not to Ko-Ko plighted . . .
> I would kiss you fondly thus (*kissing her*)
>
> . . .
>
> Let me make it clear to you,
> This, oh this, oh this, oh this (*kissing her*)
> This is what I'll never do.

More involved is the relationship in *Oklahoma!* Laurey and Curly are having a quarrel, both jealous and too proud to admit how deeply they feel. The song they sing, a list of "don'ts," has just the right tone, implying love but making no commitment. Later, when Curly seems to be flaunting his interest in other women, Laurey raises her head high and sings a song of her own independence. She is determined that "many a new day will dawn" before she sighs over a lost romance, and she feels ready for "many a new face" to please her eye. But at the party Judd's jealousy becomes too dangerous; she drops her independence to lean her frightened head on Curly's broad shoulder. The

Kinds of Plays

FIGURE 2.19 Ambitious poor girl scorned by the rich. Julie Andrews in the opening scene of Lerner and Loewe's *My Fair Lady*. New York, 1956. Photo Friedman-Abeles.

game of uncertainty and antagonism is over and they lose their separate identities in romance.

Eliza and Higgins have even more complexity in admitting their love and getting together. In the original play, *Pygmalion* (1913), Shaw kept them so free of romance, so far up on the high-comedy plane, that even at the end it was not love but a good partnership and friendship. The trivial character, Freddie, was put in to offer Eliza love and marriage. But Shaw had written many scenes where Higgins and Eliza are deeply involved in each other's lives, and in 1937 he consented to the movie ending that brought Eliza back to Higgins. The musical *My Fair Lady* sets out to express in music their growing emotional ties as well as their proud determination to keep their independence. Their joy is expressed in the triumphant "Rain in Spain," but that may be partnership in work, not love. Only when she is alone does Eliza admit her feelings in "I Could Have Danced All Night," and she has already given vent to her exasperation in "Just You Wait, 'Enry 'Iggins." To the very end, both express their determination to keep their separate ways, Higgins in "Why Can't Women Be Like Men?" and Eliza in "I Can Do Without You." Even the song Higgins sings near the end, when he really wants her to return, has a moment of anger, "But I shall never take her back . . . I will slam the door and let the hell-cat freeze." He wants her back, yet he admires her independence. Eliza will not get the adulation of an adolescent Romeo; she has moved beyond the simple dream of a warm house—"Wouldn't It Be Loverly?"—and has established an adult relation with Higgins, combining independence and love. He sings, "I'm so used to hear her say good morning

93

The Theatre of Romance

every day . . . I've grown accustomed to her face." And for the curtain, we have not an embrace or a big choral celebration but his contented sigh as he settles into the familiar relationship, with a soft "Liza, where the devil are my slippers?"

How can a musical give full romantic satisfaction if the main couple never sing their love to each other and never celebrate their wedding? The solution is simple—let the comic couple, or a younger couple, celebrate it for them. The hero of *Fiorello!*, as politician and mayor of New York, is too busy to stop for a love song, and in *The King and I* Anna has no intention of marrying a Siamese king who already has a house full of wives. But the minor couples can supply the celebration. So in *My Fair Lady* Freddie is given the conventional love song that Higgins could never sing, "On the Street Where You Live," and Eliza sings to Freddie what she really feels about Higgins: "Words, words, words, . . . If you're in love, show me." If the return of Eliza at the end is to be quiet and casual, then just before the end let Doolittle have a big song-and-dance sendoff to his wedding, "Get Me to the Church on Time." It is the most spectacular scene of the play, though the movie version subordinates it to the ambassador's ball. One can conclude that it does not matter much whether the main or the minor characters express the key emotions.

THE CHORAL ENSEMBLE

As a show moves through character songs, comic songs, and love songs, it builds to high points at beginning, middle, and end in large choral numbers. In *My Fair Lady* only one of the big choral numbers is concerned with Eliza and Higgins—the Ascot race scene, cleverly expanded from Shaw's much more intimate tea party. The big scene near the beginning shows the

FIGURE *2.20* A big production number in a musical. The determined schemer, sitting downstage at one side, dreams of a spectacular night club act. Rodgers and Hart's *Pal Joey*. New York, 1940. Photo Vandamm.

slum background Eliza is leaving, with her father's comic song, "With a Little Bit of Luck"; we return to the slums with the wedding scene near the end.

The big "production numbers" in a musical have the important effect of expanding the size and making a strong impression with crowds in gay costumes and picturesque formation, with songs and dances, and with colorful scenery and bright lights. Spectacle is a great pleasure in itself, and many a show has won an audience with little else. But a good musical uses spectacle to reinforce plot and character, as well as to shape the play by catching attention at the beginning and building a climax near the end. In Jule Styne's *Gypsy* (1959), the very orchestration develops with the progress of the story, from the tinkly piano and percussion as the girls are making their start in vaudeville to the much fuller orchestration as they gain success and come into conflict with their mother, whose last songs have a full brass setting of Wagnerian magnitude.

The main function of a large choral group is to create a sense of community. Modern realistic plays usually show the characters facing their problems alone or with a very few others, but in a musical the social group is important. In nineteenth-century romantic plays the whole band of outlaws or gypsies or soldiers came marching on with some stirring song like "We are the Royal Guards, hurray!" The aristocratic students pledged their group spirit in *The Student Prince* in a bold drinking song. One of the most stirring musical scenes in the 1920s was the "Song of the Vagabonds" in Rudolf Friml's *The Vagabond King*, with its fighting chorus:

> Onward! Onward! Swords against the foe
> Forward! Forward! the lily banners go.

Since *The Sound of Music* (1959) presents a large family of Austrian singers who acquire a new mother and escape from the Nazis, their simple fears and sentiments are naturally expressed in many choral ensembles. When the show is concerned with theatre people, the group spirit bursts out with special zest: Irving Berlin produced such a rousing number in "There's No Business Like Show Business" for *Annie Get Your Gun* (1946) that it has become the unofficial anthem of theatre people; for the Shakespearean troupers of *Kiss Me, Kate,* Cole Porter did the very lively "Another Opening, Another Show." The local color of Northwest Canada comes to life when the chorus in *Rose Marie,* dressed as Indian totems, stamp the wooden rhythms of "Totem, tom tom!" The large choral scene at the end of *Carousel* (1945) by Rodgers and Hammerstein shows clearly the social emphasis which the musical can create so well. Ferenc Molnár's play *Liliom* (1909), on which *Carousel* was based, ends with a quiet scene in which the dead Liliom visits his wife and daughter, who do not recognize him. In the musical, as Billy looks on at his daughter's graduation ceremony in front of the town school, the graduating class join in singing "You'll Never Walk Alone," giving a social dimension to the girl's realization that her dead father's love will always go with her. Put together "There's Nothing Like a Dame" for the lusty American Seabees, "Bloody Mary" for the madam, "Bali Hai" for the exotic native girls, and "Dites-

FIGURE *2.21*   The big ensemble number in a college theatre. Lerner and Loewe's *Paint Your Wagon*. Wilmington College production, directed by Hugh G. Heiland and designed by Martel Gilbert.

moi" for the French planter's tan-skinned children, and you have seen and felt the whole background for Lieutenant Cable's sad love and Nellie Forbush's more hopeful love in *South Pacific*.

DANCE IN THE MUSICAL

Dance has always been almost as important as song in the musical, and many different formulas have been tried in relating the dancing to the rest of the show. Although *South Pacific* has no formal choreography, the singers and crowds provide some rhythmic movement and grouping. At the other extreme, several Leonard Bernstein-Jerome Robbins shows have been planned from the beginning with the choreography at the center. *Fancy Free,* which Bernstein wrote for the young choreographer Robbins, made such a success with the Ballet Theatre that the two men decided to expand it: *On*

FIGURE *2.22*   The musical sensation of the nineteenth century. *The Black Crook* of 1866 started a tradition of daring display of the female form combined with many songs and dances in lavish settings, all vaguely united by a story. Museum of the City of New York.

the Town (1944) took the three brash sailors of *Fancy Free* dancing their twenty-four-hour leave all over New York City in a full-length musical. In *West Side Story,* the entire action is based on dance.

The first big American musical, *The Black Crook* (1866), was a leg show that combined a noisy romantic melodrama with a bevy of ballet dancers. Later in the century, chorus girls marched in geometrical formations, waving arms and legs, and a tradition of well-drilled lines of beautiful legs was established that has been carried down to the famous Rockettes of Radio City. The well-drilled chorus line could make a spectacular beginning or end of a song with a vigorous step and kick that kept the line facing the audience until the last dancer disappeared in the wings—an effect often satirized as a "Shuffle Off to Buffalo" exit. A new era came in just before the First World War when Irving Berlin's song "Alexander's Ragtime Band" started the craze for ragtime rhythms like the turkey trot, the bunny hug, the one-step, and the two-step. By the 1920s and 30s, in addition to such night club specialties as tap and soft-shoe, the stage used many ballroom dances—the fox trot, the Charleston, the tango, and later importations from Latin America. At the end of a song in a musical, one or two featured dancers might start a specialty number, but soon the chorus would rush in and, while the orchestra played a faster, lighter version of the melody, would fill the stage with energetic stepping, kicking, and whirling. Chorus girls were stereotyped as flashy, bright-painted symbols of attraction, to electrify tired businessmen and sex-hungry boys.

But there has been a revolution in the musical since then. Show dancing has absorbed both ballet and modern dance. Sometimes the dances stand out too conspicuously from the outline of the plot, but in most cases they have enriched the expressiveness of the performance. A number of shows have been directed by the choreographer.

Ballet made the first impact. In 1936 a quite sizable ballet, "Slaughter on Tenth Avenue," was the high point of *On Your Toes,* a Rodgers and Hart musical with Ray Bolger and Tamara Geva as show people in the raw underworld of the city. George Balanchine, the ballet choreographer, was called in to direct the dances. Then in 1938 a ballet dancer played the heroine in *I Married an Angel,* with the same combination of Rodgers and Hart and Balanchine. But for the general public, the first real ballet that seemed completely right and overwhelmingly effective was Agnes de Mille's in *Oklahoma!* in 1943. There was dance throughout the play, reinforcing the cheerful, open-air songs. But the high point of the show was the dream ballet. Laurey's fears that she had been too independent with Curly and had become too much involved with the dangerous Judd were acted out by the ballet, which conveyed her realization of the implications and dangers of what she had been doing. Here were beautiful dancing, lovely music, costumes, and lighting based clearly on the main characters and emotions of the play. After *Oklahoma!* Agnes de Mille was in great demand, and a more serious type of dancing—ballet or modern—was recognized as a major part of show business. For *Bloomer Girl* (1944), Miss de Mille created a ballet expressing the feelings of American

97

FIGURE *2.23* A specialty dance number in a large dance scene. Loesser's *The Most Happy Fella*. University of Kansas production, directed by Tom Rea, designed by Bill Birner, and costumed by Caroline Kriesel.

women as they waited for their men to return from the Civil War. Some think her richest achievement came in the dancing for *Brigadoon* (1947), which allowed a wide range of emotional expression, from the dancing for a funeral ceremony to a ceremonial sword dance at a wedding. Another choreographer, Michael Kidd, in planning the dances for *Finian's Rainbow* (1947), a satiric fantasy about Irish leprechauns, rainbow gold in the Kentucky hills, and race

FIGURE *2.24* Modern street violence danced to music. Bernstein's *West Side Story*. New York, 1957. Choreographed by Jerome Robbins. Photo Fred Fehl.

prejudice in America, made such a skillful blend of acting and dancing that it was never certain where one gave over to the other.

, Still greater achievements in dance were *West Side Story* (1957) and *Sweet Charity* (1966). Jerome Robbins opened *West Side Story* with dance, not a conventional show number of singing and kicking but a tense scene of the gang arriving suddenly in a street and looking around quickly. It was rhythmic, patterned, exact; it was unmistakably dance yet also the simplest, most direct expression of reality. *Sweet Charity* was choreographed in precise movements from beginning to end by Bob Fosse and brilliantly sung and danced by Gwen Verdon. If in story and music this musical was not quite so original as *West Side Story,* it was still a worthy successor. It was as wry and disillusioned as *Gypsy,* presenting a leading character whose innocent hopes for love had no chance in the commercial inferno where she worked. The show was no sentimental *World of Susie Wong* about a prostitute with a heart of gold, but it did make very attractive the courageous girl who could hold her own in the brassy world of a taxi dance hall or among the would-be sophisticates of a fashionable discothèque. It was an excellent song-and-dance show. The musical had come a long way from the Viennese operettas of the end of the nineteenth century, where everything was glamour and charm with a handsome prince and a beautiful woman in disguise, with sorrow and joy, anxiety and relief, even heartbreaking disappointment, but all very faraway and picturesque. It had developed into a remarkably supple form that could express a wide range of feelings, including the harsh realities of city life.

THE MUSICAL AS CELEBRATION OF AMERICA

Above all, the musical is a celebration of America, perhaps the best celebration we have. In the nineteenth century Walt Whitman celebrated in vigorous verse the energy and variety of America, but most twentieth-century poets have turned to the subjective problems of the individual or have been bitterly critical of modern America. Only a few poets have tried to speak for the positive aspects of the country—Carl Sandburg for the raw energy of Chicago, for instance, and Robert Frost for the rural moods of New England. Some novels and movies have dealt with the spread westward across the continent, but often the wide panorama has allowed for little depth of character or poetic intensity. In an age of cynicism and debunking of old values, the musical, while facing doubt, loneliness, and confusion, has searched out and celebrated the strength, the zest, and the faith that are still central in American life.

This celebration of America is evident in the range of musicals of the last four decades. Where better than in *Show Boat* (1927) can we find a picture of mid-America of the nineteenth century, with its color, its gambling spirit and quick success, its restless changes and disrupted family life? The picture is sharpened by the background of Negro workers and mulatto girls, and several of the songs—"Old Man River," for instance—suggest the vision of man helpless before large natural forces that dominated much of the thinking of the late-nineteenth and early-twentieth century. When deterministic philoso-

99

phy can be sung, a way has been found for living with it. Irving Berlin found a way to make it gay in the song "Doin' What Comes Natur'lly" in *Annie Get Your Gun.*

One of the brightest shows of the 1930s was *Of Thee I Sing,* which opened at the end of 1931 and continued through the Roosevelt-Hoover campaign of 1932. A sharp but good-natured thrust at American elections, George S. Kaufman's satire is particularly American. It points up imperfections with the utmost clarity, yet with that amused indulgence which makes fanatics despair of America's ever reaching perfection. To show a presidential election being run as a beauty contest, campaign oratory being spiced up with wrestling, nine Supreme Court Justices hopping into a football huddle to pronounce on the sex of the President's child, is to remind Americans, as Aristophanes reminded the ancient Athenians, that we often do not take public affairs seriously enough. Gershwin's music, alternately charming and raucous, emphasizes the irreverence and the satire. In the 1930s some people were shocked, but since then the political methods of Hitler, Stalin, and Castro have reminded us that people without some irreverent sense of humor do not have elections at all.

Two other shows of the early 1930s demonstrate that the musical was of first importance. One was a revue by Moss Hart, with music by Irving Berlin, called *As Thousands Cheer* (1933), which unrolled scenes based on the different sections of a newspaper. The most glamorous scene was the one set on

FIGURE *2.25*   Local color in a folk opera. The main action is reinforced by the acting and singing of the chorus. In this picturesque setting every window is an acting area. Heyward and Gershwin's *Porgy and Bess.* New York, 1935. Photo Vandamm.

FIGURE 2.26   A large painted backdrop for a singing number. The backdrop is quite far downstage to cover the setting up of an elaborate scene behind. Berlin's *Annie Get Your Gun*. New York, 1946. Photo Vandamm.

Fifth Avenue in which the famous song "Easter Parade" was sung; the most unforgettable one was the scene in which the Negro singer Ethel Waters sang "Suppertime" as she set the table and tried to think how to tell the children they would never see their father again: he had been lynched. Both American composer and American audience were learning how musicals could treat emotions never attempted in the Viennese operetta. Then in 1935 the great Negro folk "opera," *Porgy and Bess,* brought together a number of traditions. A Southern aristocrat, DuBose Heyward, created the story of a gentle cripple, Porgy, who wins the trollop Bess from the strong man only to have her lured away by Sporting Life, the high-stepping dope peddler from Harlem. At the end Porgy leaves his Negro quarters with only his goat cart to search the world for his woman. A musician from Brooklyn, George Gershwin, composer of many Broadway show tunes and of such concert works as *Rhapsody in Blue,* studied the group rhythms and melodies of the Gullah Negroes and produced the first operatic music that seems authentically American. His songs express the tenderness of love, a cheerful defiance in "I Got Plenty o' Nuttin'," a humorous reflection on Biblical stories in "It Ain't Necessarily So," and, most powerfully of all, the fears, amusements, laments, and prayers of the crowd. The opera is a celebration of American local color and a farewell to it.

Moss Hart used modern psychology in a new version of the American dream of success in *Lady in the Dark* (1941), with music by Kurt Weill. Hart, who had just been psychoanalyzed, wrote a vivid drama about a career woman who learns to follow her suppressed dreams and becomes a dependent, glamorous wife. Weill, who in the Germany of the twenties had produced the bitter songs of *The Threepenny Opera,* blossomed out in this American show with much more ebullient, cheerful songs.

The top musicals of the forties—a decade of giants like *Oklahoma!, Carousel, Annie Get Your Gun, Finian's Rainbow,* and *South Pacific*—included the sorrows of separation and death, but even when they were set in picturesque, faraway places they celebrated American strength and faith, that great "willingness of the heart" that seems peculiarly American. And the old-fashioned, brassy *The Music Man* and the almost completely operatic *The Most Happy Fella* of the 1950s continued the tradition of big, energetic productions set in the romantic America of the past. As for the West, *Annie Get Your Gun* and *Paint Your Wagon* make most of the movie or television Westerns seem pale and adolescent in comparison.

The historical mission of America—to offer a new chance and a larger world to immigrants from various limited backgrounds—has been celebrated in many ways in the musical theatre. In Marc Connelly's *The Green Pastures*, which seemed to many people in the 1930s the greatest play America had produced, the kind old preacher tells Negro children in a Louisiana parish the story of the Bible. But he is by implication telling them the dream of America. The play took on epic sweep as a black Moses showed the black Children of Israel the Promised Land, a land he would never live to see; it took on tragic depth as "De Lawd" realized that to save his people he must himself assume the human burden and suffer crucifixion. The characters did not sing their dialogue, but the Negro choir sang the traditional spirituals that so fully expressed the hope and faith of the old-fashioned rural Negro—

FIGURE *2.27*   The tough city musical. A crap game played in a sewer is given some glamour and beauty in the scenic background, here projected on a screen. Loesser's *Guys and Dolls*. University of Washington production, designed by John A. Conway.

a faith in the Promised Land that is still alive though expressed in forms less gentle and submissive.

The American dream of the European immigrants is more specifically dramatized in *Fiorello!* and *Fiddler on the Roof. Fiorello!* (1959) is set in a New York City of graft and corruption, where minority groups are struggling to find their place. They are led by that great little hero, Fiorello La-Guardia, the half-Jewish, half-Italian champion of the people, who went to Congress and then served for years as mayor of New York. *Fiddler on the Roof* (1964), taken from the Yiddish stories of Sholem Aleichem, projects the immigrant back to the narrow but colorful ghetto communities of central Europe. The old father Tevye, struggling to keep a balance between the traditions of his people and the new ideas of his children, is finally driven out of his old-world home and moves to America. Early in this century, such old-world backgrounds were the subject of broad comedy and ridicule, with clownish comedians presenting Jewish, Irish, or German caricatures. In the decades of Hitler and the Second World War, such national dialects and customs were either avoided or treated with awed seriousness. By the mid-sixties, it was possible to look with both amusement and affection at the minorities who brought local traditions and high hopes to America.

But showing admirable characters in the sweep of history is only part of the achievement of the musical in the last three decades. Equally remarkable is the use of less glamorous material—hardened city types, sardonic moods, destructive and antisocial aspects of human character. John O'Hara's *Pal Joey* (1940) was so unsentimental and sardonic that it repelled a large part of the regular audience, though it had one of the best Rodgers and Hart scores and the young Gene Kelly played the conniving hoofer who dreams of owning a fabulous night club (FIGURE *2.20*). It was a wry version of the American success story, showing up the stupid and unsavory. But it seemed a new and exciting kind of musical to many people, and when Columbia brought out a recording in 1952, the show was revived in New York and has found a real audience since then. *Guys and Dolls* (1950), with its tough-skinned but soft-hearted gamblers and racketeers, was a bit more sentimental; its sinners were softened or reformed in the end. But it, too, caught the racy vitality of America and carried the musical a long way from its aristocratic Viennese ancestors. After that *Gypsy* was the logical next step; with this production the musical reached a new maturity as it treated complexities of character that were undreamed of in the days of stereotyped heroes, heroines, and comic aunts and uncles. Ethel Merman's performance of the mother who drives her daughters to success and then to rebellion proved that the musical can be as rich in human relations as any drama.

Workers and labor unions would seem to be far from the romantic world of the theatre, but not in America. In the 1930s, the decade of the depression and the New Deal, labor and industry fought battles that did not stop short of shooting. It was a great day in 1937 when a musical revue, called *Pins and Needles,* produced and acted by the International Ladies Garment Workers Union, showed a sense of humor. Its love songs took such forms as "One

FIGURE *2.28* The informal satirical revue. Hitler and Mussolini sing an ironic topical song, "Four Little Angels of Peace Are We." Rome's *Pins and Needles.* New York, 1937. Photo Vandamm.

Big Union for Two" and "Sing me a song with social significance—nothing else will do. It must be packed with social fact, or I won't love you." An excellent recording in 1962 and television revivals have brought to life again the songs of a turbulent but idealistic period of American labor. In 1954 it seemed easy and natural that a musical should be based on the group spirit as well as loves in a labor union. *The Pajama Game* was a great success both in America and in England.

If *West Side Story* seems the most strikingly original and one of the most harmonious of all American musicals, it is yet a summary and perfection of the whole line, giving an audience almost everything it has learned to expect. There are dances and songs of group unity for the juvenile gang, songs of love and of dreams of the future, a half-comic celebration, "America," sung by girls recently arrived from Puerto Rico, and a sardonic-comic song of the delinquents, "Gee, Officer Krupke," mocking the police and social workers. There are satire, violence, gang warfare, and murder, yet such an obvious love of New York, such a strong assertion of the hope of love over hatred, that this musical must be described as a celebration of America.

MUSICAL AND OPERA

Will the popular musical develop into a full American opera? *Porgy and Bess* and *The Most Happy Fella* have a large amount of fairly elaborate music. Many composers set parts of the dialogue to something like the recitative of opera, especially in transition from conversation to song. A good example is the "Politics and Poker" song in *Fiorello!,* in which the bets

Kinds of Plays

and short remarks of the backroom politicians fall into rhythm, then into melody, and then into the full chorus of song. There are similar transitions, half-spoken and half-sung, in *My Fair Lady*. Rex Harrison was excellent in fitting a half-spoken passage against an orchestral background. Doubtless composers will make many combinations of drama and music and some people will urge them to go all the way, setting all the dialogue in music, and call it opera. That would not be too difficult, as many composers of musicals are first-rate musicians. Europeans are amazed that a musician of the stature of Leonard Bernstein, conductor of the New York Philharmonic, writes music for Broadway.

Broadway fans are glad to have their musical distinct from opera, however, as a form less aristocratic but more vital. Opera, which will be discussed in the next chapter, has its own excellence and at its best is far superior to the musical in the complexity of the music and the technical accomplishment of the singers. But a musical is often a better production than an opera. The musical has been rehearsed intensely for many weeks and has usually had a tryout of two to six weeks before opening in New York; after a month or two of playing there, it has a perfection of performance that an opera company, presenting a number of operas in repertory, seldom if ever achieves. With a half-million dollars invested in production, a musical commands better minor actors, better dancers, and better scenery and lighting than opera. The acting is usually far superior to that in opera. Opera singers commonly pay for their acquaintance with many roles by using the same conventional gestures and tricks of characterization in all. If some roles in the musical are entrusted to actors with limited voices, some are filled by excellent singers who can make clear with words and nuance of phrase the meaning of a song, where opera singers are sometimes more concerned with producing beautiful tone than with making the words communicate. Even the wider range of opera voices may be overrated. The soprano's high notes are sometimes more amazing than beautiful.

The musical can also be defended as superior to opera in expressing the moods and themes of the twentieth century. The older opera houses are museums of ancient exhibits, rarely presenting anything more recent than Puccini, who died in 1924. The most heralded composers of twentieth-century operas are the American Gian Carlo Menotti, who is only one step beyond Puccini, and the Austrian Alban Berg, whose atonal music in *Wozzeck* is too tortured and his subject matter too nihilistic to be steady diet for the modern theatre. Since the excellent comic operas of the eighteenth century, there have been very little comedy and satire in opera. The American musical comedy, on the other hand, while it is an expression of the idealism, dedication, and charm of romance, finds a place for comedy and satire, for the serious moods and anxieties of our day, and even for the bitter moods of expressionism and the drama of the absurd. If sentiment and wholesome cheer are the mainstay of Broadway musicals, they are balanced by some recognition of the difficulty of achieving them in the twentieth century.

In *Of Men and Music* Deems Taylor, a critic and a composer of several operas and much serious music, made a statement about the American musical that most theatregoers would endorse: "After all, there have only been three forms of musical stage entertainment in the history of Western culture that in their day have been huge money-makers and also perfected art forms. These three are the Italian grand opera, the Viennese operetta, and the American musical comedy. We can be proud that one of these belongs to us."

EXERCISES AND DEMONSTRATIONS

1. THE ROMANTIC HERO.   Analyze the romantic hero of a popular film or a television series. Is he a lonely, desperate man involved in violence, guilt, escape, or pursuit? What has set him apart from the comfortable, conventional world—an accident or an injustice? In what way is he superior? Does he envy conventional people or despise them? Does he hope to be able to settle down, or does he accept his desperate situation as the "human condition"? Is the story enhanced by vivid setting, costume, music, song, dance? Does the spectacle enhance some interest or ability of the main character, or does it reinforce his enemies and make him feel even more left out and alone? Does he get some glimpse of companionship and love?

2. ROMANTIC CONFLICT.   Describe the major conflict in a film melodrama or in a movie or television Western in terms of good and evil. How do appearance and incidental actions make you like the hero and hate the villain? How does the conflict develop? Are there several small provocations leading to a climax? Does the conflict lead to a chase? Is there a large battle or a secret journey to a lonely place of confrontation?

3. COMEDY IN ROMANCE.   Examine a comic moment in a romantic play or movie and ask how it is used for contrast with the serious scenes. Is the comic character a variation of the serious character, as in *Romeo and Juliet* Mercutio's coarse bawdiness sets off Romeo's sincere love? Does the comic moment prepare for or reinforce some other actions in the play, as the nurse's teasing of Juliet prepares the audience for her later treatment of Juliet, when she first offers her sympathy and help but then abandons her at the crucial moment?

4. ACTING ROMANTIC DEDICATION.   Act the scene of defiance and dedication at the end of Lillian Hellman's *The Little Foxes*. The young girl Alexandra repudiates her mother's ruthless acquisitiveness and asserts her determination to fight for a better world. The scene can be acted with another person doing the mother or as a solo, with the mother's lines omitted. Begin with "Mama, I'm not coming with you. I'm not going to Chicago."

5. ACTING ROMANTIC DEDICATION.   Act Mio's speech of dedicated triumph near the end of the second act of Maxwell Anderson's *Winterset*. Mio, who

EXERCISES AND DEMONSTRATIONS

has just found proof that his father was innocent and was executed for a crime he did not commit, is exultant. The speech begins "Then see to it! Let it rain! What can you do to me now when the night's on fire with this thing I know?"

6. SONG IN THE MUSICAL.   Analyze a song in a musical for its function in the drama, first classifying it—a philosophy-of-life song, love song, comic song, and so on—then showing how it expresses the character of the singer, how it grows out of the particular situation, how it achieves its mood and meaning through rhythm and imagery, and how it reinforces elements in other parts of the drama.

7. ACTING THE SONGS OF A MUSICAL.   A song number in a musical must be quite dramatic, the words and thoughts projected to the audience, to another character, or to both at the same time. The phrases must be very clear, the important words must be emphasized, and the descriptive words must be made vivid.

Among the most dramatic songs are those expressing anger directed at one person. In *My Fair Lady,* Eliza's "Just You Wait, 'Enry 'Iggins" and "Show Me" are very direct and can be practiced first as speech and then as half-spoken song. There is a vivid teasing, mock-tragic intention in "Pore Judd Is Daid" in *Oklahoma!*

An awareness of someone who is not on the stage but very much present in the mind can give life to a song. The songs of Nellie Forbush in *South Pacific* are excellent for practice, especially "I'm Gonna Wash That Man Right Outa My Hair" and "A Wonderful Guy," both of which require appropriate hand actions. In the Columbia recording by the original cast, Mary Martin makes the songs seem very easy. Most singers must work much harder than she seems to in order to give a sense of the character's fresh, intense feelings.

The songs of *Fiddler on the Roof* are very dramatic, often approaching speech. In the RCA recording by the original cast, the words and ideas come through remarkably well. The matchmaker's song, the young couple's "Now I Have Everything," and the parents' "Do You Love Me?" are especially good for practice.

From *Hello, Dolly!,* even better for practice than the popular title song is Mrs. Levi's self-presentation, "I Put My Hand in Here."

SUGGESTED READING

PLAYS

The crowning achievement of nineteenth-century romantic theatre is Edmond Rostand, *Cyrano de Bergerac* (1897). Maxwell Anderson in the 1930s wrote a number of romantic plays about historical characters, notably *Elizabeth the Queen* (1930), *Mary of Scotland* (1933), and *Valley Forge* (1934). William Saroyan catches some aspects of romanticism in modern setting in *The Time of*

107

Your Life (1939) and *The Beautiful People* (1941). Jean Anouilh has elements of the romantic in several plays, nowhere more than in *Becket* (1959). Perhaps the most perfect romantic drama is still the ancient Hindu play *Shakuntala* by Kalidasa.

Most epic films of history are romances or at least romantic melodramas, *Gone with the Wind* (1939) being one of the best. Like *The Red Shoes* (1948), the French film *Children of Paradise* (1944) is practically an anthology of standard romantic characters, superbly played.

CRITICAL WORKS: ROMANCE

The persistent romantic hero is traced in Lord Raglan, *The Hero** (1936), Joseph Campbell, *The Hero with a Thousand Faces** (1949), Jessie Weston, *Ritual and Romance* (1914), and many other studies of mythology.

Romanticism in the nineteenth century is studied in Mario Praz, *The Romantic Agony** (1933), and Francis A. Waterhouse, *Random Studies in the Romantic Chaos* (1923); in the American theatre in Richard Moody, *America Takes the Stage: Romanticism in American Drama and Theatre, 1750–1900* (1955), Lloyd Morris, *Curtain Time* (1958), Barnard Hewitt, *Theatre USA 1668–1957* (1959), and Howard Taubman, *The Making of the American Theatre* (1965).

A vivid account of the battle to establish romantic drama in Paris in 1830 is given in John Mason Brown, *The Modern Theatre in Revolt* (1929), and reprinted in his *Dramatis Personae** (1963).

A lively picture of popular melodrama is presented in two books of Maurice Disher: *Blood and Thunder: Mid-Victorian Melodrama and Its Origins* (1949) and *Melodrama: Plots That Thrilled* (1954). Many illustrations of settings are reproduced in *Early American Theatrical Posters* (1966). Nicolas A. Vardac, *Stage to Screen: Theatrical Method from Garrick to Griffith* (1949), shows how the nineteenth-century patterns of melodrama and spectacle influenced the early movies. Four essays on melodrama as a persistent form are included in R. W. Corrigan, *Tragedy: Vision and Form* (1965).

For a short history, see George Rowell, *The Victorian Theatre* (1956). Ernest B. Watson, *Sheridan to Richardson: A Study of the Nineteenth-Century London Stage* (1926; repr., 1964), gives an excellent treatment of theatre practice, which, for Shakespeare, can be supplemented by G. C. D. Odell, *Shakespeare from Betterton to Irving* (1920; repr., 1964), and by some of the biographies of Sir Henry Irving. Marvin Felheim, *The Theatre of Augustin Daly: An Account of the Late-Nineteenth-Century American Stage* (1956), gives details about American practice.

A quick view of stage design from the seventeenth to the nineteenth century is provided by Janos Scholz, *Baroque and Romantic Stage Design** (1955).

The religious aspects of Shakespeare's romances are treated by Northrop Frye in *Fables of Identity* (1963) and *A Natural Perspective* (1965), and by Robert Grams Hunter in *Shakespeare and the Comedy of Forgiveness* (1965). *The Arts Yearbook* (1958) is concerned with "Romantic Art" and gives illustrations of painting and architecture.

* Available in paperback edition.

SUGGESTED READING

Musical comedy has only recently received more than passing attention. For an early study, see Cecil M. Smith, *Musical Comedy in America** (1950). David Ewen has several good reference guides: *The Complete Book of the American Musical Theatre* (1958); *The Book of European Light Opera* (1962); and, in collaboration with Mark Lubbock, *The Complete Book of Light Opera* (1962). Ewen's *The Story of America's Musical Theatre* (1961) is more informal. Stanley Green has a delightful history from the point of view of the composers, *The World of Musical Comedy** (1960; repr., 1962), and an appreciative study, *The Rodgers and Hammerstein Story* (1963). Gerald Weales devotes a lively chapter to the musical theatre in *American Drama Since World War II* (1962). A very perceptive analysis of the songs is James T. Nardin, "Green Grow the Lyrics," *Tulane Drama Review* (T2, Winter, 1958).

Six Plays of Rodgers and Hammerstein is published by Modern Library, and several musicals were published in *Theatre Arts* in the forties and fifties.

* Available in paperback edition.

CHAPTER THREE

THE THEATRE OF ROMANCE: OPERA AND DANCE

The Opera

Most spectacular of all romantic dramas are the operas. Though there are intimate operas, most are "grand operas," which make the utmost use of large settings, many scene changes, crowds and choruses, ballets and specialty dances, and virtuoso feats of singing. Though there have been operas set in the time and place of the audience, even these a generation later become costume operas, and today so few contemporary operas are performed that operagoing regularly means watching a glamorized show of the romantic long ago and faraway.

THE APPEAL OF OPERA

Opera appeals to an audience in many ways—by its large effects, its romantic moods, its dramatic melodies. Some people are attracted chiefly by the spectacular scenes, in which music underscores the surge of the crowd. Especially impressive are great processions—the approaching sound of drums and trumpets, the grand entrance, the filling of a public square with marchers and spectators. Festivals with dances and choruses; public ceremonies, with the pomp of guards, rulers, and courtiers and the color of mixed groups of townspeople or peasants; special church services; rendezvous of gypsies or even of supernatural beings—these create the sense of events in which the

FIGURE *3.1*   Opera as spectacle. The magnificent scene of the return of the triumphant hero in Act III of Verdi's *Aïda* at the Metropolitan Opera House. Photo Louis Mélançon.

audience is taking part. What would *Carmen* be without the martial entrance of the guard, followed by the squad of urchins, the less orderly entry of the cigarette girls from the factory, then later in the play, the choruses of gypsies in tavern and mountain hideout and the crowd in the last act on the way to the bull fight—a procession that finally draws Carmen along and provokes Don José to kill her? What could make the lonely despair of the romantic hero more poignant than the two singing processions in the last act of *Tannhäuser,* one entering as Elisabeth watches in vain for her beloved among the returning pilgrims, then, as the forlorn Tannhäuser is dying beside her bier, another coming over the hill at dawn, singing of the miracle that means redemption for him? All successful grand operas have thrilled their audiences with such great scenes. Wagner supposed he had spectacle enough in *Tannhäuser,* with a scene in Venus' cave, processions of pilgrims, and a royal song contest, but he could not get a production in Paris until he added a ballet to the Venus scene of the first act, and then some members of the audience were furious: they had arrived late and missed the ballet, when everybody knew the ballet of an opera was supposed to be in the third act! For them spectacle was all.

In Verdi's *Aïda,* one of the most popular operas, the tragic love story is set against a spectacular background. The conquering hero, who is loved by both an Egyptian princess and an Ethiopian slave girl, is sent off to battle in a great scene in which the people sing "Return Victorious." He does return victorious to a choral song, "Glory to Egypt," which became a national hymn. The triumphal march, one of the most famous of all marches, tempts a producer to extend it with as long a procession as he can manage. There are legends of outdoor productions with dozens of chariots and with elephants

Kinds of Plays

and camels and horses by the hundreds prancing round and round the stadium as several bands play the march strains over and over. As if the pomp of royalty and the might of the military were not spectacle enough, there is an almost equal development of the ceremonial marches of priests and priestesses, with chants, prayers, dances, and display. Yet both the military and the priestly elements are necessary for the story. It is the war that brings the slave girl's royal father as a captive, tempting her to find out the hero's battle plan. It is the inflexible priests, guardians of respectability and order, who condemn the hero to death for inadvertently revealing his plan. Much of the opera is devoted to a full expression of the mood and power of these large public forces.

The descriptive power of the music is just as effective in the more quiet moods as in the noisy excitement of the crowds. The local color of a romantic setting comes alive with changing light, but even more with the color of the orchestra. What is static charm in a romantic painting casts an infinitely greater spell as lights dim up and down, characters move, and the orchestra and singers bring the picture to surging life.

One act of *Aïda* takes place at night on the banks of the Nile, the music evoking a lush atmosphere of moonlight in a strange continent. The priests are leading the princess to the temple for a vigil before her marriage to the hero while he is having a farewell tryst with the slave girl, Aïda. This tangle of love, jealousy, and betrayal is immersed in the rich blue atmosphere of the exotic night, created by lighting, setting, and music.

Although most composers of operas make extensive use of descriptive music, no one has surpassed Richard Wagner. His music depicts storm scenes and dawn scenes, murmuring brooks and lonely seashores, hunters' horns and shepherds' pipes. The four massive operas that form one sequence, *The Ring of the Nibelungs,* furnish more than a dozen hours of drama rich in descriptions of nature and its moods. The first opera of the *Ring, The Rhinegold,* starts under water with a low E-flat, and on one E-flat chord builds up the picture of the flowing Rhine waters and surface ripples. Darker, disturbing harmonies come in as the grotesque dwarf tries to win the Rhine maidens and snatch the gold they are guarding. Then, as the morning sunlight penetrates the water and the gold begins to shine, a "gold motif" on the horns bubbles up out of the sustained Rhine music. The music rises as the light reveals a lofty new castle of the gods, Valhalla, emerging on a misty mountain top. And so through the four operas, through caves and forests, rainbows and mists, the music moves on. Among the best-known passages are the "forest murmurs," in which Siegfried listens to supernatural birds, and the "magic fire music," heard as the wall of fire rises to enclose the sleeping Brünnhilde until the superman Siegfried shall come to wake her. The opera sequence ends with Siegfried's funeral music and Brünnhilde's immolation as the Rhine waters overflow to regain the stolen gold and Valhalla sinks, carrying the old gods down in flame and water to make way for a new world. There is enough descriptive music to hold an audience for hours watching a display of changing scenery and lighting and grouping, even if there were no singing.   *113*

FIGURE 3.2   Opera spectacle in the nineteenth century. Full romantic detail of trees, rocks, clouds, and sky painted on wings and backdrop, with some three-dimensional structures in the foreground. Wagner's *Götterdämmerung* at the Bayreuth Festival, 1876. Painting by J. Hoffman. Photo Richard Wagner Gedenkstätte der Stadt Bayreuth.

But some people care little for the descriptive music of opera, for the romantic moods and crowd scenes, or even for the progress of the story; they are more attracted by the melodic high points. Since opera recordings in foreign languages have become popular, offering the leading singers in favorite arias, the familiar songs are often the prime interest of a person going to a live performance for the first time, and they remain the chief interest of some people who would be glad to have the songs concentrated in concert form and would not be greatly disturbed if the last-act arias came first. The most appreciative operagoers, however, enjoy the arias all the more as part of the sweep of the drama. They learn that a good opera is not just an orchestral sound track in the background of a story, that it is not a series of songs sung in concert or even a play with songs inserted. They respond to opera as a very special theatrical form—"drama through music," as the Italians used to call it—an incomparable blend of heroic story and characters, impressive settings, and powerful music of many moods.

THE DEVELOPMENT OF OPERA

Opera was invented as an austere form in which the music was completely subordinated to the words. In the 1590s a group of aristocratic Florentine students who loved the classics gathered to discuss how they might revive the production of Greek tragedies. They knew from ancient writings that the Greek tragedies had been performed with music, but nothing was known about the music itself. Nor did the musical forms in use in their own time—neither the simple stanzaic folk songs nor the polyphonic madrigals and choral church music—seem suited to drama. They therefore invented a

Kinds of Plays

new solo form, a recitative style—*stilo recitativo*—that consisted of a heightened, intoned speech set to definite notes and accompanied by chords plucked on stringed instruments to punctuate the phrases of the speech. It had no set mode or pattern like the Gregorian chant of the medieval church, but followed freely the inflection and rhythm of the words. Early examples that have survived seem simple enough, but at the time they aroused a great deal of interest. Soon a first-rate composer, Claudio Monteverdi, saw new possibilities in the form and started opera on its amazing career. He kept the recitative for the dialogue but added *arias*—more extended dramatic passages with a more definite musical form—accompanied by an orchestra. Some of the arias were solos, some were duets, trios, or group ensembles. Thus was established a pattern for opera that remained for two hundred years and, even with the experiments of the last century and a half, has not completely disappeared. That pattern is to alternate recitative with arias, the recitative carrying the dialogue and some soliloquies, keeping the rhythm of the speech, and accompanied mainly by plucked chords, usually on a harpsichord, and the arias, with full orchestral accompaniment, expressing the more emotional moments in larger melodic patterns, with more definite rhythmic and structural forms.

In the seventeenth century, dances and changing scenery added to the sense of movement. The typical plot of a Baroque opera made a wicked magician responsible for the sudden changes of scene as the characters, usually heroes of an ancient Greek legend or a story of the Crusades, moved from stately palace to hellish cave, to enchanted grove, to stormy sea. At last, with elaborate cloud machines, a large throne-temple descended from the skies bearing Jupiter and his choir of gods to destroy the magician and praise the king, who was often in his royal box in the audience (FIGURES *2.11, 2.13*).

For two centuries or more, the dukes, kings, czars, and emperors of Europe celebrated coronations, weddings, and christenings with spectacular operatic productions. But opera was not long the exclusive property of the upper classes. Beginning in Venice in the 1630s it also became popular with the general public. The aristocrats would build the theatres and pay part of the costs, setting a pattern of subsidy that has lasted to the present. In the popular opera houses of Venice, Vienna, Rome, Naples, and Paris, the elaborate conventions of opera were established. Operas were planned to exploit the talents of the singers. There had to be soprano solos, duets, processions and dances at regular places, and large ensembles to close the acts; but above all there had to be songs, songs, songs, sometimes fifty or sixty of them, each complete in itself, usually of simple three-part musical form, called *da capo* because the third part repeated the first part *da capo*, or "from the beginning." Obviously a song with such an exact repetition could not advance the plot, but it delighted the conventional audience, which was interested primarily in the singers, dancers, and color. Of course, some people made fun of the big scenes, the showy singing, the lyrics that repeated the same words over and over. Dr. Samuel Johnson in his great dictionary gave this definition: "Opera—an exotic and irrational entertainment"; and the French play-

115

wright Beaumarchais said that opera had to be sung because the words were so silly nobody could speak them.

During the eighteenth century, new forms of opera were developed, some comic and some dealing with the sentimental concerns of everyday people. Before the end of the century Mozart was able to combine all the forms, new and old, serious, comic, and sentimental, raising opera to an expressive power it had never known. For many music lovers today, the three best Mozart operas are the high points of all music, among the highest achievements of mankind. The climax and summation of two hundred years of tradition, they stand as beacons of the good taste and perfection of the Age of Enlightenment. But people usually come to a full appreciation of them only after they grow weary of the more strident music of the nineteenth and twentieth centuries. Perhaps there is more energetic excitement in the surging chromatic harmonies in which Wagner submerges his restless gods and supermen, and there is certainly more appalling pain in the atonal harmonies that envelop the frightened little murderer in *Wozzeck*. Wagner expresses the nineteenth-century ambition to conquer the world, while Alban Berg expresses the twentieth-century nightmare of being battered by the world. When such outsize views grow tiresome or oppressive, it is a joy to go back to Mozart and his human-size view of man expressed in music that keeps a balance of the playful and the serious, of the charming and the dramatic.

Mozart was not serious enough for the anguished romantics of the nineteenth century, and his *Don Giovanni* does not please some romantics today. The comic servant dominates much of the opera, and Don Giovanni keeps a brash cynicism almost to the end. But Mozart gives several of the women much deeper emotions, and when the statue of the murdered father comes to life, the music rises to tremendous power and hell opens up to engulf the Don. Often a nineteenth-century production stopped there. But Mozart wrote a charming light ensemble ending in which the survivors reestablish order and harmony after the unfortunate disturbance. *The Marriage of Figaro* used a number of stock comic types, but the French author of the play, Beaumarchais, made the servant so superior to his aristocratic master that for years the French king would not allow the play to be shown. And Mozart deepened the feelings of all the characters, even the rake-seducer and his lonely, sad Countess, and brought the lively comedy to a wonderful finale of self-revelation and forgiveness in what may be the most perfect blend of light and sentimental comedy ever concocted. In his last opera, *The Magic Flute,* Mozart included an even wider range of characters and emotions. One of the gayest of all clowns, the bird-catcher Papageno, accompanies a young knight in search of ideal love and virtue. They overcome the wicked Queen of the Night, liberate the girl, and are initiated into Masonic rites of purification. This charming allegory of enlightened eighteenth-century ideals triumphing over old superstitions and tyranny includes fresh, naive playfulness as well as danger and dedication.

Mozart's greatest contribution to operatic music is his powerful ensembles, especially those that serve as climactic finales to the acts. He wrote beautiful

FIGURE *3.3* Romantic treatment of history. Two scenes of Nuremberg of the Middle Ages for Acts II and III of Wagner's *Die Meistersinger*. Designs by C. M. Cristini for an Indiana University production.

solo arias that fully express the thoughts and feelings of a character at a particular moment, but he advanced opera even more with his group scenes involving three or more characters. Each singer expresses a different, often changing, reaction, yet all are in harmony as the music builds to the climax. Near the beginning of Act II of *Don Giovanni,* Donna Elvira comes onto the balcony at night, angry at her faithless seducer yet still fascinated by him. From below, he hears her, disguises his servant in his cloak, and begins a serenade in order to get her out of the way so that he may pursue her maid. At first he is pretending love, the servant is laughing, and Donna Elvira is protesting, until gradually all are caught up in the spell. There is action, change, development, yet all are united in beautiful melody and harmony. If an operagoer is at first more interested in the straightforward solo songs, as he becomes more experienced he begins to respond to the passages that express many complex and changing emotions.

The Theatre of Romance

Nineteenth-century composers followed Mozart's lead and wrote some of their best music in their ensembles. Besides the famous sextet in Donizetti's *Lucia di Lammermoor,* the best-known operatic ensembles are the quartets in Verdi's *Rigoletto.* The first occurs when the hunchback jester, after hiring a murderer to kill the wanton Duke, forces his daughter to listen to the Duke making love to the other woman. The last quartet comes when Rigoletto thinks he has his vengeance by stabbing the Duke's body in the sack his hired ruffians have brought, then hears the Duke indoors gaily singing his "La Donna e mobile" ("women are fickle"). Rigoletto opens the sack to find his own daughter dying, having given her life to save the Duke. In this closing quartet, the father's song of anguish and the dying daughter's words are set against the gay song of the man and woman inside the palace.

Wagner disliked the use of the "set song" with definite beginning and ending, a musical number that could be taken out of its original context and sung as a concert piece, and he wrote a number of operas that have practically no set pieces. His ideal was a real music drama that combined all the arts, a *Gesamtkunstwerk,* or composite work of art, which moved from the opening of an act through to the end with no place for a pause, no stopping for applause. In place of opera as spectacular entertainment he wanted to substitute the idea of opera as a festival, an act of worship with a lofty ritualistic seriousness. He built a Festival Hall at Bayreuth, where his disciples and worshippers could come as pilgrims and bow down to a dedicated performance. He insisted that there be no late-comers, no frivolous social chatter in the audience, no encores. He darkened the auditorium for the performance, a radical change that was soon applied to all serious theatres. For years *Parsifal*

FIGURE *3.4* Austere staging of opera with modern lighting from high above. Act I of Wagner's *Parsifal,* as produced by Wieland Wagner at the Bayreuth Festival, 1961. Photo Siegfried Lauterwasser.

FIGURE *3.5* Austere staging of opera. The singers perform on the bare platforms of a space stage before changing backgrounds of projected light. Act III of Wagner's *Die Walküre,* as produced by Wolfgang Wagner at the Bayreuth Festival, 1960. Photo Rudolf Betz.

could not be given outside of Bayreuth, and it was usually given on Good Friday. Of course the audience does not applaud on such a sacred occasion. Today Wagner's grandsons carry on at Bayreuth with the same dedication, modifying the sacred tradition by the use of simple space settings and modern lighting.

Wagner achieved his new form by conceiving of opera as a continuous, uninterrupted symphonic poem. He enlarged and enriched the orchestra and set his voices as single strands woven with the instruments of the orchestra into a complex web. Instead of separate arias, he developed his symphonic poem with short bold melodies called *leitmotifs,* or leading motives. Each motif is associated with a particular character or idea—a very clever way of making the music carry the story and sometimes the inner drama. At the first entrance of a character, his identifying motif is heard; thereafter, whenever someone else is thinking about him, the orchestra repeats the motif. Sometimes the motif is sung, but often the voice goes its own way while one of the instruments plays the motif; thus several different feelings and ideas can be developed at the same time. The short motifs are sometimes combined and often they are repeated with variations of pitch and harmony, changing in quality and building climaxes as the drama suggests with a flexibility not possible with set arias.

Some people find the highest achievement of Wagner's operas not in the complex mythology of the four operas of the *Ring,* but in the concentrated love story of *Tristan and Isolde,* perhaps the most powerful drama of passionate yearning ever written. Here the motifs are particularly useful in building the drama. In the first act, on shipboard, Tristan tries to keep away

119

from the lovely young bride he is bringing for his king, but at the end of the act the two unknowingly drink a love potion that magically binds them together forever. In the second act the lovers meet by moonlight and sing of their love. But as day breaks the king interrupts them, and Tristan is wounded. During this scene the longings and frustrations of the lovers are built up by a long sequence of surging motifs that reach up, then move down by the chromatic scale (that is, one half-tone at a time), and are repeated over and over without ever coming to completion or rest. The form is an expression of the passionate longing that can never be satisfied in this world. Only in the last act, after the wounded Tristan has gone over his whole life in his mind, traced in the leitmotifs, and reached a new realization of the meaning of love, does he transcend the long-drawn-out pain of yearning. Isolde arrives and he dies in her arms. She completes the illumination; they are together in a *Liebestod,* a love-in-death, and the music reaches a clear, forceful conclusion. The lovers reach their apotheosis in death. In musical drama, love and the pain of longing are idealized, sensuality is transformed into art.

For the average romantic operagoer, the works of Verdi are more satisfactory than the heavy mood-pieces of Wagner. Verdi used all the old conventions, with lovely melodies and many opportunities for both choruses and solo singers to show off their voices. Except that it has only slight spectacle, *La Traviata* has the best features of the romantic drama and has been a favorite almost from the beginning, although it offended many at first. At the première in 1853 the audience could not believe that the buxom prima donna was dying of tuberculosis and laughed at the ending. Moreover, the costumes of the day made the play realistic, and the heroine was a fallen woman. But in a few decades the costumes became historical, and the fallen woman now seems so noble and self-sacrificing that it is hard to see why the Victorian audience was shocked. The opera is a dramatization of Alexandre Dumas's novel *La Dame aux camélias,* known in English as *Camille.* The first act has several of the best effects of opera, some of the best gestures of romance. At a party of pleasure-loving men of the world and their mistresses, Violetta is the center; yet her heart is untouched by the life of pleasure and she is ill with tuberculosis (the ideal romantic disease, arousing pity yet permitting a desperate, joyful intensity). The right musical effects are created by large choruses, sad soliloquies, recitative dialogue to introduce the young man to Violetta, and a love duet with some coloratura passages: high, florid runs and trills. When the crowd leaves to dance in another room, Violetta has a moment of feeling faint—the dramatic device to establish her disease and to stimulate Alfredo's tender care. In a quiet aria, he tells her of his love. Her reply is a high bit of coloratura, which, unlike such passages in many operas, is exactly right—she is laughing with forced gaiety, not daring to take Alfredo seriously. His low notes cut through her artificiality with a solid sincerity. The crowd interrupts them and she sends him away.

Alone, she is deeply stirred and begins a powerful recitative, *"e strano"* ("it is strange"), then sings an aria that makes dramatic use of the conventional two-part form, in which a meditative section is followed by a vigorous

Kinds of Plays

FIGURE 3.6 The romantic anguish of misunderstood love, sung against the reveling crowd in a large painted setting. Act III of Verdi's *La Traviata* at the Metropolitan Opera House. Photo Louis Mélançon.

one that ends on a high note and brings down the house with applause. In the first part Violetta expresses a tender longing for the one true love she has never known. But she puts that thought aside and bursts into her *"sempre libera"* ("always free"), in wild praise of freedom and pleasure. Alfredo's voice from outdoors cuts in, and again she sings her determination not to hear him. The coloratura part, just showy enough, is an excellent cover for her deeper feelings.

The rest of the opera is equally full of large romantic gestures. Violetta leaves the life of pleasure to live with Alfredo in a charming cottage in the country. They are given one ecstatic duet, and then the blow falls. Alfredo's father appeals to Violetta's better nature, telling her that she is ruining the chances for marriage of her lover's innocent young sister. Violetta realizes that she must make the Great Renunciation so common in nineteenth-century melodrama. With a broken heart, she writes Alfredo a letter indicating that she is returning to her old life and telling him a tender good-bye. In the third act, he follows her to a party, challenges to a duel the Baron he thinks is protecting her and throws at her feet, as an insult, the money he wins at cards. The short recitative phrases of the card game are set against a restless melody in the orchestra which is repeatedly interrupted by Violetta's prayer to heaven for pity. The scene ends with a marvelous ensemble in which each person sings his own thoughts yet all together build to a great climax and a big curtain.

The last act is the death scene. In a cold, blue winter dawn, Violetta wakes to anguished music of the strings. She rereads a letter she has received from Alfredo—he now understands her sacrifice and is hurrying back to take her

121

The Theatre of Romance

away with him. She sings her farewell to the past, and Alfredo returns in time for a lovely duet. Then she dies. The Victorians could indulge a woman who defied convention and who had a great passion, provided she paid—and Violetta pays, with a renunciation and *Liebestod*. So the Victorian audience could escape in song to a passion more intense and more romantic than everyday life allowed, yet their respectability was fully in control at the end. The rebel submitted and died.

OPERA IN AN AGE OF REALISM

The opera as it developed in the first half of the nineteenth century was satisfying because everything about it was large. In a large opera house, melodramatic crises and anguished decisions were sung with strong voices, acted with wide gestures, set against full choruses, and backed by spectacular painted settings. The grandiose nineteenth-century operas have been the main fare offered by opera companies ever since, but it has been difficult to adapt the operatic form to the new interests of a realistic age or to present operas in the intimate style that has become usual for stage or screen.

Bizet's *Carmen* is an interesting case in point. When it was first presented at the Opéra Comique in Paris in 1875, it outraged the audience. Although it has exotic Spanish music and the local color of towns and peasants and mountain bandits to give it romantic beauty, the main characters are common people with coarse emotions. The flirtatious cigarette girl, the toreador who fascinates her, and the man who loves and kills her are violent and crude. Bizet's spoken dialogue in the original production was later set to recitative to make a smoother transition to the arias and to move the play further from realism. The chief difficulty is the leading role, which requires dancing and acting outside the range of the standard opera singer. Carmen must have

FIGURE *3.7* Intimate staging of opera in a college theatre. Puccini's *Madame Butterfly*. University of Illinois production, directed by Kathryn Janie Sutherlin and designed by Joseph W. Scott.

FIGURE *3.8* Modern emotions in opera. The helpless little man sings his lonely anguish in a world that is absurd and cruel. Berg's *Wozzeck* at the Metropolitan Opera House. Photo Louis Mélançon.

vitality and fire and yet not be completely realistic. As a theatre piece this opera is excellent when all elements blend well, but poor when they do not.

In the 1940s Oscar Hammerstein II had the brilliant idea of turning *Carmen* into an American musical. *Carmen Jones,* with new lyrics and a new libretto, is set among American Negroes and the toreador is made a prize fighter. Stunning costumes and settings and a cast of rather good Negro singers created a show that was neither grand opera nor realistic drama but an excellent hybrid, combining Harlem night-club vitality and operatic spectacle. But the movie version of *Carmen Jones* was not a success. The realistic camera techniques destroyed the scale necessary for the old effects. When Carmen was strangled in a broom closet and then, with microphones very near, sang a grandiose dying aria, the effect was not romantic but ludicrous. Nineteenth-century opera, with its large vocal and orchestral effects, can never be intimate and completely realistic.

The several operas of Puccini and Menotti, with smaller casts, more intimate dialogue, and more realistic settings than those of grand opera, are not realistic dramas but romantic scenes of the sorrows of picturesque, out-of-the-ordinary people. A few composers have broken with the romantic tradition completely; Berg maintains a superb consistency in his use of unromantic material in *Wozzeck.* But his opera is so devastating in picturing the plight of the helpless little murderer that very few operagoers are able to listen to him at all, and few other composers are willing to move so far from the old traditions. In England, Benjamin Britten has created a stark atmosphere with fairly advanced music in *Peter Grimes* (1945). There have been vivid opera settings of several realistic plays—notably, *The Emperor Jones, Street Scene, The Little Foxes,* and *The Crucible*—but all have been performed in the regular Broadway theatres by unorthodox singers, not at the

FIGURE 3.9 Modern realistic opera. A play is set to music with little of the glamour and color of traditional opera. Weill's *Street Scene,* based on the play by Elmer Rice. New York, 1947. Photo Vandamm.

Metropolitan Opera House. At the Metropolitan, there is still not much reflection of modern realism. Fashionable operagoers in New York, San Francisco, or Dallas look for color and charm. They expect to dress well themselves and to find on the stage beautiful costumes and settings, famous personalities, some amazing high notes, and good singing with or without good acting. Above all, they want glamour, and conventional, old-fashioned emotions, enlarged and idealized. They want romance.

OPERA IN ENGLISH

An American making his first acquaintance with opera finds it hard to understand why all the good recordings and most of the performances of the best companies are in a foreign language. Must opera be kept at a distance, or can it be brought nearer to the understanding of everyone? Should opera be sung in English translation? In Italy, France, and Germany, the countries of great operatic traditions, all foreign operas are regularly translated into the language of the audience. Only in England and America, where opera is a foreign importation and where until recently most of the singers and teachers have been European, have the original languages been used.

At the end of the nineteenth century there were large numbers of German- and Italian-speaking people in New York who wanted opera in their own language. The Metropolitan Opera Company imported Italian singers for its Italian repertory and German singers for the German, and rarely did anyone attempt to sing in any language but his own. The conditions are different today, and it might seem that the only logical course is for American opera houses to present opera in English. But there are grave difficulties in translating operas and in singing them in English. The composer makes his melody fit exactly the words and syllables of the libretto. If a translation has a differ-

124

Kinds of Plays

ent rhythm, it either distorts the music or throws the accents on the wrong syllables.

Some operagoers prefer the foreign language in any case, finding the words disturbing when they understand them too well. If story, setting, costumes, and music cast a spell of distance, why break the spell? When Puccini's *La Fanciulla del West* ("The Girl of the Golden West") was presented in San Francisco in English, the audience laughed at hearing such phrases as "Dick Johnson of Sacramento" and "The Polka Dot Saloon" sung to elaborate melodies. But a decade later a performance in the original Italian, with no intelligible details to destroy the aesthetic distance, was a great success. Today, however, college opera workshops all over the country are developing young singers and opera enthusiasts who do most of their work in English; they have shown great interest in the short chamber operas as well as the full-length operas of contemporary composers, most of which call for the directness of intelligible words rather than for the distance of a foreign language.

In New York City operagoers divide in loyalty to two institutions—the more traditional Metropolitan Opera Company, which performs the large nineteenth-century operas in the original languages, and the New York City Opera Company, which performs a wide range of modern operas in English and a few traditional works. With its prestige and money, the Metropolitan can secure the most brilliant singers in the world, but some people prefer the livelier acting and English words of the New York City Opera Company. The wise theatregoer enjoys both.

Dance Theatre

Dance is an important part of opera and the musical, as we have seen, but dance theatre is also in itself one of the major expressions of romance. Of its two main branches, ballet and modern dance, ballet is much the older. Modern dance began early in the twentieth century, and for three decades its devotees set themselves against the romantic aspects of the traditional ballet. But the two forms of dance theatre have learned from each other, and both have borrowed from primitive and Asian traditions, until today both offer a wide range of theatre experience that has color and glamour and yet reflects the intense feelings of modern life.

BALLET

Perhaps the purest form of romance today is preserved in the ballet. No other form of art so directly expresses our simplest recurrent daydreams. Nowhere else is reality so refined and idealized. Nowhere else are color, setting, costuming, music, and movement combined to transport us from reality into a faraway world. Nowhere else is the human body more charmingly displayed, but the silk tights and the tutus, the precise movement so perfectly keyed to the music, and the soft lighting transform the erotic into romantic yearning. All is seen behind the veil of the imagination.

Ballet movements are abstracted from movements of real life—stepping,   *125* running, leaping, landing, kicking, turning—but they are carefully selected and simplified. In this ideal of beauty, charm, and dignity, the back is held rigid, the head is held high, the toes and legs are turned out, and feet and hands are limited to a few precise positions. Every movement begins and ends in a set pose. Such limitation permits standardization and a degree of perfection rare in the theatre. Ballet is one of the most impersonal of all arts, and the dancers perform with the precision of a machine with interchangeable parts. Only occasionally in the solo character parts does personality or emotion or even facial expression find a place. One of the pleasures of a good ballet is the exact duplication as a line of ballerinas, dressed alike and looking alike, make exactly the same movements in unison or sequence or opposition.

Like opera, with recitative and aria, the ballet has its pantomime to establish situation and story and its dances to make fuller use of movement. Many ballets have no story at all, but even when there is a strong story of rich mood and deep emotions the high points are the dances, which sometimes start with gesture but build patterns and rhythms that go far beyond the simple storytelling of pantomime.

We can see a kind of ladder of generalization or abstraction progressing from drama through pantomime and dance to music. Where drama subordinates body and voice to word and gesture in order to create individual characters in a particular time and place, pantomime omits words and uses only generalized characters—a man, a woman, a child, an old merchant—in order to suggest the timeless essence of the story. It allows a freer, more rhythmic use of movement and thrives on musical accompaniment. Where drama shows a particular character angry or joyful about a particular situation, pantomime shows a more generalized character in a more idealized time and place showing anger or joy. The dance, going further in generalization, may omit all characterization and present impersonal figures portraying anger or joy. Music, finally, carries the process of abstraction to the extreme, dealing not with the specific emotions of anger or joy but with the basic patterns underlying all emotional experience—suspense, anticipation, surprise, delay, climax, resolution. Sometimes dancers, like musicians, try to present not particular emotions but the basic patterns of consciousness, the simple feel of experience.

Ballet is one of the most traditional of the arts, with a history of more than four centuries. It reflects the three ages that have shaped it: the Renaissance courts that gave it pattern and stateliness, the classic academies of the seventeenth and eighteenth centuries that formulated its technique, and the Romantic period of the nineteenth century that gave it soul and drama. During the Renaissance it was practiced by the aristocrats themselves, who developed a number of new forms, elaborating on the formal patterns and the ceremonial bows, salutes, and flourishes of folk and social dances. Members of the court liked to dress up and act the parts of shepherds and nymphs or Greek gods and heroes. They liked a "classic" costume, derived from a soft, diaphanous "nymph" costume such as we see in Botticelli's famous painting *Primavera* ("Allegory of Spring"). During the seventeenth and eighteenth

126

centuries ballet became more strictly disciplined, calling for systematic training in the five basic positions of the feet and the most neat and elegant positions of the head and arms. The skirt was shortened to show the elaborate foot movements, and both men and women wore a stiff bodice or tunic. Soft drapery was often added to make the body look even more like a Greek statue. A theatrical dance performance consisted of a "suite" or series of separate "entries" and dances; for each one, the groups of dancers might be dressed as people of various nations, as musical instruments, as flowers, as representatives of different trades. The parts of the suite might be linked by a story or some scheme to motivate the arrival of the different groups, but the emphasis was on the variety of dances and costumes.

The Romantic period radically transformed the ballet, making it express not just the formality and elegance of the court but the dreams and longings of a new age. The vogue of the waltz gives one clue to what people wanted the dance to mean. The typical eighteenth-century dance was the minuet— slow, stately, formal, with partners more related to the whole group of dancers than to each other, their dancing very impersonal. The waltz seemed as radical and as shocking to respectable people as the French Revolution had been. The man swept his partner into a mad whirl, holding her close in an intimate embrace, and the two danced their own wild patterns with no relation to any other couple, forgetting society and the whole world in their own ecstasy.

Several choreographers at the end of the eighteenth century became enthusiastic about the new "ballet of action," which used a strong story and a central couple whose woes and triumphs could enlist the sympathy of the audience. Some choreographers began to use wires to allow individual danc-

FIGURE *3.10* Ballet as a dream of enchantment. Act II of *Giselle*. Indiana University production, designed by C. M. Cristini and choreographed by G. Reed.

ers to fly freely through the air. Then in the 1820s the ladies began to dance on their toes, completing the denial of human weight and gravity.

The romantic ballet definitely arrived in 1832, when Marie Taglioni danced in Paris a new creation called *La Sylphide* and became the toast of the town. This dance drama proved that the ballet was the perfect mode of expression for a story of the contrast between the world of the imagination and the world of reality. *La Sylphide* is the kind of romance that psychologists sometimes warn young men against. A dream can be destructive if the young man follows it instead of adjusting himself to reality. James, the young Scotsman in the ballet, follows the dream. On his wedding day, he sits by the fire dreaming of an ethereal creature, a *sylphide,* who adores him. She dances around the room, but whenever he tries to grasp her she eludes him and vanishes in the fireplace. When his earthly bride arrives, he dances with her and tries to reassure her and himself. But the *sylphide* returns to join in the dance. During the ceremony when James is putting the ring on his bride's finger, the phantom snatches it and lures him out to the moors to dance with a band of *sylphides*. Still she teases and eludes him, and when he tries to catch her with a witch's scarf, she dies. The other *sylphides* tenderly take her up in the air as the heartbroken James watches the wedding procession of his earthly bride, who has left him to marry the other man. The original ballet is rarely performed now, but a twentieth-century ballet called *Les Sylphides,* danced to music of Chopin, preserves the vision of white, ethereal creatures floating to soft, dreamy music.

A romantic ballet that does still hold the stage is *Giselle,* first danced in

FIGURE *3.11* The ballet dancer as an ethereal being from the world of dreams. Marie Taglioni, who created the first of the diaphanous charmers in *La Sylphide* in 1832, is about to lure the Scotsman James away from the world of everyday reality. Dance Collection of the New York Public Library.

FIGURE *3.12* The large ballet company. Principal dancers and the corps de ballet interweave in Act II of *Giselle*. The Bolshoi Ballet of Moscow. Photo Eugene Umnov, Moscow.

Paris in 1841. It combines three of the favorite romantic ideals: the country girl, the supernatural sylph, and the *femme fatale*. Giselle, an innocent country maiden first seen at a festival of grape gatherers, discovers that the man she loves is a prince in disguise and is engaged to a noblewoman, and she kills herself. Near her grave at night dance the Wilis, ghosts of lovelorn maidens who had loved dancing too much. They welcome Giselle to the revels, then lure a man into their midst and make him dance until he whirls to his death in the lake. Then comes Albrecht, the prince Giselle loves. At first she dances with him for joy, now eluding him, now dancing in his arms. When the Wilis pursue him, she tries to save him by having him embrace the cross at her grave. Then, under the spell of the Queen of the Wilis, who orders her to lure him away, Giselle gradually becomes a wild seductress. The scenario, by Théophile Gautier, concludes:

> At first, Giselle dances timidly and reluctantly; then she is carried away by her instinct as a woman and a Wili; she bounds lightly and dances with so seductive a grace, such overpowering fascination, that the imprudent Albrecht leaves the protecting cross and goes toward her with outstretched arms, his eyes burning with desire and love. The fatal madness takes hold of him, he pirouettes, bounds, follows Giselle in her most hazardous leaps; the frenzy to which he gives way reveals a secret desire to die with his mistress and to follow the beloved shade to her tomb; but four o'clock strikes, a pale streak shows on the edge of the horizon. Dawn has come and with it the sun bringing deliverance and salvation. Flee, visions of the night; vanish, pale phantoms! A celestial joy gleams in Giselle's eyes: her lover will not die, the hour has passed. The beautiful Myrtha reenters her water lily. The Wilis fade away, melt into the ground and disappear. Giselle herself is drawn toward her tomb by an invisible power. Albrecht, distraught, clasps her in his arms, carries her, and, covering her with kisses, places her upon a flowered mound. . . . The hunting horn resounds; Wilfrid anxiously seeks for his master. He walks a little in front of the Prince of Courland and

The Theatre of Romance

FIGURE *3.13* Nostalgia for the past. The charm of old Vienna is suggested in the ballet *Liebeslieder Waltz*. The New York City Ballet, choreographed by George Balanchine. Photo Fred Fehl.

Bathilde. However, the flowers cover Giselle, nothing can be seen but her little transparent hand . . . this too disappears, all is over!—never again will Albrecht and Giselle see each other in this world. . . . The young man kneels by the mound, plucks a few flowers, and clasps them to his breast, then withdraws, his head resting on the shoulder of the beautiful **Bathilde**, who forgives and consoles him.

Most popular of all romantic ballets has been *Swan Lake* (1877), for which Tchaikovsky wrote very appealing music. It has everything: **a prince** rejecting reality to go in search of the ideal, a union in love at the **end, a Dr.** Jekyll-Mr. Hyde pair of heroines, usually danced by the same **ballerina, a** strong pantomime story, two acts of classical dancing at the enchanted **lake,** and two acts of folk and national dancing at the prince's court. **Prince Sieg-**fried welcomes his guests at his birthday celebration, but he is **depressed** because he must choose a wife at the court ball the next night. When a **flight** of wild swans passes over the sky, he and his men take up their hunting **horns** and start after them. At the enchanted lake they discover that the **swans** are really maidens who, in the power of a wicked magician, have the **form** of swans except from midnight to dawn. Siegfried of course falls in **love with** Odette, Queen of the Swans. He begs her to come to his ball that he may choose her as his wife. But the magician brings his own daughter, Odile, looking like Odette, and after the various Spanish dances, Hungarian czardas, and Polish mazurkas have been performed by his guests, the prince dances into her power and proposes. His beautiful Odette has been hovering near,

130

Kinds of Plays

but with this betrayal she screams and vanishes as lightning flashes and thunder rolls. The prince recognizes the deception and falls to the floor sobbing. Back at the lake, the swans beg Odette not to drown herself, and finally the prince arrives to ask forgiveness. In the original version, both plunge into the lake, and his sacrifice destroys the power of the magician. As the sun comes up, an enchanted bark is seen on the lake and the two lovers are shown united forever. But some Russian productions have supplied an equally happy ending in which Siegfried destroys the magician and he and Odette are united in this world.

Thus this classic-romantic dance form, born in Paris, reached perfection in Czarist Russia, where the court spent lavishly to support schools of dance as well as dance companies and orchestras. It kept the classic aspect in the formal line of the ensembles and the large amount of pure dance, with solos, duets, or *pas de deux,* and both small groups and large. Romantic taste was indulged in the dreamlike story, the sorrows and passions of the characters, the variety of costumes, and national or character dances. Some people prefer the pure or classic ballet dances, appreciating for their own sake the patterns of the group and the leaps, turns, and attitudes of the dancers. Others find this form too cold unless a story is added, with characterization, pantomime, and a hero and heroine in whose wishes and dreams they can see their own.

The highest achievement of the ballet came when the impresario Sergei Diaghilev, with a group of Russian dancers, began to produce ballets in Paris and the West. He attracted some of the best dancers in the world, and from 1909 until his death in 1929 he brought dancing, painting, and music into a new creative union. The ballet was able to adopt new modes of modern art as Picasso, Bakst, Rouault, and Derain designed settings and as Poulenc, Milhaud, Strauss, and Ravel composed music for Diaghilev. Stravinsky wrote

FIGURE *3.14* The charm of soft skirts and classic group form. The New York City Ballet in *Symphony in C.* Choreographed by George Balanchine. Photo Fred Fehl.

FIGURE *3.15*   Margot Fonteyn and Rudolf Nureyev in a typical ballet pose, from *Romeo and Juliet*. Royal Opera House, Covent Garden.

his three most famous compositions for this ballet company. *The Firebird* (1910) was an exotic version of the romantic story of a youth in an enchanted wood who destroys a wicked magician with the help of a supernatural girl in the form of a bird. *Petrushka* (1911) was made out of a story of a sensitive puppet defeated and killed by the more successful Moor, who runs off with the ballerina—an image of the helpless "little man" struggling in vain against dull, practical, powerful men. The third Stravinsky score, *The Rite of Spring* (1913), was so shocking in its primitive movements and violent rhythms that it caused a riot. It is not often revived, but the music grows in popularity; what once seemed only noise and dissonance is now accepted as a rich symphonic poem echoing our interest in primitive rhythms.

The great contribution of the Diaghilev ballet was to create a new art of the theatre, comparable to the concepts of Craig and Appia, in which all the elements—setting, costume, lighting, movement, music—would produce an artistic unity and harmony. Audiences liked seeing several short ballets in one evening, each creating a different effect but each effect carefully controlled in movement, color, and line, every tone of the orchestra contributing to the one idea and mood. Such a concept permitted considerable freedom in the use of classic techniques; the dancer Vaslav Nijinsky, for instance, used movement in two dimensions to create the archaic Greek effect for *The Afternoon of a Faun*. More than any other man of his time, Diaghilev brought into the theatre the creative forces of twentieth-century literature, art, and music.

Ballet came slowly to America. Anna Pavlova danced her dying swan from coast to coast and the Ballet Russe and its several successors played the major

Kinds of Plays

cities to a small but devoted following. Even as late as 1940 ballet was still an exciting importation from Europe; no one would have predicted that by the 1960s America would be a world center for ballet. Yet now there are schools all over the country as well as a number of ballet companies. American audiences have come to love ballet, and ballet has taken several new directions that seem particularly American. The American Ballet Theatre, founded in 1939 and subsidized for years by the millionairess Lucia Chase, continued the eclectic, international trends of the Ballet Russe, using national folk idioms and theatrical characters. Antony Tudor devised some striking psychological ballets for Ballet Theatre, and Agnes de Mille widened the style of the company to include the masculine vigor of the American West in *Rodeo*. In her autobiography, *Dance to the Piper,* Miss de Mille gives an entertaining account of the dancers' complaints about sore muscles as they prepared that ballet, and of the delight the American audience found in the work.

Most surprising has been the creation of an American classicism in the ballet, the achievement of George Balanchine and the New York City Ballet. Balanchine fled from Soviet Russia at the age of twenty, when the originality of his choreography met reproof. He became choreographer for Diaghilev's Ballet Russe for its last five years, titillating the European smart set with ballets of romantic, fairy-story, or religious content. Then in 1933 Lincoln Kirstein, a wealthy young man who was enthusiastic about the ballet, brought him to America to found a school and from it develop a performing company. The school has lasted and is still one of the most important training schools, but the performing company survived for only a few years. For a decade Balanchine made dances for Broadway musicals, movies, and several short-lived ballet companies. Finally, in 1946, Kirstein, with an inheritance of several hundred thousand dollars, backed Balanchine in the founding of the noncommercial Ballet Society, which in 1948 became the New York City

FIGURE *3.16* A caricature of the sensational dancer Lola Montez, 1851. Museum of the City of New York.

FIGURE *3.17* A romantic drama interpreted in ballet. The New York City Ballet in *A Midsummer Night's Dream*. Choreographed by George Balanchine. Photo Fred Fehl.

Ballet, the first officially sponsored company in America. If there was no real subsidy, there was a home. The city had taken over for taxes the old Mecca Temple. Renamed the New York City Center, it was the scene of popular-priced performances of drama and opera for many seasons; dance was now added.

There was little money for costumes and scenery, but Balanchine was not greatly interested in spectacle. With a young company, mostly from his own school, he soon achieved a distinctive, brilliant style. Where other choreographers, such as Michel Fokine and Antony Tudor, had turned against the classic tradition to widen and loosen the old techniques, Balanchine returned to the strict classic forms. It had formerly been necessary to give the popular audience a romantic story with obvious gesture and pantomime, but Balanchine could now depend more on the form of the music than on literature. Many of his ballets have the charm of romantic periods of the past, and he has made his own ballets to the music of *La Sonnambula* and *A Midsummer Night's Dream* and annually revives the old favorite, *The Nutcracker Suite*. Yet he has used Japanese music, electronic music, and the music of several of the more advanced composers. Particularly fruitful has been his collaboration with Stravinsky, whose music has encouraged harsh intensities and sharp modern movements.

When the big Russian ballet companies finally came to America in the late fifties and sixties and the New York City Ballet went to Russia in 1962, it was evident how much the West had advanced. Some of the Russian critics

134

Kinds of Plays

were cold, but audiences were enthusiastic. Behind the iron curtain, the Russians had been isolated for half a century from developments in modern art—surrealism, cubism, expressionism, and others—but they were at last eager to pay attention to man's private dreams and fearful dilemmas as well as to his public duties.

Balanchine has absorbed into the strict tradition of the ballet some of the subconscious images of the surrealists, the awareness of new harmonies and disharmonies in art and music, and some of the discontinuities and disjointed rhythms of industrial life. Instead of emphasizing spectacular solo performers and static tableaux of background groups, he often uses a number of leading dancers together and interweaves them with a dynamic corps de ballet, but always keeping the precision, purity, and elegance of the classic form.

In 1964, when the New York City Ballet moved into the New York State Theater, which had been built for it at Lincoln Center, it was recognized as the leading company in America. The same year it received an impressive grant from the Ford Foundation to strengthen its performing and teaching activities, and substantial money went to other schools around the country that were using the some classic approach to ballet. Some critics complained that other approaches to ballet, not to mention modern dance, also needed support, but Kirstein and Balanchine had set such a clear direction that they won the confidence of the Foundation officials.

The Russian and the British schools of classicism were brought together in a spectacular way when Rudolf Nureyev, the rebellious young star of the Russian tradition, defected at the Paris airport in 1961 and stayed to dance in the West. He became the partner of the best English dancer, Margot Fonteyn, and the two brought to the Royal Ballet of London new heights of excellence and fame. A richly endowed dancer whose leaps are unequaled, he became for the ballet public the most dashing romantic dancer since the short career of Nijinsky early in the century. No matter how abstract or impersonal classical ballet may be, its principal appeal remains romantic assertion and erotic pursuit.

To some people the most fascinating recent development in ballet has been the psychological and surrealist ballets. Romantic ballets have always dealt with the subjective, but only through conventionalized daydreams of alluring charmers and magic powers. The ballet in the British movie *Steps of the Ballet* is of this kind: a girl is visited by four goddesses offering four suitors bearing gifts; the story would not overtax the mind of a small child. But some recent ballets have dealt with modern neuroses, nightmares, and symbolic images of the subconscious. The motivation is more compelling when dancers move under the tension of strange fears, as if they were figures inside the mind, than when they move under the command of a magician, as if in an enchanted grove.

Antony Tudor made a strong impression with ballets suggesting subjective terrors and Freudian obsessions, first in England and then in America, where he joined the new Ballet Theatre in 1940. His *Pillar of Fire*, set to Arnold Schoenberg's tense, impressionistic "Transfigured Night," is a strong study of

FIGURE *3.18* Psychological tensions developed in a modern ballet. Motifs from Greek mythology haunt the mind. The New York City Ballet in *Agon.* Choreographed by George Balanchine, to music by Stravinsky. Photo Fred Fehl.

alienation, fear, betrayal, and forgiveness, centering on the tortured life of a woman who sees the man she loves dancing off with her coquettish younger sister and, terrified of being a loveless spinster, gives herself to a passing young man. More dark and turgid is *Undertow,* which sets a modern young man, rejected by his mother and hating the women who have most attracted him, against characters and episodes from neurotic Greek legends. Most influential of Tudor's works has been his *Lilac Garden,* choreographed in England in 1936 and established in the repertory of the Ballet Theatre; it brings four central figures together in a strange garden, haunted by memories and fears, missed opportunities and frustrations. Lacking Balanchine's admiration for strict classic techniques, Tudor has used the traditional techniques to portray the sterile moments of his characters and has used much freer movements to show release toward joy and health.

Departing even further from classical tradition than Tudor, Jerome Robbins has choreographed dances dealing with modern themes and emotions. With the composer Leonard Bernstein, he produced in 1946 a ballet called *Facsimile* about lonely people desperately trying to fill their time with cheap amusements. In 1950 the same two produced a more ambitious ballet, *The Age of Anxiety,* based on W. H. Auden's poem. Four lonely strangers get acquainted and start on a journey. The Seven Ages of Man are shown in the setting of a machine-age city, and a dream journey in search of happiness is pursued among masked figures. For a moment a mechanical father image becomes leader, but then the search is carried through blaring jazz intoxication to a strong revulsion against that image and to new questioning.

In the mid-fifties, Robbins left the regular ballet companies to create his own ballet world based on jazz idioms and rhythms, on slum characters and juvenile gangs, on the violent angers and tough swaggers of the homeless

136

Kinds of Plays

switchblade set. His new dream reached full realization in 1957 in *West Side Story* (discussed earlier as a musical), which achieves a strident excitement in the dance of unglamorous, tough juvenile prowlers. Here was the wry art of an age when even Christmas and Valentine cards are grotesque and monstrous. The dancers suggest a harsh industrial world trying to find a human image for itself. In 1958 Robbins prepared his "Ballets USA" for a European tour, with a full dance company that created an even greater excitement on an extensive tour in 1960–61. He became the center of raging controversy, some hailing him as one who had raised jazz dancing to a full art, others seeing his innovation as the destruction of the idealized beauty of the ballet. When his company played a season in New York in the fall of 1961, the dance critic John Martin, who had liked Robbins' earlier work, spoke out especially violently, accusing Robbins of catering to those Europeans who wanted to see America as sick, as no longer populated with healthy cowboys and Indians but with juvenile punks who dance with the pelvis leading in sneakers, levis, and T-shirts. He called this kind of dance "an abstract classicism of the vulgar . . . to replace the scarcely more artificial swan maidens of the non-USA ballet." But many balletomanes disagree with Martin. They like the tough dance of Robbins' psychological ballets and would leave the traditional ballet to the large state companies of Soviet Russia, the subsidized Royal Ballet of London, and the classic New York City Ballet.

In spite of Robbins and a few others, ballet, even more than the opera, has been a museum of eighteenth- and nineteenth-century art. Most people expect the ballet to serve them the same charming daydreams and floating fairyland that pleased their great-grandfathers. A living museum is marvelous, but it is no wonder that ballet seems effete or childish to those who hope for a closer relation between their art and their daily life.

MODERN DANCE

It is the other dance theatre—the theatre of modern dance—that has aimed for four decades to speak directly to modern man. In recent years, as we have seen, ballet has learned to deal with modern themes, and ballet dancers and modern dancers study from each other and from many other dance traditions. But for the first decades, the 1920s and 30s, modern dancers worked in the sharpest opposition to the ballet. In their search for freedom and originality and in their focus on the common people and on liberal social and political movements, they are heirs of the large romantic movement of the nineteenth century, but for a time they set themselves against the romantic ballet—its glamour, surface charm, and playful and erotic themes. They refused to wear pretty costumes and flaunted their stark leotards. Instead of painted-picture scenery they used drapes, blocks, and abstract shapes; instead of soft string orchestras and waltz tunes they called for percussion and harsh dissonances; instead of lightness, daintiness, and delicate poses they offered struggle, weight, and strain. They broke away from the limits of the rigid back and the five positions of arms and legs by setting the body free to follow the feelings of the dancer or the particular style suggested by the subject.

137

When they needed old traditions, modern dancers turned not to the aristocracy of Europe but to the free spirit of Greece, to the ritual dances of Africa and the South Seas, and to the ceremonies of Asia.

Isadora Duncan was the first champion of freedom in the dance. Like another unconventional American, Walt Whitman, who had freed poetry from rhyme and set rhythms, she became a symbol of liberation and originality in the arts. In 1899 this charming, headstrong girl from San Francisco, having found little response in New York, took her family on a cattle boat to England, and in a few years she had European artists, musicians, and dilettantes at her feet. To the horror of conventional ladies, she danced barefoot, scorning the restraint of ballet slippers, stiff bodices, corsets, as well as stereotyped dance movements. She was just as disdainful of marriage bonds and was talked about as much for her private life as for her dancing. Life punished her enough for her daring and her loose veils. Her children were drowned in an automobile that ran into the Seine; the one man she did marry, a poet, was a spoiled child who treated her abominably; and she herself was killed in 1929 when her trailing scarf caught in the wheels of her automobile and broke her neck. It is better to remember not her life but her work—the inspiration she gave to dancers and musicians and her deep devotion to the serious possibilities of her art.

Following Isadora Duncan there was a great interest in "aesthetic dancing,"

FIGURE 3.19 The pioneer of modern dance. Isadora Duncan at the Parthenon in Athens. Photo Edward Steichen.

and "interpretive dancers" in loose robes and veils floated about while a piano or small orchestra played light classical music. Ruth St. Denis and Ted Shawn, more serious artists, developed a company of capable dancers who trouped the country in carefully prepared "numbers" based on local color with many Oriental or American Indian themes. But the Denishawn dance was still too pretty and soft for some younger members of the company. In the late 1920s three broke away and started in new directions of their own. They became the "founders of modern dance" in America, for they not only danced and choreographed but taught the new dance in their studios in New York, in college summer schools, and in master classes and lecture demonstrations throughout the country. Martha Graham set up her own school and for more than three decades remained the top performer of modern dance. Doris Humphrey and Charles Weidman together set up a school and a performing company; their style, less austere and more charming than Martha Graham's, has had a great influence. Doris Humphrey continued to choreograph for other groups long after arthritis had stopped her own dancing, and she has left an important book on choreography, *The Art of Making Dances*. Weidman continued to direct his lively satiric dances into the 1960s.

In 1931 the American movement was strengthened by the visit of the German dancer Mary Wigman, who in the bitter moods of pre-Hitler Germany had developed a more somber approach to dance. Her stark, demonic intensity demonstrated that a dance can evolve out of its own materials and does not have to depend on music, story, or surface charm. A student of Wigman, Hanya Holm, settled in this country and became one of America's important teachers and choreographers, combining the stark Wigman approach with freer American styles. No one in 1931 would have predicted that this pupil of Wigman would some day do the choreography for such glamorous musicals as *My Fair Lady* and *Camelot*.

At first the modern dance seemed as abstract as cubist painting, as violent and machine-like as an expressionist play, as wild and ecstatic as a primitive ritual, as heavy and straining as a wrestling match. Convinced that ballet positions were artificial, the dancers explored the natural relation of movement to breathing, to tension and relaxation, to strain and weight, to work and play. They were especially interested in gravity—that natural force that ballet hides or denies—and hence in falls. They liked to let the audience in on their explorations, and sometimes a large part of a program was devoted to demonstration of studio exercises.

Martha Graham was the most distinctive figure. "Martha" she was called. (The leaders became such well-known personalities that they were often spoken of by their first names—Ted, Miss Ruth, Martha, Doris, Charles, Hanya.) Martha Graham embodied the tight nervousness of the modern tempo. Her rigid lips, stiff hands, and stark costumes, her percussive movements, with sudden jerks, sharp accents, and short, broken gestures—all expressed the anxiety of modern life. She did falls, she stamped her feet and clapped her hands, she walked on her knees, she crouched, she sprang, she suddenly pulled her head between her knees. If Doris Humphrey was not so

139

FIGURE *3.20* Two explorers of new forms in modern dance. Martha Graham and Merce Cunningham dance together in *Letter to the World,* a dance interpretation of the life of Emily Dickinson. Choreographed by Martha Graham. Photo Barbara Morgan.

startling as Graham, not so angular, so taut and neurotic, she was just as fresh in her search for free, natural movements. In her falls and leaps, her off-balance tensions and recoveries, she was very much like the rise and fall of waves, smooth but elemental.

As soon as audiences got used to the new approach to movement, they realized that the modern dancers had much to say—about modern life, yes, but most of all about modern feelings, about revolt and independence, sympathy for the struggling masses, the vital sweep of America, religious idealism, the half-hidden fears in the depths of the soul that demand symbolic expression today as surely as in primitive ritual or ancient myth. Martha Graham did a major study in religious feeling which she called *Primitive Mysteries,* and Doris Humphrey developed a serious dance based on the ecstatic dancing of the Shakers. Eleanor King has done group religious dances, the touching *Mother of Tears,* and, both in group and in solo, *Annunciation Triptych.* The psychology of the modern woman has fascinated most modern dancers. Humphrey gave one of the most balanced views in her *New Dance Trilogy,* the first modern dance planned to fill an entire evening. A composition for a large group, it showed the struggle of the modern woman to work out both her own destiny and her relationships with the outside world, feeling herself now in harmony with other people, now in conflict, now loving, now torn by destructive selfish love. King choreographed and filmed a startling dance called *She,* a study of the mothers who create in childbirth but become destructive later when the adolescent boy tries to pull away to find a love of his own. William Faulkner and Tennessee Williams, both subtle students of personality, have furnished characters and feeling for a number of new dances. Graham has penetrated furthest into the terrible jungle of the subconscious, especially in her dances based on Greek myths. Her titles suggest her psychological interest: *Cave of the Heart, Dark Meadow, Night Journey.*

Kinds of Plays

Although he loves comedy, Charles Weidman has given a sharp bite to his satiric pantomimes of women of many types.

The theme of America that gave such joyous energy to the ballet *Rodeo* and the musicals has sometimes brought the modern dancer out of the dark caves of the heart into the open sky. It has found expression in several of Graham's dances, but most of all in her *Appalachian Spring,* which is available in film. The hope and strength of the pioneer bride and groom as they build their house and set up their home in the mountains is an important celebration of America. Even the demonic impulse of the sin-obsessed preacher melts as the gay young girls help him bless the occasion.

In her later work Martha Graham returned to the dark exploration of ancient myth. If some followers, like the Contemporary Dance Theatre of San Francisco, have carried the Freudian psychology and physical techniques to an extreme, her influence has also been felt in a more controlled form through Jerome Robbins and others in psychological ballets and popular musicals.

The mature techniques of modern dance can be studied in two impressive short films of José Limón. Limón, born in Mexico and a student of the Humphrey-Weidman school, became a leading dancer and choreographer in the two decades after the Second World War, taking his dance group all over the United States and to many other countries in both hemispheres. His *Lament for Ignacio* uses spoken phrases from a poem by Lorca in praise of a Spanish bullfighter who was killed in the 1930s. Limón does not mime bullfighting but instead dances the grace and vigor of a bullfighter and the sharp pain of his death. In the other film, *The Moor's Pavane,* the dignified Renaissance court dance is a vehicle for the story of Othello. Two couples pair off in different

FIGURE *3.21* New movements, new costumes, and new intensities in modern dance. Though different from ballet, modern dance can have its own elegance and precision. Eleanor King in *Four Visions.* Photo Howard Whitlatch.

FIGURE *3.22* The violent story of *Othello* told in terms of an aristocratic court dance, the pavane. José Limón and Betty Jones in *The Moor's Pavane*. Photo James Robinson Sydney.

combinations, suggesting in movement the violent emotions and strong dramatic relationships, even the strangling of Desdemona, yet the stately dance goes on. On the sound track are key lines from Shakespeare's play, setting the violence of the story in opposition to the charm and restraint of the seventeenth-century music and the etiquette of the aristocracy. These films show that modern dance, at first so spare, has rediscovered the whole range of the theatre—lights, settings, costumes, and orchestras of sound.

But modern dance, never static, has sometimes moved away from the strong emotions of Martha Graham and José Limón, seeking new complexities in the movements of the body or new theatrical effects by the dynamic use of masks, mobiles, costumes, and lights. There is even a considerable exploration of the absurd.

Erick Hawkins is one who has made a new search for basic beginnings. After receiving training in both ballet and modern dance and spending several years as Martha Graham's leading man, he started in his own independent direction, exploring the excitement of fresh, clean movement and the assertion of masculine energy. Impersonal and austere in his approach, he uses little characterization—an occasional sad clown in a solo—and no story, and he depends little on costume or setting. Reacting against the turgid agonies-on-the-floor of some modern dancers, he prefers to relate himself to heights—the morning sky or the hilltop. One is not surprised to learn that he had American Indian ancestors and that he was a Greek scholar at Harvard.

If Hawkins is all dance and little theatre, Alwin Nikolais seemed at first all theatre and little dance. His treatment of the dancers has been even more impersonal than Hawkins'. Sometimes their faces are covered as they move

Kinds of Plays

FIGURE *3.23* Dance as form in movement, with no attempt to create charm, drama, or any of the traditional sentiments. *Galaxy, A Dance Theatre Piece.* Choreographed by Alwin Nikolais. Photo Susan Schiff Faludi.

abstract forms, geometrical shapes, flexible cords, wrappings, and balloons, and they seem not human bodies but surging grotesque forms animated from within but lacking human will or desire. The choreography has been influenced by the geometrical studies of space, initiated in the Bauhaus of pre-Hitler Germany, that have influenced many architects and industrial designers. At other times, Nikolais lets the human emerge in exciting movements and groupings, with stunning costumes and settings and dynamic lighting that give the highest theatrical effect. Most theatrical of all is the Nikolais sound track on electronic tape, made up of many actual or "concrete" sounds combined with many electronic sounds that have never been heard before. The complexities of a complete orchestra are possible at a fraction of the expense, and, in addition, there is a limitless range of new sounds.

Out of the Nikolais theatre and school at the Henry Street Settlement in New York has emerged Murray Louis, an excellent dancer and choreographer who does not hesitate to create characters—lively, individual, and often humorous—or to suggest fleeting human relationships in the group, yet who is impersonal enough to allow the excitement of pure movement to come through.

But the reaction against romantic emotions and neat compositions has gone much further with some *avant-garde* dancers. They show the natural impulse of all theatre people to wake up an audience that has become accustomed to any set of conventions and is therefore passive. Why not dance among the seats, let the performers suddenly look at the audience and imitate their reactions? Instead of mounting a museum piece, complete and dead, why not invite a more active, imaginative response? Put many things on the stage and let the audience choose what it wants to watch. Bring back spontaneity for both performers and audience. Set a dozen musicians playing anything

143

The Theatre of Romance

FIGURE *3.24*   Dance as momentary encounters with people and space. *Interim.*
Choreographed by Murray Louis. Photo Susan Schiff Faludi.

they want to play, mix in a few radios, electronic sounds on very loud loud-speakers, and a siren or two. Develop a "dance by chance," leaving some movements to the whim of the performers, or let dice or cards determine the next move. Or give the audience moments of rest, with nothing whatever to see; do not Zen doctrines praise the promising empty space of a bowl more than the visible porcelain, and find more spiritual value in the empty part of a picture than in the visible details? Like the pop artists and the writers of absurd dramas we will discuss in another chapter, these *avant-garde* dancers insist that the present generation must come to terms with the banalities of daily conversation, advertising, comic strips. If experience is already chopped into fragments, break it even more. The "happenings," arranged but not planned, in which various elements of several arts are thrown into action to see what may result, promise a certain kind of excitement. A group of guests gathered at the Museum of Modern Art to watch a machine devised to destroy itself and saw the ultimate in junk and blowtorch sculpture, a collage of incongruous textures, rhythms, and antirhythmic movement—a satire on the destructiveness and meaninglessness of modern civilization.

The leader of this dance theatre of the absurd, this antidance, is Merce Cunningham, who danced for years with Martha Graham. With the *avant-garde* musician John Cage, and later with the experimental artist and sculptor Robert Rauschenberg, he has presented programs designed to shock the conservative, outrage the normal expectations of most people, amaze the young, and perhaps now and then point out a step beyond nihilism. He uses empti-ness not for Zen harmony and peace but for the shock of discontinuity, with the impudent effrontery, for instance, of having a dancer stand still for several

Kinds of Plays

minutes, then make one jump. The wonderful leaps Cunningham did with Graham's company are used for violent kinetic contrasts, as he begins by suggesting what dancing he can do, then interrupts himself and throws away the expectation he has created. Is anybody in the audience sure that his world has more order and less loud-speaker noise than the dance on the stage?

From the institutional point of view, modern dance has been at one great disadvantage in comparison with ballet. It is easy to get a large ballet company together and put on stunning theatrical spectacles. Ballet dancers, trained in standardized techniques, are interchangeable parts, easily adapted to the plans of the choreographer. But modern dance has encouraged individuality by allowing each dancer to release his own feelings and special techniques. Hence modern dancers have been inclined to work independently, creating new things for solo dance or small groups rather than settling down as performers of someone else's choreography. Only at the annual summer modern dance festival, first held at Bennington College then regularly at Connecticut College in New London, have they joined together for large-scale works. However, in recent years the New York State Theater has made room for seasons of modern dance: first briefly in November, 1964, and then for several weeks in March, 1965, large group dances in modern techniques were presented under official sponsorship. The audience response was immediate. It became clear that modern dance now has an impressive tradition, from the classics of Doris Humphrey and other choreographers of the thirties on to the host of recent dance-makers and performers. Such large group presentations will not replace solo dancing or small groups any more than symphony orchestras replace solo concerts or chamber music. But they mark the coming of age of modern dance as it exhibits a full theatre of dance, with setting, costuming, and orchestra, and a regular season of performance.

In the chapter on the various forms of realism, we concluded that realism had been able to borrow from many other traditions and even to find a place for the intensities of masks, music, poetry, and dance. The recent developments in ballet and modern dance, as we found with the musical, show that romance, formerly devoted entirely to the distant and exotic, can in its turn deal with many vital aspects of the present.

FIGURE 3.25   Modern dance as drama. The movements and costumes for *Haniwa* are based on the primitive sculpture of the Haniwa period in Japan. University of Arkansas production, choreographed by Eleanor King. Photo Howard Whitlatch.

EXERCISES AND DEMONSTRATIONS

1. ANALYSIS OF AN OPERA ARIA. Using a recording of an aria and a libretto of the opera or a printed score with both the original and the English words, show how the aria is related to the dramatic situation that leads up to it. How does it express in words and tone the character and his emotions? Is any change of thought or emotion expressed in the course of the aria?

2. ANALYSIS OF AN OPERA ENSEMBLE. Select an opera ensemble and describe the different characters and emotions that are brought together in it. How are the differences among the characters indicated through pitch, rhythm, and mood? The quartet near the end of *Rigoletto* or the serenade the Don sings to Elvira in *Don Giovanni,* both mentioned in this chapter, are good examples.

3. ELEMENTARY PROBLEMS IN CHOREOGRAPHY. Using a square dance for two couples, plan a new composition for three or five dancers with the same music and variations of the same simple dance figures. What variations of the regular movements are needed? Are some new movements needed? What floor patterns besides square, diagonal, and circle can be used? Where will symmetry appear? Where asymmetry? Where will repetition, sequence, and opposition be used in relating one dancer to the other, one movement to the next? How can a climax be built from square dance movements that regularly return quickly to rest?

4. CHOREOGRAPHY FOR STORY. Add to the last exercise a personal and emotional story, such as a competition between two people or a strong hatred. How can standard movements be made to express an emotion?

5. ANALYSIS OF A DANCE COMPOSITION. After seeing the film *The Moor's Pavane* with José Limón, describe how the stately movements of the court pavane are modified as the four characters—Othello, Desdemona, Iago, and Emilia—are swept by their changing emotions without ever stopping the dance.

6. ANALYSIS OF A DANCE COMPOSITION. After seeing the film *Lament for Ignacio* with José Limón, describe how some moments are extended and developed into a dance that is not just the mimed story of a bullfighter who comes onto the field, meets his fate, shudders in death, crawls to his coffin, and dances again in the memory of the woman. Typical dance moments are the stabbing of Fate, the series of falls, and the spasms of death.

7. DANCE MOVEMENTS FOR THE ACTOR. Taking a familiar activity of work or sport, such as digging, making something, hitting a golf ball, give it first a theatrical shape—coming on stage, getting into stride, carrying

EXERCISES AND DEMONSTRATIONS

through, coming to a close or an exit. Then give it a basic rhythm, thinking of a particular piece of music. Then give it a character and an immediate motive—a junior executive furious with his boss, a young man showing off to a new girl, and so on. Give the exercise a moment when it approaches dance by the repetition of a few movements for the pleasure of making a rhythmic pattern.

RECOMMENDED RECORDINGS AND FILMS

OPERA RECORDINGS

Ten good stereo recordings of complete operas made in the early sixties are recommended: Bizet, *Carmen,* with Maria Callas (Angel SCL-3650); Donizetti, *Lucia di Lammermoor,* with Joan Sutherland in the favorite of all coloratura roles (London OSA-1327); Leoncavallo, *I Pagliacci,* and Mascagni, *Cavalleria Rusticana,* two popular operas usually performed together, with Mario Del Monaco (London OSA-1330); Mozart, *Don Giovanni,* with Cesare Siepi (London OSA-1401); Mozart, *The Marriage of Figaro* (London OSA-1402); Puccini, *La Bohème,* with Mirella Freni (Angel SBL-3643); Puccini, *Madama Butterfly,* with Victoria De Los Angeles (Angel SCL-3604); Verdi, *Aïda,* with Leontyne Price (Victor LSC-6158); Verdi, *La Traviata,* with Joan Sutherland (London OSA-1366); Wagner, *Tristan and Isolde,* with Birgit Nilsson (London OSA-1502).

DANCE FILMS

A selected list of dance films is given in *Dance Magazine,* September, 1965.

The most satisfactory films have been those feature movies of the big studios that have included dance as part of the story. Most of the films of Broadway musicals have a great deal of dance. Several especially interesting movies were not adaptations of musicals but original scripts planned to make extensive use of dance. *The Red Shoes,* described in Chapter 2, has a long romantic ballet as its center. The film is available in 16 mm. from both Contemporary Films and United World Films. In *Seven Brides for Seven Brothers,* the vigorous open-air choreography of Michael Kidd is seen, and in *On the Town,* the urban vigor of Jerome Robbins. Both films are available from Films Inc. *An American in Paris,* with music by George Gershwin, featuring Gene Kelly and Leslie Caron, is mostly dance. It is also available from Films Inc.

The three best films of ballet, made in England on 35 mm., will doubtless eventually be available in 16 mm. One, made in 1956, presents the Moscow Bolshoi Ballet in several short ballets; another, made in 1959, presents the Royal Ballet in *Ondine,* Act II of *Swan Lake,* and *The Firebird.* Still another, released in 1966, shows the Royal Ballet with Margot Fonteyn and Rudolf Nureyev in *Les Sylphides, Le Corsaire, La Valse,* and *Aurora's Wedding.*

The best introduction to ballet is the British *Steps of the Ballet,* available from Encyclopaedia Britannica. Two short French films showing how ballet is rehearsed are excellent: *Spirit of the Dance* and *Adagio,* available from Film Images. *Russian Ballerina,* a full-length feature story of a rising star that includes several scenes from ballets, is available from Brandon Films. One of the finest filmings of ballet is the Russian *Ballet of Romeo and Juliet,* a 96-minute film with Galina Ulanova which won an award at the 1955 Cannes Film Festival. It is available from Brandon Films.

147

The four films of Martha Graham, made with far more than the usual care, are excellent. In *A Dancer's World,* which she narrates, her young company demonstrates her later, more lyric technique. In *Night Journey* she performs Jocasta in the Oedipus story, in *Clytemnestra,* the murderess-wife in the Agamemnon story, and in *Appalachian Spring,* a pioneer wife. The films are available from Contemporary Films and Brandon Films.

Good short films of modern dance are *The Desperate Heart,* with Valerie Bettis, available from Brandon Films; *Negro Spirituals,* with Helen Tamiris, available from Contemporary Films; and *The Moor's Pavane* and *Lament for Ignacio,* both with José Limón and both available from Contemporary Films.

SUGGESTED READING

OPERA

General information is available in Harold Rosenthal and John Worrack, eds., *The Concise Oxford Dictionary of Opera* (1965). Most useful for beginners are the books that tell the stories with some descriptions of performances and a few of the melodies. Those who can read a little music can study and prepare from Rudolph Fellner, *Opera: Themes and Plots** (1958), from the more thorough study of ten operas by George R. Marek, *Opera as Theatre* (1962), or from the very full treatment by Gustave Kobbé, *The Complete Opera Book* (1922; rev. ed., 1954). The casual operagoer will turn to such large books as George Martin, *The Opera Companion: A Guide for the Casual Operagoer* (1961), Frank Leslie Moore, *Crowell's Handbook of World Opera* (1961), or the very inexpensive summaries and musical notes in Stephen Williams, *Come to the Opera* (1961). Very good, fairly brief, and inexpensive is Mary Ellis Peltz, ed., *Introduction to Opera: A Guidebook Sponsored by the Metropolitan Opera Guild** (1956). Henry W. Simon, *100 Great Operas and Their Stories* (1960), is popular for quick reference. There are other useful collections of stories of the operas, for instance, those by Milton Cross and by Ernest Newman. Newman also wrote several books of vivid descriptions of performances: *Opera Nights* (1943), *More Opera Nights* (1954), and *Wagner Nights* (1949).

Of histories, Edward J. Dent, *Opera** (1940; rev. ed., 1949), is very readable. More thorough is Donald J. Grout, *A Short History of Opera* (2nd ed., 1965). Attractive is Philip Hope-Wallace, *A Picture History of Opera* (1959). Key selections from Wagner's writings are presented in a systematic arrangement in Albert Goldman and Evert Sprinchorn, *Wagner on Music and Drama** (1964). Good studies of other composers are Dent, *Mozart's Operas* (1947), Francis Toy, *Verdi* (1931), and Mosco Carner, *Puccini* (1958). A serious discussion of the problems of drama and opera is Joseph Kerman, *Opera as Drama** (1956). A good tribute to the Metropolitan is done by Mary Ellis Peltz in *The Magic of the Opera* (1960). Irving Kolodin, *The Story of the Metropolitan Opera* (1951), is a more systematic history, and Frank Merkling, John W. Freeman, and Gerald Fitzgerald, *The Golden Horseshoe: The Life and Times of the Metropolitan Opera House* (1965), gives an elaborate survey.

The problem of audience and civic support across America is discussed by Herbert Graf in *Opera for the People* (1951). For the struggles of a stage director against conventional opera acting, see Tyrone Guthrie, *A Life in the Theatre**

148 * Available in paperback edition.

(1959). A de luxe survey of world opera from 1600 to the present, with 364 illustrations, published in English in Czechoslovakia and sold in America for less than four dollars, is K. V. Burian, *The Story of World Opera* (1961).

There are good brief articles on "Incidental Music" and "Opera" in *The Oxford Companion to the Theatre* (2nd ed., 1957) and excellent articles on operas, opera houses, and performers with many illustrations in the *Enciclopedia della Spettacola* (1954–62).

DANCE: GENERAL

The best general introduction is John Martin, *Book of the Dance* (1963). Similar and equally well illustrated is Agnes de Mille, *The Book of the Dance* (1963), while a more personal brief introduction is her *To a Young Dancer* (1963). Her autobiography, *Dance to the Piper* (1952), is one of the best written accounts of the life of a dancer. Two of Martin's early books have been reprinted in paperback without revision: *Introduction to the Dance* (1939) and *The Modern Dance* (1933).

The best full history is Curt Sachs, *World History of the Dance** (1938), but Joost A. M. Meerloo has a very original and well-illustrated psychological sketch in *The Dance from Ritual to Rock and Roll* (1960).

Two good reference works are Anatole Chujoy, *The Dance Encyclopedia* (1949), and W. G. Raffe and M. E. Purdon, *Dictionary of the Dance* (1964). Romano Calvi brought out a beautifully illustrated *Dance Year* (1964).

A survey of the problem of organization and support of dance, theatre, and music is presented in the report of The Rockefeller Brothers Fund, *The Performing Arts: Problems and Prospects* (1964).

Of religious interest are E. L. Backman, *Religious Dance in the Christian Church and in Popular Medicine* (1962), and Margaret Palmer Fisk, *The Art of the Rhythmic Choir: Worship Through Symbolic Movement* (1950).

The problem of making films of dance is discussed in Arthur Knight, "Dancing in Films," *Dance Index,* VI, 8, and in "Dance in the Screen Media," *Impulse* (1960).

DANCE: BALLET

An excellent short introduction to ballet is the Penguin volume by A. L. Haskell, *Ballet: A Complete Guide to Appreciation** (1938; rev. ed., 1955). Joan Lawson is good on *Classical Ballet: Its Style and Technique* (1960). The fullest account of particular ballets is George Balanchine, *Balanchine's Complete Stories of the Great Ballets* (1954), though Roselyn Krokover, *The New Borzoi Book of Ballets* (1956), and two books by C. W. Beaumont, *Ballets of Today* (1954) and *Ballets Past and Present* (1955), are useful. Lawson has a short but good *History of Ballet and Its Makers* (1964). Olga Maynard presents both personalities and principles in *The American Ballet* (1960). Haskell has an attractive *Picture History of Ballet* (1954), and there are many illustrations in K. V. Burian, *The Story of World Ballet* (1964). Since 1947 Haskell has brought out *Ballet Annual,* with news, articles, and illustrations.

The three great choreographers who brought the Russian ballet tradition into relation with the art of the West are described in M. Fokine's edition of his

* Available in paperback edition.

father's papers, *Fokine* (1961); Haskell, *Diaghilev* (1935; rev. ed., 1955); S. L. Gregoriev, *Diaghilev Ballet, 1909–1929* (1953); and Bernard Taper, *Balanchine* (1963).

DANCE: MODERN

Isadora Duncan wrote a vivid autobiography, *My Life* (1928), and a series of essays on *The Art of the Dance* (1928). Her disciple Irma Duncan wrote a short book on *The Technique of Isadora Duncan* (1937). Two biographies are good: Allan Ross MacDougall, *Isadora: A Revolutionary in Art and Love* (1962), and Walter Terry, *Isadora Duncan: Her Life, Her Art, Her Legacy* (1964), but they cannot match the vividness of her autobiography. Mary Wigman's revolutionary ideas appeared in *The Language of Dance* (1966).

Besides the books of John Martin mentioned above, there are two excellent books on the development of modern dance, though neither deals with the last two decades. The larger is Margaret Lloyd, *The Borzoi Book of Modern Dance* (1949). The briefer book, Maynard, *American Modern Dancers: The Pioneers* (1965), is a very good introduction. Seven recent views are gathered in *The Modern Dance: Seven Statements of Belief* (1966), edited by Selma Jeanne Cohen. Louis Horst has a short but stimulating *Modern Dance Forms in Relation to the Other Modern Arts* (1961). Paul Love wrote a useful *Modern Dance Terminology* (1953).

On Martha Graham, Merle Armitage edited an excellent collection of essays by different writers, *Martha Graham* (1937). Barbara Morgan published some beautiful photographs in *Martha Graham* (1941). More recent work is covered in Karl Leabo, *Martha Graham* (1962). There is an excellent chapter on Martha Graham from the theatrical point of view in Eric Bentley, *In Search of Theatre** (1953).

Doris Humphrey set down her principles of choreography, evolved over many years, in *The Art of Making Dances* (1959). A different approach to choreography is given in Peggy Van Praagh and P. Brinson, *The Choreographic Art* (1963).

A lively profile of the *avant-garde* musician John Cage which includes an account of Merce Cunningham's new dances appeared in the *New Yorker*, XL (Nov. 28, 1964). The entire issue of the *Tulane Drama Review* for Winter, 1965 (T30), was devoted to "happenings," which often involve dancers.

Dance training for the actor is treated in two good English books and one American: Rudolf Laban, *The Mastery of Movement* (rev. ed., 1960); Lyn Oxenford, *Design for Movement* (1952); Edwin C. White and Marguerite Battye, *Acting and Stage Movement* (1963).

150 * Available in paperback edition.

CHAPTER FOUR

THE THEATRE OF EXALTATION:
GREEK TRAGEDY AND THE
MODERN FESTIVAL THEATRE

The theatre can charm the spirit, as we have seen in the last two chapters, but it can also raise the spirit to the highest exaltation. Even in a commercial theatre the play may be as powerful as a prayer or a religious ritual in bringing man into contact with the divine. The theatre may become, in Shaw's phrase, "a temple of the spirit." An even more exalted mood is created when the audience makes a special pilgrimage to see the play. Since the seventeenth century, travelers from round the world have gathered every ten years in the Bavarian mountain village of Oberammergau to witness the Passion Play put on with religious devotion by the villagers themselves. There are Wagner festivals in Germany, special Mozart performances in Austria, and Shakespeare festivals in the three Stratfords—England, Ontario, and Connecticut—and several other places. A play based on the Book of Job creates a festival shrine in Kentucky, and near Palmyra, New York, Mormons and their friends see the Hill Cumorah come alive with hosts of performers re-enacting the visions of Joseph Smith. Plays of American history, presented near the places where important events occurred, have drawn large audiences of vacation travelers over the last three decades. And England has a well-established tradition of religious festival plays, usually presented in the great cathedrals.

Religious drama, depicting the most important acts of the gods and the prophets, came into existence thousands of years ago, apparently as soon as there was religion or any concept of man's share in divine purpose. In ancient Egypt, the new king himself performed the central role in a coronation drama celebrating the victory of the young god Horus over the evil spirit Set and his own rebirth as the son of the Divine Spirit. When a king died, either the new king or his priests performed a drama before his tomb every day at sunrise to celebrate the resurrection of the spirit and its journey to the stars. This Egyptian drama, though it influenced the Greek, was completely forgotten and only recently has the story begun to be pieced together.

In Greece the drama grew up in the Dionysian festival celebrating the resurrection of the spring out of the sacrificial death of the old season. The festival opened with a wild and ecstatic procession; its high point was a series of choral dance dramas performed in a large outdoor theatre. To the traditional rowdy satyr plays, the Athenians added a very serious new form—tragedy—which combined the pain and humiliation of sacrificial death with the joy and exaltation of resurrection. Tragedy was profoundly religious, yet it put the emphasis on man and the values of this world. In accepting the defeat and death of a great hero, the audience felt pride and joy that a man had challenged the universe and measured his finite reach against the infinite. As Nietzsche pointed out, tragedy is the greatest of our affirmations of life. It is fitting that it was the principal performance at the Greek festival of spring and renewal.

The Tragic Vision

Tragedy is the most fascinating and amazing of all forms of exalted drama: fascinating because it is the most universal, carrying its appeal on stages of many different kinds to ages and countries far distant from its origin; amazing because this most serious of forms is very successful entertainment, and, while celebrating the defeat and death of the hero, one that gives pleasure to its audience. This paradox never ceases to puzzle and intrigue students of drama, and each tries to find his own explanation. We have numerous theories, involving not only problems of aesthetics and of the psychology of the audience but the deepest philosophical problems. Tragedy asks several profound questions: What is man's relation to the world, to himself, and to heaven? What is the meaning of evil and suffering, of choice and responsibility? How can man be both an individual with free will and a part of society and the universe? Those who are shaken deeply by seeing tragedy find that if the first part of the play strengthens their sense of being a rebellious individual, the ending and the import of the play reconcile them to the mystery at the heart of the universe.

The beginning student is usually startled to be told that popular conceptions of tragedy are wrong. He often thinks that the main difference between a comedy and a tragedy is that one ends happily and the other unhappily. He calls an accident tragic, and when asked to suggest a tragic plot he may think of a couple killed in a wreck on the way to the wedding or of a victim of temptation drifting into drink, degradation, and despair on skid row. He may enjoy a romantic or pathetic tale with a sad ending and even like the sharp excitement of an ironic ending. But as he explores the shocking scene of Oedipus cursing the day he was born or of King Lear raging back at the storm, he finds that he must go far beyond sadness and moral indignation to reach a spiritual exaltation that is partly aesthetic pleasure, partly a new understanding of man's destiny in the face of the infinite.

A tragedy progresses through several phases—it is not merely the turn of fortune's wheel that lifts a man to a peak, then plunges him to disaster and ruin; not merely the irony of fate that turns hopes and promises to despair and disillusionment; not merely the miscalculation, the guilt, the tragic flaw that exposes man to overwhelming punishment. It may contain any or all of these. One of the strongest patterns involves making a choice and then facing the results of that choice, but often, as in Sophocles' *Oedipus the King* and many of Ibsen's plays, the choice and the deed took place long ago and the play itself traces the long trail of results that must be faced. Tragedy, like romance, may show a quest for the secret of eternal life—a journey to a dark grove, an underground cave, or a secret place at the bottom of the sea—and a struggle with an evil monster. The hero gains his own soul, the token of his identity, even as he pays for what he has won by some dire sacrifice. The early part of the play may provoke rebellion, the isolation of the hero, while the end brings his reconciliation, his acceptance in harmony. The suffering, the struggle, may bring a cleansing. The final phase may be like a harvest, the ripening and gathering and bringing to rest after long growth, or, more frequently, like the painful sacrifice and transcendent resurrection of the rites of spring. Hence we have accumulated a number of key words, many of them dating back to Aristotle, to describe the phases of the tragic patterns: reversal of fortune, irony of fate, blind fate, tragic flaw, choice, decision, responsibility, discovery, sacrifice, redemption, catharsis, inevitability, universality, and reconciliation.

Especially helpful for an understanding of the many possible phases of the tragic pattern is Francis Fergusson's suggestion in *The Idea of a Theatre* that they may be looked at as the three P's: purpose, passion, and perception.

PURPOSE

In most tragedies the hero faces a great crisis that challenges him to the utmost. Often that challenge comes near the beginning as the hero takes on the terrible burden of action, the burden which Hamlet called a "cursed spite."

> The time is out of joint. O cursed spite
> That ever I was born to set it right.

Oedipus finds a terrible blight on the kingdom and his people turning to him to cleanse the land, no matter what the cost. In *Macbeth* the promises of the witches stir ambitions that terrify the hero. Lured on in the "swelling act of

153

the imperial theme," he knows that "to catch the nearest way" must be by murder, and murder is still against his customary nature.

> If good, why do I yield to that suggestion
> Whose horrid image doth unfix my hair
> And make my seated heart knock at my ribs
> Against the use of nature?

But yield he does, starting down the path that does not turn back. Willy Loman, the hero of Arthur Miller's *Death of a Salesman,* faces a terrifying failure he cannot understand. He is indignant. He has been displaced from his rightful place in the world. He demands justice—of his sons, of the past, of his long-lost brother, of the night. In "Tragedy and the Common Man," Miller says of tragedy: "The fateful wound from which the inevitable events spiral is the wound of indignity, and its dominant force is indignation. Tragedy, then, is the consequence of a man's total compulsion to evaluate himself justly."

Isolation is the immediate price the hero pays for taking up his burden, but it is an isolation, a rebellion, that gives him identity. Beginning with Aeschylus' Prometheus, who stole fire from heaven and succored mankind in defiance of Zeus, the heroes of tragedy have taken a stand against the accepted order, either of man or of the gods. They are men of pride and stature. They will risk destruction, even crime, in order to assert themselves, and tragedy, from Clytemnestra and Orestes to Iago and Macbeth and to the heroes of Dostoevski, Sartre, and Camus, has included many of "the great offenders," those who turn to ruthless violence and murder rather than accept the world as it is. The world may ultimately destroy them, but not be-

FIGURE *4.1* The spirit of Greek tragedy. Gordon Craig offered the simplicity and exalted nobility he found in Greek art as an antidote to the petty realism of the early twentieth century. This design for a setting for *Electra* is characteristic.

fore they have said their say. Theirs may be a limited freedom, but out of the solid rock of necessity they hew a space for freedom. It is a perilous freedom, but for a moment the hero holds it. He does choose, and choice is the very basis of identity. Antigone says to her terrified sister, "You can choose, you can be what you want to be." Nowhere in art or literature is there a fuller insistence on the importance of free will than in tragedy. Freedom is gained at a terrific price. The hero is defeated, but that particular battle will never have to be fought again. Each tragic play is a map and a deed to one little plot of freedom forever redeemed out of the dark, mysterious unknown.

In his isolation, his separation, the hero sees his values threatened. He pushes back the limits of the human farther than they have ever been pushed before, but of course he is stopped. Then he cries out against injustice. However he may find acceptance and reconciliation in the end, in the earlier phases of tragedy the hero finds the immediate gods above his head to be unjust. In Aeschylus' whole trilogy about Prometheus, Zeus, the Lord of Heaven, learns wisdom and is reconciled with Prometheus, but in the one play that has come down to us, *Prometheus Bound,* the two are apparently irreconcilable. As Prometheus is overwhelmed by Zeus's thunderbolts and as the chasm of the mountain is split open to take him far down into the earth, he cries out with his last breath, "Behold me, I am wronged." Lear does not take his treatment calmly. He lays a dire curse on his ungrateful daughters. Then, when he is thrust out into the storm and discovers that the very elements take their part, he turns his rage on the heavens. He cries foul. He may be helpless before the elements, but he is their moral superior, and he can tell them so.

> Here I stand your slave,
> A poor, infirm, weak, and despis'd old man.
> But yet I call you servile ministers,
> That will with two pernicious daughters join
> Your high-engender'd battles 'gainst a head
> So old and white as this. O, oh, 'tis foul!

Macbeth is furious at the mockery of promises and appearances, where foul is fair and whatever is, is not. At the end of O'Neill's *Anna Christie,* Old Chris sits pondering the strange ironies of life. He had tried to save his daughter from a coarse life among sailors, but she, too, was drawn into the life of the sea. He is no Prometheus who can foretell that Zeus will change in thousands of years; he controls only a very tiny realm of free will and knowledge. But he can shake his fist at "Dat old debil Sea."

To the extent that a man asserts his difference, his ability to stand apart from the universe and declare that it is wrong, he becomes a tragic hero. He is no longer a victim, a thing; he becomes a man by stealing a bit of the fire of heaven. He is no longer merely a creature; he, too, in his small way, becomes a creator. He transcends the finite even as he sinks, lost, in the infinite. We are not always sure whether it is pride, duty, arrogance, love of the good, or love of rebellion that drives the hero in his self-assertion, but we glory in his will and his choice. He takes the risk. By disobeying restrictions, he does push out the old limits.

Sometimes a tragedy is a simple study of the heroic, of the pioneer who breaks the path for the benefit of the next generation. He partially succeeds and gives his life in the battle in order that those who come after him may fully succeed. In 1945, as the plans for the United Nations were being laid, an impressive movie about Woodrow Wilson showed his struggle to establish a League of Nations in 1919. Wilson was destroyed not merely because he miscalculated the response of American senators but because as a pioneer he was inevitably ahead of his time. The bloody footsteps of the soldiers at Valley Forge trace for us a very simple path of purpose. Those men suffered for us. But purpose is only the first part of Fergusson's trilogy. Most tragedies include other complexities.

PASSION

Before they reach a reconciliation, most tragic heroes undergo tremendous suffering or struggle in which they question the basis of their own being and see the foundations of the world shaken. Like the violent convulsions of shock treatment in psychotherapy, the tragic experience tears apart all the conventional established relations. The lid is taken off the universe, opening up the great void, the deep volcano, the hidden terror. The isolation leads far away from the petty world of problem-solving. The soul is left naked, exposed to the winds from the outer spheres. Terrifying enough when there is the utmost faith in the benevolence of a deity, the glimpse over the edge often comes to the hero when he is in the strongest conflict and acutely aware of the hideous cruelty in the world. The more romantic imagination often sees evil in the very positive terms of a demonic universe. George Steiner calls it the "otherness" of the world. In *The Death of Tragedy,* one of the best of many recent analyses of tragedy, he writes, "Call it what you will: a hidden or malevolent God, blind fate, the solicitations of hell, or the brute fury of our animal blood. It waits for us in ambush at the crossroads. It mocks us and destroys us. In certain rare instances, it leads us after destruction to some incomprehensible repose." Ultimately, most tragic heroes find religious meaning in the universe, but not until they have fully faced the indifference, the malignity, and the devastating play of chance and accident.

The tragic hero cannot take the easy way out. He is fighting for his soul; his commitment is his identity. He must risk his life rather than fail his identity. He sees accident and blind determinism in the world, but that does not relieve him of responsibility. Jocasta urges Oedipus to ask no questions, to take the moments of life as they come, since all is chance and no man can predict the future. But Oedipus cannot accept this solution; he knows that not all is chance. Though the oracles predict the future, not everything is determined. Man acts, and even when blind he is responsible for his actions. Usually the tragic hero goes knowingly into his battle, with a need to face the final test, and the dimensions of the struggle give him stature. It is not a local tempest in a teapot, though there have been actors who made Lear suburban and

156

Othello a fretting husband. But these plays fail as tragedies unless the passion is of transcendent importance.

PERCEPTION

Tragedy is most significant in its final phase, that is, when meaning becomes clear, when the sacrifice is followed by a resurrection, when the trial reaches judgment and sentence, when the isolated hero is reconciled to the world he has opposed. By paying the price of suffering, he learns to be both an individual and a part of the mysterious larger entity. At last the world that seemed capricious, malignant, and unjust is revealed as moral, meaningful, and ordered, though finite man may never completely understand that order.

On the simplest level, the hero faces the result of his own actions. He had it coming. *Mourning Becomes Electra* is the title O'Neill gave his longest tragedy. His modern Electra, after being involved in avenging her father's death and in the suicide of her brother, rejects all active contact with the world and closes herself in the family mansion to live with her ghosts. Mourning is suitable to Electra. In *Sweet Bird of Youth,* one of Tennessee Williams' playboys, given the significant name Chance, finally stops running away and faces the mob he knows is determined to castrate him, saying, "Something's got to mean something." Even medieval writers, who did not guess the larger meaning of tragedy, could understand this elementary level. When Herod, in their passion plays, ordered the slaughter of the innocents, he soon found that his own son had been killed. Even the melodramas of the nineteenth century show the fitting retribution of chickens come home to roost. In the opera *Rigoletto,* as we have seen, the hunchback jester, plotting to kill his enemy, kills his own daughter. Most tragedies, though more subtle and complex, suggest that the hero had it coming. It is not easy to face the results of one's own deeds. But there is assurance that the world is not meaningless chance, that results have causes, and that fate in its indirect way has a dependable moral order. There is relief when the trial is over and the verdict is clear.

Another partial explanation of our satisfaction in tragedy is suggested by a pattern in primitive ritual. Among tragic heroes, Oedipus is the most conspicuous prototype of a scapegoat. He bears the sins of the city, and his expulsion cleanses it. Early in this century, classical scholars, accepting the ideas of James Frazer in *The Golden Bough,* built up a theory that primitive seasonal rites centered in the killing of the old king-priest as a representative of the spirit of the seasons. He had to be sacrificed in order that his magic power of fertility could be resurrected in the young heir, the representative of summer or the new year. This pattern of mixed sorrow and rejoicing may explain to some extent the paradox of our pleasure in seeing tragedy. Tragedy may rarely bring in the heir to take over (as in *Death of a Salesman*), but the sacrifice of the victim seems to ensure the preservation of the principle for which he stood.

Not a ritual purging but a metaphor of medical purging is suggested by

157

Aristotle as an explanation of the effect of tragedy. His term "catharsis" has been the most discussed term in all dramatic theory. In defining the proper reactions to tragedy as pity and terror, he adds that by pity and terror tragedy effects "a catharsis [purging or purification] of such emotions." Since we cannot know exactly what he meant, the word has been variously interpreted, from implying the repose of all passion spent to a cleansing from all selfish and petty emotions. Gerald F. Else, after years of study, is convinced that Aristotle used the word in an aesthetic sense, meaning that the poet purifies the raw material of life by putting it into artistic form.

The reconciliation of the tragic hero may take either a metaphysical or a psychological form, or both. If at first he calls the gods unjust, he finally realizes that deity is moral and meaningful, even if the meaning cannot be spelled out in exact terms. As he reaches a sense of oneness with the universe, he achieves a oneness in his own soul.

Tokens of that wider justice break into the tragic world in many ways. The Furies in the *Oresteia* of Aeschylus, Mephistopheles in Goethe's *Faust,* the Ghost in *Hamlet,* and the witches in *Macbeth* are vivid examples of supernatural forces that find an immediate echo in the psychological. In *Oedipus* the oracles and the uncanny old soothsayer are very important, and in many Greek plays the gods are brought directly on stage. Romantic writers were skillful in building up an atmosphere of terror and superstitious dread that suggested impending disaster and the fates beyond daily account. In the opera *Carmen* the fortunetelling intensifies the sense of inevitability in a primitive Spanish world used to violence, and the poet Federico García Lorca suggests an even more earthy threat of violence in the background of his Spanish tragedies. For naturalistic writers the environment is all-important; its inescapable influence is suggested by fog, storms, floods, decay, and disease.

In psychological terms, the reconciliation in tragedy is with the self. All masks have been removed as proud assertion is exhausted. Oedipus has passed beyond his Freudian conflict with his father and his ambiguous ties with his mother. He has even worked out his self-loathing by blinding himself. He finds his identity and accepts responsibility for his deeds. Broken as he is, he takes up his burden with great dignity and serenity. He has matured in facing reality. In terms of Karl Jung's psychology, the tragic hero breaks through the shell and penetrates to the deeper levels of the unconscious, where some prototypes of understanding are structured in the racial memory. There he gains important resources of strength. He integrates the different levels of personality and finds his kinship with all being. Many writers on tragedy have commented on the fact that, in contrast to the social realm of comedy, the tragic world is a lonely place, where a man comes to terms with his God, his destiny, and himself. Yet in the deep humility of suffering the tragic hero often discovers a new bond of sympathy with all suffering humanity.

Nor are the results confined to the reconciliation in the heart of the hero. As the world reverberates his shock and passion, it also shares his peace. In Shakespearean tragedy, a clear dawn follows the night, the political order is

Kinds of Plays

FIGURE 4.2 Simple dignity in a modern production of Greek tragedy. Sophocles' *Oedipus*. San Jose State College production, directed by James Clancy, designed by J. Wendell Johnson, and costumed by Berneice Prisk. Photo J. Lioi.

reestablished after the cataclysm, and the survivors find new strength. When the universe is indifferent and the individual chooses only for himself, he still finds that another person may be affected by his choice. Even in the existentialist world, as we shall notice in another chapter, no man is an island.

The tragic peace involves both a spiritual and an aesthetic balance. The audience experiences vicariously the reconciliation between the hero and his gods and between the levels of his mind. The audience also achieves an aesthetic balance in which all their own impulses are brought into harmony in the richness of the theatrical experience and in the perfection of the artistic form. Whether or not the hero gains full perception, they see the magnificence of his assertion and the inevitability of his defeat. There is magnificence because of the reassertion of choice and responsibility, hope, faith, and love, of the determination to be a person, a unique individual. The play traces the interactions between the inner self and the outer world, between freedom and necessity, interactions that are never rigid and settled. The defeat is inevitable because finite man can never reach the infinite, because in the finite world all truths are partial and imperfect, because, beyond all prophecies and revelations, man must repeatedly hew out new truths and values from the resistant rock of the unknown; the very violence of his effort creates a dangerous imbalance in himself, as his pride and arrogance set him in conflict with society and even with the old ways of approaching the gods. He defies the old gods, the minor gods, and, like Orestes in the *Eumenides*, takes his case to higher authority, where new principles must be forged and

159

his precedent considered in all future judgments. Tragedy illuminates the points of intersection of the finite and the infinite, of power and submission, of man's purposes and those of the universe. I. A. Richards calls tragedy "the most general, all-accepting, all-ordering experience known." George Steiner, though he considers tragedy almost extinct in the modern age, puts classic tragedy at the peak of human achievement. He writes, again in *The Death of Tragedy,* "There is in the final moments of great tragedy, whether Greek or Shakespearean or neo-classic, a fusion of grief and joy, of lament over the fall of man and of rejoicing in the resurrection of his spirit. No other poetic form achieves this mysterious effect: it makes of *Oedipus, King Lear,* and *Phèdre* the noblest yet wrought by the mind."

THE SCOPE OF TRAGEDY

Tragedy is not all. Important as it is—indispensable, humanists would say—it is only one of the great modes. The Greeks, who discovered it, frequently ended a group of tragedies with a triumphant play and always followed tragedies with a satyr play that celebrated a danger averted. From an early time, they also gave comedy an official place in the spring festival, and popular tradition ever since has kept the pair of masks—comedy and tragedy —as a symbol that life has complementary faces. But tragedy has some powerful enemies. We can dismiss the shallow cheermongers who do not wish to face pain, but objections from science and religion must be seriously considered. The scientist is reluctant to admit that final failure exists. So many problems have been solved, so many limitations overcome, that he keeps busy on the immediate task, studying the imperfect world in order to make it better. The preacher knows that people pray to the transcendent, to God, and identify themselves with him. Yet after all the work of science, each man must face disease, corruption, and death; all man's effort falls far short of what his mind can see. After all the promise of distant glory, man must also deal with the problematical, terrifying now. Tragedy claims an invaluable place as a humanizer and as a corrective, when both the scientist and the believer lose touch with the human dilemma, as the one gazes enraptured into the microscope and the other into the stars. Science, religion, and tragedy—the three can complement one another, reinforcing a humanistic vision of life that may avoid certain dangers peculiar to each.

Insofar as science concentrates on the finite, on the objective and measurable, scientists ignore both the infinite and the inner self. They look with skepticism at such concepts as purpose, destiny, faith, value, choice, and identity. Insofar as religion concentrates on the infinite, on God's purpose, religious devotees ignore the finite and simplify the problems of the inner self, seeing man's purpose as simply to follow the purpose of God. A humanistic vision of life encompasses science and religion and also tragedy. By science man relates himself to the finite, by religion to the infinite. In tragedy he comprehends the terrifying but invigorating interrelation between the two— between man's purpose and God's, the inner self and the outer world, skepticism and faith, purpose and fate, freedom and responsibility.

160

Kinds of Plays

Science can offer little help to the millions in the modern age who have lost any sense of purpose, of being complete and valuable as individuals. In all its concern with problem-solving and its statistics and polls of group choices, it cannot deal with choice where it is most important—in the subjective life of the individual. Religion loses much vitality if it attempts to put the infinite in easy reach, suddenly attainable by a leap of faith without any journey. The Christian doctrine of redemption—that any soul can be saved even after countless sins—is of prime importance in man's hope. But it is a stronger doctrine if the discovery of Oedipus is added to it—that no matter how blind the deed, what is done is done and each man must face the responsibility for his deeds.

Thus tragedy takes its place along with religion and science, faith and skepticism, humility and daring. Karl Jaspers in *Tragedy Is Not Enough* reminds us that there are some dangers in the tragic view if it is isolated from a wider vision. It can glorify a kind of complacent despair that is a support for nihilism. He writes, "Tragic grandeur is the prop whereby the arrogant nihilist can elevate himself to the pathos of feeling himself a hero. . . . The old beliefs are used as phrases . . . to lend a cheap aura of heroism to a life lived in comfort and security."

While tragedy is philosophical, while it invokes both religion and skepticism, it is not a generalized philosophy of life. It is an immediate experience, a particular work of art. That is why any tragedy, like any important work of art, stimulates so many different interpretations. It does not spell out a description from the outside but carries, like a budding germ, a far-reaching intuitive image. Jaspers writes that tragic knowledge "always contains the final release from tragedy, not through doctrine and revelation, but through the vision of order, justice, love of one's fellow men; through trust, through an open mind and the acceptance of the question as such, unanswered."

Greek Tragedy

Tragedy was the invention of the Greeks. In their Golden Age, the fifth century before Christ, they produced four of the world's greatest dramatists, new forms of tragedy and comedy that have been models ever since, and a theatre that every age goes back to for rediscovery of some basic principle. The Athenians had just rid themselves of a series of "tyrant" dictators and established the world's first important democracy. When the Persian armies invaded Europe, the Athenians led the confederation of little city-states and drove them back. They rebuilt their burnt city in marble and made Athens the artistic as well as the political leader of Greece.

Theatres of a sort had existed in Egypt, as we have seen, and probably in Asia Minor, for two thousand years. But the theatre in Athens was quite different. All the rich possibilities of the Iron Age were open to the Athenians—not only the new iron weapons and tools and new coinage for trading but the new alphabet and a new responsibility in public affairs. And they developed a new theatre, one for the whole city, where any talented playwright could enter his own plays in competition in the great spring festival dedicated to the god of spring and fertility, Dionysus.

On top of the fortified rock, the Acropolis, the Athenians built the Parthenon, a beautiful temple to Athena, Goddess of Wisdom, but down by the roadside on the southern slope, available to everybody, they built the theatre, a shrine to Dionysus. The center of the theatre was the round space called an *orchestra,* or "dancing place," because the drama was derived from the dithyramb, danced and chanted by a chorus. The rows of seats, built up the slope of the hill, surrounded the orchestra on more than three sides. The Theatre of Dionysus at Athens could seat something like seventeen to twenty thousand people, yet spectators in the first rows could almost touch the performers in the orchestra. The earliest plays centered in an altar in the orchestra and had only one actor, who carried on a dialogue with the chorus of

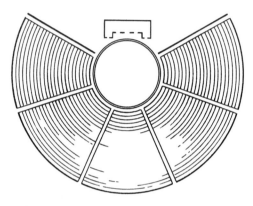

FIGURE *4.3* The general plan of the ancient Greek theatre. The actors entered from the *skene,* to meet the chorus in the circular *orchestra,* or dancing place, almost surrounded by the audience. Drawn by Don Creason.

FIGURE *4.4* Night performance of a Greek tragedy in the ancient theatre at Epidaurus. The chorus takes a formal position in the large circular orchestra. Photo by Harissiadis, Athens.

FIGURE *4.5* Tragic masks of the Greek theatre. The large dignified masks made a strong facial expression visible in a vast theatre. Between episodes they could be changed to indicate a change of emotion. Drawn by Martha Sutherland.

fifty. But soon two more actors were added, and the actors' dressing hut or *skene* was moved up to the edge of the dancing circle so that its three formal doors could serve for entrances in the action—hence the word "scene." Eventually a raised stage was built, but in classic times the actors were not separated from the chorus.

Since it derived from primitive religious rites, with masks and ceremonial costumes, and made use of music, dance, and poetry, the Greek drama was at the opposite pole from the modern realistic stage. In fact, probably no other theatre in history has made fuller use of the intensities of art. The masks, made of painted linen, wood, and plaster, brought down from primitive days the atmosphere of gods, heroes, and demons. Our nineteenth- and twentieth-century grandfathers thought masks must have been very artificial. Today, however, we appreciate their exciting intensity and can see that in a large theatre they were indispensable. If they allowed no fleeting change of expression during a single episode, they could give for each episode in turn more intense expression than any human face could. When Oedipus comes back with bleeding eyes, the new mask could be more terrible than any facial makeup the audience could endure, yet in its sculptured intensity more beautiful than a real face.

THE CHORUS

Most essential of all intensities, and hardest for us to understand, was the chorus. Yet many playwrights today are trying to find some equivalent to do for a modern play what the chorus did for the Greeks. During the epi-

163

FIGURE *4.6* Chorus used to enlarge the emotions of the main characters. The formal grouping adds stately beauty and a sense of control to the large emotions. Sophocles' *Electra*. University of Michigan production, directed by William P. Halstead, designed by Ralph W. Duckwall, Jr., costumed by Elizabeth Birbiri, and choreographed by Nancy Enggass. Photo Ouradnik.

sodes played by the actors, the chorus would only provide a background of group response, enlarging and reverberating the emotions of the actors, sometimes protesting and opposing but in general serving as ideal spectators to stir and lead the reactions of the audience. But between the episodes, with the actors out of the way, the chorus took over. We have only the words, not the music or dance, and some translations of the odes are in such formal, old-

Kinds of Plays

fashioned language that it is hard to guess that they were accompanied by vigorous, sometimes even wild, dances and symbolic actions that filled an orchestra which in some cities was sixty to ninety feet in diameter. Sometimes the chorus expressed simple horror or lament. Sometimes it chanted and acted out, in unison and in precise formations of rows and lines, the acts of violence the characters were enacting offstage. When Phaedra rushes offstage in *Hippolytus* to hang herself from the rafters, the members of the chorus, all fifteen of them, perform in mime and chant the act of tying the rope and swinging from the rafters. Sometimes the chorus tells or reenacts an incident of history or legend that throws light on the situation in the play. Sometimes the chorus puts into specific action what is a general intention in the mind of the main character. When Oedipus resolves to hunt out the guilty person and cleanse the city, he is speaking metaphorically, but the chorus invokes the gods of vengeance and dances a wild pursuit (see Exercises 3 and 4, pp 176–78).

On the printed page, the choral odes seem static and formal, lyric and philosophical, emotional let-downs that punctuate the series of episodes, like intermissions between two acts of a play. The reader who skips the odes can get the main points of the play. A few are worth reading as independent poems, notably the famous one in *Antigone* beginning, "Many are the wonders of the world, but none is more wonderful than man." Some modern acting versions omit the chorus or reduce it to a few background figures. Yet to the Greeks the odes were certainly more than mere poetic interludes: the wild Dionysian words and movements evoked primitive levels of the subconscious and at the same time served to transform primitive violence into charm and beauty and to add philosophical reflections on the meaning of human destiny.

For production today, we can only improvise some partial equivalent. In Athens the entire population was familiar with choral performances. Every year each of the tribes entered a dithyramb in the contest, rehearsing five hundred men and boys for weeks. Some modern composers have tried to write dramatic music for choruses: the most notable examples are the French composer Darius Milhaud, in the primitive rhythms, shouts, and chants of his operatic version of the *Oresteia;* George Gershwin, in the Negro funeral scenes of *Porgy and Bess;* and Kurt Weill, in the African choruses for *Lost in the Stars,* the musical dramatization of Alan Paton's novel *Cry, the Beloved Country.* For revivals of Greek tragedies we have not dared use much music, beyond a few phrases half shouted, half sung, and drumbeats and suggestive melodies in the background. We have depended mainly on our experience in choral speech and modern dance. The exercises at the end of the chapter may show that, with patience and work, a group of modern performers can make a choral ode a powerful medium of the theatre, even if it falls short of the intensities which the original must have had.

THE THREE GREAT DRAMATISTS

The three great writers of Greek tragedy saw the destiny of man in different visions. Aeschylus, the earliest, caught the heroic mood of an Athens that had just defeated the invading Persians and was reshaping old institutions and loyalties for a new age of responsible public life. Sophocles reflected the ideals of the golden time of Pericles, when men of intelligence and reason were striving for a well-balanced life in a world where blind chance and old political loyalties were constant dangers. Euripides, the last, wrote most of the plays that have survived at a time when the old ideals were fading, as Athens was being drawn deeper and deeper into the whirlpool of war with Sparta. In a world of torture, madness, and violence, he denounced old superstitions and offered a deep-felt compassion for suffering, defeated mankind. Whereas the characters of Aeschylus are superhuman—Titans, gods, and primeval kings struggling to bring order out of primitive darkness—

FIGURE *4.7* Masks for a modern production of Greek tragedy. Sophocles' *Oedipus.* Humboldt State College production, with masks by Ethelyn Pauley. Photo Peter Palmquist.

FIGURE *4.8* Greek masks as used by modern actors. These masks have the impersonal dignity of the Greek theatre yet leave the mouth and chin free for speaking. Sophocles' *Oedipus.* Humboldt State College production, directed by W. L. Turner, designed by Richard Rothrock, with costumes and masks by Ethelyn Pauley.

FIGURE 4.9   Chorus used as part of the action. Here the chorus lures Aegisthus into the palace where Orestes waits to kill him. Act II of *Dawn of Judgment,* adapted from Aeschylus' *Oresteia.* University of Arkansas production, directed by George R. Kernodle, designed by Preston Magruder, costumed by Mary Davis, and choreographed by Eleanor King.

the characters of Sophocles are very human, achieving their private identities in the midst of threatening public duties. The characters of Euripides are neurotic individuals, bursting into uncontrolled violence in response to the evil around them.

Of Aeschylus' characters, the most memorable is the great Titan Prometheus, bound and tortured on top of a mountain peak because he had stolen fire, the secret of science and the arts, from heaven and given it to man. Seeing into the future, he shouts his defiance to the upstart Olympian god, Zeus. He knows that raw power must eventually be reconciled to wisdom or it will breed upstart power forever. We do not have the last play of the trilogy, but we know that it showed the reconciliation of power and wisdom. A number of Greek tragedies have triumphant endings. Whereas Oriental philosophers taught that man is bound to the endlessly turning wheel of desire and pain and that his only hope is to escape from the wheel, Aeschylus believed that, by thought and heroic effort, the wheel itself could be changed, that even the gods could grow and learn. The Western world has never forgotten how a small band of Greeks fought back the Persian hordes to protect their budding democracies from the barbaric empire across the sea. Equally heroic, Prometheus is seen rejecting the threats of his enemies and scorning the submission of his friends, facing the thunderbolts and the flesh-tearing eagle of Zeus so that mind may prevail in the world.

Where Prometheus strove for a new order in heaven to replace crude force, the three plays of Aeschylus' *Oresteia,* the only Greek trilogy that has come down to us, trace the emergence of a new social order on the human plane. After a series of horrible murders in a guilt-ridden royal family, the goddess Athena comes down to help replace private hatreds with public order. In the

167

The Theatre of Exaltation

first play, the *Agamemnon,* the queen, Clytemnestra, and her lover, Aegisthus, conspire to murder the king on his triumphant return from Troy. Clytemnestra has not been able to forget that her husband had sacrificed their daughter Iphigenia in order to get favorable winds when he set out ten years before. The guilty pair think they will have peace, but in the next play, *The Libation Bearers,* the son, Orestes, goaded by his sister Electra, murders their mother and her lover. Nor are these avengers left in peace. The Furies, primitive underground spirits of vengeance, writhing with snake heads, come to punish Orestes. If history is nothing but neurotic violence in answer to violence, what hope is there for mankind? The last play, the *Eumenides,* finds the solution. Orestes flees to the shrine of Apollo, but Apollo cannot free him and he must take his case to Athena, the direct representative of Zeus. Knowing that a solution cannot be imposed from the outside, she establishes a new human institution, trial by jury, to hear the case and consider the motives rather than ordering punishment by old rules. Even so, the jury is divided and needs divine guidance. Orestes is acquitted, but the old forces and instinctive compulsions cannot be suppressed or destroyed—they must be transformed. Athena, goddess of wisdom, persuades the Furies to become Eumenides, "beneficent ones," and dwell in open caves near the city, helping to guard justice in Athens—a solution at once political, psychological, and metaphysical.

The Greeks would not show actual murder on stage, perhaps from religious scruples (the theatre was a sacred temple of Dionysus) or perhaps because of the difficulty of making a murder convincing, but they had many ways of carrying the audience through the shock and anxiety of violence. In the *Agamemnon* there is full preparation for the murders. The chorus sings of the departure for the Trojan War and mimes the sacrifice of the daughter, Iphigenia. As Cassandra, the wild-eyed prophetess whom Agamemnon has brought from Troy, moves toward the doorway where death waits, she expresses her terror in song and refers to terrible murders of the past, the chorus chanting with her. Aeschylus does not use the standard messenger to describe the offstage violence but brings on the murderers themselves to gloat over the mutilated bodies (doubtless artificial) wheeled in on an amazing machine, the *eccyclema.* Greek tragedy is much concerned with violence, but many elements do give it aesthetic distance: the beauty of the open-air theatre, the sacred shrine, the marble *skene* with stately formal doorways, the padded, larger-than-life actors, the boots that gave extra height almost like stilts, the large sculptured masks, the musical accompaniment of flutes and lyres and sometimes drums and trumpets, the chanting of much of the poetry, the formal odes of the chorus, the constant references to religious and philosophical principles. Violence, as we know from our old ballads, can be converted by the artist into an experience of sad beauty. Aeschylus, with a deep sense of history, showed how man could overcome violence and transform his primitive impulses by law, persuasion, and religion.

At the center in any discussion of Greek tragedy is Sophocles, for he has the clearest vision of man struggling against fate, striving greatly, suffering

168

greatly, and facing defeat with greatness of soul. While religion is always in the background, the decisions and choices are made by man. Sophocles' heroes are kings and leaders whose fate involves the health of the state, but their struggles are the inner struggles of lone souls.

Antigone and Oedipus make an interesting, contrasting pair—Antigone, the tragic heroine who sees clearly what she is doing and all its consequences, and Oedipus, completely blind. Antigone has to make a dreadful choice. When her uncle, newcomer to the throne, issues orders on pain of death that no one is to bury the brother who had attacked the city, while giving all honors to the body of the defending brother, Antigone makes up her mind that she will disobey him. She must perform the religious rites due the dead. Creon, calculating the practical politics of the state, is furious that a member of his own family would defy his orders. Against his expediency and in the face of death, Antigone sets the spiritual value of love. She cannot see that her action will make any practical difference in the world, but she has faith that the laws of the gods are beyond time. By the end of the play, Creon himself is a tragic figure. His son and the old soothsayer tell him he is wrong, and the citizens do not uphold him. Relenting at the last minute, he tries to save Antigone. But it is too late. She has already hanged herself in the prison cave, his son kills himself, and then his wife commits suicide. The broken man is finally humbled before the gods, awed that his small miscalculation could cause such suffering. Perhaps we are more touched by the suffering of the man who learns too late than by the heroic will of a religious martyr.

Where Antigone sees everything, makes her choice, and faces her punishment, Oedipus sees nothing. He was the famous problem-solver who had guessed the riddle of the Sphinx and delivered the city from that pest. In gratitude, the citizens, who had just lost their king, made him king and married him to the queen. Now they have a new problem for him to solve, a blight on the city that can be cleansed only by discovering the murderer of the old king and driving him out of the city. In one sense the play becomes an exciting detective story—the king as prosecutor interrogates each witness, piecing together the bits of story until he sees that he himself is the guilty one. Each witness has his own personality and gives a different quality to each scene as the series of episodes builds to a tremendous climax. The play is rich in irony as each witness thinks he is reassuring Oedipus, while the new fact he reveals is just one more step on the way to the final terrible certainty that Oedipus had, unknowingly, killed his own father and married his own mother. It does not matter that the audience knows the story already. More terrible than simple surprise is this suspense of watching Oedipus come nearer and nearer to the appalling discovery and seeing him respond to it.

In the nineteenth century *Oedipus* seemed a deterministic play. Malevolent fate had already settled everything. Oedipus had no chance, waking to suffering that came on him from the past. As the Victorians interpreted Aristotle's phrase about a tragic flaw, they concluded that the rash temper that led him to kill the old king and that he now turns on everybody was the tragic flaw that caused his downfall.

169

FIGURE *4.10* Tragic hero enhanced by a large bronze mask, a costume that adds size, and boots that add height. Sophocles' *Oedipus.* Shakespeare Festival Theatre production, Stratford, Ontario, directed by Tyrone Guthrie, with costumes and masks by Tanya Moiseiwitsch.

But for the twentieth century there are new meanings. Most of all, the tragedy is a study of the search for identity, an agonizing concern of our age. It is the need to find out who he is that drives Oedipus on. His wife begs him not to ask, saying that the world is chance and nothing can be predicted. Yet what she tells him only proves how right the oracles were. The problem-solver who set out objectively to discover a simple fact finds that objective facts mock him until he realizes that his inner being is involved with the world of unchangeable fact and the metaphysical problems of identity, responsibility, and fate. Freud's famous phrase, "Oedipus complex," implies a conscious antagonism of a son toward his father and an unwholesome dependence on his mother, and it is startling to realize that in Sophocles' play Oedipus does not have an Oedipus complex. He has already gone all the way to murder and incest without knowing it, and only by facing his guilt can he turn back to make the mature adjustment that Freud prescribed.

Of modern performances of *Oedipus,* the production at the Stratford Festival in Ontario was particularly impressive, and a remarkable film was made from it. Masks were used—bronze for Oedipus, silver for Queen Jocasta, and plaster-white for the soothsayer, Teiresias. If the chubby little old men in the chorus looked too much like figures from *Snow White and the Seven Dwarfs* for the highest effect of nobility, they still enlarged and reinforced the pity and terror (FIGURE *4–10*).

Unlike Sophocles, Euripides shocked his first audience and won very few

Kinds of Plays

first prizes. He was considered too sensational in depicting abnormal states of mind. He used exotic foreign melodies and dwelt on the sordid details of betrayal, cruelty, murder, and incest. Yet in later centuries when audiences got used to him, he became the most popular of all the Greek dramatists, and in modern times he has had the greatest influence. He portrayed the skepticism, rebellion, and desperation of an Athens drifting away from the high ideals, the religious devotion, of earlier times. The democracy broke down in political corruption as the war with Sparta dragged on, and disease, superstition, and hysteria were rife in the war-crowded streets of Athens. Some Athenians could joke about the situation; the comic poet Aristophanes lashed out at it in fantastical satires that are as funny now as they were at the end of the fifth century B.C. But Euripides could not laugh. He saw no hope of returning to the religious piety and civic heroism of the past. He called on the individual to liberate himself from the superstitions still clinging to religion. As Athens seemed bent on destroying her young men and trampling on any city or group that opposed her, Euripides was haunted by images of Medea in hatred killing her own children, of Agave in religious ecstasy tearing off the head of her own son, of Phaedra in madness causing the death of her stepson—women helpless in the grip of violent emotion, prodded by the unforgivable cruelty and injustice of the world. Or in another mood he pictured a king so torn by pity that he rushed out to the battlefield and took in his arms the bodies of the dead and dying, whether friend or foe. Euripides was the master of pity, the poet of the agony of Athens.

When Athens had just killed the men and enslaved the women and children of a small island that wanted to be neutral, Euripides was shocked. As he saw Athenians building a fleet to conquer Sicily—an ill-fated expedition that led to the defeat of Athens—he produced a play about ancient victims of Greek aggression, *The Trojan Women*. The military authorities could not stop him from presenting it, since they had no control over the sacred festival. He showed the goddess Athena, angry with her favorite Greeks for their impiety, conniving with Poseidon, god of the sea, to bring punishment to them on their way home from Troy. The women of Troy, in noble anguish, leave their burning city to be slaves to the arrogant conquerors. As a crowning cruelty, the Greeks kill the little son of Hector and hand his broken body on a shield to the grandmother, Queen Hecuba. A procession of doom, the play has enough indignation, enough compassion, to hold the stage today. Its different episodes are arranged with strong contrast and variety, from the half-insane Cassandra whirling a torch, gloating over her knowledge of the future of her master, Agamemnon, to the wily Helen, conniving to get back into the good graces of her husband, Menelaus.

Judith Anderson's performance in *Medea,* which fortunately is preserved in a recording, reached the summit of dramatic intensity. Robinson Jeffers, the California poet of rugged violence, made the adaptation for her in 1946, and she played it for years in New York, London, and other cities on both sides of the Atlantic. The role was made famous by her scorn, her snarling contempt for the priggish husband, the Greek hero Jason, who has used Medea,

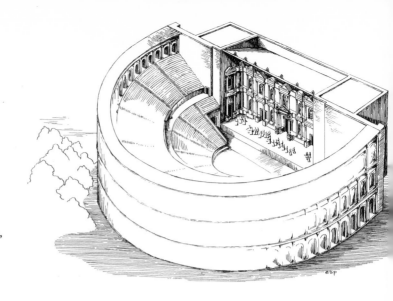

FIGURE *4.11* Roman theatre. Although it developed from the Greek theatre, the Roman theatre differed in that a raised stage and a very high scenic wall continued the structure of the large auditorium. It was used more for clowns, mimes, and spectacular dance shows than for plays. Drawn by Ethelyn Pauley.

married her, and now is abandoning her in order to marry the pretty daughter of the king. Jason has the effrontery to brag of the superiority of his race as he discards her, and then is surprised that his treatment provokes violence. She kills their children, her own children, because she hates him more than she loves them. Euripides had the sun god take her away in a splendid chariot drawn through the air by dragons. Jeffers has her leave the stage in desperate self-loathing and defiant pride.

The Modern Festival Theatre

The Greek spirit survives today in the modern festival theatre, usually a large outdoor structure on a hillside, designed like the ancient festival theatre of Athens to bring the play in contact with sky and earth. Since the plays are not about man's immediate environment but about his relation to the earth, his God, or the sweep of history, they call for a proces-

FIGURE *4.12* Religious production in a modern outdoor festival theatre. *The Book of Job* as produced in the Kentucky Mountain Theatre, Pineville, Kentucky, by Orlin and Irene Corey.

sional staging with large casts, with poetry, music, and dance, and with a breadth of acting technique to match the sweep of the stage.

In an age of summer vacations and family automobile trips, the festival theatre may become more important than the theatre of the cities. It is all the better if the festival is not in a large city but, like a holy shrine, in a place for a special pilgrimage. The audience is not looking for casual entertainment but for a renewal of the spirit in a celebration of its heritage from the past. The Canterbury Festival in England has stimulated a number of new poetic religious plays, one of which, T. S. Eliot's *Murder in the Cathedral,* we shall consider among modern tragic dramas. The Festival Theatre in Stratford-on-Avon has become one of the strongest producing companies in England, having a season in London as well as at Stratford, and has stimulated Shakespeare festivals in America at Stratford, Ontario, Stratford, Connecticut, and a dozen other places from San Diego, California, and Ashland, Oregon, to Miami, Florida. Most successful and most beautiful of all is the Festival Theatre at Stratford, Ontario, which will be described in the chapter on new space forms. Founded in 1953 to present Shakespeare and other classics, it has become, to all intents and purposes, the national theatre of Canada. The Shakespearean festivals usually follow the structure of the Elizabethan stage, but the auditorium keeps the Greek form of the hillside ampitheatre before the sacred shrine.

The festival spirit of the Greeks lives most vividly in the outdoor pageant-dramas of American history. They have usually been presented at or near the

FIGURE *4.13* A large festival theatre combining features from both the Greek and the Elizabethan theatres. The open stage, projecting into the center of the auditorium, is backed by a permanent façade of doors and levels. Shakespeare Festival Theatre, Stratford, Ontario. Photo Peter Smith.

FIGURE *4.14* An outdoor festival theatre for Shakespeare. The auditorium is a variant of the Greek theatre, but the stage is based on early twentieth-century reconstructions of the Elizabethan theatre. The Oregon Shakespeare Festival Theatre, Ashland, Oregon, founded by Angus Bowmer. Photo Dwaine Smith.

place where some great event took place—the arrival of the first colonists at Jamestown or on Roanoke Island, the trek of Daniel Boone to Kentucky, the early parliamentary battles of Thomas Jefferson at Williamsburg. Far more impressive than merely visiting a historical shrine is seeing the ghosts of the past come to life on a stage as wide and symbolic as the theatre of ancient Athens.

The most famous of these American festival plays is Paul Green's *The Lost Colony,* which opened in 1937 on the spot of the first English settlement in North Carolina in celebration of its three hundred and fiftieth anniversary, and, except during the war years, has played every summer since. The pilgrim-tourist drives down through the pines and sand of Roanoke Island breathing the salt air of the sea and enters a large amphitheatre open to the sky and the stars. The play begins with a hymn sung by a choir and an invocation of God's grace on the sacred spot and on the dream of the pioneers who first braved the wilderness. As the Indians are offering a wild dance to the corn god, they are interrupted by the arrival of English explorers. Back in England, Sir Walter Raleigh gathers his colonists to start for the New World but cannot go with them because Queen Elizabeth is preparing a fleet against the Spanish Armada. In the second part the scene is a chapel of logs set against palisades, where the whole colony gathers first for the happy christening of Virginia Dare, first English child born in the New World, then again for a Yule log as the colony wastes away, beset by hostile Indians and waiting in vain for help from England. There are patriotic and religious hymns, comic songs, battles and funerals, and finally a brave procession as the colonists, threatened by hostile Indians and a Spanish ship, choose rather to march off into the wilderness with their Indian allies than to give up their start in the New World.

Kinds of Plays

FIGURE *4.15* An American historical festival theatre. Paul Green's *The Lost Colony* at Manteo, North Carolina. This symphonic drama, produced every year, celebrates the first attempt of the English to settle in America.

Even more romantic is the experience of the pilgrim-tourist driving through the canyons of the Blue Ridge Mountains west of Asheville, North Carolina, to the isolated Indian town of Cherokee, now on a modern highway. He stops at stores filled with Indian handicraft and visits a reconstruction of an Indian village. Everywhere he sees real Indians, descendants of the Cherokees who hid out in the mountains when the rest of their tribe were forced on the "Trail of Tears" to move to Indian Territory, in what is now Oklahoma. Then he goes on to the play, *Unto These Hills,* to see the story of those Cherokees who hid in the hills for decades until Washington officials could be persuaded that they too were Americans. Tourists, young and old, thrill to both the romantic vision of Indians and the wide American struggle for liberty for all.

Paul Green called this kind of play a "symphonic drama," blending song, dance, mime, pageantry, and drama. There is some development of individual character, but the whole community is really the hero. It faces difficulties,

FIGURE *4.16* Festival drama at a religious shrine of the Mormons. *America's Witness for Christ,* presented by The Church of Jesus Christ of Latter-Day Saints at Hill Cumorah, Palmyra, New York, and directed by Harold I. Hansen. Photo Werner Wolff.

doubt, and sometimes internal division, but the leaders are persuasive, and at the end a sense of group unity gives strength for whatever trials lie ahead. The audience is deeply impressed with the hardships of the builders of America and especially moved when, as in *The Lost Colony,* the colonists face defeat. But today we know, of course, that the personal anguish was a temporary sacrifice in the march of history. There is none of the lonely terror of a true tragedy, but the audience experiences genuine exaltation through the pride they feel for the ideals of their country.

EXERCISES AND DEMONSTRATIONS

1. ANALYSIS OF THE PHASES OF TRAGEDY.   Analyze the experience of the hero in several Greek tragedies. What is his crisis and challenge? How does he assert himself and pursue his purpose? What is his "dark night of the soul"? How does he refuse the easy way? What clarity, reconciliation, peace, or humility does he reach? Good examples to use are Creon in Sophocles' *Antigone,* Admetus in Euripides' *Alcestis,* and Phaedra and Theseus in Euripides' *Hippolytus.*

2. THE PROBLEM OF TRANSLATION.   Compare two or more translations of passages from a Greek tragedy—both a choral passage and a speech—to note how the rhythm and tone of the words determine the effect and, to a certain extent, the meaning of the passage.

3. MOVEMENT IN THE CHORAL ODE.   Since many choral odes express more than the reactions of onlookers, indeed indicating action of their own, the director must plan that action, sometimes rewriting the lines to fit the rhythm and movement he has in mind. Sometimes the choral action is a parallel to some catastrophe that is taking place offstage. But in many odes we can see echoes of age-old ritual dithyrambs, with invocations at altars, tombs, or springs, exorcisms and curses, combats, sacrificial killings, laments, resurrections, ritual weddings, and bridal and funeral processions.

How would you plan the choral action and chant, sometimes using all the chorus (the Greeks used twelve or fifteen, but many modern productions on small stages use only eight or ten), sometimes dividing it into separate parts, sometimes using only one or two persons in action? What grouping will express the particular mood and the specific thought or action and yet keep some elements of stately, formal design? Are there geometrical forms—lines, circles, spirals—that can express the particular moment? How much balance, repetition, sequence, contrast, dynamic change do you want?

Take the second ode in H. D. F. Kitto's translation of *Oedipus,* after both Creon and Teiresias have told Oedipus he must drive out the hidden murderer of the old King and Teiresias has told Oedipus that he himself is the murderer. The first half of the ode, the strophe and antistrophe, are clearly an exorcism, a vigorous pursuit building to a climax. Kitto evidently

176

is thinking of very active onlookers, of an excited group watching a race or a combat. Would you give some lines or phrases to a single voice, some to two or three voices together, and some to all together?

The voice of god rang out in the holy cavern,
  Denouncing one who has killed a King—the crime of crimes.
    Who is the man? Let him begone in
    Headlong flight, swift as a horse!

(*Anapaests*)   For the terrible god, like a warrior armed,
  Stands ready to strike with a lightning-flash:
    The Furies who punish crime, and never fail,
    Are hot in their pursuit.

The snow is white on the cliffs of high Parnassus.
It has flashed a message: Let every Theban join the hunt!
    Lurking in caves among the mountains,
    Deep in the woods—where is the man?

(*Anapaests*)   In wearisome flight, unresting, alone,
  An outlaw, he shuns Apollo's shrine;
    But ever the living menace of the god
    Hovers around his head.

4. MOVEMENT IN THE CHORAL ODE.   Plan the action of the same ode using the script as it was rewritten for a production at the University of Arkansas. Four men took single lines, not merely watching but embodying the pursuit themselves, each moving on his own line like a spear or arrow or hatchet, as though pursuing the victim toward one corner at the front of the stage. The rest of the chorus followed with less movement and an underchant that continued through the lines of the individual speakers. A drum set the accented beats after the first hesitant rhythm, four strong beats to the line. The second half of the ode suddenly holds up the pursuit as the chorus refuses to accept Oedipus' guilt without proof, moving from suspended judgment, a questioning, and doubt to a strong, united reassertion of confidence in Oedipus.

UNDERCHANT   Who is he? . . . who is he? . . . where is the man?
              Where is he? . . . where is he? . . . where is the man?
        (*The underchant continues.*)
    1. The prophecy cried from the Delphian rocks
    2. Get rid of the killer. Hunt out the blood shame.
    3. His time has come. Hunt him. Hunt him. Hunt him. Hunt him.
UNDERCHANT   Hunt him down, down. Hunt him down, down.
    4. Let him fly with the speed of wild-eyed horses.
    1. Let him run with the air and race with the wind.
    2. The sons of Zeus will follow like lightning.
UNDERCHANT   Follow him, follow him, follow him, follow.

177

EXERCISES AND DEMONSTRATIONS

3. With a lightning flash, with a blinding speed
4. The furies will follow him, follow him, follow.
1. With a deadly leap, now to close him round.
2. Follow him, follow him, follow him, follow.
1. From holy Parnassus' peak of snow
2. Came a blinding flash to hunt him down.
3. Like a bull gone wild, let him run over rocks.
4. The voices of doom will din in his ears.

ALL He can't get away. He can't get away.
     Follow him, follow him, follow him, follow.
     (The mood changes—slow, fearful, drawing back.)

WOMEN'S UNDERCHANT (*High voices*) I'm afraid—for Oedipus.
               (*Low voices*) I'm afraid. I'm afraid.
1. We fear. But we cannot see what we fear.
2. That terrible thing the prophet spoke
3 & 4. We cannot believe it.
1 & 2. It may be so. I cannot deny it.

ALL MEN We do not know.
     (Each separates from group on his line, turning away, questioning.)
1. I dread the future.
2. I fear the past.
3. Was there ever a quarrel of the kings of this house?
4. Was there some dark deed cries out on Oedipus?
1. What had he to do with that long-covered death?
     (WOMEN'S UNDERCHANT *stops*.)
2 & 3. All secrets of earth are known to the gods.
3. And even a prophet can only guess.
4. Which prophet sees farther, when all is dark?
     (One moves to a strong position; others join until all are in one strong, united form.)
1. I will not blame Oedipus without sure proof.
2. At the raging words of a blind old man.
3. We all were there when the winged Sphinx, the terrible monster, faced him of old.
4. He won that test, for the public good.
5. He solved the riddle. He set the town free.
1. I cannot think any evil of him now.

ALL I will not think evil of my noble lord.
     I will not think evil of my noble lord.

SUGGESTED READING

PLAYS: GREEK TRAGEDIES

Aeschylus' *Prometheus Bound* is a good beginning. His *Agamemnon* is widely read, but it is not complete without the other two plays of the *Oresteia* trilogy: the *Choephoroi* (*The Libation Bearers*) and the *Eumenides*.

Sophocles' *Antigone* and *Oedipus the King* are his best-known works, but the final harmony of *Oedipus at Colonus* and the war bitterness of *Philoctetes* have attracted recent interest.

178

Euripides' *Alcestis, Medea, Hippolytus,* and *The Trojan Women* have been favorites, but many of his less well-known plays also seem amazingly modern.

A note on translations: Since translations fade quickly and what seemed a fresh translation to one generation seems stale and colorless to another, the reader is wise to choose one of the fairly recent translations, of which there are several good ones. First choice for some years has been Edith Hamilton's translation of *Prometheus, Agamemnon,* and *The Trojan Women,* published as *Three Plays** (1937). Many readers and actors would place next the translations made by H. D. F. Kitto and by Dudley Fitts and Robert Fitzgerald. Those by Peter D. Arnott are also good. The translations in the Penguin editions are excellent. Of the two complete collections of Greek drama, the one edited by Oates and O'Neill in 1938 now seems out of date and that issued by the University of Chicago Press in the 1950s, reprinted in Modern Library, is uneven. Scholars have been more pleased than actors with the Richard Lattimore translations.

PLAYS: MODERN FESTIVALS

Paul Green set the pattern for festival plays about American history with *The Lost Colony* (1937). His plays about early Virginia history are *The Common Glory* (1948) and *The Founders* (1957). A freer epic form was used by Ramsey Yelvington in a historical play about the Alamo, *A Cloud of Witnesses* (1959).

CRITICAL WORKS: GENERAL TRAGEDY

The classic theories of tragedy are to be found in several anthologies of literary criticism, of which the most comprehensive is Barrett H. Clark, *European Theories of the Drama,* enlarged editions with later theories in 1947 and 1965. Three recent anthologies present mostly modern theories: Laurence Michel and Richard B. Sewall, *Tragedy: Modern Essays in Criticism* (1963); Robert W. Corrigan, *Tragedy, Vision and Form** (1965); and Richard Levin, *Tragedy: Plays, Theory and Criticism** (1960, 1965). Excerpts from six theories, together with plays, are presented in Sylvan Barnett, Morton Berman, and William Burto, *Eight Great Tragedies** (1957). Good chapters on tragedy are to be found in Allardyce Nicoll, *The Theory of the Drama* (1931), in Elizabeth Drew, *Discovering Drama* (1937), and in many other general introductions.

Of full treatments of tragedy, the most stimulating are T. R. Henn, *The Harvest of Tragedy* (1956), and Richmond V. Hathorn, *Tragedy, Myth and Mystery* (1962). Herbert Muller, *The Spirit of Tragedy* (1956), and William G. McCollom, *Tragedy* (1957), are very useful.

Two valuable essays relate tragedy to the basic rhythms of life: Susanne Langer, "The Tragic Rhythm," in *Feeling and Form** (1953), and Northrop Frye, "The Mythos of Autumn: Tragedy," in *Anatomy of Criticism** (1957). Both are reprinted in Corrigan's *Tragedy,* and the Frye essay is reprinted in Levin's *Tragedy* (alt. ed., 1965). The patterns of several tragedies of the past and of the twentieth century are discussed in Francis Fergusson, *The Idea of a Theatre** (1949).

The difficulty of writing tragedy today is discussed brilliantly by Joseph Wood Krutch in "The Tragic Fallacy," a chapter in *The Modern Temper* (1929) that has been reprinted in Barrett Clark, *European Theories,* Corrigan, *Tragedy,* and

* Available in paperback edition.

SUGGESTED READING

Levin, *Tragedy*. Krutch added to his discussion in *Modernism in Modern Drama* (1953). John Gassner discusses the problem of "The Possibility and Perils of Modern Tragedy," *Tulane Drama Review,* I, 3 (Summer, 1957), reprinted in Corrigan and also in Gassner, *Theatre at the Crossroads* (1960). Karl Jaspers gives some religious objections to tragedy in *Tragedy Is Not Enough* (1952). The most extensive recent discussion of the modern climate is George Steiner, *The Death of Tragedy** (1961). Maxwell Anderson took the view that noble tragedy is possible in the modern age in *The Essence of Tragedy* (1939).

CRITICAL WORKS: GREEK TRAGEDY

The long-time favorite introduction to ancient Greek drama and culture is Edith Hamilton, *The Greek Way** (1937). More thorough and up to date is H. D. F. Kitto, *Greek Tragedy** (2nd ed., 1950). Gilbert Murray, *Euripides and His Age** (1913), is a good short book relating the plays to the events and ideas of the time. More provocative is the social interpretation of Alan M. G. Little, *Myth and Society in Attic Drama* (1942). Friedrich Nietzsche's essay *The Birth of Tragedy* (1872) has had a great influence on aesthetic theories about the Dionysian and Apollonian elements in Greek drama as well as in modern art. Interesting new interpretations are suggested in William Arrowsmith, "The Criticism of Greek Tragedy," *Tulane Drama Review* (T3, Spring, 1959). See also George R. Kernodle, "Symbolic Action in the Greek Choral Odes," *Classical Journal,* LIII, 1 (Oct., 1957).

The most thorough scholarly book is Margarete Bieber, *The History of the Greek and Roman Theater* (2nd ed., 1961), which reproduces more than five hundred pictures, but still useful is R. C. Flickinger, *The Greek Theatre and Its Drama* (4th ed., 1936). The most thorough studies of the development of drama and the theatre in Athens are three books by A. W. Pickard-Cambridge: *The Theatre of Dionysus in Athens* (1946), *The Dramatic Festivals of Athens* (1953), and *Dithyramb, Tragedy and Comedy* (2nd ed. rev. by T. B. L. Webster, 1962), all published by the Clarendon Press, Oxford. Some new ideas on the theatre are presented by Peter D. Arnott, *An Introduction to the Greek Theatre* (1959) and *Greek Scenic Convention in the Fifth Century* (1962). Gerald F. Else has written a word-by-word, sentence-by-sentence study of *Aristotle's Poetics: The Argument* (1957) and a new interpretation of *The Origin and Early Form of Greek Tragedy* (1965).

On modern revival of Greek plays, see T. B. L. Webster, *Greek Theatre Production* (1956), and John Russell Brown, "Ancient Tragedy in Modern Greece," *Tulane Drama Review* (T28, Summer, 1965).

CRITICAL WORKS: MODERN FESTIVALS

How Green shaped his historical material for *The Lost Colony* is studied by W. J. Free and C. B. Lower, *History into Drama** (1963). A thorough guide with several plays as examples is George McCalmon and Christian Moe, *Creating Historical Drama* (1966).

180   * Available in paperback edition.

SUGGESTED READING

CHAPTER FIVE

THE THEATRE OF EXALTATION: MEDIEVAL, ELIZABETHAN, AND NEOCLASSIC TRAGEDY

The Greeks shaped the first form of tragedy, and perhaps the greatest, but the Christian era brought the experience of exaltation to the theatre of Western Europe in several ways. Though much less highly developed than the Greek, the Christian drama of the Middle Ages possessed its own kind of power. The Elizabethan period in England found its chief artistic glory in the tragic drama of Shakespeare, and France reached its peak of dramatic achievement in the seventeenth century with a neoclassic tragedy that was not an imitation of Greek drama but a new creation.

The Medieval Mystery Plays

The exaltation of the religious drama of the Middle Ages has been rediscovered in the mid-twentieth century. Without regular theatres, playwrights, or actors, the monks and priests—and later the merchants—produced the separate episodes of the story of Christian salvation. The monks sang their dramas in the church, as part of the liturgy of the Christian calendar—the discovery of the empty tomb on Easter Sunday, the adoration of the shepherds at Christmas, and the miracles of the saints on important saints' days. The merchants, using many simple but vivid units of scenery, presented on the city

FIGURE *5.1* Drama as part of the liturgy of the early medieval church. The Three Marys at the Tomb, chanted by priests in Latin as part of the Easter morning service. Drawn by Ethelyn Pauley.

streets long cycles of plays that traced the story of mankind from the Creation and Fall to the Crucifixion and Last Judgment. In the language of the people and mostly in contemporary costume, with many sensational and comic details, these outdoor pageant-dramas brought Biblical history to life before the eyes of all. With only an occasional addition or revision, the same plays were put on once a year, year after year, the church plays for more than five centuries and the outdoor cycles for most of the fourteenth, fifteenth, and sixteenth centuries, until the Reformation and Counter Reformation put an end to both.

Nineteenth-century critics were very condescending about these naive *mystery* or *miracle* plays (the terms are interchangeable), calling them "pre-Shakespearean drama" and noting, as their only significance, that they mixed comic episodes with serious matter in patterns that influenced the Elizabethan stage. Only the comedy and the touches of realism seemed important. These critics had special praise for the *Second Shepherds' Play* of the Wakefield cycle, but no real appreciation for the serious devotional plays. Yet in the mid-twentieth century, as some of these old plays are revived in churches and college chapels and as large parts of the cycles are produced in York or before Notre Dame Cathedral, it is the naive devotion and the high exaltation that are most impressive.

Classic tragedy disappeared in the Middle Ages. Both comedy and tragedy had been inundated in the lavish days of the Roman Empire by spectacular shows—gladiators, animal combats, or sea fights—and by vulgar performances of comic mimes or by elegant danced pantomimes, all produced in the enormous half-circle theatres (FIGURE *4.11*). The young Christian church set itself squarely against such a vulgar theatre and put an end to it. Actors, along

Kinds of Plays

with thieves and other vagabonds, were proscribed; those popular pagan showoffs, the Roman actors, had made fun of Christian mysteries, and thus inspired so deep a hostility to the stage that to this day some churchmen smell the fires of pagan orgies in the greasepaint. The church methods of suppression were effective, and for several centuries Europe had no theatre except a few wandering mimes and minstrels.

Curiously, it was in the church itself that the theatre made a new start, some four or five centuries after the ancient theatres had been closed. In the ninth century chanted dialogue and action were added in the most sacred moment of the Christian liturgy, the Easter Mass, and drama was reborn. Three priests, their heads covered, enacted the three Marys approaching the sepulchre to look for the body of Christ. Other priests dressed as the angels showed them the empty tomb and cloth and told them to go and announce to the disciples that Christ was risen. The choir burst into an anthem of praise, adding the power of choral music to the dramatic reenactment of the sacred event. Soon a similar episode was added to the Christmas service as priests put on some suggestion of shepherds' costume to bring to the manger their offerings of gifts and song.

From the ninth and tenth centuries on, monks and priests used every means of teaching an illiterate populace the sacred history and doctrines necessary for salvation. With carved statues and stained-glass windows, they turned the churches into sacred storybooks. The Gregorian plainchant and the more elaborate anthems made the sacred words reverberate in song. But most vivid of all the artistic devices for religious instruction were the church dramas. Though sung in Latin, they made the liturgy of the day come to life.

Recently, some people have come to realize that these old Latin dramas are powerful. As modern ears become more accustomed to medieval music and the imagination learns to respond to a drama far from naturalism, an audience for a new exalted drama develops. In 1958, when the New York Pro Musica revived a twelfth-century Latin drama, *The Play of Daniel,* in The Cloisters and then in a New York church, they were amazed at the public response. They have since put on many performances in churches in this country and in Europe and have made a good recording of the work. Even in the recording, without the aid of costumes and pageantry, the play is exciting.

The occasion for the production of cycles of plays during the fourteenth and fifteenth centuries was the procession and festival that opened the summer trade fair, an important event for every growing city. The plays were given outdoors, in the language of the people, and were interpreted not just as ancient happenings in Palestine but with much local detail that brought them close to everyday life.

The procession preceded the plays, and indeed furnished the form, for from twenty-five to fifty separate plays were required to cover the whole story of the fall and redemption of man. In York some forty-eight plays were given in one long exhausting day; in Chester the cycle lasted three days; and one cycle in France, not repeated every year, took thirty days to perform. Most of the audience stood in the street, while the rich had special bleachers or raised

183

The Theatre of Exaltation

FIGURE 5.2 Early medieval Latin *Play of Daniel,* revived in a church setting at The Cloisters in New York. Directed by Noah Greenberg and performed by the New York Pro Musica. Photo National Educational Television.

pavilions. There was no proscenium stage; the action moved from one scenic unit or "mansion" to another. Sometimes a row of mansions spread down one long platform made a "simultaneous" stage or setting, as in the splendid example at Valenciennes (FIGURES 5.4 and 5.5). Sometimes the audience was in a circle, the important actors making their entrances from mansions at the outside of the circle but moving to the central playing area for the main action. An amazing picture of a drama about the martyrdom of Saint Apollonia presented in this way is redrawn in FIGURE 5.6. In most English cities, each episode was played on or around a pageant wagon which was large enough for one or two mansions, with playing room for the actors (FIGURE 5.3). The wagon for the first play was drawn to the first playing place, then pulled by men or horses to the second playing place as the second episode came to the first location, and so on until all the plays had been given in the dozen or more chosen stations. In England the separate episodes were usually assigned to different trade guilds, often with some consideration of appropriateness. The shipwrights, for instance, presented the scene of the Flood and the Building of the Ark; the goldsmiths, the scene of the Magi bearing jeweled gifts to the Christ Child; and the bakers, the scene of the Last Supper.

The medieval drama, like Dante's *Divine Comedy* and Chaucer's *Canterbury Tales,* represents a journey, a procession on the way of salvation, with a variety of experiences. In the church the standing audience moved with the

184

Kinds of Plays

actors as the Three Kings approached the simple canopied throne of Herod, then talked together on the way to Bethlehem, then came to adore the Christ Child in a simple crèche. Even in the serious drama, chanted in Latin, touches of comedy were included, such as the scene of the Marys at the spice-seller's booth and the race of John and Peter to the empty tomb.

The outdoor drama of later Gothic times became more realistic and spectacular and presented even greater contrasts. Lucifer struts and grabs God's throne. A sinuous devil flatters Eve, and boisterous devils with pots and pans hail Adam and Eve on their road or, in some plays, drive them directly into a monster hell-mouth amidst smoke and flames. Noah's wife refuses to leave her gossip friends, and has to be dragged onto the Ark, kicking and scratching. Balaam's ass appears among the prophets who predict the coming of Christ. The old Joseph is a blustering comic figure until the angel appears to him, when he becomes a devoted attendant to Mary. The shepherds, given local names, tease each other or grumble about their oppressive lords. One of them cries "Way, golly!" when he sees the shining angel. They offer their caps, toys, and an old horn spoon to the Christ Child. When Herod hears of the child, he bursts into noisy raging, even moving out among the audience. Shakespeare remembered the Herod of the Coventry cycle as a prime example of unrestrained acting and gave us the phrase "to out-Herod Herod." The women fight back with kitchen spoons and pans at the soldiers who come to slaughter the innocents; then Rachel sings a heartbroken lullaby over the body of her child. In some cycles, Herod takes on a touch of tragedy in dis-

FIGURE *5.3* A pageant wagon showing the play of the Nativity in a medieval street. As each wagon moved to the next playing place, another wagon brought the next episode, until the entire sacred history was presented. Drawn by Ethelyn Pauley.

FIGURE 5.4   Medieval simultaneous or multiple settings on a long platform. Each episode had its own mansion, though all the mansions to be used each day were set up from the beginning. From the manuscript of the Valenciennes production, 1547. Drawn by Ethelyn Pauley.

FIGURE 5.5   Six different scenes as staged one after the other on the long platform at Valenciennes. Drawn by Martha Sutherland.

FIGURE 5.6 Medieval theatre-in-the-round. The spectators stand between the central playing area and the ring of mansions. *The Martyrdom of St. Apollonia.* Drawn from several sources by Bobbie Okerbloom.

covering that he has caused his own son to be killed. Soldiers at the foot of the cross shoot dice for Christ's garments, and Judas was often given a sensational treatment that modern audiences would not endure—when he was hanged, the entrails of a hog were suddenly let down by means of a trick sack and string, as though his body had burst open, while devils, lifted by wire and pulleys, flew through the air, carrying his soul off to hell. For the burning of a martyr or the damned, not only were real flames seen but animal bones and skin were put on the flames to make the proper stench. At the Last Judgment, Christ sat with his feet on the burning world. We know that in one place four small barrels impregnated with tar were burned, one after the other, as the pageant wagon moved from one part of the town to another. The town accounts list a man who was paid for "setting the world on fire." The mechanicians who produced sudden appearances and disappearances, flights through the air, and other marvels were highly paid and guarded their secrets jealously. Yet, with all their childish details, the mystery plays dealt with the greatest of all subjects—the history and salvation of mankind—and in many scenes achieved an exaltation that still has great appeal.

The medieval principle of simultaneous settings seemed naive to Renaissance theatregoers, who delighted in their picture-frame proscenium enclosing a painted view of one city square or their Elizabethan stage façade representing a castle or a kingdom in one unified symbol. When the perspective picture stage could make a complete setting disappear and in less than a minute replace it by another, small scenic units shown at the same time seemed

The Theatre of Exaltation

FIGURE 5.7   The medieval principle of simultaneous settings used in a modern production. All the settings and playing areas are combined in one scenic structure. Design by C. M. Cristini for the opera *Carmen* at the ancient Arena in Verona.

a crude expedient. But many of the mid-twentieth-century playwrights and designers have borrowed some aspects of the simultaneous stage (FIGURES 5.7, 5.8, and 9.7). With separate pools of light it is easy to pick out one setting and its actors, while the unused units sink into shadow. For Shakespearean productions this kind of staging has become increasingly popular, offering more atmospheric detail in each unit than the more compact Elizabethan façade yet allowing the action to continue from one scene to another just as freely. We shall discuss modern simultaneous staging in the chapter on design. For epic theatre, as we have already noted, the interaction of different forces, often located miles apart, is well indicated by representing several localities simultaneously. Like the medieval religious drama, the epic treats each part of the world as real, with its own local character, but as only one aspect of a larger story.

The late Middle Ages and the early Renaissance developed two forms of entertainment that provided a transition to the Elizabethan theatre. The first was the morality play, from which playwrights developed the art of creating long plots with sustained conflict and great variety of detail. The second was the street show for a royal procession, which showed stage architects how to combine in one large scenic structure aspects of several scenic symbols.

Everyman (*c.* 1475) is the most impressive of the morality plays. In a single strong plot developed with allegorical characters, God sends Death to summon Everyman. Everyman is terrified of the journey and is not ready to present a reckoning of his life. His earthly friends Fellowship, Kindred, and Goods refuse to go with him, and Beauty, Strength, and Five Wits fall by the wayside. Only Good Deeds can go with him into the grave. *Everyman* is serious throughout, but the sixteenth century saw a large number of morality plays that included scenes of gaiety and satire on fashions, social life, and politics. One central character would undergo a series of tests as the Virtues

Kinds of Plays

FIGURE 5.8   The medieval simultaneous principle in a three-part structure for a Shakespearean play. The center section served for the throne, stage left for the tavern scenes, and stage right for the rebels. The battle scenes were played on the forestage and spread across and behind the center section. *Henry IV, Part I.* University of Arkansas production, directed by George R. Kernodle and designed by Martel Gilbert.

contended with the Vices for his soul. Some moralities included kings and princes as historical examples and, for all their serious moral concern, showed a great deal of humanistic tolerance for fun and revelry.

The street entertainments were occasioned by royal visits to a city. A king's processional entry was welcomed by a number of street shows or tableaux built along the way on triumphal arches or in front of public buildings. Actors portraying famous kings and heroes would address the king from throne pavilions or from a row of arches in an arcade screen. In a scenic castle or a triumphal arch, a curtain might open up to present a tableau on an inner or upper stage. Sometimes several symbols were combined, creating a larger, more complex scenic structure than the separate mansions of the episodic mystery cycles.

Tragedy in Renaissance England

The great task of the Renaissance was to organize a compact drama out of the sprawling episodes of the Middle Ages, to create a unified stage by combining the separate simultaneous mansions into a single symbol of reality. Two new theatres evolved, at first distinct but later combined in the main tradition of the picture-frame stage. One theatre, in Elizabethan England, put behind an open platform a symbolic structure that combined the various medieval symbols—throne canopy, castle, triumphal arch, and others—into one complex façade with formal doorways, windows, inner stages, and upper balconies. The Italians created their unified stage, as we have seen, by a very different principle, making the medieval mansions more realistic and organizing them as the separate houses on a single street dimin-

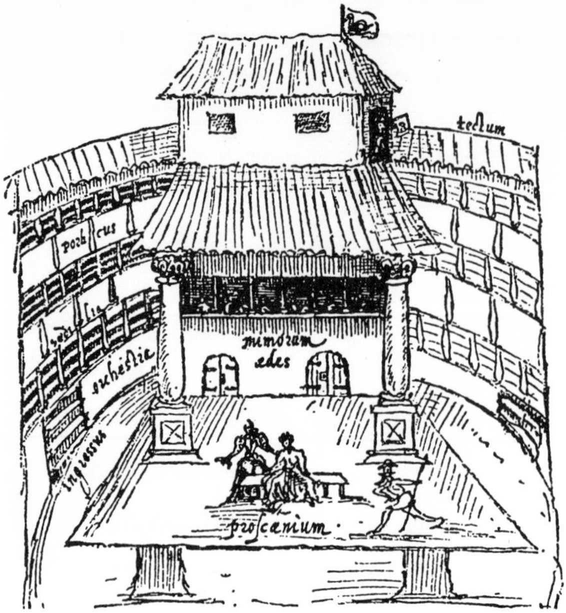

FIGURE *5.9* A Dutch copy of a contemporary drawing of the Swan Theatre of London, about 1596. Its accuracy is uncertain, but it is our only pictorial source for the interior of an Elizabethan theatre.

ishing into the distance by the laws of perspective. A proscenium frame gave finish and definition to the painted picture and set it off from the audience as an illusion of one real place (FIGURES *2.1, 2.2, 2.10, 2.13*).

DEVELOPMENT OF THE TRAGIC FORM

An even greater achievement was the creation of Renaissance drama. The Italian courts, developing both comedies and tragedies in close imitation of the ancients, achieved a great deal. But even more was accomplished in the popular, commercial theatres of Paris, Madrid, and London. In these centers an exalted drama was developed out of the tradition of the sprawling religious plays, the popular romances about adventurous knights, and the histories of kings and princes that had impressed the populace in the street shows or tableaux. From the diverse material of these several sources the popular theatres kept the multiple plots, the clowns and servants to accompany the kings, prophets, and saints, the crowd scenes, the spectacular arrival of kings, the trials and council meetings, the battles, sieges, processions, weddings, and coronations. Across the platform stage, they kept this vivid pageant moving through scene after scene with scarcely an intermission, now by bringing on thrones, beds, or tables, now by using doors, windows, and balconies, now by disclosing arranged tableaux behind curtains.

From this popular sensational drama, like modern movies in many ways, a few poets created an exalted form of art, a romantic tragedy of heroic individuals. The great heroes of history walked out on the Elizabethan platform, defied the limits of medieval society, risked terrible evil and suffering, expanded the bounds of the human spirit, threatened the very heavens, and met their deaths still fighting and striving. The medieval world had taught that fortune, controlling man like a wheel, raised him to the top and then, for no more reason, carried him on to his fall. All men must expect their fall in a world where all is meaningless change and chance; only by turning away from this world and seeking heaven could man find meaning. But the Elizabethan hero would accept no such humility. Thomas Kyd's hero in *The Spanish Tragedy* (*c.* 1589) carries out his revenge though he destroys himself and many others in the carnage. Christopher Marlowe's Tamburlaine, the shepherd who conquered the world in *Tamburlaine* (*c.* 1587), defies all limitation, even mortality. By his determination to control his own fate, he persuades even his enemies to join him.

> . . . do but join with me,
> And we will triumph over all the world.
> I hold the Fates bound fast in iron chains
> And with my hand turn Fortune's wheel about:
> And sooner shall the sun fall from his sphere
> Than Tamburlaine be slain or overcome.

In a more quiet mood, Tamburlaine describes the Renaissance aspiration that stirred the age. The Neoplatonists in Italy compared the universe and man's position in it to a ladder with man in the center, able to choose to move downward toward the beasts and base matter or upward toward the angels and God. In the political sphere it was the figure of the king at the top that drew all men upward.

> Nature, that fram'd us of four elements,
> Warring within our breasts for regiment,
> Doth teach us all to have aspiring minds:
> Our souls, whose faculties can comprehend
> The wondrous architecture of the world,
> And measure every wand'ring planet's course,
> Still climbing after knowledge infinite,
> And always moving as the restless spheres,
> Wills us to wear ourselves, and never rest,

FIGURE 5.10 Players in an Elizabethan inn yard. The inn yard probably suggested some aspects of the Elizabethan stage. A drawing from C. Walter Hodges, *The Globe Restored*. Courtesy of Ernest Benn, Ltd., London.

Until we reach the ripest fruit of all,
That perfect bliss and sole felicity,
The sweet fruition of an earthly crown.

Only in the second part of the drama, the sequel, does Tamburlaine meet limitations. His love, Zenocrate, dies, and Tamburlaine wants to wound the earth and cleave it in twain. When his son chooses a life of peace, Tamburlaine stabs him and sets out to become the "scourge of God and terror of the world." He hitches two Oriental kings to his chariot and whips them, crying, "Holla, ye pampered jades of Asia." He declares that he will "march against the powers of heaven and set black streamers to signify the slaughter of the gods," defying fate to his last breath.

Mental aspiration appeals to modern audiences more than an obsession with worldly power; for this reason Marlowe's next play, *Dr. Faustus* (*c.* 1588), is produced more frequently. In a sense *Dr. Faustus* is merely a highly developed medieval morality play. Marlowe has kept the devil and the good and evil angels, but in his drama the real experience, the conflict, is in the mind. By making a contract to ignore human limits, Faustus can explore all experience and search after infinite knowledge. He calls up Helen, the dream of immortal beauty, and sings his paean of wonder and praise:

Was this the face that launch'd a thousand ships,
And burnt the topless towers of Ilium?
Sweet Helen, make me immortal with a kiss.

. . .

More lovely than the monarch of the sky
In wanton Arethusa's azur'd arms;
And none but thou shalt be my paramour!

At the end the devil exacts the penalty, possession of his soul, and Faustus utters his curses and his remorse as passionately as he had uttered his pride and his determination to explore all knowledge. He cannot pass God's limits. But the final impression is not of death and defeat but of the magnificent individual who dared.

This is one of the patterns of Elizabethan tragedy that we call great: the overmeasure, the assertion, the tremendous bounty that expands the realm of the human spirit, pushing out limits even as it is defeated. The death of Romeo and Juliet is heightened because they have snatched their moments of ecstasy in the face of the hostility of the old feudal world. Antony and Cleopatra throw away countries and continents. But who would rather be their rival, the practical, successful, calculating Caesar? Othello is another magnificent conqueror who is defeated by the very bounty of his emotions, who loved "not wisely but too well." Throughout the best of the Elizabethans there is this great generosity, the willingness to live and love, even in the face of probable defeat. When the cautious Polonius assures Hamlet that he will take care of the Players "according to their deserts," Hamlet protests, "God's bodkins man, better. Use every man after his desert, and who should 'scape whipping? Use them after your own honor and dignity. The less they deserve, the

Kinds of Plays

more merit is in your bounty." The Elizabethans knew that such bounty left man tragically vulnerable, but they were not a cautious people. Nor did they ask assurance of reward in heaven.

TRAGIC PATTERNS IN SHAKESPEARE'S HISTORIES

It was in the history plays that Shakespeare first worked out his more subtle and complex approach to tragedy. Historians from the time of Henry VIII, Queen Elizabeth's father, saw their rulers, the Tudors, as a strong national dynasty that had replaced the anarchy and confusion of the Wars of the Roses. During the patriotic years following the defeat of the Spanish Armada in 1588, when plays of English history became popular, Shakespeare wrote four plays about the civil wars among the barons that led to the reign of Richard III, whom Shakespeare's age saw as a gloating archvillain, and finally to the accession of Henry VII, the first of the Tudors. A few years later he wrote four plays about the events at the beginning of the fifteenth century that prepared the way for the later contentions and wars. These eight plays form one of the greatest political epics of all time. While celebrating a century of struggle to become a united nation, Shakespeare examined the experience that shaped the kings and princes whose private ambitions and guilts so strongly affected their public careers. In these plays both the inner world and the outer are important, and they are constantly interdependent.

It all started with the weak, corrupt King Richard II at the end of the fourteenth century. Shakespeare makes him a sensitive, poetic soul, but not a good king. Still it was a grave presumption for his cousin Henry to revolt and to depose and kill the king. In his practical, uninspired way Henry IV was not a bad ruler, but his breach of order led to the disruptions that lasted for nearly a century. Henry soon found that the rebels who had helped put him on the throne were conspiring against him and that his own son was wasting his time in riotous disorders in taverns and on the highroads. Prince Hal is a fascinating character, and Shakespeare sets him in contrast both to the fiery Hotspur, so hell-bent on pursuing "honor" that he can never pause for love or play, and to Falstaff, so devoted to play and good humor that he has no time for anything else. As Hal accepts more mature responsibility, in a world that respects little except war, he kills Hotspur and harshly discards Falstaff to become a triumphant, if rather disturbed, king himself. The plot and several subplots are all brought together eventually, but the comic scenes have added a new dimension, a comic mirror reflecting the intrigues and robberies of the main plot—robberies and intrigues that are harmless enough in the irresponsible fun of Falstaff's group at the Boar's Head Tavern, but dangerous indeed in the lords of the land.

There are tragic undertones in all these royal leaders, very apparent in the first and last of the line—the self-pitying Richard II and the Machiavellian schemer who overreaches himself, Richard III—but almost as much in the guilt-stricken, sleepless Henry IV and in the splendid Hal, who, as Henry V, rationalizes betrayals, cruelty, and violence in becoming a national hero. We usually call these plays histories rather than tragedies, but they are far more *193*

The Theatre of Exaltation

than patriotic pageants. History marches on. Terrible are the sufferings of a nation when its rulers are wicked, or merely foolish and unbending. But Shakespeare had a very strong sense of the private betrayals, as well as generosities and ideals, of those who control public affairs.

TRAGIC PATTERNS IN *Hamlet* AND *King Lear*

Shakespeare's tragic view, suggested in these early history plays, finds its supreme expression in the great tragedies of his later years, especially in *Hamlet* and *King Lear*.

Hamlet was written at a moment of bitter disillusion in the European soul. Renaissance hopes were exhausted, the hopes that had buoyed up so many Italians a century before and so many English only a decade before, hopes of reconciling Christianity and classic culture, of creating a liberated aristocracy and an enlightened state through humanistic education, of reviving art, literature, and drama for the modern world on classic models. The liberated individual, no longer closely ruled by his trade guild or his parish parson, was free to make money and to lose it, free to rise rapidly in court or market, and free to be lonely and disillusioned. The feudal order was breaking up with the concentration of power in an absolute monarch. The old religious certainties were gone, and wars and civil wars over religious issues were more frequent and widespread. The individualism encouraged in humanistic education ran riot in ruthless murders and court intrigue. Even the heavens lost their old order as the new astronomy first banished the earth from the center, then traced the course around the sun not as a circle with one center but as an ellipse with two centers, and finally caught glimpses of other planets with their own moons. The feeling of this time of change was expressed in one of John Donne's poems as "all coherence gone."

The complex dramatic form which Kyd and Marlowe had shaped out of medieval traditions served Shakespeare well. Whereas in the comedies several different groups—servants and masters, dukes and villagers, romantic lovers and mischievous revelers—are brought together in harmony at the end, the multiple-plot scheme serves in *Hamlet* to emphasize disruption and disorder. The plots develop displacement by mirror images, where each element reflects and makes an ironic comment on the other element. Hamlet is displaced from the throne. That Elizabethan façade that so richly represents the earthly order of a throne, endorsed by the symbols of heavenly order above, stands as a solid backing of the stage. But Hamlet is not on the throne. He is out on the open platform, symbol of the free and independent individual, while a usurper king sits on the throne and from either heaven or hell comes the ghost of the dead king. In the medieval legend, the young prince Hamlet lurked around the edge after his uncle had usurped the throne, playing the privileged role of Fool. But in this play, Hamlet has to share even that role with a usurper fool, the meddling Polonius. The basic plot is mirrored in two other sons who must avenge their fathers: both Laertes and Fortinbras are reproaches to Hamlet, going to their violent revenges without hesitation or conscience. The immediate plot is what Hamlet calls the mousetrap, a scheme

194

FIGURE *5.11* A unit structure or permanent setting for Shakespeare's *Hamlet*. With minor changes, the one setting served for all the scenes. John Gielgud production, New York, 1936. Designed by Jo Mielziner. Photo Vandamm.

of using the players to catch the King. That plot is mirrored in three analogues as Polonius sets Ophelia and then the Queen as mousetraps to catch Hamlet, and the King and Queen set Rosencrantz and Guildenstern to catch Hamlet. It is further echoed in the plot of Polonius to set a spy to watch his own son. Hamlet's mock-madness that bursts over the margins of control is mirrored in the real madness of Ophelia. Ophelia, the object of Hamlet's love, is seen reflected in the distorted mirror of the Queen, and Hamlet rejects her with violent disgust and bawdy innuendoes. The multiple images include three kings, three father images, two fools, two madmen, and two women in love. The play-within-a-play is a mirror of both the hidden murder and the nephew's threat of vengeance.

Furthermore, each group makes an ironic comment on the actions of the others. Before Hamlet listens to the advice of his father, Shakespeare shows Laertes and Ophelia listening to their father advising them to beware of vows, to "give no unproportioned thought his act," to reserve judgment at other people's demands, and above all to be true to oneself. Would Hamlet have done better if he had heard this fool's advice before listening to the violent demands of his dead father? Hamlet advises the players to control their emotions, yet he does not control his, and when he interrupts the play by fooling, he is disregarding advice he has given to the players. He urges the Queen to control the blood by reason, then in the same scene lets his own blood overcome

195

The Theatre of Exaltation

his reason. He tells the Queen when her heart is cleft in twain to throw away the worser part and live the purer with the other half, then proceeds to contrive the murder of Rosencrantz and Guildenstern and later of the King. Finally, at the moment when Hamlet, free of all conscience, denies that he was responsible for the murder of Laertes' father, Laertes is setting an example of reckless determination—"Conscience and grace to the profoundest pit!/ Let come what comes"—and the Gravedigger is ironically absolving Ophelia from responsibility for her own death: it was the fault of the water for coming up and drowning her. The play is full of ironies and wry contrasts.

As many students have observed, the imagery throughout the play builds up the sense of disease and corruption. Something is rotten in the state of Denmark, and Hamlet's hope of love is blasted by the cancerous image of his mother's adultery; "Nay, but to live/ In the rank sweat of an enseamèd bed,/ Stew'd in corruption, honeying and making love/ Over the nasty sty."

Yet the total impact of the play is not despair. The murky night is shot through with flashes of light. When the armed ghost appears demanding vengeance, Horatio remembers that near the hallowed time of Christmas the nights are so wholesome that no spirits walk, and he describes the morn that comes "in russet mantle clad." Ophelia, disturbed that Hamlet is mad, reaffirms the "noble mind" that is overthrown: "The expectancy and rose of the fair state . . . that noble and most sovereign reason, like sweet bells jangled out of tune and harsh." Hamlet himself is keenly aware that the corruption is not normal. He affirms the ideal Renaissance vision of man's nobility in a splendid divine world even as he notes his own disillusionment:

> . . . This goodly frame, the earth, seems to me a sterile promontory, this most excellent canopy, the air, look you, this brave o'erhanging firmament, this majestical roof fretted with golden fire, why, it appears no other thing to me than a foul and pestilent congregation of vapours. What a piece of work is a man! How noble in reason! How infinite in faculty! In form and moving how express and admirable! In action how like an angel! In apprehension how like a god! The beauty of the world! The paragon of animals! And yet, to me, what is this quintessence of dust?

Throughout the long pageant of displacement and disruption, the stage façade stands serene and solid like a royal triumphal arch, a symbol of earthly order endorsed by emblems of heaven above. At the end, order is restored after disorder and Fortinbras stands in the center of the throne pavilion, a new king.

Each age reads its own meanings into the character of Hamlet, a baffling and enigmatic personality who appeals to everyone, the man who examines himself and keeps asking why, who curses the bloody, bawdy villain, then curses himself for unpacking his heart with words; who accuses himself of such things that it were better his mother had not borne him; who cleaves the general ear with words that make mad the guilty and appall the free. It is the magnificent intensity of the poetry that pierces our sympathy and teases us out of thought. We may not know exactly what Hamlet ultimately achieves in the holocaust that kills him as well as the guilty king or see just what he pays for

Kinds of Plays

FIGURE *5.12* A permanent setting for Shakespeare's *King Lear,* suggested by the primitive forms of Stonehenge. A design by Norman Bel Geddes.

the readiness for violent action, but we are stirred to depths we never knew we had by the magnificent terror of being a human being.

Where *Hamlet* is a play of an individual's displacement, *King Lear* is a play of the disruption and agony of a whole age. Where *Hamlet* was the favorite Shakespeare of the romantic rebels of the nineteenth century and equally of the individual rebels of the early twentieth, *King Lear* is especially fascinating to those who have watched the global conflicts and revolutionary upheavals of the 1940s and 50s. Like the twentieth century itself is this vision of an old king who turns over his authority to a calculating set of monsters who have promised him everything but who are cruel and ruthless beyond all believing. The innocent suffer, the men of good will are exiled or go underground, the world is plunged into a maelstrom of domestic, political, mental, and cosmic disorder. Yet the wicked destroy themselves, and in the end a few survivors establish order and sadly take up the task of rebuilding after the storm.

Where Hamlet feels an alien, displaced from the throne, Lear sees the roofs and clothes of the whole world torn away, leaving him and all mankind naked, exposed to the elements. Not even the turtle would give away his shell, but Lear has trusted the wrong daughters, who strip him of his attendants, of his last shreds of dignity. In the first act, Lear is thrust out by Goneril, and in the second act by Regan. The third act, continuing the rhythm in the minor plot, ends with the blinding and thrusting out of Gloucester. On the desolate heath Lear huddles with the faithful Fool, who never had a home or illusions of his own, and the fugitive Edgar, who must pretend to be a mad beggar. Lear insists on discarding his last garment, to feel desolation to

197

The Theatre of Exaltation

the fullest. He stages a mock trial of his daughters to demand if there is any cause in nature for these hard hearts. In his new sympathy with the homeless, he loses his selfish preoccupation with himself; he goes insane. Later he encounters the blinded, homeless Gloucester and in a different "reason in madness" rails at all covering up and glossing over, at hypocrites who wield authority while guilty of what they condemn. The tender love of Cordelia restores his sanity, but the machinery of violence cannot be stopped—Cordelia is killed and Lear's heart breaks.

Looking at the plot, some critics have said that Lear's only action is dividing the kingdom in the first scene and that the rest of the play is falling action, with only the plotting of Edmund keeping the suspense. But that is not at all the way the audience sees the play. There is a continuous action as Lear meets the cruelty of his daughters, fighting back and protesting at every step. His curses on his daughters are indeed moments of terror, and his defiance of the thunder of heaven is one of the major protests in all tragedy. The poet Swinburne in the nineteenth century saw nothing but the dark as Lear discovered the enormity of human cruelty, and in 1963 Peter Brook directed the Stratford production with Paul Scofield to emphasize the chaos and despair, as though Shakespeare had written for the wry absurdists of the post-Hiroshima period. Yet most readers and audiences in the twentieth century have found a

FIGURE 5.13 Sir John Gielgud and Alan Badel as Lear and the Fool in *King Lear*. Stratford-on-Avon, 1950. Photo Angus McBean.

strong line of development in the salvation of Lear. His gradual discovery of love and compassion gives the play its greatest warmth. Lear soon begins to see his mistake in judgment that has started the terrible "engine" of tragedy on its relentless course.

> . . . O most small fault,
> How ugly didst thou in Cordelia show!
> Which, like an engine, wrench'd my frame of nature
> From the fix'd place; drew from my heart all love,
> And added to the gall. O Lear, Lear, Lear!
> Beat at this gate that let thy folly in,
> And thy dear judgment out! . . .

He faces even more cruelty, and more awareness of the corruption of love in bestial adultery, than Hamlet does. It seems that evil controls the universe and his devoted friends are helpless. In the end, they cannot rescue Cordelia or Lear. Gloucester at one moment concludes that

> As flies to wanton boys, are we to the gods,
> They kill us for their sport

and tries to throw himself over the cliff. Yet Gloucester finds that the son he denounced has led him in his blindness, and Lear learns that Cordelia loves him and hence his vision of the universe is restored.

> Thou hast one daughter
> Who redeems Nature from the general curse
> Which twain have brought her to.

But more than that Lear learns to think of others, to help the Fool to a shelter he had scorned for himself. In humiliation he learns a touching compassion for all suffering humanity which he puts in the form of a prayer.

> Poor naked wretches, wheresoe'er you are,
> That bide the pelting of this pitiless storm,
> How shall your houseless heads and unfed sides,
> Your loop'd and window'd raggedness, defend you
> From seasons such as these? O, I have ta'en
> Too little care of this! Take physic, pomp;
> Expose thyself to feel what wretches feel, .
> That thou mayst shake the superflux to them,
> And show the heavens more just.

One of the most touching scenes in all literature is that in which Lear wakes and gets on his knees to beg forgiveness of Cordelia, feeling on his hand the hot tears of his loving daughter. His last long speech, a litany of prayer and forgiveness, is a strange dream of living in prison, happy with Cordelia, and watching the world "as if we were God's spies." At the end he makes one more protest at a universe that would kill Cordelia:

> Why should a dog, a horse, a rat, have life,
> And thou no breath at all?

199

The Theatre of Exaltation

The play has shown that man can fall lower than the beasts but that love (and only a fool or a crazy old king would risk love), though it cannot save, can redeem him, and hence the world, from bestiality.

Hamlet had only his friend Horatio, an uninvolved observer, as a companion in his suffering. Lear has the whole band of outcasts, primitive archetypes of lost souls—the Fool, Gloucester, Kent, and Edgar—fool and blindman, exile and mad beggar. Above all, he discovers Cordelia, steadfast in stubborn sincerity, steadfast and patient in love.

By studying chaos, by tracing the breakdown of the human personality and the destruction of order, Shakespeare affirms the necessity of order. Chaos leads to a new order, but there is enormous waste of human potentiality. Macbeth could have been a very sensitive and imaginative follower, and Othello was a great and noble general who in his private life was too easily moved by ignoble suspicion and jealousy.

THE ELIZABETHAN STAGE

To the supreme examples of tragedy created by Shakespeare the modern theatre owes an incalculable debt, but it owes almost as much to the stage on which these dramas were played. In groping for some escape from the everyday detail of the realistic theatre, playwrights, designers, and directors have learned even more from the Elizabethan stage than from the Greek or the Chinese. Although there is not a single completely dependable picture and the living tradition was lost in the three hundred years of picture-frame scenery, enough is known for the idea of an Elizabethan stage to stand as a beacon for a realistic period. To return to that stage is to enter another theatre world. There was no front curtain and no proscenium frame, no painted scenery, no pretense of creating an illusion of actual place. The actor was thrust out into the midst of the audience on a platform open to the sky and to the three rows of galleries that nearly encircled the stage and the space for standing spectators or groundlings. The actor enjoyed direct contact with the audience instead of always turning away in the strange pretense that they are not there. A splendid façade back of the open platform presented at least six openings, either for entrances and exits or for small scenes to be disclosed back of doorways or behind small curtains. That meant that the many scenes of a Shakespearean play could follow one another without interruption for scene changes but with exciting combinations of levels and playing areas. The director could close a scene on the inner stage by means of the curtain and immediately bring another group of actors onto the forestage or the upper stage. With the rediscovery of this flexible stage, Shakespeare's plays can be put on with the sequence and rhythm of the original productions, without pauses for scene change, without cutting or combining the smaller scenes, and without the distraction of a full painted setting each time a different group of actors comes on the stage.

Printed versions of the plays have been corrupted since eighteenth-century editors cut them into many separate scenes and inserted indications of place: "a room in the castle," "another part of the forest," "a corridor outside the

Kinds of Plays

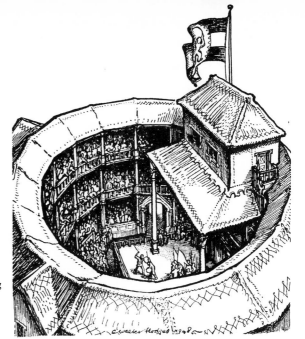

throne room," and so on. The plays published during Shakespeare's lifetime had no indications of act and scene division, much less any indication of particular place; all Shakespeare wrote was "exeunt" for one group and "enter" for the next. Only in the 1950s and 60s do some editions go back to the Elizabethan practice of letting one scene follow immediately after the other on the page, just as it did on the Elizabethan stage.

If it was necessary for the audience to know an exact place, the playwright had some character say, "This is the Forest of Arden," or "What country, friends, is this?—This is Illyria, Lady," or "What wood is this before us?— The wood of Birnam." Otherwise the action indicated all the audience needed to know. For many scenes it did not matter what the locality might be. There are a few hints that the names of places were visible on the stage, and some historians have supposed that a boy came out for each scene and either held or changed a sign on which was printed the name of the place. The film of *Henry V* shows such a boy with a sign. But other historians consider this nonsense and say that at most a tavern sign was hung out or a heraldic shield with "France," or the name of a castle was changed on the façade.

The most commonly accepted picture of the Elizabethan stage, then, is of a bare platform strewn with rushes, with a penthouse roof supported by two splendid columns, backed by an architectural façade, or "tiring house" (where the actors changed their attire), the façade pierced by two formal doorways with windows above, and at the center an inner stage with a balcony or upper stage above, which is sometimes called the "inner below" and "inner above." The basic pattern of the Elizabethan stage was apparently derived from the street shows. But on the Elizabethan stage, the throne pavilion, the arches, and the inner and upper stages were combined into one formal façade as a backing for the platform of the stage. It was left to the audience to turn that

201

The Theatre of Exaltation

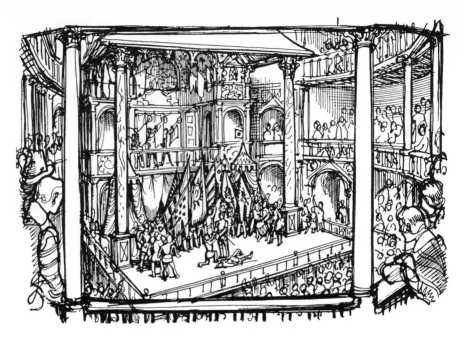

FIGURE *5.15* A closer view of the Elizabethan stage, as seen from one of the galleries. The crowd of characters, the tents and banners on the forestage, and the trumpeters on the upper stage create an elaborate spectacle. The final scene of *Richard III*. A drawing from C. Walter Hodges, *Shakespeare and the Players*. Courtesy of Ernest Benn, Ltd., London.

FIGURE *5.16* The inner stage used for a banquet scene in *Richard III*. A drawing from C. Walter Hodges, *Shakespeare and the Players*. Courtesy of Ernest Benn, Ltd., London.

FIGURE 5.17　An architectural reconstruction of the Elizabethan stage. The theatre in the Folger Shakespeare Memorial Library in Washington, D.C.

background into field, forest, cave, mountain, room, castle, or gates of a city with defenders high on the wall while besiegers from below scaled and captured the city. It has been the fashion since the end of the nineteenth century to build "authentic reproductions" of the Elizabethan stage and decorate them in the brown and tan half-timber style, the style of many medieval and Elizabethan private cottages (FIGURES *4.14* and *5.18*). Yet the contemporary references were to the splendid stage, the gaudy colors, and the painted marble columns. Further study also reveals other sources of splendor. Costumes were elaborate, actors spending as much as princes for rich garments for the stage. Then, even though there was no painted setting, many properties could be brought on—thrones, tables, beds, shop fronts, altars, tombs, tents, caves, mountains, trees. Add to these many banners, pennants, and flags, and there is colorful pageantry indeed. A small group of musicians played flourishes for the processions, accompaniment for the many songs and dances, and appropriate background music: quiet, stately tunes for sad and solemn scenes, for example, or "hellish music" for scenes of terror. That plain platform and façade stage, whether decorated like an old-fashioned Tudor cottage or in the new classical architecture, could present a splendid pageant of romantic drama.

How should Shakespeare be revived today? If full romantic painted settings are used as in the Charles Kean *Merchant of Venice* or the Katharine Hepburn *As You Like It* illustrated in FIGURES *2.14* and *2.9,* the rapid flow of the play is lost in the waits for changes and the attention is distracted by the scenery. Yet few people want to go to the extreme austerity of the Festival Theatre at Stratford, Ontario (FIGURE *4.13*). Most productions follow a compromise that offers some scenic adornment and still permits the action to flow uninterruptedly. The late-nineteenth century found one possible compromise in the "alternation" method, in which shallow scenes were given on

203

The Theatre of Exaltation

an empty forestage in front of a curtain while the full setting and properties were changed behind the curtain. Many of Shakespeare's short scenes do not need a particular locality, and audiences did not mind if actors came on through formal doors in the temporary proscenium to start the scene, then moved back into the setting as the curtain opened. Nineteenth-century producers could not imagine changing scenic elements in sight of the audience, but, as has been pointed out in an earlier chapter, a twentieth-century audience delights in such changes. The tradition set by the Elizabethan Stage Society, and in this country by B. Iden Payne, used the formal background of the "authentic" reconstruction with a few bowers and trees brought on and occasionally a bit of painted scenery in the "inner below" (FIGURE 5.18). Page boys (or more often girls with pageboy haircuts), who pulled the curtains and set up chairs and tables and other properties, gave the audience a feeling they were participating in charming old customs.

The standard, formal "authentic" stage is especially appropriate for a Shakespearean festival where several plays are alternated. It proved its worth at the Chicago World's Fair in 1933 and 1934 and then at fairs in Dallas and San Diego, where a short version of a different play would start each hour at the "Globe Playhouse," four plays in an afternoon and four in the evening.

FIGURE 5.18   A theatrical reconstruction of an Elizabethan stage for a college production. The decoration follows the half-timber style of Tudor houses, and small pieces of illusionistic scenery are changed on the inner stage when the curtains are closed. Shakespeare's *Twelfth Night*. University of Illinois production, directed by Charles H. Shattuck and costumed by Genevieve Richardson.

FIGURE *5.19*   A witty adaptation of the principles of the Elizabethan stage. While the curtains were closed and street scenes were played on the forestage, the furniture and simple settings could be changed on the inner stage. When the curtains were opened, the rooftops remained as an amusing frame. Two scenes from Shakespeare's *The Merry Wives of Windsor*. University of Arkansas production, directed by Frank McMullan and designed and costumed by Preston Magruder.

Spectators often attended three or all four in one visit, enthralled at the fast-moving drama when the gist of an exciting play was given in forty minutes. The Oregon Shakespeare Festival follows a similar tradition of one formal structure for all plays, and tourists are able to see four full plays in as many nights (FIGURE 4.14).

Where only one play is presented and there is therefore no necessity for a standard setting, many designers prefer a setting that in structure has the advantages of the Elizabethan stage but in shape and symbolism is particularly suited to the one play. Since, as we have seen, the Elizabethan stage itself is a combination of all the important medieval symbols—castle, city gate, triumphal arch, throne pavilion, and arcade screen—superimposed on one another and simplified until the abstract structure has lost the special atmosphere of any one symbol, it seems logical enough to go back to the symbols and choose those that suit the particular play, either laid out one beside the other, as in the simultaneous stage of Valenciennes, or compacted, as in the Elizabethan stage. Then, instead of being limited by one standard arrangement, the designer and the director can plan the steps, platforms, shapes, towers, and arches needed for the action. With the help of modern selective lighting, they can give a playing area the atmosphere of a corridor, bower, throne, or altar and, when the action moves elsewhere, let that area retire into shadows. Thus the best possibilities of modern, medieval, and Elizabethan

FIGURE 5.20 A permanent sculptural setting for Shakespeare's *Othello*. Free forms shape the playing areas and suggest mood. Carnegie Tech Theatre production, directed by Lawrence Carra, designed by Frank Silberstein, lighted by Steven Cohen, and costumed by John Doepp. Photo William Nelson.

staging are combined. The play progresses without a break, small changes taking place in view of the audience. Such a background creates more atmosphere than the standard "authentic" Elizabethan stage and even permits some symbolism, and the flexible arrangement of levels allows more interesting grouping and movement and a more effective use of modern lighting.

Neoclassic Tragedy

The Elizabethan dramatists achieved great vitality in a sprawling, complex form that owed much to the medieval drama. Half a century later, French dramatists went to the opposite extreme and created a new classic tragedy that surpassed the ancient Greek in compactness, austerity, and polish. The new classicism, in public life as well as in art, was a triumph of simplicity and order over complexity and turbulence. The expansive energies of the Renaissance had led to conflicts and tensions that set Catholics against Protestants and barons against the king. But in the seventeenth century men were tired of religious wars and emotional conflict, and gradually Richelieu brought the turbulent political forces of France into the tight control of a central power. Paris was ready for an age of reason and for a heroic drama in which violent personal forces and conflicting values were brought into controlled harmony. Modern students are surprised to find that in the plays of this "classic" age, the beginning of the Age of Reason, the characters almost burst with passion. But there is no real inconsistency: the age made a fetish of order for the very reason that it was aware of the violent forces just beneath the surface that might erupt at any moment.

Neoclassic tragedy was a triumph over the complex romantic form of drama that was popular in European countries. Like the London of Shakespeare and the Madrid of Lope de Vega, Paris at the beginning of the seventeenth century had a vigorous popular drama. Alexandre Hardy was almost as prolific as Lope de Vega, and year after year he entertained the Paris public with high adventure, comedy and tragedy, kings and clowns, poetry and blood and thunder. The Hôtel de Bourgogne, the chief commercial theatre of Paris, continued in a simple form the medieval simultaneous stage, with four or five mansions around a central playing area; the audience identified the place of action by the house from which the main actors entered. Often an entire act was located by one house and the other houses were ignored although they were in sight all the time. Some French producers, especially in staging operas, imitated the elaborate effects of the Italian opera, with its sliding wings and backdrops, monsters rising from the waves, angels and devils flying through the air, and whole choirs of angels and Jupiter in all his glory descending in clouds to restore order to a world in turmoil.

But when in the 1630s critical taste in France demanded a change, classical-minded men rejected alike the unconvincing, disunified conventions of the medieval stage and the extravagant display of Italian spectacle. The populace might thrill at the pageantry of the Baroque church and the absolute monarchy, and the aristocrats might delight in their splendid masques and operas,

207

but men of taste wanted an austere tragedy that would show man's solitary struggle.

When neoclassic tragedy arrived, with Corneille's *The Cid* in 1637, it was not a direct imitation of Greek or Roman tragedy; it was a distillation or condensation of the popular drama. We can appreciate the compactness of *The Cid* by comparing it with the earlier Spanish play, *The Youth of the Cid,* on which it was based. The original play is a long narrative of many episodes, including minor subplots, court ceremonies, and battle scenes. But Corneille chose only the final episode in the tale and shifted the emphasis from adventure and fighting to psychological dilemma. Rodrigue, the Cid, is called upon to fight a duel with the father of his love, Chimène. He wins by killing her father, and her anger is so strong that he rushes away to battle hoping to be killed. When he returns a national hero, intensifying Chimène's psychological conflict, she chooses another champion to fight a duel with him. Again he hopes to be killed. At the end, the king sees that Rodrigue's triumphs have almost conquered Chimène's uncertainty and distress, and he suggests that she wait a year and then accept him as a husband.

In his play, Corneille eliminated many incidents found in the earlier play as well as such supernumeraries as giants, hermits, shepherds, princes, and soldiers. Leaving offstage the battle scenes and almost all the court scenes, he replaced them with scenes between two contending characters and scenes in which a character analyzes his problem of choice. Every motive and every possible decision is carefully debated, and violent emotions are examined with utmost clarity. The Age of Reason produced not a cold debate without passion but a passionate drama of reasoning.

The Cid's choice is not between good and evil but between his love—a private good—and his duty to his father and his king—higher, public loyalties. In the end the loyalties are reconciled. Many a nobleman and merchant who sat in the audience had experienced such a conflict of personal desires and public obligations because of the tightening rule and increasing demands of an absolute monarch. The suppression of one's own desires was painful, but it was bearable because Richelieu was making Louis XIII so splendid a monarch. It was glorious to sacrifice personal inclination to follow such a ruler, as it would be later to follow his more spectacular son, Louis XIV, the "Sun King."

Even though the audience was impressed with *The Cid,* some critics thought that the refinement of dramatic material had not gone far enough. The play still contained features that were contrary to classic ideas of unity: more than one climax (though technically the action took place in one day), more than one place represented on the stage (though the different scenes were all near one another at the royal court), and more than one action (though the subplot was closely related to the main theme). The Académie Française, a council which Richelieu instituted to render authoritative judgment on both words and techniques in formal literature, condemned *The Cid* for not adhering to the classic form. In his next plays, Corneille was careful to observe the unities of time, place, and action, to include no scenes of pub-

Kinds of Plays

FIGURE *5.21* The neo-classic stage of Paris in the middle of the seventeenth century. The characters in their "antique" costumes are copied exactly from an early edition of the play. The setting is a free reconstruction from several sources. Racine's *Andromaque*. Drawn by Martha Sutherland.

lic spectacle, and to show his characters as abstract, universalized types. The neoclassic ideals of unity and decorum were thus established.

Racine, who began writing plays in the 1660s, found no difficulty in fitting his genius into the neoclassic form. Whereas Corneille stressed the triumph of the will in plays that provoke admiration rather than pity, Racine showed the appalling failure of the will. His heroes—or rather his heroines, for he specialized in feminine psychology—fall into evil, watching themselves go down helpless and finding tortuous justifications and rationalizations until time and their own deeds bring destruction. Racine's first great triumph, *Andromaque* (1667), presents four people involved in a conflict of ideals. After the Trojan War, Andromaque, the widow of Hector, is the captive of Pyrrhus, who is in love with her. But she refuses him in order to be true to the memory of Hector and to care for Hector's child. Hermione, engaged to Pyrrhus, is living in his palace, furious that he delays the wedding. Orestes, who is in love with Hermione, is sent by the Greeks to kill Hector's son. Thus each person is torn between two demands. Andromaque tries a ruse, agreeing to marry Pyrrhus in order to save her child but planning to kill herself. Then Hermione, in a fury, demands that Orestes prove his love for her by killing Pyrrhus. But when he does, she turns her fury on him. The bewildered Orestes loses his mind.

Ten years later, in 1677, Racine closed his career in the public theatre with *Phèdre,* which has provided the top acting role in classic French theatre, just as Hamlet is the top English role. It is an even more terrifying study of tragic destruction than *Andromaque*. Phèdre, in love with her stepson, Hippolytus, is spurned by him. In vengeance, she tells her husband, Theseus, that Hippolytus has attacked her. Theseus calls on the god Neptune, who sends a sea monster to destroy Hippolytus. In clear, careful debate, Phèdre analyzes her own emotions, loathing herself for her degrading passion, seeing herself caught in the fatal net, turning her frustration into destruction. Yet she remains a public figure, a queen of dignity and grandeur. The final effect is one of ma-

209

The Theatre of Exaltation

FIGURE *5.22* A neoclassic role as interpreted in the nineteenth century. Elisabeth Rachel wore rather austere Grecian draperies for her most famous part, the title role in Racine's *Phèdre.* Museum of the City of New York.

jestic sadness, for the violent passions and dark convoluted turns of the mind are all expressed in the most polished poetry, the most carefully selected impersonal diction, and the most perfectly proportioned and balanced episodes.

Setting and costume for this neoclassic drama were simple and completely removed from everyday life. By 1640, after the remnants of simultaneous setting had been eliminated, the setting was a simplified version of the perspective set introduced in Italy about 1507 but one that little resembled the elaborate fantasies of the opera. Two or three wings at the sides, all painted with dignified columns, led to a back shutter (FIGURE *5.21*). By our standards the "antique" costumes appear somewhat elaborate. The Renaissance had already developed a standardized costume for all ancient people: the tunic of the Roman soldier, with some embroidery added and a wider skirt, and the shepherdess or "nymph" costume of the pastoral plays, made a little more courtly. The men, and sometimes the women, wore wigs and plumes. But compared to the elaborate wigs of the audience and the costumes of the opera, these were simple enough. The age liked all the variety and local color of the contemporary world in its comedy, but the exalted drama had to be set in this uniform, conventionalized world of the ancients. Indeed, many portraits of the time were painted not in everyday dress but in the timeless tunics and robes of the gods and the tragic heroes. As late as the end of the eighteenth century George Washington was immortalized in marble in an "antique" robe.

To grasp the full implications of the kind of drama so much admired in the greatest period of French theatre, it is helpful to consider what *Hamlet* would be like if it had been written in neoclassic form. There would be no comedy, of course, none of Hamlet's bitter wit, no subplot or wide panorama

Kinds of Plays

of people, no public scenes, no players, no gravediggers, no ghost. The action would be concentrated on a few characters—Hamlet, the King and Queen, and possibly Ophelia—who would be drained of all individuality and whose amazing, vivid diction would be reduced to a uniform, dignified, stately language. All the minor characters would be abstracted into four confidants. Hamlet would have Horatio to talk to—there would be no soliloquies, of course. The King could not have a prime minister, like Polonius, but instead would have a friend-attendant. The scenes of Hamlet refusing to kill the King at prayer, ordering Ophelia to a nunnery, and confronting the Queen could all be retained, but each character would have his confidant present— the play would have to be impersonal even in intimate scenes. No throne would be visible, for not the public act but the private decision would be important.

By its austerity and concentration, neoclassic tragedy stands out in sharp contrast to the motley dramas of the Middle Ages and the Renaissance. The romantics of the nineteenth century despised it as cold and overrefined and compared it to the dead-white plaster casts made from ancient sculpture. But the twentieth century turns back to it with great respect for its ethical concern, its self-examination, its debates on moral issues, its direct scenes of personal conflict. From Ibsen's tight realistic plays, set in one Victorian living room, to Jean-Paul Sartre's *No Exit*, a fantasy about three people confined in one room in hell, modern drama has made frequent use of the compact neoclassic form.

The theatre can create its effect through many different means—dance, song, color, mood and local atmosphere, symbolism, spectacle—but the central impact of a play comes from the confrontation of two wills. Two people making demands on each other, shaping their mutual and separate fates, hammering out their own characters are the essence of drama. Even in the film, where so much is done with camera movement and the juxtaposition of faces, landscapes, and objects, the central scenes are often the unspectacular ones with two or three people. Background fades from view as the human drama stands out. Far more than the Greeks, who used the elaborate effects of the chorus, the neoclassic playwrights proved that an austere presentation of characters in climactic action, with all preliminary episodes, all physical action, and all public events left offstage, can be very powerful drama.

EXERCISES AND DEMONSTRATIONS

1. STRUCTURE IN MEDIEVAL DRAMA. Analyze the structure of the Wakefield *Second Shepherds' Play,* noting how the story of Mak is a parallel to, or a travesty of, the visit of the shepherds to the Nativity, with a supernatural vision in the night, the bringing of gifts to the newborn child, and the discovery of extraordinary aspects of the "lamb."

2. NAIVE DEVOTION IN MEDIEVAL DRAMA.   Analyze a medieval Nativity play or perform a speech of one of the shepherds to show how the ardent devotion is so strong that it is not weakened by the naive, slightly comic quality. Good examples are the Wakefield *Second Shepherds' Play* and the Nativity plays of the York and Coventry cycles.

3. CHARACTERIZATION IN THE MORALITY PLAY.   How might some of the minor characters of *Everyman* be cast, costumed, and acted so that they would be vivid and individual as well as fitting for the abstraction represented (Fellowship, Goods, etc.)? How might the Seven Deadly Sins in Marlowe's *Dr. Faustus* be cast, costumed, and acted?

4. CHARACTERIZATION IN THE MORALITY PLAY.   For a modern-dress production of *Everyman,* plan the modern equivalents for several of the characters, with costumes, hand properties, and stereotyped actions—for example, Strength as an exhibition boxer or wrestler or Five Wits as a fretful old-maid schoolteacher.

5. MORALITY PATTERN IN MARLOWE'S *Dr. Faustus.*   Show how the main action of *Dr. Faustus* is a morality play of the struggle of virtues and vices for the soul of Faustus.

6. CHAOS AND REDEMPTION IN SHAKESPEARE.   Considering *Macbeth* as a study of displacement comparable to *Hamlet* and *Lear,* analyze how Macbeth loses his sense of reality as appearances and promises are mocked by reality, as fair is foul and everything that is, is not.

7. STUDY OF NOBILITY IN A TRAGIC CHARACTER.   Analyze the character of Macbeth to note what possibilities of nobility are destroyed as Macbeth is swept farther on the path of evil. In what speeches does he recognize what he is losing? Where do images of light and innocence break through the atmosphere of night and evil? Where does he express his disapproval of his own evil course?

8. ELEMENTS OF NEOCLASSIC STRUCTURE IN SHAKESPEARE.   Analyze *Othello* as a structure having some aspects of the romantic play and some of the neoclassic. What elements, such as group actions, public occasions, and subplots, would have to be left out to make a neoclassic play? What sequences and scenes are already restricted to confrontation and psychological interaction of a few people? Why does Shakespeare bring in public authorities at the beginning and end of the play?

9. NEOCLASSIC STRUCTURE IN MODERN DRAMA.   Analyze a compact, well-made modern play and list all of the events, people, and forces concerned that are left offstage. Which might be brought on to make the play an epic play? Which might be developed in song and dance to make a musical? Which

212

would be shown, at least briefly, in a film play? Good examples are Ibsen, *A Doll's House, Ghosts, Hedda Gabler*; Hellman, *The Little Foxes*; O'Neill, *Anna Christie, Ah, Wilderness!*; Williams, *The Glass Menagerie, Cat on a Hot Tin Roof*; Inge, *Picnic, Bus Stop*; Albee, *Who's Afraid of Virginia Woolf?*

SUGGESTED READING

PLAYS

There are many collections of medieval or "pre-Shakespearean" plays, usually containing the serious Brome *Abraham and Isaac,* the comic Wakefield *Second Shepherds' Play,* one of the comic plays of *Noah,* and the impressive morality play, *Everyman.* The Nativity plays from the York and the Coventry cycles are especially powerful.

Useful for a better understanding of medieval plays are the following recordings: *The Play of Daniel,* performed by the New York Pro Musica, Decca DL 9402, and *Monuments of Early English Drama,* especially vol. I, Caedmon TC 1030.

Christopher Marlowe's *Tamburlaine* (*c.* 1587) and *Dr. Faustus* (*c.* 1588) and Thomas Kyd's *The Spanish Tragedy* (*c.* 1589) are representative of the drama at the beginning of Shakespeare's career, and Ben Jonson's *Volpone* (1606) and *The Alchemist* (1610) and John Webster's *The Duchess of Malfi* (*c.* 1614) are good examples of the work of his contemporaries.

Shakespeare's early tragedy *Romeo and Juliet* (*c.* 1594) is as much a romance as a tragedy. The histories, also written in the 1590s, tried out some aspects of tragedy. The highest achievements are the four great tragedies—*Hamlet, Othello, Macbeth,* and *King Lear*—written between 1601 and 1606.

There are several good scholarly editions of Shakespeare and a number of good editions in paperback. Favorite paperback editions, with clear print and good binding, are the Pelican Shakespeare published by Penguin Books and the Laurel Shakespeare published by Dell. The Pelican approaches the form of Shakespeare's lifetime in indicating how one scene flows without interruption into the next.

Of Corneille's plays, *The Cid* (1637) has had the most attention, as the play that established the anguished hero who wins his glory. But *Horace* (1640) and *Cinna* (1640) are more skillfully constructed variations of the struggle between private desires and public duties.

Of Racine's plays, *Andromaque* (1667) and *Phèdre* (1677) are studies of destruction. *Bérénice* (1670) is a tender study of the renunciation of love.

CRITICAL WORKS: MEDIEVAL

A good brief introduction to the whole period is A. P. Rossiter, *English Drama from Early Times to the Elizabethans* (1959). The possible origin of church drama in popular entertainment is suggested by Ben Hunningher, *The Origin of the Theater** (1961). A survey of social background is made in George R. Kernodle, "Six Medieval Theatres in One Social Structure," *Theatre Research,* II (1960). Two large volumes by Karl Young give a full treatment of *The Drama of the Medieval Church* (1933).

* Available in paperback edition.

The drama of the later part of the period is presented in Arnold Williams, *The Drama of Medieval England* (1961), and Grace Frank, *The Medieval French Drama* (1954). The study of staging by E. K. Chambers, *The Medieval Stage,* 2 vols. (1903), is partly superseded by the several volumes of Glynne Wickham, *Early English Stages, 1300–1660* (1959–   ). Details of the outdoor production at Mons are studied in "Naturalism—1501," a chapter in Lee Simonson, *The Stage Is Set** (1933). F. M. Salter gives a good picture of *Medieval Drama in Chester* (1955), and Richard Southern traces the development of one of the outdoor forms in *The Medieval Theatre in the Round* (1957). The drama of the tournament is described in Wickham and in George R. and Portia Kernodle, "The Dramatic Aspects of the Medieval Tournament," *Speech Monographs,* IX (1942). The medieval popular clowns and entertainers are described in Allardyce Nicoll, *Masks, Mimes and Miracles* (1931), and in Enid Welsford, *The Fool** (1935).

CRITICAL WORKS: SHAKESPEARE

An excellent introduction as well as guide to further reading is Boris Ford, ed., *The Age of Shakespeare,* vol. II of *A Guide to English Literature** (1955). New scholarship has been surveyed since 1948 in the annual *Shakespeare Survey.* Many new lives and studies of Shakespeare came out in the centennial year, 1964, but the beginner could hardly do better than Marchette Chute, *Shakespeare of London* (1956). Harley Granville-Barker and G. B. Harrison, *A Companion to Shakespeare Studies** (1934), is still useful.

Of the many essays and books interpreting Shakespeare, the following may be selected: A. C. Bradley, *Shakespearean Tragedy: Lectures on Hamlet, Othello, King Lear, and Macbeth** (1904); Harold C. Goddard, *The Meaning of Shakespeare** (1950), which discusses all thirty-seven plays; a lively book emphasizing Shakespeare's nihilistic and existentialist aspects by the Polish writer Jan Kott, *Shakespeare Our Contemporary* (1964); John Russell Brown's excellent *Shakespeare and His Comedies* (1957); Theodore Spencer, *Shakespeare and the Nature of Man* (1942), one of the best introductions to the world view of the time; two books by Welsford, who brilliantly relates Shakespeare to the popular comic tradition in *The Fool** (1935) and to the aristocratic music-and-dance tradition in *The Court Masque* (1928); and several books of G. Wilson Knight, especially *The Wheel of Fire** (1949). Three anthologies give a generous sampling of essays: D. N. Smith, ed., *Shakespeare Criticism** (1916); Anne Bradby, *Shakespeare Criticism 1919–1935** (1936); and Leonard Dean, *Shakespeare: Modern Essays in Criticism** (1957). There are two good collections of pictures: F. E. Halliday, *Shakespeare: A Pictorial Biography* (1956), and Nicoll, *The Elizabethans* (1957).

On the Elizabethan stage, the older view is expressed in John C. Adams, *The Globe Playhouse* (2nd ed., 1961). The symbolic view is developed in George R. Kernodle, *From Art to Theatre* (1944), C. Walter Hodges, *The Globe Restored* (1953), and the previously listed Wickham, *Early English Stages 1300–1660.* An ingenious theory that the stage was essentially an arena is presented in Leslie Hotson, *Shakespeare's Wooden O* (1960). The two basic reference works are Chambers, *The Elizabethan Stage,* 4 vols. (1923), continued for the period from 1616 to 1642 in Gerald E. Bentley, *The Jacobean and Caroline Stage,* 5 vols. (1941–   ). Some basic reinvestigation was started by George F. Reynolds in *The Staging of Plays at the Red Bull Theatre 1605–1625* (1940). These inter-

* Available in paperback edition.

pretations are well supplemented by Alfred Harbage, *Shakespeare's Audience* (1941).

Shakespearean productions of the past are discussed in G. C. D. Odell, *Shakespeare from Betterton to Irving,* 2 vols. (1921), and A. C. Sprague, *Shakespeare and the Actors: The Stage Business in His Plays 1660–1905* (1944) and *Shakespearean Players and Performance* (1953). Modern production problems are discussed in Knight, *Principles of Shakespearean Production** (1936), Ronald Watkins, *On Producing Shakespeare* (1950), Margaret Webster, *Shakespeare Without Tears* (1957), and Bertram Joseph, *Elizabethan Acting* (1951) and *Acting Shakespeare* (1960). Granville-Barker, *Prefaces to Shakespeare,* 2 vols. (1946–47; separate essays in paperback), has sensitive analyses for either actor or reader. See also Kernodle, "Basic Problems in Reading Shakespeare," *Quarterly Journal of Speech,* XXV (Feb., 1949).

A movie entitled *The Shakespearean Stage,* produced by the University of California at Los Angeles and following theories of J. C. Adams, using the half-timber decorations that some historians doubt, shows the great range and flexibility of the Elizabethan stage with a model in which small figures move as Ronald Colman and others speak scenes from Shakespeare.

CRITICAL WORKS: NEOCLASSIC

The French neoclassic plays are well related to the time in Martin Turnell, *The Classical Moment: Studies in Corneille, Molière, and Racine* (1948). Lacy Lockert, who has translated many French tragedies, has published *Studies in French Classical Tragedy* (1958). The 1950s and 60s have seen a large number of new translations and studies, especially of Racine; a good one is Roland Barthes, *On Racine** (1962).

The standard histories are H. C. Lancaster, *French Dramatic Literature of the Seventeenth Century,* 5 vols. (1929–36), and Nicoll, *History of Restoration Drama* (1923).

The Italian Renaissance and Baroque stage is treated in Barnard Hewitt, ed., *The Renaissance Stage* (1958), and Kernodle, *From Art to Theatre: Form and Convention in the Renaissance* (1944). The French stage is treated in *From Art to Theatre* and in T. E. Lawrenson, *The French Stage in the XVIIth Century* (1957). For the English stage, see Lily Bess Campbell, *Scenes and Machines on the English Stage During the Renaissance* (1923), Alwin Thaler, *Shakespeare to Sheridan* (1922; repr., 1964), Richard Southern, *Changeable Scenery* (1952), and Nicoll, *Stuart Masques and the Renaissance Stage* (1964). Nahum Tate's rewrite of *King Lear* for neoclassic taste is in Harrison, *King Lear: Text, Sources, Criticism** (1962). An inexpensive paperback with reproductions of more than a hundred Italian designs of the operatic tradition is Janos Schloz, *Baroque and Romantic Stage Design** (1962).

---

* Available in paperback edition.

CHAPTER SIX

THE THEATRE OF EXALTATION: MODERN TRAGEDY AND POETIC DRAMA

Modern Tragedy

It is easy to see the magnitude of tragedy in other periods—Greek, Elizabethan, and neoclassic—but can tragedy seem exalted in the twentieth century? Many critics say no, and one of these, George Steiner, has written a book called *The Death of Tragedy*. If tragedy is a heroic vision of man, celebrating the triumph of nobility of spirit over defeat and death of the body, can it exist in an age that finds in man no heroism, but only submission? No nobility, but only pettiness? This is the age of the common man, the little man in the crowd, the cog in the machine. Any exceptional quality of personality is a mark of bad adjustment or deviation. If man is biologically just another animal, how can he have nobility? How can a play deal with free will, choice, and responsibility when behaviorist psychology emphasizes mechanical stimulus and response and when it is assumed that all action is determined by social forces? Who can appeal to a pervasive moral order or comprehensive meaning when anthropologists, and even casual tourists, collect specimens of quaint customs, styles, and standards from all over the world, observing all ways but believing in none?

How can poetry have power in the theatre today? The cult of realism emphasizes the inarticulate character, his feelings too deep or too vague for words, his miseries best expressed in grunts and moans. Only a simple character speaking dialect may be poetic; we believe only in unconscious poetry. The Irish dramatists used dialect, and Ernest Hemingway borrowed Spanish idioms, quaint in English translation, in writing *For Whom the Bell Tolls.* What rhetorical intensities could survive Hitler, Communist doubletalk, or Madison Avenue's blatant advertising? Words are so debased by lies and distortions, by manipulation of the gullible masses, that nothing but propaganda remains. The scientist has a specialized vocabulary, highly technical, approaching mathematical symbols, useless for emotional expression. So what idiom can tragedy use?

As for awe or real pity or fear, how are they possible after seventy million people have been killed or deported in two wars, after bayonet drill, flame throwers, incendiary bombs, gas, chemical and biological warfare, all dwarfed by the nuclear bomb? Either the only response is horror, or there is no response at all.

If tragedy is metaphysical, what can it mean to an age of materialism? What are the myths, many people say, but childish attempts of primitive people to explain things that are now, or soon will be, explained by science? What is religion but the superstition of simple people, encouraged by those who find it profitable to keep them in subjection? Marx called religion the opiate of the people. James Frazer's encyclopedic study of folklore, rituals, and myths, *The Golden Bough,* seemed to prove that all religious practices have been based on magic fertility rites, half glossing over the older motives of blood and sex. Late in the sixteenth century Marlowe's Faustus could take Mephistopheles seriously, and Milton in the 1660s could write of archangels, but by the eighteenth century only ornamental cherubs and playful echoes of the supernatural remained to decorate poems and wall tapestries. By the nineteenth century, Nietzsche cried out: "God is dead."

In a pragmatic age that emphasizes scientific study of the "facts" and practical solving of "problems," how can there be room for tragedy? What is tragedy but a record of the unsolved problems of the past and a glorification of failure to solve them? What is this terrifying gap between the vision and the reality? It is better to keep an eye on the immediate practical goal and let the infinite take care of itself—it doesn't exist anyway. Responsibility? Of course, pay your debts. Guilt? Learn by your mistakes, then forget them. Fate? Destiny? Purpose? Love? Harmony? Peace? Reconciliation? If you can't measure them you can't deal with them. Let the preacher worry about them while you get on with the job of making the world better.

Still, whatever brash front modern man assumes, the need for tragic drama continues to exist. After all the cures of the doctor, there is still disease; after all the prolongations of life, there is still old age and death. After all the sessions with the psychiatrist, anguish and defeat still come to the healthiest minds; cosmic loneliness finds even the busiest man in the crowd. Even if man's power increased until he could shake the planets from their course, still his achievement would fall far short of his dream. Disappointment, defeat, and death, the inescapable pain and terror, are with us as surely as they were

Kinds of Plays

with Sophocles and Shakespeare—two very fortunate, successful, well-adjusted men. The reality can never equal the vision; the truly scientific man will seek some higher mathematics, create some adaptation that accepts the discrepancy between man and his fate in this world. He will turn to tragedy.

THE TRAGIC HERO IN NATURALISM

Tragedy was not congenial to the early naturalists. While they rejected the easy optimism of the Victorian age, they felt that in the long run science and reason could build an environment that would be fit for man to live in, and they thought that tragedy would only encourage a defeatist attitude. Still, when they looked at the appalling slums of the new industrial cities, many of them realized that the job of rebuilding would take generations and that in the meantime the individual in such an environment would be defeated no matter how hard he struggled. Since the ruling powers were opposed to change and the general public was indifferent, the Marxists thought that the workers would have to seize control by a violent revolution. The liberals, however, believed that if decent people could only be shown the effect of the environment on the individual they would join in the prodigious effort necessary for change. In this belief the naturalists found a possible approach to the creation of modern tragedy and of a modern tragic hero—not a hopeless victim but an individual who sees what is wrong with society and gives his life in the effort to change it. Such a hero is destroyed not because he is wrong but because more time and effort than one man has to give are needed to effect a change. There is no reconciliation or justice in the hero's defeat, as in classic tragedy, but instead the audience takes on the guilt of the injustice and the responsibility to rectify it. If the play expresses confidence in progress, it becomes a social melodrama, and we have had many good plays about the social struggle, such as *Dead End,* which we have discussed as a hopeful naturalistic melodrama. While radical social thinkers have disapproved of true tragedy, they have accepted the concept of the hero ahead of his time.

Far more deeply tragic, however, are plays that assume that progress will never solve all the social problems and that a man must struggle to define his own individuality, even in the midst of unsettled and contradictory social forces. In the mid-twentieth century, the tragic heroes are those who assert their will in the midst of a difficult environment. No Promethean defiance of the ruler of the universe but rather a very modest insistence on choice gives heroic stature to the modern individual and raises him above the helpless crowd of naturalistic victims. "Not enough to weave a banner with, but white enough to keep it from such dogs" is the heroic virtue discovered by John Proctor at the end of *The Crucible.*

Arthur Miller's *Death of a Salesman* heads the list of plays that achieve tragedy on the modest modern scale by finding dignity in the struggle of the little man. Between the two world wars the little man had been the butt of jokes about the "happy little moron," and clowns played variations on the smile that persisted no matter how much a man was pushed around. Harold

FIGURE 6.1 Tragedy of the little man. The setting takes its multiple playing areas and its open platform from the Elizabethan stage. Miller's *Death of a Salesman*. New York, 1949. Directed by Elia Kazan and designed by Jo Mielziner. Photo Graphic House.

Lloyd was one of the most popular comic little men, winning the girl or the ball game when someone else made a more stupid mistake, and Charlie Chaplin immortalized the "little fellow" with the sentiment and pathos of his clowning. In the twenties and thirties, patronizing contempt was a common attitude toward these lost souls of the cities. But when *Death of a Salesman* appeared in 1949, it was evident that a more serious attitude was possible. Postwar audiences were ready to believe that an ordinary man might suffer deeply and struggle with dignity.

Willy Loman, the salesman, displays some of the characteristics of the little man as he drifts along with the attitudes of the crowd, but Miller treats him with respect. Willy's wife, Linda, says,

> I don't say he's a great man. Willy Loman never made a lot of money. His name was never in the paper. He's not the finest character that ever lived. But he's a human being, and a terrible thing is happening to him. So attention must be paid. He's not to be allowed to fall into his grave like an old dog. Attention, attention must be finally paid to such a person.

220   As disaster threatens, Willy does fight back. He demands some explanation

Kinds of Plays

for his failure. He goes over the past to ask whether he was wrong in bringing up his sons to aim for the top, to be "well liked." He talks repeatedly to the image of his long-lost brother Ben, who made a fortune in diamonds and lumber, and wonders whether he himself was right to build a life on sales slips, appointments, and appearances. Willy does more than follow the crowd, and when he fails it is not funny.

It is Willy's decision to kill himself, in order to make his son Biff "magnificent" with the insurance money, that has caused most critical discussion. To the end, Willy is faithful to his false dream of success. Some critics say that in a tragedy the main character must reach perception. Maxwell Anderson declared that the central experience of tragedy is the main character's discovery of something important, about himself or about the world, that changes him into a better person. But Miller thought it more important to show Willy steadfast, ironically happy in his death, than to show him realizing that his whole life had been a mistake. In an essay on "Tragedy and the Common Man," Miller explains his idea:

> . . . I think the tragic feeling is evoked in us when we are in the presence of a character who is ready to lay down his life, if need be, to secure one thing—his sense of personal dignity. . . . The quality [in the great tragedies] that does shake us . . . derives from the underlying fear of being displaced, the disaster inherent in being torn away from our chosen image of what and who we are in this world. . . . The commonest of men may take on [the tragic] stature to the extent of his willingness to throw all he has into the contest, the battle to secure his rightful place in the world.

Mistaken or not, Willy is committed to his dream, and dies for it. The other characters gain the perception and clarify the issues. In the Requiem at the end, each one has his say. Biff, at last sure of his own identity, declares, "He had the wrong dreams. All, all wrong. . . . He never know who he was." The younger brother, Happy, is still sold: "It's the only dream you can have—to come out number one man. He fought it out here, and this is where I'm gonna win it for him." But we know Happy will never be happy; he is too obsessed by the symbols of success. Curiously enough, "Uncle Charley," the friend next door who had no patience with Willy's worship of success, is the one who defends Willy's dream:

> Nobody dast blame this man. You don't understand: Willy was a salesman. And for a salesman, there is no rock bottom to the life. He don't put a bolt to a nut, he don't tell you the law or give you medicine. He's a man way out there in the blue, riding on a smile and a shoeshine. And when they start not smiling back—that's an earthquake. And then you get yourself a couple of spots on your hat, and you're finished. Nobody dast blame this man. A salesman is got to dream, boy. It comes with the territory.

The wife has the final word, and it is a question: "Why?" That "why" can never be answered for any man because the life of a human being is always a mystery. He is always more than any partial explanation or sum of explanations.

221

In *The Crucible* (1953), social forces are much more important, but Miller is still able to create a drama about the choice and fate of an individual. The play has more of the traditional patterns of tragedy than *Death of a Salesman,* and some critics point to it as clear evidence that tragedy is possible in modern America. Set at the time of the Salem witch trials, the play reflects the irrational fears of the 1950s when Senator McCarthy led a witch hunt for spies and "reds" that intimidated Washington officialdom. Investigators, some of them self-appointed, made long lists of "subversives," and anyone who questioned their accusations, or their right to make them, was under suspicion. Many people found themselves out of jobs because there was some unrevealed question about their "security," and at one time Miller himself could not renew his passport for travel to Europe because his file indicated association with supposedly left-wing groups.

In this mass hysteria that prevailed in the fifties, Miller recognized a parallel to the situation in Salem in 1692, when a community was driven by its fears and by the accusations of hysterical adolescent girls to the hanging of more than a score of citizens. Some few persons were actually trying to commune with Satan, and several young girls danced naked in the woods, but most of the accused were guilty only of the great sin of disagreeing with their neighbors. Miller's main couple, John and Elizabeth Proctor, are excellent heroes for a modern tragedy. Not very articulate, not at all wanting to be rebels, each only gradually discovers the strength to be heroic, to say and do what he must in order to be himself. John is guilty of more than missing the sermons of a greedy, selfish preacher: Elizabeth has been ailing, cold, and suspicious, and he has taken the maid Abigail to the barn. Now it is Abigail who leads the hysterical girls and includes Elizabeth in her accusations of witchcraft.

Near the end, John cannot face hanging and agrees to confess to witchcraft. Elizabeth, safe from hanging because she is pregnant, admits to John that she was a cold wife and says that she will not blame him if he saves himself. But when it comes to signing his name to the confession, like Shaw's Saint Joan he balks. He will not accuse others. He says, "I have three children— how may I teach them to walk like men in the world, and I sold my friends?" When asked why he will not sign the confession, he tries, in his torment, to explain: "Because it is my name! Because I cannot have another in my life! Because I lie and sign myself to lies! Because I am not worth the dust on the feet of them that hang! How may I live without my name? I have given you my soul; leave me my name!" He tears up the paper and turns toward the scaffold. Hale, the preacher who had urged him to lie to save his life, is terrified for him.

> HALE   Man, you will hang! You cannot!
> PROCTOR (*his eyes full of tears*)   I can. And there's your first marvel, that I can. You made your magic now, for now I do think I see some shred of goodness in John Proctor. Not enough to weave a banner with, but white enough to keep it from such dogs.
> (ELIZABETH, *in a burst of terror, rushes to him and weeps against his hand.*)

Kinds of Plays

Give them no tear! Tears pleasure them! Show honor now, show a stony heart and sink them with it!

To the last, the frightened Hale begs Elizabeth to plead with John to save his life, but she is at last sure of that which transcends the dust and the worm. As the drum rolls, she turns her face into the dawning sunlight and cries, "He have his goodness now. God forbid I take it from him!"

In some ways, Blanche Du Bois in Tennessee Williams' *A Streetcar Named Desire* (1947) is a restless victim of a difficult environment. She is already badly damaged, a wanderer from the old plantation system. She finds refuge for a moment in the slums of New Orleans, where her sister has married a foreign ape-man, Stanley Kowalski, and has adjusted to the life of an animal. But Blanche has visions of finer things, and she is not too inarticulate to protest. She tries to rescue her sister and herself from the ape-man.

> BLANCHE . . . Oh, if he was just *ordinary*. Just *plain*—but good and wholesome, but—no. There's something downright—*bestial*—about him. . . . He acts like an animal, has an animal's habits! Eats like one, moves like one, talks like one! There's even something—sub-human—something not quite to the stage of humanity yet! Yes, something ape-like about him, like one of those pictures I've seen in—anthropological studies! Thousands and thousands of years have passed him right by, and there he is—Stanley Kowalski—survivor of the stone age! Bearing the raw meat home from the kill in the jungle! And you—*you here*—*waiting* for him! . . . Maybe we are a long way from being made in God's image, but Stella—my sister—there has been *some* progress since then! Such things as art—as poetry and music—such kinds of new light have come into the world since then. In some kinds of people some tender feelings have had some little beginnings! That we have got to make *grow!* And *cling* to, and hold as our flag! In this dark march toward whatever it is we're approaching. . . . *Don't—don't hang back with the brutes!*

For a moment Blanche hopes to marry Mitch, the gentlest of Stanley's rough friends, and find a secure corner in the cave. But her past finds her out and destroys that dream. If this were all, the play would be an example of the usual naturalistic defeat. But Blanche has a chance to love Mitch on the animal level of sex and refuses, keeping her dream of something finer, fighting to the last, choosing to be Blanche and be carried to the insane asylum rather than be like her sister, a companion of the apes.

Stanley Kowalski, especially as sensitively played by Marlon Brando, also has a touch of the tragic. He sees his home invaded by a difficult intruder. He suffers under her insults, and in raping and destroying her, his wife's sister, he knows he risks breaking up his own marriage. But he has his own integrity to defend. The intensity of the conflict, with important values involved on both sides, gives the play considerable stature as tragedy. It involves choice, struggle, questioning, suffering. Many of Williams' characters—Chance in *Sweet Bird of Youth,* Big Daddy in *Cat on a Hot Tin Roof*—refuse to

223

The Theatre of Exaltation

drift on in evasion and ignorance. They wrest identity and meaning even from their pain.

THE DESTRUCTIVE HERO

Not all modern tragedy has been concerned with a hero ahead of his time or a hero flying a small white banner to whom "attention must be paid." Much of modern tragedy has been concerned with the destructive hero. What help is it to the individual who has a compulsion to destroy himself and those he loves to be told that he is the victim of an unfavorable environment that will be changed as soon as a few more unfavorable facts are found out about it? What if the environment is by nature unfavorable to man, and destruction and evil are at the root of reality? Then some of the darker aspects of tragedy come to the fore. Man must explore evil, not only in order to improve the world and to solve problems, but in order to understand evil itself and come to terms with it. The old questions of guilt and responsibility, of destiny and death, become important again, and tragedy takes on new forms in exploring man's difficult psychological nature and the nature of that "reality" he is eternally trying to face.

Madness seemed the destiny of the mind itself as the psychologists explored the chaotic jungle of the unconscious. Freud himself offered no easy salvation. He believed that careful analysis, bringing up the traumas of childhood, might untangle some of the worst complexes that maimed and distorted the personality, so that the conscious mind could reduce the damage by facing reality. Freud talked about the reality principle as the bright hope, yet he was acutely aware of the dark complexities of the unconscious. He concluded that there must be a death wish, almost as basic as the drive for love and creativity.

Many dramatists have been just as fascinated by that all-too-human impulse to destroy. Ibsen wrote a study of a destructive woman, *Hedda Gabler,* in 1890. Hedda finds no constructive outlet in her Victorian society beyond complete submission to the desires of men and a smothering motherhood. Even her interference in the life of the young genius who is in love with her turns into a sordid fact, not a magnificent gesture. She is completely in the power of the very respectable Judge Brack, but she can say no. She kills herself. The optimistic naturalist may say that in the new world that's coming women like Hedda will find healthy outlets for their creative power, but the fascination of the play is not in the social problem but in the power of destruction.

That love itself, the inspiration of the romantics, could be destructive amazed and fascinated Freud as well as a number of playwrights. August Strindberg's woman in *The Father* (1887) destroys her husband, and his restless heroine of *Miss Julie* (1888), unable to resist her coachman, gathers strength enough to kill herself afterward. In Eugene O'Neill's first long play, *Beyond the Horizon* (1920), two romantic ideals, love and aspiration, set against each other, destroy the principal character. A poetic farm boy, about to leave on his uncle's ship to fulfill a lifelong dream of seeing the world "beyond the horizon," confesses his love for a local girl and gives up his dream.

224

Kinds of Plays

But love turns sour, the farm defeats him, and he dies on a hilltop reasserting the dream he had lost. A love that causes a mother to kill her own child is the theme of O'Neill's *Desire Under the Elms* (1924), a melodrama about the violent greeds and lusts seething on a rocky New England farm. Abby kills her own baby to prove that she is not just using her young lover, her stepson, to get possession of the farm. He is furious and sends for the sheriff. Yet at the end he returns to share her fate—an assertion of love and understanding and reconciliation with destiny that has much in common with classic tragedy.

In using the Greek story of Agamemnon in *Mourning Becomes Electra* (1931), set in New England just after the Civil War, O'Neill made a major attempt to recapture the Greek tragic pattern. Instead of a family curse passed on from generation to generation, he used the Freudian concept of the dangers of sexual repression. The trauma of the wedding night has created in General Mannon's wife a neurotic hatred for her husband that eventually leads her to murder him, after taking his cousin as a lover. Then the son and daughter murder the cousin and drive their mother to suicide. The mixtures of love and hate, envy and anger, involve the brother and sister too closely with each other and lead to the brother's suicide. Vinnie, the Electra, shuts herself inside the family mansion to live out the rest of her life with the ghosts. In the 1930s the play seemed a profound study of destructive psychological forces, perhaps the greatest play America had produced. The audience arrived at the theatre before five in the afternoon, went back after a dinner break, and saw the end of the play toward midnight. The event was exhausting but exalting, giving deep satisfaction through the intensity of the play and its beauty of form as well as the sense of understanding one important strain in American life through the tragedy of a single family. When the film was made two decades later, the fourteen acts were compacted into one screen play of ordinary length, and the story became a thin melodrama of no consequence. O'Neill had given the tale a scope that was lost in the condensation. One could see what Aristotle meant in demanding magnitude for tragedy.

O'Neill's later tragedy about his own family, a labor of love and forgiveness, is one of the finest plays in the tradition of naturalism. Called *Long Day's Journey into Night* (1956), it is a deep, beautiful study of that perverse need of human beings, in their shame, envy, and self-reproach, to destroy those they love. Each character, in one way or another, reveals the experiences and motivations that make him a failure, unable to love without distrusting and attacking.

THE TRAGIC DELUSION

The vision of destruction indicates a radical change from the optimism of most naturalists. The early naturalists assumed that reality is good and believed in the great myth of progress. Hence a study of reality was bound to show man how to improve his environment, if he would put aside the old romantic illusions and face the truth. But what if that hope of progress is itself a romantic delusion? What if nature is an enemy of man and the scientific pursuit of reality is bound to destroy the old faith in human values? Then tragedy takes on quite a different meaning. Such a view grew up among those people who were most impressed by science and the scientific attack on old superstitions and delusions. Equating illusion with delusion, they followed those extreme scientists who believed in nothing they could not examine or use in their laboratories.

The scientific mind could accept mathematics and maps; though unreal, they had an obvious relation to reality that could quickly be checked. But the larger, less precise constructs of the imagination were dismissed as impossible myths and fairy tales. Nature had no place for them because nature was the enemy of man. This pessimistic view was stated clearly in 1893 by Thomas Henry Huxley in a lecture he called "Evolution and Ethics." He pictured ethics and all human values as a tiny walled garden that man cherishes but that has no chance of lasting. Nature gradually breaks down the wall with powerful forces—frost, roots, sprouts sent under the wall, and seeds sent over it. Man's little illusions are really nothing more than delusions, with no foundation in the universe. From the old assumption that man was the one concern of God, the philosophers went to the opposite assumption, that man and his mind are accidents to which the universe is inimical. If that is true, then of course religion, art, and tragedy, indeed all values, are merely imaginary, invented by prescientific peoples, with no relation to reality.

In a despairing essay of 1929, *The Modern Temper*, Joseph Wood Krutch expressed the conviction that the advance of science would put an end to both faith and tragedy. While asserting that the tragic spirit, like faith, purges the soul of despair and gives meaning and justification to the universe, he concluded that it would soon be a thing of the past. He wrote, "But if it has the strength it has also the weakness of all faiths, since it may—nay it must—be ultimately lost as reality, encroaching further and further into the realms of imagination, leaves less and less room in which that imagination can build its refuge." He assumed that reality is the enemy of the imagination. In another part of the essay he stated that a world of reality is not a place for the soul of man: "The question (likely, it would seem, to be answered in the negative) is simply whether or not the spirit of man can endure the literal and inhuman truth."

If truth is inhuman and things of the imagination are lies, then one answer is "Long live the lies." Several dramatists began to talk about life-lies and to defend the illusions even if they were delusions with no relation to the real world. Ibsen, in the middle of his career, made a reversal in his attitude to the disclosure of truth. In *Ghosts, An Enemy of the People,* and several other plays, he had portrayed stupid, venal people trying to prevent the exposure of the truth, but in *The Wild Duck* of 1884 he showed the disastrous results that ensue when a misguided realist insists on telling a happy husband that his wife has been the mistress of her employer and that their daughter is not his own. In Gorki's *The Lower Depths* (1902) the truths are hunger, pain, depravity, and death, but the inhabitants of the cellar dive beguile themselves with impossible dreams of escape, and the compassionate pilgrim, Luka,

226

FIGURE 6.2 A personal tragedy in epic form. The Spanish conquest of Peru is seen as the tragedy of Pizarro's search for a new faith. Shaffer's *The Royal Hunt of the Sun*. New York, 1965. Directed by John Dexter and designed and costumed by Michael Annals. Photo Friedman-Abeles.

encourages the dreams. O'Neill enlarged on the pattern in *The Iceman Cometh* (1946), a picture of a large group of derelicts and of the painful failure they experience when someone forces them to try to make their pipe dreams come true. Most of them happily return to their lies, while the few who have acted and tried to face their hidden guilts are destroyed.

The yearning for illusion, for an impossible faith in defiance of reality, is given a romantic treatment in Peter Shaffer's tragedy *The Royal Hunt of the Sun* (1964). Pizarro, the conqueror of Peru, is a disillusioned, cynical old man, yearning for immortality of some kind. An illegitimate peasant, bitter about his struggles to rise in the world, he has little respect for the Church and for the Christians he is leading and feels drawn in sympathy to the Indian Emperor, who believes that his father, the Sun, will resurrect him if he is killed. Pizarro almost believes this too, so strong is his desire to find some faith. But when he is forced to kill the Emperor and the Sun does not resurrect the body, Pizarro is left desolate in his grief for the man he had come to love like a son. The objective reality is only death—a dying Spain gorged with gold and a blighted Peru, its men slaughtered or enslaved. Achievement is empty. All faith is a delusion, and only a bitter, compassionate sorrow is left.

If the modern view of reality cannot be reconciled with faith, it is no wonder that creative thinkers glorify the irrational, the perverse, and the destructive, inventing senseless acts to assault that inhuman objective reality, or else give up trying to make sense of the outer world and set out to establish meaning only in the subjective life. The last course is the one taken by the existentialists. If science and history can find no place for myth, purpose, destiny, or tragedy, then obviously science and history have no meaning and can be neglected, and the existentialist mind can create its own values.

The tragic writer who was influenced by early realism supposed that he had only two alternatives: to present a social reformer ahead of his time,

227

The Theatre of Exaltation

defeated by social forces, in order to make the audience take on the guilt and the responsibility for changing the environment, or to show a man rescuing some shreds of individuality and free will in the face of unfavorable social forces. But later, as he got into questions of the nature of the individual and the nature of reality—and the tragic writer is bound to raise metaphysical questions—he found many new possibilities in the modern theatre. Some of these are tragic, some are farcical and absurd, and some are tragic and farcical at the same time. We shall come back to some of the aspects of tragedy in the chapter on the existentialists and the drama of the absurd; and we must remember that Bertolt Brecht, though classified among the writers of epic realism, saw the pattern of the defeat of the individual as a form of tragic exaltation.

The Poet in the Modern Theatre

The poets as well as the naturalists have persisted in trying to rediscover exaltation for the modern world, to find intensities of language in an age of prose. They have often led in the revival or invention of nonrealistic stage techniques, hoping to create a poetry of the theatre as well as a poetry spoken in the theatre.

A direct imitation of poetry of the past has not been very fruitful. Maxwell Anderson in the 1930s was only moderately successful in giving an echo of Shakespearean verse in his romantic plays, *Elizabeth the Queen* and *Mary of Scotland,* though in *Winterset* he did write contemporary verse of some power for the protests of his existentialist characters, as we shall see in Chapter 9. The most successful strategy has been to start with an existing

FIGURE *6.3* Poetic drama with choral speech and dance. Bottomley's *Culbin Sands*. Yale University production, directed by Georgina Johnson and costumed by Virginia Roediger.

idiom, either the picturesque dialect of provincial people or the lively colloquial language of the modern city, and give it verse form and vivid imagery. Such an approach may yield interesting results even within the form of the well-made realistic play, but it has been even more effective when the fresh language is combined with songs, dances, soliloquies, debates, prayers, sermons, invocations, rituals, and many kinds of choral speech and movement.

POETIC DRAMA OF IRELAND AND SPAIN

The Irish playwrights have made the most effective use of dialect and, even in prose, have written with a strong sense of the lyrical rhythms and rich imagery of native speech. The Abbey Theatre in Dublin, soon after its inception at the beginning of the century, found in John Millington Synge a playwright who transcended the dull limits of realistic prose by catching the "wild joy" of the speech of western Ireland. He believed that "in a good play every speech should be as fully flavored as a nut or apple." Equally at home in comedy and tragedy, he was able to express a naturalistic theme in either mode. *The Playboy of the Western World* (1907) is a comedy with lively characters of whom the most engaging is the Playboy, with his bold bragging about killing his father. Fascinated by his talk, a romantic girl decides to run away with him, but she gives up her dream and turns him over to the authorities when she finally realizes that "there's a great gap between a gallous story and a dirty deed." The same author could write, in *Riders to the Sea* (1904), a powerful tragedy with the naturalistic theme of man's defeat by nature. Great dignity is maintained throughout this one-act play with the lilting Irish rhythm of such phrases as "She's lying down, God help her, and may be sleeping, if she's able" and "Is the sea bad by the white rocks, Nora?" "Middling bad, God help us. There's a great roaring in the west, and it's worse it'll be getting when the tide's turned to the wind." When the last of the sons is drowned by the sea, the old woman, Maurya, chants her somber lament and acceptance: "They're all gone now, and there isn't anything more the sea can do to me. . . . Michael has a clean burial in the far north, by the grace of Almighty God. Bartley will have a fine coffin out of the white boards, and a deep grave surely. What more can we want than that? No man can be living forever, and we must be satisfied." The poetic rhythm of the prose, like the surge of the sea, carries the heavy burden of existence and lulls the pain to rest.

Sharper pain and the anguish of disillusionment are mixed with riotous comedy in the plays of Sean O'Casey, but it is always rich language he gives his sufferers, a lyric cry for compassion that has some tragic grandeur even in sordid situations and the environment of the Dublin slums. In *Juno and the Paycock* (1924), Juno speaks this moving prayer as she and her daughter, who has been abandoned by her lover, go to identify the body of the son, who was killed for betraying a companion in the Irish underground war with the English.

> What was the pain I suffered, Johnny, bringin' you into the world to carry
> you to your cradle, to the pains I'll suffer carryin' you out o' the world to

229

The Theatre of Exaltation

bring you to your grave! Mother o' God, Mother o' God, have pity on us all! Blessed Virgin, where were you when me darlin' son was riddled with bullets, when me darlin' son was riddled with bullets? Sacred Heart o' Jesus, take away our hearts o' stone, and give us hearts o' flesh! Take away this murdherin' hate, an' give us Thine own eternal love!

In both comic and tragic scenes, it is the Irish lilt and the vivid language that raise O'Casey's plays above the dead level of naturalism.

Like Synge, William Butler Yeats started with the rich flavor of the Irish dialect and with romantic legends set in peasant cottages. A young bride dreams of a Land of Heart's Desire "where nobody gets old and godly and grave" until a fairy child comes to take her to the land of endless dancing and merriment. Later on Yeats moved away from the regular theatre of illusion: he discovered the Japanese Noh drama and decided that he wanted to write poetic plays not for a theatre but for a simple room, where musicians would sing poetic statements and the unfolding and folding of a cloth would symbolize the beginning and end of the play. His main characters are legendary figures who are heroic, grotesque, and symbolic—queens and swineherds, poets and fools, blind men and beggars, Christ and Lazarus, and the tragic princes of pagan Irish history. Typical pieces are *At the Hawks' Well* (1920), in which an old man and a young prince miss the appearance at the well of the water of eternal life because the old man falls asleep and the prince is distracted by the dancing of the Guardian of the Spring, and *A Full Moon in March* (1935), in which a queen has a swineherd beheaded when he comes to take part in a contest of song and then falls in love with the head. Not the situations but the overtones of symbolism in the verse give these plays a certain power. In *A Full Moon in March* the last part is spoken or sung by attendants as the inner curtains open and the queen dances with the head;

FIGURE *6.4* A ritualized peasant tragedy with poetic prose. Lorca's *The House of Bernarda Alba*. University of Illinois production, directed by Ned Donahoe and costumed by Genevieve Richardson.

FIGURE 6.5 A peasant tragedy with songs and symbolic figures. Behind the multiple playing areas a drawing is projected on a screen. Lorca's *Blood Wedding*. Indiana University production, directed and lighted by Gary Gaiser and designed by William E. Kinzer.

as they close the curtains, the attendants sing of the need of queens to descend to dung, "for desecration and the lover's night."

No one today knows how to handle productions of Yeats's work in the theatre. The Stanislavsky approach is not right for acting the elusive, nebulous figures Yeats created. Occasionally a modern dancer is tempted to try to bring these strange but powerful fantasies to life in movement.

From Spain has come the most exciting drama in heightened peasant idiom. The plays of Federico García Lorca have intrigued readers and directors throughout Europe and in the United States. Like Ireland, Spain has what Eric Bentley calls "the vestiges of Catholic-peasant civilization." He goes on to say that Lorca's drama "springs from this civilization, gives it amazing full expression, and is a bitter rejection of it." Lorca was executed by Franco's soldiers during the Spanish Civil War. Though Synge and O'Casey did not meet such violence in their native Ireland, several of their plays, when first produced, caused riots in Dublin.

Lorca does not paint a realistic picture of happy peasants but a lurid vision of violence, partly real and partly symbolic. His main theme is a peasant version of the theme of love and honor in the classic Spanish plays, but he expresses it in terms of Freudian suppression and primitive fertility rites. In *Yerma* (1934), a childless wife, tortured by longing for a child, tries to tease a response from her husband and then seeks out the young mothers, who enjoy their fertility. A chorus of laundresses sings of babies, of the joy of work, but also of the honor of a wife, with many hints that a woman sometimes takes another man. At a hermitage high in the hills, Yerma joins a women's primitive ritual of fertility, near a row of fig trees where men are waiting. But she cannot violate her honor, and in the end she strangles her husband, crying "I myself have killed my son!"

There is even more violence and symbolism and more singing and choral action in Lorca's *Blood Wedding* (1933). When the young bride leaves her

The Theatre of Exaltation

wedding and her bridegroom to run away with another man, the whole community pursues them, and the two men kill each other. The principal scenes are enriched with many strange songs—lullabies about horses, blood, and streams. The wedding scene, the death scene, and the Requiem are almost entirely song and movement, calling for production as elaborate as for a Greek chorus. Until the flight is discovered, tense episodes of fear and unrest are interspersed in the sequence of scenes of the wedding procession. The violent scene is presented almost entirely by choral figures—three woodcutters expressing their glee at the flight, the Moon (as a character) yearning for blood to warm himself, an old beggar woman who represents death listening to the pursuit and building up to the arrival of the lovers. The lovers pause in their flight for a moment, feeling bound together.

> Oh, it isn't my fault—
> the fault is the earth's—
> And this fragrance that you exhale
> from your breasts and your braid.

The Requiem at the end builds into a song of pain, celebrating the tiny knife:

> And it barely fits the hand
> but it slides in clean
> through the astonished flesh
> and stops there, at the place
> where trembles enmeshed
> the dark root of a scream.

If educated Americans find Lorca too exotic and do not quite recognize themselves in the atmosphere of primitive violence or the intense imagery of horses, flowers, and knives, if the pagan rituals are not quite believable—still the easy transition from lively realistic dialogue to song is amazingly effective. If Lorca does not show how poetic drama can be written for urban or sophisticated themes and characters, he does show that a theatre of poetry, music, and movement is still possible.

THE POETRY OF FRY AND ELIOT

Where Lorca and Yeats might be called writers for song-and-dance drama, the two principal poets in the modern English drama, Christopher Fry and T. S. Eliot, have kept to the spoken word. Like Lorca, they have experimented with many nonrealistic devices as part of their poetic strategy. But instead of a peasant idiom they have used the complex speech of the sophisticated world. For both religious and secular plays, Fry has developed a witty poetic style that revels in puns and alliteration. In *The Lady's Not for Burning* (1949), his bitter young hero is determined to listen to no romantic nonsense, even about the moon.

> Surely she knows,
> If she is true to herself, the moon is nothing
> But a circumambulating aphrodisiac

Kinds of Plays

> Divinely subsidized to provoke the world
> Into a rising birth-rate.

But when he finds himself a fellow prisoner with a lovely young woman condemned to die for witchcraft, he suggests they spend their last night in laughing. When she asks, "For what reason?" he gives this lively outburst:

> For the reason of laughter, since laughter is surely
> The surest touch of genius in creation.
> Would *you* ever have thought of it, I ask you,
> If you had been making man, stuffing him full
> Of such hopping greeds and passions that he has
> To blow himself to pieces as often as he
> Conveniently can manage it—would it also
> Have occurred to you to make him burst himself
> With such a phenomenon as cachinnation?
> That same laughter, madam, is an irrelevancy
> Which almost amounts to revelation.

Less wordy or witty are Fry's religious plays. In *Sleep of Prisoners* (1951), his ambiguous overlapping of words and images is appropriate for the dream state of the four prisoners of war shut up in a ruined church, enacting in their sleep not their own childhood but four incidents of the Old Testament, incidents that embody their own murderous impulses toward one another as well as toward the enemy. They go from Cain, who furiously murders his brother, to David, who reluctantly executes his son Absalom, and then to Abraham, who does not sacrifice his son. After this they dream a scene in the fiery furnace, where binding cords are burnt away. They half come up from sleep to realize dimly that forbearance in the face of hate is possible, even if it takes thousands of years to wake from the old ancestral dreams. The language achieves vividness from an elaboration of the heartiness and irony of the conventional talk of soldiers as they grope for some awareness of man's relation to God. When the fourth man is drawn to the others in the furnace, he says,

> . . . I think they forgot
> To throw me in. But there's not a skipping soul
> On the loneliest goat-path who is not
> Hugged into this, the human shambles.

And as they are waking one says, "I wish I knew where I was," and gets the answer:

> I can only give you a rough idea myself.
> In a sort of a universe and a bit of a fix.
> It's what they call flesh we're in.
> And a fine old dance it is.

Somewhat similar to this heightening of ironic anger in colloquial terms is the raising of protest to poetry in Archibald MacLeish's *J. B.,* to be discussed in Chapter 9 as an example of existentialism.

What could be done with colloquial city speech to create an ironic lyricism   *233* was indicated by T. S. Eliot in the 1920s. Soon after writing the bitter mélange of *The Waste Land,* picturing the aridity of modern life, he wrote a dramatic fragment called *Sweeney Agonistes* about the jittery pleasures of London tarts entertaining American businessmen. The gay dream of sensuous pleasures,

> *Under the bam*
> *Under the boo*
> *Under the bamboo tree*

leads to dreams of cannibalism and murder:

> Yes I'd eat you!
> In a nice little, white little, soft little, tender little,
> Juicy little, right little, missionary stew.
>
> I knew a man once did a girl in
> Any man might do a girl in
> Any man has to, needs to, wants to
> Once in a lifetime, do a girl in.

At the end, empty pleasure and violence lead to a loss of the sense of reality and a nameless terror. The play anticipates the tragic farces of the absurdists of mid-century.

But when one thinks of poetic drama in the twentieth century, one thinks first of the Canterbury Festival play, *Murder in the Cathedral* (1935), in which Eliot dealt with a theme of the highest exaltation—the dedication and martyrdom of Thomas Becket. In search of intensities outside the realistic theatre, Eliot used forms suggested by many other traditions—Greek, medieval, Elizabethan, and modern. He used the choir and music of the Anglo-Catholic tradition, a chorus of women similar to a Greek chorus, and the sharper stanzaic and rhetorical forms of medieval and Shakespearean drama. Like Lorca, he incorporated in his choruses some elements of pagan seasonal rituals of sacrifice and fertility. And after the four Knights have killed Becket, they address the modern audience directly as though they were British school debaters—a device as startling as any epic device of Brecht.

The play fits neither our usual patterns of historical drama nor those of tragedy. It contrasts sharply with Shaw's play about a medieval saint, *Saint Joan* (1923), which is an excellent historical play and a variant of the hopeful pattern of naturalistic tragedy. Joan is killed because she is ahead of her time. From the perspective of five hundred years, Shaw saw the historical forces that broke up the Middle Ages—Protestantism, nationalism, individualism—as converging on Joan. In his view, the deeper purpose of the universe—the divinity—is imminent in the whole course of history, geological, biological, and human. History is the growth and emergence of new forms to serve the divine purpose. In his preface, Shaw wrote, "The law of change is the law of God." The anguish of the individual who gave voice and leadership to that change is expressed in a prose that rises to the power of poetry.

Eliot's saint is not a historical figure but one of many timeless intercessors

Kinds of Plays

FIGURE 6.6 The chorus of a poetic religious play. The movement adds formality as well as excitement to the reenactment of the martyrdom of Thomas Becket. Eliot's *Murder in the Cathedral*. Yale University production, directed by Alan Fishburn and Edward Padula, designed by John Koenig, and costumed by Mercedes Moore.

between man and God, a saint to give meaning to life for ordinary people who see only violence and pain. Becket is not set against a Shakespearean or Shavian historical pageant but against the caution of the ordinary priests, against his own temptations, against the comic incomprehension of the Knights who murder him because in their historical view anyone who is motivated by a personal or metaphysical idea must be insane. In an anachronistic debate, the Fourth Knight insists that Thomas deliberately provoked the murder in order to become a martyr. "Need I say more? I think, with these facts before you, you will unhesitatingly render a verdict of Suicide While of Unsound Mind. It is the only charitable verdict you can give upon one who was, after all, a great man."

The real significance of the martyrdom is for the common people, the chorus of the women of Canterbury. Their life "living and partly living" is limited to the daily cares of the world—"For us, the poor, there is no action,/ But only to wait and to witness." They dread the pain of the event they are about to witness. Eliot used this chorus to relate the martyrdom to ancient seasonal rituals in which the old Priest-King was killed in order that his blood might bring the resurrection of fertility in the spring. At first the women fear the disturbance of the quiet season, not knowing how the season may be renewed.

> Winter shall come bringing death from the sea,
> Ruinous spring shall beat at our doors . . .
> Disastrous summer burn up the beds of our streams.

As the pain comes nearer, they see that it is a cleansing.

> And the world must be cleaned in the winter, or we shall have only
> A sour spring, a parched summer, an empty harvest.

235

The Theatre of Exaltation

FIGURE 6.7 The climax of a poetic religious play. The rowdy Knights kill Thomas Becket. Eliot's *Murder in the Cathedral*. Production at the American Shakespeare Festival, Stratford, Connecticut, 1966. Photo Friedman-Abeles.

While the Knights are killing Becket, the chorus expresses the ritual meaning of the act in words and dance. These common people give the earthy component to the spiritual event, feeling the event in their guts. Like all artists, Eliot knew that important human experiences are not abstract, logical propositions, that religious feelings quicken the senses, and that deep convictions are woven into the bone. As the Knights approach the murder, as Thomas makes his peace with his fate, as the priests glance into the horror of the Void, the women chant a vivid ode building up to their consent to and acceptance of the violence. The lines of the Women of Canterbury, rich in sensuous imagery and emotional power, make excellent exercises in choral speaking (see Exercises 7 and 8, pp. 238–39).

The play leaves too little place for man's will and his partnership with God to satisfy all the definitions of tragedy. It is more like a medieval miracle play of an age that was so sure of God's will and man's unworthiness that it had no place for tragedy. In *Murder in the Cathedral* as well as in *The Cocktail Party* (1949), Eliot's comedy about religious problems in everyday life, the characters are told by some superior being just what they are to do. The common people are not to expect much in their own lives but to look to their betters for meaning. Yet *Murder in the Cathedral* is a very powerful play and shows enough struggle and suffering to gain considerable tragic force.

236

Kinds of Plays

EXERCISES AND DEMONSTRATIONS

1. PLANNING A MODERN TRAGEDY.   Plan the outline of a plot turning on a character's discovery of something he has not known about himself that makes him a finer person, though it means the sacrifice of something very important to him.

2. PLANNING A MODERN TRAGEDY.   Plan an incident for a character (like Chance in Tennessee Williams' *Sweet Bird of Youth*) who refuses to drift any longer or to take the easy way out but decides to face what he has done.

3. PLANNING A MODERN TRAGEDY.   Taking the popular vision of man's fall—a once important person, now drunk, penniless, alone on skid row—plan some incident by which he regains at least a fragment of his former dignity. (Saving the life of an unknown child would be too external, too irrelevant to him.)

4. WRITING A SPEECH OF TRAGIC POWER.   For an age accustomed to rather inarticulate characters, write a speech of some power, either protesting at fate or accepting it with grim satisfaction. Can you weave the repetition of banal phrases into a rhythm of power? Can you find dialect phrases with vivid images and a strong rhythm? See Juno's passionate prayer at the end of Sean O'Casey's *Juno and the Paycock,* quoted in this chapter. In John Osborne's *The Entertainer* the down-and-out professional singer borrows for his moment of inexpressible pain an American Negro song he has heard. Can you borrow and expand phrases from some well-known source—song, hymn, prayer, poem, Bible passage, Declaration of Independence, or the like? Although a phrase too familiar, such as "Give me liberty or give me death," would probably produce a comic effect, a character can be impressive and touching even if there is something comic about his means of expression.

5. ANALYSIS OF T. S. ELIOT'S TWO PLAYS ABOUT MARTYRS.   Considering them as a religious diptych, compare *Murder in the Cathedral* and *The Cocktail Party*. Is one all heroic and the other all submissive? To what extent is the one a tragedy and the other a high comedy? Remembering the last line of the poem "The Hollow Men"—"This is the way the world ends/ Not with a bang but a whimper"—compare the martyrdom of Becket, in full color and splendor, with that of Celia, a tale told at a cocktail party about a death on an ant hill. Consider whether Edward and Lavinia correspond to the Women of Canterbury as witnesses finding strength in someone else's dedication.

6. ANALYSIS OF TWO PLAYS ABOUT SAINTS.   Compare Eliot's *Murder in the Cathedral* and Shaw's *Saint Joan.* You may compare some of their philosophical and political implications—the meaning of faith, the nature and mission of a saint, the impact of an extraordinary individual on an institution, his contemporaries, and history—or some of their dramatic and stylistic as-

237

pects—variety of characterization, comic elements, spectacular elements, realistic and nonrealistic techniques, irony, and poetic images of nature.

7. SPEECH AND MOVEMENT IN ELIOT'S MODERN TRAGIC CHORUS. The choruses of *Murder in the Cathedral* are excellent exercises in choral speaking. If they do not suggest such specific actions as some Greek choruses do, they yet demand considerable movement to illustrate both the specific image of a passage and the conflicting fears that make the women alternately retreat in isolation and cling together. Plan the staging of the following ode, in which the women sense the approach of the murderers; begin it in scattered formation and gradually form a compact group. Have some phrases taken by single voices, some by two or three together, and some by the whole chorus; some by high, light voices and some by lower, heavier voices. Give a few individuals separate movements and set some women in opposition to others.

> I have smelt them, the death-bringers, senses are quickened
> By subtile forebodings; I have heard
> Fluting in the nighttime, fluting and owls . . .
>   . . . I have tasted
> The savour of putrid flesh in the spoon. I have felt
> The heaving of earth at nightfall, restless, absurd . . .
>   . . . I have smelt
> Corruption in the dish, incense in the latrine, the sewer in the incense, the smell of sweet soap in the woodpath, a hellish sweet scent in the woodpath, while the ground heaved . . .
>   . . . Have I not known, not known
> What was coming to be? It was here, in the kitchen, in the passage.
> In the mews in the barn in the byre in the marketplace
> In our veins our bowels our skulls as well
> As well as in the plottings of potentates
> As well as in the consultations of powers.
> What is woven on the loom of fate
> What is woven in the councils of princes
> Is woven also in our veins, our brains,
> Is woven like a pattern of living worms
> In the guts of the women of Canterbury.

8. SPEECH AND MOVEMENT IN ELIOT'S MODERN TRAGIC CHORUS. Take the more positive motions of the cleansing during the actual murder. The passage should give a sense of one terrible moment of blood and pain, as well as a satisfaction in the cleansing.

> Clear the air! clean the sky! wash the wind! take stone from stone and wash them.
> The land is foul, the water is foul, our beasts and ourselves defiled with blood.
> A rain of blood has blinded my eyes . . .
> We are soiled by a filth that we cannot clean, united to supernatural vermin,
> It is not we alone, it is not the house, it is not the city that is defiled,

EXERCISES AND DEMONSTRATIONS

But the world that is wholly foul.

Clear the air! clean the sky! wash the wind! take the stone from the stone, take the skin from the arm, take the muscle from the bone, and wash them. Wash the stone, wash the bone, wash the brain, wash the soul, wash them wash them!

SUGGESTED READING

PLAYS: MODERN TRAGEDY

The hero ahead of his time, a little man struggling against reactionary social forces, is the subject of many of the earlier naturalistic plays: Henrik Ibsen's social plays, especially *An Enemy of the People* (1882); Herman Heijermans, *The Good Hope* (1900), with Dutch fishermen making the struggle; John Galsworthy, *The Silver Box* (1906), *Justice* (1910), and *Escape* (1926); Paul Green, *In Abraham's Bosom* (1926), with a Negro schoolteacher as hero, and *Johnny Johnson* (1937), with a pacifist soldier; Maxwell Anderson, *High Tor* (1937), though it is a mixture of fantasy and naturalism.

The hero has more tragic strength and individuality when he sacrifices himself to gain or maintain his identity, as in Anderson's realistic-poetic plays *Winterset* (1935) and *Key Largo* (1939); Jean Anouilh, *Antigone* (1944); Tennessee Williams, *A Streetcar Named Desire* (1947), *Cat on a Hot Tin Roof* (1955), and *Sweet Bird of Youth* (1959); and Arthur Miller, *Death of a Salesman* (1949) and *The Crucible* (1953).

The destructive psychological forces are studied in Ibsen, *Hedda Gabler* (1890); August Strindberg, *The Father* (1887) and *Miss Julie* (1888); Eugene O'Neill, *Beyond the Horizon* (1920), *Desire Under the Elms* (1924), *The Great God Brown* (1926), and *Mourning Becomes Electra* (1931); Franz Werfel, *Goat Song* (1921); Arthur Miller, *A View from the Bridge* (1955); and Friedrich Duerrenmatt, *The Visit* (1956).

Compassion modifies the impact of the destructive forces in such naturalistic plays as Paul Vincent Carroll, *Shadow and Substance* (1934); John Steinbeck, *Of Mice and Men* (1937); Williams, *The Glass Menagerie* (1944) and *The Night of the Iguana* (1961); and O'Neill, *Long Day's Journey into Night* (1956).

The "life-lie," the illusion that is delusion, is the subject of Ibsen, *The Wild Duck* (1884); Maxim Gorki, *The Lower Depths* (1902); O'Neill, *The Iceman Cometh* (1946); and Peter Shaffer, *The Royal Hunt of the Sun* (1964).

In several epic plays listed in Chapter 1 the personal tragedy stands out from the epic background enough to warrant the term "tragedy," notably in Miller, *Death of a Salesman*; Brecht, *Mother Courage* and *Galileo*; and Shaffer, *The Royal Hunt of the Sun*.

Many of the plays to be studied in Chapter 9, "The Theatre of Disruption," have tragic aspects.

PLAYS: POETIC DRAMA

The poetic plays of peasant passion are the early plays of W. B. Yeats, such as *The Land of Heart's Desire* (1894); John Millington Synge, *Riders to the Sea* (1904) and *The Playboy of the Western World* (1907); Federico García Lorca, *Blood Wedding* (1933) and *Yerma* (1934); and Sean O'Casey's many plays, including *Juno and the Paycock* (1924) and *Cock-a-Doodle-Dandy* (1949).

239

Verse in the Elizabethan tradition serves Maxwell Anderson in his historical plays, *Elizabeth the Queen* (1930) and *Mary of Scotland* (1933), and even better in his modern plays, *Winterset* (1935) and *Key Largo* (1939). Some of the best modern blank verse is in Dorothy Sayers' religious play, *The Zeal of Thy House* (1937).

Christopher Fry is at his wittiest in *The Lady's Not for Burning* (1949). T. S. Eliot combines several traditional forms of verse with colloquial idiom in *Sweeney Agonistes* (1933) and *Murder in the Cathedral* (1935), and uses a bare colloquial verse in *The Cocktail Party* (1949). Archibald MacLeish raises the modern colloquial idiom to a high intensity in his radio play *The Fall of the City* (1937) and his heroic plays *J. B.* (1958) and *Heracles* (1966). A great range of forms, traditional and modern, is used in W. H. Auden and Christopher Isherwood, *The Ascent of F6* (1937).

CRITICAL WORKS

For critical works on tragedy, including books dealing with the difficulty of writing tragedy in the twentieth century, see the Suggested Reading for Chapter 4.

SUGGESTED READING

CHAPTER SEVEN

THE THEATRE OF LAUGHTER: FARCE

The Ways of Comedy

Comedy is far more complex than tragedy and harder to define. The word is used for many different kinds of plays and for a wide range of attitudes toward them, from delight in the broad slapstick of farce to sophisticated enjoyment of high comedy, ambiguous satisfaction in stinging satire, and even enthralled absorption in romantic plays where there is no laughter at all. We see ourselves in a comic character, we like him, and then we rejoice to see him beaten. We project ourselves onto the stage and yet sit detached, watching from a distance. In some ages, all plays, whether comic or tragic, were called simply comedies. The word "play" itself implies something done for sheer pleasure.

Laughter, that noisy cachinnation, that convulsive expulsion of air and sound so like—and so different from—the barking of a dog, has never been fully explained. It brings sudden relaxation and deep pleasure. It seems involuntary and yet it can be cultivated and stimulated. It seems subjective and individual yet it takes place mostly in social groups. Does it use muscles and reactions inherited from our animal ancestors who bared their fangs and barked at what they disapproved of, who snorted to eject from the nose something tickling or stinking? Yet man is the only animal that laughs, and a mother may laugh in delight at her happy baby as freely as a running boy laughs in triumph and scorn at the grown-up who tries to catch him. Will Rogers, the cowboy humorist, said that what makes people laugh is "something funny." A person suddenly recognizes something left over, something that does not fit into his most careful calculations: "That's funny," he says, "it doesn't come out the way it's supposed to." This incongruity is at the heart of comedy—things don't fit, they're not as they're supposed to be. Henri Bergson, in his essays *On Laughter,* tells how we laugh at the conflict between living and the rules we try to impose on it. Whenever the mechanical is encrusted on the living, it is thrown off in laughter.

From very early times, festivals and holidays have been special occasions for breaking the normal pattern and returning to a tradition of disorder, freedom, and license. A temporary ruler is crowned in mock pomp to rule over the revels, and at the end of the festival his throne is torn down in wild destructive glee. Two myths known in various forms in many parts of the world especially influenced the character of the New Year or midwinter festival. According to one myth, the holiday was a time for returning to an earlier age when a trickster god ruled the world, before the later, more serious gods set mankind living by hard work and strict rules. In Rome the Saturnalia in December was the reign of the early god Saturn and a time of release from all duties and expectations. Men dressed as women, and servants ordered their masters about. After a holiday of release and reversal, people were able to take up their duties feeling a little less bound by the rigidities of their lives. The other myth gave the New Year festival an even more ancient tie, recognizing an incongruity in the very nature of the creation since the lunar calendar can be fitted into the solar calendar only if some four days—holidays— are left over. In some mythologies, creation gave form only to a finite island floating in the waters of chaos. During the new-year gap of four days, more of the surrounding primeval waters flowed into the circle of the year, renewing health and vitality. As people put on outlandish disguises to sing, dance, and act the holiday roles of revelry, they partook of that vital renewal. So, in one aspect, a comedy is a symbolic renewal of the vitality that will never be completely predicted, ruled, or controlled—the vitality of the spring of the year, the bursting of the bonds of winter, the rejection of tight patterns, the breaking of limitations.

The spirit of disorder can never be eradicated from human nature as long as man keeps a sense of spontaneity and play. In the crowds of an anonymous city, the individual may rebel against regimentation with sudden spurts of destruction. Not content with childish obscenities on back fences or practical jokes played on the guardians of respectability, he may invade buildings and pour paint on what other people take seriously or concoct a bomb scare to disrupt a school or a concert. Primitive villages provided an outlet for such dangerous impulses in the ordered disorder of a festival, with masks, costumes, songs, processions, and dramatic acts of beating, cheating, crowning and deposing, exalting and bringing low human figures as well as erecting and destroying temporary buildings. Anyone who has helped build a stage setting and then helped tear it down after the last performance knows the sensation

Kinds of Plays

Razullo.   *Cucurucu.*

FIGURE *7.1* The spirit of comic acting. The masked actors of the *commedia dell' arte* depended as much on their singing, dancing, acrobatics, and slapstick as on the words that they improvised around an agreed-upon story. Note the platform stage in the background. Redrawn from an engraving by Callot.

of being possessed by powerful supernatural forces, inherited from thousands of years of festivals that symbolized the creation of order and the destruction of that order so that a new order might begin a new year.

Civilized communities keep many of the festival outlets for fun, frolic, and disorder, but the important expression for a cultivated man is comedy. On many levels comedy makes an attack on all forms, rules, and systems. It sometimes points the way to improvement; it more often shows a way of living with both order and disorder, rule and rebellion.

To emphasize the attack on order is to see the sadistic pleasure of triumph. Punch in the old puppet show beats his Judy, his squalling baby, and finally death and the devil. Al Capp, whose comic strips have delighted people for years, has been very conscious of the cruel superiority, whether superior knowledge or luck or fate, that makes a character appealing to the public. In an article in *The Atlantic Monthly* in 1950 he wrote: "All comedy is based on man's inhumanity to man. I know that is so, because I have made forty million people laugh more or less every day for sixteen years, and this has been the basis of all the comedy I have created. I think it is the basis of all comedy." But the occasion of his writing was a renewal of acquaintance with the films of Chaplin, which had made him realize that the best comedy has another side. He went on to say: "But I had forgotten, until I saw Chaplin again, that comedy can become sublime when it makes men sorrow at man's inhumanity to man by making men pity themselves." Chaplin himself thought of his comedy in terms not of pity but of a healthy deflation of man's dangerous pretenses and pompous self-deceptions. In his autobiography he wrote, "Through humor, we see in what seems rational, the irrational; in what seems important, the unimportant. It also heightens our sense of survival and preserves our sanity. Because of humor we are less overwhelmed by the

243

The Theatre of Laughter

vicissitudes of life. It activates our sense of proportion and reveals to us that in an overstatement of seriousness lurks the absurd."

The triumph is a mixture of joy and scorn, of accepting the world yet seeing its shortcomings. James Feibleman attempted to rank eight kinds of comedy according to the proportion of pleasure and criticism: Joy, Divine Comedy, Humor, Irony, Satire, Sarcasm, Wit, and Scorn. But comedy, like life, smiles at the inadequacies of any such scheme.

The pleasure of comedy is an increase in well-being. If the pleasure is intense and sudden, it bursts out in laughter. Slow smile or quick laugh, it not only relaxes tension but unites us with the basic sources of life—the release of spring, the surge of the primitive, the triumph of the angel over the beast, of mind over matter, of vitality over calculation. The jack-in-the-box always pops up again, assertive as ever, and the clown comes back with a quip, no matter how he is beaten. With Feste in Shakespeare's *Twelfth Night*, the audience is reassured that journeys end in lovers' meeting and that all journeys end. The audience can stand, if not with the gods, at least with Puck in *A Midsummer Night's Dream,* to look down in amusement and delight at the foolishness of men and the perversity of the universe.

> Shall we their fond pageant see?
> Lord, what fools these mortals be!
>
> . . .
>
> Then will two at once woo one;
> That must needs be sport alone.
> And those things do best please me
> That befall preposterously.

Puck knows that the delusions of the night can be corrected in time.

> Jack shall have Jill;
> Naught shall go ill;
> The man shall have his mare again, and all shall be well.

Even in a world of ditches and pitfalls, man does know up from down and finds a spot in time and space. In his short essay "Comedy," Christopher Fry describes this recognition and acceptance as intuitive wisdom:

> The difference between tragedy and comedy is the difference between experience and intuition. In the experience we strive against every condition of our animal life: against death, against the frustration of ambition, against the instability of human love. In the intuition we trust the arduous eccentricities we're born to, and see the oddness of a creature who has never got acclimatized to being created.

But Fry's antithesis is not entirely accurate. Comedy is not all "intuition," with recognition and acceptance; it sometimes has its share of "experience" as it satirizes what is wrong in order to improve the world. The Greeks thought that their satyr plays derived from primitive village festivals when young men dressed as satyrs, half-goat and half-man, and were permitted to attack or ridicule publicly anyone, high or low, whose behavior during the past year

244

FIGURE 7.2 Masked comedians of ancient Greece on a platform stage. On improvised platforms or in open-air theatres, such clowns were popular all over the ancient world. After a vase drawing.

they did not approve of. Like primitive rituals, comedy may exorcise unfavorable spirits, driving out obstructors and intruders by name-calling, mudslinging, beating, and ridicule. The modern world has its drama of castigation in satire. But even as comedy attacks the ideas, institutions, and people who get in the way of the ideal, it accepts the fact that the imperfect world goes on forever. "Don't laugh at him—you only encourage him," cries the exasperated mother. Laughter does encourage man to see clearly, to attack wrongs, and yet to accept the world as it is and get along in it.

Different periods of the past have fostered particular kinds of comedy. In ancient Greece Aristophanes found ready to his artist's hand a festival of spring fertility processions, with songs and dances, competitions and contests, installation of a ruler of the festival, ridicule and expulsion of intruders and obstructors, and a final ritual wedding and feast. Through that time-honored medium, he expressed his bitter anger at the Athenians for allowing their democracy to be controlled by dictators of the war party and letting their education, law courts, philosophy, and literature be corrupted by irresponsible leaders of cults and fads. The spring festival was a privileged time, and even the war party could not censor the drama. Many Athenians still thought free speech important, and Aristophanes was not silenced when he wrote the most fantastic, and the sharpest, satire the world has ever known. In *The Knights* he even lampooned the current dictator, Cleon, as an amateur sausage-peddler selling baloney to the public. In *Lysistrata* one woman puts an end to the war by persuading the women on both sides to enforce a sex strike until their husbands make peace. *The Clouds* deals hilariously and sharply with the intellectuals who dwell in the clouds. Although these plays and others of Aristophanes laugh at the failures of little men faced with difficult public problems, they also carry the assurance that little men can do something about them. Highly original in his dramatic techniques, Aristophanes was conservative in his basic thinking and regarded Socrates and Euripides as radicals who were undermining the old faith and integrity of Athens with their "modern" ideas.

245

The Theatre of Laughter

FIGURE 7.3 Comic movements, costumes, and setting for a modern revival of ancient comedy. Aristophanes' *The Frogs.* University of Iowa production, directed by Peter D. Arnott, designed by A. S. Gillette, costumed by Margaret S. Hall, and lighted by David L. Thayer.

After Athens was overrun by Alexander the Great and then by the Romans, the citizens no longer took an interest in important public questions. The topical satire of Aristophanes gave way to the neat plots of Menander. Later, in Rome, Plautus developed from Menander's situation drama a farcical comedy that has been the standard entertainment for the tired businessman ever since. That vigorous low comedy will be discussed in detail later in this chapter.

The medieval period developed its own little farces, about a clever lawyer tricked by a simple-minded shepherd in *Patelin,* for example, or about wives dominating and cheating their husbands. Such robust tales even intruded into the great religious cycles, as we have seen, in episodes like that of Noah's wife being dragged into the Ark or that of the shepherd Mak in *The Second Shepherds' Play,* who is caught stealing a lamb and hiding it in his child's cradle just as the shepherds are summoned to adore the Christ-lamb in his cradle. Like the sculpture in a medieval cathedral, which included grotesque gargoyles and homely scenes of everyday life, the religious plays included in their grand design low characters as well as high and many elements of comedy. Medieval drama and art made a great contribution to the comic tradition, showing Shakespeare not only how to use comedy in serious plays but how to add the grim, the grotesque, and the demonic to both serious plays and comedies.

The Renaissance saw two great achievements in comedy. The first was a romantic type of comedy in which idealized young ladies and knights, engaged in the loves and intrigues of an aristocratic court, are surrounded by a variety of colorful comic characters. The appreciation of comic characters as enjoyable and even lovable was a result of the new humanistic respect for individuality explicitly taught at the beginning of the sixteenth century in

246

Kinds of Plays

Erasmus' *Praise of Folly*. Without that attitude, Shakespeare's humorous characters, from jesters, clowns, and bumbling rustics on up to the wise, playful knight, Sir John Falstaff, would never have been conceived; even to this day some overserious moralists cannot love them or indulge them in their foolishness. The second Renaissance achievement in comedy was a realistic, satiric comedy made popular by Shakespeare's young friend, Ben Jonson. Disillusioned and bitter, Jonson attacked men's "humours," or obsessions, with savage anger and took delight in exposing their greed and other vices as well as their gullibility and stupidity. His *Volpone* (1606) and *The Alchemist* (1610) still amaze and delight audiences as dramas of sharp castigation.

The high comedy of the latter part of the seventeenth century took some of the best aspects of both kinds of Renaissance comedy—the disillusioned, clear-eyed view of reality from Jonson, without his bitterness, and the charming, cultivated young lovers and the amiable fools from the romantic comedy. The Restoration Gallant, like the Shakespearean Prince, is an admirable man, much more mature than the young lovers of farce. Farce, or low comedy, is the comedy of the adolescent boy, energetic, mischievous, impatient of restraint, seeing other people as obstacles to his freedom and desires, making no attempt to understand those who differ from him. But high comedy deals with the relationships of adults who are trying to be civilized. If low comedy liberates the young man from his parents, schoolmasters, and drill sergeants, if romance opens the doors to magic journeys and enchanted castles and offers a sacred sword in the perilous clash with evil, high comedy instructs a grown man in how to get along with his neighbors, his competitors, his passing

FIGURE *7.4* Traditional farcical action derived from the *commedia dell' arte*. Scapin, a variant of Harlequin, hides the old man in a sack, ready to beat him with his slapstick sword. Molière's *The Mischief-Maker Scapin*. Northwestern University production, directed by Lee Mitchell and designed by Sam Ball. Photo Nickerson.

FIGURE 7.5 Four *commedia dell' arte* characters—Clown, Harlequin, Columbine, and Pantaloon—as they survived in the English Christmas pantomimes. From a nineteenth-century poster.

fancies, and, most difficult of all, his wife. Where tragedy records man's one ultimate clash with the universe and his humble reconciliation with the ways of the gods, high comedy records man's many clashes with his fellow men and his not-so-humble reconciliation with the ways of the world. Tragedy suggests that man's highest achievement is to find his own soul; high comedy suggests that his highest achievement is to laugh at himself, perhaps an even more important way of possessing his soul. Like tragedy, high comedy explores the more mature reconciliations with the outer world, the self, and death. But before we examine this highly developed social type of comedy, we must consider the basic, more universal type—farce.

Farce Comedy

What this world needs is a good laugh, the broader the better. After a wearing day, the busy man wants a scene of horseplay to relax him, and he turns on the TV to watch a lively comedian. The Romans on their holidays went by the thousands to see a clownish servant in a red wig and a wide-mouthed mask, who would be chased all over the enormous stage and beaten vigorously yet would always be ready with a clever remark and a new scheme for getting the money or the girl. The Renaissance clown Harlequin made his sword into a trick stick, a "slapstick" of two strips of wood which gave the maximum of sound with the least permanent damage to the rump. For three centuries, children from four to eighty have screamed with delight as the puppet Punch turns on his nagging wife, on the whining cat, and finally on the devil himself, and gives them such a fast, noisy beating that the

248

Kinds of Plays

puppet heads seem to split into splinters. It's a rough world, my masters, full of rules, officers, parents, pimples, and obstructions. There's a surprise around every corner. Nobody believes you or understands you, least of all when you speak the plain truth. Everything conspires to thwart you. There's pain, worry, accident at every turn. Maybe the whole thing has little meaning, but if you keep running fast enough, keep scheming long enough, you can win out. It may be painful at the time, but it's very funny to tell about afterwards, and it's very funny to see somebody else in a play in the same bind.

Curiously, our broadest laughs are at someone else's pain. A good farce is excruciatingly funny. It provides popular entertainment by turning the difficulties, restrictions, frustrations, and embarrassments of life into laughter. It relaxes the audience by first tying it into new knots of tension, then exploding the tension into guffaws and roars of delight.

To build that tension, a farce must seem completely real. The pain must be completely felt. Empathy and identification must be total. As far as farce is concerned, all the old sayings about "no emotions in comedy," "the mind but not the feelings involved," and "intellectual detachment" are utter nonsense. Farce has its own way of making reality ridiculous, but first it must have a strong, serious grasp on that reality. There had been many productions of Oscar Wilde's *The Importance of Being Earnest* in which Jack and Algernon were light, elegant playboys, but John Gielgud's extremely *earnest* Jack made it clear how infinitely funnier the play is when the character is dead serious.

FIGURE *7.6* Farcical costume. The popular nineteenth-century American comedian William Burton as Toodle in *The Toodles*. Museum of the City of New York.

Georges Feydeau, the very successful French author of farces, always insisted on the utmost sincerity in his actors. The settings and costumes must also be convincing. Eric Bentley in his edition of French farces points out how much is lost when the designer tries to "stylize" the lines and colors and moves the play too far into the ornamental and delicate. The joke is the tension between the face and the mask, between the everyday atmosphere and the maniacal overintensity of the situation. There is caricature, yes, but it is the caricature of Dickens or Hogarth, not the poetic distortion in Pierrot and Columbine.

With that firm hold on reality, the author and director give the production a treatment that will set it in the right farcical key. Farce acting is not stylized; in one sense, it is the most realistic of all acting. Yet it is given intensities of volume and speed, mechanical patterns of repetition or interruption, that make it very different from the realistic acting suitable for Chekhov. There are clear-cut devices and techniques that turn a real situation into farce.

THE TECHNIQUES OF FARCE

Farce is based on a three-fold compact between the audience and the play. One term of that compact is the realism: the audience must recognize themselves in farce, whether the actor is Jack Lemmon or Dean Martin in modern dress, a circus clown in fantastic costume, or Mr. Magoo in a cartoon. But another element is the built-in irony of a false situation as the playwright carefully lets the audience know that it is all a mistake or a lie. Then the third element is the kind of performance put on by the director, the designer, and the actor—the floppy hat and the glimpse of red underdrawers, the comic gesture and voice of the actor, the sheer intensity of speed and noise of the performance, the patterns of incongruity and surprise.

It is the false situation that makes the pain endurable. The moment may distress the character, but the audience knows it is all a mistake. Someone is in disguise or lying or it is a case of mistaken identity. Fate may growl like a vicious dog, but it has no teeth to bite. Everything is cleared up in the end because the situation was never real. That is one reason why the literary realists were so angry with farce; in the early twentieth century they conducted such a campaign against it that only recently have serious critics like Eric Bentley defended it as an important and respectable form of theatre. A farce may have less surprise than a melodrama, but it has great comic irony as the audience from the beginning knows something that the character does not yet know. The playwright carefully lets the audience in on the situation. He shows the putting on of the disguise, the concocting of the lie, or the beginning of the mistaken identity. In actuality, it is painful to see a husband deny his wife and upbraid her, but not in Plautus' *Menaechmi* or Shakespeare's version of the same play, *The Comedy of Errors*, because the slowest lout in the audience knows it isn't really the husband, it's his long-lost twin brother. For *Amphytrion*, Plautus apparently had actors who looked so much alike he was afraid the audience would not be sure which was which. He had one tell the audience to notice that there was a tassel on his cap but not on the cap of his duplicate. Youthful pregnancy is a serious situation in life, but we laugh freely at *Kiss and Tell*. We know Corliss isn't really pregnant; it's just a mistake that is a good joke on her parents and the neighbors who think she is. So the audience is able to watch at a safe distance, looking down on the painful antics of the low comedy. Thomas Hobbes, the seventeenth-century English philosopher, described the relation between laughter and this feeling of superiority. He wrote, "Sudden Glory is the passion which maketh those grimaces called Laughter; and it is caused either by some sudden act of their own, that pleaseth them; or by the apprehension of some deformed thing in another, by comparison whereof they suddenly applaud themselves."

It is often said that a good farce situation begins with a highly improbable premise, but that once the premise is accepted, all the rest follows with absolute logic. Only on the stage could Jupiter appear disguised as the husband Amphitryon to make love to the wife. Only in *Blithe Spirit* could the ghost of a first wife materialize, without the ability to dematerialize again. Only in *Three Men on a Horse* could a naive little man have the ability to pick the winning horses. But the opening situation is made acceptable to the audience by a completely realistic approach by the actors.

So it is not lack of empathy and emotion, it is the special treatment which turns the amazing situation into farce. First of all, the actor himself may contribute some comic qualities: a squeaky or reedy voice, a nasal tone, a peculiar inflection, or a monotone may reinforce the comic quality of a character. In broad farce, actors have not hesitated to use lisping, stuttering, limping,

FIGURE 7.7 Farcical action in a sophisticated society. The two ghosts, accidentally brought back, are not easily exorcised. Coward's *Blithe Spirit*. New York, 1941. Photo Vandamm.

and tics of voice and movement. Madame Arcati's sudden jumps and squeaks were the funniest things in *Blithe Spirit*. The costume can also add an important element. Masks, of course, set ancient comedy into a different realm, whether animal masks or clownish makeup. With more realistic characters, a floppy hat, an old-fashioned stripe, or a garment a bit too large or too short may give just the touch needed. In disguise, the incongruity may be quite hilarious. The man dressed as Charley's aunt repeatedly forgets and shows his trousers and smokes a cigar, rousing screams of terror in the audience as he almost gets caught by the girls. Moments of undress or threats of exposure cause violent laughter as they come close to breaking our strong taboos. Bright-colored underclothes heighten the effect and at the same time prevent any actual exposure.

More important than the comic qualities are the various kinds of intensities of the performance. Speed is the most obvious farcical intensity. Play anything fast enough and, as long as it carries the audience with it, it will be funny. Charlie Chaplin's Monsieur Verdoux counting money at superhuman speed can never be forgotten. Chase scenes, whether of the couples running around the restaurant tables in *The Matchmaker* or of the Keystone Cops or the automobile thieves fleeing over curb and cliff in the silent movies, are high points of delight. Beatings, fights, struggles, pratfalls—all add an enormous amount of energetic action, and of course a good farce scene must be loud. No one reading *Arsenic and Old Lace* would ever guess the tremendous effect when Teddy, who thinks he is Teddy Roosevelt, runs up a stairway yelling "Charge!" in a full, raucous voice. At the end of the first act of *The Matchmaker* the young men are jumping with delight because at last they are to run away from the store. Thornton Wilder adds a whole battery of sounds as the tomato cans in the store below explode and cans and debris fly up through the trap door. Emotions are not acted quietly in a farce but exaggerated to the fullest intensity. In a serious play, sorrow and pain are suppressed and indicated by half-hidden tensions, but not in farce. It is an interesting comment on audiences that their greatest pleasure comes from crying on the stage. While their empathy is enlisted, their own tension is released by the sheer intensity of the actors' squalling. The funniest moment in *Three Men on a Horse* comes when the wife is crying her eyes out, thinking her husband is off with other women. Doubtless the energy of the bawling reassures the audience that a character as noisy as all that is not about to die. The various intensities—speed, energy, loudness, physical action, and exaggerated expression of emotion—all illustrate the basic duality of low comedy. Characters must be convincing, yet played with such single-minded, demoniacal obsession that the empathy is spilled over into laughter. If a farce character ever stopped one moment to think, the whole situation would vanish. If the actors let the audience stop one moment to think, the whole farce would vanish.

Besides these intensities, there are many mechanical patterns: duplications, repetitions, sequences, reversals, delays, surprises, interruptions, and sudden breaks in pattern. There is a light comic effect when a young lover tries to join M. Perrichon as he is leaving on a trip with his wife and daughter in a famous nineteenth-century French farce, *Le Voyage de M. Perrichon*. When another of the daughter's suitors arrives with exactly the same excuse for going, the play moves into farce. Identical twins, two brothers dressed like two servants, or two people who find themselves in the same predicament can be the source of endless amusement as they move in unison, in opposition, or in sequence. Duplication of movement is so funny that in serious plays the director takes great care to see that two actors do not by chance sit or turn or step in unison. Duplication with variation is a highly entertaining development. Sometimes it is deliberate and derisive as one character apes another to make fun of him or express anger. Sometimes the variation depends on incongruity, as when a fat and a tall person are made to look alike or act alike. The actor T. D. Rice, who made such a success in the 1830s and 40s with his blackface comic character "Jim Crow," climaxed his program one year by having the young boy Joe Jefferson join him dressed and made up as a miniature Jim Crow. It is funny enough when Captain Fisby forgets his army regulations, adopts native costume, and starts building the Teahouse of the August Moon. His colonel is furious and sends a psychiatrist to take over. But the psychiatrist in turn has his weakness—organic gardening —and he settles down like a native, forgetting his own regulations. The colonel reacts to this surprise with a double take and a slow burn and frantically searches in his regulations, saying, "I want to see who I send to analyze an analyst." Sometimes the sequence of repetition is continued to several examples, and it is just a step to a Gilbert and Sullivan chorus, "and so do his sisters and his cousins and his aunts."

The best ending for a sequence is a reversal. Farce and melodrama take

FIGURE *7.8* Farcical action in a satiric fantasy with music. Mayakovsky's *The Bedbug*. University of Iowa production, directed by Philip A. Benson, designed by A. S. Gillette, costumed by Sandra Williamson under the supervision of Margaret S. Hall, and lighted by David L. Thayer.

great delight in the moment when the worm turns. It is all the better when the very words the offender used are thrown back. Even serious plays often include such moments of farcical retort. When he himself is favored, Shylock praises the young judge as "noble" and "wise" and taunts his victim as a "Daniel come to judgment." When the judgment goes against him, he has to listen to his own words in the repeated taunts from the bitter Gratiano. Ibsen allowed Hedda Gabler finally to turn on her fussy husband with his own constant phrase, "Fancy that . . . huh?" The quick reversal or blowing hot and cold is sure of a laugh as the audience, called on to respond alternately to opposite emotions, cannot change that fast and throws off the emotion in laughter. In *The Merchant of Venice,* Launcelot Gobbo, the shy servant boy who would like to be bold, is given an appealing scene of hot and cold as he alternately wants his father to speak for him to the prospective employer, then impatiently steps forward to speak for himself (see Exercise 1, p. 259).

Most of Shakespeare's farce scenes, like this short episode in *The Merchant of Venice,* are gentle and kind. For a full-blooded scene of changing tensions, accusations, and denials, lies and surprises, one may sample a family scene from the father of all farce, Plautus, the Roman actor-playwright who taught the tired businessmen and the soldiers on leave from Rome's world conquests to laugh at the difficulties of daily living (see Exercise 2, pp. 259–62). Without the beatings of clownish slaves or the pie-throwing of much later farce, Plautus exploited the misunderstandings and tensions of a husband and wife and the cook delivering something from a downtown store. Eric Bentley praises the French bedroom farces for releasing tensions pent up in that most basic but most difficult of all institutions—the family; in reading Plautus, we see that the tensions were no less strong in ancient Rome.

THE POPULARITY OF FARCE

In spite of its enemies, farce has been the most popular of all theatre forms for more than two thousand years. Literary critics have attacked it as trivial and vulgar, and highbrows of all periods have despised it for its use of physical action. Puritans and fanatics have despised it simply because it is funny. Being dead serious is supposed to be more profound, and entertainment is "diversion," a turning away from important things. Yet year after year, night after night, the broad laugh has been as indispensable a part of the lives of millions of people as their food and sleep.

Henri Bergson explained laughter in terms of the mechanical. Whenever something fixed, dead, and machine-like is imposed on the living, changing, adaptable human being, there is laughter; and this laughter assures us that life can never be fixed and stereotyped. Bergson's analyses throw a great deal of light on farce comedy and explain much about our delight in seeing a pattern broken. But one can go further than Bergson in search of philosophical explanation and offer at least three good reasons why farce continues century after century to delight its audience.

In the first place, low comedy is a release of pent-up dormant life, one of the surges of the springtime. For thousands of years, as we have seen, festivals

Kinds of Plays

FIGURE 7.9 Farcical action involving a group. Labiche's *The Italian Straw Hat.* Carnegie Tech Theatre production, directed by Lawrence Carra, designed by Paul Troutvetter, and costumed by Louise Duffey. Photo William Nelson.

in celebration of spring included running, jumping, racing, dancing, shouting, the stripping off of clothes and the putting on of disguises. Men set one another impossible tasks, then gave one another beatings as they failed. To make the races more exciting, they added stumbling blocks and pitfalls and laughed as many stumbled and fell. They set clowns and devils to interrupt the activities and ape and mock the solemnities of the day. Every wild intensity was stirred up as joy and vitality burst the bonds of winter.

The two boys in *The Matchmaker* break away from the store in Yonkers. They go downtown to the big city; they kiss some girls, take them out to a restaurant, and almost get arrested. They have agreed that when they are really having an exciting adventure they will cry out their signal. Dangers and surprises increase the excitement, and, even as one boy is hiding in the closet and the other under the table, in painful terror of being caught, one sticks out a head and yells their signal, "Pudding!" The old merchant himself gets into unexpected adventure and brings home a wife and a much more tolerant disposition. It is as important to thaw out his tyranny and stinginess as it is to thaw the frozen ground before new things can grow. In *Mister Roberts* the sailors on the supply ship finally get released from the tight restrictions of their ill-tempered captain. They do get a fling in the town, and Mr. Roberts smiles indulgently when he hears that they have wrecked an army officers' club. An unforgettable scene in the film made from the play shows one man returning to the ship on a motorcycle, streaking at top speed down the length of the dock and straight into the ocean. Such release is more important than all the caution and restrictions in the world.

Thus farce is one version of romance. It shows the youth leaving home to go out and kill his dragon and rescue his enchanted maiden. It also shows the older man trying to slip out and meet the enchanted maiden but running back into the house before the dragon quite gets him. The difference is that farce emphasizes the little realistic details that true romance omits. Even as the dragon is coming on with breath of flame your sword sticks in the scabbard. As you lift the veil of enchantment it catches on a nail and rips. As you mount the stairs to her tower you bump your head on a beam. As you slowly move in to kiss her you are interrupted by a sneeze. In true romance you are never interrupted, you never slip on the stair, you are never out of breath, you are never bothered by the little annoying physical details of existence. Clothes always fit and look right. You never have to worry about money or weather or broken furniture. But in farce your friend with the money is late, the wrong person shows up, and everybody misunderstands you. Farce makes the fullest demonstration possible of the breakdown of communication. Romance can soar with poetry into celestial clarity, but farce has to stumble along on the clumsiness of prose. Romance uses the large musical patterns of crescendos and climaxes and sustained anxieties leading to a full issue, then a final completeness and calm. Farce uses much faster crescendos, with interruptions, delayed climaxes, and far more sudden releases—just the pattern of our everyday efforts, irritations, surprises, and anxieties as we push toward the end of the day and the week, with the holiday as the goal. Farce reassures us that if we keep pushing the release does come.

A second reason for man's pleasure in farce is that it brings the great reassurance that all the great clowns have brought, the reassurance that man can take it. The clown takes his beating and survives; by his wisecrack and his comeback he proves his spiritual superiority to his fate. The clown has always been the butt, the victim, the fall guy, the little fellow that something always happens to. He is all of us, unlucky, put upon, mistreated. But he refuses to give up. He never admits defeat. He can always show his indifference to pain, and sometimes, just sometimes, he has a chance to snatch his own victory from his overwhelming enemies. It's a rough world, my masters, but there's many a way of getting around it.

It is that superb aplomb in the midst of danger that makes the best moments of the great clowns so memorable. At one moment in the film *A Night at the Opera,* the Marx brothers are frantically fleeing along the galleries high up in the backstage rigging in the opera house. The next moment they are serenely sailing through the air on the tie ropes as the scenery flies up and down around the performers. Or they pretend to be part of the performance, just out of reach of their pursuers. Who can forget the gravity of Charlie Chaplin as a rookie soldier in *Shoulder Arms,* left on the field marking time alone after the rest of the squad has marched away, or his quiet assertion in an early short film, *A Night Out,* when, as he is being dragged away by the collar, he picks a daisy and smells it? It is very painful to keep a bit of individuality in a regimented world, but the clown does it. Or one may remember Chaplin's unquestioning absorption in his job on a swaying ladder as he cleans the street sign each time the ladder brings him by, or the same care-

Kinds of Plays

free bravery as he walks to the other side of the room to keep the house from teetering over the cliff in *The Gold Rush*. In *The Kid* he is a proud society man refusing to bow down to poverty and rags, twirling his cane, taking off his fingerless gloves with elegance, reaching for his cigarette case (a sardine can), and carefully tapping his choice of the butts he has picked up. Charlie Chaplin in the midst of hostile surroundings can blithely follow the life and logic of his own mind in complete disregard of his enemies. While he is sweeping a pawnshop, a rope on the floor suddenly becomes in his mind a circus tightrope, and he an expert tightrope performer beloved and applauded by the crowd. While fleeing through an enormous house, he suddenly stops before a vast birthday cake to play pool and golf with bits of the frosting, making every shot count. In farce, the world may be reeling and humanity hostile, but the clowns possess what has been called the "incalculable strength of the weak."

Besides giving us strength to free the spirit and to hold up the chin, farce has a third function: it makes an important philosophical synthesis. It is a device for accepting the basic incongruity of everyday living, of spanning the ideal and the real without giving up either. It accepts the discrepancy between the finite and the infinite; it affirms the infinite and laughs at man for being bogged down in the finite. In particular, it accepts both the pattern and the impulse to break the pattern. It goes further than the Bergsonian affirmation of the living man throwing off the dead pattern, further than the spring release of pent-up energy. It is more than a romantic indulgence for the wild oats of youth or the wayward impulses of old men. Ultimately it does not demand a revolutionary change. It has no hope or wish to abolish the rules, the officers, the policemen, the parents, the wives, the jobs, the conformity that give structure to our daily lives. But it does expect to bend the rules, to get around the officer, to vary the conformity. It reaffirms order in the universe as a whole, but it suggests that on the lower levels there may be considerable incongruity. Hence it is not surprising that many famous comic figures have come in contrasting pairs—Don Quixote and Sancho Panza, the young, idealistic Prince Hal and the old, disillusioned Falstaff, the clever slave and the stupid slave in Roman comedy, Pierrot and Harlequin, Mutt and Jeff, Weber and Fields, Amos and Andy, Laurel and Hardy. These are not only symbols of different classes but of the affinity and companionship of incongruous temperaments.

Farce is a profound device for acceptance and adjustment. It lays aside the question of whether the world can or should be changed and is concerned entirely with the world as it is. And as it is, the world is full of incongruities, accidents, surprises, hostilities, and misunderstandings. Anything you undertake is likely to be interrupted and thwarted at any moment. Your emotions are frantic and sometimes noisy. The rules are very restrictive and often are enforced by stupid guardians. The institutions you are committed to—your work, your family, your moral leaders—would absorb every last minute of your life if you let them. But the very stupidity of other people is your chance. If you find the right way you can get around them. The unpredictable ele-

FIGURE 7.10 Comic costumes in the farces of Georges Feydeau early in the twentieth century. Two drawings from the magazine *Figaro*. Bibliothèque de l'Arsenal, Paris.

ment in the universe may be your opportunity. You may be slowed up in your flight at one moment because someone has locked the gate, but you find at the next moment that the demon pursuing you has fallen into an open manhole. In *The Teahouse of the August Moon,* the unexpected disaster is the arrival of the Congressional delegation. But it turns out that they are delighted with the change of plans, and the colonel must frantically try to rescue what he had ordered destroyed. He, the guardian of army regulations, cries, "Why can't someone disobey orders once in a while! What has happened to the American spirit of rebellion?" Just enough people have disobeyed; a little disorder on the lower level has saved the day. Moss Hart in his famous play *Once in a Lifetime* has his stupid director leave the lights off when a movie is taken, but the critics, even more stupid, rave about the atmospheric lighting. The sound track has picked up the director's incessant

258

Kinds of Plays

cracking of nuts in his hands, but the critics rave about the rhythmic beat and compare it to the drum in *The Emperor Jones.*

It's a mad world, my masters, but you've got two chances. One is in your own persistence. The other is in the very element of accident and unpredictability in the universe. Put those two chances together and it's a laugh. And a laugh is the one way of accepting it, better relaxation than wine, women, or song. Without the relaxation of farcical laughter, man would long ago have torn himself and his neighbors apart.

EXERCISES AND DEMONSTRATIONS

1. ACTING A SHAKESPEAREAN LOW-COMEDY SCENE. Plan the movement and emotional changes, "blowing hot and cold," of the scene in *The Merchant of Venice* in which Launcelot Gobbo applies for a place as servant to Bassanio. He gets his father, Old Gobbo, a blind, simple rustic, to speak for him, but he repeatedly interrupts and starts to speak for himself, only to become shy and push his father forward again. Bassanio's bewilderment and good-natured exasperation can add to the comic effect.

LAUNCELOT   To him, Father.

GOBBO   God bless your worship! . . . Here's my son, sir, a poor boy—

LAUNCELOT (*stepping forward himself*)   Not a poor boy, sir, but the rich Jew's man, that would, sir, (*his courage fails and he pushes his father forward*) as my father shall specify—

GOBBO   He hath a great infection, sir, as one would say, to serve—

LAUNCELOT (*stepping ahead again*)   Indeed the short and the long is, I serve the Jew, and have a desire, (*again shy, pushes the father ahead*) as my father shall specify—

GOBBO   His master and he, saving your worship's reverence, are scarce cater-cousins—

LAUNCELOT (*impatiently stepping forward*)   To be brief, the very truth is that the Jew, having done me wrong, doth cause me, (*again shy, pushing the father ahead*) as my father being, I hope, an old man, shall fructify unto you—

GOBBO   I have here a dish of doves that I would bestow upon your worship, and my suit is—

LAUNCELOT (*again forward*)   In very brief, the suit is impertinent to myself, (*again pushing the father ahead*) as your worship shall know by this honest old man; and, though I say it, though old man, yet poor man, my father.

(*Finally* BASSANIO *breaks the pattern by demanding*)

BASSANIO   One speak for both. What would you?

LAUNCELOT   Serve you, sir.

2. ACTING PLAUTINE FARCE. In a scene of misunderstanding and deception from Plautus' *The Merchant* the dialogue is rapid give and take. Lysimachus, in his wife's absence, has agreed to keep a blonde in the house for

his neighbor. His wife, Dora, has come back unexpectedly and has gone into the house.

LYSIMACHUS (*to himself*) It was bad enough that Demipho's in love, without his being a spendthrift too. I thought he'd go wild in planning the dinner. All for that little blonde. I'm glad I insisted on ordering the food myself. But it must be time for the caterer to get here with the food. But who's that coming out of my house? I'll just step over here and watch.

DORA (*coming out, in great distress, to herself*) There never was a more wretched woman than I, to be married to such a man. To think that's the man I trusted, that I brought ten talents dowry to! To think that I should endure such an insult!

LYS (*aside*) Good lord, I'm done for! My wife's come back from the country and I suppose she's seen the girl in the house. But I can't hear what she's saying. I'll move up closer.

DORA Heavens help me.

LYS (*aside*) No, help me!

DORA I'm ruined.

LYS I'm the one ruined. She has seen her. The gods damn you, Demipho.

DORA So that's why my husband didn't want to come to the country.

LYS Nothing to do now but go up and speak to her. (*Walking up very gay and casual*) Your husband bids his wife good day. Have our country folk become citified?

DORA (*savagely*) They act more decently than those who don't become countrified!

LYS (*pretending not to understand*) The country folk haven't done anything wrong, have they?

DORA Not nearly so much as the city folk, and they're not piling up nearly so much trouble for themselves either!

LYS Why, what wrong have the city folk done?

DORA You ask me! (*Suddenly*) Who's that woman in there?

LYS (*innocently*) Oh—have you seen her?

DORA Yes, I have!

LYS And you want to know—who she is?

DORA Yes, and I'll find out too.

LYS You want me to tell—who she is—she's—she's—

DORA You're stuck!

LYS (*aside*) Never a man more so.

DORA Why don't you tell me—

LYS Why, if you'd let me—

DORA You can't tell me.

LYS You interrupt me so. You jump on me as if I were guilty.

DORA No. You're not guilty. I've caught you in the act.

LYS What act? She's the girl who—

DORA The girl who—what?

LYS She's—

DORA Don't you know who she is?

LYS Oh, yes, I remember now. There was a case on her, and I've been made a referee.

DORA A referee? So that's why you have to get in a huddle with her!

LYS   No, it's this way. She's been left with me for safekeeping.

DORA   Oh, you're keeping her?

LYS   No, no, no, no. It's not what you think.

DORA   You're very quick with denials, aren't you?

LYS   This is too much for me. I'm stuck.

(*Enter* CATERER *with* ATTENDANTS *carrying baskets of provisions.*)

CATERER   (*to* ATTENDANTS)   Come on there, hurry up, you! We've got to cook dinner for a lovesick old man. But on second thought, if he's lovesick he'll be so busy gazing, hugging, kissing, he'll be eating her up, and we will have lots left over to carry home. Oh, there's the fellow who hired us.

LYS   Good God, here's the caterer.

CATERER   (*coming up to him*)   Here we are.

LYS   Go away!

CAT   What, go away?

LYS   Hush, get out!

CAT   Aren't you going to dine?

LYS   I'm fed up already.

DORA   I say there, did these men who are having you act as referee order all this too?

CAT   Is this your mistress, the one you told me you were in love with when you ordered the food?

LYS   Shut up!

CAT   (*looking her over*)   A fine figure of a woman. She's a little old, though.

LYS   Go to the devil.

CAT   Oh, she's all right if you like 'em old.

LYS   Well, you're all wrong.

CAT   (*trying to make up for his disparaging remark*)   I'm sure she's dandy in bed.

LYS   Won't you get out? I'm not the fellow who hired you.

CAT   What's that? Oh, yes, indeed you are—the very one.

LYS   (*aside*)   God help me.

CAT   Your wife's in the country, and you said you hated her like a snake.

LYS   I told you that?

CAT   Yes, indeed, you told me.

LYS   (*to* DORA)   So help me God, I never said that. (*With a meaningful wink to* CAT)   My dear wife.

DORA   Why deny it? It's plain as day you hate me.

LYS   Of course I deny it.

CAT   (*to* DORA)   No, no, he didn't say he hated you, but his wife. He said his wife was in the country.

LYS   (*low to* CAT)   This is she. Why are you such a nuisance?

CAT   Because you said you didn't know me. Don't you want to try my cooking?

LYS   No.

CAT   Give me my wages then.

LYS   Come back tomorrow, you'll get them. Now get out.

DORA   Lord help me.

LYS   Now I'm learning the truth of that old proverb: It's bad business to have a bad neighbor.

CAT   I know what you want. You want me to get out of here, don't you?

LYS   Yes, indeed.

CAT   We'll go. But give me my pay.

LYS   You'll get it. Can't you stop being a nuisance?

CAT   (*to helpers*)   Come on, set the food down at the foot of the old fellow. We'll be back—after the utensils—tomorrow. (*Running, chased by* LYS)

LYS   (*hesitating, sweetly*)   Perhaps you wonder about that caterer—why he came—and brought all—well, I'll tell you—

DORA   I don't wonder at any of your disgraceful and ruinous actions. I won't put up with it—to be married, like this, and have whores taken into the house. Syra, go and ask my father, in my name, to come back here with you.

SYRA   Yes, ma'am. (*She goes out.*)

LYS   (*desperately*)   Please, my dear, you don't understand at all. I'll swear a solemn oath that I never had anything to do with—has Syra left already? (DORA *stalks into the house.*) God damn it. Now *she's* gone. Oh dear, oh dear. May all the devils in hell ruin you, neighbor, with your mistress and love life too! He's overwhelmed me with the most unfair suspicions and stirred up my house against me. And my wife has a fierce temper. I'll go to the market and tell Demipho that I'll drag that girl out into the street by the hair, unless he takes her off somewhere from my house. (*Calling into the house*) Oh, Dorippa, even though you're mad with me, you'll have these provisions taken inside, if you're smart. We'll have a better dinner on them by and by.

SUGGESTED READING

PLAYS

Three good fantastic satires of Aristophanes are *The Frogs* (405 B.C.), about a contest between Aeschylus and Euripides, *Lysistrata* (411 B.C.), about stopping a war, and *The Birds* (414 B.C.), about starting a Utopia on a new planet. W. S. Gilbert and Arthur Sullivan wrote musical satires on the institutions of their day: *Pinafore* (1878) and *The Mikado* (1885). The best modern satire in the same spirit is the take-off on presidential elections, *Of Thee I Sing* (1931), by George S. Kaufman, Morris Ryskind, and George Gershwin. The social satire is lighter in *Finian's Rainbow* (1947) by E. Y. Harburg, Fred Saidy, and Burton Lane. Without music, Bernard Shaw satirizes international affairs in *Geneva* (1938).

The Merchant and *The Menaechmi* can introduce Plautus. The latter play was adapted by Shakespeare as *The Comedy of Errors* (1592–94). *The Taming of the Shrew* (1594) is mostly farce, and Shakespeare put low-comedy scenes in all his romantic comedies. Molière is almost pure farce in *The Doctor in Spite of Himself* (1666) and *Scapin* (1671). Good farcical scenes are mixed with romance and some high comedy in Oliver Goldsmith, *She Stoops to Conquer* (1773). Two lively nineteenth-century French farces have held the stage—Eugène Labiche, *The Italian Straw Hat,* and Georges Feydeau, *Hotel Paradise*—and Brendon Thomas' English school farce, *Charley's Aunt,* is played almost as often as it was in the 1890s.

262   The twentieth century has had many excellent farces. The nineteenth-century

continental tradition is given greater richness of characterization in Jean Anouilh, *The Waltz of the Toreadors* (1951), and Thornton Wilder, *The Merchant of Yonkers* (1940), revised as *The Matchmaker* (1953) and as the musical *Hello, Dolly!* (1963). Between the wars farce caught the harsh, wisecracking mood of America in J. C. Holm and George Abbott, *Three Men on a Horse* (1935), and John Murray and Allen Boretz, *Room Service* (1938), and especially in the plays of George S. Kaufman and his many collaborators. With Marc Connelly, Kaufman wrote *June Moon* (1927), and with Moss Hart, *Once in a Lifetime* (1930) and *You Can't Take It with You* (1936). Two of the best broad farces of the postwar period are *Mister Roberts* (1948), by Joshua Logan and Thomas Heggen, and *The Teahouse of the August Moon* (1953), by John Patrick. In the 1960s, on Broadway and on the television screen, some of the best farces have concerned the personal squabbles of young couples: Neil Simon, *Barefoot in the Park* (1963) and *The Odd Couple* (1965); Bill Manhoff, *The Owl and the Pussycat* (1964); Murray Schisgal, *Luv* (1964). These Broadway comedies have such wry characters and verbal wit that they might be called high comedies rather than farces.

CRITICAL WORKS

Several recent anthologies collect essays on comedy. Paul Lauter, *Theories of Comedy** (1964), covers past and present. Robert W. Corrigan, *Comedy: Meaning and Form** (1965), has modern essays and a good selective bibliography. For both essays and plays, see J. C. Enck, Elizabeth T. Porter, and A. Whitley, *The Comic in Theory and Practice** (1960), and Marvin Felheim, *Comedy: Plays, Theory and Criticism** (1962).

Stage comedy is related to age-old social forms of comedy—jesters, buffoons, etc.—in Enid Welsford, *The Fool: His Social and Literary History** (1935).

A philosophical theory of comedy as affirming the ideal by making fun of the actual is developed by James K. Feibleman in *In Praise of Comedy* (1939) and in a chapter, "The Meaning of Comedy," in *Aesthetics* (1949). Arthur Koestler relates humor to discovery and to science and tragedy in both *Insight and Outlook* (1949) and *The Act of Creation* (1964).

Two authors relate comedy to the rhythm of the seasons and the vital processes: Northrop Frye, "The Mythos of Spring: Comedy," in *The Anatomy of Criticism** (1957), and Susanne Langer, "The Comic Rhythm," in *Feeling and Form** (1965). Both chapters are reprinted in Corrigan's *Comedy*, mentioned above.

Anyone who deals with the films of Charlie Chaplin gets into a discussion of the perennial satisfaction of comedy. Especially good are Theodore Huff, *Charlie Chaplin* (1951), Robert Payne, *The Great God Pan** (1952), Al Capp, "The Comedy of Charlie Chaplin," *Atlantic Monthly*, CLXXXV (Feb., 1950), and Gilbert Seldes, "Here Today," a chapter in *The Seven Lively Arts* (1957). Chaplin's personal account, *My Autobiography* (1964), is excellent. Among other personal accounts are Buster Keaton, *My Wonderful World of Slapstick* (1960), and Harpo Marx and Rowland Barber, *Harpo Speaks* (1961).

Among the many books on the *commedia dell' arte*, the most authoritative and best illustrated are Allardyce Nicoll, *Masks, Mimes and Miracles* (1931) and *Harlequin* (1964). The influence on Shakespeare and English drama is studied in K. M. Lea, *Italian Popular Comedy*, 2 vols. (1934).

* Available in paperback edition.

The relation of satire to comedy is discussed in many places. An important historical study is O. J. Campbell, *Shakespeare's Satire* (1943). The best treatment of the theory of low comedy as due to conflict between vitality and a mechanical pattern is by Henri Bergson in a series of essays *On Laughter* (1900), reprinted in Wylie Sypher, *Comedy** (1956).

Eric Bentley defends farce as an attack on rigid institutions, especially marriage, in "The Psychology of Farce," in *Let's Get a Divorce and Other Plays** (1958), and in a chapter on farce in *The Life of the Drama* (1964). Some of the devices for giving farce a comic effect are discussed in George R. Kernodle, "Excruciatingly Funny; or, the 47 Keys to Comedy," *Theatre Arts* (1946).

* Available in paperback edition.

SUGGESTED READING

CHAPTER EIGHT

THE THEATRE OF LAUGHTER: HIGH COMEDY

Comedy is not limited to the antics of farce or to the enchanted dreams of romance: it can also create a vision of well-dressed people matching wits and exploring human relations in a world of fashion and sophistication. In this drawing-room comedy, business deals are made, political intrigues are sketched, plots are foiled, rivals are outdistanced, opponents are won over, friendships are made or lost, secret scandals are revealed, liaisons and marriages are arranged—all kinds of exciting situations develop through the witty conversations and wily maneuvers of urbane, charming people who are enjoying themselves and the social game immensely. In actual life, at any social level, conversation is usually one-sided, overweighted with trivia, halting, disconnected, and dull, but in high comedy every line sparkles as it hits the mark precisely in the constant excitement of retort and repartee. Where farce shows a young man bursting the bonds of restraint or a harried secretary scurrying to cover her traces before her little adventures or irregularities are found out, where romantic comedy shows an idealistic young man dedicating himself to his glamorous lady and his distant goal, high comedy shows an experienced adult picking his way skillfully and confidently among the pitfalls of a complex social world and remaining an individual while outwardly conforming to the expectations of the group.

The Social Game

One of man's greatest ambitions, often the reason he works hard for money or fame, is to be accepted in society, to "arrive," to know the language and manners of the inside group. After the adolescent has freed himself from his parents (the subject of countless farces) and has established his independence, with at least a minimum of financial and professional security, he is ready to find his role in social gatherings where he will hear not only casual gossip but comment on everything from current fashion and human behavior to the latest developments in institutions and ideas. Much high comedy is concerned with the social education of the old as well as the young as both learn, through their mistakes, to meet the difficulties of human relations, sometimes even to laugh at themselves. It is no wonder that several high comedies have been called "school"—*School for Husbands, School for Wives, School for Scandal.* Voltaire called Molière's comedy a "school for civilization." The steps of Eliza's education are carefully drawn in Shaw's *Pygmalion* and even more thoroughly in the musical *My Fair Lady,* as she learns not only the language of society but the subtle art of responding to the expectations of others.

High comedy shows people antagonizing one another, disagreeing yet somehow coming to terms. *Other* people are impossible. They presume to differ from us, yet we must live in the same world with them. They are respectable neighbors, or parents or brothers or sisters, sometimes even wives and hus-

FIGURE *8.1* High comedy. Strong conflicts become part of a social game in elegant, upper-class surroundings. Coward's *Present Laughter.* New York, 1946. Photo Vandamm.

bands. In actual life, a problem in human relations may be insoluble; but in high comedy, a few people manage, by wit and contrivance, to get part of what they want and, by smiles and patience and some sublimation of anger, to find zest in the game. They learn to be adults.

Society is the basis for high comedy, not only as drama but as a point of view. It is assumed not only that man is a gregarious animal but that his full development is social. Society has always insisted that christenings, initiations, weddings, and funerals are public events and has often even taken part in the wedding night with some kind of "shivaree." The social group establishes the norm of behavior, and the social roles—leader or clown, intruder or tyrant, exhibitionist or cry baby—or the subtle adjustments of changing roles shape the individual in his relations in the group.

Civilized society does not exist until women take part in it freely as equals of men. A mixed society adds warmth to intellectual discussion and permits the impersonal appreciation of the opposite sex. In the theatre, high comedy did not develop until women became important as characters, until Molière and Shakespeare brought them in to confront men, outwit them in deception, and stand up to them in pride and independence. Ever since Congreve's women set a classic precedent in laying down the law to their men, playwrights have put a proud, independent woman at the center of nearly every high comedy.

Unlike romance, where the woman waits for the man to pursue, high comedy allows the woman to go after the man. The most famous pursuer is Ann Whitefield, Shaw's heroine in *Man and Superman,* a modern version of the Don Juan story commented on in Chapter 1. Although Shaw's Don Juan, Jack Tanner, is attracted by Ann, he is afraid that she represents the blind "Life Force," ready to engulf him and stifle his brain in order to get the race continued. He strives frantically to keep his independence. "It is a woman's business," he says, "to get married as soon as possible, and a man's to keep unmarried as long as possible." He will not give up his independence of mind or his life purpose, and only when his dream of Don Juan in hell assures him that partnership in marriage will indulge his mind and serve his purpose does he give in to Ann.

In this play as in *Major Barbara* and many other plays, Shaw moves from personal crisis to wider social, political, or philosophical implications. Several plays of S. N. Behrman, written during the serious decade of the 1930s, are also concerned with important political and social issues. The heroine of *Biography,* a highly successful portrait painter, falls in love with the radical young reporter who is writing her biography, but she still cherishes an affection for the man from her home town with whom she once had an affair and who is now a very conservative senator. In the end she reluctantly but firmly rejects both men and their causes, for although she is interested in social problems, she is sure that the individual self and particular relationships are more important than the ideas and institutions that serve mankind. The young radical, who would sacrifice himself and any immediate relationship for his cause, cannot understand how this charming woman can tolerate people whose

267

FIGURE *8.2* Thoughtful laughter. Complex human relations are involved with love, death, art, and medicine. Shaw's *The Doctor's Dilemma,* with Katharine Cornell and Raymond Massey. New York, 1941. Photo Vandamm.

ideas she knows to be wrong. Her tolerance of people with whom she cannot agree, even when her feelings are deeply involved, is characteristic of other high-comedy heroines. Constance, the clear-eyed heroine of W. Somerset Maugham's *The Constant Wife* (1927), does not break up her marriage when she learns that her husband is having an affair with her best friend, although she is hurt. She even saves her friend from discovery by the friend's husband. And she says to her, "I think you a liar, a humbug, and a parasite, but I like you."

Where romance creates a union by the sacrifice of self, high comedy allows each character to keep his individuality. Shaw put the necessity for independence in explicit terms in one of his later plays, *The Apple Cart* (1929). King Magnus finds that his mistress is not satisfied with being at the edge of his life. It is the male this time who insists on a proper distance as absolutely essential to good relations. He says to his mistress:

> Do not let us fall into the common mistake of expecting to become one flesh and one spirit. Every star has its own orbit; and between it and its neighbor there is not only a powerful attraction but an infinite distance. When the attraction becomes stronger than the distance the two do not embrace: they crash together in ruins. We two also have our orbits, and must keep an infinite distance between us to avoid a disastrous collision. Keeping our distance is the whole secret of good manners; and without good manners human society is intolerable and impossible.

Attraction, good manners, independence—to keep these three in balance at a proper distance requires a high skill in the social game. In some encounters the game requires a mask, a protective disguise that disarms the opponent by covering the hostility in a smile. One of the most famous scenes of charming hostility is the garden scene in Oscar Wilde's *The Importance of Being Earnest* (1895), in which the two girls who think they are engaged to the same man slug it out with more devastating blows than a prizefighter ever landed. They never lose the smile that keeps communication open or the

268

Kinds of Plays

elaborate phrase that keeps it on a generalized level, above the particular or personal. When the city girl praises the garden, she adds, "I had no idea there were any flowers in the country." That gives the country girl a chance. "Oh, flowers are as common here, Miss Fairfax, as people are in London." Gwendolyn attacks again: "Personally, I cannot understand how anybody manages to exist in the country, if anybody who is anybody does. The country always bores me to death." But Cecily is ready to answer with "Oh, that is what the newspapers call agricultural depression, is it not? I believe the aristocracy are suffering very much from it just at present. It is almost an epidemic amongst them, I have been told. May I offer you some tea?"

When that protective mask is turned not toward other people but toward fate, it becomes a mask of irony. Ironic acceptance is implied in many common phrases—"Isn't that just like him?" "That's me all over." "We had it coming." "Here we go again."—and acceptance is one step toward transcending fate. In *The Second Man* (1927), S. N. Behrman sets his urbane young man, Storey, in contrast to an overserious girl, Monica, who for a moment forces him to be serious, to plan to give up his frivolity and write about suffering. But his ebullient spirit protests.

> STOREY   You're a victim of the popular prejudice in favor of agony. Why is a book about unhappy, dirty people better than one about gay and comfortable ones?
> MONICA   But life *isn't* gay—or comfortable.
> STOREY   (*seriously*)   Dear darling, life is sad. I know it's sad. But I think it's gallant to pretend that it isn't.

Irony makes each incident less grim by admitting that all life is grim.

But protection is the negative side of high comedy, the necessary but grim discipline of a sense of humor. High comedy also offers positive joys. The hard masks dissolve into our own live faces as we learn to play a game with other people, with ourselves, and with the world.

One of the delights in high comedy is to make a game of "the others." Instead of masking hostility, tease the fools, draw them out. It helps them find harmless ways of indulging their foolishness, and they may even begin to see their faults and follies. George Meredith thought that the function of the "Comic Spirit" was to correct the faults of mankind, but through gentle laughter, without the "pain of satiric heat" or the "bitter craving to strike heavy blows." In *An Essay on Comedy,* he wrote of this Comic Spirit as a "sunlight of the mind."

> If you believe that our civilization is founded in common sense (and it is the first condition of sanity to believe it), you will, when contemplating men, discern a Spirit over head. . . . Whenever they wax out of proportion, overblown, affected, pretentious, bombastical, hypocritical, pedantic, fantastically delicate; whenever it sees them self-deceived or hoodwinked, given to run riot in idolatries, drifting into vanities, congregating in absurdities, planning shortsightedly, plotting dementedly; whenever they are at variance with their professions, and violate the unwritten but perceptible laws binding them in consideration one to another; whenever they offend

FIGURE 8.3 Love as a game of both conflict and attraction. Gertrude Lawrence and Noel Coward in Coward's *Private Lives*. New York, 1931. Photo Vandamm.

sound reason, fair justice; are false in humility or mined with conceit, individually, or in the bulk—the Spirit overhead will look humanely malign and cast an oblique light on them, followed by volleys of silvery laughter. That is the Comic Spirit.

The second joy of high comedy is to laugh at oneself, a very hard thing to do. If the romantic Cyrano had had one touch of humor, the tragedy would have been avoided and he would have had his love. But a romantic cannot laugh at himself, nor can he endure being laughed at. Such acceptance takes the self-knowledge of maturity, confidence in being an individual able to play a role in society. We shall see how Sir Peter Teazle in *The School for Scandal* accepts his situation and laughs.

The third joy of high comedy depends on disillusionment, a full awareness of the limitations of man's existence. Louis Kronenberger says in *The Thread of Laughter:* "Comedy is always jarring us with the evidence that we are no better than other people, and always comforting us with the knowledge that most other people are no better than we are. It makes us more critical but it leaves us more tolerant; and to that extent it performs a very notable social function." In high comedy, disillusionment brings a triumph of balance, spanning the inner and the outer, the self and the others, independence and relationship, self-regard and friendship or love.

A good modern variation of the triumph that turns irony and acceptance into a more positive game is the conclusion of *The Constant Wife*. After Constance has forgiven her husband for his affair with her friend, she discovers that she wants to spend six weeks in Italy with a man who still adores her. She frankly tells her husband her plan, smiles as he has to say goodbye

Kinds of Plays

politely to the man he knows is going with her, and takes her own gay farewell.

JOHN   Do you think I'm going to take you back?

CONSTANCE   I don't see why not. When you've had time to reflect you'll realize that you have no reason to blame me. After all, I'm taking from you nothing that you want.

JOHN   Are you aware that I can divorce you for this?

CONSTANCE   Quite. But I married very prudently. I took the precaution to marry a gentleman and I know that you could never bring yourself to divorce me for doing no more than you did yourself.

JOHN   I wouldn't divorce you. I wouldn't expose my worst enemy to the risk of marrying a woman who is capable of treating her husband as you're treating me.

CONSTANCE   (*at the door*)   Well, then, shall I come back?

JOHN   (*after a moment's hesitation*)   You are the most maddening, willful, capricious, wrong-headed, delightful and enchanting woman a man was ever cursed with having for a wife. Yes, damn you. Come back.

The Development of High Comedy

Though there were glimpses of it in ancient comedy and in minor scenes in Shakespeare, high comedy was the achievement of the seventeenth century, the first great age that produced a *society,* a class of cultivated people with leisure time and interest to devote themselves to human relations and to

FIGURE *8.4*   A man's costume of the 1660s. With wigs, lace, ribbons, and petticoat breeches, the men who saw the beginnings of high comedy wore the most elaborate and elegant costumes in Western history.

the forms and manners that make a society possible. After a century of humanistic education, with its emphasis on classic comedy and on the social graces of good manners, eloquence, and wit, Europe was ready for attitudes of sophistication and maturity. In Paris and London, a number of men and women, gathering in the salons, at the court of the king, at the coffeehouses of the town, and in the walkways of the parks, set about exploring patterns of human behavior that are urbane, subtle, complex, and civilized. They created a new concept of ladies and gentlemen and produced a new kind of comedy.

Like the twentieth century, the seventeenth century was trying to achieve a sane, comic view of life in a period of shattering disillusion. For more than a century, religious wars had devastated France, Germany, and England, until everyone was weary of fanaticism and ready to try to achieve toleration and stability. Peace came to Germany in 1648. In England, Charles I was beheaded in 1649, but the Commonwealth lasted only a decade and Charles II was brought back in 1660. In France the absolute authority of the king was established by the 1650s, and Molière began his brilliant but short career in acting and writing in 1658. Equally disturbing as the changes in the political world were those in trade, science, and astronomy. The new astronomy

FIGURE *8.5*   Two scenes of comic deception from an early edition of Molière. A servant masquerades as a nobleman in *The Ridiculous Young Ladies,* and a young girl and her suitor deceive the old guardian in *The School for Husbands.*

LES PRECIEUSES RIDICULES

L'ESCOLE
DES
MARIS

of Copernicus and Galileo, while it made the scientific approach possible, discredited the old picture of man as the center of God's universe and the focus of his interest. While the expanding trade of a new capitalism had freed many people from the secure but limiting patterns of the medieval trade guilds, it had also left many stranded and made others cynical about a world in which human values had the uncertain freedom of the marketplace, and friendship, love, and trust became gambles.

It is no accident that modern science and the new comedy came to birth at the same time. Both required a detachment—a separation of man as objective observer from man involved in his subjective values of belief, feelings, and ethics. That detachment grew out of the painful and disillusioning recognition of multiplicity in the world: Christian and pagan philosophy, many suns in the skies, several continents across the seas, several religions side by side. The first reaction was bitterness and anguish, much like the bitterness and anguish of the twentieth century. We have noticed how that anguish found expression in Shakespeare's *Hamlet* and *King Lear*. At the same time, comedy explored gaiety in detachment. Shakespeare's clowns caught that gaiety in a form we can still enjoy, while the masked comedians of the *commedia dell' arte* made Pantalone, Harlequin, and Pulcinella popular in both court and town. By the virtuosity of their singing, dancing, acrobatic acting, broad slapstick, and witty repartee, they taught Europe to laugh at confusion.

It was Shakespeare's friend Ben Jonson who found a literary form for the new laughter. His disillusionment was bitter and cynical, but he took the first steps toward a comedy of acceptance as well as of satire. His *Volpone* (1606) presents a monstrous old schemer who bleeds his acquaintances of money and gifts by pretending to be about to die. They deserve their losses because, in trying to curry favor with him in hopes of being named heir, they are as unscrupulous as he. Jonson created laughter out of the wild competition among monsters of viciousness. It remained for the middle of the century to achieve a better balance. Though not expecting any more of human nature than Jonson, the later generation learned to accept the fact that man is an earthbound creature and to look on fools with indulgent laughter.

THE ACHIEVEMENT OF MOLIÈRE

Where Jonson was bitter, Molière was urbane. He showed plenty of fanatics completely devoted to their monstrous obsessions, and young people who with much ado eventually get around these fanatics, but what was low-comedy intrigue in Plautus here becomes more complex and subtle. In Rome, the clownish servants had to trick the old fathers, but in Molière the deception, usually played with affection and kindness, becomes a game of juggling with the basic illusions of life. The Miser will have his children marry only for money, the Bourgeois Gentleman only for title, Orgon in *Tartuffe* only for piety, the Imaginary Invalid only to bring a doctor into the family. Each one is fooled by his own obsession, held rigid in a kind of mask.

Molière brought interesting women into his farcical plays—wily old housekeepers or matchmakers—to trick the old men when necessary but also to

FIGURE 8.6 Complex farcical action raised to the level of wit. The costumes and settings of the seventeenth century are simplified for a modern college stage. Molière's *The School for Husbands*. University of Michigan production, directed by Hugh G. Norton, designed by Ralph W. Duckwall, Jr., and costumed by Zelma Weisfeld. Photo Ouradnik.

shake some sense into both old and young when their contentions passed all bounds. The Miser can be teased and indulged and led along by his obsession. The Imaginary Invalid is deceived not by a simple lie but by elaborate indulgence in his concern with his health: his brother and the able housekeeper arrange to have him initiated as a doctor, so that he can prescribe for himself. They win more freedom not only for the young couple but for the old man by freeing him from his fears and his foolish dependence on doctors.

The young girl also becomes much more important in Molière than she had been in earlier comedy. In Plautus she was merely the prize for the young man or his servant when they had got around the old man; sometimes she did not even come on stage. But Molière often told the story from her point of view and made her the active schemer. In *The School for Husbands* (1661) the young girl makes her jealous old guardian carry messages to her young man, and in *The School for Wives* (1662) the ingenue and her sweetheart tell the helpless guardian frankly how they are deceiving him. The scenes are just as funny as any classic farce scenes, but the women add variety and complexity and a light touch in the teasing that moves the plays toward high comedy. In several plays Molière set his couples quarreling; in *Tartuffe* (1664) the quarrel is over how to escape the father's plans to marry the girl to the pious fraud, Tartuffe. Finally, in *The Misanthrope* (1666) Molière moved fully into high comedy and did not bother to include the low-comedy scenes on which the other plays depend for much of the fun. Where his lovers had previously been grown children still struggling with repressive parents

274

Kinds of Plays

or wives with narrow-minded husbands, here he presents an adult couple, free from all restrictions, exploring human relations with other free adults. In the decade of the most elegant costumes and wigs, a lively, coquettish young woman, Célimène, is the center of attraction of many beaux, with whom she points out, in malicious character sketches, the shortcomings of their friends. With triumphant wit, she outdoes her smiling rival in double-edged attack. In the Richard Wilbur translation she speaks thus of a gathering at which her rival was much criticized:

> Of course, I said to everybody there
> That they were being viciously unfair,
> But still they were disposed to criticize you
> And all agreed that someone should advise you
> To leave the morals of the world alone,
> And worry rather more about your own.
> They felt that one's self-knowledge should be great
> Before one thinks of setting others straight.

The overhonest man, Alceste, who falls in love with her, objects violently to her enjoyment of the social group. Unable to see that his own obsession with sincerity is a fault, he despises flattery and even politeness. The girl refuses, at the age of twenty, to leave society and go off to a desert with him. They separate forever, unable to find a workable relationship.

FIGURE *8.7*   A stylish modern production of Molière. The setting is based on three-dimensional Renaissance wings and painted backdrop. Molière's *The School for Husbands*. New York, 1933. Designed by Lee Simonson. Photo Vandamm.

THE GOLDEN AGE OF HIGH COMEDY

Molière was a pioneer in the intricate paths of high comedy, but it remained for the witty playwrights of Restoration London, writing for a small group of sophisticates, to achieve the full realization of high comedy in the union of two proud and independent people. In their plays, the comic crudeness of the unsophisticated characters and the comic silliness of the fops and giddy women are foils for the maturity of one central couple who learn to play the roles of free, well-adjusted adults, discarding their masks of hostility and caution for the joys of love and partnership.

The characters in Restoration comedy begin where most of Molière's couples end, free from family restraints. They expect to forget their serious political and economic affairs and devote their wit and their leisure to the game of human relations. That game includes gossip and a great deal of discussion of social behavior as well as intrigue and flirtation. To most Victorian readers and playgoers these gallants and ladies seemed artificial, if not downright wicked, but a few nineteenth-century writers defended them just because they were free from such important matters as morality and duty. Charles Lamb pictured the characters of Restoration comedy in a "Utopia of gallantry," removed from all responsibility, and William Hazlitt grew ecstatic about their sparkling uselessness:

> Happy age, when kings and nobles led purely ornamental lives; when the utmost stretch of a morning's study went no further than the choice of a sword-knot, or the adjustment of a side curl; when the soul spoke out in all the pleasing elegance of dress; and beaux and belles, enamoured of them-

FIGURE 8.8   Comedy on the Restoration stage. A forestage almost as large as the Elizabethan stage was combined with Italian perspective scenery of wings and backdrop. Candles and oil lamps lit the audience almost as much as the actors. Notice the music box above the proscenium. Drawn by Ethelyn Pauley and Martha Sutherland.

FIGURE 8.9 Costumes for the famous 1936 revival of Wycherley's *The Country Wife* in London and New York. The wigs and costumes made the men more showy than the women. Ruth Gordon played Mrs. Pinchwife. Photo Vandamm.

selves in one another's follies, fluttered like gilded butterflies in giddy mazes through the walks of St. James's park!

The early twentieth century called the Restoration period an artificial society because it enjoyed dressing up, showing off, and expressing both love and hate with politeness and wit. Presumably it is more natural and honest in the twentieth century to be churlish and ill-mannered. The 1920s praised Restoration comedy because it was naughty and disillusioned and made fun of the puritans, taking special delight in the rough escapades of William Wycherley's *The Country Wife* (1675), with its double-entendres and gleeful leers. The mid-twentieth century is not much disturbed by the naughtiness and, on the contrary, finds in the best plays of Etherege, Congreve, and Sheridan an important and subtle study of the complex relationships of men and women. The fact of sex is taken for granted, as an easy relationship. The best Restoration plays are richly concerned with the more difficult relations that involve the ego.

The first fully developed hero of Restoration comedy, Dorimant in Sir George Etherege's *The Man of Mode* (1676), is sampling the casual relations of sex, insisting on freedom and variety only because he is determined eventually to find someone who is not so casual. When one mistress tries to hold him by his vows of love, he casts her off with indignant irony, saying, "Constancy, at my years! You might as well expect the fruit the autumn ripens in the spring . . . youth has a long journey to go, madam: should I have set up my rest at the first inn I lodged at I should never have arrived at the happiness I now enjoy." Only when he meets a woman as proud and independent as he is does he think of prolonged faithfulness. The cynical mood of that age, not too different from our own, is expressed in one of Congreve's songs which ends:

The Theatre of Laughter

He alone won't betray in whom none will confide.
And the nymph may be chaste that has never been tried.

In such an atmosphere there would seem little hope of finding a woman of wit and spirit who could interest a man for a lifetime. But the dramatists created a vision of such a woman—rich, independent, proud, sophisticated, but untouched by the shallowness around her. She knows nothing is certain and still she has faith. William Congreve's Angelica in *Love for Love* (1695) accepts the world as it is and revels in the joy of the game. She insists, "Would anything but a madman complain of uncertainty? Uncertainty and expectation are the joys of life. Security is an insipid thing, and the overtaking and possessing of a wish, discovers the folly of the chase . . . the pleasure of a masquerade is done when we come to show our faces."

Love between two proud, intelligent, independent people is bound to be difficult; and a great many of the best scenes of comedy, from Shakespeare's Katherine and Petruchio and Beatrice and Benedict to the couples in *Oklahoma!* and *My Fair Lady,* are built on antagonism that is both exasperating and enjoyable. Congreve gave his most famous couple, Millamant and Mirabell of *The Way of the World* (1700), several encounters where gaiety ripples in the very words and rhythm of the scene. Millamant changes her tactics from the lively to the serious at a moment's notice and leaves Mirabell with a flippant "When you have done thinking of that, think of me"—to which he can only reply with a sigh of vexation, "Think of you . . . think of a whirlwind . . . a fellow that lives in a windmill has not a more whimsical dwelling than the heart of a man that is lodged in a woman." But he accepts the fact that she is unpredictable and eventually finds that her follies are "so natural, or so artful, that they become her." Before they will consent to become husband and wife, this couple insist on a clear understanding that they shall keep some self-respect and independence. Their famous "proviso" scene is a Magna Carta of human rights in married life. Millamant speaks ironically of those rights as "trifles," such as

> . . . liberty to pay and receive visits to and from whom I please: to write and receive letters without interrogatories or wry faces on your part: to wear what I please: and choose conversation with regard to my own taste: to have no obligation upon me to converse with wits that I don't like because they are your acquaintances: or to be intimate with fools only because they may be your relations. Come to dinner when I please, dine in my dressing room when I'm out of humor, without giving a reason. To have my closet inviolate: to be sole empress of my tea-table, which you must never presume to approach without first asking leave. And lastly wherever I am you shall always knock at the door before you come in. These articles subscribed, if I continue to endure you a little longer, I may by degrees dwindle into a wife.

Millamant is sure that the best way of keeping a love fresh and lasting is to avoid childish display of affection. She will have no pet names:

> I shall never bear that—good Mirabell don't let us be familiar or fond, nor kiss before folks, like my Lady Fadler and Sir Francis; nor go to Hyde

Kinds of Plays

FIGURE *8.10* A painted backdrop for a scene in the park for the 1936 revival of Wycherley's *The Country Wife*. The actors are on the shallow forestage next to the footlights, with chandeliers above. Directed by Tyrone Guthrie and Gilbert Miller and designed by Oliver Messel. Photo Vandamm.

FIGURE *8.11* A painted backdrop for a street scene for the same production of Wycherley's *The Country Wife*. Photo Vandamm.

FIGURE 8.12   High comedy in an eighteenth-century theatre. Most of the acting was done on the forestage in front of the painted wings and backdrop. Candelabra kept the fashionable audience brightly lighted. The screen scene from Sheridan's *The School for Scandal*. Drury Lane Theatre, 1777. Drawn by Richard Leacroft. Courtesy of Methuen and Co., Ltd., London.

Park together the first Sunday in a new chariot, to provoke eyes and whispers; and then never be seen there together again: as if we were proud of one another the first week, and ashamed of one another ever after. Let us never visit together, nor go to a play together, but let us be very strange and well bred: let us be as strange as if we had been married a great while; and as well bred as if we were not married at all.

If on the page Millamant seems cruel and cold, Dame Edith Evans' recording of scenes from the play shows how sparkling and warm and affectionate she can be, even as she is clear-eyed and calm in the knowledge that all relations are fleeting and that all joy in love depends on the playful imagination to keep up the spirits.

The most famous stage duelists in love are Sir Peter and Lady Teazle in Richard Brinsley Sheridan's *The School for Scandal* (1777). One of their two quarrels is given almost complete in Exercise 4 (pp. 286–88). For all Lady Teazle's high spirits, she is very fond of her gruff old husband, and for all that he gets furious with her, he finds her irresistible when her fiery temper is up. Worsted in the battle, he has thoroughly enjoyed it. "There is great satisfaction in quarreling with her," he says, "and I think she never appears to such advantage as when she is doing everything in her power to plague me." Like his descendant in high comedy, Henry Higgins, Sir Peter has much to learn in order to be a better husband. He must learn a little humility and gain a sense of humor. He does finally laugh at himself in one of the funniest scenes in the play. When he has discovered his wife behind a screen in the rooms of the young man he thought perfect, he is outraged.

280

Kinds of Plays

The social gossips, of course, tease him without mercy, and he drives them from the house in a lively low-comedy scene. But when his two close friends begin to laugh at him, he cannot drive them out but must laugh at his own predicament, if grimly. After that he begins to see his wife in a new light and he forgives her. He realizes that he had expected too much of the young man—untempered idealism is dangerous. He concludes, "Sir Oliver, we live in a damned wicked world, and the fewer we praise the better."

Where the medieval poets had insisted that life must be dominated by love, the Restoration gallants insisted that life, and most of all love, must be a game. In some ways, the "game of love" can be compared to the "court of love" since both the troubadours and the Restoration wits demanded major modifications in the relations of men and women. Both shifted the emphasis from the union to the courtship, from the physical to the spiritual, from the family to the person, from blind instinct or moral duty to spontaneity and zest, from habit to choice. Both recognized that it was difficult to combine love with the duties and family and property considerations expected in marriage. Both taught that love comes first, even if marriage has to yield a little.

Yet the game of love differs radically from the court of love. Where the medieval knight put his woman on a pedestal—in a shrine to be worshipped, on Juliet's balcony, or in a distant castle window—the Restoration gallant met his woman on the level of everyday life. They were partners and, like partners in a game, also competitors, traders bargaining in an open market. Where the romantic lover is totally transformed by love, giving up his former self to the lady and to the new tasks she orders or inspires, the sophisticated lover expects a partner to enhance his individual life, giving up only enough to avoid the more violent conflicts. His love does not require that he lose his identity, and a sophisticated love must take its place as one among life's many demands and interests. The romantic attitude that promised everything on earth often led to disillusionment and despair or cynicism. The more modest, practical approach to love expects to outlast the romantic.

Even the minor characters in Restoration comedy confirm the higher ideal of love by despising an easy conquest. In Congreve's *Love for Love,* the old roué Tattle does not want to take a woman without some opposition. He finds that the young girl just arrived from the country is already too willing:

TATTLE Pooh, pox, you must not say yes already: I shan't care a farthing
  for you then in a twinkling.
MISS PRUE What must I say then?
TATTLE Why you must say no, or you believe not, or you can't tell—
MISS PRUE Why, must I lie then?
TATTLE Yes, if you'd be well bred. All well-bred persons lie. Besides you
  are a woman. You must never speak what you think: your words must
  contradict your thoughts; but your actions may contradict your words.

In the same play, the main couple, Valentine and Angelica, must find a relationship far above that level. She has no doubt that she loves him, but each time she thinks of admitting her love she is interrupted by one of the couples

FIGURE *8.13* A modern adaptation of the light forms of the eighteenth century. Instead of the authentic wings and backdrop, a free-standing screen is used with a playful treatment of eighteenth-century architectural motifs. The actors are playing a farcical situation in a comedy of manners. Goldsmith's *She Stoops to Conquer*. University of Iowa production, directed by George R. Kernodle, designed by Robert Burroughs, and costumed by Berneice Prisk.

who give in too easily. Her pride is stirred and she refuses. Valentine tries low-comedy tricks of deception, but they fail. Only when he openly risks all can he convince her that he is a good bet and get her consent. They must create their partnership in a world where nothing is certain, but that is their challenge.

AMERICAN SOCIAL COMEDY

After Sheridan in the eighteenth century, English high comedy was largely superseded by sentimental comedy and made no other notable appearance until the 1890s, when Oscar Wilde shocked and amused the public with his shrewdly witty plays, one of which, *The Importance of Being Earnest,* we have sampled. In this century, social comedy won great success in the work of W. Somerset Maugham, Noel Coward, and their followers until it seemed the characteristic form of English drama. It roused the special scorn of the absurdists and the Angry Young Men of the 1950s and 60s, who mocked its polite chatter as meaningless.

Americans have never felt completely at home in the parlor. While English and continental drawing-room comedies have found an avid audience in America, our own writers have not produced any of equal quality. Philip Barry and S. N. Behrman in the 1930s wrote the best this country has had. America lacks a tradition of leisure and cultivation as well as established lines of social classes. Our politicians, business leaders, and newspapermen, for instance, are never completely at leisure but mix their public activities with personal relations. Related traditions of social comedy in America have taken directions more satiric and more raucous than in Britain. For four decades we looked to George S. Kaufman and his several collaborators for timely, entertaining plays making lively comment on new fads and interests. We have already considered *Of Thee I Sing,* probably the best modern Aristophanic play, as a George Gershwin musical. Since we have in Moss Hart's *Act One* an account of the shaping of *Once in a Lifetime,* we can look back at the taste and attitudes—a mixture of satire and affection—felt in the 1930s toward such a phenomenon as the talking pictures. But most memorable is the lovable collection of American screwballs in *You Can't Take It with You,* first presented in 1936 and revived many times, notably on the New York stage in 1965.

Two American plays of two decades ago have achieved some qualities of high comedy in spite of their satiric sharpness. Far removed from the suave upper-class characters of drawing-room comedy is Billy Dawn, the heroine of Garson Kanin's *Born Yesterday* (1946). She was a sensation as Judy Holliday played her both on the stage and in the film, and she has been equally successful with the amateurs. She is a naive girl, cheap and vulgar, who is living with a gangster junkdealer. Yet she can learn. As a newspaper reporter takes over her education, she discovers Jefferson and Tom Paine and the whole liberal tradition of American thought and becomes a charming adult, with sense enough not only to leave her coarse brute but to trap him in his own game. She gains her independence and marries the crusading liberal

283

FIGURE *8.14* A robust American version of high comedy. Melodrama, wisecracks, and a moral concern over public affairs distinguish the American comedy. Judy Holliday and Paul Douglas in Kanin's *Born Yesterday*. New York, 1946. Photo Vandamm.

reporter. The play has the racy vigor of America and the suspense and action of melodrama. Yet it must be considered as partly high comedy. It even laughs at the heroine. Not quite at home in the vocabulary she has acquired so rapidly, she tells her gangster, "You're just not couth," and in a rousing speech declares that "this country with its institutions belongs to the people who inhibit it." But at the end she is a mature person who has passed gallantly the tests of the wider social world.

The emergence of the mature male ego is the subject of another very American comedy, *The Male Animal* (1940), by James Thurber and Elliott Nugent. The little professor, lowest of modern drudges, is alarmed when his wife shows interest in the go-getter businessman, a former football hero who returns to the campus at football time. The professor feels pushed around and humiliated, and when his dander is up he pokes his rival in the nose. But violence does no good whatever; it does not cause a heroic fight but merely starts a sinus pain. As a male animal the little man is a failure. But when the dean and the trustees denounce him because he proposes to read to his classes a letter written by the anarchist Vanzetti, he finds the courage to uphold his liberal principles in the face of the conventional crowd. He wins back his wife and his place in the community. He helps define the modern vision of the independent male, active and modest, keeping his own individuality.

The Serious Note in High Comedy

In our discussion of high comedy we have seen that there is usually an undercurrent of seriousness. High comedy on the stage draws a smile or thoughtful laughter. High-comedy characters, in fact, face the loneliness and discontinuity of existence as resolutely as the existentialists, who will be considered in the next chapter, but they would consider the whine of the exis-

284

Kinds of Plays

tentialist "anguish" very immature. They are as fully aware of death as Albert Camus, but they consider the fact of death all the more reason for enjoying life while it lasts. Molière gallantly made a game of the difficulties of his life by presenting in plays flirtatious young wives like his own and by dramatizing his own defiance of death. When very ill with tuberculosis, he wrote for himself the role of the imaginary invalid who played at being sick and pretended to be dead. Near the end of the fourth performance of the work, he had a convulsion; he finished the performance but died soon afterward. Noel Coward's gayest couple, Amanda and Elyot in *Private Lives* (1930), know that if philosophy dwells on death and despair life will triumph over philosophy. In the scene quoted in Exercise 5 (p. 288) they put death in its place.

The characters of Bernard Shaw are exceptional among high-comedy characters in the strength of their purposes; they are endowed with Shaw's indomitable spirit. But Shaw's religion of the Life Force leaves them to work out for themselves the ways toward their goals. Most high-comedy characters live without the frail historical support that other groups possess. The church-goer, besides his theological beliefs, has a sense of belonging to a "body" of the church, with communion with all the saints and members through the ages. The humanist has behind him the tradition of the prophets, poets, and philosophers; the liberal politician carries the torch handed on from a long line of fighters for freedom and the rights of man. The comic hero has only the vaguest sense of any predecessors and no notion that his failure or success will make a difference to anybody who comes after him. Yet high-comedy characters do not, like the existentialists, retreat into the subjective. They know that society is there, even if its patterns are changeable and intangible, and that the individuals who make it up loom solid and unavoidable in one's path, themselves living without absolutes. Some of them are too clumsy, stupid, and provincial, and others too fanatic or lost in their own obsessions, to be able to play the best comic game. Others, at the opposite extreme, are too sophisticated, affected, and superficial to make good partners. But all are part of the whole laughable pageant of man. Some may have enough maturity and sense of humor to help make a game, a fine art, of living. And their penetration and wit and light-serious philosophy will always be a special pleasure for a theatregoer who likes both to think and to laugh.

EXERCISES AND DEMONSTRATIONS

1. ACTING MOLIÈRE. For the charm and wit of Molière, take a scene from a good rhymed-couplet translation, either Richard Wilbur's translation of *Tartuffe* or *The Misanthrope* or Lawrence Langner and Arthur Guiterman's translation of *The School for Husbands*. Célimène's character sketches of her "friends" in Act II of *The Misanthrope* or the combat of wits between Célimène and Arsinoé in Act III are excellent.

2. ACTING CONGREVE'S CLEAR-HEADED LOVERS. For gaiety and teasing with serious meaning, take from Act IV of Congreve's *The Way of the World*

the speeches of Mirabell and Millamant outlining under what conditions they will become man and wife. The tone must be affectionate and playful, but also firm.

3. ACTING CONGREVE'S COMIC OLD WOMEN. Take Lady Wishfort's scene in Act IV of *The Way of the World* in which she receives the servant Waitwell, who is presenting himself to her as an ardent suitor, Sir Rowland. She gushes her elaborate language, denying that she gives in easily, while her tone, of course, is flirtatious and susceptible.

4. ACTING A HIGH-COMEDY COMBAT FROM SHERIDAN. Take the quarrel between Sir Peter and Lady Teazle in Act II of *The School for Scandal*. As a rich bachelor of fifty Sir Peter had married a lively, teasing young girl from the country, and he confides to the audience his exasperation.

> When an old bachelor marries a young wife, what is he to expect? 'Tis now six months since Lady Teazle made me the happiest of men—and I have been the most miserable dog ever since! We tift a little going to church, and fairly quarreled before the bells had done ringing. I was more than once nearly choked with gall during the honeymoon and had lost all comfort in life before my friends had done wishing me joy. Yet I chose with caution—a girl bred wholly in the country, who never knew luxury beyond one silk gown, nor dissipation above the annual gala of a race ball. Yet now she plays her part in all the extravagant fopperies of the fashion and the town, with as ready a grace as if she had never seen a bush or a grass plot out of Grosvenor Square! I am sneered at by all my acquaintance, and paragraphed in the newspapers. She dissipates my fortune, and contradicts all my humours; yet, the worst of it is, no doubt I love her, or I should never bear all this. However, I'll never be weak enough to own it.

When he tries to be firm, he strikes sparks from her lively temper. She knows how to smile at him and tease him, but she means what she says. Here are samples from the quarrel.

SIR PETER   Lady Teazle, Lady Teazle, I'll not bear it!

LADY T   Sir Peter, Sir Peter, you may bear it or not, as you please: but I ought to have my way in everything, and what's more, I will too. What! though I was educated in the country, I know very well that women of fashion in London are accountable to nobody after they are married.

SIR PETER   Very well, ma'am, very well:—so a husband is to have no influence, no authority?

LADY T   Authority! No, to be sure:—if you wanted authority over me, you should have adopted me, and not married me: I am sure you were old enough.

SIR PETER   Old enough!—ay—there it is. Well, well, Lady Teazle, though my life may be made unhappy by your temper, I'll not be ruined by your extravagance.

LADY T   My extravagance! I'm sure I'm not more extravagant than a woman of fashion ought to be.

EXERCISES AND DEMONSTRATIONS

SIR PETER   No, no, madam, you shall throw away no more sums on such unmeaning luxury. 'Slife! to spend as much to furnish your dressing room with flowers in winter as would suffice to turn the Pantheon into a greenhouse. . . .

LADY T   And am I to blame, Sir Peter, because flowers are dear in cold weather? You should find fault with the climate, and not with me. For my part, I'm sure, I wish it was spring all the year round, and that roses grew under one's feet!

SIR PETER   Oons! madam—if you had been born to this, I shouldn't wonder at your talking thus; but you forget what your situation was when I married you.

LADY T   No, no, I don't; 'twas a very disagreeable one, or I should never have married you.

He draws her a picture, which she laughingly adds to. But he is so pompous in his insistence that he provokes the half-hidden retorts she smilingly gives him.

SIR PETER   This, madam, was your situation: and what have I done for you? I have made you a woman of fashion, of fortune, of rank: in short I have made you my wife.

LADY T   Well, then,—and there is but one thing more you can make me to add to the obligation, and that is—

SIR PETER   My widow, I suppose?

She laughs knowingly. It was a standard joke of the time, but many a true word is said in jest.

SIR PETER   I thank you, madam—but don't flatter yourself; for though your ill conduct may disturb my peace, it shall never break my heart, I promise you: however, I am equally obliged to you for the hint.

LADY T   Then why will you endeavor to make yourself so disagreeable to me, and thwart me in every little elegant expense?

SIR PETER   'Slife! madam, I say, had you any of these little elegant expenses when you married me?

LADY T   Lud, Sir Peter! Would you have me out of the fashion?

SIR PETER   The fashion, indeed! What had you to do with the fashion before you married me?

LADY T   For my part, I should think you would like to have your wife thought a woman of taste.

SIR PETER   Ay—there again—taste—Zounds! madam, you had no taste when you married me!

LADY T   That's very true indeed, Sir Peter; and after having married you, I should never pretend to taste again, I allow. But now, Sir Peter, if we have finished our daily jangle, I presume I may go to my engagement at Lady Sneerwell's.

She wins that bout by keeping her temper, and her wits. Sir Peter is left breathless but smiling. She is fascinating because she has such high spirits. He muses:

SIR PETER   So—I have gained much by my intended expostulation: yet, with what a charming air she contradicts everything I say, and how

287

pleasingly she shows her contempt for my authority! Well, though I can't make her love me, there is great satisfaction in quarreling with her: and I think she never appears to such advantage as when she is doing everything in her power to plague me.

5. ACTING HIGH-COMEDY PLAYFUL SERIOUSNESS. Take the following scene from Noel Coward's *Private Lives*. Underneath are great affection and earnest concern, but on the surface there is lively, brisk cheerfulness. The scene begins with the greatest anxiety covered by smiling and builds into laughing determination that almost obliterates the melancholy thought.

AMANDA   Don't laugh at me. I'm serious.

ELYOT (*seriously*)   You mustn't be serious, my dear one, it's just what they want.

AMANDA   Who's they?

ELYOT   All the futile moralists who try to make life unbearable. Laugh at them. Be flippant. Laugh at everything, all their sacred shibboleths. Flippancy brings out the acid in their damned sweetness and light.

AMANDA   If I laugh at everything, I must laugh at us too.

ELYOT   Certainly you must. We're figures of fun all right.

AMANDA   How long will it last, this ludicrous, overbearing love of ours?

ELYOT   Who knows?

AMANDA   Shall we always want to bicker and fight?

ELYOT   No, that desire will fade, along with our passion.

AMANDA   Oh dear, shall we like that?

ELYOT   It all depends on how well we've played.

AMANDA   What happens if one of us dies? Does the one that's left still laugh?

ELYOT   Yes, yes, with all his might.

AMANDA (*wistfully clutching his hand*)   That's serious enough, isn't it?

ELYOT   No, no, it isn't. Death's very laughable, such a cunning little mystery. All done with mirrors.

AMANDA   Darling, I believe you're talking nonsense.

ELYOT   So is everyone else in the long run. Let's be superficial and pity the poor philosophers. Let's blow trumpets and squeakers, and enjoy the party as much as we can, like very small, quite idiotic school-children. Let's savour the delight of the moment. Come and kiss me, darling, before your body rots, and worms pop in and out of your eye sockets.

AMANDA   Elyot, worms don't pop.

RECOMMENDED RECORDINGS

Among the best recordings illustrating the wit and other qualities of high comedy are the following: Edith Evans in *Eighteenth-Century Comedy*, Angel 35213; Edith Evans and John Gielgud in Oscar Wilde's *The Importance of Being Earnest*, Angel 3504 B; Jean-Louis Barrault and Madeleine Reynaud in Molière's *The Misanthrope* (in French), Spoken Arts 715; Noel Coward and Gertrude Lawrence in *Noel and Gertie* (scenes from *Private Lives* and other plays), RCA Victor LCT 1156; Noel Coward and Margaret Leighton in Bernard Shaw's *The Apple Cart*, Caedmon TC 1094; Noel Coward and Margaret Leighton in *Noel*

288

Coward Dialogues, Caedmon TC 1069; John Gielgud and Pamela Brown in Christopher Fry's *The Lady's Not for Burning,* Decca DX 110; the original cast in T. S. Eliot's *The Cocktail Party,* Decca DL 9004–9005; Charles Laughton, Charles Boyer, Cedric Hardwicke, and Agnes Moorehead in Shaw's *Don Juan in Hell,* Columbia SL 166.

SUGGESTED READING

PLAYS

The ancestors of high comedy are to be found in Terence's Roman play *Adelphi,* or *The Brothers,* and Ben Jonson's *Volpone* (1606), *The Silent Woman* (1609), and *The Alchemist* (1610). Molière's *The Miser* (1668) and *The Imaginary Invalid* (1673) are available in many prose translations and are relatively easy to read in French. His wit is brought out best in translations in rhymed verse such as *The School for Husbands* (1661), translated by Lawrence Langner and Arthur Guiterman in 1933, and *The Misanthrope* (1666) and *Tartuffe* (1664), translated by Richard Wilbur in 1954 and 1963.

English Restoration comedy reached its highest achievements in William Wycherley, *The Country Wife* (1675), George Etherege, *The Man of Mode* (1676), and William Congreve's two masterpieces, *Love for Love* (1695) and *The Way of the World* (1700). The best high comedy of the eighteenth century is Richard Brinsley Sheridan, *The School for Scandal* (1777). After that there was not a successful high comedy until 1895, when Vienna saw Arthur Schnitzler, *Anatol,* and London, Oscar Wilde, *The Importance of Being Earnest.*

Bernard Shaw's use of many of the traditional elements of high comedy is especially evident in *Man and Superman* (1903), *Major Barbara* (1905), *Misalliance* (1910), and *Pygmalion* (1913). W. Somerset Maugham wrote several outstanding comedies of British high society: *Our Betters* (1917), *The Circle* (1921), and *The Constant Wife* (1927). Noel Coward seems even more the dramatist of the sophisticated gaiety of disillusioned people in *Private Lives* (1930), *Design for Living* (1933), and *Present Laughter* (1946). In 1956 Enid Bagnold proved with *The Chalk Garden* that the British tradition still had vitality.

In America, S. N. Behrman wrote sophisticated comedy, often with political overtones, in *Biography* (1932), *Rain from Heaven* (1934), *End of Summer* (1936), and *No Time for Comedy* (1939), while Philip Barry wrote warmer, less brittle drawing-room comedies such as *Holiday* (1928) and *Without Love* (1945). More robust plays of American life often have some elements of high comedy, as, for example, James Thurber and Elliott Nugent, *The Male Animal* (1940), and Garson Kanin, *Born Yesterday* (1946). A good romantic treatment of high comedy is Samuel Taylor, *The Pleasure of His Company* (1958).

CRITICAL WORKS

The classic definition of the function of social comedy as a gentle civilizing agency is in George Meredith, *An Essay on Comedy* (1877), reprinted in Wylie Sypher, *Comedy** (1956). The best description of the special qualities of wit and character in high comedies from Ben Jonson to Shaw is Louis Kronenberger, *The Thread of Laughter* (1952). The courage to live without absolute standards is the theme of great comedy, according to Bonamy Dobrée, *Restoration Comedy*

* Available in paperback edition.

(1924). The actors' approach to comedy is developed in a series of letters in Athene Seyler and Stephen Haggard, *The Craft of Comedy* (1946). S. N. Behrman explained his approach in a short article, "What Makes Comedy High," in the *New York Times* (March 30, 1932), and Joseph Wood Krutch further defined that attitude in "The Comic Wisdom of S. N. Behrman," *The Nation* (July 19, 1933), reprinted in Montrose J. Moses and John Mason Brown, *The American Theatre As Seen by Its Critics* (1934), and in Morton Zabel, *Literary Opinion in America* (1937). The difficulties of writing comedy in an overserious age, which Behrman dramatized in *No Time for Comedy,* are described briefly but pertinently by Al Capp, "It's Hideously True," and Richard Duprez, "Whatever Happened to Comedy?" both in R. W. Corrigan, *Comedy: Meaning and Form** (1965).

* Available in paperback edition.

CHAPTER NINE

THE THEATRE OF DISRUPTION

Man has always recognized disruptive elements in his world, but only in the mid-twentieth century has he become so fascinated by lack of order that much of his art is devoted to demonstrating it. Over the ages art has been primarily concerned with order, with tracing the possible paths through areas of apparent disorder. But many twentieth-century artists are so dubious of the old paths and so aware of recent upheavals in the landscape that they are more inclined to prepare the traveler for a rough journey than to try to trace a new path out of the disorder.

Most art, like most philosophy, has assumed that whatever perfection there may be in heaven, the processes of the finite historical world involve both growth and decay, both creation and destruction. Most mythologies have supposed that chaos was the original state, that an island of order had been won by a great struggle out of the sea of chaos and that it was in constant threat of reversion to chaos. In some mythologies, destruction must end each cycle so that a new order can begin. We have seen that both tragedy and comedy assume some baffling complexities and incongruities in the very nature of the universe.

Whenever man concerns himself with improving his condition, he strives to destroy the old social and intellectual order to make way for a more perfect new one, an order that will allow greater freedom for the individual. Since the late Middle Ages, most rebellions have started out with high hopes. The early capitalist traders wanted freedom from medieval trade guilds, and the humanists wanted to liberate men from narrow medieval traditions and superstitious fears. The French Revolution undertook to destroy all vestiges of the aristocratic system, the "old regime," in order to establish a new Utopia of reason, with public ceremonies for the actual worship of Reason and Freedom. Communist revolutions in the twentieth century have been dedicated to the destruction of the bourgeois world in order to make way for a classless society. More moderate reformers hope for gradual improvement of the social order and look to some form of realism as the best artistic means of making social problems seem vital. But many people, bitterly disillusioned after violent upheavals have failed to establish perfect freedom, despair of reforming the world by changing institutions and instead turn their attention to individual man and his spiritual problems, trying to show him a way to survive in a world of inevitable confusion. Modern art—on canvas, in music, and on the stage—reflects this confusing mixture of hope and despair.

Plays about disruption, understandably enough, are not easy to classify, but theatre people have been able to discuss most of them under five or six key headings. For the works of the first part of the twentieth century, *symbolism* and *dream* are the important terms, the dream techniques overlapping those of *surrealism* on the one hand and those of *expressionism* on the other. For drama since 1945, *existentialism* and the *theatre of the absurd* are the key terms. *Epic drama* deals with the world in fragments, and has borrowed much from the symbolists, the expressionists, and even the existentialists, but it tries to piece the fragments together for a real picture of the world we live in. Though it is a hybrid, it shares the constructive, objective purpose of realism, and we have considered it as one kind of realism.

Symbolism and the Inner Drama of Strindberg and Pirandello

At the very time when naturalism was getting under way in the nineteenth century, a number of poets were setting themselves against the scientific, rational view. They felt that objective, materialistic art ignored important aspects of the mind and spirit. Such poets as Arthur Rimbaud and Stéphane Mallarmé rejected both nature and reason; instead, they attempted to evoke the eternal beyond the visible by creating suggestive symbols. Like the painters, they were fascinated by symbols of man's alienation—masks and harlequins, tramps and clowns. They cultivated free association of words and images, inducing abnormal states of mind—hallucination, and even hysteria and madness—through the use of drugs and alcohol and through frantic sensuality. To them, love was only a demonic force linked with death.

The symbolist poets had a considerable influence on the theatre. Ibsen used much symbolism in his later work, even in plays that seemed realistic—the wild duck in the play of that name, the white horses seen before a death in *Rosmersholm,* the tower that was a fatal challenge in *The Master Builder.* The symbols suggested irrational forces driving man, sometimes to fulfillment but more often to destruction. The mood dramas of Maurice Maeterlinck, such as the impressionist *Pelleas and Melisande,* which Debussy made into an opera, and the poetic dramas of Yeats and Lorca made use of such symbols. But the chief importance of symbols was as images of the mind in the dream plays and expressionistic plays.

The first great explorer of the new inner geography was August Strindberg. Even Strindberg's great naturalistic plays of the 1880s, such as *Miss Julie* and *The Father,* were far from the objective studies of heredity and environment that Zola, the great champion of naturalism, had called for. *The Father,* in particular, is a turgid study of destructive hate between husband and wife, a torment no one knew better than Strindberg, whose three tempestuous marriages led quickly to angry separation and divorce. For some years after the breakup of the second marriage, Strindberg was on the verge of insanity and put himself into a private hospital for the insane. He wrote several autobiographical novels analyzing his torment and developing his mystic idea that God sends pain to men and lures them with attractive but hateful women in order to purify them. But a more important result of those "inferno" years was a new dramaturgy, a series of plays using many details of his own private life but setting them on the stage in revolutionary techniques. O'Neill called him "the precursor of all modernity in our present theatre." These plays are not easy to read; they call for stylized dream rhythms, moving phantoms, lights, colors, and group movement. But in them are the seeds of many of the effects and characteristic details of symbolism, surrealism, expressionism, existentialism, absurdist drama, and even of religious or poetic plays and epic dramas of social action.

Shifting from the prevailing emphasis on objective studies, Strindberg turned the drama inward to the phantoms and repressed images of the mind. Instead of studying the conditions of human life in the hope of gradual improvement through changing the environment, he dramatized individual suffering, guilt, assertion, struggle, and search for religious salvation. The outer world crumbles as dream images dissolve into one another. In a preface to *A Dream Play* (1902), Strindberg wrote:

> As in his previous play, *To Damascus,* the author has attempted to reproduce the detached and disunited—although apparently logical—form of dreams. Anything is apt to happen, anything seems possible and probable. Time and space do not exist. On a flimsy foundation of actual happenings, imagination spins and weaves in new patterns: an intermingling of remembrances, experiences, whims, fancies, ideas, fantastic absurdities and improvisations, and original inventions of the mind. The personalities split, take on duality, multiply, vanish, intensify, diffuse and disperse, and are brought into focus.

All the characters are dominated by one single-minded consciousness, the dreamer's.

Strindberg organized *A Dream Play* in the form of a journey of the Daughter of the God Indra to find out whether human life is as bad as human beings say. After each episode she concludes that "human beings are to be pitied." She encounters four variants of the dreamer—a lover waiting in vain for his

293

love, a lawyer whose hands are black from contact with the crimes of his clients, an ugly quarantine master impounding contaminated people, and a poet whose agonized cry for mercy she reads for the heavens to hear. Throughout the play, a castle gradually grows taller out of the muck of the earth. At the end, the castle bursts into flames and a bud at the top opens as a splendid flower. The image suggests that the poet's song has achieved a beautiful blossoming from the pain and struggle of living.

Many strange phantoms are presented briefly by choral groups—monsters, officials, ballet dancers and singers coming from the opera house, the misshapen clients of the lawyer, starving workmen watching the rich pass in the street, sailors frightened in a storm singing "Christ have mercy." Strindberg planned to keep the surface appearance of realism, with full changes of settings and costumes, but later productions became frankly theatrical: the choral group, using only suggestive indications of costume and makeup, stayed on stage and shifted from one role to another in sight of the audience. Many later expressionistic plays and many epic plays borrowed the idea of such a group; one example is found in the half-masks used by the choral group in productions of Brecht's *The Caucasian Chalk Circle*. Strindberg's method was nearer surrealism, where the dream has the surface appearance of reality. Salvador Dali's surrealist paintings of flexible watches and women whose bodies were chests of drawers were scrupulously real in every detail.

Another play of Strindberg's that has had great influence on the theatre of disruption is *The Ghost Sonata* (1907). It is also real in detail, but fantastic things happen—dead people speak and phantoms of the past come back as in the mind. Strindberg sets into opposition the dream fantasies of the hopeful young student and a bitter Old Man, Hummel. Old Hummel attempts to

FIGURE *9.1* Surrealism as a dreamlike fantasy. Both setting and characters suggest the fantasy and transformations of dreams. Cocteau's *Orphée*. Yale University production, directed by Frank M. Spencer, designed by John Koenig, costumed by Sarah Emily Brown and Frank M. Spencer, and lighted by Charles Elson.

strip off the masks and false pretenses of others and to expose their guilts and hatreds. But when they also strip him of his pretenses, he rushes out to destroy himself. The Student escapes from the room of the old guilts to seek the young Girl in a beautiful "Hyacinth Room." They try to tell each other the appalling truth about human life, but the Girl dies and the Student passionately cries out to heaven for mercy and innocence.

The other great germinal figure in the exploration of the mind was Luigi Pirandello. As steeped in pain as Strindberg, he created a more metaphysical terror in his plays. Perhaps all living is acting before a mirror, he seems to say, a mirror that distorts or gives several different reflections. Must each person keep on acting, seeing that the only reality is in the fleeting reflection? Where writers of high comedy find zest and entertainment in the idea of life as acting a role, Pirandello found only pain. Spending years looking after an insane wife, he found solace neither at home nor in the outside world. Only in the stillness of art could he make his own peace.

Several of Pirandello's plays written at the end of the First World War made a worldwide impression, and they were probably more influential than Strindberg's dream plays in causing a break in the treatment of reality. Some of them are realistic enough on the surface. The husband in *As You Desire Me* is confident that the cabaret singer he has found is the wife who was lost in the war, but she herself is not so sure. A group of sensible people in *Right You Are—If You Think You Are* are determined to learn the truth about the little wife whose husband and mother give quite different accounts of who she is. But the wife herself cannot tell them, and they find that their intrusion has only increased the pain of people who are trying to sustain the difficult interrelationships of a family.

Two other plays of Pirandello have made an even stronger impression. When modern characters appear in the medieval court in *Henry IV* (1922), we learn that servants and relatives of a nobleman have for years kept up the pretense of living in another period because, as the result of an accident while in masquerade as the German Emperor Henry IV, the nobleman thinks he is really Henry IV. When the relatives, accompanied by a psychiatrist, stage a shocking surprise in hope of curing him, he confesses that he has been sane for years but chose to remain Henry IV rather than be subjected to the illusive uncertainties of his own life. He chose to live in the past because history, like art, is settled and fixed. But in a fit of anger he kills a cynical friend, and he realizes that he must forever remain Henry IV, though now his attendants know that he knows he is acting. In *Six Characters in Search of an Author* (1921), six people interrupt a rehearsal in a theatre, insisting that the director write a play about them, and they show him painful scenes of their story, disagreeing violently over what the real relations were between the father, mother, stepdaughter, and rejected son. The suicide of the younger son provides a sudden interruption both of the unfinished story of the characters and of the contention between the director and real actors and the real-unreal characters, now never to be fixed in art and never to agree on what their reality was or is.

295

The Theatre of Disruption

FIGURE *9.2* Photographer's impression of a Pirandello play. The characters are caught in the shifting planes of reality. Pirandello's *Six Characters in Search of an Author*. University of Texas production, directed by Francis Hodge, designed by John Rothgeb, costumed by Lucy Barton, and lighted by Neil Whiting.

FIGURE *9.3* Creating reality by acting and watching others act. Pirandello's *Six Characters in Search of an Author*. Humboldt State College production, directed by W. L. Turner, designed by Richard Rothrock, and costumed by Ethelyn Pauley. Photo Peter Palmquist.

The image of acting has proved an even more fruitful image of man's uncertain condition than Strindberg's image of dream. And Pirandello went even further than Strindberg; he implied that there is no systematic reality in the world—that it is not merely a question of a dream as a disarrangement of reality in the twilight zones of the mind, but that the subjective, undependable and multiple as it may be, is prior to, and basic to, any knowledge of the "facts" of reality.

Expressionism

Strindberg's and Pirandello's disturbing explorations of the mind and of the nature of reality were soon followed by the more positively disruptive movement known as *expressionism*. Where realism and naturalism were sharp rebellions against the cheerful sentimentality of Victorian life, the new theatre forms, beginning with expressionism, have all been rebellions against realism. Realism seemed too dull and quiet, muting colors, subordinating music, understating dialogue and acting, depending on the implicit, insisting on full motivation. Expressionism went to the other extreme, reveling in sounds, colors, rhythms, and movements. Where naturalism shows a helpless victim, determined, or even overwhelmed, by his environment, expressionism shows an angry little man spitting back at a machine-made, fragmented world. In his rebellion, the expressionist has insisted that the theatre be theatrical, or at least that theatre people acknowledge more than one way of putting on plays. He has carried his point, and for several decades we have said that there are two ways of producing on the stage—representationalism, or realism, and presentationalism, frank presentation to the audience without the pretense of the illusion of reality. And all experiments in drama have insisted on some techniques of presentationalism.

Expressionism in drama was in keeping with what was happening in the other arts at the end of the First World War. Painters were smearing raw colors on their canvases, using cubistic angles and planes, paying little attention to the appearance of reality. Musicians were breaking away from the muted moods of impressionism, the controlled discords of Debussy and Ravel, to explore the multitonalities, atonalities, and twelve-tone scales, the interruptions, sharp contrasts, complex rhythms, and violent climaxes of post-impressionism. Isadora Duncan and other dancers had broken from the ritualized steps of the ballet to open the way for a freer use of body movement in dance. Why should the theatre disregard the excitement of vivid colors, strange shapes, loud sounds, strong climaxes, and machine rhythms, at once fascinating and terrifying? Stravinsky's *Rite of Spring* provided a combination of shock and pleasure. Jazz, too, was an expression of loud defiance and crude, energetic pleasure. It was the song of the modern city, brazen, monotonous, frenetic, mechanical, inhuman, yet irresistible. On the saxophone or on the expressionistic stage, the "pace that kills" or "living it up" expressed the desperate, disillusioned, intoxicated mood of the early twenties. If it smoldered in the dance halls, it exploded on the stage.

297

The Theatre of Disruption

The spirit of revolt rejected the bourgeois-imperialistic control in Europe. Even during the war, in 1917, a group of disillusioned men in Zurich, Switzerland, started "dada," an art movement that deliberately destroyed patterns and made nonsense of the conventional. It was a negative, partly satiric impulse, but it discovered possibilities of excitement as well as of shock in the juxtaposition of incongruous fragments. Its fur-lined teacups and pasted collages of scraps and objects suggested new ways of using texture even as they defied conventional thinking. If the war was the end result of bourgeois conventionality, the dadaists said, then let's destroy the whole tradition—in fact, all tradition, political, cultural, and artistic. Dramatize the insanity of a military-commercial machine age. Explode firecrackers. Paint mustaches on pretty nudes and conventional madonnas. Destroy the institutions and habits that have enslaved and misled mankind. Open the way for a new world, socialist or communist or utopian. If the false ideals that have commercialized and mechanized and militarized bourgeois society are destroyed, then the spiritual Brotherhood of Man will emerge.

It was out of this postwar spirit of revolt that expressionism was born. Some people have spoken of all revolt against realism as expressionism, but now the word is used primarily for a particular movement that took place mostly in Germany and the United States. One aspect of this movement, which followed the experiments of Strindberg, was a revolt against the objective view of the world in order to show the inner mind, especially tortured and distorted states of mind. A second aspect was a reaction to the mechanization and dehumanization of man in the industrial-military-urban complex. Thus the dream and the machine were the two poles of postwar expressionism.

In this time of artistic ferment, almost everything that could be called "experimental" was tried on the stage. Some attempts were silly and ineffective, yet a number of important techniques were invented or adapted from old forms. We can classify these techniques in four groups: first, techniques for dramatizing the inner life; second, the use of sounds, movements, and colors to build to a climax; third, the use of stylized (that is, rhythmic and sustained) voice and movement patterns to suggest the unreality of a dream or the monotony of a machine; and, fourth, generalized, as opposed to individualized, characterization.

The simplest way to dramatize the subjective was to revive the soliloquy and the aside, letting the character put into words his private thoughts, or his "stream of consciousness," an important technique in the modern novel. For a soliloquy, the spotlight became a great help, allowing one character to speak his thoughts while the background or other characters sink into shadow. The opening scene of Elmer Rice's *The Adding Machine* is a long stream-of-consciousness monologue by Mrs. Zero as she is going to bed; she reveals the resentment she feels at the empty life she has led in twenty-five years of marriage to the little bookkeeper, Mr. Zero. In the second scene, the conversation at the office between Zero and his assistant is interspersed with asides telling their hidden thoughts. The most famous use of asides is in O'Neill's nine-act psychological drama, *Strange Interlude,* a fairly realistic play in which the dialogue is interrupted repeatedly as one character utters thoughts he would not speak aloud, while the action is suspended.

The use of the dream for dramatizing the inner life was borrowed chiefly from Strindberg, but dreams and fantasies had often been used in romantic plays, in which the backdrop opened up to show the dream or daydream of a character on the forestage, and dream sequences were common in ballet. The fantasy scenes of *Liliom* and its musical version, *Carousel,* have been called expressionistic because they show the hero after death being arraigned in a celestial police court and returning briefly to his daughter on earth. But expressionism is rarely so romantic, being concerned usually with the nightmare fears and obsessions of modern man. We have already noticed the series of nightmares that come to life for the Emperor Jones in his flight through the jungle.

The central action of *Beggar on Horseback,* an expressionistic comedy by George S. Kaufman and Marc Connelly, is a dream fantasy set between realistic prologue and epilogue. The poor composer Neil decides he had better marry the rich girl rather than his poor sweetheart. The rich family visit him in the prologue, to reappear in his dream fantastically exaggerated. The mother wears her rocking chair; the father, his business telephone; and the little brother, a baseball fiend, an enormous yellow tie and bat. But here we have not only dramatization of the inner life but the distortion we call *stylization.*

The second technique of expressionism is the building of a climax, by means other than speech. Something more powerful than the soliloquy of a single actor is needed to show an inner crisis, especially since audiences have come to expect very restrained acting. The Greeks, Shakespeare, and Racine wrote long speeches with slow, rhetorical crescendos, expecting the actor to use a wide range in voice and movement. But a machine-age theatre has other resources. When Rice's Mr. Zero is fired, to be replaced by an adding machine, a crescendo of feeling grows to a climax in which Mr. Zero stabs the boss. First the soft music of a distant merry-go-round is heard, and slowly the part of the floor with the desk and stools starts to revolve. As the boss goes on with his impersonal spiel, "Sorry to lose an employee who's been with me for so many years. . . . I'm sorry—no other alternative—greatly regret—old employee—efficiency—economy—business—business—business—business," the revolutions of the platform get faster and faster, and a tremendous climax of sound is called for:

> The music swells and swells. To it is added every offstage effect of the theatre: the wind, the wave, the galloping horses, the locomotive whistle, the sleigh bells, the automobile siren, the glass-crash, New Year's Eve, Election Night, Armistice Day, and the Mardi Gras. The noise is deafening, maddening, unendurable. Suddenly it culminates in a terrific peal of thunder. For an instant there is a flash of red and then everything is plunged into blackness.

In some productions, projected streaks of red with lists and sums of figures revolve around the walls as another visual reinforcement of the climax. 299

FIGURE 9.4 Expressionism. The leaning bars of the courtroom windows suggest the terror of the inner mind as the little man, Mr. Zero, is tried for murder. Rice's *The Adding Machine*. New York, 1922. Photo Vandamm.

In the next scene of *The Adding Machine,* Mr. Zero sits quietly as his guests, Mr. and Mrs. One, Mr. and Mrs. Two, Three, Four, Five, and Six gabble the inane chatter of a stupid society. But the groups of speeches get shorter as husbands and wives compete in asserting their clichés, and smoldering feelings come to the surface in a big climax:

> SIX   Too damn much agitation, that's at the bottom of it.
> FIVE   That's it! Too damn many strikes.
> FOUR   Foreign agitators, that's what it is.
> THREE   They oughta be run outa the country.
> TWO   What the hell do they want anyhow?
> ONE   They don't know what they want, if you ask me.
> SIX   America for the Americans is what I say!
> ALL   (*in unison*)   That's it. Damn foreigners! Damn dagoes! Damn Catholics! Damn sheenies! Damn niggers! Jail 'em! Shoot 'em! Hang 'em! Lynch 'em! Burn 'em! (*They all rise.*)
> ALL   (*sing in unison*)   My country 'tis of thee, Sweet land of liberty!

The intensity of that climax enables Rice to end the scene with a striking anticlimax as a policeman arrives and Mr. Zero calmly goes out with him, saying to his wife, "I gotta go with him. You'll have to dry the dishes yourself. . . . I killed the boss this afternoon."

Stylization, the third technique of expressionism, is a deliberate break with realism. In design, it immediately indicates unreality by omitting some details and distorting others. Since the emphasis in expressionistic plays is on the insane or abnormal state of the modern world, the distortion is a direct

300

Kinds of Plays

expression of the subjective. Walls lean, posts curve, roofs hang without support, the square angles of normal life become acute angles and sharp points. Objects menace with hands, eyes, pointing fingers. In Georg Kaiser's *From Morn to Midnight,* a tree takes on the appearance of a skeleton. Scenery, usually so static a background, moves before the eyes, falling, leaning in, swinging round, taking an active part in creating the nightmare. Stylization is very important in design, giving a touch of theatricality, even when the play is not thought of as expressionistic.

In a performance, the most conspicuous aspect of expressionistic stylization is intensified rhythm. The rhythm of a realistic play is always subordinated to the atmosphere of the place, but in the dehumanized megalopolis of the expressionist, rhythm becomes insistent, often dominant. It is usually based on endless repetition of the same movement and sound, such as the monotonous flow of an assembly line or the passage of new chrome automobiles down a highway.

The fourth technique of expressionism is the generalization of character. The central character must represent Everyman, almost as in a medieval morality play. Whether he is the stupid eternal slave Mr. Zero, Yank the Hairy Ape, or just The Young Man or The Poet, he is the dream figure for audience identification, the truth seeker. O'Neill's *The Great God Brown* has two searching heroes, Dion the artist and Billy Brown the businessman, but they merge when Dion dies and Billy steals his mask of creativity. A prostitute, Cybel, becomes a figure of Mother Earth, to help the hero find that ecstatic vision of life transcendent that most expressionist heroes are seeking. When he is dying, she soothes him and helps him rediscover prayer.

> BROWN . . . Our Father . . . Who art! Who art! I know! I have found Him! I hear Him speak! "Blessed are they that weep, for they shall laugh!" Only he that has wept can laugh! The laughter of Heaven sows earth with a rain of tears, and out of earth's transfigured birth-pain the laughter of Man returns to bless and play again in innumerable dancing gales of flame upon the knees of God! (*He dies.*)
>
> CYBEL (*kisses him gently . . . with profound pain*) Always spring comes again bearing life! Always again! Always, always forever again!— Spring again!—life again! summer and fall and death and peace again!—but always, always, love and conception and birth and pain again—spring bearing the intolerable chalice of life again!—bearing the glorious, blazing crown of life again!

When the gruff police officer asks, "What's his name?" she replies, "Man." The officer, getting out his notebook, asks, "How d'yuh spell it?"

That generalized personality moves in a phantom world of even more impersonal characters. We take our name for machine men from the word used in a play by Karel Capek called *R. U. R.* (Rossum's Universal Robots), in which the few human beings still trying to be human contend with the mobs of mechanized robots. The Cashier—the hero of Kaiser's *From Morn to Midnight* who absconds and abandons his dull family so that he may try all the vices that money can buy—finds at the races a chorus of attendants

301

all alike, and then, at a cabaret, nameless guests and nameless girls in masks. The Salvation Army Lass leads him to a Salvation Army hall, where nameless penitents make their confessions against a chorus of derisive scoffers. One group of actors, of course, with quick changes of costume, serves for all the nameless mobs in such a play, because they are all part of the same dehumanized nightmare of modern life.

The short life of expressionism—about 1910 to 1925—was due partly to its weaknesses; it was too hysterical and rhapsodic, and too mechanical in its lack of real characters. But the swift loss of interest was due even more, perhaps, to a changing attitude toward the machine and modern life. The machine itself has passed through a swift evolution. Instead of the large, noisy steam engines of the first quarter of the twentieth century, there are now small, quiet electric motors. The coughing, jerking automobile has given way to the smooth V8 with a quiet muffler. The clanging metal wheels of the streetcar have made way for the rubber tires of the bus. Where the old heavy machines, with grinding wheels and clashing gears, were operated by monotonous motions of many workers, the later machines, smooth-running in streamlined casings, are more nearly automatic.

Finally, a new vision of the machine appears to be emerging, more clearly in America than in Europe. When automobiles began to clog the streets, many people were alarmed, and the proliferation of the juke boxes and automatic vending machines seemed to complete the dehumanization. As late as the 1950s Europeans could speak with real anger of America's forcing the inhuman machine on the rest of the world. But while some people do become obsessed by machinery and willingly spend hours operating slot machines, most people have learned to use the machine as an inconspicuous servant in the background of their lives. The nightmare has lost most of its terror.

Although expressionism as a large movement is past, it has left traces in realistic plays. One moment in *Death of a Salesman* reminds us that terror of a noisy machine can still be felt. Willy needs human consideration, but the young boss does not listen to him. Instead, he is fascinated by a new mechanical gadget, a tape recorder, on which he has just recorded his young son's recital of a list of the capitals of the states. When Willy has finally been fired and is left alone, he beats his fists on the desk, accidentally turning on the recorder with its mechanical repetition of a meaningless list. There is a naturalistic explanation of this machine, but the inhuman noise and its terrifying effect on Willy are a vivid moment of expressionism.

A similar moment of obsessive terror makes the inner life of Blanche Du Bois clear to the audience in *A Streetcar Named Desire*. Any new moment of panic makes her relive in her memory the dance and the pistol shot of the suicide of her poet husband. The audience hears the waltz growing louder and louder, and then the pistol shot. Yet no one thinks of *Streetcar* as anything but a completely realistic play. Both the realistic theatre and the film have so completely absorbed the incidental expressionistic technique of running a subjective experience on the sound track that no one takes special notice. Such

Kinds of Plays

a dream character as Uncle Ben moves in and out of *Death of a Salesman*, visible to some characters and invisible to others, without disturbing the sense of reality. It is not even necessary to give him artificial or dreamlike rhythms and movements.

Rhythmic group chanting to a mechanical beat reappeared, surprisingly, in 1957 in the opening scene of the popular musical *The Music Man*. The scene is a railway coach early in the century, and the train sets the rhythm as the salesmen, with jerking movements, chant their conviction that a new age of packaged commodities is coming and that the irregular salesman, Harold Hill, will not fit in. The scene is a clever means of creating interest in an old-fashioned romantic character who resists standardized city life.

This is a strange finale for expressionism. In the 1920s the machine age provoked terror, terror with fascination but with real fear that man would lose his identity in the relentless surge of the heavy beat. In 1957 an expressionistic machine scene is used in a minor part of a popular musical as a half-charming, half-satiric picture of slightly inflexible but not really dangerous semiurban fuddy-duddies.

Existentialism in the Theatre

Existentialism, the philosophy that came to dominate much of the thinking of the 1940s and 50s, especially the thinking of the playwrights, grew out of the disillusion that followed the Second World War. Thinkers turned inward in hopes of rediscovering a genuine identity, an authentic life of the self without the traditional values formerly found in nature, science, politics, and history. The sense of disruption was far greater than that felt after the First World War. Not only was there a more drastic break with the past, with old buildings destroyed, old institutions discredited, old patterns of life broken, but now a radically new element had appeared—the atomic bomb. The year 1945 seemed to put an end to all that had gone before. If the result of three centuries of science was to be the annihilation of every living thing on the globe, what gain was there in studying science? Even if destruction could be avoided, the new age of political and economic power that would follow the release of nuclear energy would be so radically different that all traditional values seemed irrelevant.

Many people were disillusioned with political action. The methods of liberalism seemed too slow, its piecemeal gains inadequate. In 1917 the Russians had turned to Communism, and in the twenties and thirties the Italians and Germans had turned to Fascism and Nazism, but it was soon clear that none of these regimes would permit individuality. Yet even in France, England, and America, where liberal institutions survived, the individual felt lost in the masses, a nameless object in a crowd. The impersonality of the city, with its constant stream of commercial advertising and political propaganda, a stream that increased with the spread of television after 1946, deprived people of a sense of authentic life; all their experiences were secondhand.

In this depressing spiritual climate, existentialism became the support   *303* of many intellectuals. Its great appeal is its rediscovery of the self, an entity with an authentic inner life, a complete being free to choose, free to create values, whether or not the universe supports them. By facing death and nothingness, the individual finds courage to be; by accepting his isolation and loneliness, he finds strength in his freedom. His anguish and uncertainty are a mark of the authenticity of his experience. Just as his death will be his own and not a statistical abstraction, his choice is his own and he creates himself in making it. The statement "Existence precedes essence" (the origin of the term "existentialism") assures the individual that his own private experience as a unique living being is more important than all the abstract studies of history and logic, more important than all the objective studies of nature. Man is not an item to be counted and classified, nor is he an object, a thing, to be studied objectively.

This reaction in favor of the inner life might have been predicted, and not surprisingly it has often gone to the extreme of denying any reality to the external world. Since the seventeenth century scientists have demanded complete objectivity and have warned against the "prejudices" and "fantasies" of the subjective. The Romantic movement was one major protest, reasserting the value of the imagination as opposed to reason and the spiritual as opposed to the material. But naturalism reestablished both the worship of the objective and scientific and the dominant power of the environment. When scientists and naturalistic thinkers have separated the "real" world of dependable, measurable facts from the "merely subjective" world of values and choices, it is perfectly simple to accept the separation but reverse the interpretation and assert that only values and choices have significance. We have already noticed in the discussion of tragedy in the modern world that some pessimistic naturalists chose an acceptance of "life-lies" in defiance of an inhuman "reality." If scientists persist in defining reality and nature as independent of human values, then clearly science is not of primary importance. Many existentialists write as though science and history did not exist and ignore nature as though they had never been outdoors in their lives.

BEGINNINGS OF EXISTENTIALISM IN FRANCE

The wider existentialist movement developed first in France, where it was especially pertinent during the long traumatic experience of the German occupation. From 1940 to 1944 each moment seemed one of critical decision—whether and to what extent to collaborate, or whether to say no and face the consequences. Character seemed purely a matter of individual decision, not a thing determined by social forces or natural environment. As thinkers developed this point of view, they discovered that such a philosophy had already been outlined a hundred years earlier by the Danish religious philosopher Søren Kierkegaard, who emphasized man's isolation and uncertainty and the anguish of choices made in fear and trembling. The Jewish theologian Martin Buber has added an important idea—that experience is not an "it" relationship, an impersonal observation of things, but an "I and thou" relationship, a personal confrontation with the universe.

Kinds of Plays

The existentialist movement since the Second World War has been developed most of all in the plays, novels, and essays of two Frenchmen, Albert Camus and Jean-Paul Sartre. Camus's novels have made a much stronger impression than his plays, though *Caligula* (1945) has interested many people because of its startling hero, who follows the logic of his idea of absolute freedom to the point of killing his friends. Camus's essay *The Myth of Sisyphus* (1942) is one of the classics of existentialism. Sartre's plays have been concerned with many problems of guilt and responsibility, from the short *No Exit,* written during the war, about three people shut up in one room in hell, to the study of a German's sense of guilt over Hitler, *The Condemned of Altona* (1959). Perhaps more important than his plays are two essays published at the end of the war: *Existentialism Is a Humanism,* probably the most widely read definition of existentialism, and "Forgers of Myths," which makes a radical redefinition of theatre, repudiating the main tenets of naturalism. To Sartre, individual differences of human beings, the qualities due to heredity and environment, were unimportant. A person or a character in a play achieved identity only as he made a decision. He could know nothing about the results of his choice on future institutions, but he had the responsibility that other individuals might also make his choice theirs. At least he could say no. A large number of plays since the war have been designed to say no.

As if to illustrate what Sartre was thinking, Jean Anouilh in 1944 wrote his own version of Sophocles' *Antigone* and actually got permission for a Paris production from the German occupation authorities. It is a political play in which a girl defies a dictator, but Anouilh presented both sides of the dilemma in a way that made his play acceptable even to the Nazis. Sophocles' Anti-

FIGURE 9.5 Existentialism. A space stage of ramps and platforms isolates the individuals who make their choices and decisions. The background suggests Greek simplicity but defines no specific time or place. Anouilh's *Antigone.* University of Washington production, designed by John A. Conway and costumed by James Crider. Photo Dorothy Conway.

gone believes that the laws of the gods are more important than the commands of men; the chorus and the prophet Teiresias endorse her, and finally Creon, the dictator himself, admits he was wrong and she was right. Anouilh, on the other hand, completely isolates his Antigone, allowing her no endorsement outside herself. She has no real belief in God, and she finds out not only that both her brothers were corrupt but that Creon is staging a splendid funeral for the loyal one merely to impress the ignorant public while actually the two bodies were so badly mangled that he could not even 'tell which was which. Hence she can find no validity for her sacrifice in external facts. Still, by saying no to Creon's world she creates a value for herself. At the end, her weak sister Ismene makes the same decision. Choice is contagious; other individuals may be influenced by example.

Anouilh changed the character of Creon even more than that of Antigone from Sophocles' conception. In the Greek play, he is a tragic figure whose pride is humbled, but the modern Creon remains set in his cold, impersonal view to the very end. He cannot understand why it is so important to Antigone to say no to his world. He compares the state to a storm-tossed ship that he has taken over because somebody has to issue orders. The mob must be led, and anyone who disobeys orders must be shot. He says, "The thing that drops when you shoot may be someone who poured you a drink the night before; but it has no name and *you* braced at the wheel, you have no name either. Nothing has a name—except the ship and the storm." In the "necessity" of carrying on, the individual has become a "thing" without identity. Creon refers to the mob as animals, moving in droves, with unquestioning, obstinate will. He cannot believe that Antigone, or any human being, would

FIGURE *9.6* Existentialist isolation of the individual. The costumes are impersonal and are not related to a particular environment, and the abstract setting offers many separate places where characters can take their stand. Anouilh's *Antigone*. Florida Agricultural and Mechanical University production, directed by Randolph Edmonds and designed by Carlton W. Molette II.

go against the herd instinct. *"No* is one of your man-made words. Can you imagine a world in which trees say *no* to the sap? In which beasts say *no* to hunger or to propagation?" But existentialism, as Sartre points out, is a humanism. An individual decision raises man above the animals.

AMERICAN EXISTENTIALISM

Leaving aside for the moment the theatre of the absurd, in which certain European playwrights carried existentialism a step further than Camus, Sartre, and Anouilh did, let us consider what impact the existentialist philosophy has had on the American theatre. Although the war caused much less disruption and much less disillusionment in America than in Europe, Americans too have been concerned with problems of guilt, suffering, and justice and have understood the lonely anguish of a questioning soul, though few of them would go so far as to deny validity to religion, science, history, and society.

In the 1930s Maxwell Anderson traced the experience of lonely American youths who had to seek their own values in a corrupt society under an empty sky. In *Winterset* (1935) Mio must tear off the mask of the social injustice that destroyed his father. He learns for certain that his father was innocent of the crime for which he was executed, but he cannot correct that injustice without destroying other people. He dies having found love and forgiveness, values that are more important than justice. This play, with its echoes of *King Lear* and *Romeo and Juliet,* was seen as a landmark in modern poetic drama—a real tragedy of a modern hero fighting in the urban underworld against gangsters and corrupt political forces. After the brave deaths of the young couple the bitter old man expresses his conviction that man's search for meaning in a cold universe makes him "emperor of the endless dark / even in seeking."

In *J. B.,* the Pulitzer prize play of 1958–59, Archibald MacLeish deals with a similar theme of modern man alone in a baffling universe. We first see J. B., the modern Job, as a successful American businessman, happy with his family at Thanksgiving dinner, secure in the bounty of the Lord. During the play his children are taken from him one by one, through war, accident, and crime. In the last act his wife leaves him after an atomic bomb explosion, and he is alone, in pain, as desolate as any European existentialist hero. He finally realizes that his cry for justice is getting no answer because there *is* no justice, only the earth and the sky.

> Cry for justice and the stars
> Will stare until your eyes sting. Weep,
> Enormous winds will thrash the water.
> Cry in sleep for your lost children,
> Snow will fall . . . snow will fall.

But MacLeish's universe is not so empty as that of the European existentialist. True, God seems much farther away than J. B. had thought, but he is there. The active functions of God and Satan in the story of Job are

FIGURE 9.7 American existentialism. A modern Job's fate is acted out in a circus ring under the eyes of two characters wearing the masks of God and Satan. MacLeish's *J. B.* University of Arkansas production, directed by George R. Kernodle and designed by Preston Magruder.

represented by two broken-down actors who put on masks as they speak the words of the Bible. They indicate two very finite ways of looking at the metaphysical. Mr. Zuss is impressed by the might and majesty of the universe; man must accept out of fear of God. Nickles has the bitter naysaying point of view of postwar disillusionment. He is sure the world is full of Jobs who suffer without reason.

> Millions and millions of mankind
> Burned, crushed, broken, mutilated,
> Slaughtered, and for what? For thinking!
> For walking round the world in the wrong
> Skin, the wrong-shaped noses, eyelids:
> Living at the wrong address—
> London, Berlin, Hiroshima—
> Wrong night—wrong city.
> There never could have been so many
> Suffered more for less.

At the end, J. B., having suffered every conceivable pain and heard his own wife say to him, "Curse God and die," is overwhelmed by the Voice out of the Whirlwind. What Nickles cannot believe is that J. B. will accept his life again, after knowing what suffering life contains.

In his speeches of disbelief, Nickles has some of the best poetic passages in modern drama, expressing his passionate bitterness in modern rhythm (see Exercise 2, pp. 327–28). MacLeish decided years ago that the classic iambic rhythm was too stately for American drama, that our rhythm is faster, with the strong initial beat of the trochaic foot: "Job won't take it." Certainly the poetry of *J. B.* makes Anderson's much smoother verse in *Winterset* seem old-fashioned.

308　　MacLeish lets the Voice out of the Whirlwind express the overwhelming

Kinds of Plays

mystery and majesty of God directly, without devising a mask or theatrical representative. In a preface to the play published in the *New York Times,* he wrote: "Job is not *answered* in the Bible by the voice out of the whirlwind. He is *silenced* by it—silenced by some thirty or forty of the greatest lines in all literature—silenced by the might and majesty and magnificence of the creation!" The playwright does not agree with those who say that science shows there is no Creator. "Does it?" he writes. "Einstein has told us that he had sometimes the sense that he was following, in his plumbings and probings of the universe, the track of an Intelligence far beyond the reaches of his own!"

In the revised acting version of the play, MacLeish made the isolation of man more complete. Though he is awed, J. B. at the end repudiates the Voice as well as both Zuss and Nickles.

> I will not
> Duck my head again to thunder—
> That bullwhip crackling in my ears!—although
> He kill me with it. I must know.

J. B. will not take his life as a filthy farce, with Nickles, or weep with the meek who question nothing, as Zuss believes man should do.

> Neither the
> Yes in ignorance . . . the No in spite . . .
> Neither of them!

In this later version, MacLeish uses a phrase from the Biblical Voice out of the Whirlwind itself to encourage J. B. to stand on his own, a phrase which gives man a metaphysical basis on which to stand.

> Deck thyself now with Majesty and Excellency . . .
> Then will I also confess unto thee
> That thine own right hand can save thee.

Love, as a symbol of life, of positive commitment, is J. B.'s choice in the end, though he knows that "nothing is certain but the loss of love." Sarah, his wife, comes back to him, bearing in her hand a tiny sprig of forsythia in blossom, a symbol of the vitality of nature, the instinctive fertility that to both Romantic poet and naturalistic playwright meant something more important than man's skepticism.

Thus J. B.'s yea is as lonely and free as Antigone's nay, but his universe is not so empty. J. B. has no positive answer to Nickles' riddle, "If God is God he is not good, / If God is good, he is not God." But the majesty of creation is not to be denied. Unlike most existentialists, MacLeish does not ignore those traditions of religion and art that give many people a strong sense of continuity with the past.

The play has been attacked from many sides. The orthodox do not like the solution by man alone, without God's help. The logical do not like leaving unsolved the dilemma of an all-powerful Creator who does not make clear

309

man's values and responsibilities. Those devoted to social purpose dislike a hero treated as Everyman, out of social context. The bohemians despise a self-satisfied American millionaire as a hero. The antiromantics dislike seeing love used as a symbol of life. The realists object to passages that are too consciously poetic. The humanists ask whether there is any real reason for a circus setting, except the fad among the absurdists for clowns and actors in their games of "now it's real, now it's playacting." Yet, in spite of adverse criticism, *J. B.* remains a play of major importance in our time—an impressive poetic drama and an example of the positive elements possible in existentialism.

The Theatre of the Absurd

Even Sartre derived a strong sense of commitment from his existentialism and worked with the Communists and other groups as he approved of their immediate aims, but the theatre of the absurd, the *avant-garde* theatre in the 1950's, discovered no values worthy of commitment. The absurdists even celebrate the breakdown of language and communication, and deliberately baffle the audience. If confusion and chaos are the human condition, then the form of the play itself must make use of interruption, discontinuity, incongruity, senseless logic, and senseless repetition. Some absurdists have gone so far as to write no play at all but to arrange a set of directions for both actors and audience in a "happening," a type of performance already noticed in the discussion of modern dance. Eugène Ionesco in 1950 called his first play an "antiplay," and absurdist playwrights delight in outraging the audience. Whereas existentialists like Anouilh, Sartre, and Camus have written carefully constructed plays which draw the conclusion that the world has no dependable order, the absurdists express disorder in the very form of their writing.

Now that the disjointed play form is established, it is possible to look back and see that several earlier plays explored some aspects of the absurd. In 1836, Georg Büchner in *Wozzeck* presented the plight of a hapless little soldier in a series of disconnected, fragmentary scenes, woven together in an impressive opera in 1926 by Alban Berg. Alfred Jarry's *Ubu Roi* (1896) and Guillaume Apollinaire's *Les Mamelles de Tirésias* (1918) expressed contempt for conventional order in a mélange of disconnected symbols, characters, and startling words. The incantatory sound of words, rather than their meaning, interested Gertrude Stein in her *Four Saints in Three Acts,* made into a charming short opera by Virgil Thomson in 1934. But the absurdist plays of the 1950s and 60s go further in their picture of man's isolation.

It is significant that three of the most important writers of absurd plays are exiles by choice, living in Paris and writing in a language other than their native tongue—Samuel Beckett, an Irishman, Eugène Ionesco, a Roumanian, and Arthur Adamov, an Armenian-Russian. A fourth, the Frenchman Jean Genêt, felt himself set apart from humanity as a criminal and pervert and has glorified his defiance of the lawful and normal. These men have chosen to emphasize the sense of alienation, which Camus has described in a much-quoted paragraph in *The Myth of Sisyphus:*

> . . . in a universe that is suddenly deprived of illusions and light, man feels a stranger. His is an irremediable exile, because he is deprived of memories of a lost homeland as much as he lacks the hope of a promised land to come. This divorce between man and his life, the actor and his setting, truly constitutes the feeling of Absurdity.

The breakdown of conventional language—the use of empty phrases that not only prevent communication but destroy the sense of identity—was the subject of Ionesco's first play, *The Bald Soprano* (1950). He got the idea from the meaningless phrases in an English phrase book for foreigners. In a social evening, the Smiths and the Martins repeat, with a spirit of affability and charm, statements that are not only inane but contradictory.

MRS. SMITH   Yogurt is excellent for the stomach, the kidneys, the appendicitis, and apotheosis . . .

MR. SMITH   Here's a thing I don't understand. In the newspaper they always give the age of deceased persons but never the age of the newly born. That doesn't make sense. . . . Tsk, it says here that Bobby Watson died.

MRS. SMITH   My God, the poor man! When did he die?

MR. SMITH   Why do you pretend to be astonished? You know very well that he's been dead these past two years. Surely you remember that we attended his funeral a year and a half ago . . . It's been three years since his death was announced.

MRS. SMITH   What a pity! He was so well preserved.

From that point, the Smiths exhaust the processes of logic in debating whether a ring of the doorbell always means there is someone there or never does. The Martins reach the amazing conclusion that since they arrived in the same compartment on the same train and live in the same room, they must, by coincidence, be husband and wife. But after a theatrical climax, the Martins take the Smiths' place and start the evening over again. Whereas the expressionist hero contended with a depersonalized, nameless crowd, in search of his own identity, here all is inanity. The characters have no hunger, no conscious desires, no identity. They are interchangeable, and everything ends where it started.

Neither action nor language carries conviction to the absurdists. As early as the 1920s the significance of man's deeds was brought into question. After the futile First World War and peace treaty and the devastating Russian Revolution, who could believe in the value of action? Burlesques of the heroic attitudes and noble gestures of nineteenth-century melodrama were popular. By the 1950s language itself had lost its validity and audiences today are amused in the absurd theatre, as in Pop Art, at obsessive repetitions of the banal. Ionesco felt that before life can recover mystery or meaning the emptiness must be fully explored. In *Notes and Counternotes* he wrote,

"To feel the absurdity of the commonplace, and of language—its falseness—is already to have gone beyond it. To go beyond it we must first of all bury ourselves in it. What is comical is the unusual in its pure state: nothing seems more surprising to me than that which is banal: the surreal is here, within the grasp of our hands, in our everyday conversation." The Pop artists bury themselves in the banal, blowing up the details of a comic strip to cover half a wall, painting forty-eight identical cans of vegetable soup or thirty-six identical faces of a movie queen, shaping a bright-colored hamburger or a three-foot piece of lemon pie out of painted plaster. If we live in a world of comic strips, neon advertising, TV commercials, and loud-speaker chatter, why not make art from this real landscape of the modern mind? But the absurd theatre is funnier than Pop Art.

Domestic inanities are the subject of Ionesco's *Jack, or The Submission* (1955), a play about Jack's revolt against his family until they find him an unusual bride, with three noses, with whom he can play his own games of sexual fantasy in terms of children's pet animals. In America a similar infantile regression is made amusing in two of Edward Albee's absurd plays, where "Mommie" and "Daddy" are lost in baby talk and the rejected, senile grandmother has to find her own death. In *The Sandbox* she finds

FIGURE *9.8*   Theatre of the absurd. The action builds up frantically to an empty announcement. Ionesco's *The Chairs*. Humboldt State College production, directed by W. L. Turner, designed by Richard Rothrock, and costumed by Ethelyn Pauley. Photo Peter Palmquist.

a kind angel of death; in *The American Dream,* she finds an emasculated muscle man, an empty dream of vitality.

Things, objects that give meaning and rich texture in naturalistic plays, become in absurd plays of the 1950s and 60s the grotesque symbols of man's emptiness or even his terror. In *The Caretaker* by England's Harold Pinter, piles of junk fill the rooms of the two insane brothers, who first show kindness to the down-and-out tramp, letting him feel a new security in the promise of becoming caretaker, then turn on him and eject him from his junk-pile paradise. In Ionesco's *The Chairs,* chairs are brought in frantically to fill a large room as an old couple welcome a world of unseen guests waiting to hear the great message the old man is to deliver to the world. When everybody is there, including the emperor, the old couple introduce the orator and jump out the windows into the sea. The orator can do nothing but mutter. In some productions, he writes the great message on the blackboard—a mass of meaningless letters, with a few single words like "angel food" or "animal crackers." In Ionesco's *The New Tenant,* the furniture is piled up until there is no room for the tenants, while in *Amédée* a growing corpse, image of dead love, crowds a couple out of their apartment. The husband drags the corpse into the street, trying to explain to others that he is against nihilism and in favor of a new humanism, until the corpse floats him off in the air like a balloon.

In his longer plays, Ionesco has used a typical "little man," called by the common French name Bérenger, as a sympathetic if ineffectual symbol   *313*

FIGURE *9.9*   Theatre of the absurd. An uncontrolled environment with proliferating detail produces terror. Ionesco's *The New Tenant.* University of Texas production, directed by Francis Hodge, designed by Robert Hedley, costumed by Paul Reinhardt, and lighted by David Nancarrow.

FIGURE *9.10* Theatre of cruelty. Hidden hatreds erupt in a cruel ritual enacted before an audience of Negro actors in white-face masks. Genêt's *The Blacks.* New York Off-Broadway production, 1961. Photo Martha Swope.

of modern man facing a baffling universe. *The Killer* is a horror story: Bérenger cannot stop the mysterious killer, though he tries all possible defenses of human values, and he finally submits to his own death. In *Rhinoceros* Bérenger defies the crowd, not entirely convinced as everybody in his town turns into a rhinoceros, even his sweetheart, Daisy.

> Daisy, don't leave me alone! . . . But they won't get me! You won't get me! I'm not joining you. . . . I'm staying as I am. I'm a human being. . . . What if it's true what Daisy said, and they're the ones in the right. . . . They're the good-looking ones. I was wrong! . . . I wish I was like them! . . . I've only myself to blame; I should have gone with them while there was still time. Now it's too late! Now I'm a monster, just a monster. . . . Oh well, too bad. I'll take on the whole of them! . . . I'm the last man left, and I'm staying that way until the end. I'm not capitulating!

At least Ionesco's little man makes an attempt to stop the reversion to the barbaric.

The compulsion to act a role, a role that becomes more real than reality, has been the theme of Jean Genêt, whose play-acting scenes conjure up more grotesque images than were ever thought of by Pirandello. Genêt follows some of the principles set forth by the French dramatic theorist Antonin Artaud in his influential work *The Theatre and Its Double,* which advocates that the theatre return to the intensity of primitive rituals, of cruelty, incantation, and dream. His plays, in various ways, act out rites,

314

Kinds of Plays

whether the social rites of maids pretending to be their mistress in *The Maids* (1947) or the ritual violation and murder of a white woman in *The Blacks* (1959). All Genêt's plays include observers watching a performance, recognizing with mixed feelings the Freudian images of their own suppressed desires.

The brothel in which Genêt's *The Balcony* (1960) is set is more than an ordinary brothel; it furnishes not only mirrors but costumes, settings, and actors so that the clients may act out their secret desires—one to be a Bishop hearing the lurid confessions of a young woman; one to be a Judge ordering a half-naked executioner to whip a beautiful girl; one to be a General riding a horse in triumph, played by an almost nude girl wearing a tail. Outside, a revolution is taking place in the town; the Chief of Police eventually puts it down by presenting the Madam as the new Queen and getting the clients to act as real Bishop, Judge, and General. The chief gets his fulfillment, the achievement of an image, when finally he sees a man come to the brothel who wants to play being Chief of Police. Everything returns to normal, and the Madam gets ready for the next clients. The indecent rites of role-playing go on in both the brothel and the real world. As in Pirandello's *Henry IV*, the pretended becomes more real than the reality outside.

Samuel Beckett, the Irishman writing in Paris, seems haunted by images of confinement and loss of freedom. In *Waiting for Godot* (1952) two tramps are unable to leave the desolate rim of the universe. In *Endgame* (1957) the two main characters are shut up in an underground dungeon, one confined to a wheelchair; a legless old couple reside in two ashcans. The Woman in *Happy Days* begins the play buried up to her waist, later up to her neck. In another play called simply *Play,* the characters are enclosed to their chins in urns. Sartre's prison in *No Exit,* the one room in which three souls are condemned to create hell for one another, has been narrowed by Beckett to more and more fantastically enclosed spaces.

Beckett's *Waiting for Godot* is the masterpiece of the absurd; of all the plays it is the most perfect in its form, the most complete in its desolation, the most comic in its anguish. Two lonely tramps are waiting for Godot, who every day sends word that he will not meet them today but surely tomorrow. The place where they wait is a desolate road, empty save for a stick of a tree not sturdy enough to hang oneself on. But the tramps are also theatrical clowns, using comic routines of vaudeville days, putting on and off their hats, boots, shirts, coats, and ties, arguing, interrupting, telling anecdotes, munching carrots and turnips, paying mock deference to each other, stumbling and falling, alternating groans with sudden squeals or grimaces. Even some of the most painful moments are exploded into laughter by the clownish antics.

To the existentialists, freedom is a challenge; to a few people, like William Saroyan, freedom is a great delight. But to Beckett's tramps, freedom is hell. They have no inner resources, no friends, no memories, and no orientation in place or time—they do not know where they were last night or indeed if it is the Saturday they were told, they think, to wait for Godot. If the audience wonders why they do not join the activities of the world, the answer appears in the arrival in each act of a new vaudeville couple, Pozzo and Lucky, a fat, active master driving his slave by a rope around his neck—a hideous but comic image of all masters and slaves, all employers and employees.

The play has a remarkably strict form, expressive of its meaning. Within each act the form is a series of moments that start an assertion, a plan, a hope, and each time quickly dissipate it. Discontinuity is both the theme and the form, deflation the theme and the comic method. The repetition in the second act of the first-act pattern, with a slight development, has a classic perfection that is like mathematics or logic or music.

At first view the play seems to be a total negation. Godot will never come. The tree has leaves in the second act, but that does not help. Where J. B.'s wife Sarah found a forsythia branch as a promise of spring and new vitality, these tramps have lost touch with nature. They know nothing of history or religion or science. When Lucky is ordered to "think," he bursts into a Joycean farrago of words, a burlesque of the traditional philosophical arguments for the existence of God, mixing in images of fire and cold that suggest the atomic bomb and the nineteenth-century theory that the sun would grow cold. The play does not point to any of the known sources of value,

FIGURE *9.11* An American play of the absurd. The constructivist setting of different levels is decorated as junk sculpture. Schocken's *The Tiger Rag.* University of Illinois production, directed by Barnard Hewitt, designed by George McKinney, and costumed by Genevieve Richardson.

yet it is a passionate cry from the depths of the night for some new faith, and in that sense it is a very religious play. The problem is certainly metaphysical. No economic improvement, no psychological adjustment, no doctor's pill, but only a new definition of man, a new relation to the universe, will serve these forlorn creatures lost in the night. In exploring the last possibility of emptiness, the play may be a turning point. If man has such a passionate need for the spiritual plane, he will find some new, or renew some old, definition of man and God.

In the meantime Beckett offers not only raucous laughter but a kind of song made of the banal. There is a touch of incantation in the short, trite phrases of Ionesco and Albee, but there is something like lyric eloquence in *Waiting for Godot*. The telegraphic short phrases in the machine rhythms and explosive climaxes of expressionism are given a more subtle, more poetic, form in the short phrases of Beckett (see Exercises 3 and 4, pp. 328–30).

The Human Condition Without Despair

Not all playwrights who deal with alienation present such utter desolation as we find in *Waiting for Godot*. In spite of artificial flowers, trees still grow; in spite of neon, the sun still shines. In spite of rockets and space ships and in spite of buildings that try, like rockets, to disconnect man from the ground, the rugged stone still feels good to the touch. Perhaps the earth is not a totally unfavorable dwelling for the spirit of man. If man is really free to choose, he is free to choose favorable values. If the universe is impartial, then the definition of the human condition as absurd is as subjective a judgment, as devoid of objective truth, as the opposite judgments of the religious prophets and the poets. If some thinkers have been paralyzed by anguish or by terror of the bomb, others have explored some limited field where communication and even action is possible. If there are moments when Franz Kafka's nameless "K" of *The Castle* seems a symbol of all of us, unable to penetrate far enough into the castle to find a dependable authority, there are other moments when we are sure about the job to be done. If Kafka's *The Trial* reminds us that organized institutional terror, the modern equivalent of the dreadful demons of romance, gets people into court so impersonally that they are never told what they are accused of, if we live in a world of iron curtains and military "security," still there survive some elements of free speech and an open market for ideas, so important since ancient Athens. If man can devise ways of killing the spirit, perhaps he can also devise ways of bringing it back to life.

The last few decades have produced several stage fantasies which, while defining man's condition as critical, have showed a triumph of the spirit. On a farcical level, in Mary Ellen Chase's *Harvey* Elwood Dowd relies on his six-foot rabbit to help him enjoy the absurdities of a world to which he doesn't want to adjust. Jean Giraudoux's fantasy *The Madwoman of Chaillot* deals with a mad world on a deeper level. When the Madwoman discovers that a group of financiers and prospectors, like invaders from another

317

FIGURE *9.12* Symbolic fantasy with several aspects of expressionism. Distorted scenery reflects the confusion of the inner mind. The characters are exaggerated types in mechanical duplication: three young lovers, three corporation presidents, three women reporters, three explorers. Giraudoux's *The Madwoman of Chaillot*. University of Arkansas production, directed by George R. Kernodle, designed by Preston Magruder, and costumed by Charles Martinelli.

planet, is about to destroy Paris to get the oil underneath, she and the Madwomen of three other sections of Paris hold a trial and condemn them, lure them into the bowels of the earth with the smell of oil, and thereby save the world. The Madwomen do not face reality; they have something better than reality—imagination and faith.

Carrying the theme of faith even further, William Saroyan wrote stories and plays that are often delightful, if rarely well organized. He is as devoted to the subconscious and the dream as any surrealist and starts with a human condition as lonely as the absurdists have portrayed. But since he reaches exactly opposite conclusions, he is dismissed as sentimental. When his characters realize and accept loneliness and the primacy of faith over facts, they discover both the love of God and kinship with all other lonely creatures. In *The Time of Your Life* when Joe assures the truck driver and the streetwalker that he believes their dream of themselves, then they have strength to be what they dream and to love each other. Saroyan's immigrants and rural characters, bringing dialect and a touch of color to the bars, public libraries, or forsaken buildings where they gather, find friendship and a racy variety in American cities. A Saroyan hero, unafraid of the machine, challenges a super-pinball machine and finally wins. Every character in Saroyan has some ability—singing, dancing, reciting, yarn-spinning, or merely believing—making much too cheerful and lively a picture for some theatregoers. Saroyan accepts a world of contradictions, life and death, inhale and exhale, comedy and tragedy. Where many young people choose Kierkegaard   *319*

FIGURE *9.13*   A touch of warmth and charm for the lonely man. Both cruelty and sympathy are found in a Texas jail. Saroyan's *Hello, Out There!* University of Arkansas production, directed and designed by Kenneth Gilliam.

and Kafka as their ancestors, Saroyan resurrects from the same past the energetic affirmation of Walt Whitman and the witty zest in dialectic of Bernard Shaw. A man is free to choose.

Much more serious is John Osborne, who has emerged in the last decade as the most versatile playwright of England. He deals in a comic way with defeat and has much in common with the absurdists, yet rescues more sense of the integrity of human character than Beckett or Ionesco. His first success, *Look Back in Anger* (1956), is almost a naturalistic play. Jimmy Porter is caught in an environment he hates, but he is not inarticulate. He spits back with racy anger that gave a name to a generation in Britain—the Angry Young Men. The welfare state is a boring fact that leaves him still frustrated. The old establishment, still intact, keeps him outside the regular social order. There is no social cause to fight for. The problem is spiritual and is worked out partly in terms of his relationship with his wife Alison. He torments her and drives her out, and he can accept her only when she, too, is humiliated and crushed by intense suffering.

The Entertainer (1957) has wider implications for England and the modern world. The run-down music-hall performer—a vivid role for Laurence Olivier on both stage and screen—is a symbol of postwar England as she has seemed at times (FIGURE *12.4*). He is facing bankruptcy and failure, but he refuses to give up his music-hall routines and move to Canada. Osborne makes brilliant use of the banality of the popular tradition of stage songs to express the cheap emptiness of modern life. Archie Rice, the entertainer, treats his father, wife, and daughter with bitter harshness, cynically planning to take on a new woman, snarling at his own lack of human feeling. Like modern man, his values are exhausted. He remembers with envy the real feeling of a Negro blues singer he heard once, and when his son is killed in Africa—an event with symbolic overtones—he finds true depth of feeling in singing the same song. Where Harold Pinter, from *The Caretaker* (1960) to *The Homecoming* (1965), has continued in the well-made-play form his psychological thrillers, comedies of menace that explore the private terror of a few passive people tortured by unaccountable intruders who are somehow in the same gray nightmare room, Osborne has moved outward. He has used epic techniques to explore historical forces of authority and doubt in *Luther* (1961), the failure of conscience in personal and professional life in *Inadmissible Evidence* (1964), and the interrelation of secret decadence and secret military intrigue in *A Patriot for Me* (1965).

Two Swiss plays became fairly popular in the late 1950s and early 60s, perhaps because their inhuman cruelty suggests much more than individual nightmare or psychological disorientation. They both become allegories of the real events of the twentieth century. Max Frisch's *Biedermann and the Firebugs* starts like a Pinter melodrama as two firebugs move into the attic of a terrified little householder and burn his house down. But gradually the audience realizes that the play is a vivid image of Europe frantically trying to appease Hitler while seeing very clearly that he is moving drums of oil into the attic. The other play, *The Visit,* by Friedrich Duerrenmatt, has

320

Kinds of Plays

had vivid performances both on Broadway with Alfred Lunt and Lynn Fontanne and in a film with Ingrid Bergman. The play is not a specific allegory but has a number of levels of appeal, both personal and political. The richest woman in the world returns to the small town in which she had grown up and offers great wealth to the run-down citizens if they will give her the life of the man who years before had seduced her. After protesting, the citizens finally kill him (in the film she lets him live) and see their town blossom, singing the praises of prosperity, for not even war is worse than poverty. The two central characters are much more interesting than those in most absurdist dramas, and there is more variety in the background figures. The personal story has the grandeur of a Greek or Elizabethan tragedy of revenge, and the townspeople suggest many of the problems of the postwar period: the weakness that may be as terrifying as evil, the price paid in war for the new prosperity, the lack of any relation between ethics and the public activities of a town. The play uses epic techniques and absurdist fantasies, but it reaches out of the subjective mists to comment on the modern world.

For all the hysterical laughter evoked from the incongruities and surprises, most of these European dramas are grim and tragic in their basic attitude. Only an Irishman was able to make a real comedy out of the absurd "human condition." In *The Hostage* (1958) Brendan Behan uses extravagant fantasies and delightful ballads to satirize warfare, group living, and Irish nationalism. Not since Aristophanes lashed out at the Athenians for not living up to their ideals has satire been so strong and racy. Behan has something very rare

FIGURE *9.14* Absurdity raised to the comic level. The Irish underground war is treated with irony and satire, slapstick and song. Behan's *The Hostage*. New York Off-Broadway production, 1960. Photo Friedman-Abeles.

among the absurdists: a sense of humor about himself. He triumphs over the grim anguish of his generation with a gay song of "Oh death where is thy sting-a-ling-a-ling."

Among American playwrights who might be classified as absurdists, Edward Albee has received the most attention both from critics and from the theatre public. His Ionesco-like one-acts have been mentioned. His superbly intense *Who's Afraid of Virginia Woolf?* (1962) combines psychological realism with the fantasy play-acting developed by the absurdists from Strindberg's dream plays. It goes beyond old-fashioned realism only in showing that the exorcism of fantasies, one of the main functions of realism in clearing the debris away from truth, may leave a character desolate and devoid of structure. Albee's *Tiny Alice* (1965) should hardly satisfy the absurdists. Out of a background of contempt and vituperation, which Albee can create superbly, a mystic young man embraces Alice as a symbol of the divine and dies happy as the lights go out in room after room of the miniature chateau, image of the world.

For characteristically American plays of the absurd, one should not turn to Albee, nor to Saroyan, whose loving characters suffer little anguish, nor to Arthur Kopit's travesty on American momism that is almost as amusing as its title, *Oh Dad, Poor Dad, Mamma's Hung You in the Closet and I'm Feelin' So Sad*. Rather, one should turn to Tennessee Williams' *Camino Real* and to Thornton Wilder's *The Skin of Our Teeth*, which in many ways is theatre of the absurd while it is also so much more.

Camino Real (1953) is a surrealist and absurdist fantasy. Kilroy, the American hero, staggers out of the desert into a tightly walled Latin-American village where various fugitives, from past and present, are trying to escape. He is beaten, made to put on a clown's nose and a clown costume, cheated by a Gypsy's daughter, and dissected by an anatomy teacher while two laughing street cleaners with a white can wait for his body. Camille, with Casanova's help, tries to get on the one unscheduled plane, while the elegant dandy from the novels of Proust gets beaten to death. No image is spared of seediness, deception, exhaustion, and cruelty. Yet these echoes of the past are reminders of the triumphs of the human spirit. The legendary Camille, the courtesan who made the mistake of falling in love, and Casanova, now King of the Cuckolds, find companionship and solace in each other. Lord Byron departs to sail back to Athens, to contemplate the Acropolis with the memory of an earlier dream of purity and freedom. At the end, Kilroy and Don Quixote go out the high gate to cross the terra incognita toward the clear mountains. It is not a futile life-lie but an indomitable courage we see in the hearts of Williams' characters.

For those who are willing to find a balanced view of the absurd human condition, recognizing disruption and destruction, the forces inside and outside that threaten man's values, and yet seeing some hope of rescuing the twentieth century from complete emptiness and destruction, *The Skin of Our Teeth* (1942) is one of the most important of all modern plays. Its theme is interruption and new beginnings, and its very form carries out this theme.

Kinds of Plays

FIGURE *9.15* Wilder's *The Skin of Our Teeth* produced with the terror of the theatre of cruelty and the earthy detail of epic realism. Mr. Antrobus comes home with the wheel he has just invented. The Tyrone Guthrie Theatre, Minneapolis, 1966. Directed by Douglas Campbell and designed by Tanya Moiseiwitsch and Carolyn Parker.

Civilization is interrupted and almost destroyed three times—in the first act by ice, in the second by flood, and in the third by war. The play itself is interrupted several times—when the scenery leans in or flies up in the air, when actors miss cues, and when they drop out of character to speak to the audience or to the other actors. These absurd occurrences are included partly for the fun of it and partly to illustrate the theme of interruption, but they also bring in another theatrical level, like the double level in *The Balcony,* as the actors make their own, often unfavorable, comments on the characters they are playing. In the last act, two actors get so carried away by their own private antagonisms that they are about to strangle each other in earnest, and the other actors have to interrupt the play. The second act, in Atlantic City, is as much a reenactment of primitive rites as Genêt could wish—the wild whoopee of the convention city, where moral habits are interrupted and old rites of seduction that almost interrupt marriage are enacted.

There is an abundance of superficial fun, as when the telegraph boy delivers a message in Excelsior, New Jersey, saying that Papa (whose name, Mr. Antrobus, is from the Greek word for man) has just invented the wheel   *323*

FIGURE *9.16* Wilder's *The Skin of Our Teeth* produced as a theatrical fantasy in the tradition of American musicals. In a New Jersey living room suggested by bright-colored fragments of walls, a mammoth and a dinosaur are family pets. Eastern Illinois University production, directed by E. G. Gabbard, designed by John E. Bielenberg, and costumed by James Koertge. Photo Bertram.

and is adding to the alphabet and the multiplication table; and the enactment in today's terms of the Ice Age, the Flood, and a modern war is much like the acting of roles in many plays of the absurd. But there are richer implications. At first the play may seem to mean that all crises in all ages are the same and that man is caught in an endless cycle; but that is not the final meaning. The first disaster, the Ice Age, is entirely external—it is out of man's control and all he can do is build fires and try to preserve a few of man's accomplishments as a help in starting over again. The Flood of the second act is not so external. Now men have earned their destruction by living for the moment, falling from their earlier dedication; Mr. Antrobus, relaxing at a convention, is about to abandon his marriage for another woman. Faced with emergency, he rediscovers his dedication to the human family and herds them and the animal representatives into the Ark waiting at the end of the pier. The third disaster, war, is entirely the responsibility of man. Where the first two crises were placed at the end of acts, the war comes at the beginning of Act III, and the main concern is how to reestablish human relationships after it is over. Mr. Antrobus faces the surviving enemy, his own son, who is also Cain, and presently the two are at each other's throats. Wilder's analysis of the psychology of conflict, written during the war, has held up very well. The son resents authority, and the father has been so sure of the importance of past achievement that he has not bothered to consider the son's own thoughts and choices.

Kinds of Plays

But even in moments of the play that have the most serious implications, absurdity reduces the tension. At the end of the first act, as the ice gets closer, the family takes in refugees: Homer, the blind singer; Moses, the judge; a doctor; and the Muse sisters, who all sing around the fire. As Mr. Antrobus is teaching Henry the multiplication table, the lights dim, and Mrs. Antrobus starts reading to Gladys from the Bible—"In the beginning God created the heavens and the earth . . . ." When tears come into the eyes of the audience, the absurd interrupts; the ushers start breaking up chairs and the maid, Sabina, says to the audience, "Will you please start handing up your chairs? We'll need everything for this fire. Save the human race." At the end of the play, after the fight between father and son has been settled and mankind is ready to start over, a parade of actors, representing the hours and the planets passing over the sky, speak passages from the great prophets and philosophers, Spinoza, Plato, Aristotle, and that same beautiful passage from Genesis. As the line "And the Lord said let there be light and there was light" is reached, the stage lights go out. When they come on, Sabina is

FIGURE 9.17 Theatre of illusion. Identity is achieved by play-acting in a brothel. One of the clients plays the role of a general with a girl as his horse. Genêt's *The Balcony*. New York Off-Broadway production, 1960. Photo Martha Swope.

starting the play again. Sabina herself, brilliantly played in the original production by Tallulah Bankhead, is an embodiment of serious meaning and absurdity. On stage almost continuously from beginning to end of the play, she is Wilder's medium for a variety of implied social and philosophical comment as she takes her several roles—comic maid of a conventional play, servant who is the confidante of each member of the family, siren who threatens family unity, and peacemaker who restores it.

The interruptions, the theatrical discontinuities, and the ritual play-acting give a full picture of the absurd human condition. The banalities of school days, of family life, of Atlantic City conventions and infidelities are all there. There is acute awareness that the thread of contact with past values is fragile and also that man is free at every moment to choose his values and create a new world. But if man remembers the dreams and hopes that carried him through the crises of the past, he will cherish every book, every formula, every scientific discovery, and every passage of sacred scripture that has come down to him. Like Mr. Antrobus, he is ready to start over again, and, unlike Beckett's tramps, he has a vision to guide him.

FROM REALISM TO ABSURDITY, from determinism to existentialism, from high exaltation to low farce, we have traced a dozen attitudes toward life and have seen how each attitude found its particular kind of play, and often its special kind of setting, acting, and audience. Yet no play completely respects such mapmaking; it is too easy to stray over the border. It was simple to distinguish a naturalistic play of the early-twentieth century from a Chinese romance or a romantic Viennese operetta, but by the middle of the century even these extremes were overlapping. Distinctions like realism versus theatricalism sometimes help in the analysis of a play, but *Death of a Salesman* is both real and theatrical. When a playwright is creating a play, he does not say, "I am going to write a modern Aristophanic satire," or "This will be a play of dream sequences like Strindberg's," or "Now I will be absurd," though Arthur Miller did say that he was conscious as he wrote *A View from the Bridge* that he was trying to give it some of the austerity and inevitability of a Greek tragedy. The playwright, as he is struggling in revision, and the director, designer, and actors, as they plan the production, do ask how this climax can be made stronger, what kind of transition is needed here, what technique or what color would make that moment more effective.

The next part of the book will be concerned with the art of the theatre—the processes of planning, rehearsing, and performing a play, the ways in which playwright, director, designer, and actors cooperate to make the play vivid and convincing to the audience.

EXERCISES AND DEMONSTRATIONS

1. AN IMPROVISED EXPRESSIONISTIC SCENE WITH MACHINE RHYTHMS. A large group arranged in a semicircle follows a leader in front, who con-

326

ducts as for an orchestra. Each actor chooses a machine he can suggest by a simple motion and sound, imitating either the machine or the operator or both. Choose a motion that can have a strong accent on a slow one-two-one-two rhythm: driving a railway spike with a sledge hammer, saying "heave-ho, heave-ho"; typing a letter repeating conventional phrases; operating an adding machine or a dentist drill, and so on. The conductor, beating the one-two like a metronome, coordinates the different machines into one rhythm. After the actors are well started as machines, one girl, the only human being, rushes in to appeal to one after the other with something like "My little brother has been hit by an automobile; please help me!" But the mechanical pattern continues. After four or five appeals the crescendo starts, led by the conductor. The others slowly move in toward the human girl, gradually speeding up the tempo, increasing the volume, raising the pitch, and making the rhythm more sharply accented. As they crowd in, the din becomes violent but remains in strict rhythm. At the climax, it could be held steady, then gradually let down, but that would require more rehearsals. It is simpler to consider the action as a nightmare that ends as the girl screams and wakes up.

The exercise must usually be done two or three times to achieve the precisely coordinated rhythm. The combination of fascination and terror creates very strong tension; it is the same combination as that developed in many expressionistic plays and some pieces of modern music and art. Stravinsky's *Rite of Spring,* Honegger's *Pacific 231,* Milhaud's *Creation of the World,* and the music of Varèse offer interesting comparisons.

2. ACTING A SCENE FROM AN AMERICAN POETIC VERSION OF EXISTENTIAL-ISM. Take the scene near the end of Archibald MacLeish's *J. B.,* where Nickles, bitter and incredulous, protests that J. B. will not accept the restored world that God offers Job. Notice that most of the lines have a trochaic rhythm, with a strong initial accent.

NICKLES   Wife back! *Wife!* He wouldn't touch her.
        He wouldn't take her with a glove.
        After all that filth and blood and
        Fury to begin again!
        After life like his to take
        The seed up of the sad creation
        Planting the hopeful world again. . . .
        He can't.
            He won't.
                He wouldn't touch her.

MR. ZUSS   He does though.

NICKLES   Live his life again?
        Not even the most ignorant, obstinate,
        Stupid or degraded man
        This filthy planet ever farrowed,
        Offered the opportunity to live
        His bodily life twice over, would accept it—

It can't be borne twice over!

Can't be!

MR. ZUSS It is though. Time and again it is.
Every blessed generation.
Time and again!

Time and again!

(*As J. B. stirs, Nickles turns to speak to him.*)

NICKLES Tell me how you'll play the end—
Any man was screwed as Job was . . . .
I'll tell you how to play it! Listen!
Think of all the mucked up millions
Since this buggered world began
Said No! Said Thank you! took a rope's end.
Took a window for a door,
Swallowed something, gagged on something . . . .
Not one of them had known what you know.
Not one had learned *Job's* truth.
Job won't take it. Job won't touch it.
Job will . . . fling it in God's face
With half his guts to make it spatter.
He'd rather suffocate in dung.
Drown in ordure . . .

Suffocate in dung,

Drown in ordure . . .

3. THE COMEDY AND ANGUISH OF ABSURDITY. Practice the following scene from Samuel Beckett's *Waiting for Godot* for rhythm and pace. The mood is grim unhappiness. Though the characters are held down by weariness and defeat, the dialogue should have a little of the irony, sarcasm, and punch of vaudeville clowns playing for laughs. The tramps are so paralyzed and absorbed in waiting that they start each unit scarcely listening to each other, with a slight wait between each speech and the answer; they build to a fretful climax and are then suddenly left empty.

VLADIMIR Well? What do we do?

ESTRAGON Don't let's do anything. It's safer.

VLAD Let's wait and see what he says.

ESTR Who?

VLAD Godot.

ESTR Good idea.

VLAD Let's wait till we know exactly how we stand.

ESTR On the other hand it might be better to strike the iron before it freezes.

VLAD I'm curious to hear what he has to offer. Then we'll take it or leave it.

ESTR What exactly did we ask him for?

VLAD Were you not there?

ESTR I can't have been listening.

VLAD Oh . . . Nothing very definite.

ESTR	A kind of prayer.
VLAD	Precisely.
ESTR	A vague supplication.
VLAD	Exactly.
ESTR	And what did he reply?
VLAD	That he'd see.
ESTR	That he couldn't promise anything.
VLAD	That he'd have to think it over.
ESTR	In the quiet of his home.
VLAD	Consult his family.
ESTR	His friends.
VLAD	His agents.
ESTR	His correspondents.
VLAD	His books.
ESTR	His bank account.
VLAD	Before taking a decision.
ESTR	It's the normal thing.
VLAD	Is it not?
ESTR	I think it is.
VLAD	I think so too.

(*Silence.*)

ESTR (*anxious*)	And we?
VLAD	I beg your pardon?
ESTR	I said, And we?
VLAD	I don't understand.
ESTR	Where do we come in?
VLAD	Come in?
ESTR	Take your time.
VLAD	Come in? On our hands and knees.
ESTR	As bad as that?
VLAD	Your Worship wishes to assert his prerogatives?
ESTR	We've no rights any more?

(*Laugh of Vladimir, stifled as before, less the smile*)

VLAD	You'd make me laugh if it wasn't prohibited.
ESTR	We've lost our rights?
VLAD (*distinctly*)	We got rid of them.

(*Silence. They remain motionless, arms dangling, heads sunk, sagging at the knees.*)

4. A LYRIC MOMENT IN AN ABSURD PLAY.   Practice the following passage from *Waiting for Godot*, more rhythmic and poetic than the passage of Exercise 3. The *"Silences"* divide the passage into sections, and in the longer sections, as well as in the scene as a whole, there is a change from sharp irony to rapt awe. The final effect is one of grim acceptance that is almost total peace. The three-line cadence might have a slight insistence, as though each speaker is correcting the other yet is equally held in the spell.

ESTRAGON	In the meantime let us try and converse calmly, since we are incapable of keeping silent.
VLADIMIR	You're right, we're inexhaustible.

329

ESTR It's so we won't think.

VLAD We have that excuse.

ESTR It's so we won't hear.

VLAD We have our reasons.

ESTR All the dead voices.

VLAD They make a noise like wings.

ESTR Like leaves.

VLAD Like sand.

ESTR Like leaves.

   (*Silence.*)

VLAD They all speak at once.

ESTR Each one to itself.

   (*Silence.*)

VLAD Rather they whisper.

ESTR They rustle.

VLAD They murmur.

ESTR They rustle.

   (*Silence.*)

VLAD What do they say?

ESTR They talk about their lives.

VLAD To have lived is not enough for them.

ESTR They have to talk about it.

VLAD To be dead is not enough for them.

ESTR It is not sufficient.

   (*Silence.*)

VLAD They make a noise like feathers.

ESTR Like leaves.

VLAD Like ashes.

ESTR Like leaves.

SUGGESTED READING

PLAYS: EXPRESSIONISM

August Strindberg dramatized the subjective in *A Dream Play* (1902) and *The Ghost Sonata* (1907). Georg Kaiser treated man's struggle with a complex urban world in *From Morn to Midnight* (1912), *Gas I* (1918), and *Gas II* (1920), and Ernst Toller showed man's revolt against machine regimentation in *Man and the Masses* (1921) and *The Machine Wreckers* (1922). Factory regimentation is treated seriously in Karel Capek, *R.U.R.* (1921), and with satire and fantasy in *The Insect Comedy* (1921), written with his brother Josef Capek. Two of the best expressionistic studies of the dehumanization of the machine age are American: the ironic *The Adding Machine* (1923) by Elmer Rice and the lighter, more satiric *Beggar on Horseback* (1924) by George S. Kaufman and Marc Connelly. Although Eugene O'Neill did not follow the German expressionistic pattern exactly, he used elements of expressionism in a number of plays, notably *The Emperor Jones* (1920) and *The Great God Brown* (1926). The Irish playwright Sean O'Casey, after other playwrights were weary of the movement, wrote two expressionistic plays, the satiric *The Silver Tassie* (1928) and the poetic *Within the Gates* (1934).

330

Later echoes of expressionism are to be found in *Death of a Salesman, A Streetcar Named Desire,* and *The Caucasian Chalk Circle.* In musicals, some expressionistic elements are to be found throughout *Stop the World—I Want to Get Off* (1963), in the opening scene of *The Music Man* (1957), and in the around-the-world scenes of *The Fantasticks* (1960). Both epic theatre and the theatre of the absurd borrowed much from expressionism.

PLAYS: EXISTENTIALISM

Luigi Pirandello was a forerunner of the existentialist playwrights in *Right You Are—If You Think You Are* (1918), *Six Characters in Search of an Author* (1921), and *Henry IV* (1922), also called *The Emperor.* Jean-Paul Sartre wrote many essays on existentialism and dramatized different aspects in *The Flies* (1943), *No Exit* (1944), *The Devil and the Good Lord* (1951), and *The Condemned of Altona* (1959), called in England *Loser Wins.* Albert Camus's plays, *The Misunderstood* (1944) and *Caligula* (1945), are less impressive than his novels and essays. Jean Anouilh's *Antigone* (1944) still seems the best play on the lonely courage of choice. In America, Maxwell Anderson dramatized anguished heroes in *Winterset* (1935) and *Key Largo* (1939), but Archibald MacLeish's *J. B.* (1958) goes further in asserting faith in an almost empty universe.

PLAYS: THEATRE OF THE ABSURD

Georg Büchner anticipated the theatre of the absurd in *Wozzeck* (1836), given new life in the opera by Alban Berg in 1926. Eugène Ionesco established the absurd form in his short plays, *The Bald Soprano* (1950), *The Lesson* (1951), and *The Chairs* (1952), and in several more extended plays, especially *Rhinoceros* (1960). Samuel Beckett, *Waiting for Godot* (1952) and *Endgame* (1957), and Jean Genêt, *The Blacks* (1959) and *The Balcony* (1960), are the strongest examples of the form. Two Swiss plays, Friedrich Duerrenmatt, *The Visit* (1956), and Max Frisch, *Biedermann and the Firebugs* (1958), have symbolic political overtones that go beyond the other plays of the movement. In England, Harold Pinter's comedies of menace, *The Birthday Party* (1958), *The Caretaker* (1960), and *The Homecoming* (1965), though written in the well-made-play form, deal with unmotivated terror. John Osborne, *The Entertainer* (1957), has much in common with the plays of the absurd.

In America, William Saroyan found faith and joy in absurdity in *My Heart's in the Highlands* (1939), *The Time of Your Life* (1939), and *The Beautiful People* (1941). Tennessee Williams finds a modicum of faith in *Camino Real* (1953). Edward Albee's short plays written in the fifties—*The Zoo Story, The American Dream,* and *The Sandbox*—are the nearest in mood to the European models, while his longer plays have moved in other directions, *Who's Afraid of Virginia Woolf?* (1962) toward naturalism and *Tiny Alice* (1965) toward religious symbolism. Arthur Kopit satirizes anguish and absurdity in *Oh Dad, Poor Dad, Mamma's Hung You in the Closet and I'm Feelin' So Sad* (1960), and the Irishman Brendan Behan makes a hilarious satire using absurd devices in *The Hostage* (1958). Plays of some hope are the French Jean Giraudoux, *The Madwoman of Chaillot* (1945), and the American Thornton Wilder, *The Skin of Our Teeth* (1942), and Mary Ellen Chase, *Harvey* (1944).

331

SUGGESTED READING

A general view of modern rebellion is presented in Robert Brustein, *The Theatre of Revolt* (1964), and Robert W. Corrigan, *Theatre in the Twentieth Century** (1963), an anthology of essays. A good view of the range of contemporary American drama is Allan Lewis, *American Plays and Playwrights of the Contemporary Theatre* (1965), and Gerald Weales, *American Drama Since World War II* (1962). A vivid denunciation of recent drama as a chamber of horrors with a nihilistic philosophy is given by R. H. Gardner, *The Splintered Stage* (1965). See also Julia S. Price, *The Off-Broadway Theatre* (1962).

August Strindberg and Luigi Pirandello are discussed by Eric Bentley in *The Playwright as Thinker** (1946), *In Search of Theatre** (1953), and his introduction to Pirandello's plays, *Naked Masks** (1952). Bentley also contributed an article, "Il Tragico Imperatore," to a Pirandello issue of *Tulane Drama Review* (T31, Spring, 1966). There is a full and exciting interpretation of Ibsen and Strindberg in Maurice Valency, *The Flower and the Castle: An Introduction to Modern Drama* (1963). Elizabeth Sprigge has a good biography, *The Strange Life of August Strindberg* (1949).

The early German expressionist movement is described by Walter W. Sokel in *The Writer in Extremis: Expressionism in Twentieth-Century German Literature** (1959), and the same author has a good introduction to German expressionist plays, with manifestos and essays together with nine plays, in *An Anthology of German Expressionist Drama** (1963).

The prevailing definition of theatre of the absurd as a disjointed form was established by Martin Esslin in *The Theatre of the Absurd** (1961), though a wider definition in terms of philosophy is offered by William I. Oliver, "Between Absurdity and the Playwright," *Educational Theatre Journal,* XV, 3, reprinted in Travis Bogard and William I. Oliver, *Modern Drama: Essays in Criticism** (1965), an anthology ranging from Ibsen and Shaw to Anouilh and Genêt. An ingenious interpretation of family relations in Albee's plays is offered in Lee Baxandall, "The Theatre of Edward Albee," *Tulane Drama Review* (T28, Summer, 1965).

Paris as the center of the later drama of disruption has been the subject of a number of good studies in English. Both Wallace Fowlie, *Dionysus in Paris: A Guide to Contemporary French Theatre** (1960), and Jacques Guicharnaud with June Bechelman, *Modern French Theatre: From Giraudoux to Beckett** (1961), pick up the threads from early in the century, while others emphasize the more recent experiments: David Grossvogel, *The Self-Conscious Stage in Modern French Drama* (1958); Michael Benedikt and George E. Wellwarth, *Modern French Theatre: The Avant Garde, Dada, and Surrealism* (1964); and Leonard C. Pronko, *Avant Garde: The Experimental Theatre in France* (1962).

Antonin Artaud, whose ideas on theatre of cruelty and ritual and on "total theatre" had great influence in France, published *The Theatre and Its Double** (1938; English trans., 1958). The *Tulane Drama Review* for Winter, 1963 (T22), devoted several articles to Artaud.

For Ionesco, see his *Notes and Counternotes: Writings on the Theatre* (1964) and Richard N. Coe, *Eugène Ionesco** (1961).

The theatre of Jean Giraudoux was featured in *Tulane Drama Review* for Summer, 1959 (T4).

* Available in paperback edition.

SUGGESTED READING

Jean-Paul Sartre glorified the rebellion of Jean Genêt in a full-length book, *Saint Genêt: Actor and Martyr** (1952; Eng. trans., 1963). See also Joseph H. McMahan, *The Imagination of Jean Genêt** (1965). The spring 1963 issue of *Tulane Drama Review* (T19) was devoted to Genêt and Ionesco.

Rosette Lamont discusses "The Metaphysical Farce: Beckett and Ionesco," *The French Review*, XXXII, 4 (Feb., 1959). William York Tindall discusses both novels and plays in *Samuel Beckett** (1965), as does Richard N. Coe in *Samuel Beckett** (1965). See also Frederic J. Hoffman, *Samuel Beckett: The Language of the Self** (1965), Ruby Cohn, *Samuel Beckett: The Comic Gamut* (1962–63), and Robert Champigny, "Interpretations de *En Attendant Godot*," and L. E. Harvey, "Art and the Existential in *En Attendant Godot*," *PMLA*, LXXV (1960).

The new wave of English drama that is often dated from 1956 soon found a lively magazine *Encore* to foster and comment. The best articles were collected in *The Encore Reader*, edited by Charles Marowitz (1965). The new drama is also described well in John Russell Taylor, *The Angry Theatre: New British Drama* (1962), revised as *Anger and After** (1965).

An excellent survey of new trends and old revivals is Laurence Kitchin, *Drama in the Sixties: Form and Interpretation* (1966).

* Available in paperback edition.

PART TWO

THE PLAY IN PRODUCTION

The finished play in the theatre, like all finished art, looks easy. Picasso's drawings show no effort; in the film about his work we see him moving his crayon through space with the greatest of ease, sure of what he is doing. As the musician plays in the concert hall, no one thinks of his years of training and hours of daily practice. Trapeze artists meet in the air perfectly coordinated with one another and with the band music. When the lights go down in the theatre and a character emerges from the darkness, the people in the audience do not stop to think that a light man is moving levers to bring on focused spotlights. As the character moves about the stage, they are not conscious of how the floor has been carefully laid out, varied in levels by platforms, steps, and ramps, and backed and shaped by vertical planes and structures which they see only as sky, tree, rock, or wall. They receive an immediate impression—a feeling of joy or anxiety, of release or enclosure—without thinking that this impression is due to the carefully planned color and texture of costumes and furnishings, the kind of lines and shapes used in the design, the quality of the

OPPOSITE   A modern space stage of sculptural forms in pools of light. Dylan Thomas' *Under Milk Wood*. Arkansas Arts Center, Little Rock. Directed and designed by Charlotte MacArthur, and lighted by Dwight Jackson. Photo Don Gucker.

rhythm and movement. The audience accepts unquestioningly the person who seems to come to spontaneous life on the stage; yet this person is an actor whose simplest movements and speech must have the concentration and control of a dance or a song. The characters were created, perhaps centuries before, by the playwright, and the words may have been interpreted in other theatres by other actors in quite different ways. But here they create the "illusion of the first time," new and surprising in the tone and stage business of these actors at home in this stage setting. The performance, now so complete and effortless, took many weeks of planning, preparation, and rehearsal by an elaborate organization of many workers with special skills, all brought into focus in one overall art of the theatre.

The theatre is a synthesis of all the arts, and yet it is a complete art in itself. It is not literature, not recitation, not painting, not music, not dance. The words of the playwright must be given life by the actor in a context very different from the author's desk or the reader's armchair. Many successful writers have failed in the theatre because they would not or could not master the art of the stage. It is a visual art, and painters and architects have made important contributions. But they have had to learn to use color, line, space, and light in a unique way. It is a time art, with rhythms and sounds, and music has always been important in the theatre. But the music for a play or a film is very different from music that stands alone. Even the dancer-actor-reciter, the center of the whole moving performance, is only one element. Each theatre craftsman must develop his skill yet subordinate it to the plan, the idea, the particular style, of the production.

The concept of a unified art of the theatre is distinctly modern. A hundred years ago people went to the theatre to see a play "put on" or performed by glamorous actors, with costumes and scenery added as a decorative afterthought. But the art of the theatre was redefined in the revolutionary decades from 1895 to 1915 by Adolphe Appia and Gordon Craig, who showed how line, color, and shape of setting, costume, and lighting must be an integral part of the play, as important as words. Craig in particular saw the need for a single creative mind, that of a director trained in all the separate crafts of the theatre, to make a central plan for the production and to see that this idea was carried out in the movement, line, color, and rhythm of the performance. It is significant that Craig called his great work *On the Art of the Theatre* and that Appia called his principal work *Music and the Art of the Theatre*. No longer was the director to "present" a play; he was to create a new work of art.

CHAPTER TEN

PLANNING THE PRODUCTION

Since many theatre craftsmen and artists are involved in the production of a play, the planning is of the utmost importance. A good team spirit is best achieved where a permanent organization has its own building, its own director, and a continuity of staff from one play to the next, as in European repertory theatres, the new American resident companies, and most college and community theatres. Such careful coordination is much more difficult to realize in the commercial theatres of New York, where each play is a completely new venture in which the entire staff is hurriedly brought together for one production. The New York producer—that is, a promoter who forms a corporation and buys an option on a play—persuades various "angels" to invest money, hires the actors, designers, press agents, and director, and rents rehearsal space and a theatre. The director supposedly has central control, but the producer, who is deeply concerned with making the play a financial success, often has a good deal to say about casting and about many of the changes that are worked out in conferences with playwright and designers during the crowded weeks of preparation.

Since the director is rarely the producer, he is not usually involved in financial arrangements and is free to take the leadership in shaping the play and bringing it to life on the stage. That creation goes through three distinct phases—planning, rehearsal, and performance. In the planning phase, the play is translated from the script of the playwright to the full plans, visualized in time, space, and color, of the director. In the rehearsal period, it is the director's responsibility to see that the play is created in the voices and bodies of the actors while the designs are being constructed as scenery and costumes. Finally, in the performance, the playwright, director, and designer step aside, about as calmly as a father during childbirth, while the stage manager and his large backstage crew help the actors deliver the play to the audience.

The planning stage involves the play and the director. For most first productions, the playwright is present and works with the director in analyzing the play, weighing its values, deciding what shape and quality it should have, and considering which techniques of directing, acting, and designing are to be used. It is said that plays are not written, they are rewritten. There may be a great deal of rewriting at this stage as the director's analysis shows possibilities for improvement. Elia Kazan, in preparing *Cat on a Hot Tin Roof,* persuaded Tennessee Williams to write an entirely new last act, making much more explicit what was implicit in the first version. It is very instructive to read the two versions, which Williams published together. The rewriting may go on up to the last minute. The writing and rewriting of *Once in a Lifetime,* described by Moss Hart in *Act One,* continued until after the out-of-town opening, when it was decided to throw away the elaborate last scene, with twenty thousand dollars' worth of scenery, and write a new, simple ending.

There may be changes at any time during the preparation, and even some improvements after the opening, but the director does not start rehearsal, nor does the designer start executing his designs, until a very careful analysis of the play has led to agreement on the main idea and to a detailed plan for the production.

As a guide in making his plan, the director has available a fairly consistent theory of play production that has been worked out in the twentieth century. It breaks down the study of a play into two phases, classification and analysis, and then considers the different techniques of directing, acting, and designing and how these serve to create the qualities and values determined in the analysis. No two directors would describe the steps of preparation in exactly the same way, but most find themselves, first, relating the play to the overall controls, asking what kind of play it is and what conventions and style will set the audience in the most receptive attitude; second, analyzing the play for the structural values of plot, character, and theme and the values of texture to be created by dialogue, mood, and spectacle; and, third, deciding on the choice and use of the basic materials and techniques of director, actor, and designer. These three phases of planning can be put in outline form.

PLANNING A PRODUCTION

I. Classification of the play in relation to overall controls
   A. Kind of play
   B. Particular theatre and audience

The Play in Production

C. Conventions
D. Style

II. Analysis of the play by the six means that create structure and texture
   A. Structure
      1. Plot
      2. Character
      3. Theme
   B. Texture
      1. Dialogue
      2. Mood
      3. Spectacle

III. Choice of materials and techniques
   A. For the director
      1. Materials: action, space, time, line, form, color, light
      2. Techniques: composition, picturization of relationship, movement, pantomimic dramatization, rhythm
   B. For the actor
      1. Materials: body, voice, thought, feeling
      2. Techniques: reading lines, movement, pantomimic dramatization, rhythm
   C. For the designer
      1. Materials: space, line, form, color, movement
      2. Techniques: cutting down from realism, building up from action, exploiting qualities of mood and atmosphere, treating scenery as idea or metaphor

The three chief workers—director, actor, and designer—must study the play carefully, make their plans together, and constantly check with one another to be sure they are creating in harmony. As we have seen in the first part of this book, there are many kinds of plays, and the director, actor, and designer will work in different ways according to just what variety of entertainment or exaltation, romance or reality, they want to create for the audience. They must agree on how to use the particular stage, what conventions of performance they will set up, and what their overall style will be. They must analyze the play for its elements of structure and texture, knowing that the techniques that create a rich mood may not be the ones to make clear the theme or the action of the plot.

The actor learns lines alone or with others in small groups, tries improvisation both alone and at rehearsal, and continues his lifelong training in body, voice, and imagination outside the theatre, but in the long hours of rehearsal he has the director with him. The designer works separately, completing sketches and work drawings, building structures, and setting lighting instruments, but he checks repeatedly with the director at the critical stages, even though he does not expect to bring all parts of his contribution together until the later rehearsals. In an art theatre with control of its own space, the designer often has the main platforms and ramps and steps, and at least practice properties and sometimes practice costumes, available for rehearsal for several weeks before the opening.

Control by Conventions and Style

Convention and style were no problem when a standard repertory of plays was presented by a company performing in one house season after season for a faithful audience. But today, when audiences see plays in many different kinds of theatre or in club rooms and churches without the regular theatre arrangements, when playwrights are trying many new forms and directors are reviving old plays in mixtures of old conventions and new, when drama overlaps with opera, the musical, and dance, it is very important that for each production one set of conventions and one consistent style be agreed on by all.

CONVENTIONS

Conventions are the accepted rules of the game, defining the relationship between the audience and the performance. At a night club, the audience expects a master of ceremonies to take charge, to talk directly to them, even to recognize particular people, and to introduce a series of separate acts. But in a small theatre for a realistic play, the audience ordinarily expects the dimming of the house lights and the opening of the curtain to begin a scene in which the actors talk to one another but never make direct contact with the audience. By the convention of the fourth wall, the furniture is arranged around three walls as if the fourth wall and everything on that side of the room had been removed. Such familiar conventions are not noticed at all, but audiences can adjust to any convention or set of conventions if the unfamiliar methods are made clear near the beginning of the performance and are used consistently throughout. Since Wilder wanted the actors to break out of character and speak their own feelings at the climax of the third act of *The Skin of Our Teeth,* he put similar breaks in the first and second acts. The solution was simpler in *Our Town,* where the Stage Manager, a main character, was used to tell the audience from the beginning exactly what method to expect.

Some conventions of arrangement are necessary even in a small theatre so that the actors may be clearly seen and heard. Even the conventions of realism allow the furniture to be turned in an "open" position so that the actors will not stand in front of one another or turn their backs completely to the audience. Many details are made large and brightly colored to project to the audience. In costume materials only large, bold patterns are used.

In the large nineteenth-century theatres, when big emotions were popular, an actor "opened up" even more than on our stage, usually standing with one foot toward the other character and one toward the audience. Movements were large, and the expansive gestures were always made with the upstage hand so that the face was never covered by the gesture. Voices were projected with full tone, inflections were wide, and actors practiced long on consonants and vowels. In defending the old style of diction that often broke a word into parts, Bernard Shaw said that at least the old stock-company actor could be heard to the last row of the gallery when he screeched, "My chee-ild!"

The Play in Production

The indication that a scene takes place at night is also a matter of convention, for practically never have night scenes been played as dark as real night. On the Elizabethan stage, if a lantern or torch was brought on it indicated night, though the performers were in broad daylight. Until electric lights came into use, only a slight lowering of stage lights was possible, but the actor's pretense was acceptable to the audience. Today, both on the stage and on the movie screen, night is indicated by leaving the edge of the picture in shadow, and the characters and main part of a night scene are often quite clearly lighted even where there is no excuse of moon or street lamp. The very stark English production of *King Lear* with Paul Scofield in 1963–64 put all the scenes—day and night, court and heath—in strong, glaring white light—a most unromantic approach but nearer the convention of the Elizabethan stage.

Some conventions have to do with defining the playing area and marking the beginning and end of scenes. In most games, a line indicates where the player steps out of bounds, and a whistle or bell or a call of the player or referee indicates "Begin," "Stop," and "Time out." The proscenium frame and front curtain are very useful to hide the actor until he comes onto the playing area of the stage, and the rise and fall of the curtain have been the standard convention for beginning and ending scenes since the picture stage began in the sixteenth century. Today the blackout or dim-out of a controlled pool of light often replaces the closing curtain. Even the arena stage, which cultivates a sense of intimacy between audience and actor, needs some subtle but clear definition, if nothing more than a rug, to mark the edge of the playing area.

The choice of the means of expression by playwright and director is also a matter of convention. Here, too, the expectation of the audience is important and a director must have a fairly consistent plan and make clear from the beginning just how he is trying to make his appeal. That actors speaking in fairly realistic dialogue should burst into song does not seem strange to audiences who know the conventions of musical comedy. That characters of a play set in a foreign land speak English is readily accepted, though a few international films have experimented with having characters of different countries speak in their own languages. As we have noticed, many Americans, trained on recordings and broadcast opera, prefer their opera at the romantic distance of a foreign language. If the realist insists that a dying man could not sing a big aria or make a long poetic speech, the musician and the poet reply that the death of an important man is significant and somebody must express that significance. Audiences have learned to accept the convention. According to the theory of realism, ordinary characters do not have beautiful voices or the gift of poetic language, or even beauty of face or body. But even in realism, the theatre must find expressive intensities of some kind, and it is not surprising that Brecht and many others have revived old conventions such as soliloquy, song, and dance, and have asked the audience to accept them in plays dealing with reality. *Waiting for Godot* requires high skill and unusual gifts in clowning. When *Our Town* amazed audiences with its unusual conventions—a stage manager as narrator, no scenery, and actors

341

miming everyday business with empty hands—Wilder reminded the public that a convention is "an agreed-on falsehood." In that sense all art is false— that is, different from reality—and even the most realistic acting is carefully contrived, artificial, and unreal. But good actors can make any conventional medium—prose, poetry, song, Shakespearean rhetoric—seem convincing and real if the audience has some understanding and acceptance of that medium.

STYLE

It is extremely important that one style be used throughout a production, uniting words, actions, movements, lines, forms, and colors. Members of an audience may not be able to describe a style or know how it is achieved, but they are aware of incongruity when one actor stands out from the rest of the cast or when the costumes or settings do not fit in with other aspects of the production. The playwright partly determines the style; a play cannot be done in just any style. But every play permits considerable latitude, as director, actor, and designer decide on a style that emphasizes some aspects and subordinates others.

If the kind of play furnishes the wider control in the choice of techniques and qualities to be emphasized in a production, and if convention controls the relation of these techniques to the habits and expectations of the audience, style determines precisely how the techniques, qualities, and conventions are to be used. It has been very difficult to define style in the twentieth century, though the better productions achieve it. The realists, as we have seen, attacked all the old styles and announced that they were creating a theatre without any style or interpretation by presenting reality itself on the stage. When realists identified their restrained, implicit acting with reality, they had to describe any other style as an artificial and useless ornament superimposed on reality and distorting or obscuring it. They labeled the melodramatic style "ham" and delighted in revivals of melodrama that burlesqued the large emotional gestures and frank playing to the audience of the nineteenth-century theatre. Even Shakespeare, if he must be played, had to be presented through realistic acting in realistic settings. The poetry was lost, but no matter: the realists had no ear for that.

Some directors, however, insisted on reviving old plays in styles similar to those of the original productions. Before the end of the nineteenth century, the Elizabethan Stage Society, under William Poel, began a tradition of playing Shakespeare on a replica (as far as scholars could guess) of the Elizabethan stage. Such revivals did not represent reality but presented the characters and speeches directly to the audience. When the term "presentational style" was introduced in 1923 by Alexander Bakshy in *The Theatre Unbound,* it was widely used to describe all revolts against realism. The term suggested the excitement of platforms on the street, with medieval mountebanks or *commedia dell' arte* clowns surrounded by eager crowds, or ceremonial Chinese characters bowing to the audience and telling them exactly who they were and what they planned to do. It suggested bright colors and flamboyant scenery moving before the audience. It recalled two mem-

The Play in Production

orable productions of *Twelfth Night,* one in Berlin under Max Reinhardt that started with the arrival of a traveling troupe of comedians and clowns who, in view of the audience, put on their costumes and set up their platforms and bright-colored hangings, and the other an American production starring Jane Cowl that presented an illustrated storybook whose twelve-foot pages were turned back and forth by a dancing Jester. Why limit the stage to the grubby and factual, the representational? Why not use a presentational style and be frankly theatrical? This distinction has been a standard part of theatre theory until very recently. Only gradually has it become clear that realism is itself one style among many and that in various ways all styles are theatrical. The director needs a finer distinction than the terms "representational" and "presentational" when he discriminates among the numerous styles possible in the theatre.

The term "stylization," which came in when the expressionists began distorting scenery and dehumanizing characters with dreamlike and machine-like movements and voice inflections, implied a style that was markedly different from realism, and a student might ask a director if he planned to "stylize" a production or play it straight. As we shall see, the term "stylization" was especially important for designers when they wanted to make a more positive use of color or line than they could in realism. But stylization is not the same as style. There are a number of stylized—that is, deliberately artificial and unreal—styles. But style in its broadest sense must have a definition that includes much more than these.

Style is the particular manner of expression of a person, a nation, or a period. The way an artist handles his lines or chooses his colors, the way a writer puts his words and phrases together, the way an actor moves and wears his costume—all may create an effect different from the style of anyone else. And a play may have its own particular style, while at the same time it follows the general style of a certain period or milieu.

Style is the expression of an outlook on the world, a philosophy, a point of view. When many people have the same social, political, or philosophical attitudes, they choose similar ways of expressing themselves and create a style for a whole period. Thomas Jefferson and the revolutionaries in France and America wanted Greek Revival public buildings because they wanted to recapture in all aspects of public life the dignified nobility of the Greek republic. The Victorians wanted for their churches and colleges the mysterious dark of Gothic architecture and stained-glass windows, and something of their point of view can still be felt in the old buildings. Our kitchens, laboratories, and automobiles must not only be clean and efficient, but they must by their very style express newness, precision, power, and speed. They do not invite us to linger in comfort or to consider them ends in themselves. When we revive an Elizabethan play, we may want a speed of movement and a streamlining of setting that has some suggestion of modern living, but we usually want also the rich splendor and dignity that we see too little of in the twentieth century. When we revive an eighteenth-century comedy, we may prefer light, free-standing screens to the picture backdrops of the period,

343

and we may adjust the rococo costumes to some aspects of twentieth-century taste, but we seek to achieve, in the curved lines of the setting and the bold stance and bows and curtsies of the actors, an appropriate elegance and a crisp combination of assertion and politeness. Style in play production is usually an adjustment between the vision of the playwright, the expectation of the audience, and the particular taste and wishes of the director, actors, and designers.

Style is achieved largely by selection: the choice of certain conventions and techniques, the choice of certain qualities in the medium, and the limitation of the expression to those few qualities. If the colors are limited to a few pastel shades, the production will have a distinctive delicacy and softness, but the actors too must then use soft, delicate movements or they will not be in harmony with the setting. *Carmen Jones,* the Negro version of *Carmen,* was designed with each scene limited to two colors; one scene, for instance, was done in red and gray, and another used orange-tan against magenta-purple, with soft transitions to temper the harshness. In the ballet *Rodeo* and the ballet in *Oklahoma!,* Agnes de Mille achieved an outdoor Western style very different from classical ballet by giving the dancers more energetic jumps and leaps. Although the prominent designer Jo Mielziner has a wide range in style, he has designed a number of settings with his own distinctive emphasis on sharp outline of structure and thin or transparent walls.

While each play must have its own particular style to express the exact nuances of what the director considers to be the play's meaning, it is useful to set up a half-dozen or so general classifications of common styles. In addition to period styles, there are several broad styles that playwrights and producers are aware of as they plan. Although the Moscow Art Theatre has been known primarily for the realism of its style, one of the original directors, Nemirovitch-Dantchenko, taught his actors to consider six other styles which he called heroic, Homeric, epochal, comical, farcical, and lyrical. At Yale, both Alexander Dean and his successor, Frank McMullan, have had their students distinguish six major styles: classicism, romanticism, naturalism, realism, expressionism, and impressionism, with some subclassifications, such as neoclassic for seventeenth-century versions of tragedy. Their definitions of these terms are derived from the characteristics of historical periods or from such general attitudes as have been described in Part I. In their definition of classicism, for instance, they emphasize control, order, polish, simplicity, majesty, grandeur, dignity, nobility, and exaltation.

Style is not something added to a play as decoration; it is the basic manner of expression, and its control is one of the most powerful means of achieving unity in a production.

Analysis of Structure and Texture

When the director and the staff have decided what kind of play they are dealing with, what scenic format and conventions they expect to use,

The Play in Production

and what style they will try to achieve in the production, then they are ready for a more detailed analysis of the form and values of the play itself. Every play has six possible dramatic values, and all six may help in different ways to give the play organization and unity. Aristotle long ago listed them as plot, character, theme, dialogue, music (interpreted as mood for modern drama), and spectacle. The first three values have to do with the structure of the play, the last three with texture. The structure is the form of the play in time. The texture is what is directly experienced by the spectator, what comes to him through his senses, what the ear hears (the dialogue), what the eye sees (the spectacle), and what is felt as mood through the entire visual and aural experience. In analysis of structure and texture, the director retraces systematically the steps that the writer took with less conscious thought. Often, by showing the playwright the structure he has created intuitively and by pointing out the possibilities of the play in dialogue, mood, and spectacle, the director can help him strengthen or clarify the play in rewriting.

In examining a play, the director and his staff must choose the values that they wish to emphasize. Some plays are rich in all six of Aristotle's values. Certainly the Greek plays were, and most productions of Shakespeare are, though Shaw thought Shakespeare very weak in theme. Some productions have held an audience with emphasis on one value and only the slightest attention to the other five, but in general the larger the number of values, the better. Spectacular movies are likely to follow the same formula as nineteenth-century melodrama, emphasizing plot and spectacle, with little attention to characterization and theme, and providing no dialogue that is interesting or beautiful in itself. On the twentieth-century stage, character portrayal and mood are valued highly; dialogue is often flat and commonplace, and poetry or witty or poetic prose is fairly rare. The director and his staff must note the values most emphasized by the playwright and then consider whether they may make a better production by reinforcing other values even if that should mean not exploiting all the obvious values to the full.

PLOT

A drama means something happening—the very word in Greek means something done, an act. It is not narrative, not description, not analysis. It is a fearful becoming before our eyes, a present moment but one full of promise and threat, pregnant with the future. There is delay, with terrible suspense, but the critical moment does arrive and a fate is determined, a choice is made, a door is closed forever. William Archer called drama "the art of crises, as fiction is the art of gradual development." In his playwriting classes, George Pierce Baker liked to call a play the shortest distance between two emotions. Perhaps the most concentrated and intense of all the arts, drama derives much of its intensity from the plot. The audience is caught up in beginning, middle, and end, carried from crisis to crisis in a rhythmic pattern of tension and relaxation, swept to a climax by irresistible propulsion, then left at the end changed and thrilled, with a

345

sense of having gone through a great experience. Susanne Langer's statement that the theatre creates a sense of destiny is true in more than one sense. Every moment of a play links past and present in a terrible compulsion to see the outcome. That outcome is fraught with the significance of a lifetime. It is a destiny.

Aristotle considered action primary, not only in a play but in life. He wrote, "But the most important of all is the structure of the incidents. For tragedy is an imitation, not of men but of an action and of life. And life consists in action, and its end is a mode of action. Now character determines men's qualities, but it is by their actions that they are happy, or the reverse." Although many writers today distrust action and see man as a victim of blind circumstance, incapable of free will, thought, or decision, audiences usually agree with Aristotle that action is the essence of drama.

Dramatic action is not just running around on the stage. At first glance some readers have said that *Prometheus Bound* has no action. At the beginning of the play three henchmen of Zeus fasten the great Titan by chains to a rock on top of a mountain. He stands in the one spot, talking to a series of visitors, until a thunderbolt from Zeus rends the rock and buries him underground. But the play is full of dramatic action. Each visitor challenges Prometheus, and each makes him all the more determined to defy Zeus. Acts of the mind and the will, even thought, are exciting and dramatic whether they issue in visible movement or not. The interaction of two minds may be conflict as tense and exciting as a physical fight on the stage.

Plot is the arrangement of the incidents that take place on stage. A drama is therefore all in the present, a present calling forth the future. Much of the actual story may already have taken place. A complete narrative about Oedipus would begin with his birth and his rescue from the mountain where he was left to die. It would include his leaving his supposed parents, killing the unknown man who was really his father, and marrying the Queen. But Sophocles' play starts after all that; it is not the story of how Oedipus got where he is but an action showing how he finds out who he is and what he has unknowingly done—a dramatic plot. The past is retold incidentally, but every piece of the past becomes dramatic as it makes a present impact on those who have got to hear. Ibsen's characters are very much concerned with the past; they are at each other's throats forcing each other, at last, to tell the long-hidden truth about the past. Discoveries explode like carefully placed time bombs, one after the other, shaking and sometimes destroying those forced to hear. A drama is not narrative, not mere dialogue or conversation; it is interaction. Each speech of each character makes a demand, provokes a reaction from another character. Even in monologue the character is struggling against a memory or trying to make a choice. Each speech makes us watch moment by moment, eager to see what will come next. Whether it is a violent fight or a quiet decision in the inner mind, a drama is an act, a plot.

A plot may be called a metaphor of action as it follows the pattern, literally or figuratively, of a real-life action. The pattern may be a fight to the

The Play in Production

finish between a good hero and a villain, rousing our basic fighting instincts as well as our moral indignation. It may be a race or a contest between worthy opponents, involving the same suspense as first one side and then the other gets ahead. It may be an actual or metaphorical journey, in which the young hero, like a medieval knight, searches for his Holy Grail, now getting closer, now distracted and delayed. Courtship is a variation of the journey. "Boy meets girl, boy loses girl, boy gets girl"—there is the structure of a three-act play. The film *Tom Jones* combines journey and courtship. Another pattern is the invasion of the lives of stay-at-homes; an intruder or a guest in the house may disturb the peaceful equilibrium and cause all kinds of complications before peace is restored. The formula "Get the character in hot water, then get him out" has been stated by George Abbott in a three-act form: "In the first act get your hero up a tree; in the second throw rocks at him; in the third get him down." A prophecy calls for fulfillment, and reckless behavior creates an expectation of downfall.

The trial is one of the most powerful patterns for a play, concentrating deeds of the past into the suspense of the judgment—the long-awaited destiny. Sometimes it is in the formal setting of a courtroom, but there is much the same excitement when Oedipus serves as his own prosecuting attorney and his own judge, calling up witness after witness to find the murderer of the old king, only to discover that he himself was the murderer and the old king was his own father. In other plays, other ceremonial occasions—a procession, funeral, wedding, dance, banquet, homecoming, or even ritual acts, exorcism or sacrifice—may set the pattern of action. Think of *Oedipus* as an exorcism, a scourge to drive out the old pollution, the crime, and you give it a strong propulsion toward the agonized departure of Oedipus at the end. The sorrow at his suffering is made bearable in the acceptance of the cleansing that had to come. Compare Desdemona to a human sacrifice on an altar and you give the last scenes of *Othello* a ritual dignity that lifts the play above the physical horror of the killing.

Many plays follow some pattern of nature—the rhythm of the day or of the seasons or of a storm leading to the dawn, clear and calm and reassuring after the terrifying night.

Sometimes the conclusion of a play is a sudden revelation of that which was hidden: the discovery of the lost papers, the clearing up of the mistaken identity, the finding of the child that had been stolen, the true heir, the real prince, the unknown benefactor. There is an unmasking, like the end of a masquerade party. Eric Bentley points out that a play has some things in common with a striptease, taking off layers of concealment. The revelation may be spiritual, like the enlightenment sought in Zen and other Oriental religions. The main character in a Japanese Noh drama sheds the dull robes of the present and appears in the full, colorful identity of his youth in order to exorcise his deeds of violence and find a new spiritual peace.

Several writers on playwriting see structure as the phases of the will of the protagonist. Paul Goodman defines plot in terms of narrowing of choice: in the beginning, everything is possible, and there is great suspense; by the

347

middle, the movement gets faster and choice is narrowed as certain things become probable; by the end, everything is necessary—there is no choice and no suspense. Samuel Selden used to tell his playwriting students to check by the five letters P A S T O whether they had developed the five aspects of Preparation, Attack, Struggle, Turn, and Outcome. As we have noted in Chapter 4, on tragedy, Francis Fergusson thinks of the three phases of a play as the three P's—Purpose, Passion, Perception. Marian Gallaway finds much meaning in the three simple words "and," "but," and "therefore." "And" indicates the logical sequence growing out of a situation, "but" the conflicting developments, and "therefore" the conclusion.

In making the ground plan for the structure of the play, the director carefully outlines his plot. Sometimes he consciously divides the play into parts, which, for the benefit of his actors, he gives conventional labels. The opening part is the *exposition,* which makes clear to the audience what has gone before and what the present situation is. Then at a certain *point of attack* the *inciting force* appears. There comes *complication* after complication. The tension increases in a *build,* or crescendo, to a *minor climax,* followed by a *let-down.* There is *anticipation* or *foreboding* of future conflict, and with delay or continued threat comes great *suspense.* Each confrontation of opposing forces creates a *crisis.* Usually there will be a point of no return, when the fight comes out in the open in the *major crisis,* which may be the point of highest tension, or the *major climax.* After that comes the *conclusion* or the *dénouement,* the French term for "untying" the plot. Aristotle gave us such terms as *discovery,* when that which was unknown comes clear, and *peripeteia,* the turn of the plot.

The plot is the basis for the overall rhythmic pattern of the play. Whether a play is broken up into acts and scenes by intermissions and scene changes, or whether it flows continuously without interruption like an Elizabethan play or a movie, it is organized in time. It cannot be experienced all at once but, like a symphony, must have a pattern of tensions and relaxations, of builds, climaxes, and let-downs, of units of different sizes and intensities. As we come to the analysis of dialogue, mood, and spectacle, we will see how they can reinforce the large patterns—how a change in mood, for instance, can emphasize a change in suspense in the story, or a spectacular setting add power to the climax. And we shall see how the designer, in planning the format of scene changes, must consider the overall rhythmic pattern. But the pattern depends most of all on plot. The conflict of forces in a play finds release in much the same way as a physical force finds release, either in vibrations or in spurts, or *quanta.* An electric current is smooth when it flows through a wire of low resistance, but if it meets high resistance—a space of air, for instance—it is discharged in rhythmic spurts of sparks. A river through a valley does not cut a straight course but eats too far on one side until its impulse is exhausted by the mounting resistance and it is turned with new force against the other side. Similarly, in the structural rhythm of a play, each new complication sends the plot moving until that pulse is exhausted and resistance is built up to stop it. Then suspense grows and

The Play in Production

grows, to be discharged finally in a new spurt of action. In such rhythmic alternation of tension and relaxation, the play moves on to its climaxes and then to the end, when the forces are exhausted or have reached an equilibrium.

Although nine out of ten plays are organized by plot, the director must still decide whether the plot is merely a thread tying together many episodes and characters, to be made evident only at the major crises and the conclusion, or whether it is all-important and must dominate at all times. The nineteenth-century theatre throve on strong plots. Popular melodramas were little else but spectacular scenes of heroines pursued by villains and rescued by heroes. Even Shakespeare was often played for the strong scenes of conflict. We have Clement Scott's exciting review of Sir Henry Irving's *Hamlet,* which describes in detail Hamlet's whirlwind energy in the Play Scene as he lured, tempted, and trapped the King, drove him out conscience-stricken and baffled, and then, with a hysterical yell of triumph, sank down on the throne himself. Irving left no doubt that the play was a fight between two men and that he had won that round. Our generation is not so sure of triumph. After a world war "to end all wars" that only led to another world war more devastating than the first, after a stalemate in a prolonged cold war, and after conflicts and compromises in many labor revolutions, audiences today are not so fond of the clear-cut fight to the finish. *Hamlet,* as we have seen, may still have conflict and suspense, but usually it presents a more complex web of baffling intrigue and checkmate. There is less combat in our vision than in Irving's, but the action seems more complex and subtle.

CHARACTER

If plot is what happens, character is why it happens. The motivation is the basis of the action. Plot may be what gives the play its immediate sense of excitement, but plays are remembered for their characters. Lear on the Heath, Lady Macbeth rubbing blood from her hands, Cyrano helping the other man with his love, the undefeated Amanda of *The Glass Menagerie,* the defeated Blanche of *A Streetcar Named Desire*—characters like these can never be forgotten. It is through the creation of character, the evocation of the nuances of personality, the immediate and the deeper motives of the soul, that actors win their audiences. Even the minor characters come to life to give the play variety and vitality as the actors find a distinct personality and an inner meaning for each.

The director, both alone and with the actor, makes a careful study to create each character with a particular tone and quality—not just the recognition traits of age, size, occupation, appearance, dress, tempo, rhythm, roughness or softness, but characteristic attitude. Is he naturally a doubter, a kidder, joyful or morose, ardent or disdainful, playful or serious? Is he conceived according to the conventional idea of his role in society—father, judge, pedantic schoolteacher, or go-getting young executive? Or does the character violate the conventional picture, such as a mother who is an executive and smokes cigars? Can he be explained by some of the Freudian con-

349

cepts—repressions that burst out in unpredictable compensations, inferiority complexes, destructive obsessions and neuroses, nervous tics and compulsive gestures? Is he introvert or extrovert, or does he overcompensate by over-reacting? The actor may bring to this study his own observations from life or from research in books, newspapers, and other plays. Within the play itself director and actor carefully note what the author says, what the character does and says, and how the other characters speak of him and react to him. Does he play a different role with each character he meets? Is there a strong central "spine" that gives shape and support to the charac-ter throughout his adaptation to different people and changing circumstances? Is there a pattern of change as the character develops or discovers himself in the course of the play?

It is the deeper motives—how he stands up for the higher values of life—that give a character his real quality. The superego, in the long run, is far more important than the ego, absorbing as the ego may be. For most charac-ters, the director and the actor must ask not only what his tones and rhythms are, his likes and dislikes, quirks and neuroses, but what he ultimately re-spects. The answer to this question will relate the character to the theme of the play as surely as the motivation ties the character to the plot.

Whether it is conscious choice, as Sartre and the existentialists demand, or unconscious natural bent that gives the outline of the character, that outline is filled in by the actor. He brings to the part his own natural tones and qualities, and, according to the skill and range he has developed, he adds or emphasizes those qualities that he and the director think the character should have. A good actress can make a scene seem very cold or she can fill it with warmth and happiness. The lines of the play may assert over and over again that the heroine is charming, but the audience will not believe it for one second unless the actress is attractively dressed and can add charm to every-thing she says and does. Even murder on the stage is vicious only if the actor brings out a vicious quality: he might kill with mindless apathy or with agonized reluctance. Often the director is glad to cast somewhat against the type, using the native qualities of the actor to add other dimensions, to counterbalance some of the words and actions. This is particularly true of characters that are vicious or odd. It might be too ugly and painful to double the effect with real coarseness or some eccentric quality from the actor him-self. Where some later actresses have made emphatic the hard, cold, destructive aspects of Mrs. Phelps in *The Silver Cord,* Laura Hope Crews, in the first production in 1926, made her a warm and vivacious mother. It was far more terrifying to see such an appealing woman fight, using all her feminine, weak-seeming strength to destroy her sons. Of course, the actor must have enough of the right qualities to make the role credible. A scene in which a cruel husband browbeats a mistreated wife is hardly believable if the wife obviously could pick him up and spank him. The director has to decide, as he looks over his possible casting, how much he hopes to indi-cate by action, how much by the basic qualities of the actor, and how much by the acting itself. In rehearsal he will help the actor enrich his part by

The Play in Production

finding unexpected moments when a strong character shows weakness and a weak character strength and by giving an evil character some moments of sympathy and a good character contradictory moments when he seems not so good. People are not all of one piece and are all the more fascinating for their complexity.

In addition to understanding individual characters, the director must see clearly the playwright's scheme of characters. A play is not a solo by one character but a complex composition. Not only do the characters change each other but each character is defined in comparison and contrast with all the others. The playwright has added other examples to reinforce, to explore variations of, to oppose and contrast with, his central characters. The director and the actor must know exactly how each character fits into the whole scheme.

If two characters are exact duplications—two brothers, two young men in love, two servants, two angry fathers—the play offers the possibility of broad farce, a subject already discussed. Such a mechanical scheme we cannot take seriously. But if the second is a variation, he can add a very telling development. Theme and variation is as important in theatre as in music. The situation of two brothers given different treatment and growing up in different ways was apparently the subject of one of the earliest Greek comedies we know of; it was then dramatized by Terence in *The Brothers* and has been used in hundreds of plays since. Two different people reacting to the same event have given some of the best contrasts in drama. Shaw takes his Liza in *Pygmalion* out of the slums and watches her blossom as she becomes a lady in the richer, wider world. To a Cinderella romance he adds both educational and psychological interest in the process of Liza's development. Liza's father, Doolittle, is also by chance broken away from his slum pattern, but he cannot grow at all and is comically unhappy as he tries to adjust to the moral demands of his new situation.

Variation on a different level and in a different key is frequent in all kinds of plays, especially in romantic comedy. A comic pair of lovers sets off the serious pair, and obviously it is easier in any class-conscious society to make lower-class characters more comic. The humble characters are funny for seeming to repeat somebody else, but they serve another function in romance. Like a lightning rod, a comic servant can deflect from the romantic hero not only the jealous blows of fate but the realistic skepticism of the audience. The ancient Hindus understood this very well and regularly set a clownish servant as the companion to the romantic king. The servant could feel fatigue, hunger, fear, and pain, but the king never could. The servant could stub his toe, tear his trousers, suffer all the indignities of finite existence, leaving the hero to dwell in the realm of ideal perfection, knowing only the sunset sorrow of separation from his love.

As in all art, contrast is vital in drama. The hero and the villain enlist our interest in their fight because they are so different. Every protagonist is defined by the nature of his antagonist. The devotion of Sophocles' Electra to the memory of her murdered father is turned into smoldering fury by the

351

brazen assurance of the mother and her paramour. Antigone faces her hard, practical uncle, the new king, and quietly defies him by honoring her brother's funeral rites. Both these strong heroines are given weak, indecisive sisters for another kind of contrast. Hamlet contends in quite different ways with the King, his mother, Ophelia, and Polonius, and finally with Laertes, and is provoked into a different role with each. He tries to a degree to imitate Laertes, who recklessly moves to his revenge without conscience or regret. Hence Laertes must be cast and played as a presentable young man who can be fiery and ruthless. But Horatio offers a contrast of another kind. He does not contend with Hamlet at all but offers a point of rest—something every complex work of art needs. His serenity and quiet strength are above the battle. With him Hamlet can drop his guard and show how much he dislikes all the contention. Hamlet envies him for not being "passion's slave." Hence he must be cast, not for his first scene, which helps build up the terror at the beginning of the play, but to offer Hamlet glimpses of sympathy, serenity, and sturdy sweetness. Romeo is defined by contrast with his enemy, the hot-tempered, angry youth of hate, Tybalt, but also by contrast with his close friend Mercutio, who is raucous, bawdy, and cynical about love. Prince Hal in *Henry IV* is defined partly by contrast with Hotspur and provoked into proving he can meet Hotspur and surpass him in deeds of valor; but he is defined even more, in his carefree moments, by his friendly companionship with Falstaff, a generous friendship he knows cannot last beyond his youth, since serious responsibilities are bound to overtake him.

Sometimes a more elaborate scheme of characters provides one character for each aspect of a problem, each different from the rest and all together making a complete arrangement. The medieval allegories abounded with such schemes—the Seven Virtues, the Seven Sins, the Seven Liberal Arts, often pictured as personalities as distinct and visible as the Greek Muses. Modern playwrights are rarely so obvious in naming each character according to what he represents, but they use schemes equally precise. In the early part of the twentieth century, before the freer epic form was developed, authors interested in political and social problems—John Galsworthy, for instance—would bring together at a crisis a character for each important point of view or nuance of attitude. In Shaw's *Saint Joan*, each institution—the Church, the Inquisition, the Feudal Lords, the State of England—has a champion, and some more than one, to bring out the several attitudes in the large debate at Joan's trial. To create a kind of epitome of New York as a melting pot, Elmer Rice in *Street Scene* brought into one New York block representatives of all the principal nationalities in that cosmopolitan city, just as O'Neill in several of his plays of the sea had brought on shipboard all nationalities from both sides of the Atlantic. The character scheme may be as important for the theme of the play as what happens or what conclusion any of the characters reaches.

The way in which a character changes in himself may be the major action of a play. Growth, self-discovery, learning, and conversion can be fascinating to watch and very dramatic. *The Male Animal* takes on excitement when the

The Play in Production

little college English teacher decides he has been pushed around enough, discovers his strength, and hits back. Billy Dawn in *Born Yesterday* needs not only a new boy friend but an education in the meaning of freedom in America before she can get rid of her crude junkman and emerge as a free person. She learns to wear glasses and read books, and she creates a new personality as she learns self-respect. The belief in growth, learning, and self-realization is among the most sacred beliefs of the western world. Even naturalistic studies of the erosion and defeat of character by environment reaffirm, by ironic contrast, our belief in the value of growth and identity, the basic values of characterization.

It is often remarked that Greek drama showed little interest in character development. In one sense that is true. What the Greeks found important was revelation, the discovery of true identity. And we have seen how Oedipus, through discovery, gained a new dignity and humble strength and Creon, in Sophocles' *Antigone,* a new humility. After two decades of playwriting, Maxwell Anderson came to the conclusion that discovery was the most important element in tragedy, or in all drama. He did not mean the discovery of hidden facts, as Aristotle did, but the discovery by the main character of something about the world or about himself that made him, even as he lost, a better person.

Thus development in character is seen as one of the most important forms of dramatic action and, of course, as the closest tie between character and theme. Too, it is one way in which character can give unity to a play. Laurence Housman's *Victoria Regina* traces the career of Queen Victoria from her girlhood to her Diamond Jubilee, through many different episodes that have no connection in plot and little continuity of minor characters. The play does not have a dominant theme to give it unity. But it does show the gradual development of a fascinating human character. The creation of this role marked the climax of Helen Hayes' career—an unforgettable character.

In planning an absurdist drama, the director and the actor need not discard all the concepts of motivation and development that have enriched the drama over the centuries. But for some plays they must be ready to plan a character that takes on a sudden obsession without continuity with previous motives. As in expressionism, many actors are used not to create rounded characters but to present fragments or merely to add exciting sounds and movements in a larger composition. Actually there is a great deal of continuity in most dramas of the absurd. Sabina is the same character throughout *The Skin of Our Teeth,* though she takes on a slightly different personality as she sets out to seduce Mr. Antrobus in Act II. In Ionesco's *The Lesson,* the Professor has a strong drive to teach the girl. There is no sudden change as the drive gradually becomes more intense and demonic until he attacks and stabs her. An absurdist play may require that the character be conceived as fragmented or distorted, but even in the most dehumanized or mechanized dance drama the theatre deals with an image of the human race, and that image will always deal with some aspect of character.

THEME

Theme is so closely related to the other dramatic values that the full meaning of a play may not be clear until we have thought it over for some time. The meaning may be so implicit in the characters, in what happens, in the rich texture of the actors, the setting, and the performance that it cannot be put into words, though we may know that the play stands for certain values of living. We know more about life for having seen it. Only in a very few plays can the theme be called a moral, for a moral is a neat external conclusion *about* life. Some people call the theme "thought," but thought may suggest the argument or conclusion of a particular character, and this may or may not be the meaning of the play as a whole.

Theme may be interwoven in the play in many ways. Sometimes the basic unity of the play depends on theme. In both *Our Town* and *The Skin of Our Teeth* there is practically no continuity of plot and far from complete consistency of characters from one act to the next. But each play has a strong unity of theme. In *Our Town* there is very little story, no antagonist, no conflict, and not even much contrast. The first act has continuity through a day from dawn to bedtime, but it jumps about and is interrupted as the Stage Manager builds up piece by piece his picture of the daily life of the town. The second act starts again at breakfast, but it soon loses the time sequence, even including a flashback to the drugstore scene. Yet it has a tight unity since all the scenes are about marriage and build up to the impressive scene of the wedding. Though the last act has echoes of the first and second, it is completely independent, tied to the others only as it completes and perfects the theme of the infinite value of human life seen against the infinite scope of time. In *The Skin of Our Teeth* the three acts are even less closely connected, with no plot sequence at all. But each act is concerned with a new crisis, and the theme of how man meets his crises ties the play together.

If the theme is fully stated in dialogue, the director must make sure that the words are clear to the audience. But words will not be remembered unless they sum up and make explicit what the audience already sees. Medieval drama, intended to teach a wide illiterate public the events of the Bible and the steps of salvation, often made use of an Expositor, who, in the character of a learned doctor of theology or sometimes of an Old Testament prophet, introduced the play in a Prologue and sometimes also explained the meaning in an Epilogue. In some modern plays an external character talks directly to the audience and comments on meaning; the chatty Stage Manager in *Our Town* is the most memorable example. In the nineteenth-century problem play a minor character, called a *raisonneur,* explained the theme. But the play seems stronger if the main character comes to a realization and states his conclusion—the "discovery" already commented on. In the discussion of modern tragedy, we have raised the question of whether *Death of a Salesman* would be a better play if Willy Loman had seen clearly where he had been wrong. In the older tragedies, from *Oedipus* to *Othello,* the main character reaches his own clear knowledge about himself and to a large extent puts his discovery into words.

The Play in Production

We must be careful, however, not to assume that a single statement of one character must be the meaning of the whole play. At one point in *King Lear,* the blinded Earl of Gloucester comes to the conclusion that "As flies to wanton boys are we to the gods./ They kill us for their sport." But that is only the momentary conclusion of one character. The actor must make clear that Gloucester is in deep despair, but later he must make even more emphatic that Gloucester, after trying to commit suicide, finds a new patience and acceptance of his condition.

Sometimes what is said in the dialogue offers an ironical contrast with what actually happens. Life is more complex than any man's attempt to sum it up. Several modern critics have noted that soon after Portia in *The Merchant of Venice* delivers a splendid sermon on mercy, she shows something less than mercy when she has Shylock in her power. In *Hedda Gabler,* Judge Brack seems a wise commentator, quietly watching Hedda, sure that he understands her and has her in his control. But he is the most surprised of all when she kills herself. He ends the play with the famous tribute to the unpredictability of human nature, "Good God!—People don't do such things."

Whether brought out by direct statement, by ironical contrast, or by implication, the theme is an essential part of a play. Even the most trivial farce implies certain philosophical attitudes, and the great playwrights from Aeschylus, Sophocles, and Euripides to Shakespeare, Molière, Goethe, Ibsen, and Shaw have made large contributions to human thought. But the best plays offer more than philosophical understanding: they create a sense of vital renewal as the characters move in the driving rhythms of action and destiny toward a more profound spiritual harmony.

DIALOGUE AND SPECTACLE

Plot, character, and theme, which we have been considering, are the elements of structure. Equally important are the elements of texture—dialogue, mood, and spectacle. Indeed, modern theatre people, like modern painters and musicians, have been particularly interested in texture. The word is derived, like the word "textile," from the Latin word for weaving. We say a cloth has a fine texture, a coarse texture, or a ribbed texture. Our strongest sensation of texture comes from touch, from feeling the difference, for instance, between roughhewn granite and polished marble, but we extend the word to the other senses. In music there is a difference between the clarity of a single-voiced texture and the thicker texture of polyphonic music, in which several lines of melody are interwoven to produce harmonies or contrapuntal complexities. In painting, texture adds considerable surface interest as the painter gains depth and vibrancy by interweaving brush strokes, smears, and spots of color in applying his oils or even by pasting pieces of cloth, paper, wire screen, or rope to his canvas. In the theatre, texture is created by the sounds and images of the language, by the subtle but powerful hold of the mood, and by the materials, color, and movement of setting and costume. We will discuss mood in detail, but language and spectacle have great importance, not only in themselves but in their contribution to mood.

355

In Part I, we discussed the various kinds of dialogue or language, from the realistic language based on the broken phrases of everyday speech, which the actor enriches with deeper feelings, to the poetic flights of language of romantic or exalted plays. Most modern plays have limited poetic language to local dialect, as we have seen, and have subordinated words to other elements such as background sounds or movements, clothes, and furniture to create a rich composite effect of local color, leaving lush language to romance, wit to high comedy, and poetry to the outdoor festival plays and a few dramas in verse. Even so, the director and the actor must study the dialogue of any play very carefully, for it is chiefly through the sound, and particularly the rhythm, of the dialogue that the playwright indicates the basic mood of the play and the changing moods of the scenes in sequence.

Which should receive greater emphasis—language, mood, or spectacle? As with the three elements of structure, the answer has varied from age to age. Aristotle's statement that spectacle had the least connection with the poet's art has been taken as giving it least value, but his words may have been no more than a reflection of theatrical conditions of his day, when not the poet but a separate worker took care of the scenery. Aeschylus a century before had been poet, musician, chief actor, choreographer, and director and had taken care of the masks and scenery as well. He did not despise spectacle, he made it serve him. In our own time, some critics deplore the emphasis given to spectacle on stage and screen. It is true that it sometimes gets out of hand, and a night club act may be all rhinestones and pink feathers, a TV spectacular all lines of shouting singers, or a film all sunsets, dawns, fires, battles, chariot races, or floods. As one *Cleopatra* or *The Crusades* follows another on the screen and all blend together in memory as a conglomerate mass of meaningless scenery, we understand why Aristotle put spectacle last on his list. We remember that three of the greatest theatres in history—the Chinese, the Japanese Noh, and the Elizabethan—while making much use of poetry, dance, and song, had no painted settings and used colors only for splendid costumes and a few portable symbolic indications of place.

Yet spectacle does belong in the theatre. It is important to see Macbeth and Lady Macbeth in splendid robes sitting on splendid thrones, with attendants, trumpets, banners, tapestries, and canopies—the full panoply of royalty—to mark their triumph. And the banquet scene must be made an impressive spectacle, showing Macbeth in a closed circle of friends and councilors when his hopes are dashed by Banquo's ghost and the circle of order dissolves. In order to feel completely the tragic fate of the archbishop in *Becket,* the audience must see him in the pomp of his investiture. In order to know the magnitude of the desecration wrought by the Spaniards in Peru as Peter Shaffer has conceived it in *The Royal Hunt of the Sun,* the audience must see the Sun-King of the Incas splendidly enthroned in a huge sun-medallion and the glittering procession of his subjects bearing the golden treasure that is to fill the royal chamber. Both in such romantic dramas and in naturalistic scenes we expect most characters to be shown involved in the larger world around them, the world of nature, history, or society. Our pres-

The Play in Production

ent ideal of a unified art of the theatre is nearer the ideal of Aeschylus, who included spectacle, than that of Aristotle, who isolated it. How the director and the designer create this scenic element and make it serve the total impression will be discussed in the chapter on design.

MOOD AND RHYTHM

For his fifth value in the theatre, Aristotle used the term "music," but although music is still of major importance in opera and musicals, in most plays we make little use of melodies or instruments. Hence we substitute the word "mood" for "music." Mood in the theatre depends upon a blending of many elements, including spectacle and language, but it is created chiefly by rhythm, which is communicated directly, as the audience sees the actor moving in rhythm and hears him speaking in rhythm and feels the rhythmic changes in intensity of the lighting.

The universe is organized in the rhythm of alternating patterns—dawn and sunset, day and night, summer and winter, rain and sunshine, birth and death. Primitive man expressed through dance his sense of being part of that natural rhythm, most particularly the rhythm of seedtime and harvest, preparation and fulfillment. In this way, he gave order to his life, defining the basic order that underlies the disconnected moments of living. By means of rhythm he coordinated the activities of the whole tribe, just as a hive of bees must be set into a new dancing rhythm when it is time to hunt a new home, then brought back into the rhythm of daily work. For modern man, rhythm is still the great coordinating principle, as powerful and indispensable in the theatre as in dance or music. Movement without rhythm is clumsy, jerky; only when the muscles and the lower nerve controls are organized in a rhythmic pattern can a movement get in stride. Rhythm creates a relationship between the parts of the body and between one person and another. Sailors pulling a rope or hauling a sail sing a chanty with a strong rhythm, in order to pull together. The coxswain coordinates the crew of a racing shell by calling out the rhythm. Men work far more easily if they are held by one rhythm for the whole group. Spectators at a play follow the rhythm of the actors as closely as a marching army follows the band or a crew the coxswain; the rhythm reverberates through the audience, tying stage and house together under one spell.

John Dewey defined rhythm as "ordered variation of changes" and pointed out that when there is a uniform flow, with no variation of intensity or speed, there is no rhythm; nor is there rhythm when variations are not "placed." He found a wealth of suggestion in the phrase "takes place" in reference to an event that not only happens but belongs, that has a definite place in a larger whole. The rhythm of walking is an alternation of the terror of falling with the promise of recovery, and the same alternation is visible in a row of columns supporting an architrave and pediment. Rhythm is not mere repetition but the recurrence of relationships; each point of balance completes the previous relationships and leads the expectation on to the next.

We have already spoken of the larger rhythmic patterns of the play, the

357

large surges of tension and relaxation, and noticed how they are related to conflict when one force, like a winding river, pushes on in one direction until the accumulating resistance stops it and sends it in another direction. We have noted that this seems to be the basic interaction pattern of physical energies, each going for a time, compressing the opposing energy until the latter can overcome the first, which has been relaxing as it extends. The release of energy takes place in rhythmic spurts. In the same way the tiny vibrations and spurts of each actor seem to take a similar rhythmic pattern as each one reacts to the environment and interacts with the other actors. Each short "beat," or unit of a few lines, has its own rhythm, though it may be only a part of the large surges of the plot. Just as a sequence of moods can mark and reinforce the large structural rhythm of the play, so the mood of each moment is created by the rhythm of the actor, occasionally reinforced by background music and sounds.

The poet can illustrate his rhythm in a sentence, the drummer can beat out a pattern, the orchestra conductor can demonstrate by the movement of his baton and hands, the dancer by movements of the whole body. The actor communicates the rhythm of the scene directly and instantly to the audience, not merely as an abstract pattern of beats but with subtle feelings and qualities. The director can guide the actor just as directly, controlling the rhythm by his own tone of voice or gesture of the hands, suggesting modification by such simple terms as "quieter," "sharper," "gentle and slow," "both gay and flippant." Often the actor does not need to be conscious of the rhythm if he is thinking of the mood itself. But the director must know exactly what mood he wants and what rhythm will produce it. The student can increase his response to a play if he knows some of the ways that rhythm is achieved. Instead of trying to describe the rhythms of the theatre, let us note how the theatre shares some of the qualities of rhythm found in music, in dance, in poetry, and in the natural environment, and how these rhythms are adapted to the stage.

Measure, tempo, accent, pause, rest, legato, staccato, double and triple, offbeat, syncopation, downbeat, march—such musical terms are borrowed by the stage director because musicians define their rhythms in great detail. Most music combines a flexible, living melody with a steady pattern of accented and unaccented beats. Drums set a continuous march beat of ONE-two, ONE-two to hold the band and the marchers together. But with the drums alone the 2/4 or 4/4 meter is intolerably monotonous. Against it the other instruments play a melody that has short and long notes, statements and answers, beginnings and endings, and yet that fits its complex pattern into the basic steady pulse of the drums. Or, having once set the regular beat, the drum itself may play variations while the regular pulse continues in the minds of musicians and listeners. The expected pattern in Western music has an accent on the first note of the measure, but for a change the composer may accent an offbeat, an effect called *syncopation*. Some music, especially jazz, may use a syncopated pattern throughout.

358   The ONE-two, ONE-two rhythms, or their more frequent ONE-two-THREE-

four variants, are steady and driving, while the triple meters, the ONE-two-three rhythms, seem lighter, faster, and more delicate or playful. Old-fashioned waltzes have a very charming sweep and lilt, very different from the heavy, pounding dance in 3/4 time called a waltz in the 1960s.

Many scenes in the theatre have as strong and definite a beat as a march or a dance. In *The Emperor Jones,* a driving, relentless rhythm is created by a drumbeat that starts slow but gets faster and faster as the natives pursue Jones through the jungle, stopping only with the pistol shot that kills him.

Most theatres in history have made rich use of music, at least as background if not in song and dance, and an orchestra was a regular attraction in commercial theatres until the Second World War. Even though the naturalistic directors banished conventional musical instruments, they used many other sounds, from nature, from human activities, or from the mechanized city. In a movie or TV drama the voices are almost as richly supported by background music as the singers in a Wagnerian opera.

If there is no music in the play to build the rhythm and mood, the director often turns to music for his actors. The silent films were regularly made with background music, often from a single violin, to help the actors get into the right mood. In the theatre, many a rehearsal is started with music, recorded or live, to set the tone and rhythm for a scene. In period plays, this can be as helpful in creating a style and atmosphere as the heels, skirts, and bodices or the bows and curtsies of the age. In teaching directing at Yale, Alexander Dean had his class listen to the preludes of Chopin and attempt to find terms, direct or suggestive, to describe the qualities distinguishing each prelude from the others. Frank McMullan, who has continued Dean's use of the Chopin, has described the results in *The Directorial Image:*

> The interesting thing about this experiment was the general agreement among the students about the evocative and connotative qualities of particular preludes which suggested the moods of certain plays. For example, the tenth prelude has a playful, impish mood quality similar to that of Sherwood's *Reunion in Vienna.* For many students, the eleventh prelude evokes a general feeling of physical activity and conflict of a melodramatic sort. Its mood seems like that of many early American melodramas, Gillette's *Secret Service,* for instance. The twelfth prelude has a sweet, sad, sentimental, and meditative quality reminiscent of *East Lynne.*

The pervasive rhythm that gave a lilt to the film *Lilies of the Field* was set in one group song, "A-men," and echoed throughout the sound track on banjo or harmonica. It was carried out by the movement and posture of the actors—the five German nuns and the American passer-by, played by Sidney Poitier. All held their heads high and stepped with a high lift, proud, assertive, and jaunty, yet all showed full respect for one another. They could meet exasperations with an ironic flick of the head because of that mutual respect and because they were all dedicated to building the new chapel. The rhythm created a basic spirit that gave unity to the film.

Even for the musician the notes on the staff cannot indicate all aspects of 359 performance. Besides the marking of tempo, of loud and soft, crescendo and diminuendo, the composers have developed a vocabulary, mostly Italian, to indicate the general tone they want, whether broad, gentle, lamenting, impassioned, solemn, majestic, vigorous, lively, with fire, and so on. Still, much has to be left to the performer. Every concert player makes some use of suspension, pause, interruption, bunching and spreading out, speeding and slowing, and strong dynamic contrasts, though far less now than in Victorian times. The theatre director uses many terms and concepts from music, but he finds that some aspects of rhythm in the theatre cannot be described in musical terms. In order to deal with these, he learns much from the rhythms of dance, of poetry, and of the natural and social environment.

Some folk dances have a pattern of movement as rigid as a march or waltz. But freer, more expressive dances cannot be described in terms of duple and triple meter or measures and accents. Both the dancer and the actor may do many practice exercises that start with walking, then make the walk heavier as in marching and stamping, or lighter for swinging or lilting, go on to prancing, skipping, jumping, and leaping, and finally give the walk a new quality by adding an intention or an emotion—responding to the sky and wind of a hilltop, strutting in front of someone in pride or defiance, or slipping around while someone else sleeps. A simple movement is studied in different dimensions—small and large, high and low, straight and curved, diagonal and spiral—while the movement itself acquires different qualities, such as tenseness or relaxation, smoothness or jerkiness. The dancer discovers many qualities of movement that are just as pertinent for the actor.

Rudolf Laban, who has worked with factory workers in time-motion studies as well as with dancers and actors, has made in *Movement for the Stage* a very provocative analysis of some of these factors of human movement, all of which contribute to the rhythm of a play. Taking a set of everyday words for kinds of movement, such as *punch, slash, press, flick, dab, float,* and *wring,* he started to analyze the difference in the movements suggested. He saw that some were gentle or light while others were much heavier. Some were quick and short and some were slow and sustained. Likewise some movements, like *punch, dab,* and *press,* come to a definite end in space, while others, like *slash, float,* and *pull,* may continue without a final goal or direction. Some of these movements imply strong resistance or inner restraint while others, like *float, glide, smear,* and *stroke,* imply much less resistance. Such active verbs may suggest to a director and an actor that at one moment the character might use, in speech and movement, the sustained, strong, flexible qualities of wringing and stretching, while another character might need the light, quick directness of dabbing and patting or the gentler, smoother qualities of floating or gliding.

But more immediate to the theatre than rhythms suggested by music or dance are those supplied by the playwright, especially the poet-playwright. The rhythm of his phrases, the sounds of his words, and the rich suggestion of his images give the actor a chance to create a mood that may be the most compelling power of the play.

The Play in Production

Shakespeare's characters, without the help of scenery or lighting, cast a spell over the scene by the power of movement and words. Just before his murders, Macbeth fills the air with suggestions of all the dark terrors of the night. After the shock of seeing the dagger, he suddenly changes his rhythm and, with the slow, thick stab of short words, describes the dark which possesses him.

> Now o'er the one half-world
> Nature seems dead, and wicked dreams abuse
> The curtained sleep.

In the next act Macbeth has just sent the murderers after Banquo and is eagerly waiting for night.

> Ere the bat hath flown
> His cloistered flight, ere to black Hecate's summons
> The shard-borne beetle with his drowsy hums
> Hath rung night's yawning peal, there shall be done
> A deed of dreadful note. . . .
> . . . Come, seeling night,
> . . . Light thickens, and the crow
> Makes wing to the rooky wood;
> Good things of day begin to droop and drowse,
> Whiles night's black agents to their preys do rouse.

Much of the dark anguish of *Hamlet* is created in the opening scene of the changing of the guard at midnight and the brief remark of the guard who is relieved, " 'Tis bitter cold and I am sick at heart." The moonlight balcony scene of *Romeo and Juliet* is built up in the phrases of Romeo, who sees Juliet as brighter than sun and moon, her eyes twinkling for the stars. He addresses her as "bright angel . . . thou art as glorious to this night, being o'er my head/ As is a winged messenger of heaven." He speaks of "night's cloak to hide me," of the blessed moon "that tips with silver all these fruit-tree tops," of "how silver-sweet sound lovers' tongues by night," evoking a spell of idealized love in the sustained light rhythms and sounds. For the violent scene of the fights and deaths, a hot noon atmosphere is quickly created with sharper rhythms and images:

> The day is hot, the Capulets are abroad,
> And if we meet we shall not 'scape a brawl,
> For now these hot days is the mad blood stirring,

a passage in which the air is stabbed by short phrases, monosyllables, and seven accented syllables in the last line. For the storm scenes in the third act of *King Lear,* Shakespeare devotes a whole scene to two minor characters describing their struggle against the wind, rain, and lightning before bringing on Lear and his Fool. Lear answers the thunder with the trumpet tones and slow, heavy rhythms of "Strike flat the thick rotundity of the world." But in the next storm scene the mood is more quiet and eerie as Lear begins to go

361

mad, and the new tone is set by the strange mock madness of the outcast Edgar: "Through the sharp hawthorn blows the cold wind."

Not only the actors but the designers listen to the rhythm of the dialogue, whether the imagery of the poet or the prose of local color, so that their sounds, lighting, and changing scenery and costumes may enrich the rhythms indicated by the words.

The spell of the geographical or historical environment may set the rhythm as the characters are shaped by local color and caught up in the mood and purpose of a particular situation. The romantics have always been interested in moods of time and place, from enchanted caves and forests, solemn all-night vigils of medieval knights, and moonlight trysts of lovers to the witches' caverns, smugglers' dens, and village festivals of nineteenth-century melodramas. In musical and opera, much time is used in creating a rich mood of local color and time of day. *Pelleas and Melisande* evokes its ghostlike lovers out of dim night and twilight to drift through strange forests and old castles, beside pools of water in deep caves—helpless, lonely wraiths who fade back into the mists whence they come. The dialogue of Maeterlinck, made up of short hints and phrases, suggestive and evocative, never strong or assertive, finds its perfect expression in the impressionist music of Debussy, who made an opera of the play, with delicate fragments of melody half emerging from a rich orchestral web.

Modern directors are extremely aware of the rhythms of different places at particular seasons and times of day. In directing classes much time is spent on how to set the movement and stage business by which the actors establish the rhythm of place. There can be a wide range in detail as each actor falls into a variation of one basic rhythm. Dean used to start with evening in a cabin on an old-fashioned southern plantation. He would put the grandmother in a rocking chair to set one slow, straightforward, basic two-four rhythm. After the beat was established, firm and cheerful, he would bring on the mother, who would iron at a beat twice as fast but synchronized with the grandmother's rocking. Then he would bring in the granddaughter bouncing a ball, with four beats to the grandmother's one. All were united in one rhythm, expressive of the place, the time of day, and the attitudes and qualities of the characters. Then, to show the difference between tempo and rhythm, he would ask the actors to increase the tempo, the speed of the basic beat. Either adding a faster variation of the basic rhythm or increasing the tempo will create a build, a sense of rising step by step to a climax.

Rhythm of place may be set by the temperament of the people. A Mexican village differs from a Scandinavian or an Irish town, a Spanish festival from an American square dance or a court minuet. Card parties in different localities vary as widely as the people differ in basic rhythms.

The intent of the characters may also set the rhythm. Hope has a brighter, lighter rhythm than despair. A character will set different tones when he is dreading, when teasing, urging, begging, or threatening, when weary, exasperated, suspicious, quizzical, or puzzled. If a character has brought some very alarming but uncertain news and has left, the other characters will start

The Play in Production

a new beat of puzzled suspense with sharp, light rhythm. Inflections will be mostly upward and unfinished, the speech and movements restless, coming in sudden slight spurts with frequent interruptions and pauses. Worry and anxiety and tension will continue, sometimes suggested in slight irritations and disagreements but not released into full clear action and not relaxed into rest and harmony. All the characters will be caught in the same rhythm though they may each play a variation on it.

The overall texture is a blend of many elements—the spectacle, with its colorful settings, changing lights, and moving masses of costumes; the dialogue, with its rhythmic phrases, suggestive images, and vibrant sounds; and the mood, created by the qualities and rhythms of the actors. For each play the director must determine just what texture is needed so that later, in rehearsal, he can communicate this to his actors now by words, as he describes the overall texture and the particular mood, and now by rhythmic movements, as the conductor of an orchestra leads his players through the subtle nuances of the music. McMullan, in *The Directorial Image,* describes the style, mood, and emotional quality of Arthur Miller's *All My Sons:*

> . . . homespun, durable, rough cut, without gloss, dark brown streaked with black and green, with threads that, criss-crossing and intertwining in depth, form a pattern of meaning. Its fabric does not tear easily, but once torn it unravels quickly and permanently.

In a similar way he hunts for the adjectives, figures, and suggestive colors to describe the quality of Shakespeare's *Henry IV, Part One:*

> . . . a tapestry of rich and vibrant colors, with three main warm colors dominant. The design is Gothic in spirit: it soars and it moves leisurely but always with virile heartiness and swagger. It is not lacking in grace and wit, though the latter may be larded o'er with unblushing references to "country matters." Here is little delicacy but a great deal of fiery feeling circumscribing duty and honor. It is a procession of banners flapping to the warm but fresh wind blowing off Elizabeth's England.

Throughout the analysis and the preparation, the director, the actor, and the designer must keep in mind this overall effect. Where the director is aware of builds and let-downs, character schemes and rhythms, the audience must see only characters in action, a colorful image of human destiny.

EXERCISES AND DEMONSTRATIONS

1. DISCOVERY IN AN IBSEN PLAY.   Take one of Ibsen's social plays—for example, *A Doll's House, Ghosts,* or *Rosmersholm*—and examine it to see how a character finds out something very shattering about the past.

2. PLANNING A PLOT BASED ON DISCOVERY.   Outline the steps by which one character, accidentally acquiring a piece of information, follows it up or

363

how he blunders into knowledge that changes his relations with someone else. Does he find out new things about himself—about his deeds or his character?

3. PLANNING A PLOT BASED ON DECISION. Starting from a strong decision, either to do something or not to do it, plan several preparatory episodes that will lead up to the decision. Include both episodes showing a developing situation that will require action and episodes indicating aspects of character that will determine the decision.

4. PLANNING AN ENDING. Take a play, a movie, a TV drama, or a story, and plan a new plot with a similar situation but a quite different ending. What changes will be necessary, what different characters with variation, contrast, or conflict will reinforce the new plot, and what episodes will build toward the new ending?

5. PLANNING A PLOT BASED ON A TRIAL. Plan an informal hearing or trial, that is, one character in a family, an office, a club, or any other group demanding an explanation or action.

6. ANALYZING A CHARACTER. Take a character from a play and write an analysis such as an actor might make in studying the role. Include appearance, manner of speaking and moving, rhythm, main objective, and such points as how the character has reacted to his environment, how he reacts to other characters and they to him, what function he has in developing the plot and the theme, and how he fits into the scheme of characters, as variation or contrast, reinforcement or opposition.

7. PLANNING A SCHEME OF CHARACTERS. Start with a character who wants something and plan a whole cast of characters for a play by surrounding him with such other characters as (1) a foil to give strong contrast or opposition, (2) two variations—one who has a weaker drive toward the same objective and one who has a much stronger, perhaps even fanatic, drive, and (3) several background characters to tie the play into a real place and add texture and mood that can reinforce the main character or provoke opposition from him. Plan incidents to show the variation of intensity and show how differences in intensity bring two characters into opposition.

8. PLANNING A PLOT TO REINFORCE THEME. Devise a love plot that depends on theme by making the choice of a girl mean the choice of one way of life. One kind of love plot exploits disagreement as the two discover or develop their disagreement after they are in love. Does she come over to his side or he to hers? Do they discover a third and better way, or do they accept disagreement, either together or forever separate?

364

EXERCISES AND DEMONSTRATIONS

9. ANALYSIS OF INTERACTION OF PLOT, CHARACTER, AND THEME. Analyze John Steinbeck's *Of Mice and Men* to find out how the elements of structure reinforce each other.

For plot, ask these questions: Why is there a separate scene for the exposition of the dream of George and Lennie? How does the end of the play tie up with the beginning? What complicating forces are introduced by Curley and his wife? What different reactions do they have to Lennie? What are the episodes that prepare for the killing of Curley's wife? How does the killing of the dog prepare for the killing of Lennie? Is anybody to blame? Should Candy have killed the dog himself?

For character scheme, ask these questions: What are the variants of loneliness? Of attempts at companionship? Of dreams of security? Of loss of companionship? Is Curley's insecurity and need for companionship different from that of his hired men? Is this a sociological study of conflict between owner and workers or a study of isolated, if universal, loneliness?

For theme, ask these questions: Who is to blame? What is to blame? What rouses your interest and sympathy? What do you conclude about life? How far is the capitalist system to blame? How far is this farm owner to blame? The title is taken from a line of Robert Burns's poem "To a Mouse": "The best-laid schemes o' mice an' men gang aft agley." What does this tell you about both plot and theme? What is the effect of repeating the examples of lonely men reaching for security and meeting defeat? Why are there so many helpless people in the play—old Candy, the crippled Negro, the slow-witted Lennie?

10. RHYTHM AND MOOD IN MUSIC. Study the different moods in Moussorgsky's *Pictures at an Exhibition*. How does the dignified walking theme differ from the various descriptive sections? How far do the titles of the pictures help the listener to imagine the mood? What other pictures might fit the music equally well? Devise groups of characters with movements and sounds to fit particular sections of the music. Are there scenes from plays that have similar moods?

11. GROUP RHYTHM AND LOCALE. Plan a group scene in pantomime as Alexander Dean planned the scene in a plantation cabin, showing several people who belong in one locale engaged in different but related activities, moving at different speeds but united by one basic rhythm. Then give the performance a dramatic form by creating an event that causes a change in tempo and intensity—for instance, the entrance of a new character.

12. GROUP RHYTHM AND MOTIVATION. Plan three different group scenes, either in pantomime or with improvised brief phrases, showing the people of a particular locale on three different occasions—for instance, a bank on an average day, on the day before the Fourth of July, and at a time of rumors of financial panic, or the booking office of a steamship company on an average spring day when summer trips are being planned, on a day when refugees

are trying frantically to get passage, and on a day when there have been rumors of a disaster at sea.

SUGGESTED READING

Many books have dealt with the analysis of the play from the playwright's point of view, beginning with William Archer, *Playmaking: A Manual of Craftsmanship* (1912), and George Pierce Baker, *Dramatic Technique* (1919). Kenneth Rowe's two books, *Write That Play* (1919) and *A Theatre in Your Head* (1959), are helpful on analysis. John Howard Lawson, *Theory and Technique of Playwriting* (1936), has detailed analyses of the structure of recent plays and insists that man's relation to social institutions is the subject matter of drama. Later revisions bring the book up-to-date and include television drama. Two brief books—Samuel Selden, *An Introduction to Playwriting* (1946), and Kenneth Macgowan, *A Primer of Playwriting* (1951)—are useful. Studies of the theory of drama include Fred Millett and Gerald E. Bentley, *The Art of the Drama* (1935), Alan R. Thompson, *The Anatomy of Drama* (1946), and Allardyce Nicoll, *The Theory of Drama* (1931) and *The Theatre and Dramatic Theory* (1962).

Ronald Peacock, *The Art of the Drama* (1957), deals especially with symbolic and nonrealistic forms, and Eric Bentley, *The Life of the Drama* (1965), has many new ideas about action and other aspects of the play.

There is a good short chapter on "Dramatic Structure, Form and Style" in O. G. Brockett, *The Theatre: An Introduction* (1964), and a good introduction to play analysis in Marian Gallaway, *The Director in the Theatre* (1963).

Excellent examples of play analysis are given in Michael Chekhov, *To the Director and Playwright* (1963), and Frank McMullan, *The Directorial Image* (1962). Analyses by Stanislavsky and the post-Stanislavsky directors Elia Kazan and Harold Clurman are given in Toby Cole and Helen Krich Chinoy, *Directors on Directing** (1963).

Style, a recent problem in an age of eclectic theatre, has not been extensively treated. The fullest discussions are in Michael St. Denis' brief book, *Theatre: An Analysis of Style* (1960), and George R. Kernodle, "Style, Stylization, and Styles of Acting," *Educational Theatre Journal* (Dec., 1960). Style in the other arts has been more freely described—in art, by André Malraux, *The Psychology of Art,* also published as *The Voices of Silence* (1953), one passage of which is reprinted in Morris Wentz, *Problems in Aesthetics* (1959); in literature, by Eric Auerbach, *Mimesis** (1953); and in architecture, by Sigfried Giedion, *Time, Space and Architecture* (1952; rev. ed., 1959). A good article on style in relation to culture is Meyer Shapiro, "Style," in A. Kroeber (ed.), *Anthropology Today* (1953).

366   * Available in paperback edition.

CHAPTER ELEVEN

THE REHEARSAL:
DIRECTOR AND ACTOR

When the director is sure just what attitude of comedy or tragedy he is aiming for, what style he needs as control, what patterns he wants in plot, character, and theme and what qualities in dialogue, mood, and spectacle, he starts to put the play on the boards. After he and the designer have worked out the ground plan and know where the doorways, steps, and levels are to be and where the walls and furniture will shape the playing areas, he lets the designer and his assistants go their own way for a time while he concentrates on putting the actors on the stage. Now he makes use of the five techniques of the director listed in the outline of play production in the last chapter—composition, picturization, movement, pantomimic dramatization, and rhythm. The first two—composition and picturization—are techniques for controlling the picture in space and the last three set the play into movement in time. The director considers how he can make the play clear and meaningful to the eye, as though the spectators were deaf, and to the ear, as though they were blind. In the early rehearsals, he looks at each moment of the play as though it were a still photograph, to see that the composition is clear and the relationships in the picture are meaningful; later, he watches and listens as the large movements, the reading of lines, and the small reactions propel the play through its rhythmic patterns in time.

Controlling the Picture in Space

The director's first step in putting the play on the boards is to visualize it in space. He is not putting a single orator on a podium or a preacher in a pulpit. He is not placing a beautifully dressed manikin in a store window, though the stage and the show window have much in common. He is visualizing an action involving people with people and people with the world they live in. If he left the actors to themselves, they would get in front of one another and muddle the composition, and each would move without regard to what the others were doing. The grouping would be meaningless, and the attention of the audience would be scattered. The composition of the picture and the picturization of relationships must be planned and controlled completely by someone outside the picture; hence these two techniques belong very logically to the director.

Where the movie and television director has a camera with which to select and control what is to hold the attention, the stage director has only the actor and the space of the stage for his picture. In placing and moving his actors in the various areas of the stage, he has many ways of changing the picture to give different meanings and to shift the attention from one character to another. He may subordinate one character by turning him away from the direction of the audience while he gives prominence to another by asking him to "open up" (that is, turn more toward the audience), to stand up, to step out from a group, or to move from a weak area to a stronger area of the stage. Or he can throw the emphasis on one character without moving him by moving the characters around him, so that they give him more space and contrast, and by having them turn their eye-focus on him. In deploying his actors, the director divides the stage into six areas (sometimes nine) and labels them up right, up center, up left, down right, down center, and down left (FIGURE 11.1). Stage left and stage right indicate the sides as viewed by the actor facing the audience; upstage is away from the audience and downstage is toward it. For four centuries—in some places well into this century—upstage was actually higher than downstage, as the old picture stage had a

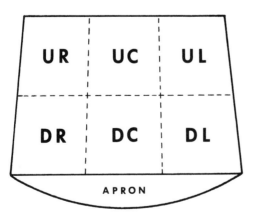

FIGURE 11.1 Stage areas. The director divides the stage into at least six areas, to lend variety and to use the relative strength from the soft up left or up right to the very emphatic down center.

FIGURE *11.2* Extremely formal composition for a religious performance. The stylized costumes and makeup suggest stained-glass windows. *The Book of Job*. Pineville, Kentucky. Adapted and designed by Orlin and Irene Corey.

sloping floor to give a forced perspective effect to the wing-and-backdrop setting.

Not only are some areas stronger than others but different areas have different qualities. The soft distant areas up left and up right are good for lyric moods, for longing, dreaming, brooding, and for some delicate love scenes. Scenes in those areas are so soft that they do not assure us that action will follow. For instance, a lonely, isolated person, hearing other people talking unfavorably about him, could smolder up left or up right in suffering and anger, but not until he came into the area down left or down right would we believe him capable of taking revenge. Decisions and quarrels often need the strength of the down center position after a climactic move from one of the weaker areas. But scenes of violence—murder, for instance—are too shocking if brought downstage. A stabbing or strangling is usually played in a weak area; it will be strong enough upstage left, behind a sofa, with other actors covering the body, and more convincing than it would be if the audience could see how the blow is faked. Even a film usually omits the final impact, showing only the arm or the shadow of the murderer or the horrified face of an onlooker.

The director devotes the first rehearsals to "blocking"; that is, he goes through each scene speech by speech, telling the actors when to come in, where to stand or sit, on what lines to move or carry out such "stage business" as handling the properties or eating, and how to perform many of the

369

The Rehearsal

small reactions that go with the lines. As they go through the actions, they write the directions down in their scripts. If a commercial acting edition of the play is used, the director tells them to disregard the printed stage directions. He has usually worked out carefully new movements and actions that will fit the particular stage, the design, and the dramatic concept he has in mind.

Blocking of the first act may take one three-hour rehearsal or longer, and then three or four rehearsals may be necessary to get the act set before the next act is blocked. Directors vary a great deal in the extent of their blocking, some giving full directions immediately, others leaving much of the detail to be worked out later as the actors try out their lines and their reactions to one another. Bernard Shaw was for a very full blocking, insisting that actors had as much right to know from the first walking rehearsal where they were and what they were doing as to know the words they were to speak. But almost any director makes adjustments in later rehearsals, modifying the original blocking by adding or simplifying as he and the actors discover better ways of moving and reacting. He must constantly make sure that his picture has clarity, focus, and variety. The form of his composition, its formality or diffuseness, hardness or softness, will add meaning to the play. At the same time, the grouping creates a web of interaction as the picture tells the story.

The drawings in FIGURE *11.3* show some differences between formal and

FIGURE *11.3*   Formal versus informal composition. A formal throne scene with many vertical lines is contrasted with a more relaxed, informal scene. A formal duel, symmetrical, vertical, parallel to the front, is contrasted with a more dynamic fight on a diagonal floor pattern. Drawn by Don Creason.

FIGURE *11.4* Trial scene with formal lines on a diagonal ground plan. Primary emphasis is on the officer on the stand and secondary emphasis is on the prosecutor. Wouk's *The Caine Mutiny Court Martial.* Mankato State College production, directed by Ted Paul and designed by Burton E. Meisel.

informal composition. The king's throne placed up center commands a symmetrical scene of formal vertical lines, which contrasts with the more informal scene. The formal, symmetrical duel scene set square to the front is not nearly so dynamic as the informal fight set on a diagonal line.

Most actual scenes on the stage are more complex than these drawings. FIGURE *11.4* shows a tense moment in a college production of *The Caine Mutiny Court Martial.* In considering the overall controls, the director has decided that this is a very strong situation play with romantic, even melodramatic, interest in conflict, threats, fears, and concern over justice. With the designer, he decided to bring the action far downstage but not actually to break the fourth-wall convention. Since the concern about justice is abstract and the people are removed from the actual ships and storms where the mutiny took place, the setting and composition can be rather abstract and formal. But since conflict is so important in the play and is not resolved into an unquestioned justice at the end, the ground plan is placed on the diagonal; the court is not square to the front, and the judge is not so dominant as in a civil courtroom. The designer has provided several levels for playing, and in this scene the director is making good use of them to give the prosecutor an uphill handicap in his assault on the witness. The isolation of the two figures at the front, with considerable free space, and their dynamic interaction make them stand out clearly from the seated figures. Of the two, the officer on the stand easily dominates, even without the special lighting, because of his higher position and because his face and body are turned more toward the audience than toward the others. Furthermore, in contrast to everybody else he is relaxed, and contrast, like isolation in space, adds a   *371*

The Rehearsal

FIGURE *11.5* Informal scene in naturalistic style. Curved lines hold the compact group together. Though the characters are emotionally isolated, they indicate many potential loyalties and conflicts. Miller's *A View from the Bridge*. University of Oregon production, directed by William R. McGraw and designed by Karl Kaufman.

powerful emphasis. If attention should wander to the judge or his associates, it is sent right back to the officer because they are looking at him. The director constantly uses such "eye-focus" of the characters on stage to point to the center of interest. If the attention is to go to the judge or one of his seated associates, the director will need to turn several people to look at him and subordinate the forestage men by turning their faces away from the audience.

For a very informal composition, let us consider the scene from *A View from the Bridge* shown in FIGURE *11.5*. Although the space used is fairly shallow, the characters are very much at home and the environment is important. The play is a naturalistic drama that has strong conflict under the surface, but in this scene the little conflicts and changing interactions are more important than any one thread of action. Character and mood, at least for this scene, are more important than plot. The curved lines of the composition create informality and warmth and bring all the characters into a close circle. Yet the director keeps nearly all of them isolated from one another. All belong to one family, yet they cannot come together. There is a great deal of variety, with two standing, two seated, and one sitting on the floor, and the director creates many different relationships. The boy sitting on the floor has one thought—his love for the girl he is with—and both his humble position and his eyes are begging for her love. He is safely enclosed between the two women, but he is isolated from the men, and the line of their faces, with conflict brewing, leads directly to him. The woman standing could easily take the attention—her position gives her a high level, she is near the center of the stage, and she is facing front in contrast with the two

372

The Play in Production

seated men—but she subordinates herself by dropping her eyes. At this moment she will not tie herself to anyone, though the lines of the picture tie her closely in three directions. The curved lines and her nearness to the young couple in love show her sympathy for them; her position at the table ties her to her husband sitting at the table, though she separates herself from what he is saying; her standing shows her implicit sympathy with the young man standing at stage left. The man sitting at the table is obviously the man of the house and all the others are closely tied to him, but he keeps his isolation and is slightly hostile to the young man at his left. Nobody is completely subordinated, and each could easily be given the center of attention. For instance, if the boy sitting turned his face more toward the audience, he would be stronger, and if one or more of the three other characters turned an eye-focus on him, he would be the center of action.

Sometimes the director has the problem of setting one person against a crowd. In FIGURE *11.6,* a scene from *The Bridge at Rio Campana,* the intruder is a surprised girl facing five rather hostile young men. The one girl standing, reinforced by the vertical line of the archway, can easily balance five men sitting close together in one mass. The director has achieved a great deal of variety in their sitting positions. Their relationships to one another have disappeared as they are united in a not quite shapeless mass by the arrival of the intruder. In FIGURE *11.7,* a scene from *Brand,* the one speaker completely dominates the crowd, which is subordinated almost to anonymity. The director, wanting an almost chaotic mass, has let some actors momentarily cover others, yet a few groupings and relationships give some form to the

FIGURE *11.6* Informal composition. The five boys in a variety of positions are united in mild hostility to the intruding girl. Gorostiza's *The Bridge at Rio Campana.* Northwestern University production, directed by Marshall Mason and designed by Elise Morenon.

FIGURE *11.7* Composition dominated by one speaker on a platform. The mob is shapeless except for a few listeners who relate themselves to one another in groups or pairs. Ibsen's *Brand*. University of Oregon production, directed by Preston Tuttle and designed by Judith Wolf.

FIGURE *11.8* One character in contrast to a group. Seats at the dining table are staggered to the limit of credibility to enable upstage characters to be seen. O'Neill's *Ah, Wilderness!* Theatre Guild production, New York, 1933. Photo Vandamm.

FIGURE *11.9* Formal, balanced composition on an open stage. Characters are evenly spaced for aristocratic stateliness at a wedding that is suddenly turned into a scene of violent accusation. Shakespeare's *Much Ado About Nothing.* The Euclid-Seventy-Seventh Street Theatre of the Cleveland Playhouse. Directed by Kirk Willis and designed by Paul Rodgers.

crowd. This picture shows very forcibly how height, space, and a position facing the audience give emphasis. The actors in the lower group are made mere listeners by being turned away from the audience; the ones whose faces are partly toward the audience are subordinated by being crowded close into the group, without contrast or space to let them stand out. The scene from the 1933 production of *Ah, Wilderness!* in FIGURE *11.8* gives the one contrasting character, the drunk showoff Uncle Syd, full emphasis without separating him from the family group.

Two quite different styles of directing a scene of violent accusation may be compared in the scenes from *Much Ado About Nothing* and *Look Homeward, Angel,* FIGURES *11.9* and *11.10.* On the open stage of the Euclid-Seventy-Seventh Street Theatre of the Cleveland Playhouse, the wedding scene of *Much Ado* is given very formal treatment, with exact symmetry. The even spacing of the characters would give aristocratic stateliness to the beginning of the wedding. But when the bridegroom suddenly accuses the bride of misconduct, the isolated figures, leaning forward, seem to threaten her from all sides. An everyday squabble is picturized in the scene from *Look Homeward, Angel.* The young man at the steps is apprehensive, wanting to come to the defense of the accused couple at the center, as the other characters look on or join in with varying degrees of interest.

In all these pictures, we see the director much concerned with the effect of his composition, using straight lines and formal groupings for one play and curved lines for another, setting the action parallel to the front of the stage for formal balance or on a diagonal for more dynamic conflict. We see that the director is even more concerned with controlling the center of action, moving the attention of the audience from one point to another by making

375

FIGURE *11.10* Strong story emphasis in an informal group. The main characters, given emphasis by space, are balanced against the mass of boarders. Within the mass the boarders show many degrees of interest and involvement. Note in the setting how the roof, treated as an outline in a drawing, blends with the realistic scene. Fring's *Look Homeward, Angel.* University of Michigan production, directed by Claribel B. Baird, designed by Ralph W. Duckwall, Jr., and costumed by Elizabeth Birbari. Photo Ouradnik.

one actor emphatic and the others subordinate. We see that, other things being equal, bringing a character from the side toward the center or from upstage toward the audience will make him stronger. But it is easy to subordinate characters, even in strong areas, by turning the face and body partly away from the audience, for the actor whose face is turned more nearly to the front will hold the greater interest. The higher face will dominate the lower, a character standing will dominate one sitting, one on a step or platform will dominate one on a lower level. Eye-focus of the actors is one of the easiest means of controlling the attention of the audience, since we tend to look at what someone else is looking at. As we see in several of these pictures, a single figure with space around him can, like a small weight on a long lever, counterbalance a whole mass. An element of the scenery that repeats the line of the actor, or a guard or attendant, can give him more importance. Contrast is such a powerful element that it can counteract any of the other methods of controlling attention. One figure sitting, bent over, with his head turned away from the audience, is weaker than a figure standing and facing the audience, but if there are three or four straight standing figures, the weak bent figure takes the attention by contrast. It is the whole picture that the audience sees, and each actor, each property, each part of the setting must take its place in the controlled context or it distracts the attention and destroys the illusion of the scene.

376   The audience is rarely aware of the composition in itself, unless it is clut-

tered or confused. What they see is the story in the picture, told through the action and interrelation of the characters. Alexander Dean called this storytelling arrangement "picturization," and it may even more precisely be called "picturization of emotional relations." It is a visual language, a medium as powerful as words, by which the director communicates with the audience. It is one means by which a play, so short in comparison with a novel, can make as strong an impression, sometimes even stronger. The actor, the designer, and the director can show the audience at a glance complexities and qualities of relationship that may require many pages of a novel to describe or suggest. For the novelist can present only one detail at a time, and must depend on the reader to add the details into a total impression, while the director can present a whole group in action at once, in full color, tone, and texture. In a well-directed scene of an accident in the street, for instance, the audience can tell by the position of the actors which is the wife of the victim, which the mother, the father, the friend, the wife's friend, and which are mere passersby, adding their own groupings and emotional reactions in the background. Even the manikins in a store window or the drawn figures of a dress advertisement do not line up as on parade but are arranged to simulate actual people aware of their environment, listening, talking, responding to one another. We naturally turn toward and keep near those we like or trust or feel something in common with. We keep at a distance from those we dislike, or turn away from them. If a girl is in the center, halfway between two boys who are turning hopefully toward her, we know she must make a choice. If she sits or relates herself to some piece of furniture, we know that she will not make the decision and that it is up to the boys to break the equilibrium. Move her nearer one and we know she has chosen him. Turn her feet and body toward one and her eyes toward the other, and her eyes tell us which she is thinking about while her feet and body tell what she will actually do. If the men are facing each other and making a demand on each other or opposing each other, have her close to one and we know she belongs to him, even if she is also opposing him. If she and one of the men are making the same demand, they will stand in the same position facing the other person, she ahead if she is taking the lead or behind if he is taking it. They may lean toward each other slightly, out of a feeling of being together. If a woman is sitting or standing and a taller man is standing behind her so that the audience sees the two as one, we know they belong to each other, in a far stronger relationship than brother and sister or two friends. There are many other relations that are clearly indicated by the picture—one person asking, refusing, suspecting, accusing, protecting, or disdaining another. Farewells will be different if casual or before a long absence, if someone is leaving for a picnic, or for war, or to prison. If the director finds a title for the scene in terms of its basic action, he can see more clearly how to arrange his picture.

In many ways the director makes visible basic attitudes, secret thoughts, and even unconscious desires of the characters. As the play progresses and certain chairs, sofas, doors, or small properties become associated with people in the play, other characters react to the objects as if they were the people themselves. After one character goes out, the one left may express his anger at the door or at the chair where the other sat, and the audience will see his thoughts. A playwright in the Middle Ages wrote the specific direction, "When anyone speaks of paradise, let him point to it." The mansion representing paradise was, of course, visible at the end of the long simultaneous-mansion platform (FIGURES 5.4 and 5.5). The modern director wants more complexity than simple pointing, but he is just as much interested as that medieval director in making the inner life of the play visible.

Moving the Play in Time

For the director, even more important than the control of the picture in space is the movement of the actors and the progression of the play in time. As Gordon Craig has said, "The art of the theatre has sprung from action—movement—dance." As we saw in the discussion of plot, the action may be a decision or the failure to make a decision, but even Chekhov's drifters are busy with the little activities of daily life and little responses to one another. On the stage people don't just talk, they do something, and as they carry on daily business they are constantly changing their relations with one another. The dialogue of the playwright is the surface expression. It is the director's job to find the inner life of the play and see that it, too, is expressed, in the changing moods, the larger movements, and the smaller business and reactions of the actor, which Dean called "pantomimic dramatization."

Movement is picturization in action. Those relationships that the student works out so carefully in terms of still pictures are never still on the stage. As relationships and attitudes change, the movements are as important as the words—indeed, often more important since they can modify, even contradict, the words and add other meanings and nuances. Hence the director makes sure that the actor understands the motivation and begins his action with the thought; then the movement will express his intention and the words will be part of a total response. The tone of the voice will follow the strength and tension of the movement. The audience believes the voice tone it hears and the muscle tone it sees, let the words say what they will. It usually takes many rehearsals for the actor to achieve a good integration of intention, speech, and movement, and in the early stages improvisation may be helpful to bring movement and words spontaneously from the thought. For the actor, there is the added complication that the director, in watching for clear composition while creating a build, may require him to make some movement not obviously motivated by the lines. Then, in order to make the movement convincing, the actor must find an acceptable motivation in the general situation, if it is no more than crossing the stage to get an ash tray.

An actor never crosses the stage in a straight line unless he wants to indicate that the character is abstracted and unaware of his surroundings. Not only is the curved approach more pleasing and useful in opening up the actor as he comes toward his objective from an upstage direction, but it also

378

shows his awareness of the other persons or objects on the stage. You never move abruptly past someone you know. You move around him, acknowledging him, and he makes a countermove, acknowledging you. The feeling is similar to the interaction of the dancers in a square dance. They never merely move past each other on a straight line to opposite places but always turn slightly toward each other as though bowing, or swing each other by the arm. No actor on the stage moves alone. Any movement is part of a readjustment that gets at least a slight acknowledgment from all the rest. The actors are all bound in one web of interrelationships as if invisible rubber bands were stretched between them. As they follow curved paths around one another and around the furniture, the actors create a sense of depth in a stage picture that otherwise looks rather flat.

Sometimes the basic action of the play is made clear by a change from the initial picture to one in sharp contrast, or in some cases a return to the first picture after a change in the middle part of the play. The action may begin at one side of the stage and push the opposition out the other side, like a football team pushing down the field over the goal line at the opposite end. If the seat at the head of the table or a dominant chair is occupied by one person at the beginning, the person who defeats him will take his place. In *Mourning Becomes Electra,* at first the mother is central, dominating the picture, with the tortured daughter coming at her from the side. After the mother is driven to suicide, the daughter stands in front of the main door, dominant in her turn.

In early rehearsals, while watching the composition and picturization and blocking the movement, the director works only in the most external way with the actor. He could almost use dominoes or stand-in actors, so little acting is involved. As the play moves forward, the actor takes the center and the director stands at the side, planning, suggesting, stimulating, controlling. But first the director must help the actor to understand the structure of the play as a whole, to see the waves of tension and relaxation building with crescendos to the climaxes where plot, character development, and theme come together.

In order to build that overall rhythmic structure, the director must make a chart of the play, breaking it up into units in time. In some plays the act structure is clear and distinct, each act forming a complete unit, a large section of the whole, and the author or director may give a descriptive title to each act. In addition, an act may already be broken up into scenes by scene changes and interruptions to indicate the passage of time. But the director needs smaller units than the acts and scenes. In France, publishers regularly mark a new scene every time a character enters or leaves the stage; hence we sometimes speak of "French scenes." But most directors want still smaller units, feeling that a new unit begins with each new intention or change of relationship, which may or may not coincide with an entrance or an exit. John Dietrich, in his book on directing, calls these subdivisions "motivational units," while followers of the Stanislavsky method speak of "beats." Sometimes a beat covers only two or three lines, while again it may run for pages

379

before the objective or relationship is changed. Each beat has a shape of its own, and the series of beats gives form to the larger units, which in turn give form to the play.

Sometimes the experienced director, with experienced actors, can be sure that the shape and quality of each beat and the sequence of beats will take care of themselves, but a beginning director usually works out the sequence in great detail, marking a line in the script where each new beat begins, defining in words the impetus of the new direction, the main objective of the beat, and the mood and the pattern, and asking whether there is an even tension, a build, or a let-down during the beat. Then the director describes to the actor the relation of each beat to the other beats and to the play as a whole. Some examples might be "even, terrifying suspense, where nobody dares speak real feelings," "a moment of playful diversion before she starts her campaign," "an interruption that brings on a new kind of complication," or "a complete drop after the first climax—you are numbed, and not yet thinking of any action." Sometimes the beat is described in terms of the desire or objective of the active character: "trying to quiet his suspicions," or "beginning to be afraid, he tries to delay." Thus the director, whether he writes it down or not, must have in mind exactly what is happening in each unit, what the mood should be, and how he wants the unit to follow the previous beat and lead into the next. Even if he believes that the actors can take care of most changes and developments, he often has to interrupt rehearsals to make the actors more sharply aware when a new unit starts. For instance, he may say, "Look, we need to show a stronger change here. Let's try a new piece of business. Have him go all the way over to the sideboard to put his cup down, find there's hardly room, push the other cups with a little impatience, then take more time answering her, with a deeper bite in his patient inflections. That way we see he has realized for the first time what a difficult person she is. She keeps on and on, not realizing how much she is irritating him, until the new beat starts with . . . ." Thus motivation, feelings, interactions, movement, and lines proceed under careful guidance and control.

Movement in the group is one of the director's ways of creating a build. When he decides that a beat or a sequence of beats needs to increase in tension, he does not depend entirely on the voices, the increasing tempo and volume, and the higher pitch and sharper quality. Like a choreographer with a group of dancers, he must also create a build for the eye. That means adding movements for the stimulation of the audience, sometimes called "breaking up the scene." A long talky scene needs some breaking up even if no great build is required. The first part of a beat will usually carry itself, and the director will conserve his power, adding few movements and only those that are casual and related to the background. As the scene progresses, he will add more and more movements, timing them closer together and increasing them in size and intensity, always careful that they are so placed and motivated as to reinforce the scene and not distract from it. If one character is telling a long story to several others, the director may not want to give any

The Play in Production

noticeable movement to the teller, but he can gain the needed breaking up or build if some listeners, at first very relaxed, get excited and move in closer, while others interject audible reactions and nod agreement with one another after vivid moments in the tale.

To the audience, all movement, large or small, is action. But in the theatre there is a distinct difference between the large movements, which take the actor from one part of the stage to another and which are mainly the concern of the director, and the smaller reactions of hands, arms, face, and body—the pantomimic dramatization, which is the most intimate concern of the actor. The director may contribute much of this dramatization as part of the larger movement, as he blocks the action and helps the actor see the relation between inner feeling and the words, action, and rhythm that express it. For instance, he may say to the actor, "After her line, cross to the window, uncomfortable, uncertain how to answer. Look out a second. Begin 'Mary' uncertainly, then turn and spurt the rest of the speech to her." Actors found that Joan Littlewood, whose London company became famous for fresh spontaneity, would not tell them "Here you move from right to left," but rather suggested images that described the feeling of the character: "In this scene you're coming out of a cellar, and fighting your way down a long, dark passage. You can't see, but you just know you have got to get out and through the door at the end."

In the coaching rehearsals, directors differ widely in their ways of stimulating the actor. Those who follow the Stanislavsky or the Actors Studio methods spend a great deal of time discussing the motivation of the character, comparing the character's experience with previous experiences of the actor, becoming almost amateur psychoanalysts in hope of discovering and releasing the actor's inhibitions. Other directors believe there is nothing like rehearsing the play. Sir Laurence Olivier, director of the National Theatre of England, expressed his impatience with the New York methods to an interviewer of the *New York Times:* "I'd rather have run the scene eight times than have wasted that time in chattering away about abstractions. An actor gets the right thing by doing it over and over. Arguing about motivations and so forth is a lot of rot. American directors encourage that sort of thing too much. . . . Instead of doing a scene over again that's giving trouble, they want to discuss . . . discuss . . . discuss. . . ."

Repetition in rehearsal seemed enough for Sir Laurence's professional actors, but directors of amateurs often find they must go to great effort to stimulate the actor. The actor may make the largest gesture he has ever made or utter the loudest shout, and it may still be very small. The director may stop the rehearsal and have the whole cast practice singing full tones and swinging and thrusting the arms like a fencer, until full voice and gesture seem easy and natural. Joan Littlewood found that even professional actors needed preparatory exercises to get both the imagination and the muscles limbered up. For the opening scene of *A Taste of Honey,* a weary mother and daughter arrive in their squalid new lodgings. Miss Littlewood had the two actresses spend an hour dragging heavily laden suitcases around the stage, trying to get on buses, arguing with landladies, struggling with rain, even imagining they were dragging the suitcases down long, dark, filthy tunnels. They learned how to feel worn out and fretful. When she was directing *The Quare Fellow,* a play about prison life in Dublin, she rehearsed the actors a week before she gave them the playwright's scripts. She had them march round and round on a slate and stone roof, improvise scenes of breaking from the line for a quick smoke and furtive conversation, wash out the cell, stand at attention, respond to the warder, the chaplain, and the cook carrying food to the man about to be executed. In early rehearsals of any play she would have the actors put much more action into a scene than was to be retained in performance in order to get a full surge of muscular response. For instance, she had the actor pace out in four forward steps Macbeth's line "Is this a dagger which I see before me? Come, let me clutch thee." All through the run of the satiric revue *Oh, What a Lovely War,* she rehearsed the actors every day, sometimes in order to rework and improve a particular scene, sometimes just to see that voices and bodies were kept flexible, and, above all, to see that the eager, imaginative response to the scene and to one another, which is especially important in this type of play, was not lost.

Just as singers spend some time in vocalizing and dancers in stretching and limbering up the muscles, actors are often put through warming-up exercises before rehearsal begins. The director has them sing full tones and pronounce consonants sharply, extend and limber muscles, and, often in pairs, practice watching, listening, and responding to each other to increase their awareness of other people. Especially for period plays, such a preliminary warmup is very useful not only for practicing bows, curtsies, and all the little actions with dress and hand properties, but for stimulating the imagination of the actor and getting him into the mood and rhythm of the play.

The final coordinating rehearsals are generally considered to be nightmares, and in the days when amateurs brought everything together—costume, scenery, properties, and lighting—at one last frantic dress rehearsal, they were just that. The performance could not possibly be as bad as that night, and the legendary saying was repeated that "a bad dress rehearsal means a good performance." But today school theatres and community theatres are much more serious and usually have from three to five dress rehearsals, besides working out many of the details before the first dress rehearsal. The company of an art theatre with its own building has a great advantage over casts playing in commercial theatres where they cannot get on stage until the last minute. It is a great help to actors to have platforms and steps, doors and windows to practice with and to have scene changes and much of the lighting worked out ahead. For a period play, the director and the designer often have a dress parade, bringing all the actors on stage in costume and makeup to try the key moves and see what changes and adjustments are necessary. If actresses have been rehearsing in long practice skirts, they will be ready for the full costume.

The first coordinating rehearsal will be mainly for practicing the cues for light changes, sounds, and the beginning and ending of scenes. There may

The Play in Production

be so many interruptions and repetitions and such consciousness of costumes that the overall structure and tempo, and even the actors' characterizations are lost. Yet for the moments of correlating the actors with the other elements, the director is keenly aware of the tone and rhythm he wants. David Belasco, who worked for the utmost perfection of detail, claimed that he had "sometimes experimented with a curtain fifty times, raising or lowering it rapidly, slowly, or at a medium speed. The curtain men must be taught to feel the climaxes as keenly as the actors and to work in unison with them."

After the strenuous coordinating dress rehearsals, it is a good idea to have several full rehearsals that run through without interruption. If some details must be corrected, the director often repeats a whole scene to relate the detail to what comes before and after. But most of his suggestions he makes to the actors after each act or after seeing the play as a whole. He is free to watch the flow of the play, to feel the surges toward the climaxes. He may make many notes, some of them on details that can be improved next time through, but at this point he is chiefly watching the overall effect. Is the style maintained consistently? Is the plot clear? Are the characters believable? Do the important ideas come through in words and actions? Is the texture rich and controlled, not too soft or too harsh? And, finally, do all the elements—setting, lighting, movement, tones, words—move together to carry the play to its big climaxes and give it structure and shape? By this time the actor is free to follow without interruption the secret life of the play in the hundred and one little reactions that give the play vitality. He is ready for that one final spark that will set the performance into flame—direct contact with a living audience.

EXERCISES AND DEMONSTRATIONS

1. FORM AND VARIETY IN A STAGE COMPOSITION. Direct a still tableau of six men in a crap game, using a circular ground plan with an opening for the audience to see the throw of dice. Place the six at six different levels, from lying flat with elbows on the floor to standing. Next rearrange the order to get variety and to break up the formal line. Then add variety by individual reactions: one bored, two angry with each other, one afraid that the police or the parents may catch them.

2. VARIETY AND EMPHASIS IN THE TRIANGLE. Place three people casually related to one another in a still tableau. Show how a change of eye-focus of one or two of the three can shift the emphasis. How many different relations can be shown by the three? First vary the distances within the group and the stage areas in which they are placed, then the body positions of one or two—sitting, lying, half-turned away, on different levels, and so on.

3. TECHNIQUES FOR EMPHASIS. Study the illustrations in this book to find examples of creation of emphasis in composition by (1) stage area, (2) body

383

position, (3) level, (4) space, (5) line, (6) eye-focus, (7) repetition either by another character or by an element of the setting.

4. MOOD AND QUALITY OF THE COMPOSITION. Find examples in the illustrations in this book in which the quality of the composition—formality or informality, straight or curved or broken lines, and so on—adds meaning to the scene. Distinguish between the quality created by the setting or lighting and the quality created by the arrangement of people.

5. CHANGE IN EMPHASIS BY MOVEMENT. Put a still tableau on the stage with emphasis and interest concentrated on one character. Then shift the emphasis to a different character by moving him from a subordinate place to a place of great emphasis, not necessarily at the center. He could move to a place where height or space or some other factor gave him the emphasis. Then achieve the same change of emphasis by moving only the other people. Then make the same change of emphasis by moving only heads and eye-focus.

6. STORY RELATIONSHIPS WITH THREE PEOPLE. Taking one girl and two men, try on stage the many variations of relationship suggested in this chapter, p. 377.

7. STORY RELATIONSHIPS IN THE STAGE PICTURE. Taking six or eight actors, direct on the stage a still tableau of the scene of an accident described in this chapter, p. 377, showing which is wife, mother, passer-by, and so on.

8. CHANGING THE PICTURE TO CHANGE THE MEANING.
a. Direct a tableau of a newly eloped couple arriving to tell the girl's parents. Show first that one of the parents is unforgiving, then that the parents are surprised but not really opposed.
b. Direct a tableau of a father helping the children play with toys on the floor. Show first the arrival of some relatives they do not like, then the arrival of the mother home from a trip.
c. Direct a tableau of the family telling the son good-bye. Show first that he is going on a vacation trip with friends, then that he is going to prison, and then that he is going to his first job, a glorious opportunity.

9. AN ORIGINAL PICTURIZATION. With four to seven students, plan and direct a still tableau that tells a story. Then let the rest of the class analyze the tableau, noting which character gets the most emphasis, who the characters are, where they are, what their relationships to one another are, and what they are doing. Can you give a title to the central situation? What is the relation of each character to what is happening? How far is each involved?

In planning, consider (1) the place and each character's relation to it, (2) the most appropriate areas of the stage, and (3) the overall quality ·of the composition—formal or informal, compact or diffused, with straight or broken or curved lines, clear-cut and melodramatic or enriched by many incidental details of place and character. Consider also (4) which character must get the emphasis and how, (5) how the main characters will show their reactions and relationships, and (6) how the secondary characters will show their relation to the others.

SUGGESTED READING

The systematic theory of Alexander Dean is presented in *Fundamentals of Play Directing* (1941), revised and brought up-to-date by Lawrence Carra under the same title (1965). The elementary parts of the Dean theory are presented in vivid form in Ruth Klein, *The Art and Technique of Play Directing** (1953).

All of Stanislavsky's writing, both on analyzing the play and on coaching the actor, is pertinent to directing, but especially useful are his separately published analyses of *Othello* and *The Sea Gull*. His *Building a Character* (1949) is concerned with shaping the actor's performance from the outside. An excellent account of his work is Nikolai Gorchakov, *Stanislavski Directs* (1954).

The very practical approach of John Dietrich, *Play Direction* (1953), and Curtis Canfield, *The Craft of Play Directing* (1965), can be supplemented by the more imaginative general discussions of Hugh Hunt, *The Director in the Theatre* (1954), and Michael Chekhov, *To the Director and Playwright* (1963).

Rehearsal techniques are well outlined in Hubert C. Heffner, Samuel Selden, and H. D. Sellman, *Modern Theatre Practice* (1959). Vivid descriptions of rehearsal conditions on Broadway about 1930 are found in Moss Hart, *Act One** (1959), and Joseph Verner Reed, *The Curtain Falls* (1935).

John Gassner, *Producing the Play* (1941; rev. ed., 1953), includes separate chapters by several authors on different kinds of directing—for arena, for musical, for television, and so on. A full anthology of statements about directing, with a history of directing and an excellent bibliography, is Toby Cole and Helen Krich Chinoy, *Directing the Play: A Source Book of Stagecraft* (1953), enlarged with a new title, *Directors on Directing** (1963).

Stark Young's essays on acting and directing, published in the twenties and reissued in various forms, are extremely sensitive and suggestive.

The most thorough examination of play analysis and the techniques of production is H. D. Albright, W. P. Halstead, and Lee Mitchell, *Principles of Theatre Art* (1955).

---

* Available in paperback edition.

CHAPTER TWELVE

THE PERFORMANCE:
ACTOR AND AUDIENCE

When the audience arrives for the excitement of opening night, it is the finished performance they have come to see. They know nothing of the hours of analysis and planning; they care nothing for the long days of rehearsal. Playwright, director, and designer disappear from view, and the backstage workers are mere assistants helping with costume changes, lights, musical instruments, or background sounds—all to enable the actor to create the play. The members of the audience lose themselves in the imaginary event and only afterwards marvel at the intensity of the emotions and at the technical control of the actor who can sustain that intensity throughout the play and repeat his performance night after night. The actor is the heart of the theatre, as it was from the beginning.

The naive theatregoer tends to identify the actor and the character, supposing that actors must have the same qualities offstage and on. Some parents are alarmed to see their children act convincingly the roles of worldly and even criminal characters. The more experienced playgoer sees the character that the playwright has created but, paradoxically, also enjoys the art of acting for its own sake, as the actor uses his charm, his sensitivity, and his skill to make the audience identify with the feelings and motives of the human being created on stage.

The Actor's Art

New York playgoers of the 1940s, 50s, and 60s saw some remarkable acting performances, clear and forceful, expertly controlled, that were repeated night after night, month in and month out, and yet each time the curtain rose were as fresh and delightful as if the event were taking place on the stage for the first time. Such performances defy complete analysis, but some of the actor's techniques can be recognized, and a description of the character and the emotions he creates can give some idea of his artistry. The playwright's work and the shaping and movement the director has given the play are absorbed and transformed in the creative work of the actor.

Some of the best acting of the 1940s was seen in Tennessee Williams' *The Glass Menagerie*. It is easy to describe the technique of characterization, the "psychological gesture," of Laura, the daughter, as played by Julie Haydon. She was an exquisite shy girl, as vulnerable as the glass animals she cherished, wincing, withdrawing, expecting to be hurt, trying to get behind a chair, a post, a doorway, then, for a moment, as the Gentleman Caller warmed to her, reaching forward in tentative hope. But the performance of Laurette Taylor as Amanda, the mother, was a marvelous combination of technique with the charm and personality of the actress, perfectly controlled and projected yet suffused with that glow of sensitivity that gives vivid reality to the best performances on the stage. Some of her techniques were clearly visible. Both her despair at learning that Laura had dropped out of business college and her sobbing when she was reconciled with her son Tom had a definite note of play-acting, that extra push at the beginning of phrases and the wide inflection of the voice of the conscious martyr that were unmistakable. Yet the audience realized that Amanda was really in despair, and the play-acting became part of her brave determination to do something. By sheer willpower she summoned her strength to insist that Tom invite some friend to the house, a Gentleman Caller, as a possible husband for Laura. Her loud contention with him left her exhausted, her shoulders drooping. But she pulled herself together and in a very different key started selling magazine subscriptions over the telephone. Again in this small scene her body and voice were ready to collapse, but she resolutely turned on her Mississippi charm.

Amanda's petty Southern vanity, her contemptible conventionality, her relentless drive—all made life unendurable for her children. Yet both in her scenes of anxiety and in her long scene dancing around the room with daffodils in her arms, invoking the nostalgia of the old plantation society, she showed that within that nagging, driving mother was a wounded, baffled, romantic soul, a glow of warmth, a tender solicitude, a fragile triumph over disaster, heroic resolution that could never be held down, the incalculable power of the defenseless and weak. When she learned that the friend Tom had brought would not be a husband for Laura, the enthusiastic, ebullient tone faded out, the wide warm inflection dropped to an almost voiceless, wanly cheerful farewell to the caller. She still did not give up, and at the

388

The Play in Production

very end her voice rose again in irony and anger. The acting was carefully calculated, but the voice and body were so delicately responsive to the wide range of feelings and the feelings were so perfectly controlled by the mind and imagination of the actress that no one thought about the technique. Audiences laughed and cried at the same time. Laurette Taylor had pierced the tight protective shell of unfeeling to create an evening of intense pain and joy, an understanding not only of Amanda and her wounded children but of all mankind.

Playgoers of the 1950s will never forget the acting in O'Neill's *Long Day's Journey into Night,* with its tortured family—father, mother, and two sons—all needing one another yet destroying one another. A worn-out actor who has betrayed his talent, a mother who is a drug addict, and two sons drinking themselves to death do not seem very promising as characters to enlist the deepest sympathy of the audience. But Fredric March made the gruff father a puzzled, suffering old man who would do anything for his family—anything but change the habits of a lifetime. Jason Robards, Jr., showed all the ugliness and self-loathing of the older brother, but his characterization projected such understanding of the thwarted idealist that when in a drunken confession he told his younger brother how he had hoped to destroy him as he had destroyed himself, the audience could forgive him. But most exquisite of all was the performance of Florence Eldridge as the mother who wandered in and out of sanity as she was repeatedly forced to remember that her indulgence in drugs drove her men to excessive drinking and that now the younger son was about to die of tuberculosis. The actress knew exactly how

FIGURE *12.1* Laurette Taylor as Amanda in Williams' *The Glass Menagerie.* She gave the role a combination of stubborn determination and southern charm. Photo Culver Pictures.

to begin a sentence with a clear intention, then drift into uncertainty, how to flare up in anger if her family turned suspicious eyes on her, how to bring up from the past what she knew would hurt them and then, in shame and regret, try to express the love that was mixed with her need to hit back at a world she found painful. Throughout the early part of the play she reached tentative hands toward her husband and sons. At one point she hoped to find a moment of understanding and self-justification with the maid. At the end she gave up reaching out, pathetically clutching her old wedding dress as she clutched memories of her girlhood ambitions and her baffled love for her family. The words on the page are pale beside the suffering image of humanity that Florence Eldridge created on the stage.

More recently, playgoers saw remarkable performances by Uta Hagen and Arthur Hill in Albee's *Who's Afraid of Virginia Woolf?* (FIGURE *19.2*). On the page these characters are cruel, vindictive, and obscene in a play that seems never to end. But the actors gave the words such vibrancy of tone, so many nuances of thought and feeling, that the audience sat spellbound, forgetting the time. There was none of the fragile beauty that Laurette Taylor, floating delicately in a soft party dress, gave her cruel Amanda; none of the tender, withdrawn suffering that Florence Eldridge, dreaming of long-lost hopes, gave her Mary Tyrone. This was a vicious fight with no holds barred, a final showdown between husband and wife who had tortured each other for more than a dozen years. Now reaching the age when they had to admit their failures, in cascades of vituperation they bitterly tore away the last shreds of pretense. At the end the angry sadism was exorcised, and the wife, especially, was left bare and barren under the wind off the dark side of the world. The plot and theme offer little shelter to hide a hope under, yet the actors gave such vitality to the roles, such depth, such a profound revelation of the strange combination of love and hate, resentment and dependence, that the violence and obscenity did not matter; here were two human beings revealing themselves fully. The clarity was a beauty, the perfection of performance a joy. Much of that searing intensity, if not all the subtlety of the stage performance, is caught in the recording.

It is possible to recapture something of the power of the actors of the past as theatre historians compare descriptions and pictures of performances with texts of the plays. In *Rip Van Winkle* the words alone give just the slightest hint of what Joseph Jefferson must have made of the leading part. For four decades his performance was the delight of the English-speaking world. Nineteenth-century playgoers went to the play over and over again, and took their small children so that they might tell their envious grandchildren that they had seen the great Joseph Jefferson. The ne'er-do-well Rip, who accepted his exile, who teased his wife even as she drove him out, who came back years later to find a crumb of domestic happiness at the edge of his daughter's family, seemed, with his Dutch dialect, the most amusing and lovable man they had ever known. Jefferson must have given a superb technical performance. But the audience did not see the technique. Through their tears and laughter, they saw a fully revealed human being.

The Play in Production

FIGURE *12.2* The beloved
ne'er-do-well Rip Van Winkle
as created in the nineteenth
century by Joseph Jefferson.

Any theatre enthusiast would give his choicest possession to be able to
see the virtuoso clowning of the *commedia dell' arte* performers who delighted Europe for more than two centuries, both at the cultivated courts
and at noisy street corners. Each performer was a star, perfecting one role
in a lifetime of practice. Yet the troupe took great pride in the way they
played together. With no playwright and no director, they made up the words
as they went along, following an outline of a plot tacked up behind the
scenes by the manager to indicate what episode was to come next. They memorized witty sayings and had at the tip of their tongues clever entrance and
exit speeches and riddles and retorts, and the lovers memorized songs and
love sonnets and poems of complaint; but the good performers were well-
read people who could improvise and adapt their dialogue to the immediate
situation, making references to local affairs and taking advantage of any response of the audience or accident on the stage.

The company presented a whole family of stereotypes that had been established through hundreds of repetitions of the same plots and relationships.
The young lovers were constantly interrupted and thwarted by the two old
masked fools. The Pantalone, the rich magnifico from Venice, was either
the girl's father or himself a suitor for the girl. The other old man, the
pedantic Doctor from Bologna with a gallimaufry of learned words, was
always in the way or causing trouble. The two zanni, or comic servants, came
to the rescue, at the same time causing other complications. Even when the
lover sang a charming serenade to his Lucinda in a window, Pantalone was
around a corner mocking him, waiting to rush out and beat him. Or perhaps it was not Lucinda at all but Harlequin disguised in her cape, showing

391

The Performance

his black devil-like half-mask to the audience. Or Pedrolino, the country servant, jumped through a window and interrupted the lovers, or the Spanish captain came strutting, bragging, down the street.

Commedia performers were acrobats, mime experts, singers, jugglers, as well as improvising actors, and even in foreign countries they could make their movements and gestures so vivid, their inflections so lively, that nobody needed a translator. Sometimes the plot was serious, but it did not remain so for very long before the comic performers started one of their famous running gags known as *lazzi.* Many of the *lazzi* were so well known that the manager would merely indicate in the scenario that at this point Pulcinella tries to delay the Doctor with the *lazzo* of the broken leg, or of suicide, or of "which would be better," "spill something on his cloak," or "pretend he sees ghosts." Patterns of repetition were set, then broken, reversed, or interrupted. Doubtless some performances did not work—an entrance was made before another actor reached his gag line or the expected lead cues got jumbled. But when the teamwork was right and the comedians were in good form, the *commedia* was one of the highest delights of theatre history. The actor as performer, without playwright or director, has left us a goal and an ideal. We get glimpses of that ideal in a few single performers at their occasional top form—Bob Hope, Red Skelton, Danny Kaye, Jack Lemmon, and several others—when there is sheer joy in watching their high skill, their dazzling virtuosity.

Glimpses of some remarkable modern performances can be had in records and films. Shakespeare has been given a new vitality. For the Victorians he was the touchstone, and any important actor had to be tested as he showed his skill in the best-known roles. Sometimes, especially at the end of a season, he would present an evening of favorite scenes from several plays, and he expected to repeat the most dazzling speeches as the audience demanded an encore. The Victorian audience responded to a wide range of acting styles, from the quiet melancholy gentleman of Edwin Booth's Hamlet to the raving maniac of Tommaso Salvini's Othello, performed in Italian, usually with a local company performing in English. Sir Henry Irving, the first English actor to be knighted, brought acting down to a more respectable subordination of the actor to the production, and after Irving the newer actors, realist or "new school" performers, took the virtuoso dash out of Shakespeare. It is no wonder that Maurice Evans was able to make a sensation of *Richard II* and *Hamlet* in the 1930s when he put a singing tone back into Shakespeare. His recordings may seem too operatic for some tastes, but in performance it was thrilling to hear a beautiful voice used with superb technical skill. Sir John Gielgud achieved a better balanced reading, adding a wider range of characterization to a rich use of voice tone and poetic rhythms. Besides several early recordings, he made in the 1960s two anthology recordings—"Ages of Man" and "One Man in His Time"—of key passages from a number of Shakespeare's plays.

The triumph of magnificent intensity in acting of the 1940s is captured in the recording of Judith Anderson's Medea—not the strong, queenly dignity

392

FIGURE *12.3* Violent emotions in the grand manner. Judith Anderson in Jeffers' adaptation of Euripides' *Medea*. Photo Bachrach.

of her movement but enough in the voice for listeners to sample the range, power, and technical control of a great performer. It is a vivid part for her, a climax to a long career of acting strong, suffering women. But the play hardly matters; such a virtuoso performer is herself a show. As Sir Tyrone Guthrie writes, "In politics, in the pulpit, and above all, in the theatre, the supreme thrill is the thunder and splash of a great personality as, like a wave, it surges over the audience and slaps the back wall of the house."

The screen has given some idea of the virtuoso acting of Sir Laurence Olivier. Of his Shakespearean film roles, his dashing young Henry V and sly, sarcastic Richard III are perhaps of more lasting interest than his blond, raw-boned, brooding Hamlet. His *Othello,* not produced as a film but recorded electronically as the scenes from the stage production were run in an enlarged studio setting, catches some magnificent glimpses of his power as an actor, though the audience perspective is sometimes all wrong. In many scenes both the camera and the microphone are too close for makeup and acting that were designed for an audience at the distance of a large theatre. Even more astonishing than Olivier's portrayal of Shakespearean characters is his performance of Archie Rice, the seedy music-hall singer in Osborne's *The Entertainer.* Though the film cannot give the full dynamic contact of singer and audience that the stage performance gives, it does capture the controlled abandon of a weary, heavy-drinking man who has lost all reason for going on yet makes ironic songs and witticisms about his fading ability and keeps up the show. A supreme performance of an entertainer who is losing his ability to perform is an extraordinary feat. In spite of the twentieth-century emphasis on the play and the ensemble, such acting reminds us what it means to love a star.

393

The Performance

FIGURE *12.4* The versatile actor as a seedy modern character. Laurence Olivier in Osborne's *The Entertainer.* Photo Friedman-Abeles.

One of the top performances of classic comedy in recent decades is partly caught in records and film. The revival by Sir John Gielgud of Wilde's *The Importance of Being Earnest,* played in London in 1939 and then for several years with various casts on both sides of the Atlantic, presented in Gielgud the most earnest Earnest the audience had ever seen, in Dame Edith Evans the most proud and haughty Lady Bracknell, in Margaret Rutherford the most crotchety Miss Prism, and in George Howe the most amazed Reverend Chasuble. To superb reading of lines, with a range of pitch and inflection rarely achieved, each actor brought nuances of feeling and resources of personality which were controlled and projected by skills acquired in a lifetime of acting. Gielgud and Dame Edith Evans come through well on both the short early recording and the complete later one. The movie is worth seeing, though Michael Redgrave replaced Gielgud and Edith Evans took a pace so slow for the camera that she is not nearly so funny as she was on the stage.

Fortunately, one of the best twentieth-century performers, Charlie Chaplin, after a short career on the music-hall stage in England, developed his career of four decades for the screen and his films can be seen directly, not in an adaptation. All but his last films were made in America and were extremely popular in the twenties, thirties, and early forties, yet many Americans have never seen his major pictures. In the 1940s he made new enemies. During the war he had spoken too enthusiastically for cooperation with Russia, and several of his films satirized business barons and generals. Finally the irony of his *Monsieur Verdoux* (1947) cut too deep for some patriotic minds; his debonair hero, who murdered a half-dozen wives for

394

The Play in Production

money, cheerfully went to his execution insisting that in a world that killed millions in war he was not so bad. Involved in a personal scandal and a paternity suit, Chaplin won in the courts but lost in the newspapers. When he left the country disputing his income-tax bill, several superpatriotic organizations accused him of being subversive and prevented the showing of his films. Chaplin countered by withdrawing his long films from circulation in the United States (he did not control the early short ones). He long ago settled his income tax and withdrew his objection to having his films shown here. As common sense prevails, Americans are getting a chance to see the greatest of all clowns. There is nothing subversive in his films, unless it is subversive to laugh at pomposity and pretense.

Like the *commedia dell' arte* clowns, Charlie Chaplin began by improvising his actions and much of the plot as he went along. Those early short subjects, made at one speed in the days of silent films and now run at the faster speed of sound films, show only glimpses of the later Chaplin in feats of running, falling, balancing on ladders, or handling properties. But the clownish character, elegant in his down-and-out condition, was already formed. Chaplin made some variations as he put the little tramp in different situations, but, like the *commedia* actors, he played essentially the same character all his life. In all the longer films, in the midst of satiric comment on some aspect of the world—the circus, the army, the Gold Rush, the Depression, the factory, Hitler, and human massacre—there are scenes of clowning that show amazing skill, that require a skill in balancing or miming or dancing on which is superimposed another sequence of comedy. In *City Lights,* as night watchman in a department store, Chaplin skates superbly

FIGURE *12.5* Comedy and sentiment. The elegant tramp as created by Charlie Chaplin in *The Kid*. Museum of Modern Art.

through the aisles, a fallen lamp shade over his head blindfolding him as he boldly skirts the edge of the stairwell with the clown's supreme disregard of danger. In *The Great Dictator,* as Hitler dreams of possessing the whole world, he embraces a balloon globe and dances with it. In his public speeches he spouts German doubletalk, an amazing farrago of Teutonic syllables that almost make sense. In *The Gold Rush,* as a starving gold prospector boiling and eating an old shoe in the style of a rich epicure, or, in the lonely shack, imagining his dream girl dining with him, performing a dance with forks stuck in two rolls, Chaplin's little fellow bravely carries on the business of living. To the sensitivity of a poet and the daring of a prophet, Chaplin adds a technical facility and control equal to that of a circus performer or a concert pianist.

The Actor's Training

Chaplin and most of the other actors whose work has been described here have that elusive quality called genius, but it would have availed them nothing without skillful technique, and certainly no actor of less native ability can dispense with the discipline of intensive training.

Most of the actor's basic training is designed to give him more flexibility and more control of his voice and body. An actor using the narrow range of tone of everyday life would be limited and monotonous on the stage. He needs voice exercises to develop a full, resonant tone that will carry strength and emotion and be heard throughout the theatre. The usual exercises of a singer will widen his range of pitch, but he needs many other qualities of voice, some of them less smooth and more emotional than the impersonal tone many singers strive for. Since it is possible in using rough, husky tones to tighten the vocal cords and damage the voice, the actor needs coaching and supervision. He practices constantly to get a sharp projection of consonants and a clear distinction between vowels. If not so intensive as the training of an opera singer, the voice training of an actor is more complex and almost as important. Many of the better actors continue the study of voice and movement long after their training period, just as opera singers work with a coach on every role. Even after three decades of acting star roles, Vivien Leigh takes several months of intensive voice training before each new play.

The actor must also learn to use voice and body together, to use the muscle tone of movement or potential movement to support and shape a speech. In simple voice practice most people can get a fuller, more interesting tone when lifting a chair or other weight. It may take a great deal of practice to make words come out of a total body response. Such a phrase as "I said no" will sound very different if spoken with a stamp of the foot, or a clenched fist pulled against the body, or a shrug of the shoulders, or an arm being twisted. One reason some opera singers are poor actors is that they learn to produce tone without body response, forgetting that in animated conversation people speak with the whole body, not only hands and

The Play in Production

FIGURE *12.6* Oriental dance training for the actor. *Manohra,* a classical dance drama from Thailand, adapted by Ubol Rakbamrung. University of Hawaii production, directed by Wallace Chappell.

shoulders but torso muscles that respond to every thought, and above all with an animated face, raising the eyebrows, thrusting out the chin, tossing the head. The lips and chin are very active in snarling, sneering, disdaining, or mocking, in smiling, savoring, teasing, or laughing; facial movements reshape and color the tone of the voice in many ways. At the end of the chapter are some simple exercises that actors use to increase their response to the implication of the dialogue and to help coordinate the body with the voice.

For plays of naturalism, particular ways of using the voice and body were worked out. Whereas the nineteenth-century actor used elaborate inflections, rich voice tones, and large round gestures, the naturalistic actor has used the central muscles more than the peripheral, the abdomen more than the hands, the neck and shoulders more than the face, the grunt and the interrupted monotone more than the inflection. Such acting needs only a very limited kind of training. Nor have the relaxed patterns of modern living made different demands on the voice and body. Many people have never learned to move or speak with self-respect and authority. For characters that are not so inarticulate and passive, a wider training is required. Acrobatics and sports are a good beginning in body training, but dance can produce a more supple, responsive body. Modern dance, because it is more spontaneous, varied, and emotional than ballet, is better training for modern plays and for the plays of ancient Greece and other rather elemental periods, but for the aristocratic plays from the Renaissance to the eighteenth century ballet training is very useful.

While expressionistic plays were popular, actors learned with little difficulty to stylize their movements in order to emphasize the wooden, stiff-jointed, doll-like quality of dehumanized robots and to move and speak in unison or in a mechanical sequence. Some awkwardness did not matter. But for other stylized effects, the required techniques are sometimes more exacting. Phantoms in a dream are stylized by moving in a sustained, weightless manner, obsessed with one purpose or ideal. The ghost in *Hamlet* needs some

397

The Performance

stylization to make him supernatural. Just as definitely, the play-within-the-play must be set apart from the rest of *Hamlet* with exaggerated, sustained gestures and overelaborate, sustained voice inflections, yet it must at no moment suggest a burlesque of nineteenth-century melodrama.

The many period styles that are neither realistic nor stylized require very specific techniques. Gordon Craig was so opposed to the strutting of nineteenth-century actors and the petty realism of the newer actors that he advised the actor to think of himself as a supermarionette and study the noble artificiality of a mask rather than attempt to copy the everyday life of people around him. To speak poetry clearly and beautifully, to build a long speech in Greek tragedy or Shakespeare to a full climax, to wear the costumes and use the bows and curtsies and the postures of command and challenge of various periods—all require a high degree of technical control and training. The director may coach the reading, but for songs and movement he often calls in a specialist. Oriental dance techniques are useful for many modern plays as well as for the Oriental plays that are becoming increasingly popular. Fencing practice is helpful not only for dueling but for the precise movements of many styles. Renaissance court dances can set the style for Shakespeare's noble characters who move with pride and boldness yet with grace and ease. For the more precise, more showy and dashing characters of seventeenth- and eighteenth-century comedy, ballet positions, with head high, back straight, and legs and feet turned out in ostentatious pride, can set a vivid style, while some of the movement around the stage may have the zest and lilt of a traditional square dance. Bows and curtsies can express many different attitudes of deference and response, even impudent mock respect. It takes long training in voice and body to develop such techniques.

European acting schools have given much broader training in styles of acting than American schools. Since the French regularly include the classics of many periods in their national repertory companies, their actors must develop a variety of styles. English actors likewise have training and experience in many kinds of plays; especially in the revival of period plays and in modern drawing-room comedy they often surpass American actors. Only recently, since American colleges and the new repertory companies systematically produce a wide range of modern and classic plays and since the plays of disruption have introduced new styles, have American students become aware of the need for thorough technical training. Musicians expect to practice technical exercises hour after hour each day for years, but many actors, seeing a pretty face win a Hollywood career with little or no training, think that they are born with all it takes or that a costumer and a coach can show them style in a few easy lessons.

Technique and Feeling in Acting

Stanislavsky's attack on nineteenth-century acting technique and his emphasis on inner feeling and the fresh approach to character have been described in the chapter on realism. Impressed by the Stanislavsky approach,

FIGURE *12.7* Nineteenth-century acting. The audience-oriented style of acting was characterized by large voice and large gesture, with little relation to properties or to other characters. A caricature of Edwin Forrest, who made his robust acting quite convincing. Museum of the City of New York.

some actors are very suspicious of training in technique, calling it "mechanical," "external," or "puppet-like imitation." Forgetting that Stanislavsky wrote several books on external techniques and that his own students spent many hours a day on voice and body exercises, some American students of acting think it enough to delve into their own souls, bring up their own feelings, and trust their God-given talent to do the rest. They want to be "creative" and not merely repeat "technical performances." Let piano students practice technical exercises for fifteen years—they are interpretive performers. Let ballet dancers worry about technique—they expect to be identical puppets following the choreographer through the traditional patterns of the classical ballet. The assumption of this group is that if the feeling about the character is right, the performance will take care of itself. The director is merely an amateur analyst who helps release emotional memories on the stage.

To this question of whether feeling or technique should guide the actor, the only sensible answer is "both." While no one defends technique without feeling, yet feeling by itself is not enough. The evocation and use of feeling becomes itself a technique, for there are inner as well as outer techniques.

Techniques of projection, precision, and clarity are absolutely necessary. The audience would not see or hear without some clarity and projection. The coordination of the cast would be impossible, the repetition of a play impossible, without the precise control that enables each actor to depend on another actor's speaking at a certain spot at a certain time with a certain tone, speed, and emphasis. Stanislavsky in *Building a Character* and *Creating a Role* and in his analyses of several plays describes the planning of a role in precise mechanical detail, with little left to the inspiration of the moment. Yet there is danger that the external techniques will seem empty, that the imaginative re-creation of the motives of the character will not be strong enough

399

The Performance

FIGURE *12.8* Modern acting. Even in the midst of properties and intimate interrelations among characters, acting still has moments of full intensity and wide extension. Harry Ellerbe and Madame Nazimova in Ibsen's *Ghosts*. Photo Vandamm.

to make the emotions of the play convincing. Hence modern actors have become very much interested in the inner techniques by which the outer expression can be integrated with the inner resources of the actor. The early realists discovered that a great deal of business with properties could make the actor seem genuine, but he would not necessarily be acting from strong inner compulsion. Much more analytical and thorough than other early directors of realistic plays, Stanislavsky found that the actor had several ways of calling up his own feelings, of searching for the "inner flow," the "deeper content," the "inner musical score" that lay hidden behind the words of the play. Stanislavsky recognized, as Freud did, that although the subconscious could not be forced to reveal its secrets directly, there might be indirect ways of unlocking its treasures. The actor must develop psychotechniques for teasing the unconscious to create for him. Most important of the psychotechniques was the appeal to emotional memory. If the actor thought back to an experience of his own that had created a feeling similar to that of his situation in a play—a childhood experience, for example, perhaps trivial in itself but important to him at the time—he might rediscover the tone and texture that accompanied the original experience. The second psychotechnique was improvisation. Treating the words of the play script as only a surface component of the full experience, the actor might go behind the words, imagining other moments in the life of his character and improvising appropriate actions and words for them. When he returned to the play itself, he would possess the inner flow, the hidden life, of the character and present a whole person.

Followers of the Stanislavsky system spend long hours analyzing their roles. What was the childhood of the character? What experiences have made him what he is? What did he do the day before the opening scene of the play? What is he thinking as he speaks his lines? As a director, Stanislavsky would

The Play in Production

often "prompt" the inner feeling while the actor was speaking his lines so that the tone might tell more than the lines. While one young man was chiding his girl, Stanislavsky stood nearby and spoke the true feeling—"Oh, how beautiful she is!"

More directly, Stanislavsky helped the actor to become sharply aware of simple sensation—the feel of velvet or of damp stone, the smell of straw or of scorched bread—that might re-create in his imagination the texture and mood of the environment of the play. By the use of emotional memory from specific experience of his own, he might fill the dramatic situation with personal feelings. Stanislavsky and a number of other theatre people—we have mentioned Joan Littlewood in the chapter on rehearsal—have felt that the actor, even in playing a long run, must try to keep some elements of spontaneity in the performance. They have even devised small changes to keep the actors alert.

The question of how much the actor feels is more complicated than the question of how much the poet or the painter feels while he is creating. Clearly all artists express their own emotions, at least the emotions they imagine, but in a symbolic form that sets them apart from everyday life. The poet deals not with raw emotion but, in Wordsworth's phrase, with "emotion recollected in tranquillity." In the words of Shakespeare's song, the details of actuality "suffer a sea-change."

> Of his bones are coral made;
> Those are pearls that were his eyes:
> Nothing of him that doth fade
> But doth suffer a sea-change
> Into something rich and strange.

A work of the imagination is not a faded copy of reality but a transformation into the more beautiful material of art.

Since his own voice and body are his instrument, the actor may be a little closer to using his own emotions than the poet is with his pen and paper or the painter with his brush and canvas. At least in rehearsal many an actor has turned loose his own emotions in the slightly disguised emotions of the role. There is no doubt that Edmund Kean, who had had a miserable life from infancy, was expressing his own bitter resentments when he burst on the London scene in 1814 and made his Shylock and Richard III as vivid expressions of the rebellious assertion of the Romantic Age as his contemporaries Lord Byron and Napoleon were. He became so keyed up in a performance that often after getting home at midnight he would ride a fast horse over the countryside for hours before settling down to sleep. An actor does get keyed up, and even after years of playing he may shake with stage fright just before going on. Yet after weeks of rehearsal he can control his performance and is not overwhelmed by the emotions he is simulating for the audience. In one sense he experiences vicariously the emotions of the character, and in another he stands aside watching, controlling the character. Just as he memorizes every movement and inflection of a responsive body and

401

FIGURE *12.9* An older character created by acting and makeup, including slices of apple to enlarge the cheeks. Helen Hayes in Housman's *Victoria Regina.* Photo Vandamm.

voice, so he memorizes every mood and motive stirred in a sensitive imagination, though never so well that he can be completely sure. Perhaps more than any other artist, he worries that he will not be in good form and is unhappy when he falls short of what he would like to do.

Some roles are much more congenial to the actor than others as they strike a note of sympathy or express feelings the actor shares. Paul Muni, whose family had known the persecution of the Jews in Europe, was drawn to champions of progress and science fighting entrenched conservatism. In the movies, he made his reputation playing the fighting journalist Émile Zola and won an Oscar for his role as the embattled scientist in *The Story of Louis Pasteur.* In the 1950s he returned to the stage to play the lawyer Clarence Darrow, who defended the teaching of evolution against the Tennessee hardshells in *Inherit the Wind.* José Ferrer felt a special affinity for Iago and for the tortured husband in *The Shrike.* "I don't know what it is," he told an interviewer, "but somewhere along in my background, I had sufficient insecurity to understand this trapped man and this trapped feeling. I don't know why, because there's nothing in my life that's parallel to it, but I sure as hell—I was out on that wave length, boy, very close, very, very close. It wasn't an invention, that performance. That performance was a true identification." Helen Hayes found herself attracted to the role of the queen in *Victoria Regina* out of sheer respect and admiration for the little English queen of the play "because she did her job well. She didn't have anything else that was exciting about her, did she? She was little, a kind of dumpling of a woman, and she wasn't a bit amusing. She just didn't have one ingredient of an exciting human being about her but that one thing—that she saw her

The Play in Production

duty and she did it, and she did it well. She did it untiringly, and she triumphed over everything in herself and in the world in which she lived."

The Actor in Character

In addition to voice and body exercises and improvisations and exploration of his senses—training that may go on all his life—the actor makes special preparation for his role in a particular play. He searches for the key, the driving idea, the "spine" or central motivation that carries the character through the whole play, though it may be modified, disguised, or reinterpreted in each small beat.

If the play is realistic, the actor studies the environment that shaped the character. He visits the place of the action or one like it or he reads up on the qualities of the surroundings, for the character may take his rhythm, along with his dialect, his costume—even his paleness or sunburn, his sweat, dirt, or hayseed—from his surroundings. The actor can usually find some element of that environment, partly re-created in the stage setting and properties, on which to concentrate at each performance and so recapture the feelings and compulsions of his character. Morris Carnovsky tells what a great help he found the properties and business at his first entrance in *An Enemy of the People.* The business enabled him to forget himself and the audience as he came into his brother's house and put down his hat and umbrella, saying to himself, "Here is my hat. It is my hat," and, looking at the room, "Here is the room. There is that lamp, that expensive lamp that my foolish brother bought. Here is a tablecloth. I don't have any such tablecloth in my house. This carpet is probably much finer than anything anybody in town has. What right has he to have a tablecloth and stuff like this around?" Thus, before a word was spoken, Carnovsky had his character established and his hostility to his brother stirred up in his imagination.

To make the dramatic situation more vivid in his mind, the actor may conjure up some element from his own life. José Ferrer tells of how difficult it was to keep up the intensity of the last scene of *The Shrike,* when the character he was playing gave himself up to the scheming wife he hated. "You should know some of the things I did to myself in my own mind. At one point or another, I think I killed every single person that I loved—and I saw them lying there bleeding before me on their deathbeds—to work myself up to the point where I was moved. Because along about the third or fourth month of eight times a week, I can't be as stimulated by the situation as I was the first month; and I killed my father and my daughter and my best friend and his wife and my pet dog and my rabbit and my canary. Anything."

Sometimes a picture, a drawing, an anecdote, or a bit of conversation in dialect will give the actor a suggestion for the right mood. Helen Hayes tells of the difficulty she had had in getting into the role of the old duchess in Anouilh's *Time Remembered* until one day, listening to the radio, she heard "some music written by Giles Farnaby for the virginal—you know, one of those sixteenth-century instruments. I listened for about half an hour, and

403

suddenly the idea came to me. That old duchess, I told myself, is like the music, light, dainty, period, pompous, tinkling. And, poor me, I'd been playing her like a bass drum."

Sometimes the actor finds an expressive body stance or movement, a key gesture, that captures the essence of the character. Michael Chekhov, nephew of the playwright Anton Chekhov and a follower of Stanislavsky, who long acted, taught, and directed in America, provided a useful term, "psychological gesture," or "P.G.," for the characteristic gesture or stance that would make the objective of the character more vivid and integrate the inner motives with the outer action. He wanted the actor to find an inner glow or excitement that would motivate the impulse to project to the audience. To ensure a more effective response to the impulse, he devised exercises that would enable the actor to explore the use of his body, starting with a hand, then an arm, then eyes, neck, and finally the whole body in full extension. If the character is suggested in condensed form by a grasping or catching gesture of greed, the actor practices the gesture until it involves the whole body in movement and relates him to the other characters, to the properties, to the sky and earth, and involves him in the rhythm and the changing tempo of the various scenes. If a character's objective is to dominate, the actor may practice standing wide and strong, his hands pushing downward, until he finds the feel of the body actions that he can carry over into the part. If his character is to fear and dread the dominance of others, he may practice cringing, running, and dodging.

In such existentialist dramas as Anouilh's *Antigone* and MacLeish's *J. B.,* where the properties are not important, the character can be expressed in quite clear psychological gestures of defiance or refusal. In those plays of Ionesco and Pinter where the properties are overwhelming, the actor can find persistent psychological gestures to express the senseless obsession with things. Even in the disconnected and illogical sequences of scenes of the absurd that use melodramatic terror or comic repetitions of inanities, the quick technical changes are not merely mechanical. They are expressions of some concept of character, fragmented, divided, or twisted though it may be.

The spine of the character is not a large abstraction, a skeleton without flesh. Like the structure of the play, the audience is aware of it only in retrospect. The actor must have it in the back of his mind in order to keep control and give a clear direction to his emotional drive. But he constantly embodies the drive in the little actions and reactions of the moment. The large movements show the big changes of relationship as the characters are directed to move about the stage. The larger gestures and big speeches add operatic high points, especially to the more exalted kinds of plays. But it is the little pantomimic dramatizations—the snarl on the lips, the clenching of the fist, the flinching of a shoulder—that give punctuation and color to the spoken phrases and are a visible expression of the inner life of the character. The playwright may suggest some of the small reactions in the business of handling properties and in the interrupted rhythm of the dialogue. The director may suggest much of the business and coach the actor in trying for both

404

The Play in Production

richness and clarity. But pantomimic dramatization is the special responsibility of the actor; it is the heart of the action, the magic that turns a package of printed pages into a living drama.

EXERCISES AND DEMONSTRATIONS

1. COMMUNICATION BY TONE OF VOICE.   Suppose that you are standing at a window. Describe some vivid action to someone who cannot see out the window. Or create a radio announcer's description of a street scene or event. Make the emphatic reactions in the voice at least as important as the words.

2. COMMUNICATION BY TONE OF VOICE.   Suppose you are reciting a well-known poem or story to a child or an invalid in bed. You see something disturbing outside the window or door but keep right on reciting, letting the audience know by changes of tension the pattern of the action seen. The actor must imagine very specific action, for instance, a dog about to be run over by a car or someone scolding, then repeatedly slapping, a child.

3. COMMUNICATION BY TONE OF VOICE THAT CONTRADICTS THE WORDS. Use a sentence that says one thing while showing by the inflection, tension, and rhythm of the voice that the truth is something quite different. A comic effect is created when the words insist that all is quiet and calm while the voice and jerky rhythm of speaking and breathing clearly betray fear or excitement.

4. THE RESPONSE OF THE VOICE TO BODY REACTIONS.
  a. To practice creating a sense of action, color, and emotion in the tone of the voice, start with a list of verbs of action like *jump, trudge, stumble, slide*. Use each in a sentence, with strong action involving the whole body. Then use the same sentence with the same muscular intensity but with movement of less than an inch.
  b. In the same kind of practice, use words of hand action like *pound, twist, smear, tickle*.
  c. Do the same with words of sensation like *cold, warm, gritty, slimy*. The reaction of mouth and face may be especially strong.
  d. Do the same with words of attitude like *puzzled, growling, snarling, delighted*.

5. PSYCHOLOGICAL GESTURE (P.G.).   Present one character in a series of emotional attitudes, changing in reaction to other people, using improvised words, movement, small reactions, and business with properties. For instance, a young man gives an account to his friends and relatives of something he has just done that he thinks is wonderful. Then, as each one tells him off, he reacts in degrees of disappointment, distress, depression, and defiant anger, taking a different psychological gesture for each change.

405

6. CONTRASTING STYLES IN PSYCHOLOGICAL GESTURE. Develop the P.G. for a naturalistic character who feels menaced, frustrated, and confused. Use tensions in the muscles of the torso and have the hands seem clumsy and useless; mutter confused phrases and grunts in a broken rhythm. For contrast, develop the P.G. of a romantic rebel chieftain, proud, bold, and daring, reassuring his band and planning a raid, using his hands in large gestures and his voice in strong inflections as he describes and commands.

7. PSYCHOLOGICAL GESTURE IN A PLAY. Describe and demonstrate the P.G. of a particular character in a play. First take the simplified abstract stance and movement; develop it from small movements to large, relating it to things, to people, to earth and sky. Then show how the P.G. can be adapted and applied in particular moments of the play.

SUGGESTED READING

A comprehensive anthology with bibliographies is Toby Cole and Helen Krich Chinoy (eds.), *Actors on Acting: The Theories, Techniques, and Practices of the Great Actors of All Times as Told in Their Own Words* (1949). The comprehensive history of acting is Edwin Duerr, *The Length and Depth of Acting* (1962), which has a very thorough bibliography. A good sampling of earlier discourses on acting is Brander Matthews, *Papers on Acting** (1958).

The books by and about Stanislavsky are listed at the end of Chapter 1. Most twentieth-century books on acting are derived from Stanislavsky or are at least influenced by him. Richard Boleslavsky, an actor and director under Stanislavsky, wrote *Acting: The First Six Lessons* (1933); Michael Chekhov wrote *To the Actor: On the Technique of Acting* (1953). Other books are Charles McGaw, *Acting Is Believing* (1955), F. Cowles Strickland, *The Technique of Acting* (1956), H. D. Albright, *Working Up a Part: A Manual for the Beginning Actor* (2nd ed., 1959), and Stanley Kahan, *Introduction to Acting* (1962). Morton Eustis' interviews with a number of New York actors, first published in *Theatre Arts,* are gathered in *Players at Work* (1937). Even more lively recent interviews, including the ones quoted in this chapter, are published in Lewis Funke and John E. Booth, *Actors Talk About Acting* (1961), and Lillian and Helen Ross, *The Player: A Profile of an Art* (1962).

Bertolt Brecht's approach to acting, almost the exact opposite of Stanislavsky's, is developed throughout his writing and quite specifically in "On Chinese Acting," *Tulane Drama Review* (T13, Autumn, 1961). The relationship is discussed in Eric Bentley, "Are Stanislavski and Brecht Commensurable?" *Tulane Drama Review* (T25, Autumn, 1964).

Of all critics, Stark Young was the most interested in acting, and he developed his own theories, rather independent of Stanislavsky. Young's early essays were published in the 1920s in several books, and a selection from his reviews appeared in *Immortal Shadows** (1948). Young influenced Edwin Duerr, whose important historical work, listed above, searches for other bases than Stanislavsky.

A wide view of acting is taken by the English actor Michael Redgrave in *The*

406 * Available in paperback edition.

Actor's Ways and Means (1953) and *Mask or Face: Reflections of an Actor's Mirror* (1958).

The acting of comedy, especially high comedy, is discussed by Athene Seyler and Stephen Haggard in *The Craft of Comedy* (1957). Bertram Joseph's books examine the Shakespearean tradition of acting: *Elizabethan Acting* (1951), which looks at the time of Shakespeare; *The Tragic Actor* (1959), which surveys tragic acting from Burbage into the twentieth century; and *Acting Shakespeare* (1962), which offers principles to the present-day actor. Rosamond Gilder made a detailed record of *John Gielgud's Hamlet* (1937).

The important books on movement for actors come from England: Rudolf Laban, *The Mastery of Movement* (1960); Joan Lawson, *Mime* (1957); Lyn Oxenford, *Design for Movement: A Textbook on Stage Movement* (1952) and *Playing Period Plays* (1955), which has also been published in four separate paperback parts. The extremely live French mime movement is described in Jean Dorcy, *The Mime* (1961). The Delsarte approach to movement got a bad reputation from its elocutionary followers, but Ted Shawn, in *Every Little Movement Has a Meaning All Its Own** (1963), presents the elements of the Delsarte theory that he finds still valid for both dancers and actors.

Biographies and autobiographies of actors make some of the best reading about the theatre, often giving insight, if fragmentary and unsystematic, on the art of acting. First on any list would be the vivid *Autobiography* of Joseph Jefferson, reprinted many times and recently in a scholarly edition edited by Alan Downer (1964). In the eighteenth century David Garrick and Mrs. Siddons dominated the English scene. The two most vivid romantic actors were Edmund Kean in England and Edwin Forrest in America. The melancholy Edwin Booth, best Hamlet of all, and Henry Irving, first actor to be knighted, made actors respected. Sarah Bernhardt and Eleanora Duse brought two contrasting temperaments from the continent. Fanny Kemble was the most glamorous of a large family of actors. Constance Rourke gives an account of Lotta Crabtree and other early actors in California in *Troupers of the Gold Coast* (1928).

---

* Available in paperback edition.

CHAPTER THIRTEEN

DESIGN FOR THE THEATRE

The design creates an environment for the actor—a pedestal, a showcase, a picture, a machine for acting. It gives the actor form, creating a space in which he can move. It adds color, change, contrast, and mood as it shapes the play in both space and time. As we have seen, the designers of scenery, costume, and lighting must be in on the basic planning of the production. The locations of entrances and exits and the shaping of the playing areas will determine the patterns of movement the director can use. The kind of setting created and the changes of costume and lighting will determine how one scene flows into the next and condition the rhythmic structure of the play. As much as the playwright or the director, the designers are responsible for the unity of the production.

The Setting

In the nineteenth century, the main function of scenery was to indicate time and place. The painted backdrops, along with the costumes, told the audience they were in Spain or China, ancient, medieval, or modern times, prince's palace or peasant's kitchen, summer garden or winter snow. No matter whether the mood was comedy or tragedy, satire or fantasy, the designer brought on the stage the results of careful "research." Going to the theatre was as important a way of learning facts as a guided tour through a museum or a social survey of how the other half lived. The historian, the

409

FIGURE *13.1*   Abstract design of platforms and columns. Lunacharski's *Faust and the City*. State Dramatic Theatre, Leningrad.

sociologist, the journalist, and the designer were equally interested in presenting local color. The designer used gaily colored landscape backdrops or box sets with realistic detail, according to whether the piece was a romantic opera or a realistic character play. He was glad enough if he created a mood, but mood was a by-product. His first thought was of the actuality of time and place.

Modern design, in protest, has gone to the other extreme. Designers have denounced the attempt to put interior decorating on the stage, to illustrate the story with painted pictures. They insist that design should not be something just put behind the actors as an afterthought but an integral part of the movement of the play. To indicate time and place is far less important than to create mood and atmosphere, to shape the movement of the actors and to give a unifying idea, and many designs do not indicate place at all but present imaginative, atmospheric abstractions or arrangements of playing ramps, platforms, and steps. Adolphe Appia in 1899, in one of our most famous theatre books, *Music and the Art of the Theatre,* distinguished the "expressive" from the "symbolizing" functions in a work of art. He said that the symbolizing details that indicate the particular locale should be kept to a minimum—just enough to orient the audience, as a signboard might—in order to allow the expressive functions more play. Mordecai Gorelik in our day makes a similar distinction between the "reminiscent" and the "immediate," between the setting that is merely a documentation of the outer world of history or geography and the more imaginative treatment of line and form that gives an immediate impact to the play. By 1919, Kenneth Macgowan defined the aims of the new stagecraft as simplification, suggestion, and synthesis: simplification to get rid of all Victorian ornament that might distract attention from the actor; suggestion to evoke a mood by sim-

The Play in Production

FIGURE *13.2* Abstract geometrical patterns in design. Shakespeare's *Antony and Cleopatra*. State Dramatic Theatre, Leningrad.

ple means—"a single Saracenic arch can do more than a half dozen to summon the passionate background of Spanish *Don Juan*"; and synthesis to create a unity and consistency whereby actor, setting, lights, and action would express the essential inner quality of the play and change as the play progressed.

The new ideal had first been given clear form by Appia when he analyzed the stage into its abstract components: (1) the horizontal plane on which the actor stands, whether floor, step, or platform; (2) the vertical screens behind the actor; and (3) the living, moving actor. The only thing that could unite the living actor with the inanimate setting, he declared, was plastic lighting, light that could change shape and give form to the horizontal planes and vertical screens. The traditional backdrop with painted details was too flat and hence must be discarded for screens and pylons, ramps, and shapes that could take three-dimensional form in the new controlled light. The emphasis was shifted from the unmoving painted setting to the moving actor. For the scene in which Wagner's Siegfried hears the voices in the forest, Appia wanted to discard the nineteenth-century flat strip of cloth, painted and cut in holes to represent leaves and jogged up and down by means of a rope over a pulley, and show no leaves at all, but only Siegfried standing in a light that casts moving shadows on his face as he listens.

In a sense, the new ideal means the complete abdication of the designer, for the modern design must not stand out as a beautiful picture. Robert Edmond Jones describes the new challenge in an inspired book called *The Dramatic Imagination*.

> A setting is not just a beautiful thing, a collection of beautiful things. It is a presence, a mood, a warm wind fanning the drama to flame. It echoes, it enhances, it animates. It is an expectancy, a foreboding, a tension. It says

411

Design for the Theatre

FIGURE *13.3* Design for unity, mood, and idea. The groups of actors on the steps are dominated by one great leaning street lamp. Robert Edmond Jones's drawing of a Berlin production by Leopold Jessner of a play about Napoleon. From Macgowan and Jones, *Continental Stagecraft.*

nothing, but it gives everything. . . . The designer creates an environment in which all noble emotions are possible. Then he retires. The actor enters. If the designer's work has been good, it disappears from our consciousness at that moment. . . . The actor has taken the stage; and the designer's only reward lies in the praise bestowed on the actor.

How does the designer achieve the actual design for the play? How does he find the form that will fit the theatre, serve the actor, create the mood, and reinforce the basic idea of the play? He may not be sure just what method he uses, and he may use several approaches simultaneously. But looking at the results one may say that there are four rather distinct ways of creating a design. A design may be cut-down environment, built-up action, a mood piece, or a metaphor, according to whether the designer starts with the actual place and selects from it, or with the actor and builds up space around him, or with the mood and creates evocative lines and colors, or with some metaphor or symbol, treating the setting as idea. Sometimes it is obvious which one of these ways has been followed, but often a good setting looks as if several approaches might have been used at once.

THE DESIGN FORMAT

First of all the designer and the director must find a format—a scheme of settings and transitions that will give the play a smooth and meaningful progression from one scene to the next. The overall texture and the rhythmic progression in time depend on the shape and quality of each setting and on the rhythm of the changing of scenery. This fact is most obvious

The Play in Production

FIGURE *13.4* Design for mood. The impressive dignity suggests the classic form of Greek tragedy in a New England setting. O'Neill's *Mourning Becomes Electra.* Drawn by Robert Edmond Jones. Museum of the City of New York.

in the progression of the many scenes in a musical. The alternation of large scenes and small scenes and of choruses and solo songs, the transition by blackouts or fade-outs, curtains or partial curtains, small fill-in scenes on the apron or on one side to cover scene changes on the other—all these must fit in with the mood and rhythm and give the show a propulsion in a single line.

The old wing-and-backdrop format was simple. The drops could be lifted up into the flies by ropes and pulleys and the side wings could be slid out in grooves to show another set of drops and wings already in place—a change easily made before the eyes of the audience. The heavy box sets with many realistic details take several minutes to change. Even when the designer has an elevator stage to lift a section or an entire setting up from a lower level or a wagon stage to roll in scenery from the wings, the shift usually means letting the curtain down, a kind of interruption that limits the playwright and the producer to a very few scenes. Most productions of several scenes use some combination of these two formats, making some changes in sight of the audience by raising and lowering drops or turning small turntables or rolling in small wagon stages and hiding some upstage changes with a curtain or painted drop while another scene is playing in the shallow downstage space. Even so, a change may mean a complete break in the sequence of the show. It is no wonder that designers prefer lighter, more flexible forms that are not only cheaper and easier to construct and to handle than a series of full settings but are also less demanding on the attention of the audience.

In designing any play, the designer must find a format that will fit both   *413*

Design for the Theatre

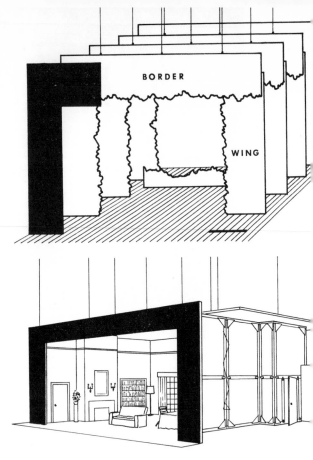

FIGURE *13.5* The two scenic formats inherited from the nineteenth century—the wing-and-backdrop set and the box set. Drawn by Don Creason.

the producer's idea and the limitations of the particular stage. If, for example, he is to do *Boris Godunov,* an opera of many scenes, he first makes a chart showing which are interior and which exterior scenes; which are Russian and which Polish and what differences the two must show; which are intimate scenes and which crowd scenes; what contrasts must set the palace scenes off from the church and inn scenes; how the crowd can be shown off; how and to what degree the coronation scene should be made a climax to the others. He examines pictures of the architecture and decoration of the period and listens to the music of the opera to catch the mood. He constantly considers how his ideas would work on the stage. If he plans to fly several painted backdrops or sections of wall, does the theatre have enough lines to hold these and still leave lines for a few rows of lights? What space is there at the sides for moving more solid structures? Can some platforms, steps, and ramps be left on as part of several scenes? Can some small scenes be set in front of larger scenes that are not moved? Can the format show a meaningful sequence in the order of the scenes?

This last question is very important in designing any play. Mozart linked the scenes of *The Magic Flute* by a sequence of related keys, expecting each scene to follow another so quickly that the ear would retain one key as the music progressed into the next. Should there be a corresponding sequence

The Play in Production

of colors and tone in the setting? In Ibsen's *An Enemy of the People,* Dr. Stockmann begins his attack on the corrupt officials of the town in his sitting room, then moves his fight to wider arenas, first the office of the newspaper, then a public gathering of the townspeople. When he is defeated there, he is shown in his small private study, disheveled by the mob, doggedly setting out to train a few disciples to go out and re-educate society. The sequence of scenes in Chekhov's *The Cherry Orchard* is just as meaningful and more subtle. The first act is full of hope as the members of the family arrive in the early morning to pick up the threads of their old life. Appropriately, the reunion is in the old nursery. In the second act the darkness is falling as the wistful family gathers near a wayside shrine, beyond which can be seen glimpses of old tombstones and the telegraph poles of the new age (see FIGURE *1.8*). The third act carries the laughter into the night with wild dancing and news of the sale of the estate. The last act shows a new dawn, cold and pitiless, as the family say farewell. The designer must find a format that will give unity to the play and a meaningful progression from one scene to the next.

To keep a play of many scenes moving without interruption, the designer may abandon the front curtain and picture stage and base his format on some of the older forms of theatre—a formal architectural "unit set" like the Elizabethan, which permits minor changes in small openings or panels; a simultaneous placement of small settings side by side or compacted into a continuous structure like the long medieval platform; or the processional way of bringing on mobile units with the actors, as the medieval pageant wagons were brought on or the properties on the apron stages of the Orient. When the New York Theatre Guild in 1928 wanted to alternate performances of Goethe's *Faust* and O'Neill's *Marco Millions,* both plays with many scenes, Lee Simonson built as a unit set a solid structure of columns and arches with a central opening and smaller side openings. Small scenic elements could be inserted into the openings quickly, either while the curtain was down for intermission or during a blackout. The format imposed an austerity and a tight unity on both plays, and, of course, limited some of the movement and grouping for the director.

Epic theatre, as we have seen, demands a format that permits easy flow from one scene to another, with many direct presentations to the audience, such as characters speaking from podium or forestage, and movies, slides, slogans, or symbolic ideograms displayed or projected onto a screen. Brecht was wary of romantic color and mood lighting, preferring the clear open effect of a lecture platform or a sports arena. Yet even with simple background and mobile units of epic scenery, a great deal of texture and atmosphere can be created. The tents, medical laboratories, and tropical costumes of *Yellow Jack* gave a rich sense of time and place in the struggle with yellow fever. The slum tenement house towering over the forestage scenes gave rich texture to *One-Third of a Nation,* as did the wet black umbrellas of Emily's funeral to *Our Town* and the skeleton of a small house dominated by tall apartment buildings to *Death of a Salesman* (FIGURE *6.1*). 415

For *Death of a Salesman,* the excellent format was devised after the play was written. Miller had written thirty-five scenes, hoping that the designer, Jo Mielziner, would help him find a scheme to bring them into a simple unity. Together with the director, they settled on three elements. Instead of full stage pictures frequently changing, they planned a format with no interruptions except one intermission. At the center they put a skeleton structure of Willy's house, with three rooms cut down smaller than actuality—the kitchen, the bedroom, and the boys' room upstairs. Then they brought all the memory scenes and even the city scenes onto the forestage, with the few props carried on by the actors. To get the boys down from the bedroom and into the wings for the downstage scenes, hidden elevators were built under the beds. Amateur productions using the same kind of setting find that a hidden stairway serves as well. The third element, to add atmosphere and to help indicate when Willy is remembering the happy past, was a painted transparent gauze curtain at the back of the house structure and a painted drop back of that. One lighting showed the high brick apartments crowding in on the house; another lighting caught up the green trees of the happy past when the family had first moved in.

DESIGN BY OMISSION

The first method of design is to start with the real place, the full actual scene, and select from it, cut it down, and reshape it for the particular stage, building materials, methods of changing scenery, and moods needed. By leaving off the ceiling and most of the side walls and cutting down the back wall, the designer can suggest a room without overwhelming the actor in naturalistic detail and can create a simple sculptural form that is a welcome change from the splashy backdrops and ponderous box sets inherited from the nineteenth century. A pool of light from spotlights above the stage can concentrate the attention on the actor almost as intensely as the camera close-up. By lighting the cloth or plaster cyclorama at the back of the stage instead of filling out the picture with a painted backdrop or painted walls, the modern designer can set his actor and his streamlined setting against the expanding space and hypnotizing lighting of the sky. As Oliver Smith puts it, "Design is principally the elimination of everything which is not absolutely

416

FIGURE *13.6* Three sketches showing the development of a scenic idea from the outside shape to a stage form for actors. Ardrey's *Thunder Rock.* Drawn by Mordecai Gorelik. From John Gassner, *Producing the Play.*

Thunder Rock, 1   *Thunder Rock,* 2   *Thunder Rock,* 3

FIGURE *13.7* Cut-down setting with wit and fantasy. Hochman's *Margene and the Messiah*. University of Arkansas production, directed by Virgil Baker, designed by Preston Magruder, and costumed by Mary Davis.

necessary. A beautiful set should be a skeleton allowing air for the other participants of the theatre to breathe in."

Soon after *Our Town* startled audiences by omitting the scenery, Mielziner had the job of redesigning *Abe Lincoln in Illinois* for a popular-priced run in a larger theatre (FIGURE *13.8*). The first consideration was to save money: Mielziner left out most of the doorways for entrances, keeping only the few features necessary for the action. But in the end he decided he liked the cut-down production better than the more lavish one. In the tavern scene, the jibes at the famous Presidents who were all dead were all the more powerful when the audience saw only the actor, not the pictures he pointed at. In the lavish production, the desolate Lincoln had shuffled up a heavy stairway after telling his friends of the death of Ann Rutledge. In the cut-down setting, the

FIGURE *13.8* Cut-down scenery. The platform, railing, and a few leaves indicate an outdoor setting. Sherwood's *Abe Lincoln in Illinois*. New York, 1938. Designed by Jo Mielziner. Photo Vandamm.

friends left the room, carrying the lamp, as Lincoln's head dropped down in anguish in the last dying pinpoint of light. The final scene, his farewell to Illinois, needed only the rear platform of the train, and only a few feet of that.

DESIGN BY ADDITION

The second method is just the opposite of the cut-down method. It is to build out—to start with the actors and the few most important events of the play and add space, platforms, shapes, and voids around that action. Gorelik tells his students to start with the action of the play, ignoring locale, season, weather, time of day or night, and time lapses; all that can be put in later. First must come what the actors are doing. He has students write an outline of the action in two hundred words, then boil the outline down to sixty words, then choose the most important moments of action and draw that action, using stick figures and including props only when they are important —a suitcase if someone is leaving, a boy outside a door with a bouquet of flowers and a box of candy, the girl inside the door. When the student sees clearly what the actors are doing, he can start designing. Norman Bel Geddes was equally sure that no matter what the nature of the play the designer should disregard any period concept of architecture or locale and think only of abstract "solids and voids." "The voids," he explained, "are spaces where entrances from nowhere to within the sight of the audience can be made," while "the solids are the areas between these voids."

A setting designed with close attention to stage movement is sometimes called a machine for acting. Lee Simonson calls it a plan of action, as important in controlling the movement of the actors as the architect's ground plan for a kitchen or a railway station is in creating and shaping lines of

FIGURE *13.9* Setting as a "machine for acting" in which levels suggest a ship. Coxe and Chapman's *Billy Budd*. University of Minnesota production, directed by David Thompson and designed by Lyle Hendricks.

FIGURE *13.10* Formalism. An architectural screen of large Renaissance arches gives dignity and unity to the play. Slight changes are made behind the arches by letting down simple elements such as leaves for an orchard or a panel for an altar. Shakespeare's *Much Ado About Nothing.* University of Arkansas production, designed and drawn by Don Creason.

traffic. In *The Stage Is Set,* he gives a detailed analysis of the opening scene of Shaw's *Arms and the Man,* in which a girl's bedroom is invaded by a frightened soldier. He shows the dramatic consequence of five simple centers of action—a door, a window, a bed, a table, and a settee. "But until the director visualizes them," he writes, "and places them so that he is sure of their effect on the movement of his actors, no amount of characteristic detail of Bulgarian architecture is of any importance whatsoever." Suppose the play shows a murderer coming toward the victim, who is trying to reach the telephone to call the police. It makes all the difference in the world whether the phone is at hand or across the room, and whether there are pieces of furniture or steps between. Whether it is playwright, director, or designer who decides on the setting, it is a basic part of the action of the play. Bel Geddes did not want to know anything of what the playwright had planned for the setting, but to read a script with only the words and basic interactions of the characters. Then he could start fresh in devising an arrangement of entrances and acting areas. In several instances he persuaded the playwright that he had a better plan than the original. Kingsley had thought of the action of *Dead End* in a slum street that led to the river at the back of the stage. But Bel Geddes visualized the action turned the other way, with the boys jumping off over the line of the footlights into the river in the orchestra pit. The result was one of America's most stirring productions of social realism (see FIGURE *1.5*).

How far must different groups of characters be separated? Juliet on her balcony is an object of worship just out of Romeo's reach. Should two groups be as officially separated as the jury in a courtroom watching but protected by a railing? Or should there be easy passage, either up or down steps or between pieces of furniture that tend to define and separate? What the designer does will largely determine what the director must do. The two must work in close rapport. Two of Shakespeare's plays, *Romeo and Juliet* and *Much Ado About Nothing,* have large ballroom scenes from which small

419

Design for the Theatre

FIGURE *13.11* Constructivism. A machine for acting that emphasizes the machine construction. Setting for Tairov's adaptation of *The Man Who Was Thursday*. From Mordecai Gorelik's *New Theatres for Old*.

groups or individuals must emerge for short scenes, then join the crowd again. A row of arches will enable the small groups to come forward into sharp focus while the dancing continues more quietly back of the arches (FIGURE *13.10*). Or the director may prefer to give full display to the dancers in a large open area, then take most of them off stage or stop the dancing while, in a separate alcove, Romeo whispers his poem to Juliet and takes his kiss.

The ultimate of the machine-for-acting approach was *constructivism,* which was a rage with some Russian producers in the 1920s (FIGURE *13.11*). Using no walls at all and little or no indication of location, the designer broke the stage floor into different levels with platforms, ramps, steps, and ladders to allow the actors many positions. The supports were frankly exposed, to gain the excitement of posts, beams, towers, scaffolds, pipes, and guide wires. The constructivist sculptors had led the way in abstract compositions, borrowing in wire, string, glass, and metal from both mathematics and machine structures. Vsevolod Meierhold led the movement into the theatre, frankly brought his lighting instruments into view, and even worked out a machine approach, called "biomechanics," to a very acrobatic acting. He liked to make his props and scenery move, with beds flying through the air and walls sliding, and to have real automobiles and motorcycles run down the aisles, up over the orchestra, and onto the stage. We have Norris Houghton's description in *Moscow Rehearsals* of how a lover expressed his abandonment and joy at a reunion with his love: "Meierhold places the lady at the foot of a tin slide, the lover climbs up a ladder to the top of the slide, zooms down it, feet first, knocks the lady off onto the floor, and shouts something that sounds like Russian for 'Whee!' "

The Play in Production

Such extremes, useful for satires on the Machine Age, have not often been seen. Far more popular have been the styles called *formalism* and *abstractivism*. Remembering that the Greek, the Elizabethan, and the Chinese classic stages used permanent architectural structures with little or no realistic scenery, designers have turned to modern abstract structures which, with flexible lighting and a few portable cloths and props, can serve for many different scenes. For a number of years Jacques Copeau at the Vieux-Colombier in Paris put on a variety of productions, with slight additions and changes, in a basic architectural form of steps, platform, and upper level. The Festival Theatre in Stratford, Ontario, is now the best-known theatre that uses one architectural structure for all plays (FIGURE *4.13*), but there have been many other variants. Theatre people still talk of the Bel Geddes production of *Hamlet* with Raymond Massey in 1931 and the plain dark structure of platforms and levels, steps, and corners that changed freely with the lighting and the movement of the action (FIGURE *13.12*). The more abstract forms serve well the timelessness of some of the existentialist plays, as we have noticed in Anouilh's *Antigone* (FIGURES *9.5, 9.6*) and some of the absurdist plays, which resemble the constructivist settings in breaking the elements of reality into fragments (FIGURE *9.11*). An interesting synthesis of realism, fantasy, and constructivism is indicated for the metaphysical circus of *J. B.,* whose religious existentialism we have already examined in the chapter on the theatre of disruption (FIGURE *9.7*).

The building-out of a theatre machine may meet and overlap with the

FIGURE *13.12* Space stage. Steps and platforms are given form and meaning by the actors, the lighting, and a few cloths that can be changed. The Players' Scene from Shakespeare's *Hamlet*. New York, 1931. Directed and designed by Norman Bel Geddes. Courtesy Hoblitzelle Theatre Arts Library, The University of Texas.

FIGURE *13.13* Setting cut down from reality or built out from actors' playing areas.
Levy's *Gold Eagle Guy*. Group Theatre production, New York, directed by
Lee Strasberg and designed by Donald Oenslager. Photo Vandamm.

opposite method, described above, the cutting down or selecting from reality
to make a machine for the theatre. The one process starts from a real center,
the actor, and adds on a basic structure of platforms, doorways, beams or
rafters, fragments of reality. The other process starts with a real periphery,
the environment, and cuts down. If the shingles are torn off, the walls pared
down, and the illustrative details reduced to a few suggestions, then the
girders, beams, and posts—the ribs of reality—take on an independent form,
an organic form like a piece of sculpture.

In the 1920s the most exciting development was the very abstract, cubistic
settings of Appia and Craig, with steps, platforms, towering doorways, and
pylons. The very trademark of the new age was Bel Geddes' fantasy, for
Dante's *Divine Comedy,* of a crater of hundreds of steps with hundreds of
actors, caught by long beams of light, descending or climbing. Some people
found such abstraction too bare and cold, and Eugene Berman, who liked
elegance and color, recently expressed his contempt for it. "The Appia, Craig,
Bel Geddes, and other schemes of colossal nude platforms, of massive for-
bidding columns or steps have always seemed gloomy, rigid, and depressing
in their puritanistic primness and intellectual intolerance."

DESIGN TO CREATE MOOD
The third method of designing is to start with the mood of the
play, forget the details of actuality, and find the lines, shapes, and colors
that will create the mood desired. Of course, both the romantic picture setting and the naturalistic scene sought to create mood, but they did so by
borrowing directly the moods of reality—the flowers and clouds of the
sunny day, the texture of the slum kitchen. The modern designer wants to
make more direct use of the expressive power of line, form, and color. Nature
may be used, but the detail is far less important than the mood. In Robert
Edmond Jones' words, a setting aims to be "not descriptive but evocative."
The designer should omit the "prose of nature" and be a poet.

The Play in Production

Gordon Craig long ago made the same point and, in a famous passage in his first book, *On the Art of the Theatre,* suggested how the designer should go about reaching a design for *Macbeth:*

> We take *Macbeth* . . . I see two things. I see a lofty and steep rock, and I see the moist cloud which envelops the head of this rock. That is to say, a place for fierce and warlike men to inhabit, a place for phantoms to nest in. Ultimately this moisture will destroy the rock; ultimately these spirits will destroy the men. Now then, you are quick in your question as to what actually to create for the eye. I answer as swiftly—place there a rock! Let it mount up high. Swiftly I tell you, convey the idea of a mist which hugs the head of this rock. Now, have I departed at all for one eighth of an inch from the vision which I saw in the mind's eye?
>
> But you ask me what form this rock shall take and what color? What are the lines which are the lofty lines, and which are to be seen in any lofty cliff? Go to them, glance but a moment at them: now quickly set them down on your paper; *the lines and their direction,* never mind the cliff. Do not be afraid to let them go high; they cannot go high enough; and remember that on a sheet of paper which is but two inches square you can make a line which seems to tower miles in the air, and you can do the same on the stage, for it is all a matter of proportion and nothing to do with actuality.
>
> You ask about the colors? What are the colors that Shakespeare has indicated for us? Do not first look at Nature, but look in the play of the poet. Two; one for the rock, the man; one for the mist, the spirit.

Craig warns of the dangerous attempt to "tell of the moss of the Highlands and of the particular rain which descends in the month of August." But this is no mere picture independent of the actors. He continues, "You have to

FIGURE *13.14*   Mood of feminine gaiety created by exaggerated curved lines in hats and furniture. The Millinery Shop in Act II of Wilder's *The Matchmaker*. Redrawn by Don Creason from a sketch by a University of Arkansas freshman.

consider that at the base of this rock swarm the clans of strange earthly forces, and that in the mist hover the spirits innumerable . . . clearly separate from the human and more material beings."

In another passage Craig describes how the designer uses both his inner eye and inner ear as he reads the play,

> to see the whole color, rhythm, action of the thing. He then puts the play aside for some time, and in his mind's eye mixes his palette (to use a painter's expression) with the colors which the impression of the play has called up . . . colors which seem to him to be in harmony with the spirit of the play, rejecting other colors as out of tune. He then weaves into a pattern certain objects—an arch, a fountain, a balcony, a bed—using the chosen object as the center of his design. Then he adds to this all the objects which are mentioned in the play, and which are necessary to be seen. To these he adds, one by one, each character which appears in the play, and gradually each movement of each character and each costume.

In designing for a ballet, the earlier designer thought of the scene and the story. Now a designer such as Horace Armistead goes first to the music and listens to it over and over again. Gradually his fleeting impressions begin to emerge in terms of shapes, colors, rhythms, and texture as the strings whisper or the French horns murmur, or the shimmer of woodwinds is followed by arpeggios on the harp, or trumpets and brass burst forth like blazes of light.

FIGURE *13.15* Setting for a mood of hysteria in a superstitious backwoods community. The fragmented two-dimensional structure suggests a tumble-down church. Richardson and Berney's *Dark of the Moon*. Indiana University production, designed by Richard L. Scammon.

In his notes on "Designing for Ballet" he writes:

> A smooth, melodic phrase of music can create nostalgia—moonlight—soft, misty green, and silver. A crisp, brilliant phrase of sharp contrasts can create feelings of conflict or happy exaltation. Fear, tragedy, and despair, all of these reactions can be aroused by music and have their forms and colors. . . . We must convey the right emotion even if we cannot put an exact name to that emotion.

In the same way, the designer listens to the rhythm of a play in order to create mood and atmosphere, not merely because they are appealing in themselves but because the mood of the setting can reinforce important aspects of the play. Early in this century, Joseph Urban decided in designing Wagner's *Die Meistersinger* that it was less important to show the whole of Nuremberg with all its Gothic details than to give the impression of joy, of the radiant splendor of sunshine as the people greeted Hans Sachs. The pagan element in *King Lear,* so strong in the imagery and in Lear's oaths and curses, would be enormously reinforced by the setting, designed by Bel Geddes but never used, of an arc of Stonehenge rocks bursting into flames at the top (FIGURE *5.12*). Different interpretations of Hamlet may be given character as much by the setting as by the acting. Before dark curtains and shapeless cloths, Hamlet is a lone existentialist wanderer in a nightmare empty world. Before a throne-tower and a Christian altar, he has ample reason, in his respect for political order and his Christian conscience, for hesitating to murder the King. In the London production of *Waiting for Godot,* the desolate wasteland and the forlorn stick of a tree left the two tramps in an empty universe. In the University of Iowa production, bright-colored puffs of smoke from behind the earth-banks punctuated every pause. That universe was not empty at all. A bright demon, with circus-candy taste, was laughing at mankind, just out of sight. In the original Gielgud production of *The Lady's Not for Burning,* the misunderstood girl and the adventurous, suicidal young vagabond win their acquittal in a very solid, neatly designed, semispherical Gothic home, and go out to their honeymoon wanderings through a solid Gothic door. In another design, the open spherical ribs indicating a house not only suggest the metaphor of an astronomical instrument but expose these terrified questioners to the bleak winds from the chartless skies. Sometimes the designer must restore the epic quality that ancient heroes have lost through the passage of time. As Lee Simonson writes, "The palace doors behind Clytemnestra or Jocasta must have the quality of majesty and the scale of doom that these queens can no longer convey wholly by their presence."

DESIGN TO EXPRESS IDEA

Metaphor—scene as idea—is the fourth method of design. The scenic metaphor was an obsession of the expressionists. They not only distorted natural lines to indicate the nightmares of the disturbed mind and to make lines express mood directly, but constantly searched for some symbol,

425

FIGURE *13.16* Setting for a mood of exotic Oriental violence. Puccini's opera
Turandot. Design by C. M. Cristini for an Indiana University production.

some visual image, to catch the inner meaning of a play. A tree was not only
barren and desolate, it had suddenly to look like a skeleton, or, in O'Neill's
Desire Under the Elms, to let down grasping fingers from brooding heights.
For Andreyev's *Life of Man,* Lee Mitchell designed geometrical forms with
opening lines for the birth scene and forms with closing lines for the death
scene, while he symbolized the crowning scene of worldly success by a gilt-
edged screen with a large dollar sign on it. Few people would want to go as
far as the designer who tried to make every setting in a play about the
French Revolution, whether doorway, lattice, courtroom, or trees, somehow
suggest a guillotine. But sometimes a dominant image gave a strong unity to
a play. Simonson's *The Stage Is Set* describes two famous productions of
Richard III in the 1920s:

> I have seen Richard III storm up and down the blood-red stairway pro-
> vided for him by Jessner and Pirchan at the Berlin State Theatre, but his
> malignity was as successfully dramatized by Arthur Hopkins and Robert
> Edmond Jones in New York where a reproduction of the gate at the
> Bloody Tower backed every scene like a fanged jowl that alternately
> menaced and devoured. The single background of the prison that was the
> background of every character's fears and ambitions became as effective a
> symbol as a single stairway.

Gorelik calls such a symbol a "visual metaphor" and points out that while
it can be excellent it can also be very limiting if the image is too narrow.
When one of his students suggested that the first scene of Shaw's *Man and
Superman* should be played not in a living room but in a bank vault, Gorelik
showed him that it would be better to design a living room with some of the
qualities of a bank vault. In Roger Furse's designs for *King Lear,* the open-

426

The Play in Production

ing palace scene was made of nursery blocks. Such an approach reinforces the fairy-story atmosphere, with the king acting like a spoiled child, but makes it very difficult to raise the latter part of the play to the grandeur we expect of Lear. Albee wanted the setting for *Who's Afraid of Virginia Woolf?* to suggest a cave or a womb, but the designer, William Ritman, kept the impression quite realistic. *Tiny Alice,* however, is a much more symbolic play, and Ritman made the toylike miniature of the chateau dominate the large room of the actual chateau, the detail realistic but the miniature serving as a symbol of the wider metaphysical realm.

Gorelik describes his own need for a metaphor, whether the audience is conscious of it or not. While telling all the necessary facts of locale and atmosphere, the setting must suggest the essence of the action. Thus "the attic bedroom of *The Three Sisters* is not only an attic, not only a bedroom, not only a girls' room, not only a European room, not only a room of the period of 1901, not only a room belonging to the gentlefolk whom Chekhov wrote about. On top of all that, and including all that, it may be, for the designer, the scene of a *raging fever.*" When Gorelik was designing scenery for Odets' play about a modern Noah, *The Flowering Peach,* the author himself said, "This opening setting [a living room] is a gymnasium in which the characters perform verbal gymnastics and it has a breakfast nook which is an icon, because there is a feeling of holiness about it."

This search for an image of action takes the designer right back to the director's analysis of the basic action of the play. Even when the play requires that the setting and costumes emphasize the period or the local color,

FIGURE *13.17* Setting for a mood of brooding conflict. The contrast between the exotic, shadowy foliage and the neat interior creates not only a mood but also a metaphor for the conflict of a princess from southeast Asia with a New England husband and family. Space-stage forms are enclosed in a proscenium. Anderson's *The Wingless Victory.* University of Illinois production, directed by Ned Donahoe, designed by Warwick Brown, and costumed by Genevieve Richardson.

FIGURE *13.18* Idea and mood in an expressionistic setting. The platform for the confession suggests both a cross and a gallows. The broken fragments of houses suggest anguish and disintegration of personality. The high central figure and the bright light and radiant lines expanding from the center create an exciting release and exultation. Kaufman's opera *The Scarlet Letter*. Design by C. M. Cristini for an Indiana University production.

the designer can make sure that the appropriate mood is created and the theme clarified. The design becomes much more than a decoration to cover the backstage void or indicate time and place. It creates mood, style, and metaphor; it becomes an organic part, not only in space but in time, in the rhythmic progression of the play. The setting must shape the action, reinforce the meaning, and propel the play to its destiny.

The Costumes

The costume continues the design into the characterization and movement of the actor. It even becomes part of his instrument—he makes his costume act. As much as the setting, the costume must express the mood, atmosphere, and style of the play. It must reinforce both action and meaning.

Like the setting, the costumes carry the audience into the world of imagination. They belong to the theatre and never to life, even if they are the same as everyday clothes, as they rarely are. For they must be as carefully planned and integrated with the actor and the action for a realistic play as for a period play or a fantasy of men of Mars. Most costumes in life are made to be seen close up, but the stage designer must see to it that the costumes project, that they are selected, or created, with the line, shape, color, and texture that can make an impact on an audience at a distance. For the stage they are given a theatrical flair, a boldness, simplicity, and brightness. They are often made of special theatrical materials, painted or dyed and put together in ways quite different from everyday clothes.

The nineteenth-century tradition of costuming, like that of setting, put

428

The Play in Production

great emphasis on historical and geographical authenticity. The producer and designer spent great effort in "research," and the costume departments of our large libraries, and of Hollywood, collected shelves of books of pictures and descriptions of the costumes and accessories of all ages and countries. Costume rental houses grew up as every repertory theatre or amateur club or high school production expected to show the audience an authentic costume for King Henry V or for a Palestinian shepherd of the time of Christ. It mattered not whether the play was a comedy or a tragedy, or whether the king was frivolous, dignified, or evil. For contemporary plays, the actors haunted secondhand shops if the play was about a lower class or fashionable dressmakers and tailors if it was a play of high society. Seamstresses and ladies' maids for the women and dressers for the men were important servants in the theatre, but there was little consideration of what we call "design." Today in the art theatre and the college theatre, the costume shop is a major part of the building, and the design and making of costumes is as much respected as a creative art as the writing of the plays or the acting or singing.

Costuming today is not a historical reconstruction; the designer usually takes only a few hints from the silhouette or some special effect of the time and place represented. He has no wish to put a costume museum on the stage. He considers it much more important to catch the inner spirit of each character and the inner spirit of the play—its special style, mood, and meaning. Even for a historical play like *Henry IV*, Hotspur's costume may tell us that the time is the beginning of the fifteenth century, but still more it must tell us that here is a proud, fiery rebel who despises elegance, subservience, and compromise.

FIGURE *13.19* Theatrical costumes, exaggerated and varied for projection to the audience and for musical-comedy gaiety. *Singing Jailbirds,* New York, 1928. Photo Vandamm.

FIGURE *13.20* Costume for a period farce. One costume suggests undress with bright-colored underwear, the other pretentious elegance made incongruous by the body position and expression of glee. Labiche's *An Italian Straw Hat*. University of Kansas production, directed by Gordon Beck, designed by Virgil Godfrey, and costumed by Herb Camburn.

This reaction against slavish dependence on historical research was stated very emphatically by Gordon Craig in *On the Art of the Theatre* early in the century. He wrote:

> Do not trouble about the costume books. . . . Doubt and mistrust them thoroughly. If you find afterwards that they contain many good things you will not be so far wrong; but if you accept them straight away your whole thought and sense for designing a costume will be lost.

Craig defined the new ideal of creative design as follows:

> Remain clear and fresh. If you study how to draw a figure, how to put on it a jacket, coverings for the legs, covering for the head, and try to vary these coverings in all kinds of interesting, amusing, or beautiful ways, you will get much further than if you feast your eyes and confound your brain with [the history books]. [Even the best history] is more a book for the historical novelist, and one has yet to be written about imaginative costume. Keep continually designing such imaginative costumes. For example, make a barbaric costume; and a barbaric costume for a sly man which has nothing about it which can be said to be historical and yet is both sly and barbaric. Now make another design for another barbaric costume, for a man who is bold and tender. Now make a third for one who is ugly and vindictive . . . it is no easy thing to do. . . . Then go further: attempt to design the clothing for a divine figure and for a demonic figure.

If modern costumes for historical scenes shock us by having too little aesthetic distance, a really authentic costume would distress us by having too much. A good historical costume is a compromise, adapted to the taste of the audience and to their idea of the period. The good designer has always

The Play in Production

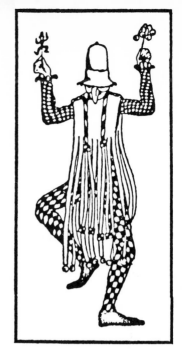

FIGURE *13.21* Costume project for a professional puppeteer, not based on any historical period but designed to suggest a clown or jester in bright-colored squares. From Gordon Craig's *The Mask*.

instinctively made that adaptation, and we can tell at a glance whether a medieval dress for the stage was made for an audience wearing dresses with hoop skirts or bustles or styles of the present day.

COSTUME FOR THE ACTOR

How does the designer go about the actual process of planning the costumes? He may be aware of five things costume can do: it can enhance the actor, create the character, set the style, tie the individual into the scheme of characters, and show the progress of the play.

Just as the scene designer starts with the moving actor and the stage space, creating the areas, levels, and shapes that enhance the action, so the costume designer starts with the moving actor and the costume material, creating new shapes, colors, and movements. Material may be fitted or draped. Some dancers' costumes are entirely fitted, with color and texture but nothing added to the shape, allowing the movement of the body to be seen in its simplest form. The bullfighter is almost as austere, with a little flow in his bolero jacket and several sharp accents of ribbons and color contrasts. Most Greek and Roman costumes were entirely draped, as are some ceremonial robes today. But more often the designer makes a combination of fitting and drape, a tight bodice leading into a flowing skirt, a tight upper arm leading into a flowing sleeve, a fitted body partly covered by a cape, arms and legs partly seen between the panels of sleeves and skirts. An accent such as a belt, a band, or a ruffle is most interesting at the transition from a fitted to a draped section. Accents sometimes mark the joints of the body, especially the shoulders and sometimes the hips but, except for comic effects, not the elbows and knees.

Whether fitted or flowing, with accent or accessory, the costume trans-

431

FIGURE *13.22* Costume for characterization. A draped ceremonial costume turns the soldier Joan of Arc into a more dignified leader at the coronation, yet the scallops suggest vulnerability. The king's long cloak and fur cape and his sceptre and crown are a little too large, suggesting that he is scarcely equal to the position. Anouilh's *The Lark.* University of Texas production, directed by Francis Hodge, designed by John Rothgeb, and costumed by Lucy Barton.

forms the appearance, the movement, and indeed the soul of the actor. An actor in underwear or a dancer in a leotard is very different from a performer in makeup and costume. A warrior in plumes and war paint and a chieftain in mask and ceremonial decorations take on roles already shaped by the design. In Brecht's *Galileo,* the Pope receives the scientist in his dressing chamber with sympathy and understanding. But as the attendants dress him, adding robe after robe, he is transformed into an official representative of the Church, with a very different attitude. In one sense costume creates the actor.

Psychologically the costume is very important. Looking in a mirror, the actor gets a vision of what he is supposed to be; he must live up to that vision. Some directors say that in many situations no makeup is needed. But what actor would be willing to plunge into a role without watching himself transformed into a different being as he puts on his costume and makeup? Dance teachers find that a mask is a stimulation to a dancer, giving him a vision of the character he is to create in movement. In sophisticated society a dark, impersonal mask is used at a ball to hide the identity, but in primitive societies a mask is the embodiment of identity. Like a primitive tribesman, the actor must put on his *persona,* or mask, before he becomes the personality to play his role.

The actor knows that the costume will enhance him. If he is doing a glamorous role, the designer can reshape him considerably, building out where he is too slight, emphasizing his good points and hiding his weaker ones. If he is doing a character role, the costume is an integral part of his stance, quality, and movement. A firm, tight bodice or stiff, tight waistcoat forces a very erect body. High heels shift the stance forward, while large, sloppy shoes invite a collapsed droop in standing and walking. Heavy boots slow the walk.

432

The Play in Production

In movement the actor soon learns why the designer gave him a cape or a long sleeve. As he turns his shoulders, lifts his elbow, or raises his arm, the cape or sleeve sweeps on beyond, extending the movement and giving it accent. The longer and heavier the cape, the slower the sweep. That extra material is not a hindrance but a tool he can use if he learns its feeling and makes the costume act. At the end of a speech he can swing the cape across his body as he turns to walk away, with an impressive gesture of finality. The actress learns to give her full skirt a swing that expresses the character

FIGURE *13.23* Fantastic costume and makeup for an animal fable. The characters are Noble the Lion, Reynard the Fox, and Tiecelin the Crow in Fauquez's *Reynard the Fox*. Centenary College and Kenlake State Park Amphitheatre, Hardin, Kentucky. Directed by Orlin Corey and designed and costumed by Irene Corey.

and just what she is thinking. A cane, a pipe, or an umbrella in the hand becomes a telling extension of the personality, and no one has exhausted the possibilities of the fan for indicating changes of thought or feeling.

If the costume makes the actor, it no less takes the actor to make the costume. No amount of beautiful fabric or dashing style can affect the audience unless the actor feels and projects the beauty and the dash. When the actress feels beauty, she gives life to the beautiful silks and velvets. Some actresses can get the right feeling through imagination. With others it may help to put lace and ribbons on the petticoat that the audience never sees.

COSTUME FOR THE CHARACTER

But the costume designer not only enhances the actor, he creates the character. The costume must tell the audience at a glance if the character is young or old, rich or poor, doctor, beggar, or thief, brassy bar maid or kind old grandmother, arriving from a cold journey or off to play tennis in the sun. It can show character change. The hard-working clerk of the first act becomes the president of the corporation in the second. The eager girl in her plain school clothes and simple makeup blossoms into the leader of society in elegant evening clothes and sophisticated hairdo. The dashing young spendthrift becomes a drunkard in untidy clothes. The costume may characterize by not fitting. The king's garments on Macbeth "hang loose about him like a giant's robe upon a dwarfish thief." Not only the traditional insignia—the king's crown, the bishop's mitre, the priest's collar, the scholar's dark-rimmed glasses—but the whole range of caps, canes, fans, gloves, and other accessories indicate immediately who the character is or what impression he is trying to make.

The costume designer goes further than such tokens of identification. He

FIGURE 13.24 Stylized makeup. The makeup, wig, and beard create the effect of Romanesque sculpture. With Greek-like padded clothing and raised buskins, the actor stood more than seven feet five inches. Saint Paul in Corey's *Romans by Saint Paul*. Kenlake State Park Amphitheatre, Hardin, Kentucky. Adapted and produced by Orlin Corey and designed by Irene Corey.

cotton lace over white plus mourning veil

white ruffle at neck and wrists - with black lace edging

black embroidery on stomacher silk

cut steel trim on hanging sleeve

corduroy 6' long velvet

French hood. taffeta - pearl trim

sleeves: black organza with black glitter

very low decolletage

white gloves

"mourning" dress

black taffeta skirt velvet tubes come in?

Tubes fly when she turns.

Ellen Bloodworth   LADY ANNE — I

Miss Gail Jaffe   OLIVIA — I

FIGURE *13.25* Two costumes for women in mourning. The costumes are based on the same period, but one is designed for tragedy and one for romantic comedy. Soft flowing lines and heavy corduroy material convey the dignity and sorrow of Lady Anne in Shakespeare's *Richard III,* while the shiny taffeta bodice and skirt, the crisp glittering sleeves, and the low decolletage suggest that bright energy is more important than mourning for Lady Olivia in Shakespeare's *Twelfth Night.* Designs by Paul Reinhardt.

is a collaborator with the actor and director in creating the inner character. How the character feels can be indicated by what he wears and how he wears it. Does he keep the costume neat or neglect it? Is she dowdy or chic? Would she show off in bad taste by choosing flashy colors or putting on too many jewels and ornaments? The comic pretentiousness of the spick-and-span inspector in a murder mystery may be created by the too-tight coat that pulls apart between the buttons. The little man in a plain costume who bursts forth proudly with a new hat, or the Cinderella who has rough, itchy stockings with her unaccustomed new clothes—who can say how much is suggested by costume and how much by the pantomime of the actor? A good costume becomes one with the actor, suggesting, reinforcing, extending the movement. The Queen and the long cape hanging from her shoulders become one tall figure of dignity. The peasant girl and her horizontal stripes on skirt and sleeves become one wide earthy image of health and jollity. Even more than the setting, a costume that is excellent in performance attracts no separate notice; only the good performance of the actor is remembered. That is why we know even less about stage costumes of the past than about scenery. Nobody thought it important to mention them.

Some attitudes and feelings are more easily expressed in contemporary costumes than in costumes of the past. Audiences recognize the difference   *435*

Design for the Theatre

FIGURE *13.26* Lines that create character.
Vertical lines create queenly dignity
and horizontal lines create robust earthiness.
Drawn by Don Creason.

FIGURE *13.27* Two interpretations of Lady Macbeth's costume for the sleepwalking
scene. One, designed by Lemuel Ayers for Judith Anderson in the New York
production, emphasizes soft, drooping lines to suggest sorrow. The other, by
Mary Davis at the University of Arkansas, emphasizes vertical lines for queenly
dignity and jagged lines to suggest tortured anguish.

between sophisticated eastern clothes and small-town provincial or rural garments, even the subtlety separating a Madison Avenue suit from a Continental cut. Tyrone Guthrie's modern-dress *Hamlet* at Minneapolis was able to indicate many aspects of character that are usually lost in historical costume. For instance, Laertes was characterized as an impetuous college boy. When his father was trying to break through the surface and put some sense into his head, there the callous boy stood, in madras sport coat and Tyrolean hat, tennis racket under his arm, restless, eager to be off. The scene took on a fresh meaning, due largely to the costume.

Many societies conventionalize the outer expression of the inner state—mourning dress, for instance, expressing grief and marking the ritual isolation of the family. Tearing the clothes and letting down the hair are accepted indications of a distraught mind. Shakespeare inherited the medieval conventions, by which each rank in the church and the feudal order and each craftsman in the town—cook, doctor, carpenter, or painter—had a special costume, and these costumes have not entirely disappeared. The installation into a new rank required the "investment," or putting on of the official vestments of that rank. Equally accepted was an indication of change of spiritual state. When the Prodigal Son in the plays returned to his home he had to have new clothes to mark his restoration to the family. Though modern actors have ignored the passage, Ophelia's description would indicate that Hamlet's distraught mind was expressed by disheveled clothes, and we have detailed descriptions in the dialogue of how Ophelia and King Lear looked when mad.

COSTUME FOR SPIRIT AND STYLE

The third consideration of the costume designer is the spirit and style of the play. Costume can add dignity to tragedy, charm to romance, and playful variety to light comedy. Instead of merely reproducing the fashion of a particular period, the designer searches for a particular point of view, sometimes looking to views of the period shaped by contemporary or later artists. Watteau, for instance, painted in rather light pastel colors only the charming aspects of the eighteenth century—carefree couples in soft satins departing for a dream island of picnics or watching slightly sad comedians. Hogarth, in contrast, selected out of almost the same period a much more robust vision, a comic caricature of energetic, if scarred and diseased, lower classes catering to the rich, who quarreled with their brides or sprawled in crowded houses of ill repute. The designer searches for all the variants he can find in the period, and takes suggestions from those details that express something of the spirit and style he feels he wants for the play.

In costume design, selection is a very powerful means of creating style. To limit the color scheme for the entire cast to pastels, to earth colors, to two or three primary colors, or to black and white makes a strong, unified impression. A variety of heavy, dull textures, or of shiny taffetas and satins, creates a particular feeling and style while allowing for considerable adaptation to individual characters. We have already noticed that musical comedy thrives on bright colors and sparkling materials. Yet *The Pajama Game* made

FIGURE *13.28* Style and unity in costume created by lines and materials. Costumes are limited to a few lines and patterns and are set against sculptural scenic elements that suggest casual sketches. The two quarreling couples at the end of Shakespeare's *The Merchant of Venice.* University of Illinois production, directed by Clara Behringer, designed by John Ahart, and costumed by Genevieve Richardson.

FIGURE *13.29* Comic costumes using the sturdy, rough texture of canvas as a unifying element throughout the production. Shakespeare's *The Taming of the Shrew.* University of Washington production, designed by John A. Conway and costumed by Lucy Barton.

very successful use of everyday fashions, in simple prints and light materials, while *West Side Story* achieved a high excitement out of plain faces and harsh, tense movements of men dressed in dark slum clothing.

In the play and the opera *Pelleas and Melisande,* the shadowy, twilight mood is all-important, as we have noted in the section on rhythm. The costume designer will keep all the characters in a narrow range of blue-gray and green-gray tones, with soft, flowing lines. Many plays, such as *Hamlet, Lear,* and *Macbeth,* are more psychological dramas of a vague land of legend than historical plays, and no one medieval or Elizabethan period style has special pertinence. No wonder it is tempting to settle for modern costumes or for rehearsal costumes as Richard Burton did in his *Hamlet.* Several designers for *Lear* and *Macbeth,* in seeking a bold, primitive effect, have borrowed more details from the South Seas and the Bronze Age than from early Britain, and in 1955 Gielgud startled Stratford and London with an abstract, vaguely Japanese *Lear* designed by Isamu Noguchi.

For comedy, sharp contrast is startling. That is why stripes and bright spots are so often used (FIGURE *13.19*). Incongruity is even more comic: the small vertical hat over the big round face; the sleeve or cape too small or too large, out of proportion to the rest of the costume; the color or texture that does not match. The costumer may emphasize the peculiarities of the charac-   *439*

FIGURE *13.30*   A satiric view of human coarseness and folly. Dame Overdo is contrasted with the brawling people of the fair. Some variety is achieved even though the overall style limits the designer to coarse materials and untidiness in design. Jonson's *Bartholomew Fair.* University of Texas production, directed by James Moll and costumed by Paul Reinhardt.

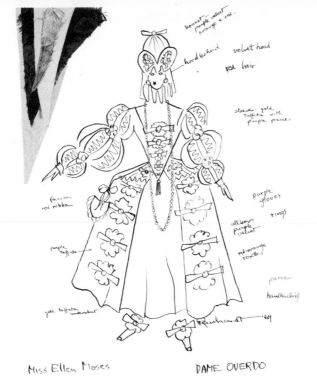

Miss Ellen Moses

DAME OVERDO

FIGURE *13.31* Costume to match the name—Dame Overdo. Purple, red, and gold are used in velvet and taffeta. Jonson's *Bartholomew Fair*. Design by Paul Reinhardt.

ter—the fat stomach of Sir Toby Belch and the thin lines of his companion, Sir Andrew Aguecheek—or may accent an awkward place, such as an elbow or a knee. Droopy, baggy, and floppy parts of the costume are as comic as a limp wrist, a chin hanging down, or a collapsed gesture.

COSTUME FOR THE SCHEME OF CHARACTERS

The fourth consideration of the costume designer is the scheme of the characters, their relations with one another and with the setting, already analyzed as part of the structure of the play. The costumes must give harmony to the picture by a unified color scheme and be closely related to the setting yet stand out from the background. They must look well together, and they must be so planned that in large scenes the colors are well distributed. Yet the costumes must control the spread of attention, indicating which are subordinate characters and which important, and must make many fine distinctions within the large picture.

The designer can do more than the actor or director in making clear how the characters line up in loyalty or opposition, in similarities and differences. The scheme is simple in *Romeo and Juliet,* where the feud sets two groups apart. The audience should know at a glance who belongs to which: Mercutio should be in a mixed costume and the Friar and the Prince should be seen to be completely above the quarrel. Some designers use two quite different colors for the two sides. Similarly, in the back-and-forth fighting in *Macbeth,* it is important to know at a glance who is fighting for Macbeth and who for Macduff. *King Lear* is more complex. Not only are there two families—the King's and Gloucester's—but there are good and bad children in each. Lear's

440

The Play in Production

FIGURE *13.32* Style and unity created by costume and makeup. Five insane characters are distinguished from the Marquis de Sade, who sits upright. Touches of bright decoration assert a note of cheerfulness in defiance of the coarse, dirty texture of cloth and hair. Weiss's *Marat/Sade*. Royal Shakespeare Company production, London. Photo Morris Newcombe.

two wicked, flattering daughters are united against the honest, plain-spoken Cordelia. The costumes can make that clear even if the designer does not go quite as far as a Munich production in which the wicked daughters were in identical scarlet dresses unbroken from neck to wrist to toe and Cordelia was in pure white. The same opposition between flattery and honesty is extended to the servants, in a quarrel between Lear's plain-speaking, plainly dressed servant (Kent in disguise) and Goneril's sycophantic, elegantly dressed servant Oswald. In any play the characters must be vivid enough to stand out from the environment, but those who are at home will be in close harmony with it and with one another, while intruders will be set apart. If a son brings a noisy girl into a dignified home, the costume should signal the conflict as she enters. In the next act we should know immediately whether the environment has changed her or she has changed it.

COSTUME FOR CHANGE

The fifth approach to costume design concerns the progression, the change and development in the course of the play. Katherine in *The Taming of the Shrew* is transformed from a high-tempered, aristocratic girl

441

to a disheveled, almost-beaten-down wife and then to a gracious, compliant wife who is knowing in her gesture of obedience. Her costumes should show the changes; at the end they should be softer and more matronly but still have some lines and colors of assertion and self-reliance. Sometimes the tone of the play must change when it is impossible to change the set. To brighten the middle scenes in *Hamlet,* the Players can bring on bright hangings and cloths to throw over chairs and even over the floor, but such a change is not possible in many plays. Then changes in costume and lighting can create the desired effect. Carnival hats and streamers at a party can quickly add gaiety, while putting on, or merely closing and buttoning, dark raincoats can cover and dampen the previous brightness. The meaning of the sequence of scenes in Verdi's *La Traviata* is more dependent on the costumes than on the setting. The four acts alternate between large party scenes and small intimate scenes. In the first act, at Violetta's lively gathering of her rich friends, sophisticated and daring but warm, friendly, even cozy, the setting and the harmony of the color scheme should bring them close together. The rural cottage happiness of the second act needs not only a flower garden but costumes indicating a rustic simplicity almost, but not quite, achieved. In the gambling party in the third act, where the same friends that appeared in the first act are separated into small groups, hostile and suspicious, the costumes must be harsh, suggesting a brazen note that was absent from the first party. The last scene is all tenderness and forgiveness as the dying Violetta waits in a cold blue dawn and rises in a soft blue or white negligee to greet her love and die in his arms.

Like the setting, the dress should be more than charming or spectacular decoration, more than style and mood. As an instrument for each actor to play on, it becomes part of the action. For the whole group, the costuming helps organize and clarify the picture.

The Lighting

> Now the dark stage begins to burn and glow under our fingers, burning like the embers of the forge of Vulcan, and shafts of light stab through the darkness, and shadows leap and shudder, and we are in the regions where splendor and terror move.

> Robert Edmond Jones, *The Dramatic Imagination*

The audience is held spellbound as the house lights go down, the curtain disappears, and the lights bring form out of nothingness. Both the actor and the setting emerge in bold relief, creating highlights and shadows in the controlled plastic light of the spotlights. Then, as the action moves from one part of the stage to another, the light gets stronger there and the rest of the stage recedes into the margin of attention. For light, even more than setting, shapes the action and exerts a hypnotic control over the interest and emotions of the audience. As Norman Bel Geddes describes it, "Good lighting adds space, depth, mood, mystery, parody, contrast, change of emotion, intimacy,

The Play in Production

FIGURE *13.33* Space stage within a proscenium frame. Three beams of light make a light pool on a pyramid of steps. Space is defined by light and actors. A sketch by Robert Edmond Jones of a Berlin production of Toller's *Man and the Masses*. From Macgowan and Jones, *Continental Stagecraft.*

fear." The basic idea of adding light at the center of the action seems simple enough. Max Reinhardt is quoted as saying, "I am told that the art of lighting a stage consists of putting light where you want it and taking it away where you don't want it." But now lighting is a major creative art, and the designer of the lighting of a play is given full recognition with the author, the director, the designers of setting and costume, and the actors.

THE DEVELOPMENT OF LIGHTING

In theatrical lighting, the age of electricity can boast of its superiority to all other ages. It has perfected an art that started when primitive actors thousands of years ago danced with flaming torches in the flickering firelight. While the Greeks and the Elizabethans used the open sky and most medieval performances took place in the daytime, many kings and princes knew the impressive effect a processional entry into the city could have at night, with torches and pageants sparkling with lights. When the Renaissance princes created the first modern stages in their palace ballrooms, they started a tradition of bright chandeliers for the well-dressed audiences, bright chandeliers for the actors, and lights back of the scenes for stunning effects of moving clouds and sunrises and sunsets (FIGURES *2.11, 2.13*). Renaissance architects made their perspective settings of three-dimensional houses sparkle by putting glass bottles of colored water in round and diamond-shaped openings in the walls and lighting them from behind by lamps (FIGURE *2.10*). Sometimes they would start a tragedy in bright lights with

443

FIGURE *13.34* Dramatic
lighting as conceived by a
seventeenth-century painter.
Strong contrast between
highlights and dark
background. The source of
light, a candle, is included
in the picture. Honthorst's
Christ Before Pilate.
Photo copyright National
Gallery, London.

FIGURE *13.35* Dramatic lighting similar to lighting in seventeenth-century
painting. Faces are highlighted against dark background and dark clothing by
light coming from directly above or from very low. Note the Queen's shadow
on the backdrop and the two spotlights on the floor near the audience.
Hamlet in modern dress, the Old Vic, London. Directed by Tyrone Guthrie.
Photo Angus McBean.

visible flames on the roofs, suggesting the gaiety of a festival. Then at the catastrophe they would suddenly darken the stage by letting down shields over the flames by means of cords over small pulleys. In his paintings, Rembrandt explored the excitement of highlighting a face and hands and leaving most of the canvas very dark, but on the Baroque stage there was not enough technical control of light to get such contrast between highlight and shadow. Now that almost any lighting effect is possible on the stage, theatre people find those paintings very suggestive. The faces seem to glow from within, and while Rembrandt and other painters often indicated the source of light in a window or a candle, they showed that selective dramatic lighting could be convincing whether or not it had an obvious source (FIGURE *13.34*).

Gas lights introduced at the beginning of the nineteenth century concentrated much brighter light on the stage and permitted some degree of control because the footlights, the border lights above the actors, and even the house lights could be turned down separately. But still stage lighting consisted of the flat general glare from long rows of open flames. Only when the limelight and the carbon electric arc were introduced in the middle of the century was it possible to concentrate a strong light in a narrow space by the use of a lens. When it was discovered that a piece of calcium or lime heated to   *445*

FIGURE *13.36*   The lighting control board under the front of the stage at the Paris opera. The prompter's box is set in the footlights. The border lights are open striplights with bulbs substituted for the earlier gas flames.
From *L'Illustration,* June 18, 1887.

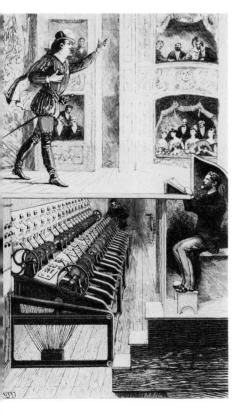
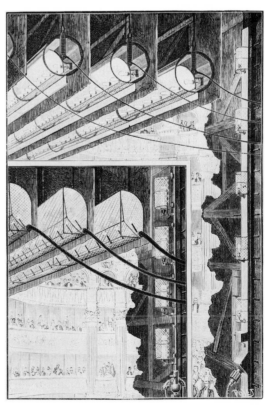

incandescence in a gas flame produces a very strong, concentrated light, "in the limelight" became a new term in the English language. Even brighter is the light from the spark that arcs between two rods of carbon when a strong electric current is sent across the gap. If a metal box is placed around that arc with a lens at the end, it will send down a bright spot to make one or two actors stand out from all the rest. This "follow spot" is still sometimes used for specialty numbers in a revue, though it is rather crude in comparison with the subtle equipment possible today.

It was with the invention of the incandescent lamp in 1879 that the real development of modern lighting began. The incandescent lamp is safe and noiseless, available in many sizes, and easily controlled by a dimmer. The filament is so concentrated that a spherical or ellipsoidal reflector and a lens create a pool of directional, not diffused, light. It is easy to put a sheet of colored gelatin, acetate, or glass in front of the lens. Today light has shape, direction, and color and can easily change from bright to dim.

Light not only gives the actor and setting shape but also gives the picture a new dimension in time. By the end of the century, London and New York were being impressed by the changing moods of twilight, sunset, moonlight, and dawn of Sir Henry Irving's Shakespeare and David Belasco's ultra-realistic, sensational scenes of the Wild West, exotic foreign lands, and city slums. With Irving and Belasco the spotlight controlled by dimmers had already become the basic modern form of lighting, yet as late as the middle of the twentieth century ignorant architects and builders continued to install clumsy, expensive footlights and borders in school and city auditoriums— mere electrical adaptations of nineteenth-century gas lighting. The one important development in the use of spotlights in the last several decades has been the use of the reflector lamp, a light that has the whole spotlight—reflector, lens, and filament—built into the bulb. Too small for the main lighting of a large stage, it is extremely useful in smaller areas, and it is the main instrument for window displays and most architectural and landscape lighting.

LIGHT IN SPACE

The great prophet of the new art of lighting was Appia, whose book of 1899, *Music and the Art of the Theatre,* as we have seen, has been invaluable to stage designers. He might have called it *The Music of Light,* for light was the new element to express the soul of the drama that was so well created in Wagner's music but impossible to express with the painted backdrops and flat lighting of the nineteenth century. "Light is to production," Appia wrote, "what music is to the score: the expressive element in opposition to the literal signs; and, like music, light can express only what belongs to 'the inner essence of all vision.' " The new use of light meant a radically new approach to the plastic form of the stage. Instead of drawing the third dimension on the backdrop, Appia wanted to set his actor moving in three dimensions on ramps and platforms and to create the third dimension by catching both actor and the plastic setting in highlights and shadows. That required sculptural forms with very little painted detail and little color;

446

The Play in Production

FIGURE 13.37 The same scene in work lights and in stage lights. What is dull and flat in diffused general light takes life and form under spotlights. Marlowe's *Dr. Faustus.* Indiana University production, designed and costumed by Richard L. Scammon and lighted by Gary Gaiser.

the form, the intensity, and even the color were to be created by the mobile, focused light.

Appia made the first analysis of the kinds of light to be derived from the different instruments. He defined the basic difference between general and specific lighting, or "diffused light" and "living light," in the four kinds of lights and lighting:

1. The fixed border lights, which light the painted flats, supplemented in the wings and on the stage floor by the movable striplights.
2. The "footlights," that peculiar monstrosity of our theatres, designed to light both the scenery and the actors from in front and below.
3. Movable spotlights that throw focused beams of light on playing areas or projections on flat screens.
4. Light within the settings, that is, light intended to reveal the transparent parts of the setting by lighting from behind.

The third type, which he called "living light," was most important, for it could create form-giving shadows. The first two, giving general or diffused light, could have only a subordinate function, to soften and blend the sharp contrasts of the living light.

How that plastic living light could shape the play Appia shows in detailed light plots for Wagner's operas. The scene could change as the thoughts and emotions of the characters change, showing the world largely through their eyes. In the second act of *Tristan and Isolde* the terrace of the castle shows only a torch lighted at the center of the stage—the torch set as a warning for Tristan to stay away—as Isolde sees nothing but cruel empty space: no trees, no form to the castle, only the torch and the sharp shadows of the figures. She moves to the torch and extinguishes it, and Tristan comes to her in deep shadows. For a while the music dominates the scene; time and space cease to exist. Gradually the lovers move together down the ramps to another area more sheltered, closed in, "deluded." Then a pale light appears in the upstage entrance arch as King Mark and his followers rush in. Daylight increases, cold, severe, revealing the whole portico-like section of the castle. Then only one area, the sheltered space in front of the terrace, is left invisible, spared by the dawn. Day, the enemy, has come to destroy the lovers. Without any movement of scenery, the picture makes dynamic changes as the light follows the action, reshaping it, opening up one area and closing another, changing the mood, revealing the meaning of the action.

THE LIGHT PLOT

To create and control this dynamic, revealing light, the lighting designer works out a *light plot,* a chart of the placement of all the lights and a list of all the changes. The light plot is actually a complete lighting score comparable to the musical score or the text of the play.

The spotlights are planned first. Since the general lighting will be only
448 supplementary, striplights used mainly for blending and for lighting the

FIGURE *13.38* Lighting from one side, creating the excitement of sharp, rather harsh contrasts between highlights and shadows. Molnar's *Liliom*. Carnegie Tech Theatre production, directed by Lawrence Carra, designed by Lloyd Weninger, lighted by William Nelson, and costumed by Douglas Russell. Photo Regis Cejrowski.

background and the sky cyclorama, the main lighting will be by spots—spots from the bridge or from a pipe just back of the curtain, and spots from the beams in the auditorium. Since evenly diffused lighting would take away shadows and hence form, the spotlights are not spread everywhere but grouped to form pools of light. The stage is divided into areas, either the six playing areas defined by the director or whatever areas the setting suggests. Usually two spotlights are focused on each area, aimed from the two sides about ninety degrees apart and casting light down at an "angle of throw" of about forty-five degrees. Each side of a face will get some shadowing, but not too much. If one light is stronger than the other, or, better yet, if one is of a warm color and the other cool, the plastic effect will be richer.

Side lights and back lights are used for special effects. Light from the side or from straight above gives very sharp shadows, far too strong for most realistic scenes unless subtly blended with some front lighting (FIGURE *13.40*). Back lighting, from above but from upstage of the actors, adds a highlight on head and shoulders, a halo effect (FIGURE *13.39*) frequently used in television lighting to make an actor stand out from a dark background. For most plays only the more subtle tints of colors are used: fresh pinks and very light ambers if the scene is warm and sunny, lavender or light blue if a colder mood is needed. But for dance and for less realistic plays, strong colors and sharp angles of throw from the sides that produce extreme shadows can give excitement (FIGURES *13.35, 13.38*).

General illumination for the sky cyclorama usually comes from standard strips both above and below, wired in three circuits. In lighting, the three primary colors that mix together to produce other colors are not the red, yellow, and blue of the painter but red, green, and blue. Dimming these three colors up

449

FIGURE *13.39* Back lighting in two consecutive, related scenes. A strong light from above and upstage of the actors catches the top of their heads and shoulders with a halo effect, while they are left dark enough to be silhouetted against a bright background. *Rain,* from a story by Maugham. University of Wyoming production, directed and designed by Richard L. Scammon, lighted by Scammon and Soller, and costumed by Charles Parker.

or down will produce almost any sky effect, from night to sunrise to daylight to fire, as well as all the unnatural colors of red and purple. Scenic effects projected onto the background are becoming increasingly popular. We will have more to say about them in discussing new concepts of space in the next chapter.

Appia's fourth kind of lighting, from inside the setting itself, has had very little use in the theatre so far, though it has long been used for commercial signs and juke boxes that glow from within. Architects have begun making use of it to illuminate buildings at night; more exciting than general illumination from floodlights is the effect produced when a building is treated like a piece of sculpture, with sequences of dark and lighted spaces set against the dark of the night through the use of luminescent panels and small coves and ledges lighted from hidden sources. The theatre has the same opportunity. Not all the light has to come from far above the stage area. In an age of transistors, of miniature control and illumination units, and of three-dimensional sculptural forms on the stage, a revolutionary, very exciting lighting could be built into the setting.

The nerve center of the lighting is the switchboard that controls the dimmers. The early kind of dimmer was the resistance dimmer, a long handle that pulled the contacts around a heavy plate-shaped coil. The early dimmer board might occupy a whole wall and need several strong-armed

The Play in Production

workers to manipulate, though master handles and large master dimmers were developed so that several circuits could be dimmed together by one handle. Basic and dependable, the resistance dimmer is still used in many places. But many new systems have been invented, each making the last seem old-fashioned and clumsy. Instead of perfecting the old, inventors have often become enthusiastic about the new. The autotransformer, especially a neat model called the Variac, was the rage in the 1930s. Then electronic systems of control captured the interest of designers. But they now seem enormous, clumsy, and very expensive in comparison to the small silicon rectifier invented in the late 1950s. Since the designer has available small sensitive dimmers and small spotlight lamps, each with its own reflector built into the bulb, it has become common practice to supplement the large spotlights with a large number of sources of light around the stage, with many circuits all controlled from one console smaller than an organ console. At this board an expert follows the light plot and at each cue moves small levers or punches small buttons that control a number of changes. If the board is even further mechanized, he puts a punched IBM card in a slot which, at the right cue, may bring one set of lights up fast, one set down fast, and other sets up or down at different speeds. Most lighting designers feel that the human element must never be lost, however, and that the man at the switchboard must be as fine a player of his instrument as a concert pianist. He must have a light plot worked out in the greatest detail, but he must make fine, intuitive adjustments as he watches the play. Hence it is very important that the switchboard be located where the operator can see the entire stage.

In the overall format of the production, the scheme of lighting, with its

FIGURE *13.40* Lighting from above. Sharp lighting from directly above catches the inside of the group and increases the excitement of a singing, shouting mob. Lawrence and Lee's *Inherit the Wind*. Eastern Illinois University production, directed by E. G. Gabbard and designed by John E. Bielenberg.

FIGURE *13.41* Architectural lighting. Architects and theatre lighting designers are both learning to use sculptural lighting to add another dimension to an interesting form. A shopping mall in Miami Beach. Lighting by Feder.

conventions, becomes part of the rhythmic progression of the show, now punctuating with blackouts, now blending one scene into the next, changing the mood, shifting from dream to reality, revealing and concealing different playing areas. Old conventions of vaudeville often persist in musicals. Setting and lighting are realistic for dialogue, but as the actors begin a song, the realistic lights are dimmed out and a follow spot cuts them away from reality in their own pool of light. As solo song or duet gives way to the chorus for a full dance, the follow spot gives way to the fantasy lighting of a dream. Thirty years ago most lighting for drama was fairly realistic, and a window or a lamp always provided at least a nominal source of the light. Almost imperceptible changes might be made during a scene, but any marked change was justified by the dawn, or by clouds, or by putting on a light or blowing out a candle. But today, even in realistic plays, audiences accept bold changes if they are well integrated with the movement or feelings of the characters.

Like setting and costuming, lighting is an integral part of the play, serving many functions. It highlights the center of action and subordinates the less important areas. It reveals form, giving plasticity to each actor and each background structure and shaping the playing areas to reinforce the composition of the director. It not only suggests local color and time of day but creates mood through color, intensity, shape, and angle. Perhaps most important of all, dynamic changes of light do as much as the dialogue, the plot, the actors' movement, and the incidental music and sound to propel the play to its destined goal.

The Play in Production

1. DESIGN TO CREATE MOOD BY LINE.   Draw a tree to suggest a mood for (1) a scene of moonlight and roses for a young couple in love; (2) a scene in which an old person returns in autumn to a place where he had been happy in love; (3) a scene of murderers waiting to catch the victim; (4) a scene in a wide desert with a lone cactus tree; (5) a scene in a graveyard where a boy must pass alone; (6) a scene of mock fright at Halloween; (7) a caricature of hillbillies.

2. DESIGN TO CREATE MOOD FROM CONVENTIONAL FORM OR MATERIALS. Start with some familiar building form or a material that has been handled in a traditional way, such as the openwork steel structure we see in bridges and towers, primitive stone shapes such as those at Stonehenge, wooden beams, Oriental bamboo, molded concrete or plastic. Design a setting from this conventional form or material in such a way as to create a mood: tortured and twisted; fantastic and playful; light, high, and aspiring; heavy and oppressive, with horizontal lines and low ceilings. Or design from the conventional material a setting to fit a particular idea or image, such as a small, painful prison cell, a gay and expansive night club, a decorated birdcage that is charming but offers no escape, or a threatening structure partly seen over a hill or a wall.

3. DESIGN OF A STREET TO CREATE MOOD.   Draw a street with houses on both sides to fit the mood of each of the following situations: (1) a frightened boy from the country visits the city hoping to make his fortune; (2) a couple pass through the street on their way to a lively party; (3) the couple, weary and rather drunk, pass through the street on their way home; (4) a weary murderer who knows that people are waiting to get him passes through the street. Make the lines of the houses, rather than the people, express the mood.

4. DESIGN FOR AN EXPRESSIONISTIC SCENE.   Draw an expressionistic design for the scene in *Death of a Salesman,* described in Chapter 9, where Willy Loman hopes for a human response from his young boss but instead gets fired. The design should suggest how the room might appear to Willy after he has accidentally turned on the tape recorder and is maddened by the inhuman mechanical sounds.

5. DESIGN TO CREATE SYMBOLIC OR ABSTRACT SETTING FROM CONVENTIONAL BUILDING FORM.   Take a familiar building form, such as a nineteenth-century Gothic church, a Roman-temple bank building, an old-fashioned state capitol or court house, a Greek-column southern plantation mansion, or a skyscraper. Treat it in either of these ways: (1) as a simplified symbol that could be sketched in a cartoon or flashed across a screen in

453

a movie montage or projected on a back screen as a dream or fantasy; (2) as a three-dimensional skeleton of a building with acting areas within it.

6. DESIGN FOR FANTASY. Take a familiar setting, such as a kitchen, a dining room, a bedroom, a barn, a garden with a pavilion, and treat it from the point of view of fantasy: (1) as a scene in the style of a thirteen-year-old girl's dream of a bride and groom like the figures on a bridal cake; (2) as a scene for the "Munsters" or some other monstrous people of reversed values; (3) as a tumbledown scene for a dirty, bearded old hermit; (4) as a poor boy's dream of lavish wealth.

7. COSTUME FOR CHARACTER. In the illustrations in this book, find examples of costumes that suggest at first glance a distinct characterization. Is the actor standing or moving in a way that reinforces the impression?

8. COSTUME SCHEME. Plan a costume scheme for two quite distinct college groups in a musical comedy. Possible groups are the beatnik set, the tennis set, the pencil-and-sliderule engineers, the rich playboy set. Plan the costumes for the two choruses of distinct, exaggerated types, with slight variations of color and line for each. Then plan three variations of each choral prototype—one character that is greatly caricatured, one that has only a suggestion of the prototype, and a romantic lead that can be recognized as belonging to one of the two sets.

SUGGESTED READING

DESIGN

While there are excellent books on the planning, construction, and handling of scenery and lighting, too little has been written about the creative process of design. Gordon Craig wrote the most exciting suggestions in *On the Art of the Theatre* (1911, 1958) and in scattered comments in his other books. Arnold S. Gillette makes a systematic presentation of the problems and processes of the designer in *An Introduction to Scenic Design* (1967). The best statements that other designers have made—all too brief—are brought together by Orville K. Larson in *Scene Design for Stage and Screen* (1961). The quotations in this chapter from Jones, Simonson, Smith, Berman, and Armistead may be found in Larson's book.

The ideas and drawings of several top Broadway designers can be examined in books. For Robert Edmond Jones there is not only his own exciting little book of essays, *The Dramatic Imagination* (1941), but his earlier *Drawings for the Theatre* (1925) and a volume of designs edited by Ralph Pendleton, *The Theatre of Robert Edmond Jones* (1958). Donald Oenslager presents some of his designs, especially for classic plays, with comments on his approach, in *Scenery Then and Now* (1936). Lee Simonson publishes his own designs in *Part of a Lifetime* (1943) and some of his own with those of others in *The Art of Scenic Design* (1950), and he writes a brilliant account of past scenery and the conditions and problems of modern design in *The Stage Is Set** (1932). Jo

454

Mielziner presents his designs, with valuable discussion, in *Designing for the Theatre* (1965). Mordecai Gorelik writes trenchantly on the processes of design, beginning with the book *New Theatres for Old* (1941) and continuing with a number of articles, notably "Designing the Play" in John Gassner, *Producing the Play* (1941; rev. ed., 1953), "The Setting and the Image," *Drama Survey*, II (Winter, 1963), and the several articles collected by Larson in *Scene Design for Stage and Screen*. Norris Houghton interviews four Broadway designers on their approaches to design in *Theatre Arts*, XX (Oct., Nov., Dec., 1936) and XXI (Jan., 1937). James H. Clay shows how atmosphere and symbolism shape a play in "On Chekhov's *The Cherry Orchard*," *Players Magazine* (Feb., 1965). Arch Lauterer's ideas on design are presented in "Design for the Dance," *Magazine of Modern Art* (March, 1938), and in the entire issue of *Encore* for 1959.

A large number of pictures of designs and productions have been published in book collections. Most theatre histories are illustrated, but especially rich in visual material are Sheldon Cheney, *Stage Decoration* (1928), Allardyce Nicoll, *The Development of the Theatre* (4th ed., 1965), and George Altman and others, *Theatre Pictorial* (1953). Twentieth-century designs are lavishly illustrated in Samuel J. Hume and Walter René Fuerst, *Twentieth Century Stage Decoration* (1928, 1965), Leon Moussinac, *New Movement in the Theatre* (1965), and René Hainaux and Yves-Bonnat, *Stage Design Throughout the World Since 1935* (1956) and *Stage Design Throughout the World Since 1950* (1964).

Much has been written on executing the design—building, painting, and changing scenery. Some important books are Samuel Selden and H. D. Sellman, *Stage Scenery and Lighting* (1930, and many later editions), Harold Burris-Meyer and Edward Cole, *Scenery for the Theatre* (1938), Philip Barber, "The New Scene Technician's Handbook," in Gassner, *Producing the Play*, Arnold S. Gillette, *Stage Scenery: The Construction and the Rigging* (1959), Oren W. Parker and Harvey K. Smith, *Scene Design and Stage Lighting* (1963).

The general student can use several shorter books on scene construction and backstage practice or find good chapters, with drawings, on "Scene Design," "The Crafts," and "Stage Lighting," in Frank Whiting, *An Introduction to the Theatre* (1954), and the same chapters slightly abridged in the revised 1961 edition.

COSTUME

As is the case with scene design, little has been written about the creative aspect of costume design, but much has been written about the execution of costumes. The best recent book, by three Englishwomen who design stage costumes under the name Motley, is *Designing and Making Stage Costumes* (1965), which says a good deal about both designing and executing. Gordon Craig and Robert Edmond Jones consider costume as well as scene design. Tanya Moiseiwitsch expresses a good deal in a brief interview, "Problems in Design," *Drama Survey*, III (Spring–Summer, 1963), and Tyrone Guthrie makes an excellent case for "Hamlet in Modern Dress" in the same issue of *Drama Survey*. A personal account is Virginia Volland, *Designing Woman: The Art and Practice of Theatrical Costume* (1966).

The designer discovers that theatrical costume has often been quite different from the costumes worn in life. Any illustrated history of theatre will confirm

* Available in paperback edition.

this, but several books concentrate on the theatrical conventions, notably Theodore Komisarjevsky, *The Costume of the Theatre* (1932), and James Laver, *Costume in the Theatre* (1964) and *Drama: Its Costume and Decor* (1951).

Most costume books are historical studies or studies of particular groups. When the main approach of the designer is to adapt historical designs, history and dressmaking are all-important, and for three decades the indispensable book has been Lucy Barton, *Historic Costume for the Stage* (1935). An excellent brief handbook on history and construction, with a useful bibliography, is Berneice Prisk, *Stage Costume Handbook** (1966). A good selective bibliography is provided in A. E. Santaniello, *Theatre Books in Print* (1963).

LIGHTING

Adolphe Appia's basic theories are stated in *Music and the Art of the Theatre* (1960), edited by Barnard Hewitt, and they are summarized in more readable form in Simonson, *The Stage Is Set.*

Good books on the practice in England are Harold Ridge and F. S. Alford, *Stage Lighting* (1935), Percy Corry, *Lighting the Stage* (1958), and Rollo Gillespie Williams' two books, *Lighting for Color and Form* (1954) and *The Technique of Stage Lighting* (1960).

An early American book by Louis Hartman, who lighted David Belasco's realistic productions, is *Theatre Lighting* (1930), but more comprehensive are Theodore Fuchs, *Stage Lighting* (1929, 1965), and Selden and Sellman, *Stage Scenery and Lighting.*

The most popular simple plan of lighting is presented in Stanley McCandless, *A Method of Lighting the Stage* (1932; rev. ed., 1958). McCandless also published an outline of his course at Yale, *A Syllabus of Stage Lighting* (1958). A number of new ideas are developed in Joel Rubin and Leland H. Watson, *Theatrical Lighting Practice* (1954).

Lighting equipment, past and present, is described and illustrated in Whiting, *An Introduction to the Theatre,* and the purposes of light from medieval times to the present are discussed in George R. Kernodle, "The Magic of Light," *Theatre Arts,* XXVI (Nov., 1942). The relation of lighting to modern art, especially Impressionism, is suggested in Kernodle, "Wagner, Appia, and the Idea of Musical Design," *Educational Theatre Journal,* VI (1954).

For scenic effects projected by light, Thomas Wilfred, *Projected Scenery: A Technical Manual,* published in the twenties and reprinted in 1965, is good. Stark Young describes Wilfred's experiments in projecting moving color in "The Color Organ," *Theatre Arts,* VI (Jan., 1922). A recent book is Edward F. Kook, *Images in Light for the Living Stage: A Survey of the Use of Scenic Projection* (1963).

* Available in paperback edition.

SUGGESTED READING

CHAPTER FOURTEEN

NEW STAGES AND
THEATRE AUDITORIUMS

The concept of stage space has been radically altered by the invention of the electric lamp, which makes it possible to define the playing area with light. For four centuries the playing area had been defined by a proscenium frame and a full painted picture. As spotlights were developed at the end of the nineteenth century and as their possibilities were explored in this century, they made obsolete the old painted picture and its frame; the picture space became a sculptural space. Instead of standing in front of a distant cloth painting, the actor moved on and around a three-dimensional structure. The painted backdrop with its finite trees, clouds, and birds gave way to the infinite space of the sky cyclorama. The proscenium frame and the wings and side walls of settings faded into the darkness at the edge of the picture as the stage space was defined by pools of light from invisible sources above the stage.

This *space stage* was developed within the traditional proscenium arch, sometimes with a specially designed inner proscenium to frame the sky cyclorama and hide the equipment that sent down the pools of light. But once the space was established as complete in itself and independent of the proscenium picture, it was easy to accept the idea of a space stage outside the proscenium entirely, in the middle of the audience as an arena or theatre-in-the-round or on the stage apron with the audience only partly surrounding it. The three forms that have evolved in recent years—the space stage set up behind a regular proscenium arch, the arena stage, and the open or thrust stage—are closely related.

The Space Stage

The space stage is the logical development from Appia's analysis of the elements that create a living three-dimensional form on the stage: the floor levels and screens, the moving actor, and the changing beams of light that unite the actor and the setting. For most of his designs, Appia wanted a sky cyclorama as a backing, and he did not question the use of the proscenium frame to mask his lighting instruments and the edge of the picture. As his light plots show, however, he expected to use the pools of light to isolate one action at a time, and the acting levels and abstract forms required the audience to create the illusion in the imagination. Thus Appia can be considered the father of the space stage.

A space stage usually has several acting levels, to which may be added simple scenic pieces, either completely abstract or merely suggestive of reality, lightweight enough to be brought on by hand or let down from above. It is seen in its simplest form in the sketch by Robert Edmond Jones of a Berlin production of *Man and the Masses,* which shows a lone woman and the mass caught up in pools of light (FIGURE *13.33*). Two other examples can be seen in the pictures of a production of *Lamp at Midnight* at Brigham Young University (FIGURE *14.1*). In one, an informal group on several levels is kneeling to authority; a heraldic symbol hanging above them reinforces the theme without reference to a particular place. In the other, the steps are arranged in more formal symmetry while metal grilles, one small arch, and praying figures create the atmosphere of a church. The treatment of space is so free that a character standing in front of the island of steps may be thought of either as in the particular church or as somewhere else but aware of the church in general.

Robert Edmond Jones in *The Dramatic Imagination* suggested a permanent structure for the stage that could be adapted to many scenes and plays by the addition or removal of small elements and variation of the effects through light and the grouping of the actors:

> . . . A structure of great beauty, existing in dignity, a Precinct set apart. It will be distinguished, austere, sparing in detail, rich in suggestion . . . [creating] a high mood of awe and eagerness. Like the great stages of the past, it will be an integral part of the structure of the theatre itself, fully visible at all times . . . continually varied by changes of light . . . animated through the movement of its actors . . . related to the particular drama in question by slight and subtle indications of place and mood, by ingenious arrangements of the necessary properties, by the grouping of the actors, by an evocative use of sound and light.

Jacques Copeau created a permanent stage which he could modify, in a small theatre in Paris early in this century, and a permanent background

The Play in Production

FIGURE *14.1* Space stage in a proscenium theatre. Two scenes show how changes are made by rearranging the step units, letting down a heraldic symbol, and bringing on a grille and arch. A large sky cyclorama for mood lighting is framed by formal elements at the sides and above. Stavis' *Lamp at Midnight*. Brigham Young University production, directed by Harold Hansen, designed by Charles Henson, and costumed by Beverly Warner.

is used in the large Festival Theatre at Stratford, Ontario. But most designers, whether working on a proscenium stage or on an open stage, like to create a different structure for each play.

The space stage is a happy solution for the revival of old plays. In using modern lighting and sculptural forms it is more dynamic than any supposedly authentic reproduction of the stages for which the plays were written, yet not so heavy as a series of realistic settings would be. Many earlier theatres resembled the modern space stage, and often some important aspect of the original stage is incorporated into a free-standing structure, which is given decorative details to suggest the milieu of the play and is set in front of a cyclorama or plain curtain or an appropriately decorated curtain or screen. A space-stage setting for *Antony and Cleopatra* may achieve the panoramic sweep of Elizabethan staging with its several levels and playing areas but at the same time in its shape and decoration suggest Egypt rather than the Elizabethan period, and in its simplicity and dynamic lighting please modern taste. For *Othello,* Robert Edmond Jones designed a splendid Renaissance screen which, with a few changes, suggested a Venetian throne room, a street, or the bedroom. For a production of *King Lear* at the University of Iowa, William Molyneux designed an imposing medieval tower and parapet that, by the drawing of a curtain, the hanging of a tapestry, or the arrival of attendants with banners, changed readily for the various scenes in and around the several castles (FIGURE *14.2*). The sky

FIGURE *14.2* Space stage for Shakespeare. The steps and platforms of the modern space stage are combined with the inner and upper stages of the Elizabethan theatre in a setting that vaguely suggests a castle. *King Lear*. University of Iowa production, directed by George R. Kernodle, designed by William Molyneux, and costumed by Ethelyn Pauley.

FIGURE *14.3* Space stage for a classic play. One sculptural form against a dark background is used for the entire play. Sophocles' *Oedipus*. State Theatre production, Darmstadt, Germany, designed by Franz Mertz. Photo Pit Ludwig.

above indulged the modern feeling for openness and its changes of color and intensity, from blood red to tempest green, helped to create mood. The witty setting designed by Preston Magruder for Frank McMullan's production of *The Merry Wives of Windsor* at the University of Arkansas is illustrated in FIGURE *5.19*. The complex structure, with much more suggestion of an actual Tudor street than the Elizabethan stage would have shown, had formal entrances and an inner stage curtain, and it provided a series of interiors that allowed one scene to flow into the next as easily as in any "authentic" antiquarian production.

For Molière and Restoration comedy, designers in the early twentieth century liked to use an antiquarian reproduction of the apron-proscenium stage, with footlights and chandeliers, an inner proscenium with formal doors, and, on the inner stage, wings that slid out and a backdrop that rose out of sight to disclose the next setting (FIGURES *8.10, 8.11*). But recent designers have felt that they could catch as much of the period charm in free-standing screens shaped and decorated to suggest the period, set against either the sky or in front of a draped curtain (FIGURE *8.13*). Revivals of Chinese plays may imitate the canopy and decorative background of the Chinese stage (FIGURES *1.24, 1.25, 1.26*). But when Magruder designed a setting for *Lady Precious Stream*, he preferred to dramatize the formal entrances as moon doors and set a lightly decorated, free-standing screen behind the acting areas, which were shaped by the actors and the pools of light.

The triumph of the space stage is the scenic projection. Instead of lighting the rounded cyclorama to show the vast space of the empty sky, the designer may use the large cyclorama or a smaller reflecting screen as a backing for a projected photograph or image. The projection box, a simple device with a strong light behind a piece of transparent plastic, may

461

FIGURE *14.4*   Projection of a shadow design as a background for dancers.
A lighting demonstration at Yale University.

be hidden above or below, either in front of the screen or, if the screen is translucent, behind it. The image can fade in or fade out and can be changed as quickly as the piece of plastic on which it is drawn can be slid out and in or the current turned on for another box. The image may be a simple decorative shadow, as in FIGURE *14.4,* or it may be a phantom of the mind, as in Robert Edmond Jones' sketch in FIGURE *14.5*. We have seen how a projection added bizarre grandeur to the sewer crap game in *Guys and Dolls* (FIGURE *2.27*). The projection may even be extremely realistic, as in the Seattle street scene of FIGURE *14.6,* where the building seems to be just behind the men on the platform. Yet the projection, by being obviously a picture and not actuality, may easily serve as an ideogram or symbol rather than an immediate background. For instance, the University of Illinois production of *All the King's Men* showed characters in a room in the state capitol, but the projected background, shown only at the beginning of scenes, was a sketch of the whole State House (FIGURE *14.7*).

Once the space stage had been accepted, the standard theatre with front curtain and picture frame for box sets or painted drops, and even the cyclorama, seemed obsolete. If a pool of light can begin a scene by bringing form out of darkness and end it with a blackout or fade-out, there is no need for a front curtain. If the pool of light can define the edge of the playing area, then a box set needs no ceiling and no side walls, but only enough of a wall to suggest a place or provide the doors, pictures, and furniture essential in the action. If there is neither painted landscape nor realistic wall to be lifted out of sight into the flies but only

The Play in Production

FIGURE *14.5* Projection to fade in or out. Richard sees the ghost of Lady Anne in Shakespeare's *Richard III*. Sketch by Robert Edmond Jones for a New York production. From Ralph Pendleton, *The Theatre of Robert Edmond Jones.*

FIGURE *14.6* Projected realistic background. *The Dream and the Deed,* a civic pageant-drama of Seattle, designed by John A. Conway.

FIGURE *14.7* Projected scenery as a symbol. An exterior view of the state capitol
building establishes the location, although the scene on the stage takes place
inside the building. Warren's *All the King's Men*. University of Illinois production,
directed by Wesley Swanson and designed by Joseph W. Scott.

light sculptural pieces, there is no need for the vast space above the stage
nor for the elaborate machinery of ropes and pulleys, fly lines and counter-
weights. Even the cyclorama, that lighted vision of the vast sky, is changing in
function and form. It too has been an enclosing element, framed by the
proscenium or seen through openings in the picture setting, showing no
edges of its own. But as the action is brought forward in free space, the sky
can be indicated by a pool of light on a wall of the theatre building or
seen as a free-standing screen. James Hull Miller has on some occasions
divided that free-standing screen into several panels presenting framed sections of sky, like a Japanese screen or a Renaissance arcade. If in freedom of
time and place the modern theatre is approaching the conventional theatre
of China, it differs radically in having dynamic lighting and expressive
sculptural forms.

It is no wonder that new theatres now being built differ widely from the
traditional theatre of the picture frame. Convinced that the actors should be
brought into close relation with the audience, the advocates of new theatre
forms have denounced the proscenium theatre as a relic of Victorian conventionality. They point out that most of the great theatres of the past—the
Greek, the medieval, the Elizabethan, the Chinese, the Japanese Noh—
were open stages, not overwhelmed with scenery, that set the actor in an
easy relationship to the audience. Even for the first two centuries of the
picture stage, the actor came forward on an apron, and the scenery was kept
back on an inner stage as symbol rather than as enclosing prison. Only in the
nineteenth century, with the turn toward realism, was the actor pulled back
into the setting and cut off from the audience. The traditional theatre

464

The Play in Production

FIGURE *14.8* Projection from rear on a translucent screen. Both diffused colored light from floodlights and a cut-out pattern are projected on the same screen. Drawn by James Hull Miller. Courtesy of Hub Electric Co.

seems perversely devised to make the actor hard to hear; the tall loft for lifting scenery is a sound trap, the proscenium and inner framing units cut off sound and bounce it back into the wings, and realistic convention does not even permit the actor to face full front. Sean O'Casey called the picture-frame stage "the stage of the time of the sedan chair, the stage-coach, the candle, the silk-and-satin-clad ladies and gents that had become wholly separate from the people." Sean Kenny, a young English disciple of Frank Lloyd Wright who advocates open stages, has denounced the "shocking, chaotic mess" of the proscenium theatre, "those hysterical Victorian Birdcages." Such advocates are ready for the more open forms of the stage that bring the actor out close to the audience. It is, after all, but one step from the space stage behind the proscenium to a space stage outside the proscenium.

The Arena Stage, or Theatre-in-the-Round

Abandoning the proscenium theatre makes it possible to put the play right in the center of the audience, with the actors almost touching the first row. On the movie screen and in television the audience can see full facial expression in close-up. Arena is the theatre's own close-up. The audience foregoes spectacular effects and elaborate sets in exchange for a more direct contact with the actors.

When people first attend a performance in the round, they tend to avoid the front row and try to look away if the actors are close and facing their way. But they soon get used to the form, and their response, especially laughter, is often reinforced by the audience responding on the other side of the playing area. In the eighteenth-century playhouse, the spectators sat under bright lights, in gilded boxes, and turned and smiled at one another as they responded to the play. They enjoyed belonging to a secure "society." They enjoyed themselves at the theatre. The audience around an open stage recaptures something of that eighteenth-century social glitter, in

465

New Stages and Theatre Auditoriums

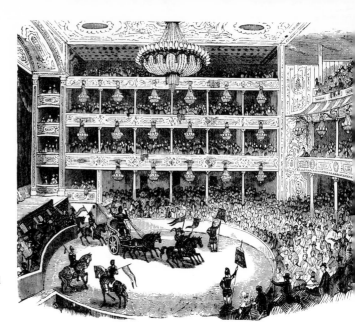

FIGURE *14.9* A large nineteenth-century proscenium theatre converted into an arena theatre for spectacular shows. Astley's Amphitheatre in London.

sharp contrast to moviegoers, who, alone or in couples, like to lose themselves and forget the world in a dark auditorium.

Glenn Hughes, who started the whole movement in college theatres in the early 1930s, saw the arena stage as primarily a form for drawing-room comedy, and his first theatre, called the Penthouse, had only three rows of seats—172 in all—and a playing area little larger than a twelve-by-eighteen-foot rug. For most plays he used different arrangements of one specially built set of light-colored, low-backed sofas and chairs. Others have used the form with much larger audiences and with almost all kinds of plays. Margo Jones, who in the 1950s ran a successful professional theatre-in-the-round in Dallas, thought the only type of drama not suited to it would be scenes of violence and horror that would unnerve an audience sitting so close to the actors. Her theatre seated only 198, with a playing stage of twenty-by-twenty-four feet. But the splendid Arena Stage in Washington has a stage thirty-by-thirty-six feet and seats 752 in eight steeply banked rows. The Lambertville Music Circus seats 1,300, and Casa Mañana, the music circus in Fort Worth, seats 1,832 under its aluminum dome.

There are special problems in producing in the round. With the audience on all sides, every actor has his back to part of the audience at any moment. It is as hard for him to send his voice around back of him as to project it in the larger, standard theatre. Arena is not a theatre of whispers. Only occasionally can the actor make the rear as visually expressive as the front; Margo Jones tells of the actress playing Lady Bracknell in *The Importance of Being Earnest* who reacted to Jack Worthing with a false smile on her face and a bounce to her bustle. She got the same laugh from both sides of the house. In most scenes the one who listens is as interesting as the one who speaks, and there can usually be some face to watch even for those directly back of the speaker. But the director must move the actors around more

466

The Play in Production

than on the regular stage. No actor whose reactions are important can be left
sitting very long, and arena performers are on their feet during most of
the play. To make sure that all parts of the audience see some of each scene,
the characters do what Margo Jones called "making the rounds." The
stage area is like a wheel with imaginary spokes, and a director hopes that
he is not being too obvious in moving characters in toward the center on
one spoke and out on another. With more than two or three characters, the
problem of attention gets more complicated. As there are no weak areas,
no one can be subordinated unless he is seated very low or pulled back into
the entrance aisle. Attention is achieved mostly by movement and animation,
and of course the listeners on stage must be moved occasionally before one
part of the audience gets tired of having a particular character block the
others. For large groups it is helpful to have different floor levels on the
playing area, with important people stepping to the top (FIGURES *14.10,
14.11*). At Casa Mañana there are steps down from the acting platform,
on which minor characters often sit, still part of the scene but allowing the
audience to see over them. A musical chorus is turned outward from the
center, with part of the chorus playing in each direction; for smaller group
specialties, the rest of the chorus is taken offstage or brought to the floor
while three couples easily fill a large playing area with choreography in
three dimensions.

FIGURE *14.10*   Arena staging with the rich texture of local color suggested by fragments
of scenery. A small-town yard and back porch are suggested by the flowers and the
low board fence built into one corner. The steps and platform give a variety of levels.
Inge's *Picnic*. Eastern Illinois University production, directed by
E. G. Gabbard and designed by John E. Bielenberg.

FIGURE *14.11* Variety in a large group in arena staging. The acting is realistic but no attempt is made at scenery beyond abstract blocks for sitting and standing.
At the moment two centers of action are competing for audience attention, and characters are given emphasis by their degree of involvement in the action.
Première of Arzoomanian's *The Trespassers*. University of Iowa production, directed by Philip Henson.

FIGURE *14.12* Scenic decoration for the arena stage. Period details, suggested by the medieval paintings of Giotto, are held above eye level by slender columns. Shakespeare's *Much Ado About Nothing*.
University of Washington production, designed by John A. Conway.
Photo Dorothy Conway.

FIGURE *14.13* Scenic decoration for the arena stage. Chinese pavilions in two corners can be used either as entrances or as canopies for a judge's bench or an emperor's throne. Note the bridge in one corner for entrances. *The Circle of Chalk*. University of Arkansas production, directed by George R. Kernodle, designed by Preston Magruder, and costumed by Charles Martinelli.

More scenic decoration is possible in theatre-in-the-round than might be guessed. Columns, arches, and pavilions and light, cut-out outline forms can be used even in the center and still allow action to be seen (FIGURE *14.12*). At the corners there may even be rather realistic walls, windows, and doors, if they are indispensable to the action. For the Chinese play *The Circle of Chalk* at the University of Arkansas, Preston Magruder created atmosphere and color with simple structures in the corners: the orchestra box in one corner and a tall entrance bridge opposite it; a canopied niche for the judge and the emperor in a third corner; and opposite the niche, on several curving steps, a lovely open gateway for the front of the house (FIGURE *14.13*). Interior scenes easily spilled out into the center from that gateway. Built-up levels in the center are possibilities few designers have yet explored, and the Arena Stage in Washington has trap doors in the floor for trenches, openings, entrances, or even an orchestra pit (FIGURE *14.14*).

Various methods have been used for opening and closing the scene on the arena stage. To bring actors on in the dark as if by magic and have the lights go up suddenly seemed very important to Glenn Hughes, but others have objected to this method. There is noise, confusion, and danger of bumping into the audience unless the actors are drilled to perfection, and too much trickery if they are. It seems like trying to achieve the old effect of opening a curtain on an arranged tableau. If the curtain is

469

New Stages and Theatre Auditoriums

FIGURE *14.14*   A well-equipped, fairly large arena theatre seating 752 in steeply banked rows. The Arena Stage, Washington, D.C.

discarded, the innovator should have the courage of his conventions. Nine times out of ten a little rewriting will make the scene start with an entrance and end with an exit. Audiences also accept easily the convention of low lighting for the actors to get into position and full lighting for the action to begin.

FIGURE *14.15*   Arena stage arranged with the audience on three sides and a scenic unit at one end. Saroyan's *The Time of Your Life*. Eastern Illinois University production, directed by E. G. Gabbard and designed by John E. Bielenberg.

The Open, or Thrust, Stage

The exciting new theatres of the last decade have followed a form somewhere between the arena and the proscenium stage, called variously thrust, open, apron, or three-quarter-round. Like the arena, the open stage can bring a large number of spectators fairly close to the actors, with the acoustical advantage of having the actors and audience in the same room. It offers the economy of building and operating a stage without heavy scenery, but it permits much more interesting effects of scenery, grouping, and lighting than the arena.

To read Tyrone Guthrie's book, *My Life in the Theatre,* is to follow a prophet who has caught a glimpse of a distant goal. The vision that gradually came to Guthrie was the open stage. In his years as director of the Old Vic in London and as visiting director for many theatres all over the world, *471*

FIGURE *14.16* Ground plans showing the relative distance of the last row of an audience of 350 from the actor in four kinds of theatres—regular proscenium, proscenium with apron, thrust or open stage, and arena. Drawn by Don Creason after a drawing by James Hull Miller.

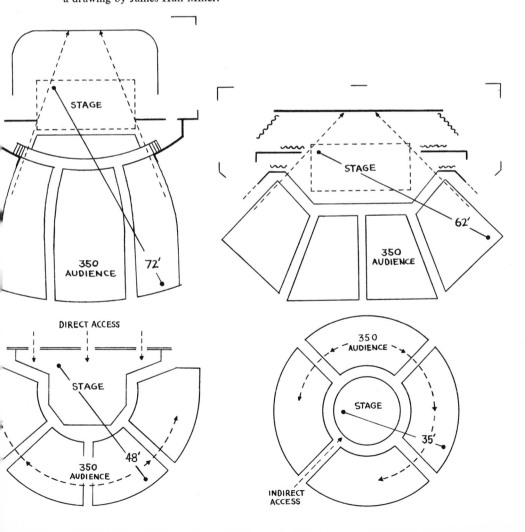

FIGURE *14.17* Open stage in the Presbyterian Assembly Hall, Edinburgh. Lindsay's
The Satire of the Three Estates. Edinburgh Festival production, directed by
Tyrone Guthrie. Drawn by Richard Leacroft. From Helen and Richard Leacroft,
The Theatre. Courtesy of Methuen and Co. Ltd., London.

he was vaguely feeling for a new form more open than the proscenium
theatre. His crucial experience was his discovery in Edinburgh of the Presbyterian Assembly Hall, a room with seats and balconies on four sides of a
central platform, much like the Elizabethan theatre. There he produced
a late medieval Scottish morality play, *The Satire of the Three Estates,* closing
one side of the room for stage entrances and background (FIGURE *14.17*). The
results were exciting. A few years later Guthrie, with the help of Tanya
Moiseiwitsch, designed a large Shakespearean theatre for the new festival
in Stratford, Ontario, and directed several of their productions (FIGURE *4.13*).
The form has been so well liked that it has inspired the Festival Theatre
of Chichester in England, which Sir Laurence Olivier opened in 1962
(FIGURE *14.19*), and also the plans for the new National Theatre in London,
designed in this open form after a half-century of discussion. When Minneapolis wanted to mark its arrival at maturity as a city, Guthrie was asked
to help plan a theatre and become its first director. The Tyrone Guthrie
Theatre is built on the model of the Stratford theatre, with a slight concession to the picture stage behind the apron.

The theatre at Stratford, Ontario, makes no concession to scenery but
offers a dark-colored, formal background of entrances, doors, and steps,
with a pavilion and columns supporting a podium above. Color and life are
supplied by the actors, who can enter from several directions, including
ramps or steps from below the stage. The auditorium extends in more
than a semicircle, like the Greek amphitheatre, and has a balcony above,
providing a total of 2,254 seats, the farthest only seventy feet from the
stage, closer than the back row of some theatres a third the size. The Minneapolis theatre is smaller, seating about 1,400, with no seat more than
fifty-four feet from the platform, which is a little off center. It has no formal

The Play in Production

FIGURE *14.18* Realistic scene on the open stage. A strong sense of enclosed reality is created without walls. Chekhov's *The Three Sisters*. The Tyrone Guthrie Theatre, Minneapolis.

FIGURE *14.19* The large open stage. Sir Laurence Olivier helped to plan the Festival Theatre, Chichester, England, for the company that became the National Theatre Company of England.

FIGURE *14.20* Open stage with three centers of action—a sloping platform built on the central turntable and two side platforms. Kalita Humphreys Theatre, Dallas Theatre Center.

façade but does have a shallow fly loft which permits a change of painted backdrops to be combined with movable three-dimensional structures in front. The theatre is planned for a wider range of plays, classic and modern, than the Ontario theatre.

The open form was used by Frank Lloyd Wright for the Dallas Theatre Center, an intimate theatre he designed near the end of his life (FIGURE *14.20*). It has a revolving stage, and the entire stage area is built on the same curved line, with side stages and upper balconies to extend the playing areas. The loft permits small units of scenery to be lifted out of sight, but the

FIGURE *14.21* The small open stage. The extension of the stage along the walls of the auditorium is sometimes called a "caliper stage." Swarthmore College. Rebuilt to designs by James Hull Miller. Courtesy of Hub Electric Co.

theatre is intended primarily for plastic elements of setting to be brought on or turned around on the revolving stage in front of sky or drapes.

The most daring American advocate of the open stage is James Hull Miller, who has created a number of free-form theatres in a variety of styles. Instead of two rooms, one for the audience and one for actors, he thinks of a theatre as a single architectural space, with entranceways for the actors and flat walls or screens for projected backgrounds. The ceilings are acoustical canopies common to actors and audience and are provided with slots that may be used for lighting or for curtains. Miller believes that decor should be free-standing central accents about which the characters move—scenery not as perimeter but as nucleus. Instead of painted wings and backdrop or box set to enclose the actors and fill out the picture up to a frame, he uses scenic islands such as a tower or small platform with properties and a window or doorway, or a fragment of wall. Sometimes a shape or an object can serve as a signal of the locality or as an ideogram. Instead of a cyclorama to enclose and fill out the picture, he uses slabs of the theatre wall cut by openings for actors' entrances. He projects scenic elements and colors, either on the walls or, preferably, on portable self-standing screens set up in front of the wall. Since there is no elaborate rigging to fly heavy scenery, the instruments for scenic projection may be housed overhead or behind the translucent screens. Miller's plans have been particularly useful for low-cost public school theatres.

The neatest summary of the open stage has been given by the English theatre historian, Richard Southern. After observing that most of the great theatres of the past—Oriental, Greek, and Elizabethan—have had audience on three sides and a conventional scenic backing for the fourth, he gives this formula for the ideal and universal theatre: take any room and put a stage against one wall; open the four traditional access ways to it in the wall (left, right, and center doors, and an "above"); add the "booth," or players' rooms behind the stage; rake the seating floor; provide for a gallery for looking diagonally down on the stage.

The strongest protests against the open stage have come from the British drama critic Kenneth Tynan. He calls the open stage a "stuck-out stage," a "peninsula," a "promontory," or the stage that "sticks out its tongue at the audience." He strongly attacked the festival hall at Chichester on the grounds that the stage was so vast that even the proximity argument failed: the wide stage put the actor on the opposite side of the stage farther away from the first row of spectators than he would have been from people in the twelfth row of a proscenium theatre. Tynan felt that the large open stage was wrong for any play that made use of verbal nuance and that Olivier's own style, developed on the proscenium stage, was lost on the large open stage. Tynan was aghast when it was announced that the new English National Theatre would have a large theatre of the open-stage form and a small one of the proscenium type. When the Mermaid Theatre of London produced Ibsen's *John Gabriel Borkman* on its Elizabethan-type stage, he felt justified in his objection. "You cannot," he wrote in his review in *The Ob-*

server, "take a play that depends on an atmosphere of imprisonment and claustrophobia and stage it without walls or ceiling. Like the prospect of being hanged, the proscenium stage concentrates one's mind wonderfully, and Ibsen the realist is lost without it." He maintained that "the more-or-less straight-edged stage (preferably stripped of its proscenium framing) remains the most cunning and intimate method yet devised for transmitting plays to playgoers."

Yet the open stage has been quite successfully used even for very realistic plays. Tynan himself found Olivier's production of Chekhov's *Uncle Vanya* at Chichester extremely effective, and the illustration of the Cleveland Playhouse production of *The Deadly Game* on an open stage shows that it is quite possible to give a strong suggestion of enclosure and rich realistic atmosphere with a free-standing setting of a wall, even with no ceiling and very limited depth (FIGURE *14.23*). When some of the productions of Max Reinhardt were being discussed in 1936, one London critic wrote angrily, "The Reinhardt gang has never realized that to venture one inch beyond the proscenium arch destroys the whole illusion so laboriously created. This is the age of the picture stage and even if you are twelve German producers rolled into one, you cannot put the clock back. You may put something in illusion's place, but that isn't what I want." The critic himself was the one trying to put the clock back. Now it is completely acceptable, even in forms of realism, to bring the play into a more direct relationship with the audience. Then what could be better than to build the kind of stage that encourages such a relationship?

FIGURE *14.22* Open stage of an outdoor festival theatre. Delacorte Theatre, Central Park, New York. A rehearsal of *King Lear,* directed by Joseph Papp. Drawn by Claude Marks. Museum of the City of New York.

FIGURE *14.23* Realistic setting on an open stage. A small three-dimensional unit is used where background is needed, and the rest of the area is backed by black masking wings or black drapes. Duerrenmatt's *The Deadly Game.* Euclid-Seventy-Seventh Street Theatre of The Cleveland Playhouse.

The Multiform Theatre

Since there is so much disagreement about the ideal form for the theatre, since some directors prefer a proscenium and some an open stage, since some plays seem better suited to one form and some to another, the best solution might be a compromise, a multiform theatre that could be used in more than one way. There is one obvious difficulty: the side seats of the auditorium, if spread around a thrust stage, will have impossible sight lines when the setting and actors are behind a proscenium. It is not easy to cut the side seats off with screens or curtains, and it is very bad to leave them empty—nobody likes to see empty seats. Is some compromise possible? Many suggestions have been offered for a multipurpose building. But the protests at most of them have been loud: "An all-purpose theatre is a no-purpose theatre"; "A compromise theatre has no form of its own"; "If you try to please everybody, you please nobody."

The most ingenious solution is to make whole sections of the auditorium mobile. Several projects were drawn in the 1920s, notably one for a convertible theatre that would become a proscenium theatre or an arena as the circular center section of the building revolved. Now the Loeb Drama Center at Harvard offers a similar solution, with electronically controlled machinery to make the change. A large center section of the floor holds seats when the proscenium stage is used. These seats can be rolled off and the floor raised to make a thrust stage. When the seats are placed on the proscenium stage, the   *477*

FIGURE *14.24* The large convertible theatre. Electronically controlled changes
in the platforms and seating can make either a proscenium theatre or an open stage.
Notice the many openings in the ceiling for lights. The Vivian Beaumont Theatre
in the Lincoln Center for the Performing Arts, New York City. Photo Ezra Stoller.

floor becomes the center of an arena. The new Vivian Beaumont Theatre at
Lincoln Center in New York is likewise convertible. In one arrangement it is
a not-quite-semicircular amphitheatre with a balcony, facing a proscenium
stage. But it is equipped with a large lift and turntable system that can replace
about sixty orchestra seats with an open stage of extreme thrust (FIGURE
14.24). Such equipment is extremely expensive, costing sometimes almost as
much as two theatres would cost.

All theatre people agree that the multiform plan is excellent for the small
studio theatre, especially as an experimental theatre for students. Several
universities have small studio theatres with sections of the floor mechanized
to change quickly in level, providing many different combinations of levels.
For the small room that would seat a hundred or less it is possible to make
many changes by hand, to move platforms, steps, and ramps for the acting
areas, and to put tiers of audience seats down one side, all at the end or
on two or three sides, or even to change between scenes to provide whatever
audience-actor relationship the director wants to try. Such a room should
be neutral in wall decoration, with beams visible above for lighting equipment. For such a functional room many directors would want to use plain,
flexible screens and pylons to suggest environment. But there is nothing to
prevent the designer from providing portable sculptural forms or even self-
standing painted pictures as scenery. At first it may be a pleasure to see

478

The Play in Production

the crude, unadorned lighting equipment, but some designers like to plan more pleasing sculptural forms to contain the sources of light.

The only complete solution, it seems, is to have more than one theatre and to use each one for the kind of play and production it best serves. Many schools and communities need an auditorium seating two thousand or more for large meetings, concerts, operas, and spectacles. But that size is virtually impossible for plays and even for the more intimate operas. The ideal lyric theatre for musicals, small operas, dance programs, and some plays should not seat more than 1,500. For amateur actors, dramatic theatres are being built to seat from 300 to 600, and the most popular arena theatres are even smaller. Lincoln Center in New York is merely an extension of the interest, developed in many colleges and community centers, in having a number of theatres, each devised for a special purpose. Lincoln Center offers in one planned area Philharmonic Hall for concerts, the Metropolitan Opera House, the New York State Theatre for operetta and dance, and the Vivian Beaumont Theatre, containing not only the changeable-form theatre just described but also "The Forum," a small open-apron stage planned especially for readings and tryouts of new plays. The Kennedy Center for the Performing Arts in Washington is planned to contain four theatres in one building: a large concert hall, an opera house, a proscenium theatre seating 1,100, and a 500-seat convertible experimental theatre.

New generations try new forms of theatre. The proscenium was a new frame for a magic picture in the sixteenth century, a picture made more amazing when in the seventeenth century ways of changing the entire setting

FIGURE *14.25* Four theatre buildings and a school in the Lincoln Center for the Performing Arts, New York City. Philharmonic Hall for concerts is in the foreground, and the New York State Theatre for operetta and dance is at the left. The Metropolitan Opera House, with an arched portico, is in the back. The Vivian Beaumont Theatre is in the center, and the Juilliard School is at the right. Photo Bob Serating.

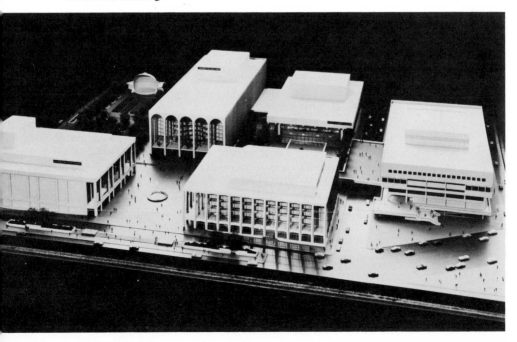

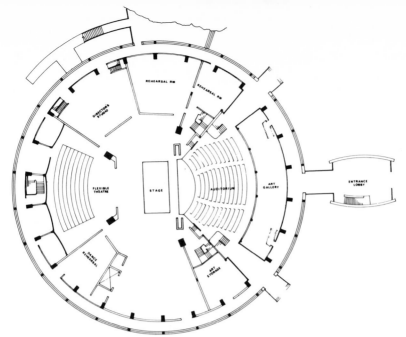

FIGURE *14.26* One theatre building with a small, flexible theatre, an auditorium with an open stage, and several rehearsal rooms. Ground plan of the theatre building at Brandeis University.

were invented. In our age electric lighting is the new means of giving shape to the acting area, while movies, recorded sound, and electronic tapes have opened up further possibilities. Epic theatre has made interesting combinations of old processional forms and new machines for projecting movies, words, and images. Just as the movies and then television created a separate form of theatre, so there may sometime be a theatre of electronic sounds, projected images, and mobile forms changing in mobile light.

SUGGESTED READING

European arena productions received high praise in Kenneth Macgowan and Robert Edmond Jones, *Continental Stagecraft* (1922). The intimate arena for comedy, as developed by Glenn Hughes, is described in his *The Penthouse Theatre* (1935; rev. ed., 1958). The techniques and hopes of Margo Jones are described in her *Theatre in the Round* (1951).

Good chapters on directing in the arena may be found in John Gassner, *Producing the Play* (rev. ed., 1953), and Lawrence Carra's revised edition of Alexander Dean, *Fundamentals of Play Directing* (1965), and on designing for arena in Orville K. Larson, *Stage Design for Stage and Screen* (1961). Richard Southern traces some early arenas in *The Medieval Theatre in the Round* (1957) and some modern British ideas for both arena and three-quarter-round in *The Open Stage* (1959), and he compares the open-stage forms of many countries in *The Seven Ages of the Theatre* (1961). Lee Mitchell wrote "The Space Stage Defined" for *Theatre Arts*, XX (July, 1936). An account of the experiments in the Bauhaus in Germany that influenced new plastic and streamlined forms was

480

Oscar Schlemmer and others, *The Theatre of the Bauhaus,* published in German in 1924 and translated in 1961. The political and philosophical purposes of the open platform stage are discussed in George R. Kernodle, "The Open Stage: Elizabethan or Existentialist," *Shakespeare Survey,* XII (1959), and in Mordecai Gorelik, *New Stages for Old** (1940).

The main theme of Tyrone Guthrie's *A Life in the Theatre** (1959) is his search for a theatre outside of the proscenium. The many ways of rearranging audience and playing space in a small room are discussed in Walden P. Boyle, *Central and Flexible Staging* (1956).

The experience at Stratford, Ontario, is described in Tyrone Guthrie and Robertson Davies, *Renown at Stratford* (1953), and in Guthrie, *A Life in the Theatre.* The plans for the Tyrone Guthrie Theatre in Minneapolis have been published in many places, beginning with *Drama Survey,* I (Spring, 1961). How the plans were made and how the first plays were produced are told by Guthrie himself in *A New Theatre* (1964). The open-stage productions in Cleveland are the subject of Frederic McConnell, "Using the Open Stage: A Ten-Year Experiment at the Cleveland Playhouse," *Theatre Annual,* XVII (1960). The new building of the Washington Arena is presented in "New Image, Old Plan for Arena Stage Theatre in Washington, D.C.," *Architectural Record,* XLIII, 2 (Feb., 1962). Percy Corry, *Planning the Stage* (1961), summarizes many ideas. Discussion of the new theatres at Minneapolis and at Chichester, among others, at an international symposium in Manchester is recorded in Stephen Joseph, *Actor and Architect* (1964). An international symposium in London in 1962 is reported in a paperback pamphlet, *Adaptable Theatres,* published by the Association of British Theatre Technicians.

James Hull Miller's plans and ideas have appeared in many articles in, for example, *Progressive Architecture,* XLIII (Feb., 1962; Sept., 1962), and the *Journal of the Royal Institute of British Architects* (April, 1963; May, 1963). A profile on Miller appeared in the *National Observer* (Feb. 17, 1964). Miller himself has published *An Open-Stage Technical Manual* (1964). The Hub Electric Company has published *The Open Stage: Based on the Designs of James Hull Miller* (Bulletin No. 109, 1965).

The design and models made for the Ford Foundation project in 1960–61 are published by the American Federation of Arts, *The Ideal Theatre: Eight Concepts** (2nd ed., 1965), and they have been reproduced and commented on in many magazines: for example, *Architectural Forum,* CXVI, 1 (Jan., 1962), and *Progressive Architecture,* XLII (Dec., 1961). A number of designs for theatres under construction are presented in "The Changing Practice: Theaters," *Progressive Architecture,* XLVI (Oct., 1965). Maxwell Silverman and Ned Bowman, *Contemporary Theatre Architecture: An Illustrated Survey* (1965), present and describe some fifty recent theatres, with a full list of references to new theatre plans from 1946 to 1964.

* Available in paperback edition.

PART THREE

THE MASS MEDIA

Theatre through the camera eye is a new kind of theatre, requiring new kinds of plays for cinema, radio, and television and new conventions for their presentation. These new kinds of plays and new conventions are determined partly by new patterns of attendance and viewing. Going to the legitimate theatre is a special occasion, with a distinct social pattern, but going to the movies offers little chance for sociability and watching television offers even less. Far from being a special event, a drama on the home screen is just another daily diversion mixed in with news events, songs, chatter, and commercials. Drama in the mass media has an audience much larger than the theatre has ever had before, and it has an influence over the mind and imagination perhaps greater than any traditional art has ever had. But to gain that audience it has had to adapt to the commercial patterns of mass entertainment.

The problems of mass entertainment are part of the general problems of mass culture. For the first time in history it is possible for almost the entire population to share in a culture at

OPPOSITE   The drama of Joan of Arc performed before the camera eye. The moving camera creates images to be rearranged and reproduced on screens for audiences of millions. CBS studio.

a high level. But too few people use the new leisure and wider means of communication to enrich their lives, and every thoughtful person is aware of the cheapness and vulgarity of much that is offered in the name of popular art. Do popular programs merely exploit low taste, or do they create and perpetuate it? Will the packaged, synthetic product in time drive out all genuine art? Is there no escape from uniform mass mediocrity? Is excellence gone from the modern world?

As the movies drained off part of the audience of the legitimate theatre, the quality of stage drama improved, and as television drained off a large part of the movie audience, the quality of screen drama improved. But is good drama possible only for the minority? If so, how can better programs be paid for in the mass media? Is popular art necessarily cheap and vulgar, or can something finer be created in a popular tradition?

All three of the mass media began by fascinating the public as mechanical gadgets. In the late 1890s and early in this century, audiences crowded into rented halls and nickelodeons to watch the marvelous new moving pictures—horses, boxers, trains, anything that would move. In the 1920s Americans sat up long into the night, dialing from one radio wave length to another, listening to song, talk, or static long enough to get a station identification and then move on, eager to see how many distant stations they could find. In the late 1940s it mattered little what was broadcast, the TV screen was a fascination in itself. Out of that flickering snow emerged vague forms of distant singers, speakers, events. But as we examine the movies, the oldest of the mass media, we shall see that what started as technology has become an art—the one new art created in modern times. Is it possible that broadcast drama, too, will become an art? It is not yet entirely clear how broadcast drama differs in technique from cinema and what its possibilities are. The fact that it has a quite different relation to its audience suggests a development distinct from the older forms of theatre.

In the mid-twentieth century an American's experience of theatre begins with television and the movies. Since these media are familiar to everyone, taken for granted, we have all the more reason for examining them closely and considering what contributions they have made to dramatic art and what may be expected of them in the future.

CHAPTER FIFTEEN

FIFTY YEARS OF MOTION PICTURES

A film play is not a stage play caught by a camera and projected on a screen. The inventors of cameras and projectors were not theatre people, the promoters of the new toy were not theatre producers, and the audiences were not regular theatre patrons but people who were fascinated by the illusion of real life on the screen, the glorious animation of the photograph. Before we consider the techniques of this new art, we must see how it developed, especially as promoters found the motion picture one of the greatest moneymakers of all time.

The Early Years

The motion picture is the crowning achievement in the development of photography. Still photographs, popular though they were by the middle of the nineteenth century, were not real enough. Devices were invented for deepening the picture and giving it perspective; a stereopticon viewer became an indispensable item in the Victorian parlor. Projection of photographs on a screen by a "magic lantern" increased the reality in the 1890s and the first decade of the twentieth century. Travel lectures with projected slides were popular, and almost up to the First World War, the standard final number of a vaudeville bill was the singing of a popular song while appropriate pictures, drawn or photographed and often colored, were flashed on a screen.

FIGURE *15.1* The strong man of the West. William S. Hart, greatest of the many Western heroes of the screen.

By the 1890s it was possible to make the photographs move on the screen with a sense of reality that outdid all other kinds of pictures. Early films were advertised as "pictures, so natural that life itself is no more real" and "life motion, realism, photographed from nature so true to life as to force the observers to believe that they are viewing the reality and not the reproduction." In April, 1896, at the first public projected film performance in New York City, Edison's Vitaphone showed surf breaking on Manhattan Beach, a boxing match, a couple of vaudeville dance numbers, and the finale of a popular stage play. A few months later the American Biograph Company made its debut with a few terrifying feet of film in which the Empire State Express bore down upon the audience.

From the first, the movies captivated the public imagination. Anyone with a projection machine and a few feet of film could be sure of attracting an audience to a town hall or country schoolhouse. In 1905 the first regular movie house, or nickelodeon, was opened, and in the next five years hundreds of these places for the showing of one-reel films at a nickel a head were scattered over the country. During the early years, thousands of people who had never gone to the theatre saw the new motion pictures, and most of them quickly became addicts. Best of all they loved full-length stories with exciting action and glamorous stars.

FAVORITE TYPES OF PICTURES

Three types of pictures became special favorites of the popular audience: the Western, the spectacle, and the slapstick comedy. All were full of fast action, suspense, and excitement, and all made frequent use of the chase.

486

The Mass Media

The Western dates from 1903, when Edwin S. Porter of the Edison Company directed *The Great Train Robbery,* the first important story film made in America and the prototype of all Westerns: it had a dance-hall scene, a chase that shifted back and forth from pursued to pursuers, and a startling close-up of a bad man pointing his pistol at the audience. Only the cowboy hero was missing, and he was introduced to the screen in 1908 with "Broncho Billy" (G. M. Anderson), who appeared in many Westerns in the next few years. The strong man of the West had been popular for decades on the stage, but he seemed much more romantic on his horse in a wide landscape on the screen. Some Western movies were made in New Jersey, but the dry hills of the West offered the ideal locality to show man's dominance of the wide-open spaces. Thomas H. Ince in 1910 built Inceville on an eighteen-thousand-acre tract near Santa Monica, California, and by 1914 he had established William S. Hart as the greatest of all screen cowboys.

Since that day the popularity of the Western has never wavered. The Western hero as a pioneer in new territory and as a champion of simple right against wrong had immediate appeal in other countries as well as in America. The Western offered the audience one thing that Hollywood could do superbly: outdoor action. As the choreographer George Balanchine said in an interview in the *New York Times* in 1961:

> If you were to say to me, "What's the best thing in America, artistically the best thing?" I would reply, "Cowboys! Westerns!" The people are right for it, they know how to do what they're doing, and to me it all rings true. When I see on the screen that wonderful Nevada or Arizona space and horses galloping beautifully across it, I am instantly satisfied. I find no fault in it at all.

Screen spectacle began almost a decade after the Western. When the Italian film *Quo Vadis* in nine reels was shown at the Astor Theatre in New York on April 21, 1913, a new way was opened for the American moviemaker. No such length of film had as yet been tried by American producers, and they were impressed when a fashionable crowd paid an admission of $1.50 and sat for two hours. Three other long features made in Europe were soon shown in the United States: *The Last Days of Pompeii, Cleopatra,* and *Les Misérables,* the last a film of twelve reels released in this country in four sections.

The first American to follow this trend was David Wark Griffith, a rising young director who made a long feature of a Biblical story, *Judith of Bethulia,* in 1913. His employers, the Biograph Company, became aware of what he was doing in distant California too late to forestall him and were surprised when the picture more than paid for itself at the box office. The following year Griffith filmed *The Birth of a Nation,* the first American screen masterpiece, which had its première in February, 1915. Based on a mediocre novel, Thomas Dixon's *The Clansman,* the film owes little to the novel except the simple love story set in the South during the Civil War and the Reconstruction period. Today we are shocked at some of its content, which includes vivid scenes of the Ku Klux Klan coming to rescue white families

487

FIGURE *15.2* The big screen spectacle. The Italian film *Quo Vadis,* shown in New York in 1913, stirred the ambition of directors like D. W. Griffith. Museum of Modern Art.

from dangerous Negroes, and the film as originally shown was even more inflammatory than the version we see. Demonstrations occurred in some northern cities, notably Boston, and the film was not shown in Ohio for two years, though Lillian Gish, a star of the film, was a native of that state. Griffith, a Kentuckian whose father had been a Confederate Army officer, was surprised at the outcry. Though he denied accusations of racial prejudice and pointed out that his picture criticized the carpetbaggers and "scalawag whites" who incited the Negroes, he did cut the scenes that had been found most objectionable. The experience rankled, however, and he developed his next picture on the theme of intolerance. For most people who flocked to see *The Birth of a Nation,* it was simply an enthralling story of unsurpassed vividness and excitement. The more discriminating saw in it the marks of genius and the promise of a great artistic future for films. In *The Birth of a Nation* and *Intolerance* (1916), Griffith made great advances in the art of editing, which will be discussed in the next chapter.

One obvious effect of Griffith's films was to ensure the future of screen spectacle. After his demonstration of the possibilities of storytelling on a grand scale, the whole line of spectacles, through Cecil B. De Mille's Biblical epics of the twenties and thirties on down to the spectacles of the sixties, became inevitable.

Spectacular action had long been familiar to patrons of stage melodrama, but the old theatrical effects could not compete with the realism of the movies. Races run on a stage treadmill before spectators painted on canvas could hardly fail to seem crude if one had seen motion pictures of real horses on a real racetrack with a real crowd in a real grandstand. Who would ever again want to see the heroine lashed to a piece of track on a stage floor with a miniature cardboard train bumping toward her once he had seen her on the screen on a real track with a real locomotive bearing down, or on the edge of a real cliff ready to plunge into a real canyon, or, by the skillful use of a dummy, actually seeming to do so to escape the pursuing villain? Stage spectacle that aimed at a reproduction of reality was doomed. The stage version of *Ben Hur* of 1899, which has been described in the chapter on the romantic play, was already almost an anachronism.

Similarly, the chase as the thrilling climax of a story of action was not a discovery of the moviemakers, but they did it so well that chase sequences of the nineteenth-century stage were better forgotten. In 1874, the entire last act of the stage version of *Oliver Twist* presented two chase sequences, the first between Nancy Sikes and the Fagin crowd and the second between the Fagin crowd and the law. Throughout the second half of the nineteenth century and even the first decade of the twentieth century, Eliza crossed the ice, pursued by bloodhounds and ruthless men, in hundreds of stage productions of *Uncle Tom's Cabin*. But in being able to photograph pursuit in actual country and to work with film that could be cut and spliced instead of with clumsy stage scenery to be shifted, the moviemakers had an insuperable advantage over producers for the stage. To this day, even in rather sophisticated films, the chase, whether for thrills or laughter, remains one of the greatest pleasures of moviegoing.

Slapstick comedy made equally good use of the fast action, the spectacular dangers, and the chase that were characteristic of the silent film. In 1912 Mack Sennett, who had been working in pictures for several years, set up his Keystone Company and created the Keystone Cops, the most popular comic figures of the early American films. Sennett was ingenious in concocting variants of simple formulas, and he developed remarkable teamwork among his comedians. To see a dozen Keystone Cops tumble out of a car too small to hold them and scramble after an offender, all falling over the same obstacles, rolling down hill or piling up in a ditch, delighted the popular audience. Sennett's Bathing Beauties added sex appeal, winking, giggling, and fleeing in mock alarm from their admirers with almost as much action and speed as the cops. Sennett's cameramen found a rich field in trick photography, slowing, speeding, suspending, or reversing action and creating all possible illusions of peril—falling from high places, being buried in the debris of buildings, or being run over by vehicles of all kinds.

It was not until the movies were well established that they began to borrow extensively from stage drama or the novel. At first New York actors were contemptuous of the popular form, but by 1912 there was enough money in film acting to attract them, and two movie companies, headed respectively by Adolph Zukor and Jesse Lasky, were formed to present famous actors and actresses in their stage successes. The two joined in 1916 to form the Paramount Company, with the avowed purpose of bringing to the screen the best dramas played by the greatest actors. Many nineteenth-

489

century fiction classics were filmed with just enough adaptation to fit the popular patterns of love, heroism, sacrifice, and a triumphant happy ending. It was only gradually that moviemakers came to realize that a good play or a good novel could become a good film only if the director knew how to use the special possibilities of the screen.

The greatest shortcoming of the movies was the superficiality of the vision of life they provided. The screen gives physical reality; in fact, no other medium can do it so well. But reality of the story is another matter. In moving pictures there was until the last three decades comparatively little effort to achieve psychological, ethical, or "literary" truth. Susanne Langer calls the cinema the "dream mode" among the arts. Swinging with the camera freely through time and space, the moviegoer experiences events in the unhampered manner of the dream. Movement of camera and of objects and people gives a sense of freedom, and, like the dreamer, the spectator readily identifies with the hero or first with one and then another character as the action dictates. In the darkened theatre, immersed in undemanding atmospheric music, the spectator finds an outlet in this daydream for his desire for luxury, power, independence, or adoration. It early became the business of Hollywood, which has been called the "dream factory," to supply the tales that fit the frustrations and yearnings, largely unconscious, of the masses.

THE MAKING OF THE STARS

A very important part of the dream was the stars with whom the audience could identify. The first producers did not think of advertising particular actors; their names were not even given on the screen. But soon the public demanded the names of their favorites, and of these the list was soon headed by the Biograph Company girl with the long curls: Mary Pickford. By 1913 she had made 125 one-reel pictures and was one of the three or four greatest drawing cards on the screen. She left the film company that year to play on the stage in David Belasco's *The Good Little Devil,* thinking she was leaving the screen forever. But she found that the admirers who hung around the stage door were people who had seen her in pictures, and she was swept back into the movies by her fans. She made a film of *The Good Little Devil* and embarked on her long career as "America's Sweetheart" and one of the most highly paid stars. Her forte was sentimental roles like Pollyanna or Little Lord Fauntleroy, but she was often cast in tomboyish parts in which the show of physical energy was all the more effective because of her soft features. She was remembered as the dream girl of an innocent public, portraying domestic virtues and noble ideals whether her stories were set in western plains, city slums, or the homes of the wealthy. At a retrospective showing of her films in Paris in 1965, some critics were surprised to discover that she was an extraordinarily gifted entertainer with not only the pathos but the humor of Dickens and a flair for slapstick.

Among the stars to win fame before the First World War, even more important than "Little Mary" was Charlie Chaplin. When Mack Sennett re-

FIGURE *15.3* Mary Pickford on her way to stardom. "Little Mary" plays the oldest of the three children, an appealing young girl with curls. *The Lonely Villa,* 1909, directed by D. W. Griffith. Museum of Modern Art.

placed one of his comedians with a member of an English music-hall troupe that had been touring the United States, he could not know that he was launching one of the greatest careers of motion pictures by bringing a genius to the screen. In his second assignment with the Sennett Company, Chaplin adopted on the spur of the moment the costume that was to become his trademark. It was put together, as he tells in his autobiography, out of oddments that were too large or too small—baggy trousers and tight coat, big shoes and small derby hat—with small moustache and cane for the finishing touches, and the little tramp character to go with the costume was gradually created. Chaplin had left the music-hall company at a salary of $60 a week to take $150 a week with Sennett. A year later he joined the Essanay Company at a salary of $1,250 a week, and in 1917, at the age of twenty-eight, he signed a contract for a million dollars to deliver eight films in eighteen months. The costume, the walk, and the personality of the little tramp were copied in dolls, toys, and a dance called "The Chaplin Walk." Chaplin's status as a star was demonstrated in a striking way when in 1916 he went by train on a vacation trip to New York. At Amarillo, Texas, he was dragged out of the dressing room with lather still on his face to be greeted by the mayor and a crowd the police could hardly handle. Telegraph operators, relaying a message he had sent to his brother in New York, had passed the word to the press. Crowds even larger awaited him in Kansas City and Chicago, and in Chicago he received a wire from the chief of police in New York asking him to get off the train at the 125th Street station, since people   *491*

Fifty Years of Motion Pictures

were already gathering at Grand Central Station a day before his expected arrival. The New York newspapers had issued regular bulletins since he left Los Angeles. Later, when he made a world tour, equally enthusiastic crowds greeted him in London, Paris, and Tokyo.

Many other stars became objects of adulation during this early period. Wallace Reid was one of half a dozen actors of romantic roles who acquired a large following of women fans. Most of the female stars played "good" women, some of them more sophisticated than "Little Mary," but Theda Bara made the "vamp" type popular and in 1917 reached the climax of her career in the portrayal of the historical prototype of the *femme fatale,* Cleopatra (FIGURE *17.1*). In the end the star system gave the film business security. The price paid for a popular actor was high, but once the contract was signed, he ensured high box-office returns for any film in which he appeared.

Motion Pictures as Big Business

The expansion of the American film business was phenomenal. What had started with several small companies in New York, Brooklyn, Philadelphia, and Chicago became a major industry, with a new center on the West Coast. Hollywood was a peaceful stretch of citrus orchard in 1907, when the first feature film was made there. But half a dozen companies built their main studios in the land of gold and sunshine, and many eastern groups used California for some of their operations. In the scramble for profits new producers got their equipment by whatever dubious methods they could devise. It was said that one great advantage of Hollywood was that it was near the Mexican border in case a film-maker had to flee a court summons for infringing on patent rights. But soon able business men came into control. Although many of them had had no experience in moviemaking— Adolph Zukor left the fur business to make more money in films—they knew how to create a big business organization. By 1920 they had settled their patent suits and merged many companies into a few. They bought control of the movie houses so that regular countrywide distribution of their films was assured. Their only reverse came in 1919, when Mary Pickford, Charlie Chaplin, and Douglas Fairbanks, together with director D. W. Griffith, formed their own company, United Artists, and won a place of respect for all actors. The big producers were now forced to devote a considerable portion of their profits to fabulous salaries for their stars, but long-term contracts brought the actors under effective control of the organization, and with large studio staffs the producers were able to turn out hundreds of films a year.

Meanwhile Europe's early lead over America in film-making was lost because of the interruption of the First World War. After the war the European studios continued to make good films, but in the mass market they could not compete with the organized efficiency of American movie production. From 1920 to about 1950, Hollywood was the movie capital of the world. The result was one of the largest commercial enterprises of the modern age, for years America's number two industry, second only to meat-

492

packing. The actors, designers, and directors themselves spoke of "The Industry."

In the early days the studios had been modest establishments, sometimes little more than an old warehouse. But the studios of the twenties were handsomely equipped. Production was organized as on a factory assembly line, with many people working on each film. In the thirties, Louis B. Mayer listed the number of professions, vocations, and crafts required in making films at 117. He administered 5,000 employees in forty-nine departments. From the first discussion of a script or the need for a script to the moment when the film went to the distributor, several dozen persons had their say about it. The script writer had little influence, though he might have a huge salary. The director was in no stronger position, and if he wanted to do anything unusual, he might have to fight the front office. Few men in the top positions had strong convictions about what films should be. They watched their competitors and followed what they supposed to be the taste of their ever increasing public. If a company got out of line by becoming "artistic" and producing a failure, the loss might run into millions.

In the 1920s some twenty thousand movie theatres were built, in the last wild fling of nineteenth-century "period" architecture, before "modern" set in. Banks might be Roman temples and stores Renaissance villas or French chateaux, but something even more exotic was required for moviegoers— Chinese, Aztec, or Arabian Nights palaces with Gothic rooftops and interiors provided with thickly carpeted staircases, huge, gilt-encrusted mirrors, heavy draperies, ceilings adorned with heavenly or classical figures painted or in bas relief, and crystal chandeliers. The Capitol Theatre was one of the show places of New York until it was surpassed by the Paramount, more elegantly rococo than Versailles, and then by the still larger Roxy, with taller twisted Baroque columns and more impressive Spanish arches and tiled roofs than might have been seen in the whole Spanish Empire. But the spree ended with Radio City Music Hall. Though it was the largest of all, seating more than six thousand and offering a combination of moving picture, organ and orchestra music, and a "presentation" with acres of scenery and spectacular song and dance numbers, the building was modern in design. The public was ready for simplicity in architecture, and, as the name of the theatre suggested, radio was taking its share of popular attention.

During this movie theatre boom, the aim of "The Industry" was to get everybody to the movies, not once a week but several times a week. The nickelodeon had appealed to a mixed lower class, but now all social classes were movie-conscious. Every film, no matter if it duplicated the last, had to be publicized as unique, better than anything that had gone before, "colossal, daring, unforgettable." Openings in Hollywood became dramatic productions of the first magnitude; fan magazines, general periodicals, and newspapers were fed startling releases, and the private affairs, real or imagined, of the stars were exposed to the public to increase the value of their screen personalities. Stars traveled about the country with impressive entourages for personal appearances in houses where their latest films were being shown. In

493

the twenties Hollywood was one of the richest and most celebrated spots on the globe.

To please the masses and keep them coming to the theatre, the producers wanted new ideas, but only safe ones. The market salesmen sat in on the conferences as the many advisers and "idea men" laid plans to repeat the appeal that had brought millions to see the last picture, hunting for a new sensational effect yet constantly fearful of offending some group. Films in the twenties did not deal with social problems, though some early films had done so. The big business men of Hollywood wanted no disturbing plays. When the screen was not portraying highly colored events of the past or dealing with adventure, horror, or the ludicrous, it was giving an image of life as a continuous social game in which wealthy, well-dressed playboys and glamorous women engaged in daring flirtations, drinking, and orgies.

THE THREAT OF CENSORSHIP

In dealing with sex and violence, the businessmen who controlled the film industry were torn between the box-office appeal of such material and the fear of provoking official government censorship or informal censorship by organized groups.

Until the twenties the film industry was almost free of censorship. In the first year of American public movie projection (1896), a five-minute film strip called *The May Irwin-John C. Rice Kiss,* made from a scene in a then current stage play, upset a few puritans, though it would seem innocuous in the 1960s. Except for a few such single instances of protest, there was no demand for censorship until 1907. By that time it had become obvious that movies were not a passing fad to be ignored but a growing influence on American youth, and some protests about sensational content were made by newspaper editors, juvenile court judges, clergymen, and other responsible persons.

In 1909 the National Board of Censorship was established by the People's Institute of New York City in cooperation with the organization of movie producers called the Motion Pictures Patents Company. With a change of name to the National Board of Review, this group certified all motion pictures that were shown in commercial houses until the 1940s. Before the National Board was formed, half a dozen states had established their own censorship, no two of them with exactly the same strictures. But until 1922 the censorship of the National Board was nominal, and though the producers might have misgivings from time to time, they felt no real constraint.

The First World War was followed by a period of social change when the younger generation scandalized their elders with short skirts, bobbed hair, wild dances, and new patterns of uninhibited behavior. Among the young-married groups, drinking parties, scandalous flirtations, and divorces were more common than before. The moving pictures often presented such behavior, and if what was said about the stars was true, they were no better than the characters they portrayed on the screen. When in 1920 the idolized Mary Pickford divorced Owen Moore and almost immediately married

Douglas Fairbanks, the fans were shocked. Then in 1922, within a few months three Hollywood scandals outraged the public. William Desmond Taylor, an English director, was murdered in his bungalow in Los Angeles. The murderer was never found, but the investigation of the crime disclosed another scandal: narcotics were being peddled in the movie colony and Wallace Reid, one of the most popular romantic actors, was an addict. Then came the Fatty Arbuckle case. A minor actress died at a drinking party in Arbuckle's suite in a San Francisco hotel, and, although the popular comedian was acquitted at the trial that followed, much sordid information about movie people was played up in the papers. The beloved Fatty of the old Sennett company was never able to appear on the screen again. Many ministers and some newspaper editors preached against the sin pit of Hollywood. The studios sent Will Rogers and other popular stars of unsmirched reputation to speak around the country in defense of the morals of the movie colony.

Frightened enough to make common cause, the competing producers set up a central organization to establish standards of decency and morality for the screen and to assure the public that the industry could regulate itself without government censorship. As "Czar" they secured a national figure of respectability, Will H. Hays, a Presbyterian elder who had been chairman of the Republican National Committee and was at the time Postmaster General in the Harding administration. The Hays Office, taking into consideration the attitudes of various state, city, and religious censorship bodies, worked out a code and undertook to advise their producing members, both when scripts were first submitted and after the films were finished, what scenes had to be cut or modified. The Hays Office did forestall national censorship and went to great effort to assure the public that, whatever the movies might have been in the past, they were now clean and moral.

The "code of decency," in trying to avoid the more objectionable appearances of evil and to placate the puritans, became a curious hodgepodge of regulations, compromises, and evasions. It prohibited showing scenes of unnecessary violence and barbarity, treating any religion irreverently, treating "explicitly" or "attractively" adultery and illicit sex, showing scenes of passion, seduction, or rape, and using the themes of sex perversion, white slavery (quite a popular film subject in the decade before the First World War), miscegenation, venereal disease, and childbirth. The camera could not even show a double bed. The code not only encouraged American filmmakers to avoid mature treatment of sex or suffering but made it possible to cater to adolescent dreams of glamorous passion and sadistic excitement, always with the recognition that such indulgences are forbidden in everyday life.

The restrictions of the code could be circumvented and often were. A considerable amount of forbidden material might be included, for instance, if before the end of the picture it was specifically condemned by a good character as immoral, if those involved were punished, or if the hero or at least the heroine remained pure in the midst of vice. Such evasions, however, were not likely to improve the movies as an honest picture of life.

495

FIGURE *15.4* Heroic action in romantic spectacle. Douglas Fairbanks fights against great odds in *The Three Musketeers,* 1921. Museum of Modern Art.

Though the producers were not legally bound by the restrictions of the Hays Office, they adhered to them, at least nominally, avoiding situations in stories and plays that might give offense. When a producer was accused of "emasculation" of the novel or play for which he had paid perhaps as much as a quarter of a million dollars, he would defend himself by saying that he was not manufacturing entertainment for a small minority of liberal-minded readers or theatregoers but for the vast movie audience of unsophisticated families. Producers admitted frankly that they were "servants of the box office, trying earnestly to satisfy the ticket-buying masses."

A new outbreak of criticism in the thirties was directed chiefly against violence and the attractive presentation of underworld characters in gangster films and against the pictures of Mae West, who, in *Diamond Lil* and several other films, created an amusing image of a seductive Gay Nineties woman. Her husky-voiced, insinuating "Come up and see me some time" became a popular phrase. The new code that resulted in 1933 was somewhat more restrictive than the earlier one but could still be evaded. Commenting on a change of personnel in the Hays Office in 1946, James Agee, film critic of *The Nation,* wrote with some asperity, "It remained possible, as before, to say almost anything if it was prurient, childish, or false enough in the first place and sneakily enough said in the second. It remained impossible, as before, to say anything whatever, without sneaking it, which might move or interest anyone past the moral age of five."

The fear of censorship was a curb on the film-makers, since the producer could use it as an excuse for not trying anything the mass audience was not

The Mass Media

used to. Apparently any amount of cheap, sensational material could be shown as long as it followed the old conventions, inherited from Victorian times, of what could properly be seen by the whole family. Characters treated according to modern ideas of psychology and human behavior could be shown on the stage and portrayed in the novel, but they could not be seen in the American movies. Only in the fifties and sixties, as we shall see, was censorship relaxed, or restricted by the courts, so that directors had greater freedom and could make more adult films.

THE LAVISH TWENTIES

With a rich industry in control, it is not surprising that the twenties were a decade of lavish pictures. Of these the most colossal were the Biblical epics directed by Cecil B. De Mille. De Mille had made his mark as a director in the year of Griffith's great success—1915—when, following a trend of presenting prominent stage stars on the screen, he produced *Carmen* with the opera singer Geraldine Farrar and with Wallace Reid, an actor who already had a screen following. As patriotism mounted before and during the First World War he produced a series of popular patriotic films, and when the war was over he was ready with another kind of film guaranteed to please: the daring sex comedy whose sophistication suited the postwar mood of relaxed morals and the pursuit of pleasure. But he found an even more popular and remunerative formula in films based on the Bible, in which scenes of fascinating wickedness could be combined with piety. *The Ten Commandments* (1923) and *The King of Kings* (1927) brought huge crowds to the theatres.

But De Mille did not have a monopoly on colossal offerings. Douglas Fairbanks, the most athletic star the screen had known, scaled walls, leaped from parapets, and fought his way through crowds of armed men in one tale of adventure after another—*The Three Musketeers* (1921), *Robin Hood* (1922), *The Thief of Bagdad* (1924), *The Black Pirate* (1926). Horror was created on a large scale by the actor Lon Chaney in *The Hunchback of Notre Dame* (1923) and *The Phantom of the Opera* (1925). If a tale was contemporary, the sets might be scarcely less elaborate than for a period film. Erich von Stroheim, an Austrian actor and director who had come to the United States in 1909, spent $200,000 on a replica of the Casino at Monte Carlo for an ordinary feature film, *Foolish Wives* (1922). The same director did the Viennese musical *The Merry Widow* (1925) on a grand scale; it was a great box-office success and a subject of scandal since some of the "orgy sequence" was so realistic in detail that it had to be cut to appease the censors.

Rudolph Valentino was the great male star of the early twenties. Born in Italy, he had lived in the United States since 1913, working as landscape gardener, dishwasher, and dancer in vaudeville. An unknown actor when he was selected for the principal role in *The Four Horsemen of the Apocalypse* (1921), he was an immediate success as a picturesque Argentinian gaucho, and he became one of the greatest screen lovers and romantic figures that

497

Hollywood, a place of romantic figures, has ever known. In all his pictures he was an exotic character—bullfighter, sheik, eighteenth-century adventurer, army officer in the court of Catherine the Great of Russia—presented in some lavish setting, and if the picture allowed even the slightest excuse he danced the tango that had set off his slim figure in *The Four Horsemen*. The legend of Valentino remains largely unimpaired because, unlike other romantic Hollywood figures, he did not live to grow old or be replaced. After a star's career of only a little over five years, he died in 1926 after an emergency appendectomy.

Among female stars, a more sophisticated type than Mary Pickford was popular in the twenties. Clara Bow, famous for her interpretation of flaming youth, was the supreme possessor of "It," the new term for sex appeal taken from the title of a third-rate novel by Elinor Glyn. Gloria Swanson had perhaps the most extraordinary career of all the stars of the twenties, and it was fitting that she should appear three decades later in *Sunset Boulevard* (1950), a nostalgic piece about an aging screen star who tries to recapture the old lavish days of Hollywood. A member of Sennett's Keystone Company, Gloria Swanson left low comedy in the twenties for woman-of-the-world roles. In 1925, when she returned to the United States after filming *Madame Sans-Gêne* in Paris, she brought with her a new husband, the Marquis de la Falaise, and made a triumphal entry with him into Hollywood, accompanied by the mayor of Los Angeles, a motorcycle escort, brass bands, and swarms of fans.

To the glamour of such sparkling American women was added the exotic appeal of foreign stars. Among the most famous were Vilma Banky (Hungarian), Alla Nazimova (Russian), Pola Negri (Polish), and Greta Garbo (Swedish). Garbo proved herself an actress of real worth in the twenties and thirties. Nazimova was an accomplished actress who had been a member of the Moscow Art Theatre company for years. Her *Doll's House* was a memorable silent screen play, and she appeared in one of Hollywood's rare experiments in the "artistic" film, an unusual production of Oscar Wilde's *Salome,* with costumes copied by Valentino's wife from Aubrey Beardsley's drawings of the 1890s.

The dominance of Hollywood was overwhelming. Whenever new talent appeared in other countries it was bought and brought to Hollywood. Although the exotic foreign stars were a success in American films, many of the directors failed. Often they had made their mark with a stark realism that was quite different from the glamour of Hollywood scenes. When they were required to give the characters in their Hollywood films what was considered the correct moral tone and the stories the right optimistic ending, the quality that had distinguished their earlier work was lost. The German film had a very creative period in the 1920s, when Berlin studios made several realistic films of city life (often referred to as the "street films") that reflected the dark mood of the depression years of the twenties in Europe. Not only were the extraordinary new camera effects impressive but the characters showed wide box-office appeal in America. One of these films, *The Last Laugh*

(1924), made by the German director F. W. Murnau and starring Emil Jannings in the principal role, is a pathetic tale of an aging doorman at a fashionable hotel who is reduced to a job as a lavatory attendant and suffers deeply from lost pride. Jannings and Murnau were both brought to Hollywood largely on the strength of the reputation they acquired from this picture, but neither was able to create anything of equal quality in America.

An interesting exception to the common fate of foreign directors was Ernst Lubitsch, who was brought to this country in 1923 to direct the costume drama *Rosita* for Mary Pickford and directed American movies until his death in 1947. To *So This Is Paris* (1926) he brought a twinkle of sophisticated Continental wit, and his reputation for deft handling of European gaiety and worldliness grew with each new picture.

THE ARRIVAL OF SOUND

Before the flush times of the twenties were over, radio offered a threat to the monopoly of the movies in popular entertainment, but until television at a much later date added the visual element to home entertainment, the competition was not overwhelming. Even though the depression affected all business by the end of the twenties, the introduction of sound to the movies added the new element that made them irresistible even to the very poor.

The impetus for the introduction of sound was economic. Warner Brothers, on the verge of bankruptcy, made a desperate effort to recoup by using synchronized projected sound for *The Jazz Singer* with Al Jolson. This "singing picture" was first performed on October 6, 1927, and public enthusiasm was immediate. The company went on to make *The Lights of New York* (1928), the first "all-talking" picture, and the other companies were forced to convert to sound. Fox made the first all-talking picture filmed outdoors, *In Old Arizona* (1929). For several years some silent films were still made, but there was no doubt about the trend. In five years, in spite of the depression, the change had been made, and the silents had become a thing of the past. In July, 1928, only 220 theatres in the United States were equipped for sound; by the end of the year there were 1,000 and in 1929, 4,000. Attendance at the movies increased nearly fifty percent between 1927 and 1929. The most obvious business and technical problems—getting theatres converted to sound, improving the sound itself, synchronizing sound and image more effectively, finding suitable material to film, sorting out silent screen actors whose voices could be used—were solved in a comparatively short time. The industry reached the end of the decade in a mood of triumph.

With the introduction of sound, the filming of stage plays, which had been common practice even in silent pictures, was greatly stimulated. Just as European screen directors had been imported in the twenties, both European and American stage directors were now in demand in Hollywood, since it was presumed that they would know how to deal with dialogue in pictures. Even more in demand than directors were stage actors and actresses who could be counted on to speak well. Stars who had had stage experience

499

before their movie careers were fortunate, but many who had acted only for the screen found that their voices were not suitable or that they were hampered by the sound track in their accustomed style of performance.

Achievements of the Twenties and Thirties

In screen material, each decade from the twenties to the fifties shows a similar pattern. Westerns, spectacles, sentimental tales, society dramas, mysteries and thrillers, and farce comedy were the staples, but fads in locale, plot, character types, and theme or social attitude varied in response to public interests or to the arrival of a new screen personality. As in popular fiction, one success set off a chain of imitations, and so there were flaming youth pictures in the twenties, gangster and G-man pictures in the thirties, and pictures of fighting in jungles and on beachheads in the forties. The many hundreds of second-rate and third-rate films produced on low budgets with a minimum of time and effort varied little from one decade to another. Yet a few films in each decade did achieve some distinction.

The twenties saw the climax of what is now spoken of as the "Golden Age of Comedy." Several very popular comic personalities had emerged from the midst of the gadgets and falling debris of the Mack Sennett slapstick. Today we revive with great delight and considerable nostalgia the films of Harry Langdon, Buster Keaton, and Harold Lloyd, aware that such superb clowning was at its best in silent films and faded out with the coming of sound. Harold Lloyd was scarcely less popular than Chaplin in the twenties, and his *Safety Last* (1923) was a great comic thriller. In one breathtaking sequence, Lloyd crawls along window ledges and up the side of a tall building and gets mixed up with the hands of a clock far above the street. Lloyd was his own stunt man, and if he was not the twenty stories above the street that the camera showed, he was two or three stories above the nearest landing place if he should fall (FIGURE *15.5*).

An exceptional serious film is Erich von Stroheim's *Greed* (1924), made from Frank Norris' naturalistic novel of 1899, *McTeague,* a tale about a stupid dentist, his marriage, his murder of his miserly wife in order to get the money she has hoarded, and his flight and death. Directed with painstaking attention to every realistic detail, the picture was so long (some forty reels) that it was never shown to the public in its entirety. It marked the beginning of Von Stroheim's ruin as a director. The producers saw no box-office possibilities in this grim tale, they were shocked by the cost in time and money, and they were not impressed by its artistry. But the picture stands, even in its mutilated state (for much of the film was destroyed), as probably the greatest masterpiece of American film realism.

The twenties also saw the creation of a very successful new kind of Western. Westerns by this time had become formula pieces, often filmed entirely on sets in the studio. However, in 1923 Paramount sent the director James Cruze with a company on location in the Snake Valley, Nevada, to film a

The Mass Media

FIGURE *15.5* Film comedy. Trick camera work and cutting greatly extended the possibilities of farce comedy. Harold Lloyd climbs up the outside of a skyscraper. *Safety Last,* 1923. Museum of Modern Art.

story taken from a novel about the Forty-Niners crossing the plains to California. The film that Cruze made, *The Covered Wagon,* not only was beautiful in natural background but had an epic sweep, the important theme of pioneer ambition and hardship, and the vigor and humor of frontier types. Although the love interest consisted of the usual shallow romance, the picture had a sense of reality and grandeur that captivated not only the regular patrons of Westerns but also discriminating moviegoers. It was followed the next year by *The Iron Horse,* directed by John Ford, which dealt with transcontinental railroad building. The two are ancestors of many western epics, among them *Union Pacific* (1939), another railroad picture; *Wells Fargo* (1937), a saga of the early express service in the West; and *Cimarron* (1931), a film about the opening of Oklahoma to settlement, remade in 1960.

During the twenties and thirties, Chaplin made his most important films, creating long silent comic scenes with a musical background years after everybody else had converted to the talking film. He ended the decade of the thirties with *The Great Dictator* (1940), a scathing comic comment on Hitler and Mussolini. W. C. Fields, the team of Stan Laurel and Oliver Hardy, and the Marx Brothers, all successors of the comics of the silent era, provided in the new era of sound their own variety of zany antics and inspired nonsense.

Most American films of the 1930s gave little indication that this was a decade of economic depression and international tension, the period of Franklin D. Roosevelt's New Deal, the Spanish Civil War, and the rise of Hitler. Geared to mass production, Hollywood was more likely to offer es-

501

cape from pressing political, economic, and social problems than to disturb patrons by dealing directly with painful or controversial issues. A considerable part of the public was made happy by sentimental pictures with the child actress Shirley Temple and by the pseudonature tales of Tarzan, played by a succession of muscle men. But some merely entertaining pictures of the thirties were excellent. The musicals with the dancer Fred Astaire and the witty "Thin Man" mystery-comedies in which Myrna Loy and William Powell played are examples.

Though they were not the rule, some pictures did deal seriously with current problems. *The Big House* (1930) exposed bad prison conditions, and *I Am a Fugitive from a Chain Gang* (1932) carried enough impact to cause an investigation and the alleviation of brutal treatment of prisoners. *Fury* (1936), directed by Fritz Lang and starring Spencer Tracy, was an impressive film dealing with the danger of mob violence, showing not conventional villains and bad men but ordinary good citizens giving way to cruelty and revenge. Other pictures exposed rackets, political corruption, and the methods of newspaper scandal sheets; instead of recognizing these as national problems, however, they followed the usual screen pattern of placing the blame on individuals and implying that a change of heart or some simple plan of reformation would correct the situation. *The Grapes of Wrath* (1939), made by John Ford from John Steinbeck's novel, was a thoughtful and moving screen play with an epic sweep, dealing with the acute conditions of farmers in Oklahoma and transient workers in California during the mid-thirties. Less serious and more popular were *Mr. Deeds Goes to Town* (1936) and *Mr. Smith Goes to Washington* (1939), in each of which one man overcomes corrupt businessmen or politicians with simple, naive goodness supported by a large bank account. Gary Cooper's millionaire Longfellow Deeds, lovable, reassuring, and only superficially credible, was related to other dream figures of the screen. Yet the pictures were very well done and rank among Hollywood's best in storytelling, directing, and acting.

The gangster films of the thirties were more symptomatic of the times, reflecting public restlessness, dissatisfaction, and cynicism. Fifty gangster films were made in 1931 alone. They not only pleased the popular audience with their suspense, excitement, and violence but satisfied the moviegoer-who could appreciate the clear telling of a credible story, together with fine camera work, directing, acting, and editing. Tough characters and, with the new sound track, tough language were presented in raw reality and sharp directness by new actors with irregular, individual features rather than romantic good looks—Paul Muni, George Raft, James Cagney, Edward G. Robinson, and others. The type of story and character was one of Hollywood's most original contributions to the screen, a new artistic creation of script writer, director, and actor. Although the gangster appeared in *Public Enemy* (1931), *Scarface* (1932), and many other pictures as the twisted, cruel, amoral personality that he was, the screen life he led was thrilling, and the script writers, often taking their material from newspapers, did not always follow the approved practice of showing, at any cost to veracity, that good

The Mass Media

FIGURE *15.6* The underworld of violence and power. In a typical gangster film the criminal leader and his men defy the law and threaten the wealthy. *Little Caesar,* 1930. Museum of Modern Art.

would overcome evil. In spite of the sadism of many scenes and the melodramatic clichés of gang loyalty and betrayal, the gangster films showed awareness of the problems of a modern city and the conflict of economic and political forces.

Gone with the Wind (1939), a romantic spectacle based on Margaret Mitchell's popular novel, was one of the most widely acclaimed films of the thirties, and although some critics described it as just another oversized sentimental Civil War tale expressing conventional political and ethical views, it has held up well with the public in numerous reruns. It was the best American spectacle, for storytelling, acting, and editing, since Griffith's *The Birth of a Nation* twenty-five years before. The story and the characterization were of better quality than Griffith's, color increased the romantic glamour, and sound heightened the interest of character. The acting of the four principals—the English actors Vivien Leigh and Leslie Howard and the Americans Clark Gable and Olivia de Havilland—and of several others was excellent. If the film said little about the causes of the Civil War, it said a great deal about how people adjust themselves as they see the destruction of the kind of world they have known. A claim could be made for calling it the best American epic of all time.

Only a few of the outstanding films of the twenties and thirties have been mentioned here. If to these are added two important new film developments to be discussed in the next chapter—the documentary and the animated cartoon feature—the record is not undistinguished.

Mature Films in the Forties

The forties were not a time likely to encourage the more daring moviemakers. The world war of the first half of the decade was followed by the anxieties and caution of the cold war, as Russian-American hostility

FIGURE *15.7* The romantic hero on the screen. When the lonely actor finds his love in a popular dance hall, he is threatened by the rough man of action. *Children of Paradise,* 1944, with Jean-Louis Barrault. Photo Culver Pictures.

reached a fearful stalemate. In America the cold-war hysteria led to a strong attack on Hollywood by Senator Joseph McCarthy's Un-American Activities Committee, and producers became more reluctant than ever to make films that might be considered radical or unconventional in any way. Nevertheless in several countries films of distinction were produced that may be called adult entertainment. If they did not touch on the immediate problems of a confused world, they showed a high order of artistic excellence. Of these, five are of special interest, covering a wide range of theme and style: *Children of Paradise* (1944), a French film that had considerable popularity in this country; Laurence Olivier's brilliant *Henry V* (1945); *Citizen Kane* (1941), *The Ox-Bow Incident* (1943), and *The Treasure of the Sierra Madre* (1947), the last three made in Hollywood.

Children of Paradise was made by Marcel Carné during the German occupation of France, when it was not possible to deal honestly with current themes. If it has a contemporary element, it is the tone of melancholy and near despair, but this tone is entirely suitable to the romantic substance of the picture. Set in the mid-nineteenth century, the story concerns the worshipful love of Baptiste, a man of humble spirit, for a woman who is elusive for him but very accessible to more worldly men. The cast includes hundreds, for this is romance, with crowd scenes in street carnivals, theatres, salons, or underworld hideouts alternating with intimate scenes in lodgings, backstage dressing rooms, and boudoirs. As the Pierrot in a troupe of entertainers, Baptiste has several scenes of pantomime beautifully performed by Jean-Louis Barrault. On a street platform he mimes the actions of a pickpocket he can see among the spectators, and in the theatre he mimes a wistful Pierrot longing for an ideal lady but bound by loyalty to his wife—a scene that represents his own dilemma in real life. The screen has not had a better piece of modern romantic theatre.

The British-made *Henry V*, the other romantic piece in this group of five, is a fine blend of scenes of pageantry with a strong characterization by

504

The Mass Media

Laurence Olivier of the energetic, personable young king, the intelligent man of action. The picture proved that Shakespeare could be made not only palatable but exciting for popular audiences in the twentieth century and paved the way for Olivier's *Hamlet* (1948), *Richard III* (1955), and *Othello* (1965) and Richard Burton's *Hamlet* (1964).

The Ox-Bow Incident, filmed by William Wellman from a novel by Walter Van Tilburg Clark, is as stark as any picture that has been made in this country. It is a tale of rough men and rough injustice, set in 1885 in the cattle town of Bridger's Wells, Nevada. A man named Kincaid has been reported killed and some cattle have been stolen. A posse setting out into the mountains finds the cattle and with them a stranger, Martin, and two companions, a half-crazy old man and a Mexican of dubious reputation who has Kincaid's gun. Martin insists that he bought the cattle and knows nothing about the murder and that the Mexican found the gun. But he is not believed, and he and his two companions are hanged. After the lynching Kincaid appears and confirms that the cattle had indeed been bought by Martin. A lynching on circumstantial evidence is not original material for a tale, but the treatment of the characters and of the moral implications of their actions and motivations is very unusual in an American film. The men who do the lynching vary in kind and degree of human weakness. The leader of the posse is a sadist who wants to kill; his son sympathizes with the victims but is brutally forced by his father to take part in the hanging.

FIGURE *15.8* Character in the epic film. With a vivid portrayal of the English king, Laurence Olivier dominates the spectacle in his *Henry V,* 1945. Photo Arrow.

Among the other men some are unwilling to take a stand, doubtful or even indifferent, easily led. The one man who is strongly convinced of the innocence of the principal victim is too cowardly to force a showdown with the leader. The materials are potentially melodramatic but are handled with restraint. There is no violence merely for the sake of violence, and there is a sense, as in a tragedy, that the victim is being carried by the inexorable progress of events to the catastrophe. Nothing could be less like the usual Westerns with their simple scheme of morality and action too fast for thought. Clark's novel is very compactly and convincingly written, and the film follows it more closely than a film usually follows a novel. Although the final view of man's nature is not quite so harsh as Clark's and although one character, played by Henry Fonda, is allowed more humane feeling and perception of moral values than he is in the novel, no real violence is done to the tale or its meaning. The film is an impressive piece of screen art.

Citizen Kane, made by Orson Welles at the beginning of the forties, is the most brilliant cinematic achievement among the five films we are considering, a picture that has been almost as influential on other film-makers as Griffith's *The Birth of a Nation.* Twenty years after its release it won an international critics' poll conducted by the British Film Institute as the best picture ever made, and directors are still using many of the techniques it introduced. Orson Welles was only twenty-four years old when he signed a contract with RKO that assured him $150,000 for every film he made for the company, in addition to a percentage of the receipts. He was free not only to direct but to write the scripts and to act in the pictures, and he was not to be interfered with in any way during the making of a film. The generous terms were the more remarkable because, although Welles had made a name for himself as actor and director for the stage and for radio, he had never made a motion picture. At least for the first production, *Citizen Kane,* the company observed its promises. *Citizen Kane* is based on the life of newspaper magnate William Randolph Hearst, and in part the sensation caused by the picture was due to this fact, but the film was also one of remarkable inventiveness and technical ingenuity. It achieved a sense of great breadth and depth without the wide screen, which had not yet come into use. Close-ups, once so original in film, had become a fetish of moviemakers, and the many wide, distant shots in *Citizen Kane,* prolonged for an unusual length of time without movement of the camera, brought a sense of fresh experience to the viewer. When close-ups were used in the film, it was in an unusual way, as when, early in the picture, Kane's lips almost filled the screen as he made his dying comment on life. Narration to introduce and bind the sequences together, dialogue in which voices overlap, and the use of music to enhance dramatic effects, not just to provide background, were fresh techniques that have since become familiar. The picture opens with a view of Xanadu, Kane's estate; it is followed by a quick shot of his last moment of life and then, in newsreel technique, a rapid survey of his public career, before the film begins the story of his life—his business successes, his two marriages—and the unfolding of his personality. An example of the economy of visual

506

means is the short sequence in which Kane's estrangement from his first wife is indicated by successive shots of the breakfast table with the two sitting farther and farther apart and appearing more and more indifferent to each other until finally they are shown at opposite ends of a long table, each reading a newspaper. Changes of dress and of the decor of the room indicate the passing of time. Not half a dozen lines of dialogue are used in the sequence. The picture is sometimes given a retrospective showing, and it has not lost its power.

Although Orson Welles was too original to survive very long under the commercial control of Hollywood, a few directors did succeed in putting their own impress on their pictures in spite of the caution of the executives and the routine of script conferences that usually eliminated any distinctive ideas. Alfred Hitchcock, an English director who in the thirties had acquired a reputation for distinctive thrillers, came to Hollywood after the war and applied his own techniques and his special treatment of murder and moral ambiguities in films that bore a personal stamp. Elia Kazan was able to carry into his films the same intense treatment of psychological conflict that had made his reputation as a stage director. John Ford, who had made *The Iron Horse* in the twenties and *The Informer* and *The Grapes of Wrath* in the thirties, continued his impressionistic control of mood in man's struggle with his environment and created an audience that eagerly looked forward to the next Ford picture. But John Huston's experience is an interesting example of the difficulties the front office could put in the way of the director who wanted to do something unusual. The studio executives supported Huston for a popular crime film like *The Maltese Falcon* (1941), and he made several successful war films, but when in 1947 he wanted to go to Mexico to film a little-known novel, *The Treasure of the Sierra Madre,* the executives protested that the story seemed very unpromising. It had no women and no romance and took a very harsh view of human character in a harsh landscape. But Huston persisted and made the film a timeless fable of all men's striving for an elusive goal. The plot concerns three American bums of the 1920s who are lucky in a lottery and use the money to strike out into the Mexican Sierra Madre mountains in search of gold. They run into real Indians (not the stereotyped actors of the Westerns), a Texan who wants to get in on their scheme, and a gang of Mexican bandits with a terrifying but convincing leader called Gold Hat. But it is their mutual suspicion and fear of one another as they push into desolate country that in the end is their undoing.

Huston cast his own father, Walter Huston, a distinguished stage actor, as the oldest bum and Humphrey Bogart as one of the younger adventurers. Bogart was then a top-ranking box-office attraction in romantic leads, and the image he created in this film—he is the least stable and least admirable of the three unheroic principals and even more suspicious of his companions than they are of him and of each other—did not please the studio. At one point Bogart saved the picture from being modified by insisting that he would play his role only as Huston had written it.

Huston met even greater difficulties as he set out in 1951 to film Stephen

507

FIGURE *15.9* A more realistic and more adult Western. A group of unheroic, greedy men hunting gold in the mountains of Mexico are destroyed by their own suspicion and fear. John Huston's *The Treasure of the Sierra Madre,* 1947. Warner Brothers Pictures.

Crane's short realistic novel about a soldier terrified in battle, *The Red Badge of Courage.* More is known about this picture than about most Hollywood pictures because the journalist Lillian Ross watched the preparation of the film in Hollywood and her articles written about it for the *New Yorker* appeared in book form in 1952 as *Picture.* Besides having a cowardly hero, the film had little plot and no love interest, and therefore could not, so the film executives thought, be a box-office success. The director was blocked at every turn, and it was only through the most dogged persistence that he managed to finish the film. It made more money than had been expected, and Huston did not give up his fight for better films. He was one of several distinctive directors who flourished under the greater freedom of the 1950s and 60s when, as we shall see, the movies became a minority art and the studio executives lost their tight control.

The five outstanding films of the forties that have been described show that if the general quality of pictures was low the film world was not entirely a wasteland. The three films that were made under Hollywood conditions—*Citizen Kane, The Ox-Bow Incident,* and *The Treasure of the Sierra Madre*—demonstrate that in spite of the caution of the studio executives an occasional director could create a work of distinction. Starting as an entertaining gadget, the movies became not only an industry of enormous size but an art form of great variety and breadth, sometimes showing deep perception and almost always demonstrating great technical skill. Some elements of the art will be examined in the next chapter, and we shall then go on in the following chapter to show how the movies entered a new era of maturity in the fifties and sixties.

The Mass Media

EXERCISES

1. COMEDY OF THE "GOLDEN AGE." Compare some comic star of the silent screen with a recent comic star. What techniques are similar? What differences do you note? What *individual* characteristics do you find in each performer? What image of human bravery, pluck, or misfortune does each create? To what extent is the comedy the creation of the actor and to what extent is it the creation of the director and the cameraman?

2. THE MOVIE SPECTACLE. Analyze a spectacle (not a Western epic) you have seen recently for elements that make it popular: glamour of the actors, excitement and suspense in the story, interest in some period or episode of the past, beauty of landscape and other background, and so on. What faults do you find?

3. THE WESTERN EPIC. Compare a Western epic of the twenties or thirties with a recent one in treatment of history, ending of the story, pictorial quality, and other pertinent elements. A comparison of an early and a later version of the same picture would be especially interesting—for instance, *Cimarron* as made in 1931 and as remade in 1960 or *Stagecoach* as made in 1939 and as remade in 1965.

4. STUDY OF *The Birth of a Nation* OR *Gone With the Wind*. Can you account for the popularity of the film at the time it was made? Do you find the picture interesting now? In what ways would it be different if it were made today? Where does it make good use of action, spectacle, camera movement?

5. ROMANTIC STARS OF THE SILENT SCREEN. What romantic stars of the silent screen have you become aware of from seeing old movies on television or in special showings? Compare one or more of them with some star or stars of the present.

6. THE MATURE FILM. What is your own concept of a mature film? Give recent examples of mature films and of films that are not mature. When is a happy ending justified? When is it an avoidance of a problem? Is the immaturity in the examples you cite due to an overromantic or conventional attitude toward sex? Is it due to an oversimple view of evil? Is it due to a conventional view of social problems? To what extent is a film that is not mature acceptable to an intelligent moviegoer?

7. STUDY OF AN IMPORTANT FILM OF THE FORTIES. If you have a chance to see any of the five pictures described in the last section of the chapter, make your own analysis of plot, characterization, theme, and mood. Is the picture a good piece of drama? If you study *Children of Paradise* or *Henry V*, apply the criteria of the romantic play; if you study one of the others, apply

509

the criteria of the serious realistic play. What scenes or sequences in any of the pictures seem to you especially effective as *screen* drama?

SUGGESTED READING

Suggested reading for films is given at the end of Chapter 17.

SUGGESTED READING

CHAPTER SIXTEEN

THE ART OF THE SCREEN

The American motion picture industry, as we have seen, was established by hardheaded businessmen. The directors they employed were concerned with turning out the required number of entertaining pictures. Working pragmatically with crude settings, lighting, and camera and with actors who were inexperienced in the new medium, the directors obtained more or less satisfactory results according to their talents. But eventually, just as grammatical principles are derived from a language already established in usage, the artistic principles involved in film-making were explored and explained after years of hit-and-miss practice. In 1915 the poet Vachel Lindsay, approaching the subject intuitively, devoted a book to *The Art of the Moving Picture*. By the 1920s even the businessmen in the motion picture industry talked about "art," and since then there has been an increasing amount of critical attention to cinema art. In France, considerable aesthetic consciousness existed from the beginning, and Russia provided its great theorizers in the 1920s and 30s.

Cinematic Principles and Techniques

Cinema is theatre and involves all the arts of writing, planning, directing, designing, and acting we have discussed in Part II. But a movie-goer sees only a series of pictures flashing on the screen. To understand screen drama as an art form, he needs to know how the director or editor   *511*

FIGURE *16.1*   Realism in the movies. A small, crowded street is arranged for a
candid-camera impression of reality in the filming of *Hard Bargain*. Even in daylight
some extra lighting is needed. Twentieth-Century Fox.

assembles the series of pictures, how the writer shapes the screen play to
take advantage of camera techniques, how sound and color are used, and
how the work of the actor is affected by the work of the cameraman and
the editor.

THE ART OF EDITING

Basic in the art of the motion picture is motion. The movement
of the actor and the movement of the camera become part of the movement
of the pictures as the film is run through the projector. Hence the most important art in film-making is editing—the arrangement of photographs in
sequence as they are projected on the screen. A moving picture is a succession
of still photographs of moving actors and objects taken at close intervals and
run through the projector at a standard rate of twenty-four to the second.
On the screen the illusion of motion is created because the eye is so constructed that it retains an image of an object for a fraction of a second after
the object has been removed. Successive photographs thus overlap just
enough to seem to flow continuously. As one sequence of pictures follows
another, a complex composition is built up just as a poem is built up from a
series of words and images grouped in phrases, lines, and stanzas.

Each still photograph in a film is called a *frame,* but the basic unit in
editing is a series of frames taken without interruption, called a *shot.* The
length of the shot affects the tempo and rhythm of the film; a succession of
very short shots gives an effect of speed while very long ones create a slow

The Mass Media

tempo. The form of transition from one shot to another also helps create the rhythm of the film. Dramatic excitement is created by the *direct cut,* a sudden shift from one place or one line of action to another as the film strip of one shot is attached to the film strip of another. A softer transition is made when one scene gradually disappears in a *fade-out,* leaving the screen empty momentarily, and a *fade-in* gradually introduces another scene. A slow fade-out gives a sense of finality to one sequence and is used to prepare for an important shift to another place or another aspect of the story. A transition may also be made by the *wipe,* in which the black of the screen disappears as if a piece of masking paper were being torn off and the picture "underneath" is allowed to appear, or by the *lap dissolve,* in which one scene fades into another superimposed upon it. The superimposition may indicate a symbolic link between scenes, as, for instance, in *The Greatest Story Ever Told* (1965), where a scene of special significance sometimes persists in the background of less important events. In the shift from shot to shot and in the linking of one series of related shots to another, the film-maker manipulates the rhythm of the movie just as the writer manipulates rhythm in poetry or prose or as the director of a stage play chooses a slow curtain or a fast blackout to end a scene.

In a feature film there are hundreds, even thousands, of shots, which have usually been taken at widely separated times and places. The editor, or cutter, must spend many days, weeks, or even months in preparing the film as it is to be printed for distribution, cutting the strips of film, discarding some, and fastening the rest together in a meaningful order. Ideally the director edits his own film, but in practice the editing is usually done by someone else. Sometimes a director and an editor form an effective sympathetic team, but in the days of the big studios the director often found that he could hardly recognize his film when it came from the cutting room. Now it is a mark of a director's recognition as an artist that he has the "final cut," that is, approves the final form of the film.

Editing is the most vital artistic tool of the cinema, a process unique to the screen. The performance on a stage or on live TV will be seen as presented and can be altered only in another performance. A performance for film, on the other hand, is only the initial step in a long creative process. In the 1890s, one-reel films of fifty feet, and a little later of 200, 250, or 400 feet, were photographed with consecutive action (that is, in a single shot) and shown just as taken, with all the imperfections. But moviemakers soon adopted the practice of retaking a scene or portion of a scene until a satisfactory result was obtained, and the best sections of the different takes were then pieced together to make up the film. Such elementary editing sufficed until photography became more complex. In early pictures the camera was set in one position commanding a large stage area, across which the actors moved back and forth, facing front, but as soon as the camera became mobile, photographing was interrupted and editing became more complicated. Shots might be made at long range or very close up or anywhere in between, or the camera might be fastened to a car or other moving object

FIGURE *16.2* The dream fantasy in the movies. Cinematic techniques and cutting offer new possibilities for fantasy. The dream ballet in *Oklahoma!* 1955, directed by Fred Zinneman. Magna Pictures Corp.

and follow the action of a rider or vehicle. It could be mounted on a movable framework called a dolly and pushed about indoors or out, or on a crane to be swung high in the air. Eventually equipment was devised that could swing the camera horizontally through 360 degrees in the action known as "panning," or up and down on a vertical axis.

The first great film editor was D. W. Griffith, whose *The Birth of a Nation* (1915) was discussed in the last chapter. Griffith began his movie career as an actor in the Edison studio in 1907 and moved to the Biograph Company in 1908. Since specialization had not yet developed in the film world, it was easy for him to shift from actor to director. Between 1908 and 1915 he made an average of two one-reelers a week, in all more than 700. These films were his work in every respect: he directed them, he sometimes acted in them, he worked out the story—not as a full script but as a rough outline, which he developed as he went along—and, most important, he did the editing. The experiments of these years, which led to his masterpieces, *The Birth of a Nation* and *Intolerance* (1916), included every device possible at that stage of technical development in photography and lighting. Some of these devices he used for the first time, and all of them he used more effectively than his predecessors had—the flashback to show action prior to the time of the story, close-ups for facial expression, abrupt shifts from one situation to another at a distant place, parallel development of two story lines by crosscutting from one to the other, the use of some visual object as a focus of interest, the use of a moving camera, and shooting on location for authentic atmosphere.

514 For *The Birth of a Nation,* Griffith followed his usual method—remarka-

The Mass Media

ble in so extended a piece of fiction—and used only a rough outline of the action, improvising as he went along. The relative complexity of the picture is indicated by the fact that there were 1,500 shots in the print of the twelve-reel picture at its première, whereas *Queen Elizabeth,* a four-reel picture with Sarah Bernhardt made three years before, had only twenty-eight shots. Griffith had studied *Quo Vadis* and other Italian spectacles, which were like large stage dramas performed on a vast platform viewed from one vantage point, and he knew he could surpass them in excitement if not in magnitude. His film had the rapid narrative flow of a first-rate historical novel, cutting from intimate scenes to crowd scenes, from one locale to another, following with the camera the battle movement, Sherman's destructive march through Georgia, and the ride of the clansmen. His expert cameraman, Billy Bitzer, obtained a collection of Civil War photographs made by Mathew Brady that furnished many authentic suggestions for groups and settings, notably the interior of Ford's Theatre, where Lincoln was shot.

Griffith used all the resources of the camera: he moved it freely, tilted it up and down, panned it to encompass the battlefield, and mounted it on the rear of an automobile to precede a ride of the clansmen. But it was his work in the cutting and editing room that gave the film its strong emotional and dramatic impact. He used the dissolve as a linking device and fade-ins and fade-outs to open and close scenes. He created vignettes—scenes covering less than the full screen area—to emphasize some small significant action or to give an emotional effect, either blacking out the rest of the screen or showing a related scene. He split the screen to show two actions at once. In this picture for the first time the close-up was used for full emotional effect, to the horror of some of Griffith's associates, who protested that he was decapitating an actress whom people expected to see entire. Griffith used crosscutting from one line of action to another for excitement and suspense, and he selected and combined individual shots in such a way as to suggest a striking similarity or contrast and to make people or objects serve as symbols.

The second Griffith epic, *Intolerance,* in which 60,000 players appeared, was one of the most colossal and expensive films ever made. Using continual crosscutting, it interweaves four stories in different periods of history, all illustrating the evil of intolerance: the fall of ancient Babylon, the Crucifixion, the persecution of the Huguenots, and a contemporary story of social injustice. The linking device of a mother figure rocking a cradle, suggesting the continuity of life and the generations, is not completely successful. But although this picture, like *The Birth of a Nation,* is over-sentimental and has other flaws, it is admired by film enthusiasts for its technical expertness.

An intuitive worker, Griffith developed his skill as director and editor without much theorizing about film art. Like any artist, he often achieved more than he had aimed at, suggesting implications that he had not anticipated and perhaps did not even recognize in the finished product. In particular, he seems not to have realized the full significance of his visual imagery and sym-

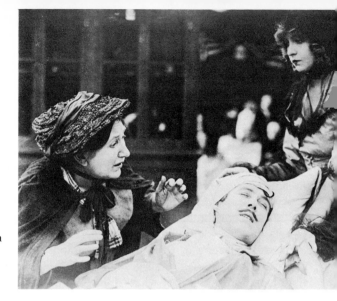

FIGURE *16.3* The emotional power of the close-up. Into his sequences of crowd spectacle and heroic action, D. W. Griffith cut intimate emotional scenes like this one of the death of a soldier. *The Birth of a Nation,* 1915. Museum of Modern Art.

bolism. But it was partly on the basis of the possibilities he had demonstrated that the Russians built their theories of cinema technique and illustrated them in some of the most remarkable films of the 1920s.

The principal achievement of Russian directors was the development of what they called *montage,* the juxtaposition of shots in such a way as to produce emotional effects or even to convey abstract ideas, through visual images. Griffith and other American directors and editors employed it, but from the time when Lenin saw Griffith's *Intolerance* during the Russian Revolution of 1917 and was struck with the power of the screen to present ideas with emotional coloring and move men to conviction and action, the Russians made much fuller use of it.

The Russian directors, of whom Sergei Eisenstein, Vsevolod Pudovkin, and Alexander Dovzhenko are best known, found inanimate objects and scenes from nature particularly useful in conveying meanings. They discovered that, to the extent that a film can suggest meanings beyond the immediate visual image, it approaches the lyricism of poetry or painting. Eisenstein noted that a piece of film that seems emotionally neutral may suddenly acquire a new meaning when joined to another piece. An expression on a face may be interpreted very differently according to what is pictured in juxtaposition to it, and the viewer tends to accept the association provided for him. Applying this idea, Russian cutters reedited German films in the 1920s to make them conform to Russian political views, and often a slight alteration of the film changed the meaning completely.

Eisenstein found inspiration for his theories of montage in the work of Charles Dickens, especially in Dickens' sharply drawn characters, each with some outstanding physical characteristic, and his well-sketched visual images in description, his quick shifts of time and place, and his use of parallel action. Other sources for Eisenstein's ideas were the nineteenth-century melodramas, the conventions of the Japanese stage, which reduce characterization to essentials and vivify it by masks, and Japanese poetry, in which a

516

The Mass Media

succession of visual images (which Eisenstein called a "shot list") creates an emotional impression or intellectual concept.

In his most famous scene, the Odessa steps sequence of *Potemkin* (1925), Eisenstein created excitement and emotional montage not by camera movement but by the way in which he edited the film, cutting from one brief shot to another. Troops descend a long flight of wide steps without breaking the rhythm of their march, shooting at the common people of Odessa as they go and stepping over the dead bodies. Shots of the advancing soldiers, usually showing only the rhythmically moving legs and feet, are intermingled with glimpses of the panic-stricken people, their abandoned possessions, and the bodies of the dead or dying. Especially remarkable are the shots of a baby in a carriage rolling wildly down the steps after the mother has been killed.

Pudovkin's *Mother* (1925) illustrates only a little less strikingly how shots may be combined in editing to give meaning beyond the immediately visible. The plot concerns the effort of a mother to free her son, a political agitator, who is in prison. The season of the year is established as spring by successive shots of a swollen stream, geese waddling through pools, a boy laughing and splashing in puddles, the mother walking across a muddy field on her way from the prison. In his prison cell the son receives word of a plan for his release. The shots that follow (all very short, from four to thirty-nine frames each) express, in the same visual images that were used to establish the idea of spring, the prisoner's feeling of joy and anticipation at the thought of his release. Later, scenes of broken ice blocks carried along by the flow of the river and jamming against a bridge are introduced among

FIGURE *16.4* The Odessa steps sequence in *Potemkin,* 1925. Eisenstein's direction of nonprofessional actors and his use of montage made this a vivid depiction of ordinary citizens destroyed by tyrannical authority. Photo Culver Pictures.

scenes of the crowd coming to rescue the son, suggesting the surge of chaotic emotions and then the blocking of the crowd's progress by the Cossacks. It is evident that such material, in the hands of a creative director and editor, can enrich the screen with a level of emotion and idea above mere photographic realism.

The term montage has been applied in Hollywood chiefly to methods of showing passage of time (as by fast-moving hands of a clock, turned pages of a calendar, a dissolve from a scene with carriages in the 1890s to the same scene with automobiles in the 1920s) or of giving a quick summary of a period of history, a locale, or a milieu, as when a series of short shots of landscape, villages, ceremonies, city streets, or public events provides an introduction to a picture set in Rome or Venice, India, Africa, or medieval France. A good example of effective montage is the opening sequence of *The Magnificent Ambersons* (1942), directed by Orson Welles. The film was made from a novel by Booth Tarkington about the decline of an Indiana family from a position of social eminence. In the first sequence, to establish the period (about 1900), the status of the family, and the personalities of the principal characters, Welles combines a background of narration with montage shots of the things mentioned—everyday episodes of small-town life, the different social classes, the women gossips, the mode of dress, the custom of the serenade, and so on.

The Russian practice of montage undoubtedly made film-makers in all countries more keenly aware of the emotional and symbolic power of the visual image. Landscape is rich in poetic suggestion, and it is the business of the director and the cameraman to sharpen this suggestion and of the editor to give it maximum power in the film sequences. In *The Greatest Story Ever Told,* George Stevens relies on wide views of the natural formations in the Nevada desert, where much of the film was shot, to suggest the grandeur and awesomeness of the theme of the picture; the few constructed settings are simple by comparison with the elaborate structures in Cecil B. De Mille's religious epics. The plains of the West, the moors of England, deserts, jungles, and oceans—all have given to many a film the suitable atmosphere of repose, confinement, joy, sorrow, desolation, or terror. A man-made environment—a garden, a slum back yard, a deserted room, a narrow alley—may be used in the same way. A single natural or man-made object may be brought into meaningful relationship with a man and enhance his story. Small objects, almost negligible in the theatre because only spectators in the first rows can see them clearly, are effective on the screen because the camera can focus on them in close-ups. A life history may be suggested in a broken shoe or a frayed collar. The symbolic focus of a screen tale may be a commonplace object like a child's crib, as in *Baby Doll* (1956), where it is a constant reminder that the girl has never grown up.

Close-ups of objects as well as of people are used with special purpose and power in *The Passion of Joan of Arc,* made in France in 1928 by the Danish director Carl Dreyer. In giving a full, accurate account of the last day of Joan's trial, based on the actual records, Dreyer wished to suggest an occur-

The Mass Media

rence of great historical significance, but at the same time he wanted to reveal every shade of emotion in all the people involved. He filmed the scene of Joan and her judges almost entirely through close shots of objects like books, weapons, and instruments of torture, of hands, and of faces in which squinting eyes, frowning forehead, compressed lips, slack mouth, or thrust-out chin revealed a character's nature or attitude. The many close-ups of the actress Renée Falconetti convey every nuance of Joan's agony.

The same scene was filmed very differently by the French director Robert Bresson in 1962 for his *Procès de Jeanne d'Arc*. Wishing to present a record of fact, to interest his audience in following a historical event step by step without emotional involvement, he used few close-ups. The viewer is made to view the entire situation, to see the different characters and groups in relationship to one another and to the background.

It is the editor who gives the final structure and texture to the film. By cutting in the different threads of action, he creates exciting narrative that builds to the climax; by cutting in suggestive images and symbols or juxtaposing different actions, he creates emotional overtones and sets his main action in a meaningful context. By controlling the length and sequence of shots he creates the rhythmic patterns of the film.

THE SCREEN PLAY

The main source of continuity in a film drama is the story. Even the visual images or montage sequences have as their purpose the telling of the story or the reinforcement of some aspect of it. Where story may be incidental to the stage play, serving merely to guide the main characters to the scenes of confrontation, the story is the chief interest of the film play, emphasizing the developments that lead up to the important situations more than the situations themselves. The film play usually follows the loose dramatic structure characteristic of the epic play or the romantic play, rather than the compact structure achieved in Greek and neoclassic tragedy and in Ibsen's naturalistic tragedies.

Ideally, the play developed in a film should have been written expressly for the screen, but it is not surprising that in a new art a very large number of films have been based on stage plays, short stories, or novels. Many original screen plays have been filmed, but in the commercial studios they have usually been concocted by a team of writers trying to devise a variation of a popular formula or to adapt an idea to fit a particular star. But a screen play, like a stage play, should be the creation of one mind, a work of the imagination carefully constructed and developed in detail. After years of improvising or working from brief notes, Chaplin in creating his full-length features wrote his shooting scripts in the greatest detail.

Some original screen plays have been written by good writers of fiction or drama. The novelist and critic James Agee wrote film plays for several excellent pictures, notably *The African Queen* (1951), and William Inge's screen play for *Splendor in the Grass* (1961), as carefully prepared as one of his stage plays, was followed very closely in the filming. The Swedish director Ingmar Bergman considers an original film play absolutely necessary because "film has nothing to do with literature." A film, he says, "is mainly rhythm . . . inhalation and exhalation in continuous sequence." Nevertheless, film writers have constantly used adaptations, which may also be creative works, and most of the techniques of creating a story on the screen have been worked out in the process of recreating a stage play or a work of fiction.

We have noticed how Corneille in the seventeenth century simplified the medieval story of the Cid, omitting the romantic episodes that led to the day of decision. When a writer adapts a stage play for the screen he does exactly the opposite. He cuts the dialogue of the big scenes to a very few words and adds the earlier episodes and related actions that the playwright left offstage. The added scenes may merely give variety, or they may develop the feelings and motives of the characters or the mood and atmosphere, using visual images where the playwright depended on words. If the social or political background is important, the added scenes may create an epic play that presents man in his wider environment with much more visual detail than an epic play on the stage ever can.

Inherit the Wind, by Jerome Lawrence and Robert E. Lee, is an example of effective adaptation. The stage version (1955) takes place entirely in the Tennessee courtroom where Bertram Cates is being tried for teaching evolution. The screen version (1960) opens with the meeting of several citizens who are to investigate the rumor about Cates' teaching. The spectator follows the men into the classroom, hears with them a portion of the lesson, sees the teacher arrested. Throughout the trial there are sequences showing other people and other events around the town. Moving the camera and cutting in other sequences are so easy that it is natural to spread the story out in time and space. In this film the result is particularly effective because the whole town is involved and many small scenes lead easily to the climactic scenes in the courtroom, where all threads of interest are pulled together.

Merely spreading the action, however, does not necessarily make a good screen play. In fact, it may dissipate the basic tension of the original play. The screen adaptation of *Twelve Angry Men,* filmed in 1957, kept the tension of the original television play by confining the action to the one jury room and provided variety by taking shots from many angles and alternating close-ups with group scenes. The screen version of *Five Finger Exercise* (1962), however, lost all of its power in the spreading of the action. The stage play, by Peter Shaffer, was a little masterpiece with four members of a middle-class English family and one outsider presented in subtle, shifting relationships. There was plenty of movement between the one downstairs room and the two upstairs rooms and hallway, all visible in one confined setting. In the film version the characters, changed to restless Americans, were shown wandering about on a California beach and motoring back and forth between Carmel and Oakland. The tight structure that playwright, director, and actors had woven on the stage in London and New York was destroyed and no meaningful substitute was found. Shifts of background from one room to another, to the garden, to the highway, to the beach, were a distraction without artistic point.

A Broadway hit is a challenge to a film-maker, but he knows he cannot merely transfer the play to the screen. He must completely rethink the play in cinema terms, using much less dialogue and much more visual action than the stage version had. He must decide where to use long shots and where to take close-ups of faces, hands, and objects, where to cut in visual images that create atmosphere and add other meaning, when to show the speaker and when the listener, whether to show the face in thought or the thought behind the face. He is not filming a stage play but creating a new work, a movie based on the stage play.

The adapter of a stage play has a great advantage in the flexibility of point of view offered by the screen. The audience in the regular theatre usually sees an objective presentation of people and events. Even as they sympathize with some characters and hate others, they see and hear them all equally. Various devices are used for revealing the inner being, as we have seen in *Strange Interlude, The Adding Machine,* and other plays, but the stage norm remains an objective presentation. The screen, however, permits many shifts in point of view within a single film without psychological or aesthetic incongruity. The spectator may be the objective observer, like any bystander at a real event, and he may look at the action from the point of view of first one and then another character as the camera, by concentrating on the characters in turn, enables him to identify with each of them. A narrator's voice may be that of an unidentified observer or of a minor or major character in the story. A character's subconscious may be revealed with more scope and detail than on the stage, as it was in the screen versions of *Beggar on Horseback* and *The Emperor Jones.* Tricks of photography, bizarre lighting, or unrealistic color values may be used to suggest psychological states. The sound track may carry a sequence of subjective impressions while the visual narrative proceeds objectively. Although much of the action in films is objective, audiences are so accustomed to shifts in point of view that subjective scenes or sounds may be introduced at any time.

Among many recent films that treat the subjective, *The Pawnbroker* (1965), directed by Sidney Lumet, is notable. The film opens with a sequence in slow motion, establishing the mood of the idyllic past that preceded the imprisonment of a Jewish family in Auschwitz and suggesting one level in the emotional memory of the surviving father of the family, now a pawnbroker in Harlem. A memory flashback of the death of a friend in the concentration camp is photographed in sharp outline. Parts of the same scene are among the lightning-quick flashes in memory sequences later in the film, when the pawnbroker is in an agitated state of mind. The searing memory of the journey to Auschwitz is shown with complete realistic detail as the pawnbroker looks from a car of a subway train into the cattle car that took him and his family to the concentration camp twenty-five years before. Indelible impressions from the past are mingled with the sequence of present

521

events convincingly, frighteningly, and beautifully. The visual imagery, supported by an excellent sound track, carries extraordinary emotional power.

Since the novelist can also present his episodes from various subjective points of view and since he usually develops the wide range of scenes that the playwright must leave offstage, it is easier to create a screen play from a novel than from a stage play. The novelist has created a variety of characters and has gathered information on social and political background. It remains for the movie scriptwriter to sharpen the story line, to choose the characters to be retained and simplify them, eliminating subtleties that cannot be portrayed on the screen and making the characters approximate the types the available actors are accustomed to play, to enlarge the episodes in which pictorial values are strong and eliminate discursive dialogue, and to supply new scenes where needed. One critic has said that a novel being adapted for the screen must be contracted in dramatic magnitude—the number of characters and incidents must be reduced—but expanded in dramatic detail —each incident must be fully developed, whereas in the novel it is sometimes summarized in a few sentences. Again, a screen play is not a novel put before the camera. It is a new work, based on the characters and episodes of the novel but reconceived in cinema terms. To make it so presents a difficult problem: if the film departs too far, it will outrage those who like the novel; if it is merely an attempt to illustrate the work of the novelist, it may lose all the qualities that distinguished the novel without gaining the power of a good film play.

Most of the movies made from Dickens' novels have been extremely effective, because, as Eisenstein discovered, his characters and scenes are cinematic. Some of the pictures made from works of Tolstoy and Dostoevsky have been good enough as films, but no one remembers them as vividly as the novels themselves. The skillfully woven texture of political and social ideas, personal and historical narrative, perceptive analysis of character, philosophical speculation, and more intangible elements is exceedingly difficult to reproduce on the screen or to match in cinematic materials. *The Informer* (1935) is an example of a highly successful adaptation. From a good but not superior novel by Liam O'Flaherty, John Ford made a distinguished film as he developed visually the mute suffering of a tough who had betrayed his friend and who wandered stumbling to his death in the Dublin night. George Bluestone in *Novels into Film* analyzes in detail the way in which Ford converted verbal description and suggestion into visual symbols.

A brilliant example of adaptation from the early 1960s is *Tom Jones* (1963). This screen play, directed by Tony Richardson, is not Henry Fielding's eighteenth-century classic. Fielding wrote a tale of contemporary though imagined events. His attitude toward his material was determined not only by his own vigorous mind and personality but by the social conditions and moral standards of his time. His readers had approximately the same background, experience, and attitudes as his own. His writing, though original in style, was addressed to a public who would readily follow him, a public of leisurely reading habits, with expectations from the printed word very different from those of twentieth-century readers. A movie audience of the 1960s must look back two hundred years. Styles of living, thinking, writing, and reading have changed. Moreover, the film medium is different from the fiction medium even of our own day.

Wisely, the makers of *Tom Jones* adopted an attitude toward the material that would capture the audience, and they maintained this attitude clearly and consistently throughout. What for Fielding was a "real-life" tale they treated frankly as storybook romance. Without contempt, they smiled at the plot, taking the audience into their confidence in the opening sequence and emphasizing the improbability of Fielding's happy outcome by adding the stereotyped, theatrical rescue of Tom at the gallows. They shortened and tightened the plot, omitting not only historical background and philosophical and aesthetic commentary but many incidents and characters, and dealt freely with time and place, bringing into one long sequence in the Inn at Upton all the principal characters, some of whom are not there in the novel. Characters are changed to fit the scheme of what is actually a new tale: Tom is not the polished though sexually careless young gentleman Fielding created, but an uneducated, lusty, likable young rustic; Squire Western is not only ignorant, unpolished, and profane, as Fielding made him, but slovenly, bawdy, and wild; Sophia is less restrained in behavior than Fielding's heroine, nearer the twentieth-century concept of an independent young girl in love. But the zest, cheerfulness, and essential optimism of the author remain. And, in addition to excellent acting, the movie contains richness that only a film can give. There are scenes of a fox hunt across wide stretches of the English countryside; scenes of eighteenth-century London, well realized in both its narrow streets and its diverse human types; scenes of barnyard and churchyard, manor and inn. There is a delightful musical background, suggestive of period and mood but also of playful twentieth-century mockery. There are color, rapid movement, and many effective filmic devices. Occasionally, for example, an actor looks directly at the audience through the camera eye. The camera performs its task like a veteran actor, with confidence, precise technique, and dash, and the editing is brilliant. John Osborne, an English playwright whose stage plays we have discussed, wrote the script, but the film is of the screen, not the stage.

THE ART OF SOUND

The introduction of sound in the late twenties created a major crisis in Hollywood. Broadway playwrights and actors were imported, and speech and acting classes were set up in every available space. Producers had to solve new business problems, and directors had to take a new view of cinema art. The total confusion was amusingly reported in the lively comedy *Once in a Lifetime* (1930) by George S. Kaufman and Moss Hart. Since audiences were entranced with hearing the shadow figures speak from the screen, almost no one but Charlie Chaplin dared produce another silent film. With mime language of the silent actors discarded, the relation of camera to action had to be reconsidered. It seemed to some critics that the art of the movies had been set back thirty years. For a decade and more such critics looked back with nostalgia to the days when simple disembodied images larger than life floated across the screen, unencumbered by earth-bound dialogue. Rudolf Arnheim, writing on the art of the film, deplored the loss of that "cinegenic species of tale, which was full of simple happenings," for, he said, "this meant replacing the visually fruitful image of man in action with the sterile one of the man who talks."

Some of the first talking pictures were completely static; the characters sat still and talked interminably, and the cutting back and forth from speaker to listener did not help. Not even with a sound track could a good movie be made by photographing a stage play. Soon the old screen writers and the more adaptable of the new playwrights imported from New York discovered that the basic principles of cinema action still held, and they learned to sub-ordinate the dialogue by reducing it to casual, everyday phrases muttered in the midst of action. For realistic drama that method worked well, but some playwrights protested at being made "hacks of the director and slaves of the camera." According to the English playwright Terence Rattigan, writers and producers should realize that the screen play is not only the child of its mother, the silent film, but also of its father, the drama. Another critic, in discussing the fiery tirades in John Osborne's *Look Back in Anger* (1956), has written, "If we're going to have talking pictures, let us acknowledge the glory of talk, and be grateful for rhetoric which has the splendor of wrath and wit." Orson Welles has made full use of lively talk, and even such fast-moving films as *Tom Jones* and *Becket* (1964) have climactic confrontations that are fully developed in dialogue. Yet in any film the main continuity is carried by the visual movement. This does not mean merely that the actor walks while he talks or that the camera constantly moves, but rather that attention is focused clearly on the developing intention and response of each character as he becomes the center of the action.

Directors and cameramen soon discovered that there could be many com-binations of sight and sound besides cutting back and forth between a face speaking and a face listening. The camera can show not only what the characters are doing while talking but what they are seeing, or by indirect association—the use of a photograph, a glove, a chair—what they are think-ing of, or by flashback what they are remembering or dreaming of. Just as the editor can cut in segments from different sequences of action, he can make the sound track jump from one fragment of conversation to another, picking up only the important words. The confessional monologue, which had such rich development in radio plays of the thirties, became equally important in the sound movie as one character, alone or talking to another, narrated while the camera showed silent scenes of what was being described. If radio had the advantage of creating in the imagination far more than the literal camera could show, the sound movie had the advantage of being able to portray simultaneously the present and the past and often two points of view as well, for the camera could either confirm what the voice was recalling or show that what actually happened in the past was quite different from what was being narrated.

Sound can be manipulated in many ways. The tone, for instance, can be changed by electronic control to light or dark, smooth or rough, jittery or sepulchral, childish or pompous. A different voice can be substituted, or *dubbed,* not only for foreign languages but often for songs. We see Audrey Hepburn as Liza in *My Fair Lady* (1964) and hear a better voice than her own singing her songs. Some critics object to such a synthetic product, remembering that one of the first appeals of the film was the sense of honest reality caught unawares. But if the dubbing is smooth and subtle, the audience accepts the manipulation of voices as an aspect of cinema art that is just as legitimate as the arrangement and editing of sequences of pictures.

Other sounds, musical or natural, placed before, during, or after a speech can modify the audience reaction, creating an aural image comparable to visual imagery. A mechanical noise or a musical instrument may replace the voice. In Eisenstein's *Thunder over Mexico* (1932), the captured peasant rebels are buried up to the neck and horses are ridden up and down the row of heads. The camera catches the screaming face, but the scream is put on the sound track by a clarinet. In *The 39 Steps* (1935), Alfred Hitchcock showed a terrified woman open her mouth to scream; then he cut to a shot of a locomotive coming out of a tunnel, the piercing train whistle merging with her voice. In *The Ox-Bow Incident* (1943), when the horse is whipped from under a man to be hanged, the screams come from orchestra strings— a sound at once more piercing and intense than a human voice and removed into the realm of art and beauty.

Chaplin had great difficulty in accepting the talking pictures and was depressed by the thought that the art of pantomime was becoming obsolete. "I had thought of possible voices for the tramp," he writes in his autobiography, "whether he should speak in monosyllables or just mumble. But it was no use." As late as 1936, when he produced *Modern Times,* he did not speak or use the casual conversation of others. In the factory scenes, a full-

FIGURE *16.5* Charlie Chaplin in one of his most successful feature-length pictures. In a mechanical age the dauntless Little Fellow contends with the machine. *Modern Times,* 1936, produced and directed by Chaplin. Museum of Modern Art.

wall television screen lights up and a tyrannical voice over a loud-speaker orders the workers to speed up. When the salesmen demonstrate the time-saving feeding machine, they bring a phonograph to play their sales spiel. Only near the end of the picture is the tramp's voice heard, singing a song in a night club. Later, when Chaplin got the idea for a Hitler story based on mistaken identity, he saw a brilliant solution of his voice problem. As the little barber in *The Great Dictator* (1940) he need speak only a few words, and the Hitler character he could treat with satire and burlesque, finding plenty of opportunity for pantomime. The parodies of Hitler's speeches were virtuoso performances in German doubletalk. Chaplin had gradually found a place in his films for the human voice and made it wonderfully effective. Yet his great love was for visual action—acting, pantomime, and the many kinds of dancelike movement he did so well, whether skating, playing with a globe map as if it were a balloon, or running around corners with one foot sticking out.

Whatever the problems of using the voice in films, the great advantage of the sound track for musical background was immediately clear to all, for at last a complete musical score could be recorded on the margin of the film and played in perfect coordination with the action. Audiences must have something to listen to or they get restless. Music with no relation to the action is better than nothing, and even the shabbiest nickelodeon of the early days had a mechanical piano. But music that underscores actions and moods is far better, and the honky-tonk pianist soon moved from the melodrama stage to the movie house with "Hearts and Flowers" for love scenes, the theme from "William Tell" for galloping horses, a passage from Schubert's "Erl-King" for restless suspense, and a slow triumphant passage for the "Came the dawn" scene at the end of a sentimental film. In the movie palaces of the 1920s the music was more carefully planned, and it was played by a skillful organist alternating with an orchestra. For a few feature pictures an entire score might be prepared. The critics had high praise for Joseph Carl Breil's score for *The Birth of a Nation,* made up of some original themes and a large number of folk tunes and symphonic excerpts. But for the routine picture the movie company sent out a cue sheet, which listed the episodes and the timing for each and gave the first few measures of a suggested piece of music, which the organist played with one hand while with the other he opened the music that he had placed in readiness on his music rack. The organist usually had only one run-through for practice, and had to be very resourceful in improvising and making transitions.

With the coming of sound the local musician lost his job, for a musical background was an integral part of each film. But the music of the sound track was very different from the musical background of a silent film. Since natural sounds could be recorded directly, it was no longer necessary to illustrate each separate action, and audiences had grown tired of familiar descriptive melodies anyway. It became standard practice to compose large orchestral pieces in the tradition of Wagner and Debussy which carry the

526

sweep of the drama through many episodes to its large climaxes. Occasionally a composer may set a mood with a melody on a popular instrument and repeat it several times during a movie. A simple ballad gives a lonely, melancholy mood to *High Noon* (1952). The spiritual that the passing Negro workman teaches to the nuns in *Lilies of the Field* (1963) is echoed throughout the film on banjo and harmonica. *Cat Ballou* (1965) is based on a ballad, and not only the song itself but recurrent shots of two men playing and singing the ballad are essential to the structure of the film.

The older function of film music, that of illustrating the action, has been followed by Charlie Chaplin and Walt Disney. No one has been more aware of the integral part of music in film than Chaplin, a musician and dancer himself. He confesses in his autobiography that in preparing a film he often started from music:

> Even in those early comedies I strove for a mood; usually music created it. An old song called *Mrs. Grundy* created the mood for *The Immigrant.* The tune had a wistful tenderness that suggested two lonely derelicts getting married on a doleful rainy day. . . .
>
> Simple little tunes gave me the image for other comedies. In one called *Twenty Minutes of Love,* full of rough stuff and nonsense in parks, with policemen and nursemaids, I weaved in and out of situations to the tune of *Too Much Mustard,* a popular two-step in 1914. The song *Violetera* set the mood for *City Lights,* and *Auld Lang Syne* for *The Gold Rush.*

When everyone else was making talking films, Chaplin refused to join in and produced *City Lights* in 1931 without voices but with a musical score, which he composed himself. He refused to let the arrangers give it a complex orchestral texture, insisting instead that they keep to a clear simple treatment of his melodies. Nor did he want the music to be a separate source of comedy. "They wanted the music to be funny," he wrote. "But I would explain that I wanted no competition, I wanted the music to be a counterpoint of grace and charm, to express sentiment, without which, as Hazlitt says, a work of art is incomplete." His music does not descend to the grubbiness of the tramp but offers an elegant, romantic contrast to the tramp character. What distinguishes Chaplin's music in all his films is that he fits a melody exactly to the rhythm and pattern of the action. He was fascinated by the Chinese theatre music he heard in Singapore and of course he was familiar with the use of music in the old melodrama, and he found a similar musical pattern of his own to add a dimension to the action.

The same approach of melodic underscoring, so different from the big Wagnerian orchestral background, has been used for some of the cartoons and many of the nature features of Walt Disney. In one delightful scene in the short feature *Bear Country,* a bear scratching his rump on a tree is accompanied by a melody that catches exactly the rhythm and the climactic pattern of the scratching. When the rhythm and movement of a film are created mostly by camera movement and cutting, the big orchestra can give unity and sweep to a series of episodes. But when the actor's movement is rhythmic, as with Chaplin and the animals Disney photographed, the method

527

of following the actors closely with music works well. While the orchestral sea of sound is usually dead serious, the imitative method can enhance either melodrama or comedy, keeping the audience aware that it is watching a play. But it is possible to combine several methods in one film. For *The Informer,* the composer Max Steiner used orchestral mood pieces for some sections, a haunting Irish song sung by a blind beggar for others, and imitative music for some specific actions—a chord for a door slamming, a few notes for coins falling on the floor, a run on the harp for the blowing of cigarette smoke, rough music when Gypo rips a poster from the wall.

THE ART OF COLOR

Color became established as a regular part of film-making just a little later than sound, but there had been experiments in color almost from the beginning, usually with the idea of making pictures prettier or more real than the black and white. More rarely, experiments were inspired by a desire to create mood. Many of the early short films from France were colored by hand, frame by frame. A three-color process known as "Kinemacolor," introduced in England in 1908, was used to photograph the Coronation of George V in 1910, but the color values were false and the outlines were fuzzy. In the original print of Griffith's *Intolerance,* the four stories were printed on film of four different colors—gray-green for the Babylonian story, blue for the Judean, sepia for the French, and amber for the modern. For *Broken Blossoms* (1919), besides using tinted sequences, Griffith had beams of pastel-colored light thrown on the screen while the film was run, to add to the soft, romantic atmosphere.

In 1923 a two-color process was marketed in which the red-orange-yellow portion of the spectrum was photographed on one negative and the green-blue-purple on another, and the two were laminated together. It was used for *The Black Pirate* (1926), with Douglas Fairbanks, and added to the film an atmosphere of the romantic past. By the time sound arrived several years later, a good color process was also ready, and several major studios used it. But the manufacturers were not prepared to process color film as fast as it was needed, and sound was creating problems enough to be solved in a period of depression, so within a year color had virtually disappeared. Laboratory experiments with color continued, however, and in 1935 *Becky Sharp,* directed by Rouben Mamoulian, was shot in the improved Technicolor, awakening a new interest in color that has never flagged. Ever since the Second World War color has been expected in spectacles and is frequently used in feature films.

Purists object to color because it destroys the clean-cut outlines and forms of black and white. As it has been used it tends to romanticize or sentimentalize, and that is why it seems so satisfactory in musicals and period pieces. But it should be possible to control color as effectively as sound is controlled, sometimes with a completely unrealistic treatment. Interesting experiments have been made in using color in this way. In *South Pacific* (1958), the musical numbers were shown in heightened color to set them apart from the

The Mass Media

narrative sequence. The picture made of *Oedipus* (1956) at Stratford, Ontario, in which grays and subdued blues and yellows predominated, was not at all realistic, but the color was well suited to the tragic feeling of the play. In filming *The Greatest Story Ever Told,* George Stevens used grayed tones in some sequences to increase the effect of melancholy and foreboding. In *The Cincinnati Kid* (1965), Norman Jewison eliminated the primary colors, using mainly faded green, soft browns, and beige as appropriate to the back streets, grubby hotel rooms, and smoke-filled gambling houses of his story.

Some of the most important European directors, among them Federico Fellini, Michelangelo Antonioni, and Ingmar Bergman, did not use color until the middle sixties, and they have been interested primarily in its psychological effects. An extreme example is Antonioni's *The Red Desert* (1965). As the heroine, a mentally disturbed woman, walks in the street, her depression is suggested by the uniform dull gray of the surroundings, not only the buildings but the people, the face of a man selling fruit, the fruit itself. When her lover thinks of her, everything in the scene takes on a blue tone, a color he associates with her. When the two meet in a hotel room, the walls change color as the woman's mood changes from hope to distress, then to disappointment. The color symbolism in this film is extremely obvious, and some directors prefer more subtle effects.

A few years ago it was commonly thought that a picture was shot in black and white only to save money, but film artists have always known that black and white is preferable for some pictures. The harsh texture so important for *The Pawnbroker* would have been softened and sentimentalized in color. For *Cleopatra* (1964), a lush color was effective, but when Elizabeth Taylor and Richard Burton planned *Who's Afraid of Virginia Woolf?* (1966), they decided that black and white was far more suitable for that particular subject. One does not disdain drawings or etchings because they have no color. A connoisseur of the film should be glad of a variety of treatment: gaudy color for some cartoons, rich Renaissance colors for historical spectacles, subtle grayed soft colors for mood plays, changing colors for films that attempt a subjective treatment of character, and good sharp black and white for farcical situation comedies and harsh studies of man and his environment.

SCREEN ACTING

Whether the picture is *Tom Jones, Thunderball, The Sound of Music, Ship of Fools,* or *The Collector,* it is the star that draws the crowds. The audience may be amused, thrilled, or deeply moved by the story, fascinated by new plot devices, property gadgets, and camera angles, charmed by backgrounds that are exotic, or captivated by those that are familiar and real, but it is the people on the screen, and especially the faces, that command the center of attention. Ingmar Bergman is quoted by his producer, Jörn Donner, as saying:

529

There are many film-makers who forget that the human face is the starting point in our work. To be sure, we can become absorbed by the esthetic of the picture montage, we blend objects and still lifes into wonderful rhythms, we can fashion nature studies of astonishing beauty, but the proximity of the human face is without doubt the film's distinguishing mark and patent of nobility.

On the screen as on the stage, the actor counts most.

Acting for the screen is not completely different from acting for the stage. Though there are some actors who prefer one and despise the other, there are many who move back and forth between stage and screen, enjoying the special challenges of each. For the camera close-up the actor cuts down his scale to small movements, subtle facial expression, and an intimate tone of voice. For the stage he uses large movements and more fully projected tones of voice.

At first the stage actor feels lost in acting before a camera without the stimulation of a live audience. The movie lot does not have even the half-genuine audience situation created by "guests" in a television studio. Every experienced actor in the theatre feels his audience and responds to it, adjusting his speaking of lines to make room for the laughs, which are not in the same places or of equal duration at all performances; on a good night he knows that he has the audience in the palm of his hand. For stimulation and guidance the screen actor, surrounded by mechanical apparatus, subjected to interruptions and delays, must rely on his imagination and on his director. But the stage actor, too, must rely to a great degree on his imagination and on his director, and stage performances, too, have their distractions—backstage bustle, complicated stage settings, quick costume changes, minor accidents on stage and the missing of lines or cues, intense heat from the lights, restlessness in the audience, and many others. One of the first disciplines an actor acquires is concentration, which may be achieved in the movie studio with only a little more difficulty than in the theatre. And if an audience is a stimulant, it is also a hazard. The screen actor does not pay so heavily as the stage actor for a cue missed, a line forgotten, a movement clumsily made. Total disaster is not possible for the actor in the studio: the scene can be shot again.

The conditions that make it impossible to act a screen play straight through with the scenes in proper sequence require a more difficult adjustment by the actor. A stage actor well rehearsed has a feeling for the development of the plot and for the growth of his character. In his performance, he usually begins in a low emotional key and builds to his climaxes. It is not customary to rehearse a screen play in its entirety before shooting begins, though this is sometimes done. Instead, scenes are commonly rehearsed separately, each one just before it is shot. The actor goes over and over one bit until the director is sure he has a good "take," or enough takes so that he can piece together from several. If the "rushes" developed at the end of the day are not satisfactory, the actor must do the same bit the next day. The sequence of shootings is arranged according to convenience in construc-

530

tion of sets, arrangements for going on location, commitments of actors to other assignments. As a result, the screen actor may have to play his biggest scene first. If he is a serious artist, however, and has studied his role, with the help of the director and on his own, he knows how the particular scene fits into the total pattern and is able to summon the right feeling. An actor lives by his imagination, and he becomes used to applying it in the ways the screen requires.

In keeping spontaneity of performance, the screen actor has one advantage over the stage actor: he may have to repeat a scene many times before the cameras roll and even after, but once the completed film has gone to the cutting room, the projector, not he, repeats the performance. Unlike the stage actor who performs the same part night after night for months or years if a play is successful, the screen actor moves into a new role. A successful screen actor may create many more parts than the stage actor, even when the stage actor is a member of a repertory company.

The director's control has been irksome to many screen actors. Some autocratic film directors have little regard for the art of acting. Robert Bresson, a French director who has made several of the most original films of the last decade, is quoted by John Russell Taylor in *Cinema Eye, Cinema Ear* as saying:

> Acting is for the theatre, which is a bastard art. The film can be a true art because in it the author takes fragments of reality and arranges them in such a way that their juxtaposition transforms them. Art *is* transformation. Each shot is like a word, which means nothing by itself, or rather means so many things that in effect it is meaningless. But a word in a poem is transformed, its meaning made precise and unique, by its placing in relation to the words around it; in the same way a shot in a film is given its meaning by its context, and each shot modifies the meaning of the previous one until with the last shot a total, unparaphrasable meaning has been arrived at. Acting has nothing to do with that, it can only get in the way. Films can be made by by-passing the will of those who appear in them, using not what they do but what they are.

The good actor is exasperated to realize that so much can be done by using only the actor's face and not his versatility as an actor. But that is one of the particular powers of the screen; both the camera and the editing can create the illusion of changing emotional reaction when the actor has actually done little or no acting. A strong face may give quite different impressions when it is photographed from different angles. If a scene is shot by several cameras from different angles, the director may find that one of them has caught just the expression he wants. Then in the cutting room the inexpressive moments are thrown away. Further, as Bresson notices, the context can define the meaning of a shot. If a close-up of a face brightly lighted is suddenly cut into the picture, the face looks startled, surprised, assertive. If a scene that should produce joy is put next it, the assertive face looks joyful; if a scene that should produce anger is cut in, the face looks angry. Shown in soft light, slowly approached by the camera, the same

531

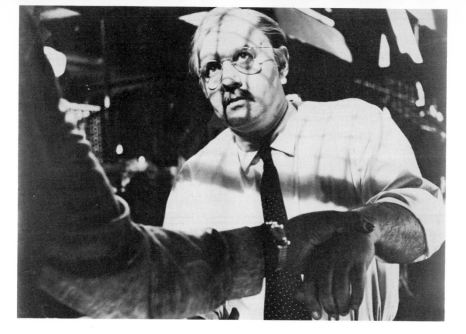

FIGURE *16.6*   A high point in acting for the screen. In Sidney Lumet's
The Pawnbroker, 1965, Rod Steiger plays the role of the victim of Nazi persecution
who finally allows himself to feel. The Landau Company.

face looks quiet and tender, but the particular meaning of its quiet tenderness is defined by the shots the editor puts next it. The face does not have
to change very much. All the cameraman and editor need is a mask, like a
Greek or Japanese Noh mask, an Egyptian statue of Nefertiti, or a Gothic
statue of the Virgin—a superdoll endowed with personality that satisfies
some deep need of the public: the exotic lure of Theda Bara or Pola Negri or
Jean Harlow, the wistfulness of Greta Garbo, the proud imperturbability of
Elizabeth Taylor, the vital defiance of Sophia Loren.

It takes good actors, however, to give that mask its great vitality, its power
to sustain a character throughout a film. The camera can create expressive
moments, but the actor, whether he makes his scenes in sequence or not,
must create the action as a whole, making every inch of footage live in every
reaction he makes, every gesture and every step. Rod Steiger in *The Pawnbroker* is much more than a series of close-ups made from well-calculated
camera angles. He is an actor.

Most directors therefore disagree with Bresson about the art of acting.
John Huston is only one of many who rely greatly on the imagination of their
actors, their improvised action or accidental inspirations, their considered interpretations. A film director may talk over the situation of a scene with his
cast, make general suggestions, and depend on the ingenuity of the actor to
work out details of voice, gesture, and movement as much as a stage director
does.

In character parts good acting has always been important. If actors of
straight roles may depend on personal charm and good looks and the power
of lighting and photography, character actors have to work to create their

The Mass Media

roles, using the qualities of their own personalities but seeking variety in makeup and performance from one role to the next. Alec Guinness has had big box-office appeal for more than two decades, and a large part of the interest of the public has been the fascination of his amazing transformations from one role to the next, not only in makeup but in rhythm, psychological gesture, and speech. Anthony Quinn has created many strong character roles, whether the rough man of inarticulate emotions in *Requiem for a Heavyweight* or the life-loving Zorba the Greek, with his hearty enjoyment of work, drink, love, and companionship and his warm laughter, big gestures, wild dancing, and moments of quiet sentiment. When the annual presentation of Academy Awards is made, the public is glad to see good acting recognized in smaller roles as well as in starring roles. Even in films where the glamour of stars is outrageously exploited, good acting may emerge. If little is demanded of Elizabeth Taylor in *Cleopatra* besides cold serenity, some use is made of that austerity in the quarrel scene. If Richard Burton has only a narrow range in *Becket,* that range has quiet power set against the mercurial instability of Peter O'Toole's vivid King Henry. Many people have decided that the living theatre is a more dependable place to find good acting, but the camera can and often does present good acting and sometimes great acting. When all is over, it is the actor, not the camera angle or the editing, that is remembered.

Screen Art in Special Kinds of Pictures

Important as he is in the fiction films that are the bulk of movie fare, the actor is *not* always of primary interest. In three kinds of pictures —the animated picture, the documentary, and the experimental film—he may yield the center of interest to animals, machinery, streets and other man-made environments, the operation of industries or institutions, drawings, and all sorts of camera effects. In the development of two of these kinds of pictures—the animated picture and the documentary—the United States has had a very important part.

THE ANIMATED PICTURE

The animated cartoon and the animated or partly animated feature, associated the world over with the name of Walt Disney, are notable examples of commercial development of experimental techniques. Disney was not the inventor of the animated cartoon. Early examples are *Humorous Phases of Funny Faces* (1906), made by J. Stuart Blackton, and *Gertie the Dinosaur* (1909), a film of 10,000 frames drawn by Winsor McCay, a New York newspaper cartoonist who took the picture on a vaudeville tour. But Disney elaborated the known techniques of animation, created vivid animal characters of great popular appeal, and above all developed an organization that made large-scale production possible and profitable.

The simple process of animation is not difficult to grasp. Each frame of the film requires a separate drawing photographed by a stop-motion camera

533

FIGURE *16.7* Charming fantasy in the animated cartoon. Both animals and men are fantastic in Walt Disney's *Alice in Wonderland,* 1951. Walt Disney Productions.

that takes one picture at a time. Each drawing moves the action ahead or cuts to a new sequence. There are devices, such as drawing on transparent plates and changing only part of the picture for each successive frame, which reduce the amount of labor, but making an animated film requires extensive equipment and a large team of workers. Since in normal movie projection there are twenty-four frames to the second, a five-minute film will need five times sixty times twenty-four frames, or 7,200 drawings. The sound track is usually made with live voices and musicians, and the sounds are sometimes distorted, as, for example, for Donald Duck's squawky voice. The synchronization of sound with visual image is approximately the same as for ordinary film. Instead of live music, some producers use electronic sounds or even draw lines and shapes on the sound track that produce extraordinary effects.

Disney's first films, a series called *Alice in Cartoonland,* which combined real actors and drawn figures, made no great impression, but when Mickey Mouse made his appearance in *Plane Crazy* (1928) and in the same year in *Steamboat Willie* with synchronized sound, he was a sensation. The first Silly Symphony was *The Skeleton Dance* (1929), still one of the best of Disney's many short fantasies. In 1932, *Flowers and Trees,* the first colored Silly Symphony, won an Academy Award.

Since his first animated features, *Snow White and the Seven Dwarfs* (1937), *Pinocchio* (1939), and *Fantasia* (1940), Disney has made several other animated features and several other kinds of pictures: combinations of human and animated figures, a wildlife series with real animals, straight live-action story pictures, and live-action fantasies using trick photography. In *Mary Poppins* (1964) he combined most of his devices in one film.

For three decades Disney's experimentation has been carried on within a very large commercial organization, and the pictures lack the freshness and

534

The Mass Media

spontaneity of the films that were more completely his own creations. Most of his story films in the cartoon technique are oversentimental, and his straight story films, without animation, are undistinguished, offering colorful, lively images suitable for family viewing. His nature studies, however, are superb, the real quality of rocks, plants, and animals coming through in spite of the silly love stories he superimposes through the words of the commentator. With all reservations, Disney's accomplishments are considerable. Mickey Mouse, Pluto, Donald Duck, The Three Little Pigs, and for that matter the penguin waiters in *Mary Poppins,* are inspired creations. Disney's human animals have become part of American folk tradition and have delighted audiences in all countries. None of the many other experimenters in animated cartoon techniques have as yet surpassed Disney.

THE DOCUMENTARY FILM

The documentary in a crude form has existed ever since the first man with a movie camera filmed a street parade, but it was not recognized as a separate genre until the twenties. It was developed by men who had tired of the conventional storytelling film or found it false, and the documentary has always appealed to experimental film-makers.

The documentary exploits reality, or what John Grierson, the most important figure in the development of the British documentary film, calls "the film's power of imaginative observation." When the documentary concentrates on fact and shows social purpose, as it often does, it is comparable to the Living Newspaper and other forms of epic theatre on the stage. Paul Rotha, an associate of Grierson in the thirties, defines the documentary as "the creative dramatization of actuality and the use of the film medium to interpret creatively and in social terms the life of the people as it exists in reality."

The creator of the documentary was an American, Robert Flaherty, a naturalist and explorer. He became an original, even revolutionary, figure in the film world of the twenties. While Hollywood was producing De Mille's colossal spectacles, the superromantic Valentino films, and the equally unreal pictures about the social game of wealthy people, Flaherty filmed *Nanook of the North* (1922), a true-life picture about Eskimos, showing the people themselves, not actors, and the interest, excitement, dignity, and beauty of everyday life, without heroics or romance or even story. In this film, as in all his pictures, Flaherty used actuality to develop the theme of man's relationship to nature in gaining a livelihood or in developing a culture. *Moana of the South Seas* (1926), with more exotic material than *Nanook,* was equally honest and revealing. But when Flaherty got financial support from Hollywood producers, they tried to add a Hollywood gloss to his pictures. Showings of *Moana* were advertised with posters representing the conventional hula dancer, and in some large theatres glamorous and synthetic South Sea scenes were set up in the lobby. When Flaherty was sent to make another South Sea documentary in 1930, a director of fiction films, F. W. Murnau, was sent with him. The resulting picture, *Tabu* (1931), has

FIGURE *16.8*   The American documentary. A scene from Flaherty's
Louisiana Story, 1948. Museum of Modern Art.

only traces of Flaherty's honest, poetic work. In his next piece, however, he
was his own master. *Man of Aran* (1934), perhaps the best of all his films,
shows simply and impressively the life of fishermen on an island off the
coast of Ireland: the struggle against sea and storm, the victories and defeats,
the disasters stoically met. Memorable are the real faces, with lines etched by
toil and the elements.

Flaherty continued his documentary work into the forties, producing
The Land (1942) and *Louisiana Story* (1948) only shortly before his death.
The latter, financed by the Standard Oil Company, is about the discovery of
oil in a Louisiana bayou and its effect on a Cajun family, but the film is
memorable chiefly as an idyll of an adolescent boy's life on the bayous. All
of Flaherty's films are poetic in their loving observation of nature and people. It is said that, unlike most other makers of documentaries, Flaherty
always began his shooting without a preconceived idea of what he wanted the
finished film to mean. He recorded landscape and people on many hundreds
of feet of film and then spent months studying what he had taken, cutting
and arranging, in order to find the core of meaning. He did not think of his
work as a means of bringing about changes in any way of life he pictured.

In the 1930s Flaherty's lead was followed by several directors, among them
Pare Lorentz, who added to the natural poetry of Flaherty the element of
social purpose. *The Plow That Broke the Plains* (1936) dealt with problems
of the dust bowl, and *The River* (1937) with the natural history of the
Mississippi Valley and man's mistreatment of the land by deforestation. With
poetic language on the sound track as well as poetic images on the screen,
The River is one of the most beautiful of all documentaries. *The City* (1939)
dealt with city planning, now a commonplace topic but fresh in the thirties;
it was based on Lewis Mumford's *The Culture of Cities* and was prepared

The Mass Media

specially for showing at the New York World's Fair of 1939–40. Other distinguished American documentaries of the thirties are a film inspired by the Spanish Civil War, *The Spanish Earth* (1937), with narration by Ernest Hemingway, and *The Four Hundred Million* (1938), directed by Joris Ivens, a factual and sympathetic film about China and its democratic revolution.

The actuality and the poetry of the documentary were already important elements in many storytelling films, especially Western epics like *The Covered Wagon,* and some city films of the thirties. In the forties and fifties, city streets became a milieu for many realistic films of Europeans and Americans.

In England, under the influence of Grierson, the documentary became a movement in the thirties and forties. Grierson was a sociologist, and although he was an admirer of Flaherty, he believed that honesty and poetry were not enough. He thought that a film should be used to show people the defects and the potentialities of the world they lived in and that for this purpose a modern country was a better field of observation than a remote spot in the Arctic or the South Seas. After spending three years (1924–27) in the United States studying modern means of communication, including the film, Grierson returned to England fired with the possibilities of using the cinema for public enlightenment and social improvement. He succeeded in having a film unit set up in the Empire Marketing Board, a minor government agency, and in getting public money to make *Drifters* (1929), a film about the herring fisheries in the North Sea. Several other films dealing with industries, including one directed by Flaherty, were made before this agency was dissolved, and by that time Grierson was able to get films made by other government departments. *Night Mail* (1936), showing the activities of the postal department, was one of the best. Throughout the thirties and forties Britain made distinguished documentaries, and in the war years films became an indispensable means of informing and influencing the public.

Flaherty was not the only influence in the development of the English documentary. As we have seen, the Russians used brilliant techniques in giving their political and social ideas a visual impact, and for three decades almost no Russian film deviated from the propagandist purpose. In addition to story films, the Russians also made documentaries about industries or special projects comparable to the Grierson films in England. *Turksib* (1929), an early example, presented the full story of the building of the Turkish-Siberian railroad. And finally the Russians began in the twenties to make a full camera record of the news with Kino-Eye, directed by Dziga Vertov. This project and comparable ones in other countries—in the United States, for example, *The March of Time,* which began in 1934—gave the most complete visual news coverage before the days of television.

Continental Europe felt the influence of both the American and the Russian documentary. Even before Flaherty had made his *Man of Aran,* Jean Epstein, an *avant-garde* artist and experimentalist, made *Finis Terrae* (1928), about kelp gatherers on the coast of Brittany. Other experimentalists in France and Germany had already made city documentaries: Alberto Cavalcanti, *Rien que les heures* ("Only the Hours," 1926–27), picturing a Paris day from dawn to night in its various moods; and Walter Ruttmann, *Berlin* (1927), also called *Symphony of a City*. A treatment of a city that showed the growing interest in social criticism was Jean Vigo's *À Propos de Nice* (1929), which is not merely a study of mood but a piece of caustic social comment, using the camera to emphasize extremes of wealth and poverty in the resort city.

Many documentary films were made in Europe and America during the Second World War. Important American examples are John Ford's *The Battle of Midway* (1942), William Wyler's *Memphis Belle* (1944), and John Huston's *The Battle of San Pietro* (1944). Since the war, documentaries have been used in the armed forces, schools, and industry as well as for the general public, to explain processes and industrial or social developments or to give the background of important current events. In making them, directors have learned much about photographing real places and people and using things, especially machines, for a combination of pictorial effect and social meaning. They have learned to select the significant object or the revealing face and to create dramatic effects with crowds or with movement in nature and in machinery.

The treatment not only of background but of people in story films of the forties, fifties, and sixties owes much to the documentary, and the first films of many of the best directors, like John Huston in this country, Alain Resnais in France, and Michelangelo Antonioni in Italy, were documentaries. Many films of our time are described as "semidocumentary." An example is *Synanon* (1964), a film about drug addiction that uses activities in an actual home for addicts and adds a few professional actors and a thread of story. Several films directed by John Frankenheimer have a strong element of the documentary, notably *Birdman of Alcatraz* (1962), based on the real story of a prisoner in a Federal penitentiary, and *The Train* (1964), concerned with the effort to save valuable paintings from the Germans during the Occupation; in the latter film, the operation of French trains, railroad stations, and signal systems becomes almost as interesting as the plot itself. Sidney Lumet, who directed *The Hill* (1965), a film about a British prison camp in North Africa during the Second World War, thought that its strongest asset was its "rough-grained, almost documentary quality." In *The Slender Thread* (1965), the story of an attempted suicide and its prevention, a great deal of footage is devoted to the "crisis clinic" to which the potential suicide appeals and to the operation of the city telephone and police systems. The moviegoer often acquires information while he is being entertained.

Most popular with moviegoers are the biographies of real people. Several impressive Hollywood films in the thirties dramatized the lives of famous men, giving a sense of historical forces through techniques that were influenced by the documentaries. Some of the best biographical films—*The Life of Louis Pasteur* (1936), *The Life of Émile Zola* (1937), and *Juarez* (1939)—made use of the versatile actor Paul Muni. For recent important figures it is possible to produce more authentic documentary-biography,

538

with photographs, news films, and television tapes taken from life. Three brilliant examples are *The Finest Hours,* about Winston Churchill, made in 1964 while he was still alive; *The Eleanor Roosevelt Story* (1965); and *John F. Kennedy: Years of Lightning, Day of Drums,* released in the United States in 1966 after having been shown abroad through the United States Information Agency.

While films concerning historical events such as *The Longest Day* (1962), about the allied landing in Normandy in 1944, *Is Paris Burning?* (1966), about a plan of the Germans to destroy Paris before abandoning it after the Occupation, and *The Last Battle* (1967), about the last days of the Hitler regime, have made use of documentary research, some films consist entirely of still photographs and moving pictures made in the past. *To Die in Madrid* (1965) draws on almost-forgotten files of actual pictures of the Spanish Civil War of the thirties in recreating a piece of modern history. Documentary is the most important means of holding the motion picture to the reality that was its first aim, though the concept of the reality has been greatly extended.

THE EXPERIMENTAL FILM

The documentary and the animated picture were originally "experimental," but the term *experimental film* has usually been applied in a very restricted way. It refers to a film that has been made without the expectation of wide distribution, although the film may actually have some commercial success and may influence producers and directors in large film

FIGURE *16.9*　Fantasy in an early French film. The Gigantic Mushrooms Grotto in Georges Méliès' *A Trip to the Moon,* 1902, was created in the studio. Photo Culver Pictures.

companies to adapt its striking effects to more conventional patterns. The experimental film has most commonly been abstract in form or highly subjective in content, sometimes expressing so exclusively the film-maker's consciousness that it has not been intelligible to the viewer, and it has often used extraordinary camera techniques or tricks. It has usually been created by and for the *avant-garde* who reject the conventional film patterns of the moment. Such groups have been more influential in Europe than in the United States, where most film experiments have been fitted into the routines of the large companies and have therefore been less free or erratic.

Though he belonged to no *avant-garde,* Georges Méliès, one of the first French film-makers, may be called the first experimentalist, not because he was the first to create stories in film (his *A Trip to the Moon,* made in 1902, and several other story films preceded Porter's *The Great Train Robbery*) but because, unlike many other early film-makers, he used the camera to create fantasy rather than to record the real world. He had been a stage magician, and in the movie studio he worked out comparable scenes of transformation, showing great ingenuity in devising unusual effects with the camera. Although his productions were not entirely cinematic, since the staging was like that in the legitimate theatre, he had the experimentalist's impulse to make the screen a medium for something besides closely observed reality.

The first radically experimental motion picture to be widely noticed in the United States was an expressionistic film, *The Cabinet of Dr. Caligari* (1919), made in Germany. Streets, walls, houses, and furniture are distorted;

FIGURE *16.10* Expressionism in the movies. Setting, costumes, and movement are treated as seen in a distorted mind. *The Cabinet of Dr. Caligari,* 1919, directed by Robert Wiene. Museum of Modern Art.

FIGURE *16.11* A vision of a mechanical world. Men are machines, the slaves of inhuman masters, in the underground passages of the city. *Metropolis,* 1926, an early experimental film directed by Fritz Lang. Museum of Modern Art.

makeup and acting are stylized; and the photography is in the sharpest contrast of black and white. At the end it is revealed that the entire action is in the imagination of a madman obsessed with the idea that the head of the mental hospital is a demonic Dr. Caligari who controls a somnambulist by witchcraft and causes him to commit murders. Another favorite theme of German expressionism, the mechanized city, is the subject of *Metropolis* (1926), directed by Fritz Lang, who later did *Fury* and other good films in Hollywood. The picture represents a future state run by an industrialist dictator. The masses—a race of robots artificially created—live in underground factories, producing wealth for the privileged class. The settings show above the surface a clean, mechanized metropolis. The workers revolt, but they are eventually reconciled with the dictator, and the play ends with the promise of an ideal future. The story is somewhat lame in social thinking, but the film is imaginative and effective. The mechanization theme was given a cubist treatment in *Ballet Mécanique* (1924) by the French artist Fernand Léger, one of the first cubist painters. It resembles his canvases with its succession of shafts, gears, and wheels, to which are added eggbeaters, pots and pans, and other metal objects as well as people with mechanized movements.

Two German abstract painters of the twenties, Hans Richter and Viking Eggeling, were amateur experimentalist film producers. In trying to find means to develop visual themes in painting as musical themes are developed in a symphony, they hit upon the use of film. Richter's *Rhythmus 21* and Eggeling's *Symphonie Diagonale,* both made in 1921, used animated abstract

541

forms moving in sequences to give visual ideas the dimension of time. Richter called some of his creations "absolute film," using masks and cut-outs and double exposure and other camera devices. Oskar Fischinger, also a German artist, in 1928 made a film using cartoon technique to create visual accompaniment to standard orchestral works, an idea like that developed later in Walt Disney's *Fantasia* (1940).

In France, many people, both professional directors and amateurs, were interested in applying to film the principles of new movements in the other arts. The Dadaists, artistic anarchists interested in absurdities for their own sake, liked to startle, shock, or outrage the public. Man Ray, the American artist of still photography who lived in Paris in the twenties, made his first moving picture for an evening of mixed entertainment by a Dadaist group. Called, ironically, *The Return to Reason* (1923), his picture was made partly by sticking bits of unrelated objects to raw film. A more orderly though still absurd piece was *Entr'acte* (1924), made by the professional film director René Clair on commission from Rolf Maré for an interlude for his Ballet Suédois. The actors included the leading dancer of Maré's company, Maré himself, Man Ray, the composer Darius Milhaud, and other artists. The absurd "story" includes an accidental murder and the funeral procession of the deceased. The hearse breaks loose, and there is a mad chase at frantic speed to recover it. When the hearse finally stops, the coffin falls out and the corpse pops up smiling. The whole picture is a mixture of many ingenious incongruities created partly through camera tricks, and there is no total meaning.

Surrealism, partly an outgrowth of Dadaism, was somewhat less chaotic. Most of the surrealists were radical in politics, they all rejected conventional concepts in manners, morals, and art, and they were influenced by the current craze for Freudian concepts and dream imagery. The most famous films of this movement are *Un Chien andalou* ("An Andalusian Dog," 1929), made by the painter Salvador Dali and Luis Buñuel, both Spaniards who played minor roles in the film, and *L'Âge d'or* ("The Age of Gold," 1930), made by Buñuel. *Un Chien andalou* has several shocking images that are often cited as examples of surrealist fancies—an eyeball cut by a razor, a fist enclosing a nest of ants, and the carcass of a donkey draped on a grand piano.

L'Âge d'or, a masterly picture of imaginative incongruities, caused a double scandal. The Vicomte de Noailles, who had commissioned it but had not been told what the completed film was like, invited a select group of guests for the première, and they were outraged. After the film had run for several weeks in a Montmartre public theatre, a demonstration was staged against it as a "Bolshevik piece," and after other protests it was banned by the police. The demonstrations and protests were not surprising, for the picture is a denunciation of the church and society. The film opens like a documentary with a scene of barren rocks and a discourse on scorpions, then cuts to a scene of priests celebrating Mass among the rocks. Later, at a social gathering, tumbrils carrying peasants pass through the room and a fire breaks out in the kitchen without causing any interruption of the festivities. When it is reported that a gamekeeper has killed his son, there is a momentary stir, but the explanation that the son disobeyed his father settles the matter. No other surrealist film was so sharp in social comment. After producing only two or three unimportant films in the next twenty years, Buñuel resumed his cinema career in Mexico in the late forties and produced several remarkable films that will be considered in the next chapter.

The best known of the early French experimental films is Jean Cocteau's *Le Sang d'un poète* ("The Blood of a Poet," 1930), made on commission from the same man who commissioned Buñuel's *L'Âge d'or*. Somewhat like *Un Chien andalou*, it juxtaposes incongruities, follows unexplained transformations, and tries such camera tricks as looking through a keyhole and seeing people walking on walls or ceilings. It anticipates Cocteau's more sophisticated film fantasies of the 1940s and 50s, *La Belle et le bête* ("Beauty and the Beast," 1946) and *Orphée* (1951), in which he uses the fairy tale and the Greek myth of Orpheus in the underworld to express in modern psychological terms his theme of the ambiguity of desire and fear as man is lured and controlled by irrational forces.

The United States has usually followed rather than led in the more radical artistic movements in cinema. In the 1920s there were a number of American admirers of the advanced European movements, film aesthetes who rejected the current Hollywood offerings in favor of foreign films. There was even an American expressionist film, *The Fall of the House of Usher*, made in 1928, and a semiabstract film, H_2O, directed by Ralph Steiner in 1929. But the United States made its important artistic contributions in the documentary and the animated cartoon rather than in the experimental film.

Since the Second World War interest in unusual aspects of film-making has increased. The principal figure in the forties was Maya Deren, who tried to suggest through the film medium elusive states of consciousness. Her *Meshes of the Afternoon* (1943) introduces several figures and incidents that impinge on the consciousness of a woman, then traces the recurrence of these figures in various combinations in the free play of the mind. The images and the slow movement of the film create an empathic response of illusion.

Some American experimentalists of the last decade have been especially interested in the use of abstract forms in rhythmic combination with music, recalling some of the experimental work of the twenties. The development of electronic music suggests new dynamic combinations of the visual and aural. Many films are the work of amateurs, who have their own publications and gatherings for viewing films, most of which are made on sixteen-millimeter or sometimes eight-millimeter stock to be shown on small screens. It has been possible in the last decade for amateur or semiprofessional film-makers to rent studio space in Hollywood with the best facilities.

Like some of the "New Wave" French, a group of New York directors in the sixties (sometimes called the "New York School") became interested in improvisation. *Shadows* (1960), directed by John Cassavetes, is entirely improvised. Amusing and fresh as a single specimen made by imaginative people, it remains an actors' exercise. One of the principal members of the New

543

FIGURE *16.12* Absurd duel in an "underground" film. Experimentalists delight in incongruities. Adolfas Mekas' *Hallelujah the Hills,* 1963. Vermont Pictures.

York group is Jonas Mekas, whose *Guns of the Trees* (1961) and *The Brig* (1964) have received wide attention. Jonas helped his brother Adolfas with *Hallelujah the Hills* (1963), which has been shown in several foreign film festivals. The substance of *Hallelujah the Hills* concerns two young men's reminiscences of a girl they both loved, but the fun for an in-group of cinema experts lies in the visual allusions to the work of Chaplin, Sennett, Griffith, Eisenstein, and others, and to Ma and Pa Kettle (comic characters of the forties). Jonas Mekas is also known for his film reviews, for the founding of a quarterly magazine, *Film Culture,* as a forum for young people, and for his connection with other projects of experimental film-making and viewing. These activities outside the large film companies are sometimes referred to as "underground cinema," and the movement has attracted many amateurs with cameras. The catalogue of the Film-Makers' Cooperative, which rents and releases works of this new American cinema, lists several hundred films and nearly a hundred film-makers. San Francisco is a center for similar experimental and amateur activity on the West Coast. Such a lively interest in cinema outside the large studios is one sign of vitality in the art of film.

EXERCISES

1. CAMERA MOVEMENT. Analyze some of the camera movement of a particular film. What is the purpose of a move—to follow the moving actor, to bring in an actor from a long shot to a close-up for greater sympathy and identification, to create a faster tempo, a restless mood, or a sense of dynamic action, or to bring a sequence to a quieter ending by moving away? What are the purposes when writer and cameraman have spread into several

EXERCISES

places action that a stage playwright would keep in one spot? Does the movement from place to place add variety and a sense of action? Does it put each moment in a surrounding appropriate to it? Does it add anticipation before a climax or reaction after one, or does it merely dilute the dramatic tension by unnecessary change?

2. CUTTING AND MONTAGE. Analyze a movie for narrative cutting. Is there crosscutting of different groups of characters or different parts of the story? Are the shots cut in decreasing length so that there is an increase in tempo towards a climax? Analyze scenes that show the cutting in of objects, parts of the environment, or faces to create symbolic imagery, or "montage," as the Russians use the term. What meaning and what mood is added by bringing the object or fact to the center of attention so that it can be associated with the main characters of the scene?

3. ACTING IN MOVIES. Describe the acting in particular scenes of some movie. To what extent do makeup and lighting create glamour? How much is the appearance of emotional reaction created by the movement of the camera, how much by what is shown just before and just after a close-up, and how much by the acting itself?

4. ACTING IN MOVIES. Analyze a particular star. How far does the star correspond to one of our conventional prototypes of hero or heroine, and how far does he add an individual quality or suggest a new variation of an old type? How much does the star vary from one film to another?

5. ACTING IN MOVIES. Analyze some character actor. How much does he vary from one film to another? Is the difference created by makeup, costume, characteristic movement, basic attitude to life, or what?

6. THE USE OF SOUND IN FILM. Analyze some treatments of sound in particular films. What natural sounds are used? Are they brought in as part of the background to create mood? Are they used subjectively as the memory or imagination of one character? Is music used throughout or only in certain places? Is there a consistent plan for using music with some scenes and not with others? Is there a song or particular theme for the film? Is it associated with a particular character or action? Is there a characteristic instrument, as flute, horn, guitar, harmonica, and so on? Is there a large, sustained orchestral background, or does the music at some points illustrate or underscore a particular movement of the actor? Is dialogue kept to a minimum or is it sometimes interesting in itself? Are there long sequences of dialogue? Some sequences without any words? Has the dialogue mood, local color, rhythm, wit, poetry, strong rhetoric, or other intensities of its own?

7. COLOR IN FILM. Analyze examples of the use of color in film. Is the treatment suitable to the particular subject, or would black and white or

545

a different range of color values have been better? How far is color used for mood? Is it used to indicate the subjective experience of one character? Is there a difference in the treatment of color from one part to another? Consider a black-and-white film and ask what would have been gained and what would have been lost if some parts or all of it had been in color.

8. A DOCUMENTARY FILM. Study a documentary film and ask what organization and continuity it has. Does the narrator give it continuity? Is a character who asks and learns used for audience identification? How are touches of human interest brought in? Is the interest mainly in a poetic mood and local color? Has the film a social purpose, urging a particular change? Would you call the film good propaganda?

9. A FICTION FILM WITH DOCUMENTARY BACKGROUND. Study a story film that has real backgrounds. To what extent are the studio interiors consistent with and integrated into the real scenes? What mood is created by the location shots? To what extent are the backgrounds informative and interesting in themselves?

SUGGESTED READING

Suggested reading for films is given at the end of Chapter 17.

CHAPTER SEVENTEEN

MOVIES AS A MINORITY ART

In the last two decades the movies have reached a new maturity. The resistance of directors in the 1940s to the tight control of producers was a true forecast of change, and the development of television greatly stimulated the change. With television providing a new medium of casual entertainment for the masses, the cinema soon became an art for a minority, though a large minority, and the new status brought new freedom.

Between 1946 and 1956 attendance at the movies dropped fifty percent. If people could have routine screen entertainment at home, why go out? Many movie theatres were closed, and with the decreased demand for pictures, some of the large studios in turn were closed or converted to rental property; others turned to making standard weekly programs for television. Furthermore, the big Hollywood producers could no longer rely on guaranteed bookings for their films because of court rulings that brought about a separation of distribution and production. The independent producers who operated on a small scale could now compete in marketing their films. And although the large film companies might help finance pictures by the independents, they did not have complete control over the content. With the loosening of the power structure, the independents often broke away from the formulas that had dominated the films of the twenties and thirties, and the large producers sometimes followed their example.

The conformist pattern of mass entertainment that had been set by Hollywood was also modified during this period by the increasing practice of making pictures outside the United States. When European countries placed restrictions on sending money out of the country and, to protect their own film companies, set limits on the showing of foreign-made films, American producers were tempted to make films abroad to use their impounded funds and to take advantage of low costs of materials and labor, unlimited distribution in the country where a film was made, and an atmosphere of experimentation. As American tourists and military personnel traveled all over the world, the audiences back home took increased delight in pictures set in Paris, Rome, Switzerland, or the Greek isles.

Thus, changes took place in the film world, but those who predicted in 1950 that the cinema would disappear were wrong. In spite of television there are still nearly 20,000 movie theatres in this country and 100,000 in Europe —no small market for commercial production. Nor are all the theatres drive-ins or neighborhood houses where anything goes. Most producers have held the movie audience by doing things television cannot or will not do. A few producers took advantage of a relaxation of censorship to exploit sensationalism, but the more responsible producers used it to give a large minority audience an adult treatment of screen material, and some even pushed into experimentation that could be acceptable to only a very small part of the public.

In our examination of the survival and growth of the movies, two lines of development will appear—the conformist and the nonconformist. Conservative producers, or producers in their conservative moods, have made a bid for a large part of the mass audience with variations of old film patterns, using new stars with the old glamour. The more daring independent producers, or the big producers in their daring moods, have created original pictures for a limited audience, which has sometimes become a large minority.

Variations of Old Patterns

Among the types of story and character that had pleased the movie audience for half a century, three were successfully adapted to new conditions in the film industry and to changes in public taste—the spectacle, the Western, and the picture of youthful rebellion. Resourceful producers and directors were able to find some new element in each type to make the old seem fresh.

THE WIDE SCREEN AND THE SPECTACLE

In the 1950s producers who saw the audience melting away looked to the large screen to save their business. It was something television could not provide, and they hoped to dazzle the public with colossal effects. The wide screen was not a new idea. Experiments go back to a French Cinéorama of 1897, a movie projected on a circular screen by ten projectors. An outstanding experiment was made in 1926 by Abel Gance, a French director, with *Napoléon Bonaparte,* made for projection on a triple screen four times as wide as high. But this and other experiments were isolated

FIGURE *17.1* Two cinematic treatments of the story of Cleopatra. ABOVE: The 1963 filming, with Elizabeth Taylor, was the ultimate in postwar scenic spectacle. BELOW: The 1917 version, with Theda Bara, was produced with less lavish spectacle and more emphasis on Cleopatra as siren. Photos New York Public Library.

examples. In 1929, just before the depression, the large American studios were almost ready for mass production for a wide screen, and several pictures were actually made on film wider than the standard thirty-five millimeter, but producers and exhibitors decided that adaptation for sound was as much as they could cope with at that time. Processes for taking pictures to be projected on a wide screen and the size of the screen were not standardized until the fifties. There were many incongruous results before filmmakers learned what could be done effectively. CinemaScope was introduced with Fox's five-million-dollar adaptation of Lloyd C. Douglas' pseudo-Biblical best seller *The Robe* (1953). By 1957, 17,500 theatres in the United States were equipped for CinemaScope.

The Robe was a great success, and Hollywood put more and more money into the big epics; *Cleopatra,* by the time it was finished in 1963, had cost more than forty million dollars. With great sums of money, the whole world as a studio, and big screens and loud-speakers to astound the audience, the movies blew up to colossal size all the old spectacular effects. Cecil B. De Mille's formula of spectacle combined with religion, sex, and violence, which had attracted millions to the theatres in the twenties and thirties, was still potent, and De Mille himself was still active, bringing in new fortunes with *Samson and Delilah* (1949) and a wide-screen remake of his 1923 success, *The Ten Commandments* (1956).

Some moviegoers seemed never to tire as *Ben Hur* was followed by *The Fall of the Roman Empire,* as *The Ten Commandments* led to *The King of Kings, The Greatest Story Ever Told,* and *The Bible,* and as battles of Alexander and the Caesars alternated with scenes of the Crusades or modern land, sea, and air battles. But although it was exciting at first to see large images of chariot races and gladiator fights, once the eye had grown used to the wide screen most people found the scope less impressive, and now the grand effects often seem pretentious or even ludicrous. Many of the stories from which spectacles are made have little literary value, and when the scriptwriter tries to supply real characterization the results are sometimes worse than when the tale is treated as a straight adventure story. In *Spartacus* (1960), Stanley Kubrick, a resourceful director, attempted to give psychological depth to his characters, but the Roman lovers never seemed more than dressed-up Hollywood actors, the dialogue was dull, and the attempt to suggest inner conflict slowed down action that might have been more acceptable if the audience had not had time to think.

A number of the better directors tried their hand at spectacle. The chance to command an enormous budget, to work with good actors and technicians in interesting parts of the world, and to have considerable independence in putting the stamp of their own personality on the film has great appeal. *Ben Hur* (1959), under the direction of William Wyler, became an absorbing story without the worst inanities of spectacular shows. The old clichés were there: the persecution and civil strife in Judea, the fight on the galley slave ship, and the chariot race, with its long shots of crowds and horses and its close-ups of the mangled flesh of the villain who had been dragged by his own overturned chariot. Wyler did not create real people or elicit real acting, but he did keep his glamorous actors and his story from being lost in the spectacle. The director Richard Brooks had a better story for *Lord Jim* (1964) in the novel of Joseph Conrad, as well as an excellent actor in Peter O'Toole, but he all but lost Lord Jim's personal crisis of responsibility and guilt in intrigues and exotic spectacle. Even a good director cannot always keep spectacle in its place.

The top achievements in spectacle have been the films of the British directors Peter Glenville and David Lean. For *Becket* (1964), Glenville had in Jean Anouilh's stage play two far better characters than are found in most of the novels used for the big films, and he had two excellent actors to play them: Richard Burton, as the quiet Chancellor who is transformed into a dedicated Archbishop, and Peter O'Toole, as the volatile King Henry, fascinated by Becket but perversely driven to contrive his murder. The film is a spectacular show, with castles, royal audience chambers, crowds, and processions, but the spectacle is made to serve the characters and the story. The installation of Becket as Archbishop, for instance, is magnificent spectacle, but the attention is constantly on Becket as he is transformed by the ceremony and gradually takes on the new resolution that will remove him from Henry's control.

David Lean produced three very large shows—*The Bridge on the River Kwai* (1957), *Lawrence of Arabia* (1963), and *Dr. Zhivago* (1965)—in which he kept the spectacle in proper proportions. In *The Bridge on the*

FIGURE *17.2* Spectacle with a dominant hero. Peter O'Toole as Lawrence greets a crowd of Arabs in David Lean's *Lawrence of Arabia,* 1963. Columbia Pictures.

River Kwai the episodes of the deprivation and torture of British prisoners in a Japanese camp, of the construction of a bridge for a Japanese railroad, and even of the escape and return of an American soldier are all made to serve Lean's study of the existentialist dilemma of the English engineer, played by Alec Guinness, who cannot resist pride in his building job though its purpose is to aid the enemy. *Lawrence of Arabia* shows expanses of desert, Cairo army headquarters, the exotic pleasures of Bagdad, and battles between the Allies and the Turks, but the focus is constantly on the complex personality of the European who loves the desert and the Arabians and can meet the most extraordinary situations with uncanny understanding of others but little understanding of himself. *Dr. Zhivago* suggests the sweep of the Russian Revolution, with a setting of the city of Moscow built on a movie lot in Spain and snow scenes taken in Finland and the Canadian Rockies, but it keeps a focus by showing the impact of events on the character of Dr. Zhivago, played by Omar Sharif.

TRANSFORMATION OF THE WESTERN

The "adult Western" has been almost as successful as the spectacle in keeping a large audience coming to the movies, by using better actors and a fresher approach to characterization than television Westerns do. We are not considering now the historical epics with western settings that have been popular since *The Covered Wagon* (1923) and have been seen in such recent examples as *How the West Was Won* (1962) and *Cheyenne Autumn* (1964). In the 1950s a type of Western less ambitious than the epic was developed, concentrating on one heroic figure and telling a personal story rather than one of broad social or historical significance.

Although the adult Western has many of the conventions of the "B Western," as routine Westerns have been called, it uses better screen actors and shows more realism in setting and story and more imagination in photography. The early star William S. Hart made a specialty of portraying convincingly the man of the West, capable of heroism and fine feelings but on the whole realistic. But in the commercial decades, as routine Westerns were turned out by the hundreds, the image of the cowboy became less rugged and more conventionally romantic through successive portrayals by Tom Mix, Ken Maynard, Hoot Gibson, Hopalong Cassidy, and finally Gene Autry with his guitar. Some B Westerns are still made for the movie screen, but television supplies most of the entertainment for addicts who want the same hard-riding, sharp-shooting figure.

We have already commented on *The Ox-Bow Incident* and *The Treasure of the Sierra Madre* for their intelligent use of dramatic material in a western background. But the first movie to establish the adult Western with a wide public was *High Noon* (1952), directed by Fred Zinneman. Its strong man was played by Gary Cooper, who had already played a number of Western roles, usually creating a more credible hero than the stereotype. *High Noon* takes place in the 1870s in a cattle town with a population of four hundred, about the same period and environment as in *The Ox-Bow Incident*. The

552

marshal, played by Cooper, learns that an outlaw whom he had sent to jail in a nearby town has been released and is returning on the noon train to take his revenge. When the marshal tries to raise a posse to deal with the outlaw, everyone has an excuse for not becoming involved. In the saloon, bets are made that the marshal will be dead at five minutes after noon. As the story builds from mid-morning to noon, suspense is created through repeated camera shots of the railroad tracks and the deserted streets and through a crescendo of ticking clocks and the plaintive "High Noon" ballad, with its note of impending doom. In the end the marshal gets his man, but the figure of the tired, reluctant gunfighter in plain, dark, worn clothing, doggedly stalking through the streets, is not the stereotype of the man of the West, and the theme of failure of community responsibility is an unusual one for a Western.

Shane (1953) has a hero nearer the conventional pattern—a stranger who has killed a man and who rides into frontier country to escape from the law. In helping a homesteading family to defend their rights against villainous cattlemen, he is forced to shoot a hired killer, and he must ride on again, a lonely outcast. The part is played with unconventional honesty by Alan Ladd, the other characters and the life of the family and community are portrayed realistically, and there is a freshness in details chosen for both the sound track and the camera that makes the picture superior to the routine Western.

Other directors followed a promising lead, among them Marlon Brando, who not only directed *One-Eyed Jacks* (1961) but played the leading role of a lonely young man involved in western violence and vengeance for

FIGURE *17.3* The lonely stranger as a savior figure in an "adult Western." In the wide open spaces of the American West the champion fights evil to protect the settlers who are opening up a new continent. George Stevens' *Shane,* 1953. Paramount Pictures Corporation.

complex personal reasons. George Stevens in *Giant* (1956), John Huston in Arthur Miller's *The Misfits* (1960), and Martin Ritt in *Hud* (1963) used the wide spaces of horse and cattle country where conflict was settled as in the early days through personal violence, but all three indicated that a new social attitude had penetrated the legendary West, making personal violence a gross violation of human relations rather than a clear-cut fight with evil. In these films distinguished actors gave the characters some of the complexity they had learned from playing other roles—Gary Cooper and James Dean in *Giant,* Clark Gable, Montgomery Clift, and Marilyn Monroe in *The Misfits,* and Paul Newman and Raymond Massey in *Hud.*

Psychological values in the adult Western should not be overstressed. No matter how honest the attempt at characterization in depth, the chief interest for many viewers of Westerns is beautiful scenery and pictorial effects of men and animals against a great expanse of plains, mountains, or sky, made all the more spectacular on the wide screen. The better Westerns take their place alongside the historical, religious, and literary epics as old forms that compete successfully with television because of their better acting, better directing and camera work, and occasionally their more adult approach to characterization.

There have been many humorous Westerns, including one made by Buster Keaton called *Go West* (1925), but *Cat Ballou,* a hit of 1965, is a particularly amusing lampoon of the Western, and *The Hallelujah Trail* (1964), in which Burt Lancaster is a harried army officer trying to get a trainload of whiskey to Denver in spite of thirsty soldiers and Indians, is an uproarious tale of Western life filmed on an almost epic scale.

THE NEW IMAGE OF REBELLIOUS YOUTH
In the 1950s, Hollywood's darkest years, when the mass audience turned to television, when many American writers and directors made films in other countries, and when foreign-made pictures became popular with

FIGURE *17.4* The Dean image of troubled youth. Caleb cannot find security in himself, his family, or the girl he loves. *East of Eden,* 1954, with James Dean and Julie Harris. Directed by Elia Kazan. Warner Brothers Pictures.

American moviegoers, producers in this country created one new image that caught the attention of the world—rebellious youth. Young people have usually idolized an image of independence and assertion in a popular singer, from Bing Crosby of the thirties to Elvis Presley and the Beatles of recent years. But the alienated young hero treated seriously and acted realistically is something quite different. Marlon Brando struck the chord of lonely rebellion in *The Wild One* (1954), *On the Waterfront* (1954), and *The Fugitive Kind* (1960), giving an appealing portrayal of the rootless young man with black leather jacket and motorcycle, but the more youthful James Dean created in the fifties the perfect image for American young people, and indeed for the youth of other countries. It was an image of a "rebel without a cause" (the title of one picture), for many young people an image of their own insecurity and unfocused frustration, their lack of dependable standards, and their lack of meaningful relationship to parents, school, and society. For people of all ages it was an image of the isolation and alienation of the individual that spread over the western world at the end of the Second World War.

Dean died at twenty-four (speeding in a racing car) after having made only three important pictures—*East of Eden* (1954), *Rebel Without a Cause* (1955), and *Giant* (1956)—but he left a deep impression. A product of the Actors Studio in New York and a discovery of Elia Kazan, who directed his first picture, he riveted attention with his casual stance and natural movement, creating that exciting current between actor and audience that is one mark of dramatic talent. In *Rebel Without a Cause* he portrays a boy, the son of middle-class parents, who gets drunk, draws a knife, and finally accepts the challenge to play chicken with another boy by dashing to the edge of a cliff in their cars, the first to jump before his car goes over the cliff to be "chicken." The other boy is killed, and the "rebel" shows that he has sounder principles than his parents by insisting, against their wishes, on going to the police. In *East of Eden,* an adaptation of John Steinbeck's lengthy novel telling a modern Cain and Abel story, Dean plays the younger brother Caleb. His search for his mother and his efforts to win his father's esteem lead to pain and frustration. A family crisis develops from the father's failure in a business venture and the two brothers' interest in the same girl. In his torment, Caleb drives his brother to near madness and causes his father to have a paralytic stroke. The plot is melodramatic, but the film, an early wide-screen color picture, is well directed, well acted, and technically excellent. The identification of James Dean with his role seems complete, and the troubled boy makes an irresistible appeal.

The American image has had counterparts in other countries. Since 1956 the Canadian director Sidney Furie has made several goods films in England dealing with youths and their problems, of which *The Leather Boys* (1963) is best known. The title refers to the leather jacket that became the uniform of a certain young set, as the motorcycle was their means of transportation. In this picture, a fresh, talented young actress, Rita Tushingham, created an unglamorous but effective image of the lonely, homeless girl, fit companion

555

for the motorcycle set. In a Canadian offering at the New York Film Festival in 1965, *Nobody Waved Goodbye,* the hero is a rebellious high school boy, played by Peter Kastner, a new screen figure, who was himself a high school boy with problems not unlike those of the hero of the film. Curiously, the Dean image had an impact in Eastern Europe. The Russian *I Am Twenty* (1965), portraying an embittered older generation, unhappy factory workers, and troubled adolescents who seek release in rebellion and American rock-and-roll, is very different from many other pictures that have come from the Soviet Union. Both *Ashes and Diamonds* (1958) and *Knife in the Water* (1961) from Poland show a strong Dean influence in restless young heroes, alienated, not daring to trust the impulse to love, ready for violence and death. In the Czechoslovakian *A Blonde in Love* (1965), the teen-age factory girls in a town near Prague and the wide-eyed pianist of a visiting dance band who forms an easy attachment with one of them might be young people of any western country. Most of the actors in this film are nonprofessional, and much of the action and dialogue is improvised. Just as American films caught some of the freshness of the Stanislavsky "method," the Czech film caught some of the freshness of the impromptu "happenings" that have fascinated recent directors.

In *Breathless* (1959), under the direction of Jean-Luc Godard, the French actor Jean-Paul Belmondo created a more aggressive young rebel, restless, not expecting genuine emotion or real meaning in the world. This variation of the rebel may be considered a transition figure between the much softer Dean rebel and the completely ruthless, unfeeling hero or antihero James Bond, as played by Sean Connery. It seems significant in American social history that the irresistible movie hero of the mid-fifties was the sensitive character played by James Dean, painfully trying to reestablish relationships with family or friends, protesting that a world of indifference and cruelty was wrong, while the popular movie image of the mid-sixties was Connery's James Bond, who accepts as normal his identity as a number—double-0 seven —and a world of indifference and violence and proceeds ruthlessly to dominate that world with all the gimmicks and gadgets imaginable by the makers of science fiction. In answering objections to violence in the Western, some people say that there can be no bad influence on viewers since everyone knows that a pioneer period is being portrayed. The same defense cannot be made for the Bond kind of violence, which is strictly contemporary. The Bond movies enabled the audience to play it both hot and cool. They could identify with Bond and get the satisfaction of a ruthless triumph over personal opposition, resistant women, and international evil. At the same time, as the fantastic gadgets and the outrageous clichés piled up one after the other, they could laugh with both pleasure and derision. The public that could delight in "camp," in *art moderne* because it is so bad and so quaint, in the TV program of Batman because it is so outrageously corny and infantile, could enjoy the Bond movies. In a time of uncertain standards of taste a faddish crowd likes to protect itself from asking whether something is infantile and foolish by expressing derision. The Bond movies are produced with

The Mass Media

superb finish. Again the mass medium, with worldwide distribution, can present its daydreams and glamorous actors with technical perfection and an aroma of modernity.

The International Trend

Since Hollywood's dominance of the world market has been broken, the cinema has become truly international and has gained freedom, variety, and vitality as it has escaped the confines of commercial control. The lead in many new trends has been taken by film-makers of Europe and even of Asia, and both American directors and American audiences are aware of the films from many countries.

The focus of international interest is the annual film festival. Festivals are largely a postwar phenomenon, although the one in Venice was established by Mussolini in 1932. The Cannes festival in May, the most important one, dates from 1947, and New York held its first festival in 1963. Other festivals occur annually in Edinburgh, Berlin, and other European cities, in Montreal, San Francisco, and several other cities on this continent, and in several South American cities. At all the festivals new directors have a chance to show their work, and any film-maker who gets an award has received the best possible advertising for himself, his picture, and his actors. Festival awards have brought fame to such directors as Akira Kurosawa of Japan, Satyajit Ray of India, François Truffaut of France, Michelangelo Antonioni of Italy, and Michael Cacoyannis of Greece, to name only a few.

POSTWAR NEOREALISM

The first postwar development to attract international attention was the neorealism of Italy. In fact, it began before the war was over, with the street scenes and documentary social backgrounds of *Open City* (1945), made by Roberto Rossellini. A print of the picture was brought to the United States in 1945 by Rod Geiger, an American G.I. who had bought the American rights for $13,000, and in seven years the film grossed more than three million dollars in this country. Harsh photography caught the sun-drenched Roman streets. The violence of the conflict as the Germans were leaving the city was treated frankly, casually, without sentiment or charm. Rossellini's *Paisan* (1946), Vittorio De Sica's *Shoeshine* (1946) and *Bicycle Thief* (1949), and Luchino Visconti's *La Terra Trema* ("The Earth Will Tremble," 1948) reestablished the Italian film in the theatres of the West. The characters in the stories were city slum dwellers or peasants, the actors were nonprofessionals, and the pictures were made with limited photographic equipment. When an Italian bricklayer's face caught De Sica's fancy, a man who had never acted before became the star of *Bicycle Thief*. Italian audiences were not much interested in seeing a frank presentation of their impoverishment, but American audiences were fascinated by people without Hollywood glamour and by action without soft lights and romantic charm. Here were real people, real streets, real economic

557

problems, real political passions. In comparison, Hollywood's film about veterans adjusting to a postwar world, *The Best Years of Our Lives* (1946), seems a synthetic set-up of personal problems that nice people can solve in time for the happy ending, in spite of realistic scenes and the acting of a real veteran who had lost both hands in the war.

The British new realism did not come until the late fifties, when a group of playwrights and novelists who became known as the Angry Young Men discovered the back streets of England's northern industrial cities and the resentment that struggling young people felt toward the "establishment," the genteel, well-educated upper classes who had dominated England for centuries. John Osborne's *Look Back in Anger* (1958), Shelagh Delaney's *A Taste of Honey* (1962), and *The Loneliness of the Long Distance Runner* (1962), adapted from a short story by Alan Sillitoe, which were all made by a talented young director, Tony Richardson, brought to the screen complexity of characterization and freshness of treatment. In *A Taste of Honey,* the lonely young girl, pregnant from a passing affair with an American Negro sailor, finds she would rather turn in her need to the homosexual boy with whom she has formed a platonic friendship than to her own irresponsible mother.

The best film story to come out of the new British realism was John Braine's *Room at the Top* (1958), with Laurence Harvey in the role of a young man of the working class who is determined to get ahead in the industrial city, using any means to reach the top. He seduces the boss's daughter and before marrying her spends a few days in a lonely cottage with a neglected married woman, poignantly played by the French actress Simone Signoret. The country idyll and a bloody fight by the canal bank are variations of old clichés, but as a whole the story is treated with complexity, honesty, and vitality that made an impression in both England and America. The central characters took such strong hold of the imagination of the author that he wrote *Life at the Top,* which was filmed in 1965 with Laurence Harvey playing the same role.

The British neorealists were greatly influenced by the documentary movement discussed in the last chapter and were very conscious of social purpose for a realistic art. In launching the "free cinema" movement in 1956, Lindsay Anderson and Karel Reisz stated in their manifesto that they would make films "which share an attitude: a belief in freedom, in the importance of the individual, in the significance of the everyday." But their social purpose inspired almost as strong a rebellion against the established social and political order as the anarchy of the absurdists. Their emphasis is on the freedom of the individual. In the 1960s they have produced films with comedy and even fantasy that are far from the grim realism of their earlier work. *Tom Jones,* directed by Tony Richardson, has period charm and racy comedy, but it shows its kinship to the movement in its frank treatment of sex and the reality of country roads, pigs, and kitchens. Karel Reisz, after directing a grim study of an angry young working man in *Saturday Night and Sunday Morning* (1960), brought out in 1966 an extravagant movie

Morgan!, much of which is the "black comedy," half funny, half horrifying, that has appealed to recent film-makers. The hero (or antihero) makes outrageous attacks on everything conventional and is obsessed with fantasies of gorillas and old Tarzan movies. As we discovered in the first chapter of this book, the tradition of realism has reached a point where it is capable of including almost anything.

The realistic approach has been continued in Italy by Vittorio De Sica, Pietro Germi, and Luchino Visconti, members of the original group of neo-realists, while, as we shall see, several new directors have gone in a very different direction. But Italian realism of the sixties is not the same as the realism of the forties. We see on the screen a more prosperous Italy and the most advanced cinematic effects. Most of the stories, often comedies, deal with the middle or upper class rather than with the working class, and they are in general more sophisticated. But there are still scenes of ordinary city streets, ordinary people, and small towns. Although Germi's *Divorce Italian Style* (1961) has a fashionable touch of cynicism, the setting in the home of a provincial family gives the impression of complete authenticity. The sense of reality in Italian films has not been lost, and the earthiness that American audiences have liked is still there, especially in the acting of Sophia Loren. Marcello Mastroianni has been equally competent as an actor in these pictures and in the more complex spiritual milieus of the director Federico Fellini. The director Mario Monicelli has offered amusing variations of the sophisticated and more-or-less real film in *Casanova 70* (1964) and others. Visconti has continued in the realistic tradition with popular films like *Rocco and His Brothers* (1960) and *The Leopard* (1963), but his *Sandra* (1965), a partial parallel to the Electra story, emphasizes psychological relationships rather than external realism.

AN ITALIAN *Avant-Garde*

The Italian leaders in European screen developments in the sixties are Federico Fellini and Michelangelo Antonioni. Fellini's *La Dolce Vita* (1960) has had international success. The title, implying both "high life" and "living it up," is an ironic reminder that modern life is not sweet. The photography catches the sharp detail of city streets, luxury hotels, and night clubs, showing a more affluent Rome than *Open City.* The film uses many symbols, often ironically; it opens with a statue of Christ dangling precariously from a helicopter over Rome and ends with revelers finding a huge dead fish on the beach at dawn. The scenes are presented in fragments, without clear sequence of time or place and without explanation of the background or motivation of the characters. The central character, a reporter played by Mastroianni, touches on the lives of a number of people, each one almost, but not quite, giving him a real human contact and helping him find meaning in life. In one sequence he escorts a movie queen in and out of hotels and night clubs. For a moment he is drawn to a young girl from the country. His father comes to Rome for a visit and the young man is about to renew contact with his childhood, but the father is distracted

559

by a woman, becomes ill, and goes back to his small-town life. At one point the reporter believes that an older friend, a serious scholar and poet, has found the answer, but presently he hears that his friend has killed his children and himself. After an all-night party of drunkenness and childish exhibitionism, the revelers walk out at dawn onto the beach, where they find the monstrous dead fish. The young man sees at a distance the young country girl waving to him, but he cannot get over the strip of water to her, and, as the film ends, wind and surf drown out what she is saying. In spite of the objective approach of the director and the fragmentary effect produced by short scenes without transitions, Mastroianni stimulates the identification of viewer with screen actor that gained the commercial movies their mass audience, and *La Dolce Vita* has had a wide appeal all over the Western world. John Russell Taylor, an English film critic, has written in *Cinema Eye, Cinema Ear*: "All these elements are found in life, everything that appears in the film may well have been seen somewhere in the streets or clubs of Rome, but this unremitting concentration on the peculiar, the exceptional, the larger-than-life gives the film, within its superficially realistic coating, a feverish, expressionistic quality which takes it in effect farther away from reality than anything Fellini had previously done. . . ." The influence of the film on other directors has undoubtedly been very great, but John Schlesinger's *Darling* (1965), which has been called an English version of the same modern attitudes, lacks the rich texture of Fellini's film.

Fellini's *8½*, which followed *La Dolce Vita*, is the story of a director of films who is trying to make a picture without a definite script. Memories, dreams, and waking fantasies and hallucinations of the director mingle with

FIGURE *17.5* Modern man's fruitless search for identity. Marcello Mastroianni plays the successful but lost film director in Federico Fellini's *8½*, 1963. Embassy Pictures Corporation.

the "real" so that it is sometimes hard to tell which is which. The strange title derives from the actual number of films Fellini himself had directed, and the film is partially a piece of spiritual autobiography. It is an outstanding example of the film that shows the personal touch of the creator to a degree that was not possible in the Hollywood of the twenties and thirties, when scripts were worked out by teams in conferences.

The most appealing of Fellini's earlier films, several of which deal with tramps, is *La Strada* (1954). A coarse wandering entertainer, Zampano (played by Anthony Quinn), takes on a young, innocent, not very bright girl, Gelsomina, played by Giulietta Masina, Fellini's wife. He buys her, in fact, from her impoverished mother. She learns to play a trumpet, to dance, and to take her part in making the living, accepting Zampano's rough treatment and infidelities. They join a troupe of carnival people, and an acrobat befriends her. When Zampano kills the acrobat and he and Gelsomina are outcasts on the road, he decides to abandon her. Obsessed with the memory of the girl, he eventually finds the village where she had wandered and died. In the last sequence he stands on the shore of the gray sea in grief and despair. As in all Fellini's pictures, the camera regularly emphasizes the extraordinary and unpredictable rather than the ordinary and typical, and the vision of life is highly individual.

In *Juliet of the Spirits* (1965), Fellini's first film in color, Giulietta Masina plays a very different character from the waif of *La Strada,* but the housewife who becomes aware of her husband's philanderings and goes through a mental crisis of fantasy, externalized on the screen in visual images, is no less sensitively created by the actress and the director.

Michelangelo Antonioni is the only other Italian director whose reputation approaches Fellini's. He too has his own personal style. His early work in documentaries, one of them about the miseries of life in the villages of the Po Valley, trained him in close observation of landscapes, common activities, and large groups of people, but he is particularly noted for his cinematic studies of individuals, especially of women. His best-known films are *L'Avventura* ("The Adventure," 1959), *La Notte* ("The Night," 1960), and *L'Eclisse* ("The Eclipse," 1962), all with the background of a wealthy bourgeois society. In *L'Eclisse,* a scene of hysterical people in a stock-market crisis emphasizes the modern obsession with money to the exclusion of love. In *L'Avventura,* a young woman disappears on an island, and her fiancé and her best friend wander over the island and then the mainland, searching for her and developing a growing interest in each other. But in the end their relationship fails; they know that the emotional bond between them is tenuous. Any love will be lost, the film seems to say, as the girl was lost among the rocks of the island, with no trace, no explanation. *La Notte* shows the same kind of lost people, drifters finding no real fulfillment, only temporary distraction in casual eroticism.

Although alienation is a frequent theme in recent stage drama, Antonioni gives the dilemma a new poignance. *The Red Desert* (1965), his first film in color, shows a woman definitely separated from reality, on the verge of

561

madness. Antonioni has found in Monica Vitti the ideal actress to portray his lost women, and he instructs her to the smallest detail, for he is a director who manipulates his actors like puppets.

The Italian *avant-garde* has moved away from the realistic film of the forties. Uncheerful as the new outlook is, it has resulted in some arresting and beautiful motion pictures that are not without their moments of exhilaration and, in Fellini's films, hilarity.

THE FRENCH NEW WAVE

In France new developments have occurred since the war not only in the work of Robert Bresson, whose few fine films have not been widely shown in this country, but in that of a "New Wave" of film-makers who created a sensation in the late fifties. Although they have been bracketed together, they do not form a cohesive group, and it is impossible to apply to their work a single epithet like "absurdist." All of them, however, have been closely associated with the *avant-garde* magazine of film criticism, *Les Cahiers du Cinema*. They subscribe to the *"auteur* theory," which, simply stated, is that the director is responsible for a film. Scornful of the conventional story film and the standard methods of characterization, they are fascinated by camera techniques and like to improvise and experiment. Like Fellini and Antonioni, they give an accurate picture of any portion of the world they choose to observe, but their attitude toward it is far different from that of the realist with a social conscience. They want no sentimental identification with the characters but a cool objectivity that often has shock and horror near the surface. They are fascinated by the films of Alfred Hitchcock, not only because of his cinematic skill but because of the *univers hitchcockien,* where terror is close to laughter. They find in his films elements of his own religious and psychological autobiography and admire the way in which he puts his personal stamp on his work. These *avant-garde* Frenchmen have operated on much more limited resources than the new Italian directors; all of them began in a small way, almost as amateurs. Much the most important figures are Alain Resnais, François Truffaut, and Jean-Luc Godard.

Resnais was an actor, and his first films were sixteen-millimeter shorts about painters and their work. His training in the documentary is evident in *Nuit et Brouillard* ("Night and Mist," 1955), an impressive forty-five-minute documentary about concentration camps of the last war. By interweaving shots of camp sites as they appeared in the 1950s with still photographs or moving pictures taken in the same places during the war years, and by using an unemotional but inexorable voice for the narrative, Resnais fascinates the spectator and stirs the social conscience. In the story film *Hiroshima mon amour* (1959), which aroused the interest of film enthusiasts throughout the western world, there are bold and effective sequences of shots taken shortly after the atomic blast, but the interest is chiefly psychological and metaphysical. The central figure is a Frenchwoman whose love affair with a German soldier during the occupation of France and her subsequent dis-

562

The Mass Media

FIGURE *17.6* An elusive "New Wave" French film. A Frenchwoman and a Japanese, psychological victims of the upheavals of war, try in vain to make a commitment to each other. Alain Resnais's *Hiroshima mon amour,* 1959. Photo Culver Pictures.

grace in her village hang over her as, years later in the haunted atmosphere of Hiroshima, she tries to form a relationship with a sensitive Japanese. Feelings are suggested but not defined, and no moral judgments are passed. *Last Year at Marienbad* (1961), the other film for which Resnais is best known, is not topical but personal, and more elusive than *Hiroshima.* At a resort hotel, a man and a woman meet who did or did not meet in this same place the previous year. The man says that they did and that the woman agreed to go away with him after a year had passed. The woman seems not to remember, but perhaps she does. This is a Pirandello situation. Does the man imagine the earlier meeting, or is he deliberately trying to sway the girl by a pretense? And what happens at the end: do they go away together or do they not? The author of the screen script and the director, when questioned, have not agreed in their answers, and viewers of the picture do not. The hotel, with interiors of great rooms and long empty corridors and an exterior of endless terraces and walks, is not quite real, a proper setting for characters without clear identity and events that may or may not actually have occurred. As an atmospheric piece the film is very effective, but it has little characterization or emotion. Resnais's more recent films, *Muriel* (1963) and *La Guerre est finie* ("The War Is Over," 1965), are scarcely less elusive.

Truffaut and Godard, born in the early thirties, are a decade younger than Resnais. Truffaut's *Les Quatre cent coups* ("The 400 Blows," 1959), *Tirez sur le pianiste* ("Shoot the Piano Player," 1960), and *Jules et Jim* (1961) established his reputation in Europe and among connoisseurs in the United States. *The 400 Blows* has the ingredients for a social purpose film or a psychological study or just a sentimental tale about a wronged child, but it is none of these. Antoine, a Parisian boy of eleven or twelve, is in trouble at home and at school. When he is caught with a stolen typewriter, he is taken to the police station by his father, is interviewed by a psychiatrist whose voice is heard during the interview but whose face is not seen, is sent to a reformatory and escapes. In a last long sequence he runs to the sea, then turns and faces the camera. He has known the deep experience of confinement; this is freedom. The beauty in the film is the objective treatment that nevertheless conveys the feelings of the boy. He is not presented as over-

563

Movies as a Minority Art

whelmed at first by an unsympathetic environment, as a naturalistic writer might have shown him. His parents are not blamed for lack of understanding, as they might be in a sociological film. The film-maker is not interested in what caused the trouble or how it might have been avoided or what other boys might be affected in the same way. This is a completely objective and perceptive portrayal of an experience of one individual.

The usual kind of storytelling, with analysis of motivation, development of character, and self-revelation, does not interest these French film-makers. As Penelope Houston, an English critic, has written of the New Wave films in general, "We have a cinema of personal relationships, private worlds, and anti-heroes engaged in splicing together the broken and rough ends of personality, or in pursuing illusions half-recognized as such; an amoral cinema, or one endeavouring to construct its morality through a series of *ad hoc* judgements."

Shoot the Piano Player is very different from *The 400 Blows*. It is a tale with several underworld characters and a plot of vengeance, but little time is spent on motivation, and the melodramatic ending with a death in a beautiful snowy landscape cannot be called "convincing." Truffaut is fascinated by a tale as a tale and by pictorial effects and film techniques. *Jules et Jim* is closer to reality with its story of two young men, one French and one German, who are friends and in love with the same girl, but the relationships are not developed in a conventional way. The film is set in the period before, during, and just after the First World War and echoes the old silent movies in many situations and techniques. The point of view blends sympathy and detachment in a way that is characteristic of the New Wave film-makers. Just as the viewer is about to become involved in the emotions of the characters, a narrator's voice breaks in with a dispassionate summary of action, or some incongruity in the images or absurdity in the situation restores the objectivity.

Of the New Wave group, Jean-Luc Godard has proved the most prolific. His first full-length film, *Breathless* (1959), which we have already mentioned, is still one of his most arresting pictures. The city environment is

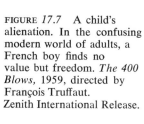

FIGURE *17.7* A child's alienation. In the confusing modern world of adults, a French boy finds no value but freedom. *The 400 Blows,* 1959, directed by François Truffaut. Zenith International Release.

FIGURE *17.8* The eternal triangle with a difference. François Truffaut used scenes and film situations and techniques of the twenties in portraying the lives of two men and a girl in the decade after the First World War. *Jules et Jim,* 1961. Janus Films.

treated realistically, but the motivations of the characters remain largely unexplained. The antihero, played by Jean-Paul Belmondo, is a thief; the girl is an American vaguely and unconvincingly connected with the press in a European city. The love scenes of this pair and their movements about the city are absorbing in themselves but do not add up to much. When the law is about to catch up with the man, the girl at first protects him but later calls the police. As he is trying to escape in a stolen automobile she runs into the street and sees him shot down. It is a story in real surroundings which is not quite real. There is no moral issue; lawlessness, violence, betrayal, and death are treated casually. The film is an action, more tantalizing than absurd drama, which at least implies a philosophical attitude of despair.

Since *Breathless,* Godard has made two or three films a year, most of them enigmatic. *Le Petit soldat* ("The Little Soldier," 1960), a picture about the Algerian war, was so uncompromising in its exposure of the follies of the war that no faction found it acceptable. *Les Carabiniers* ("The Soldiers," 1963) is another searing view of war. *La Femme mariée* ("The Married Woman," 1964) portrays a woman who can find no meaning in her frag-mented life, an Antonioni kind of woman but treated far less solemnly. *Alphaville* (1965) concerns a woman of the year 2000 learning to feel in a world without emotions, a world much like the mechanized fantasies of expressionism. The English critic Kenneth Tynan describes Godard's *Pierrot le fou* ("Pierrot the Madman," 1965) as "a free-wheeling holiday movie, an assault on narrative continuity, a surrender to free association and chance encounters . . . full of puns, songs, aphorisms, literary allusions, topical gags, quotes from ads, spasms of cruelty, interludes of mime." The director stated in an interview that many scenes in the film were improvised. Godard has not exhausted his capacity for astonishing, and, like Antonioni, he has found an actress, Anna Karina, whom he can mold to the image of the woman he wants for his films.

BERGMAN, BUÑUEL, AND CACOYANNIS
No other European country has produced as many makers of un-usual films in the fifties and sixties as Italy, England, and France, but there are several important isolated figures who have achieved a wide reputation. *565*

FIGURE *17.9* The chess game between the Knight and Death. The strong man plays for postponement of his end so that he may seek the meaning of his life. Ingmar Bergman's *The Seventh Seal,* 1956. Janus Films.

Ingmar Bergman of Sweden was one of the earliest of European postwar directors to show a distinctive personal style and is perhaps now the best known of them all. By working in the regular theatre during the winter and limiting himself to a low budget and a small company of actors, he has been able to survive as an independent producer-director and to make more than two dozen films without concession to the commercial point of view. He has gained a considerable audience and the most articulate following among advanced film enthusiasts. No one since the war has been written about more than Bergman. His symbols have been catalogued and explained, from the chess game of Death and the Knight in *The Seventh Seal* (1956) to the spring that gushes from the ground where the girl was raped in *The Virgin Spring* (1959). If Bergman is cold and objective in part of a film, he usually varies his dark scenes with scenes of sunshine and happy youth. He is objective in his treatment of character, but some of his characters in *The Virgin Spring* come through with great warmth, from the young girl whose independence invites the rape to the maid who sends her jealous curse on the girl and the anguished father who deliberately and ritually washes himself before killing the men who raped and killed the daughter. Sometimes a cold character emerges as a human being, like the gentle old professor of *Wild Strawberries* (1957), who on a journey to receive an academic award half finds or just misses the illusive tokens of his past life. In *The Devil's Eye* (1960) a serious theme is treated with playful irony. When Don Juan, a breaker of hearts who is now in hell, returns briefly to the world, he falls in love himself and must face an eternity of despair. But three films made by Bergman between 1960 and 1962 that constitute a trilogy—*Through a Glass Darkly, Winter Light,* and *The Silence*—offer no humor to relieve the depressing atmosphere of doubt, guilt, and destructive emotions. It is not sur-

566

The Mass Media

prising that most people not only do not want to give the attention necessary for a subtle, unconventional film technique but prefer most of their films to show a healthy balance between the bleak and the more positive. Bergman's audience is a special one.

Totally unlike Bergman except in his independence, the Spaniard Luis Buñuel, though not a new figure, is interesting for several reasons. A member of the European *avant-garde* of the twenties, maker of the sensational *L'Âge d'or* (1930), which was described in the last chapter, he has continued to make films that are distinguished and often controversial. Strongly opposed to political developments in his native Spain, he has spent most of his adult life away from that country. In spite of radical political and social ideas, he managed to make a living in the film world for many years by dubbing films or editing documentaries. In the last two decades he has been able to make his own films, and he has attracted both high critical acclaim and a fairly large popular audience, especially in Mexico. It was *Los Olvidados* (called in English "The Young and the Damned," 1950), made in Mexico, which set him going again on his interrupted career. It is a powerful semidocumentary about delinquent boys in Mexico City who are under the influence of vicious older boys. The social message is not conveyed by a moralizing commentary but by the vivid shots themselves—heaps of rubble, squalid hovels, mounds of garbage where people dig for food like animals, the body of a murdered boy carried on muleback to a public dump. There is a thread of story in which the principal figures are the vicious teen-age Jaibo and his younger victim Pedro, who has seen Jaibo commit a murder and who is himself finally killed by Jaibo.

The more than twenty story films Buñuel has made in Mexico and France and the one he made recently in Spain are strong and individual, and most of them have disturbing implications for those who see below the surface, for he has not essentially altered in his attitudes toward the world and its accepted values since he filmed *L'Âge d'or*. The Spanish-made film *Viridiana,* considered by some to be Buñuel's masterpiece, shared the major prize at the Cannes Film Festival in 1961. On the point of entering a convent,

FIGURE *17.10* A pious girl in an imperfect world. In *Viridiana,* 1961, Luis Buñuel works a variation on his central theme of the weakness of saintliness in the face of corruption. Kingsley International Release.

Viridiana pays a visit to a widowed uncle-by-marriage, who falls in love with her and hangs himself in despair when she rejects him. Feeling responsible for his death, she stays at the farm and makes it a gathering place for tramps, whom she clothes and feeds, making them pray and live an apparently holy life. When she returns after a short absence, she finds her protégés in the midst of a drunken orgy and is herself nearly raped. Disillusioned, she abandons her attempts at good works and seems at the end to accept the materialistic attitude of her uncle's son. The picture was held up indefinitely in the censor's office in Spain, but it has been shown all over Europe and in some places in America. When he was past seventy, Buñuel could still be counted on to produce at least one arresting picture a year. His entry at the Venice Film Festival in 1965 was characteristic—*Simon of the Desert,* a forty-minute satire on saintliness.

A much younger international figure is Michael Cacoyannis of Greece. Since he produced a low-budget comedy called *Windfall in Athens* (1954) that was chosen for the gala première at the Edinburgh Film Festival, he has had several unusual successes on the stage and on the screen, both in Greece and in the United States. His staging of Euripides' *The Trojan Women* in New York in 1961 was extremely successful. The film *Electra* (1962), made in outdoor settings near Athens and at Mycenae with a distinguished Greek cast, gives a fresh view of a well-known classic. His *Zorba the Greek* (1965) is an adaptation of Nikos Kazantzakis' novel of life, love, and violence among ordinary people in a village in Crete, with Anthony Quinn as the untamed citizen at the center of events. The film is notable for its expert direction of peasant scenes in which the people *are* peasants and for the close-ups of the

FIGURE *17.11*   Greek tragedy in an outdoor production. Sophocles' *Electra,* 1961, directed by Michael Cacoyannis, has tragic grandeur in the wide landscape of Greece. United Artists.

faces of actual people. No actress could be made up to convey the sense of absolute reality that is given by the black-clad ancient crones who sit near the bedside of the dying Frenchwoman, ready to utter their mourning cries and to plunder her room when she expires. Like the Italian neorealists, Cacoyannis has an eye for interesting faces and a sure touch in directing non-professionals. He was born on the island of Cyprus, studied for the law in England, directed the BBC Greek program during the war, and afterward acted in London till 1950. His international background stands him in good stead in the present climate of the film world.

ORIENTAL FILM-MAKERS

The Orient, and in particular Japan, now has an important part in the film world—in 1955 alone, Japan produced 422 feature pictures, more than Hollywood produced in the same year—though only a small percentage of the total production is shown widely in the West. Most Japanese movies deal with contemporary life and problems, but the films that have held the greatest interest for Europe and America are those that draw on Japanese history and tradition or show people in a village or country environment different from our own. Attention was drawn to the Japanese period film by several awards at European festivals. In 1951 *Rashomon*, directed by Akira Kurosawa, won the grand prize at Venice, and in 1954 *Gate of Hell*, directed by Teinosuke Kunugasa, was awarded the grand prize at Cannes. Since then a Japanese entry at any western festival has been a significant event.

Kurosawa is the Japanese director best known in the West, largely because of *Rashomon* and *The Seven Samurai* (1954). Although *Rashomon* has an eighth-century setting and is Japanese in tempo and pictorial beauty, it is not concerned primarily with an action in the past but with the timeless theme of the nature of truth. It begins and ends with a scene, at a public gate during a rainstorm, that might almost be a framework for a tale of contemporary realism. One of the persons huddled together for shelter from the storm tells the story of a murder he has seen. The main sequences of the film show not only his version as an onlooker but those of the three participants—the lady who has been raped, the brigand who attacked her, and her husband, who has been killed but who speaks through a medium. The fascination of the film, like that of a Pirandello play, is the question, never resolved, of whose version is true; even the man who saw the murder may not be completely believed. The elusive theme is reinforced by lovely images of sun-flecked woods and distant views of the beautiful lady, played by Machiko Kyo, and the contrasting pictures of the outlaw, played by Toshiro Mifune, one of Japan's finest actors. Kurosawa's *The Throne of Blood* (1957), the Macbeth story in a medieval Japanese setting, concludes with a striking scene of the Macbeth character transfixed with arrows to the wall of his castle. Some of Kurosawa's more recent films, like *Redbeard* (1965), are more realistic than the films with which he made his reputation in the fifties.

In spite of excursions into realism, however, and even into a kind of   *569*

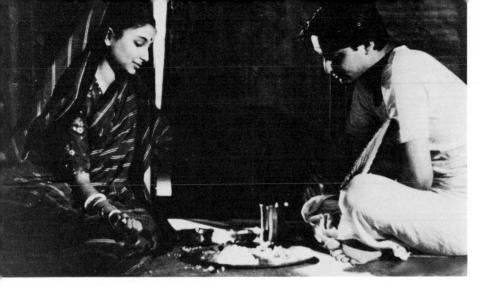

FIGURE *17.12* Oriental study of fine feelings in a real world. Apu falls in love. *The World of Apu,* 1959, the third film in a trilogy directed by Satyajit Ray. Harrison Pictures.

symbolic drama comparable to the absurd drama of the West, as in Hiroshi Teshigahara's *Woman in the Dunes* (1965), Japan still produces fine films of fantasy and of the past. A beautiful color film of 1965 was Masaki Kobayashi's *Kwaidan,* based on three supernatural and metaphysical tales by Lafcadio Hearn, a late nineteenth-century American writer who spent many years in Japan.

Although India has a large film industry, Indian films were almost unknown in Europe until Satyajit Ray's *Pather Panchali* ("Lament of the Path") was judged "the best human document" at the Cannes festival in 1956. The film had been made under extraordinary difficulties. Ray was an ardent student of the cinema who had watched the French director Jean Renoir when he was making *The River* in India and had received some encouragement from the older man. But he could get no backing for the film he wanted to make, an adaptation of a realistic Bengali novel. Films in India had followed a stereotype of romantic story combined with song and dance, and the film companies had no confidence in a picture about real people in everyday surroundings. An employee of an advertising agency, Ray worked on his film for two years in his leisure hours and financed it mostly with his own savings, though before the film was finished he received a government subsidy. Partly through the influence of John Huston, who saw some of Ray's film on a visit to India, the young director was invited in 1954 to send the film for a showing at the Museum of Modern Art during an Indian exhibit, and thus *Pather Panchali* had its première in New York. After this recognition and the award at Cannes, Ray was assured of a career in film-making. He next made *Aparajito* ("The Unvanquished"), which won the grand prize at Venice in 1957, and in 1959 he completed his trilogy with *Apu Sansar* ("The World of Apu").

570   The first two films are about Apu's childhood in a village in Bengal and

The Mass Media

his experiences in Calcutta, where he goes to become a modern man and a writer. In *The World of Apu* he is a struggling writer in the slums of Calcutta, but he is drawn into a new way of life when he is invited to a provincial wedding. The bridegroom proves to be insane, and to save the bride from the curse that will fall on her if she is not married at the appointed hour, Apu marries her and brings her home to his shabby rooms by the railroad tracks. Though the marriage is accidental, he loves her, and when she dies in childbirth he is so distraught that he no longer wishes to write and for a time becomes a wanderer and common laborer. Five years later he discovers his son and a new reason for living. The story is simple enough, but the director handles its subtle relationships with skill.

The international trend continues, with film writers and directors, rich or poor, recording their visions in almost all parts of the world. Even from eastern Europe, as the pressure for state propaganda is relaxed, have come independent and original films. The range of Russian films is wide, including an extraordinary filming of *War and Peace* and a *Hamlet* that impressed even the British audience, as well as realistic films about contemporary life like the one on youthful rebellion mentioned early in the chapter. Czechoslovakia provided one of the best films of 1965, *The Shop on Main Street,* which was shown widely in the United States. The picture was notable not only for fine acting but for the honest treatment of the theme of Jewish persecution, and this in a country where many people had cooperated in the persecution. Not only at the international festivals but more and more in cinema clubs and commercial theatres, moviegoers have a chance to share the lives and dreams of people all over the world.

Nonconformist American Cinema

American film-makers have been aware of the recent developments in Europe and the East, have been influenced by them, and have even participated in them. They have also pursued their own course toward a larger freedom. The independent producer in particular has tried to create films which are not merely variations on old themes and patterns but which offer a new approach, bidding not for a large audience but for an intelligent, informed minority. He has profited from foreign example, new attitudes of American moviegoers, and an altered status of censorship.

RELAXATION OF CENSORSHIP
Film censorship is not what it was in the twenties and thirties. An equivalent of the Hays Office has been maintained, but the code has been relaxed and producers have tended more and more to ignore it. In the last two decades legal decisions have made such a code innocuous if not absurd.

The New York stage won its freedom from censorship in the twenties, when it had almost ceased to be the main source of mass entertainment, but all through the thirties and forties New York plays when adapted for the screen were regularly made to conform to conventional ideas of propriety and morality. In the first filming of Lillian Hellman's *The Children's Hour,* renamed *These Three* (1936), the element of lesbianism was omitted. In 1962 the play was filmed under William Wyler's direction with its original psychological complexities. The light comedy *The Moon Is Blue* had aroused no scandal on the stage, but when Otto Preminger filmed it in 1953 the Hollywood censors refused to pass it because it had a playful discussion of the heroine's determination to remain a virgin. He released the film without approval and got by with it. He filmed *The Man with the Golden Arm* (1956), defying the code ban on showing drug addiction. He had to go to court to defend his right to use clinical details about rape in the film *Anatomy of a Murder* (1959), but he won his case.

Legal censorship has been dealt one blow after another. One of the most important early rulings came in 1933, when the U.S. District Court declared that James Joyce's novel *Ulysses,* which had been banned in this country, was not obscene. In the 1950s the cinema won its wider freedom. When New York officials banned *The Miracle,* a film by Rossellini, the fight was carried to the Supreme Court, which ruled in 1953 that the screen shares with the press the protection of free speech guaranteed by the first and fourteenth amendments to the Constitution. In 1959 the Supreme Court declared illegal the New York State ban on the French film made from D. H. Lawrence's novel *Lady Chatterley's Lover.* Since then some states have abolished censorship or liberalized their attitude, sometimes merely insisting that exhibitors label certain films as not for children. But a film can still be subjected to boycott and even legal action, and it can have trouble in getting a Production Code seal, as *The Pawnbroker* did in 1965, though the nudity objected to was certainly not used for sensational effect.

NEW MATERIAL AND NEW ATTITUDES

If the greater freedom has made it easy for some producers to exploit sex and violence and for exhibitors to profit from a sly sensationalism by using the label "for adults only," it has given others the chance for serious treatment of modern problems. In the late forties and fifties several topics that had been avoided in the days of mass entertainment were brought to the screen, among them anti-Semitism, race prejudice, alcoholism, and drug addiction. *Advise and Consent* (1962) is one of several serious treatments of political situations. If the characterization of the Senators and members of the Supreme Court is superficial, if the plot is overmelodramatic, and if the point of view is childishly malicious, the film still offers an unusual complexity of political motives and dares to treat blackmail for homosexuality.

The new freedom is most evident in the exploration of the disruptive aspects of personality. Movies for mass entertainment seldom admitted complexity in psychological problems, but in recent years a number of Eugene O'Neill's plays, with their studies of how love and creativity can turn to hate and destruction, have been filmed with little concession to conventional caution. Movies made from the plays of Tennessee Williams, using such popular actors as Paul Newman, Richard Burton, Elizabeth Taylor, Katharine Hepburn, and Geraldine Page, have been favorites with many moviegoers, partly because they include such sensational elements as cannibalism, castration, and homosexuality, but more because they offer some understanding of the complexity of human desires, fears, and frustrations. The climax of the interest in tortured mental states came in 1966, when Edward Albee's play *Who's Afraid of Virginia Woolf?* was filmed with Elizabeth Taylor and Richard Burton. Without such popular romantic stars it is possible that no producer would have dared to film the play. Though it had been played in theatres all over the world and widely read, it is stronger fare than most moviegoers are yet accustomed to.

The view of the modern world as a nightmare of unexplained terror, a commonplace of the theatre of the absurd and of some of the European *avant-garde,* has found an occasional place in the films of established moviemakers. Duerrenmatt's play *The Visit* was softened as a film vehicle for Ingrid Bergman in 1963, and its ending was changed by the revelation that the rich woman had relented, that she did not really intend to have the townspeople kill her former lover. But there was no softening in Orson Welles' filming of Franz Kafka's novel *The Trial* (1962). Welles caught the nightmare terror of a modern man (played by Anthony Perkins) accused and dragged into court but never told what he is accused of. Through vast outdoor ruins and under the low ceilings of arched underground passages he is haled to a fantastic courtroom to face tier on tier of accusing faces. Welles suggested more than the actual terror of the modern police states and the widespread fear of subversives: he caught the modern cosmic insecurity and sense of intangible guilt.

The more intense psychological studies have been favored by the new directors doing low-budget films. A film of low cost used to be thought of as an inferior production turned out to supply the second-rate movie houses, but though this kind of product still exists, there is also a totally different kind. European directors long ago discovered that good pictures could be made without high-priced stars or elaborate settings. Americans have learned the lesson late. Several of the absurdist plays that were produced in off-Broadway theatres were filmed by members of the "New York School" of directors, notably *The Connection* (1960), directed by Shirley Clarke, and Genêt's *The Balcony* (1963), directed by Joseph Strick. But the surprise came when *David and Lisa* (1962), written and directed by Frank Perry, achieved wide notice and considerable financial success. This is a poignant study of how two psychotic adolescents in a small institution learn to trust each other and to trust reality. After *Lilies of the Field* (1963), made by Ralph Nelson for $250,000, a fairly small budget, achieved a very wide response, the Hollywood companies were more willing to take chances on low-budget pictures made by independent directors, and a half-dozen were produced in the spring of 1965 through Metro-Goldwyn-Mayer, Columbia, and United Artists, among them *A Patch of Blue*. The story in *A Patch*   573 *of Blue* is about a white girl, blinded in early childhood, who responds to the kindness of a Negro. Related to these modest films are two unspectacular but very powerful British films that took an unconventional view of human nature as it may be revealed in children. *Lord of the Flies* (1962), made by Peter Brook from William Golding's disturbing novel about lost boys reverting to savagery on a tropical island, and *High Wind in Jamaica* (1965), adapted from Richard Hughes's novel about children who become captives of pirates and in their lack of feeling are more ruthless than their captors, could scarcely have been produced before the more liberal time of the sixties. Such visions of callousness and evil in the young are far removed from the many saccharine screen stories of childhood· in the past.

Comedy, too, has shown some developments in the sixties worthy of an adult mind, and several films have even shed the clarity of a comic light on such difficult subjects as race relations and atomic warfare. Since the fifties American moviegoers have delighted in a wild and foolish comedy, with elements of crime and detective fiction, a touch of satire, eccentric characters, and much slapstick action, that has been a specialty of the British. *Kind Hearts and Coronets* (1948), *The Lavender Hill Mob* (1951), *The Ladykillers* (1955), and others in which Alec Guinness appeared have been succeeded by a somewhat different type of comedy in which Peter Sellers has specialized. A recent example, better than many of his pictures, is *What's New, Pussycat?* (1965), in which Sellers plays the most absurd psychiatrist of all time and Peter O'Toole the most distraught of sex-obsessed comic heroes. The film is satiric slapstick, with scarcely any plot but a succession of ridiculous situations, with many "sight gags" and a chase on scooters in the last sequence, but there is enough pointed satiric reference, absurd fun, and unusual camera work to please an intelligent adult. Even more brilliant camera work is used in the Beatles' *Help!* (1965), directed by Richard Lester. The film is in part a take-off on exotic pictures about heathen temples, sacrifices, jewels, and charms, but the entertaining features are the many incongruous combinations of reality and absurdity, the complete aplomb of the musical Beatles in the midst of every conceivable deadly danger, and an extraordinary display of ingenuity in mechanical devices and camera tricks—multiple images, a human figure reduced to miniature size hiding in an ash tray, human beings standing horizontally on the screen, and bewildering montages. *The Knack* (1965), a dramatization of Ann Jellicoe's offbeat comedy that was also directed by Richard Lester, was equally effective and the sequence in which a huge brass bed is propelled by the three principal characters through the streets of London is considered as funny as anything that has been seen in movies.

America has provided in the last few years specimens of a comic satire with more point than such absurdities. The postwar mood, with the cold war, the long, inconclusive campaign in Korea, and the tense concern over Communism, was too serious for satire. To disagree with an officer was serious mutiny, dramatized in the films *From Here to Eternity* (1953), *The*

Caine Mutiny (1954), and *Billy Budd* (1962) without a trace of humor. The fantasy of a mad general is a real fear in an age when military leaders have wide power and influence. That fantasy was dramatized as straight melodrama without comic perspective in John Frankenheimer's *Seven Days in May* (1963), Sidney Lumet's *Fail Safe* (1963), and James B. Harris' *The Bedford Incident* (1965). But hilarious satire and a wise view of responsibility and danger appeared in Stanley Kubrick's *Dr. Strangelove, or How I Learned to Stop Worrying and Love the Bomb* (1963). Borrowing from science fiction the idea of a Third World War and using tricks of the international spy stories, this fantasy shows a mad general starting American bombers toward Russia and the futile efforts made in Washington, on an army base, and in Moscow to get them stopped. The film ends ironically with an uplifting hymn on the sound track as a greeting to eternity.

More relaxation is achieved in *The Americanization of Emily* (1964) than in previous satires, and a finer discrimination between what is foolish and what is sane. An amiable young American officer makes his own adjustment to a war-torn world, catering to the whims of his superior officer, an admiral heading an American naval group in London during the last war, as long as the admiral's wishes are regular, but when the admiral gets a private romantic mania, he considers it his duty as a subordinate officer to persuade, delay, and if possible circumvent his superior until sanity returns. When he is swept into the madness, he goes along, scrambling for cover as best he can. The English Emily, a girl of high principles, is finally converted to his kind of not-unpatriotic individualism. The wry irony of Chaplin's *Monsieur Verdoux,* with its good-natured little hero who killed only a few in an age of mass killings by war, was unendurable to American audiences in the 1940s, and they turned against the little fellow who had been a favorite comedian for so many years. But in the late 1960s they could enjoy such black comedies as George Axelrod's *Lord Love a Duck,* with its wry fantasy of a supernaturally bright adolescent who will murder, if necessary, to indulge his girl in whatever she wants. Even the extravagant American funeral rites are satirized in Tony Richardson's *The Loved One* (1965), though with little of the light touch of the Evelyn Waugh novel which the film dramatized.

The movies mentioned here are only a few of the films that show independent enterprise and a general sense of freedom from business and conventional restrictions. They are enough to demonstrate that some freedom exists and that it has been used for the making of some films that do not conform to set patterns. The future should see a more extensive use of a freedom that has been hotly contested at times and not easily won.

THE SPECIAL AUDIENCE

These new developments have stimulated the growth of small theatres and special audiences. French ciné clubs were organized in the early 1920s for showing films of unusual artistry, but the first American audiences for such films did not develop until the 1930s, after sound was introduced and it became clear that only the foreign movies of great mass appeal would be given sound tracks in English. Then in the larger cities a number of "art theatres" sprang up for the showing of foreign language film with the English dialogue in subtitles superimposed at the bottom of the picture. Gradually these small houses have added not only the films of the newer European directors but the more unusual American films, especially those that bear the label "experimental."

Another selective audience has been created for viewing films of the past. Movies developed so fast as lively entertainment for the public and big money for the producers that for a long time no one thought of saving old films or systematically studying and comparing the better productions. But schools and art centers now regularly show series of films and offer lectures and courses on the film. In the early 1930s the Museum of Modern Art in New York began to collect and preserve films, many of them found on forgotten shelves, to show them in its own theatre, and to duplicate them in sixteen-millimeter copies for schools, art centers, and cinema clubs across the country. Several other organizations, notably the Eastman Kodak Company, began to collect films, and finally Hollywood established a museum of film art. The Gallery of Modern Art in New York has regular series of showings of film classics. A number of commercial companies rent sixteen-millimeter copies of fairly recent films to schools and clubs. Now the commercial distributors sometimes bring out a "retrospective" series of old movies, either a composite of excerpts from several films, like "The Golden Age of Comedy," or a series of films starring a particular actor or made by a particular director. What with the drive-ins showing one- to five-year-old pictures, television presenting many films of one or two decades ago, and special examples of early products made available to the public in the Museum of Modern Art series, it is possible to get a wide view of the history of this remarkable art, to see movies in perspective, and to see favorite films more than once.

The real movie enthusiast willingly joins the crowd for popular current pictures. Hollywood has such resources of skilled technicians that even a routine picture may be effective or interesting in some aspects—good photography, interesting scenery, one or two lively actors, a fresh point of view in a few scenes. Occasionally a film like *Mary Poppins* comes along, so skillfully produced, so effective in every way that it does not matter that it is conventional, childish, synthetic, and glossy. Julie Andrews and Dick Van Dyke handle its sentimental clichés smoothly, the sprightly musical numbers have clever words and easy tunes, the spectacle includes a cinematic ballet of chimney sweeps on rooftops, with dancers popping in and out of chimneys, as well as several sequences in animated cartoon technique, and the family scenes are romantic and charming. A big hit in 1964, the picture wins new audiences each time it is shown, and discriminating moviegoers are not ashamed to admire it.

The adult moviegoer enjoys a variety of films. If one week he goes along with the masses who respond to the lush music and thick sentiment of *The Sound of Music,* the next week he will join the much smaller audience that responds to the strong acting and bitter compassion of *The Pawnbroker*. He can enjoy a good thriller, especially if it is done with the cinematic skill and individual touch of an Alfred Hitchcock, an occasional spectacle or a good lively Western, a wild farce or a sprightly comedy of the battle of the sexes. He wants to see the latest offering of a director of wide reputation and almost any picture with one of his own favorite stars. If he waits and watches, he can find even in the commercial houses a piece of earthy realism, a picture of psychological depth, a film that deals with a political or social problem, an impressive picture made from a fiction classic, a good documentary. Then in his cinema club or in a museum or art center he will find the film classics of the past, a selection of the new foreign films, and some of the *avant-garde* and experimental work that is not seen in the popular theatres. The lament of many film critics each year that films are not so good as last year's or the pictures of one, two, or three decades ago, is not discouraging, for it shows that there is a strong, live interest in screen drama. Broadway critics utter a similar lament each year about the offerings on the legitimate stage. Such critics of stage and screen are doing the theatre a service if they prevent producers, directors, actors, and theatre-goers from becoming complacent. Theatre thrives on criticism.

To follow the best in motion pictures in the mid-twentieth century is deeply rewarding. In spite of much inferior material, the movies must be considered our most sophisticated entertainment, a lively popular art with moments of inspiration and vision that bring it within range of the fine arts.

EXERCISES

1. COMPARISON OF AMERICAN AND FOREIGN FILMS. Study a foreign-made film for its particular techniques and its attitudes toward character. Does it have a texture quite different from the Hollywood gloss? How does it differ from American practice in photography, in camera movement, in cutting? Has it a characteristic pattern of continuity or discontinuity? How do the attitudes toward character and the motives of behavior differ from what we expect in American films? Is the attitude more grim, pessimistic, ironic, or less sentimental than conventional American attitudes?

2. THE EXPERIMENTAL FILM. Analyze a film you have seen recently that departs from standard practice, for instance, one that makes extensive use of fantasy, that uses sound or color in an unusual way. Describe one that uses abstract forms rather than objects and people. To what extent could any of the techniques you describe be incorporated in the standard picture? Could a picture of feature length be made with only abstract forms?

3. THE EXPERIMENTAL STORY FILM. Analyze a film that uses a set of characters but does not try to give consistent continuity of story. How much motivation is suggested? Do the characters win your sympathy? Does the

discontinuity create excitement? A sense of the complexity of modern life? Irony? Cruelty? Immediacy of experience?

4. CARTOON TECHNIQUES. What cartoon films have you seen that are not standard in subject or in color or other techniques? Cite examples of the incorporation of cartoon techniques in credit titles (as, for instance, in *The Pink Panther* with Peter Sellers).

5. CREATING PERSONAL HISTORY AND FLASHBACK SCENES TO EXPLAIN CHARACTER. Write a scenario for a film about a student who is facing a critical situation in college. Write directions and dialogue for scenes as he visits his home, with flashback scenes to show episodes that shaped his character in his youth. Then write an episode after he gets back to college and confronts his situation, and indicate what brief flashback shots you would cut in to show how the earlier experience is affecting his present action.

6. VARIETY OF EXPERIENCE IN MOVIEGOING. List as many of the pictures you have seen in the last year as you can. To what type or category does each belong? Have you had a varied experience? What are the opportunities in your community for widening the experience?

FILM RENTAL

Because movies of the past on television are not always well selected, are often cut considerably, and are interrupted by commercials, it is desirable to arrange for special viewing of films from one of the many rental services. Five are listed below.

Brandon International Films (Brandon Films, Inc., 200 West 57th St., New York, 10019; Film Center, Inc., 20 East Huron St., Chicago, 60611; Western Cinema Guild, Inc., 381 Bush St., San Francisco, 94104) has the most extensive list, including the United States, Canada, Europe, Latin-America, Australia, and the Orient.

International Film Classics (Audio Film Center, 2138 East 75th St., Chicago, 60649; 10 Fiske Place, Mount Vernon, N.Y., 10550; 406 Clement St., San Francisco, 94118) has an excellent listing, including not only important European, Oriental, and Latin-American films but some good American films of the last decade and many silent classics, among them Griffith's films and *The Great Train Robbery* and other very early pictures, sometimes with several combined in one package. This is one place to find the work of the early French film-maker Georges Méliès. Pictures of the twenties include *The Cabinet of Dr. Caligari, The Covered Wagon,* the Valentino films *Blood and Sand, Son of the Sheik,* and *The Eagle* (with Vilma Banky), *The Thief of Bagdad* with Douglas Fairbanks, *Dancing Mothers* with Clara Bow, and *The Hunchback of Notre Dame* and *The Phantom of the Opera* with Lon Chaney.

Janus Film Library (The Wellington, 55th at 7th Ave., New York, 10019) lists the principal films of Ingmar Bergman and a few other Swedish films, some Italian films (including Antonioni's *L'Avventura*), some French films (including

578

Truffaut's *Jules et Jim*), some Spanish, Indian, and Polish films, experimental American films, and a number of interesting "short subjects."

Contemporary Films, Inc. (614 Davis St., Evanston, Ill., 60201; 1211 Polk St., San Francisco, 94109) has good recent films and some that go back to the forties and fifties.

The Film-Makers' Cooperative (414 Park Avenue, South, New York, 10016), a division of the New American Cinema Group, Inc., provides an outlet for "underground cinema," the work of noncommercial independent film-makers. Jonas and Adolfas Mekas' films as well as those of many little known film-makers are listed.

SUGGESTED READING

For a general view of the American film, two pictorial histories are excellent: Deems Taylor, *A Pictorial History of the Movies* (1943), and Arthur Mayer, *The Movies* (1957). Thomas Wiseman, *Cinema* (1964), has fewer but excellent illustrations and gives much attention to European film. Liam O'Leary, *The Silent Cinema** (1965), covers both American and European cinema. See also Paul Rotha, *Movie Parade* (1936; rev. ed., 1950), Ernest Lindgren, *A Picture History of the Cinema* (1960), and Daniel Blum, *A Pictorial History of the Silent Screen* (1953).

Arthur Knight, *The Liveliest Art** (1957), is the best concise critical survey of film from the beginning into the fifties. Standard early histories are Benjamin B. Hampton, *A History of the Movies* (1931), Terry Ramsaye, *A Million and One Nights: A History of the Motion Picture* (2 vols., 1926), Maurice Bardèche and Robert Brasillach, *The History of Motion Pictures,* translated from the French by Iris Barry (1938), and Lewis Jacobs, *The Rise of the American Film: A Critical History* (1939). For a recent critical history, see A. R. Fulton, *Motion Pictures: The Development of an Art from Silent Films to the Age of Television* (1960). Edward Wagenknecht, *The Movies in the Age of Innocence* (1962), gives an account of Griffith's work, with a detailed description of all his pictures, and personal recollections of Mary Pickford and the Gish sisters and other stars of the silent screen. Gilbert Seldes in *The Seven Lively Arts* (1924; rev. ed., 1957) and *The Movies Come to America* (1947) expresses a judicious enthusiasm; in *The Great Audience* (1950), he expresses less confidence in the movies and other mass media. Kenneth Macgowan, *Behind the Screen: The History and Techniques of the Motion Picture* (1965), gives a good account of what actually goes on in a movie studio and has excellent comments on the screen play, sound, color, and acting. See also Gary Jennings, *The Movie Book* (1963), William K. Everson, *The American Movie* (1963), and Ivor Montague, *Film World: A Guide to Cinema** (1964). The history of cinema before 1897 (that is, the steps in the invention of the motion picture) is given in C. W. Ceram, *Archaeology of the Cinema* (1965).

The social significance of motion pictures is suggested in Margaret F. Thorp, *America at the Movies* (1939). Interpretations of Hollywood attitudes and influence are found in Leo C. Rosten, *Hollywood: The Movie Colony, The Movie Makers* (1941), Parker Tyler, *The Hollywood Hallucination* (1944) and *Magic and Myth of the Movies* (1947), Leo A. Handel, *Hollywood Looks at Its Audience* (1950), Hortense Powdermaker, *Hollywood the Dream Factory: An An-,*

* Available in paperback edition.

thropologist Looks at the Movie-Makers (1951), Ezra Goodman, *The Fifty-Year Decline and Fall of Hollywood* (1961).

An interesting study of character types in the movies is Martha Wolfenstein and Nathan Leites, *Movies: A Psychological Study* (1950). For the psychology of star worship, see Edgar Morin, *The Stars** (1960), and Richard Schickel, *The Stars* (1962). Interesting studies of Marilyn Monroe, Marlon Brando, and other stars are found in Hollis Alpert, *The Dreams and the Dreamers* (1962). Ray Stuart, *Immortals of the Screen* (1966), is profusely illustrated. See also Norman J. Zierold, *The Child Stars* (1966).

For the serial, see Kalton C. Lahue, *Continued Next Week: A History of the Moving Picture Serial* (1965). George N. Fenin and William K. Everson, *The Western* (1962), comment on variations in the Western formula. For comedy, see John Montgomery, *Comedy Films* (1954), and William K. Everson, *The Bad Guys* (1964). Lillian Ross, *Picture* (1952), gives a full account of John Huston's filming of *The Red Badge of Courage*. Terry Southern and William Claxton, *The Journal of "The Loved One"* (1965), gives the production log of the film, with text by the director and candid shots.

The art and techniques of film are discussed in Roger Manvell, *Film** (1944), Ernest Lindgren, *The Art of the Film: An Introduction to Film Appreciation* (1949), Raymond Spottiswoode, *A Grammar of the Film: An Analysis of Film Technique* (1950), Rudolf Arnheim, *Film as Art** (1958), and Siegfried Kracauer, *Theory of Film: The Redemption of Physical Reality* (1960). The theories of the Russian directors are presented in Sergei Eisenstein, *Film Form* (1949), edited by Jay Leyda, and *Film Technique and Film Acting: The Cinema Writings of V. I. Pudovkin* (1949), with an introduction by Lewis Jacobs. See also Sergei Eisenstein, *The Film Sense* (1942, 1947), edited by Jay Leyda, and Jay Leyda, *Kino: A History of the Russian and Soviet Film* (1960). Griffith's techniques are discussed in Iris Barry, *D. W. Griffith: American Film Master* (1940). A very early aesthetic comment is Vachel Lindsay, *The Art of the Moving Picture* (1915; rev. ed., 1922). Leslie Howard and Lionel Barrymore comment on "The Actor," in *Behind the Screen: How Films Are Made* (1938), edited by Stephen Watts.

Allardyce Nicoll in *Film and Theatre* (1936) is concerned with the way in which movies differ from stage drama. A historical approach to film art that emphasizes similarities of popular stage and film is Nicholas A. Vardac, *Stage to Screen: Theatrical Method from Garrick to Griffith* (1949). George Bluestone, *Novels into Film* (1957), analyzes a number of screen adaptations of novels.

Film: An Anthology (1959), edited by Daniel Talbot, has articles presenting special points of view, including Susanne Langer, "A Note on the Film," Margaret Kennedy, "The Mechanized Muse," James Agee, "Comedy's Greatest Era," Robert Warshow, "The Westerner," and Pauline Kael, "Movies: The Desperate Art." Also useful is John Sutro, ed., *Diversion: Twenty-Two Authors on the Lively Arts* (1950).

Agee on Film, vol. I (1958), is a collection of reviews by James Agee, an excellent film critic of the forties. Pauline Kael in *I Lost It at the Movies** (1965), a collection of her articles and reviews from several periodicals, expresses in a lively style very positive opinions on American and foreign films of the fifties and sixties.

* Available in paperback edition.

SUGGESTED READING

Murray Schumach, *The Face on the Cutting Room Floor: The Story of Movie and Television Censorship* (1964), comments on the anomalies of censorship and gives some illustrations. The Motion Picture Production Code as of December, 1956, is given in an appendix.

A good introduction to foreign films is Michael F. Mayer, *Foreign Films on American Screens* (1965). Thomas Wiseman, *Cinema* (1964), gives an excellent critical survey of developments in European and American film. Georges Sadoul, *French Film* (1953), is a concise but fairly complete survey of French cinema. Penelope Houston, *The Contemporary Cinema** (1964), is especially good on the French New Wave and European developments of the early sixties. John Russell Taylor, *Cinema Eye, Cinema Ear** (1964), has excellent critical discussions of Fellini, Antonioni, Buñuel, Bresson, Bergman, and Hitchcock and a good section on the New Wave and other experimentalists. Since Alfred Hitchcock has been so much admired by the new directors in Europe, his work may well be studied in connection with foreign films. Robin Wood, *Hitchcock's Films** (1965), has very full analyses of the principal pictures. Written by devotees, the following are very subjective treatments of important European directors: Peter Cowie, *Three Monographs: Michelangelo Antonioni, Ingmar Bergman, Alain Resnais* (1963); Pierre Lerpohon, *Michelangelo Antonioni: An Introduction** (1963); Ado Kyron, *Luis Buñuel: An Introduction** (1963). Cocteau makes interesting comments on his own work in *Cocteau on the Film: A Conversation Recorded by André Fraigneau* (1954). Ingmar Bergman and his films are interpreted by his producer, Jörn Donner, in *The Personal Vision of Ingmar Bergman* (1964).

The script of Cocteau's *The Blood of a Poet* (1949) and Alain Robbe-Grillet's script for Resnais's *Last Year at Marienbad* (1962) are worth reading. *Screenplays of Michelangelo Antonioni* (1963) gives some insight into the director's work. Bergman gives a brief but revealing introduction in *Four Screenplays of Ingmar Bergman** (1960). John Osborne, *Tom Jones, a Film Script* (1964), is good reading for anyone who has seen the film.

A survey of Polish film is *Contemporary Polish Cinematography* (1962). For a history of the German film, see Siegfried Kracauer, *From Caligari to Hitler* (1947). See also Forsyth Hardy, *Scandinavian Film* (1952), and Vernon Jarratt, *The Italian Cinema* (1951).

Joseph I. Anderson and Donald Richie, *The Japanese Film: Art and Industry* (1959), makes a careful survey. Donald Richie, *The Japanese Movie: An Illustrated History* (1965), makes comparisons between Japanese films and those of other countries. Donald Richie, *The Films of Akira Kurosawa* (1965), is a handsomely illustrated account of the Japanese director who has been most acclaimed in the western world. In Parker Tyler, *The Three Faces of the Film* (1960), there is a helpful discussion of "*Rashomon* as Modern Art." Erik Barnouw and S. Krishnaswamy, *Indian Film* (1963), has a full history of Indian film and a good account of Satyajit Ray's career.

For the documentary, see Forsyth Hardy, ed., *Grierson on Documentary* (1947), Paul Rotha, *Documentary Film* (3rd ed., 1952), Jay Leyda, *Films Beget Films* (1964), and Arthur Calder-Marshall, *The Innocent Eye: The Life of Robert J. Flaherty* (1966).

Robert D. Feild, *The Art of Walt Disney* (1947), gives an account of Disney's

* Available in paperback edition.

early career and a description of animated cartoon techniques that is intelligible to the layman.

The many biographies and autobiographies of important film figures—producers, directors, actors—give insight into the problems of the movie world, and most of them have interesting anecdotes. Arthur Mayer, *Merely Colossal* (1953), is an autobiographical account of the film industry. Bosley Crowther, *Hollywood Rajah: The Life and Times of Louis B. Mayer* (1960), is an account of the career of one of the most successful Hollywood producers. Josef von Sternberg, *Fun in a Chinese Laundry* (1965), relates interesting experiences in the author's directing of Marlene Dietrich in the thirties. Cecil B. De Mille (with Donald Hayne), *Autobiography* (1960), and Peter Noble, *The Fabulous Orson Welles* (1956), deal with directors. Biographies of comedians include: Charles Chaplin, *My Autobiography* (1964); Mack Sennett (written with Cameron Shipp), *King of Comedy* (1954); Buster Keaton and Charles Samuels, *My Wonderful World of Slapstick* (1960); John McCabe, *Mr. Laurel and Mr. Hardy* (1961). See also Mary Pickford, *Sunshine and Shadow* (1955), and Maurice Zolotov, *Marilyn Monroe* (1961).

Agee on Film: Five Film Scripts by James Agee, vol. II (1960), contains the screen play of *The African Queen.* For other American screen plays, see John Gassner and Dudley Nichols, eds., *Twenty Best Film Plays, Best Film Plays of 1943–44, Best Film Plays of 1945* (1943, 1945, 1946). Clifford McCarthy, *Bogey: The Films of Humphrey Bogart* (1965), has many photographs of Bogart and production notes on his 75 feature films. Gerald McDonald, Michael Conway, and Mark Ricci, *The Films of Charlie Chaplin* (1965), presents in pictures and text 80 films made by Chaplin since 1914.

SUGGESTED READING

CHAPTER EIGHTEEN

THEATRE FOR THE
MASS AUDIENCE

The Art of Broadcast Drama

A broadcast drama is not the same as a movie. It grew up as a distinct form, and it has quite a different relation to its audience. The millions of listeners to broadcast drama have not gone out for a special occasion. Sitting relaxed at home, singly or in small groups, they expect a continuing program, with the same characters or even the same story pattern every week or every day. The performer, whether actor or announcer, speaks confidentially and directly to the home group. Though many movies are broadcast and some people have considered the television screen as primarily a device for showing movies, the home audience in its habits and expectations is quite different from any other.

The pattern of listening to half-hour or hour programs, continued every week or every day, was established early in the days of radio, and although some radio techniques were made obsolete by video, many of the basic techniques had a great influence on the emerging television drama. It seems worthwhile, therefore, to take a look at radio drama.

RADIO DRAMA

It was not clear at first that radio drama was possible, that people would listen to voices and sounds with neither actors nor settings to look at.   *583*

Would the audience know who was speaking and where? Would long passages of narration or description be necessary? Should a radio drama be actually a radio short story? But writers soon found that different voices for the dialogue create a dramatic present rather than a narrative past and that a few descriptive words could indicate the place, as Shakespeare's characters did on the Elizabethan stage. More powerful than words are sound effects. Footsteps, turning doorknobs, creaking hinges, slamming doors are not usually heard on the stage, but in radio drama they can not only enrich the background but become as much a part of the action as the words. Rain, wind, birds, insects—the offstage sounds of the environment which on the stage can only be hinted at through words—can be brought to the center of attention. Early enthusiasts overdid the sound effects, marking every time a spoon touched a dish or a book touched a table and following into the distance every departing car or airplane, but they gradually realized that sounds are important only as characters become conscious of them and that automobiles, sea waves, rain, and wind sound so much alike over loud-speakers that they are not effective unless the dialogue tells what is being heard and how the characters are reacting to it.

The sound, whether from the action, from the environment, or from musical instruments, is even more powerful for radio drama than for the theatre, serving now as a bridge, to emphasize the impact of the last episode and create a mood for the next, now as a background for poetic, dreamy, and meditative scenes, now as an irritation for an outraged character to fight against. The music may pick up the rhythm of some spoken phrase, echoing or mocking the speech, elaborating the emotional intent.

Sometimes as important in a radio play as dialogue, music, and sound effects is an announcer who takes the listener into the midst of action. An impersonal station official was always present to give the station identification and start the program, and a lively news reporter was familiar in on-the-spot sports broadcasts and newscasting. But no one had realized how effective an announcer could be in creating the action of the play until Archibald MacLeish wrote the poetic radio play *The Fall of the City* in 1937. MacLeish declared in his preface, "The Announcer is the most useful dramatic personage since the Greek Chorus . . . an integral part of radio technique. His presence is as natural as it is familiar. And his presence . . . restores to the poet that obliquity, that perspective, that three-dimensional depth without which great poetic drama cannot exist."

The Fall of the City is a parable about a city welcoming a conqueror who is a product of their imagination and fear; when he arrives he is discovered to be an empty suit of armor, a figure created by the mob who want to be mastered. The poet makes vivid use of the announcer, taking the listeners into the square of an imaginary city and having him describe the scene as though it were a real news event. First the Studio Announcer sets the scene, the daily terror and foreboding in a distant city:

> Ladies and gentlemen:
> This broadcast comes to you from the city.

. . . . .
For three days the world has watched this city—

. . . . .
Each day for three days there has come
To the door of her tomb at noon a woman buried!

. . . . .
We take you now to the great square of this city . . .

Then, after the hum of a vast crowd fills the background, the matter-of-fact Voice of the Announcer takes up the play:

We are here on the central plaza.
We are well off to the eastward edge,

and so on, with a description of the surging mob waiting for the dire predictions of the dead woman. The dead woman and various voices in the crowd are heard, then the orator, the priest, and the general debate, with exhortations to the people to make no resistance, to think of heaven, or to fight. Several messengers arrive and finally the new master himself. The mob welcomes him, free of its freedom, the long labor of liberty ended. The Announcer, like a Greek Chorus, both involved in the events and above them, makes clear the significance of the city's fall.

Creating the environment was not the only problem of the new medium. It was evident from the first that putting a microphone or a row of microphones in front of a performance or bringing the actors to the microphone was not the same as performing a play before an audience in a theatre. Without the visual element, not only scenery and lighting, facial expression and gesture, but even the relationship of the characters to one another was lost or confused. In fact, a new perspective of space and relationship was created by the microphone. The listener could tell which voice was very close to it and which more distant, when a face was turning away or turning closer. The difference in sound was a matter of quality and not volume, for the amplifier could easily make the more distant voice just as loud as the nearer. The actor deliberately uses a different tone if he is talking at a distance, and the microphone picks up a different tone when the voice is distant. When the actor comes very close to the microphone and speaks very quietly, a new intimacy is created that makes radio very different from the stage. That close, intimate voice, talking only to itself or confiding private feelings to the audience of listeners at home, was far more subjective than anything familiar in realistic drama. And it was evident that radio could jump from objective to subjective, from outer action to inner feeling, from present to past, in a fraction of a second. Not only could place be changed instantaneously but the level of reality could be shifted, from memory to expectation or reality to fantasy. As Arch Oboler wrote, after a decade of writing for radio,

. . . only the radio medium permits the lightning shift of scene from past to present to future, from air to earth to water. . . . The most flexible form in the history of artistic expression, radio offers great, exciting opportunities. There are no limitations of stage or movie set, there are no

585

Theatre for the Mass Audience

boundaries of time and space; a word, a sound effect, a strain of music, and in a split second the listener is emotionally part of the dramatic thought of the author.

In his radio drama *Baby* (1938), Oboler uses a single character who talks to the audience between the time she leaves the doctor's office and the time she arrives home to tell her husband they are going to have a baby. It is the depression decade and she fears he will be angry. Expressionistic voices echo the sound of her steps with "ba - by, ba - by." As the steps hesitate in dread, the voice chants, "slower, slower," and as they quicken in hope, "faster, faster." She is repeatedly wakened from her thoughts by the traffic or a policeman, by passers-by, then by the neighbors in the apartment house. After she has spoken aloud, she shifts, by the slightest drop in tone, speaking very close to the microphone, to the quiet intimacy of the subjective. Enlarged and sent across the nation by the amplifier, the voice still has a quiet intimacy, clearly set off from the words spoken to another person. In her daydreams she remembers how happy she and her husband were as sweethearts and then as newlyweds in an amusement park. We hear memories of her mother's warning that she would cry set against sounds of her husband's laughter, followed by her present thought, "But how can he laugh now!" and echoing voices calling out, "Rent, Gas, Dentist, Lights, Carfare . . . Bills . . . Bills . . . Bills."

Orson Welles had great success in the late 1930s with a form that was particularly well adapted to radio. A strong central character tells the full story directly to the audience as though it were a narrative monologue, but when other voices come in or the main character speaks to other people, the narrative past becomes dramatic present.

The most imaginative use of all the best techniques of radio was made by the poet Dylan Thomas in a play for voices, *Under Milk Wood,* finished just before his death in 1954, when radio drama was about to yield to the television screen. It has had a number of full stage productions, but it is far more effective as a radio play or when staged as a dramatic reading with six or eight readers. It is unsurpassed in its use of vivid language and of radio's lightning-quick creation of character and evocation of situation in the shift from description to dialogue, to dream, to song. Some thirty-odd characters are developed fully while many others appear briefly as the listener ranges the high street and shops of a seaside village in Wales, overhearing the public conflicts and private hopes. Sometimes two narrating voices invoke the dreams of the sleeping and the dead, from before dawn through the day to sleep again. Or the voice is blind Captain Cat's as he dreams of his long-dead sailors, who ask, "How's it above? . . . Is there rum and lava bread? Bosoms and robins?" or as he remembers his women or the children of his childhood. Sometimes there are women gossiping at the pump, or we hear the voice of postman Willy Nilly, carrying letters and gossip from house to house. A girl dreams of her lover "tall as the town clock tower, Samson-syrup-gold-maned, whacking thighed and piping hot, thunderbolt bass'd and barnacle-breasted, flailing up the cockles with his eyes like blowlamps and

586

The Mass Media

scooping down over her lonely loving hotwaterbottled body." Mrs. Pugh calls her husband a pig—"You should wait until you retire to your sty"—while he dreams of poisoning her—"Sly and silent he foxes into his chemist's den and there, in a hiss and prussic circle of cauldrons and phials brimful with pox and the Black Death, cooks up a fricassee of deadly nightshade, nicotine, hot frog, cyanide and bat-spit for his needling stalactite hag and bednag of a pokerbacked nutcracker wife." Polly Garter, who takes on all the lonely farm boys or drunk husbands, sings her wistful song:

> But I always think as we tumble into bed
> Of little Willy Wee who is dead, dead, dead.

Thus the imagination creates from words and sounds. As MacLeish said earlier, "Over the radio verse has no visual presence to compete with." Many an old-time radio listener remembers with nostalgia the fantastic scenes conjured up by suggestion—lonely roads, dismal swamps, the dark side of the moon, the inside of the brain. A few words, a strange scrape or rustle—the imagination did the rest. The suggestive power of words and sounds, so recently discovered, was one of the radio techniques that were not preserved in the new medium.

Most radio dramas were shallow, routine anecdotes to hold the attention for a passing moment. A few ballad plays showed distinction, combining snatches of song with dialogue. Norman Corwin wrote some good impressionistic sketches of American scenes and some good patriotic war plays. The form of radio drama seemed promising enough, offering depth in the subjective confession and atmosphere through sounds and the power of words, but, except for the plays of the poets MacLeish and Thomas, not many of the thousands of radio plays devised over a twenty-year period seem worth hearing again—a few of the action serials, perhaps, for sheer virtuosity in telling a conventional story. Some people blame the limited time; most radio dramas were a half-hour in length, including time for commercials, and even the hour play was much shorter than a movie or stage drama. Certain kinds of development need scope to be convincing and many a stage play has lost its vitality when abbreviated for movie or broadcast. Still, time is not an impossible handicap. Although a playwright cannot be expected to create in a few lines a work of great intensity and wide implications as a poet can, he ought to be able, by avoiding subjects that involve many characters, to find material that can be developed honestly and forcefully in the half-hour spot. But both playwrights and sponsors were afraid to risk losing the mass audience. Again and again they chose to try for the easier, stereotyped response.

Even Arch Oboler, the most original of the popular radio playwrights, pulled his punches and resorted to the conventional happy ending. His play about unemployment in the depression years, with an honest, touching subject, is an example. The title, *This Precious Freedom,* is bitterly ironic. A man in his fifties finds he is free to be fired, to be driven out of his home by his son, and to be deserted by his wife. There is no villain or sudden violence, only the little day-to-day changes in human relationships that stage

587

naturalism had presented so well and that radio, in its freedom to move easily through many short scenes, could indicate even more effectively. But Oboler would not let his honest situation move to its natural ending. His man gets a job on a farm, and, passing a church where the congregation is singing a hymn about casting false gods to the ground, has a quick uplifting revelation: "I'd . . . I'd lost things that were—were false, too! A—a wife who was no *real* wife—a son who was no son—and—a house that wasn't a home! I'd lost them—yes!" Such a quick acceptance, with strong religious music in the background, is an evasion of the problem of the family disintegration that followed unemployment, which is so honestly presented in the rest of the play.

When the video screen was added, broadcast drama continued most of the patterns of radio: the commercial sponsorship, the continued day-to-day or week-to-week programing, and most of the techniques. But the two most distinctive developments of radio have been neglected in television plays. The poetic element has had few echoes, being too verbal for visual-minded producers and too highbrow for mass-minded authors. As with many movie directors, the emphasis has been on the mime and movement inherited from the silent screen, with rich incidental sounds and music but with words kept to a dull minimum. Curiously, even the character telling his own story, with quick flashbacks, has not been frequently used. The cutting in of brief scenes from another place or time has been much slower because television directors, less willing than radio directors to depend on the subjective, have felt they must show at least a corner of a real setting and not just flashes of faces, as would be necessary if the speed of similar radio action were to be maintained. The stream of consciousness, so powerful in fiction, poetry, and even stage drama and a mainstay in radio plays, has had little use in television drama. "The Fugitive," the series that caught the sympathy of the youthful television audience from its beginning in 1964, might have been even more powerful with an occasional glimpse into the feelings behind the round innocent face of the pursued man. Radio techniques proved their worth, and will be available when imaginative directors want to go back and explore them.

REALISM ON THE TELEVISION SCREEN

While providing light entertainment for the nation, television in its first decade created a very serious realistic drama, and seriousness and realism dominated the continued weekly shows about doctors, lawyers, reporters, and detectives in the 1960s long after the first period of intimate individual television drama was over. Even the tearful soap operas, family situation comedies, and Westerns, popular with radio listeners since the 1930s, were given solid realistic settings and glimpses of streets or mountains to add validity to the conventional situations. The new plays written for television in the 1940s and 50s did not borrow from their popular screen neighbor, the variety or personality show, in which the customary short skit, tailored to fit a virtuoso performer, makes use of song and dance and easy

The Mass Media

contact with the audience, in the light-travesty tradition of vaudeville or stage extravaganzas. Instead, full-length dramas went in the opposite direction and sought the authenticity of the documentary—a documentary more solid and real than the radio documentary, for instead of depending on an announcer to give a sense of an actual place, they could bring the camera directly to the spot.

Television inherits and combines the cinema sense that the camera is showing the actual fact and the radio sense that this is news direct from the event itself, not a fictional plot. From the beginning, radio seemed to its listeners to have a kind of official dependability. When an English station in 1926 presented a parody of an announcer describing a supposed riot, it was taken seriously. When Orson Welles in 1938 produced a dramatic program about an imaginary invasion from Mars, using some of the techniques of announcers and interviewers, listeners were disturbed and many ran out of their houses in terror. Even some who had heard from the beginning that the program was a dramatization of H. G. Wells's novel *The War of the Worlds* were caught by the sense of reality. Television carries the same sense of reality. In a movie house, the viewers knew that even the newsreels they were watching were something arranged for them out of pictures made a number of days or even years ago, but news broadcasts keep the home audience feeling that they may well be seeing something which is happening almost at that moment.

Watching a good news program may be better than seeing the event in person, as the camera team spreads over several advantageous spots to take the viewer inside or outside, alternating wide views with close-ups of small groups, objects, or single faces. If to the direct shots of the event are added shots of other people and facts important in the background of the event,

FIGURE *18.1* Broadcast of a real event. Elaborate equipment is needed for a simple presentation of public personalities. Candidates John F. Kennedy and Richard M. Nixon debate the issues in the Presidential campaign of 1960. Photo NBC.

the result combines the immediacy of a news story, the emotional involvement of a drama, and the explanation in depth of a feature article or a historical essay. Robert Flaherty in his documentary films showed how the camera could catch the poetic texture of everyday lives, and Pare Lorentz caught both a poetic mood and an urgency for social action in *The River* and *The Plow That Broke the Plains,* produced in the 1930s. In the same decade the Living Newspaper and other epic productions brought to the theatre dramatizations of public problems, and the March of Time brought to the movies and radio a combination of newsreels and background information to present a current topic in some depth. But the television documentary has far surpassed its stage, movie, and radio ancestors.

Some documentaries have made history by giving public definition to an urgent concern in political and international affairs. When in 1952 the much-admired Edward R. Murrow devoted his "See It Now" program to an examination of Senator Joseph McCarthy's campaign against supposed Communists, the public saw clearly for the first time how unreasonable and vindictive the campaign of the Senator had been. At the height of the Cuban crisis in 1962, a program devoted to the missile sites, with Secretary of Defense Robert McNamara as narrator, was more than news; it was an official explanation and reassurance to the nation. Also in 1962 American newsmen in Berlin, gathering information from refugees about conditions in East Germany, made contact with the young men who were digging a tunnel under the wall dividing East and West Berlin and financed the photographing of many aspects of their work, including the actual digging. The newsmen had the planning stages reenacted and added a sound track in America. The results combined a factual program with an adventure story which had suspense, terror, and escape to freedom. Officials of the State Department were fearful for months of the effects of disclosing how much American newsmen were involved in the escape operation.

Even the most factual documentary has some elements of fiction and dramatization. The first space flight cost the three networks an estimated ten million dollars, but that sum paid not only for televising the launching and the recovery of the capsule from the ocean but for many shots of similar structures, some of them created in the studio, showing not the actual men in the actual space capsule but how the equipment probably looked in use. Some critics thought that the announcers did not indicate clearly enough which shots were "prerecorded" and which were actual shots. But audiences trust newsgatherers to keep them close to reality and of course want to know much more than they can learn from glimpses of the particular event. Perhaps in the case of the first space-flight broadcasts, drawings would have been more honest than models that could be supposed real.

Some very interesting questions arise in connection with documentary programs, important not only in public policy but in the matter of the relationship of drama with fact and truth. On the stage there is no question. All is representation of truth, on a particular level of honesty or fantasy but not actual fact. But the camera introduces a new element. How complete and just a picture does the camera present? Does the cameraman change the event by his presence or even create "pseudo-events" by asking people to reenact a happening? Judges and congressmen have been very reluctant to allow a television camera in court or Congress, trusting the summary made by a reporter but not the facts selected by the camera or the effect the presence of the camera might have on the participants. It is not clear whether the newsman or cameraman has the right to be present on all occasions and to expose everything. Sometimes a fictional representation is wiser and more just than the raw facts.

Most documentaries use a guide to introduce and comment on the factual material, often a familiar personality whom everyone knows and trusts—a Huntley, Brinkley, Cronkite, or Sevareid. From there it is just a step to the story drama that combines a fictional central character with a real background. Such a candid-camera realism has dominated the broadcast drama. Whether in the intimate drama of Paddy Chayefsky and Horton Foote, with bedrooms and kitchens, dance halls and buses, or in more recent city-situation dramas about lawyers, doctors, and social workers, the main characters are seen in the midst of real places, crowds, and professional activities.

THE GOLDEN AGE OF TELEVISION DRAMA

Although it has almost disappeared from the air in America in the 1960s, the individual television play had a remarkable development in the 50s. It was a live studio drama, using television techniques but retaining much of the freshness of a stage performance. It could be recorded by

FIGURE *18.2* The many intimate settings of a TV drama set up in one large studio. This view from above shows the lighting instruments as well as the cameras. While most of the settings have solid or painted detail, the translucent screen in the foreground shows a scene of windows projected on it.

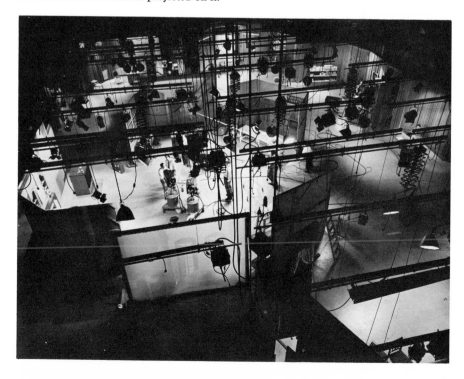

kinescope on film and shown again, but a kinescope broadcast was not so clear as a live one, and until the tape method of recording was perfected in 1957, the country had a feast of plays that were both live and lively. Playhouse 90, the Philco-Goodyear Playhouse, Studio One, the Kraft TV Theatre, and several others brought to the home screen new plays on the average of once a week. Some were adaptations from stage plays, novels, or short stories, but many were the work of a new school of playwrights who explored the documentary realism and quiet intimacy of radio drama to develop a new form of broadcast drama that was especially effective on the home screen. Looking back at the genuine characters created by these playwrights, critics call that time of the late forties and early fifties "The Golden Age of Television Drama."

Intimacy was the key word of the new drama, the final development of the intimate realism that had appeared late in the nineteenth century and had dominated most stage productions since. Not even the small theatres of stage realism were as intimate as the "theatre" of the TV audience in their homes. With a microphone and a camera very close to the face, actors attained the ultimate in quiet subtlety and casual expression. Properties, so important in stage realism, became even more important as the camera focused on a single chair or table or hand. Later television drama, recorded on tape, could wander outdoors and, if the sponsor was willing to pay, include spectacular effects. But this early blossoming of TV drama was in the studio, in a few interiors of homes, and now and then in a corner of some public place. Recently the dramatic value of that emphasis on intimacy is disputed as television production includes long shots and large open spaces. But the early workers, convinced that realism was the true mode for the home screen, thought that movie long shots were too indistinct and that close-up and medium shots were the essence of television drama.

The new playwrights of the air, interpreting realism rather differently from the way writers of sentimental romance and melodrama for the movies did, followed one of the main streams of the theatre. Avoiding the drastic naturalism of Gorki or the violence of O'Neill, they preferred the quiet, implicit realism of Maeterlinck and Chekhov, using the kind of suggestion to be found in impressionist painting. Their quiet characters are in conflict with their environment at many little points, trying to find a small area of freedom while accepting the web of fate that holds them. In Tad Mosel's television play *The Haven,* when a middle-aged woman finds out about her husband's infidelity of years ago, she does not shoot him or leave him. She is too closely entangled in the web herself and must work out a new adaptation as life goes on. As in Ibsen, bits of the past may break into the present, but in this gentle drama of the home screen, people "do not do such things"—they do not commit suicide. Such adjustments and decisions as are possible are made out of sight. In Paddy Chayefsky's *The Mother,* the major decision is made between scenes. The old mother, discouraged in trying to maintain her independence, gives up and goes to her daughter's apartment, wondering what she will do with her furniture and dishes and what she will do with her life.

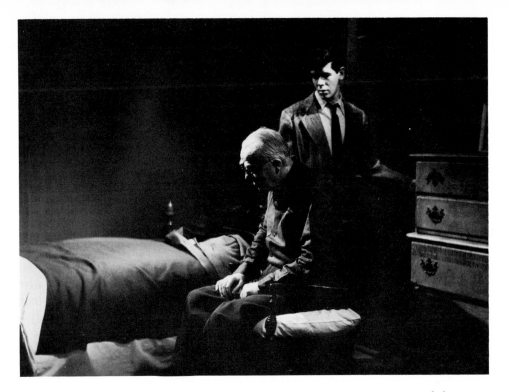

FIGURE *18.3* Muted conflict at close quarters. The intimate TV drama of the "Golden Age" of the 1950s took place in small rooms or old-fashioned workshops. Chayefsky's *Printer's Measure.* Wagner International Photos.

Instead of going to bed, she sits exhausted in a chair. Then as the thin morning sun comes in the window, we see her still sitting in the chair. But the decision has been made. She puts on her hat and coat and starts out, determined to maintain her independence a little longer. Habits, things, the little relations with home surroundings—all these give texture and meaning to human lives.

When there is rebellion or an attempt to escape, the prisoner finds the outside world is no better and comes back to his chains. In Chayefsky's *The Bachelor Party,* the husband feels crushed by his routine job, his wife and home, and the endless struggle to make ends meet. Now a baby is expected. He envies the bachelor at the office who always has several girls on the string and money to spend on parties. The office group decides to have a wild fling at a bachelor party, a farewell for one of them who is to marry the next day. They go from bar to bar, getting higher and higher, until the groom calls up his girl to tell her he won't get married, he's having too good a time as a bachelor. But presently the evening palls. The husband takes the bridegroom home, persuades him to apologize to the girl, to tell her frankly he's afraid. "Everybody's scared, Arnold," the husband explains.

> Everybody's got things in them they're ashamed of. That's what a wife's for. To make you feel you don't have to be ashamed of yourself. Then she tells you what makes her feel miserable. . . . Then that's your job. It's

593

Theatre for the Mass Audience

your job to make her feel she's not as bad as everybody makes her think she is. That's what marriage is, Arnold. It's a job. You work at it. You work at it twenty-four hours a day.

The ending is more subtle than this explicit moralizing. The husband goes home, knowing he is glad he has his burden. There is no gesture of decision. He looks at his wife asleep in bed and quietly goes into the bathroom. We hear a fragment of song from the bathroom and a sliver of light touches the wife's face. We see a trace of a smile as she half-wakes. The rebellion is over. The husband is back in his groove, and glad of it.

Flight is made literal in Horton Foote's *Trip to Bountiful,* a story of a little old Texas lady who leaves her son's house and makes her way back to her old home in the farm community she had left to move to the city. Pursued in her flight by her son and daughter-in-law, she finally gets to the deserted house, only to find that her closest friend has died and that the farm is overgrown with woods. She is found by her irate daughter-in-law and her distressed son and gives in, but she has had her glimpse of the place that had some meaning for her. "You go tell Jessie Mae I'm sorry," she says. "I won't fight any more. I've found my dignity and my strength." As Foote was getting a group of his plays ready for publication, he noticed that they had all been about the small town in Texas where he had grown up and about people who after a protest had accepted their fate.

The high point of the intimate drama, the miniature television masterpiece of the 1950s, was Chayefsky's *Marty,* put on the air in 1954 with Rod Steiger in the title role and later made into a successful movie with Ernest Borgnine as Marty. The play is significant both as the high point in the study of casual human relations and even more as a new version of the old pattern of revolt against the environment. Here the outer environment is the dehumanized world of city drifters, unmarried men trying to live up to the cheap ideal of the crowd, while the home environment is created by a mother-son relationship that cannot be fully resolved. Marty is a short, fat worker in a butcher shop, a homely man in his thirties who spends much time with a group of younger men in bars and public dance halls. One night he meets a lonely, unattractive girl who is ignored by the other men. The two, in their loneliness, find they are congenial. Marty's companions make fun of his girl, and his mother disapproves. For a moment Marty hesitates. But after getting another glimpse of the life led by his rootless young friends with their ideal of flashy feminine beauty and cheap popularity, he rebels, and asks the ugly duckling for a date. He has a chance for a family of his own on the back streets of the big city.

At most there was muted sadness on the Golden Age screen, never such sharp defeat as in the realism of O'Neill or Tennessee Williams. One of the finest plays was Tad Mosel's dramatization of the James Agee novel *A Death in the Family,* called on the television screen, as on Broadway and in the movie, *The Long Way Home.* The family, faced with the sudden accidental death of the husband and father, finds new strength through deep and uncomplicated affection for the departed and for one another.

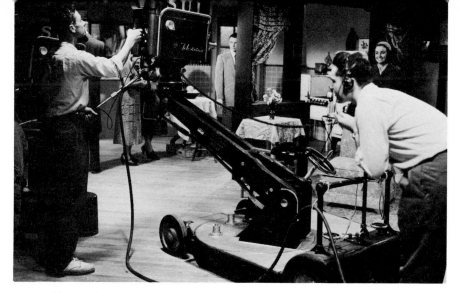

FIGURE *18.4* Intimate TV drama in a college studio. The cameras easily turn to several rooms in a house in succession. University of Iowa.

Looking back at the intimate domestic drama, one can find in it a number of realistic insights—conflict of mothers and sons, jealousy of sisters, frustration and anger in crowded apartments and boarding houses, conflict between the values of the big city and the small towns or old city neighborhoods. But these insights were not enough to save it. Before the fifties were over, this drama had gone, leaving a few echoes and some slight influence on the series and serials that replaced it. There are at least three reasons for its disappearance.

The first reason was the change of methods of production that came about with the perfection of recording tape in 1957 and the subsequent shift of production from the television studio to the movie studio. At first the movie producers looked on television with fear and contempt and the broadcasting studios created most of their own shows and ran such old movies as the Hollywood companies would sell. But by the mid-fifties the movie studios saw the enormous possibilities for making television shows themselves, and the recording tape gave them their opportunity. When the only way of recording a performance was by the kinescope, there was every advantage in broadcasting a show live from the studio. But when the impulse that is sent over the air can be recorded and broadcast from a tape, it is as clear as a live performance. To record all the impulses of a television broadcast in one line would have meant running the tape extremely fast and would have required a tape of unmanageable length. But by 1957 a method was perfected of recording zigzag back and forth across the two-inch-wide tape, with a separate sound track on one edge of the tape. A tape is a great convenience to the producer, who can show it at different hours across the country to suit the different time zones, and of course he can reproduce it and sell it to various stations and even to other countries for many later broadcasts. Moreover, prerecording frees the director from having to do the play con-

595

Theatre for the Mass Audience

tinuously in one studio of limited space. He can make various sequences in any location he chooses and cut and splice the tape exactly as in film-making. The special intimacy of the broadcast studio and the freshness of a live performance were gone. Sponsors were more interested in plays with wider backgrounds and cinematic techniques.

A second reason for the abandonment of live studio drama was that several of the writers of the intimate plays lost interest. Chayefsky, most praised of all the television playwrights, not only stopped writing for television but turned in a different direction in his writing for the stage. Weary of the low intensity of realistic episodes and everyday prose, he tried a more poetic style for a reluctant but powerful hero in the Biblical play *Gideon* (1961). The dialogue between Gideon and the Angel of the Lord rose to rhetorical intensity as the roused, stubborn man demanded an independent place somewhere between heaven and earth. Chayefsky moved even further from the quiet rebellions of television intimacy in trying the epic sweep of Russian revolutionary history, with songs, monologues, and satire, for *The Passion of Joseph D.* (1964).

The third reason for the disappearance of the television drama of the fifties was that the attitudes of the public and the advertisers changed. Hubbell Robinson, who was head of production for the Columbia Broadcasting System in the years of the intimate drama, said recently,

> Remember that in the mid-fifties, television wasn't really a mass medium. There were only some ninety stations operating throughout the country, and mostly in the cities: the cost of TV sets was still high. In effect we enjoyed a brief period when we could program for something resembling an elite audience.

But with the expansion of the economy in the late 1950s and 60s, the television audience expanded and the wider, more affluent audience was not interested in little plays about little people or in the theme of frustration and the acceptance of limitation—the central theme of intimate realism since Chekhov. The advertisers, for their part, did not want the public to dwell on acceptance of the limitations of small towns and grubby back streets but to dream of the glamorous elegance of new automobiles and hair sprays. Although television realism softened defeat and indicated plenty of sentiment beneath its muted discords, the values it expressed were in sharp contrast with the new pattern of free spending. The characters created by Chayefsky, Foote, and Rod Serling, trying to hold on to the ways of the small town or foreign neighborhood, were bewildered or repelled by urban ways. The slick city idlers who are Marty's companions are shown to be empty and sterile. The daughter-in-law who tyrannizes over the little old lady in *Trip to Bountiful* is cheap and vulgar, interested only in soft drinks, glamour magazines, and beauty parlors. Yet American economic expansion depends partly on the buying of luxuries—chrome-encrusted automobiles, smart kitchen equipment, and cosmetics.

596   As a substitute for the individual television play, producers and advertisers relied upon the packaged drama series with the same familiar characters and the same pattern of action continued week after week. It held the unthinking mass audience better than the individual plays and it was more likely to set the audience in a mood for buying. Like the commercials themselves, it portrayed rich, successful people. In "Peyton Place" there were old crimes, prison records, and misunderstandings that might have come from nineteenth-century novels or daytime soap operas, but the women had beautiful hairdos and, for a small town, rather up-to-date homes. Doctors, nurses, and psychiatrists in other series had mostly rich patients. "The Beverly Hillbillies" retained their rural twang but had money to throw away. The Cartwrights of "Bonanza" were not first settlers struggling to build a home in the wilderness but owned the finest ranch in the world and defended an established security against evil intruders and eccentric wanderers. In TV series, poor people with foreign accents were merely passing problems for the lawyers, social workers, or legislators to do something about. Small-town characters might survive, but they were usually given a comic treatment, as in the farcical gossips of the general store and post office at "Petticoat Junction," the high school group in "Mr. Novak," or the people in Andy Griffith's more genial comedy. So the anthologies of live drama dropped out, leaving fresh spontaneity only with the Jack Paars and Johnny Carsons and other M.C. personalities.

The Weekly Series Dramas of the 1960s

The vitality of broadcast drama in the 1960s has been almost entirely in the series. The few original single plays that have been produced on such programs as Alfred Hitchcock or the Kraft Suspense Theatre have been as stereotyped as the continuing series and less vital. The Hallmark Hall of Fame has brought some excellent actors in stage classics—Maurice Evans in *Macbeth* and *The Tempest,* Ingrid Bergman in *Hedda Gabler,* and Alfred Lunt and Lynn Fontanne in *The Magnificent Yankee.* Ed Sullivan and others have presented selections from the new musical hits as well as opera and ballet performers. Camera Three on its small budget has showed sample scenes from some of the more unusual new plays or dance programs. These are mere scraps, welcome to people of taste and acceptable to the average viewer because they stir his curiosity without exhausting his patience. There is no point in regretting the loss of new plays each week or in looking with envy to England, where many authors, some of them American, find producers for original broadcast plays. The American screen seems to be committed to the standard package.

There are differences of quality among the series, of course, and in watching "The Defenders," "Dr. Kildare," and a few others, the viewer may wonder whether some day a series will develop the richness of a good long novel, with challenging roles for actors, designers, and cameramen. Meantime he can add to a casual absorption in repetitive formula drama some pleasure in a special performer, a wispy Elizabeth Montgomery as the fretful but devoted witch wife in "Bewitched," or Dan Blocker's homespun Hoss Cart-

597

wright in "Bonanza." Or he can turn to the real virtuoso actors, the specialty performers—Jackie Gleason, Bob Hope, Jack Benny, Danny Kaye, Lucille Ball, and the others whose skill in song, dance, mime, or comedy adds a glory to any art, no matter how shoddy or repetitive the material they have to use.

Repetitive formulas and tested routines have been used by popular actors since the beginning of drama. Under Aristophanes' leadership, Athenian comedy for a short time dealt with important current topics, and his actors followed every new fancy of his fertile brain, but after him comedy soon reverted to the conventional antics of sputtering old men and a clever-stupid pair of slaves. For several centuries Rome delighted in companies of clowns in standard comedies involving absurd old men and slaves in a legendary village of Atella. One Atellan character, Maccus, a country lout always in trouble, became so popular that he was put into new situations in a series of plays: *Mack in the Army, Mack in a Convent, Mack the Bartender,* and so on. The series was under way.

Like the Atellan clowns, the *commedia dell' arte* troupes regaled Europe for three centuries on the streets and at court by repeating the same characters, the same stock situations, and the same repertory of verbal and sight gags, even using standard costumes and masks. Some superb performers raised the stale routines to the level of a fine art. In the seventeenth century Molière was able to transform the stereotypes of the popular *commedia* troupes into histrionic and literary masterpieces, but in the eighteenth century Goldoni felt he must discard them in order to create a comedy he could respect. A popular stereotype cannot always be galvanized into life.

From the Sherlock Holmes of Conan Doyle to the James Bond of Ian Fleming, readers of suspense fiction have watched for the next book to see their mastermind detective tackle a new case. Moviemakers soon discovered the appeal of repeating the same character in new situations. The most famous early film serial was *The Perils of Pauline,* which had a new episode each week that left the heroine suspended over a cliff or surrounded by stalking villains and left the audience in almost unbearable suspense until the following week when they could see Pauline get out of that dilemma and into the next. Feature-length films have followed the pattern of a complete story in each, but for the neighborhood houses producers are quick to try a sequel when a character makes a hit. Tarzan went on through movie after movie, a new muscle man taking over when the star died or grew too fat or became tired of the cave-man stereotype. In the 1930s a teenage character, Andy Hardy, and his likable small-town family won a movie audience that followed them through a long series of films, a series on a higher level than the horror films spawned by *Frankenstein* and *Dracula* that brought childish minds to the cheaper movie houses time after time. Ma and Pa Kettle were a great success in a series of pictures in the 1940s. Comedians, especially, have been expected to repeat the same character in film after film. Such famous comedians of the great age of film comedy as Harold Lloyd and Buster Keaton followed virtually the same character pattern in all their

The Mass Media

FIGURE *18.5* Violence, amiability, and high principles in a TV Western. The three likable members of the Cartwright family help a Mormon rancher fight off the prejudiced mob. "Bonanza," the most popular Western series of the 1960s. Photo NBC.

films, and there is the same impulse to show Jack Lemmon and Jerry Lewis repeating their triumphs. The greater artistry of Chaplin is seen in the subtle variations he makes in his little tramp in each successive film.

Broadcast drama, especially in America, has thrived on the series. If singers were the first radio favorites, they were soon surpassed in popularity by Amos and Andy, and ever since then it has been largely the continuing characters that have peopled the popular mind. When Charles Correll and Freeman Gosden, who had been in show business several years, got together in 1926 to do dialect sketches for radio, their Negro characters Amos and Andy caught on immediately and were used on as many as forty-five stations. In 1929, NBC contracted to put them on live for $100,000 a year, and presently they were as indispensable to the American evening as dinner and sleep. Meals, committee meetings, suburban train schedules, social engagements had to be arranged so that people could hear Amos and Andy. Through the depression and wartime, Americans could relax when the organ playing the familiar theme, "The Perfect Song," assured them that they would hear the same characters worrying about the same petty problems. The pair continued without interruption for fourteen years. In that time they created some 550 characters, the two men doing all the male roles. It was said that sometimes the actor of Amos did the entire show when Andy was sick. After 1943, they continued intermittently and in 1952 played their ten-thousandth show.

It has been said that this series set American race relations back for decades by perpetuating a stereotyped attitude of superiority to ignorant Negroes who got their words mixed up in trying to put on airs. But the fan

599

Theatre for the Mass Audience

had no such thought. Correll and Gosden had created a world as far removed from reality as the town of Atella or the Venice of Pantalone and Harlequin. That imaginary world, filled with clowns and comic-strip caricatures, was a simplified image of an urban world of business enterprise, status seeking, bluff, rivalry, and pretense that appealed strongly to the large number of Americans who had only recently left the farm or country store for the city. The laughter of bourgeois white America was not at the Negro but at a comic treatment of the new attitudes in its own business and social world.

A broader vision of provincial America was created by Fred Allen in the 1940s. In his "Town Hall Tonight," he brought together vivid types— Down Easterner and Southerner, Jew and Irishman, politician and housewife—making Americans more familiar with Senator Claghorn, Titus Moody, Mrs. Nussbaum, and Ajax Cassidy than with their own neighbors. Then they laughed at Mollie Goldberg's Jewish family, recognizing the strength of the local flavor that was tending to disappear in the colorless "mainstream of American life." By the end of the decade of the fifties, most dialect comedy had disappeared, to survive only in such isolated comics as Cliff Arquette's Charlie Weaver of the "Tonight" show, whose hillbilly home, Mount Idy, was so vague that no actual local group need be self-conscious. The Beverly Hillbillies were equally uprooted, bringing the clichés of dialect comedy into conflict with the vagaries of urban America. The popular audience found in the familiar characters an easy way of looking at their own situation, that of old-fashioned provincials trying to live in a big city.

Series of the 1960s may be divided into two classes. One is action drama, ranging from Westerns to science- and space-fiction to the exploits of rescue champions—detective, reporter, lawyer, social worker, or high school teacher. The other class, usually called situation comedy, may center in a family with an exasperating husband or wife or difficult children. The wacky wife was made popular for the radio audience in the 1930s by Fibber McGee and Molly and by the lively scrapes of George Burns and Gracie Allen, who rang all the changes on troubles a wife could get into through ordering the wrong thing for the house or jumping to the wrong conclusion. The scatter-brained wife has been kept perennially alive in the last two decades by Lucille Ball in "I Love Lucy." Children of various ages have dramatized their little surprises and misunderstandings several times a week in "Leave It to Beaver." There is always available on the home screen a high school set which gets into trouble, whether the naive sixteen-year-old Corliss Archer and her friends, popular for a decade, or youth seen from Mr. Novak's point of view. The young married set must be represented by such plays as those on the "Dick Van Dyke Show" and "Please Don't Eat the Daisies" or in the fantasy world of "Bewitched." Samantha, the wife who is a witch, keeps close to the petty realism of other situation comedies, with only an occasional miraculous disappearance in order to get little things done faster than the ordinary way permits. By breaking the limitations of the live studio drama, a recorded situation comedy like "Bewitched" can intersperse with the home scenes glimpses

600

The Mass Media

of the husband's business world or of his glamorous adventures in night life or travel.

More important for home consumption, however, has been the action drama of bringing rescue or aid to suffering humanity. In the 1930s, radio listeners from eight to eighty, hearing the *William Tell Overture* and the sound of pounding hooves, settled down comfortably for another episode of "The Lone Ranger." They knew the formula. Some questionable character was threatening the rights of the good settlers, and it was time for the masked stranger to appear on his horse Silver. He arrived with the Indian Tonto, spoke in a deep rich baritone, and shot the gun out of the hand of the villain. Although he had supposedly been a Texas Ranger, nobody really knew who he was. Accepting no thanks for his services, he called "Hi-ho, Silver!" and rode off into the mysterious void, to be seen again only when his help was needed. On other nights, the Lone Ranger of the Machine Age, the Green Hornet, arrived in a purring roadster with his house boy Kato to the theme music of *The Flight of the Bumblebee*. He could put a villain to sleep with a green whiff from a nontoxic gun. With a modern urban rhythm, he embodied the same primitive dream of a savior hero who arrives from the outside to overcome evil.

Besides these rescue melodramas, the 1930s discovered the appeal of hearing real people in trouble advised by an expert, Mr. Anthony. A Bronx cab driver, who was incidentally very unsuccessful in his own marriage, set up a Marital Relations Institute and went on the air as John J. Anthony. Every Sunday night husbands and wives wept as they reviewed their quarrels for the gaping ears of most of America. It was the newspaper advice-to-the-lovelorn column come alive. Psychologists and social workers might be contemptuous of the simple clichés "Mother knows best" and "Follow the Golden Rule," but Mr. Anthony knew how to draw out the confessions and guide the squabbles so that the audience had a sense of seeing into human misery and was given reassurance that some solution, some magic advice or unexpected financial aid, could be found.

In the early sixties a number of high-quality series attracted the respect of serious people. They were a surprising but very strong hybrid combining the Lone Ranger with Mr. Anthony and adding the baffling complexity of naturalism. The modern rescue hero—doctor, lawyer, reporter—gave mature, professional advice and undertook to face complex problems that could not easily be solved. A fair amount of realism appeared in the courtroom dramas about Perry Mason, but the people he came to rescue from the district attorney were involved in conventional situations of deception or misunderstanding and the interest centered in the clever devices of courtroom strategy. Mason never lost a case. But the helpful high school teacher, Mr. Novak, found that many students had problems he could not solve. The social worker in "East Side, West Side" dealt with difficult problems of slum children and old people, with poverty, greed, even abortion and insanity—problems too serious and too genuine to win the top rating for the program. It was dropped after one season. Other rescue series that were less disturbing to the average viewer but still honest and serious managed to survive a little longer. "Slattery's People," showing an idealistic young statesman working on public problems in a state legislature, had a rich, smooth social setting, but it gave a sense of a rescue figure in a real world. In "The Defenders," the two lawyers, father and son, had to explore all aspects of the modern city in order to help their clients. If Dr. Ben Casey knew very quickly how to handle his patients, there was much more complexity in the cases of "The Doctors," "The Doctors and the Nurses," and "Dr. Kildare." "The Reporter" gave a strong sense of reality, though often the rescue was not much more subtle than the swift leap of Superman through the air. Danny the Reporter would counterblackmail the blackmailer or trap the schemer who had overreached himself. Even some of the lighter, more sentimental series of the early sixties had a touch of reality. "The Andy Griffith Show" was set in a conventional small town, where family and community problems were solved not by a legal or medical expert but by an old-fashioned, good-natured sheriff.

The problem television series was a major attempt to create serious social drama for a wide public, offering the continuity of a few appealing characters the audience could identify with, a repeating pattern that made understanding easy, and considerable variety and complexity in the cases that needed help. The attempt partly succeeded, promising a second "Golden Age." It found an audience of many millions, and "East Side, West Side," "Slattery's People," and "The Defenders" won high praise from thoughtful people. But the mass medium had no place for the taste of even a large minority. By 1965 the interest in the serious problem drama was gone, leaving only a few echoes. As Peter Falk played O'Brien in "The Trials of O'Brien" (1965–66), a rather tough, cool lawyer brought some rich texture into the investigation of mysterious crimes. The small, crowded offices and workshops of lower-middle-class business people suggested the intimate realism of the television dramas of the 1950s, and the atmosphere was a little like that of the gangster movies of the 1930s, but the situations were derived from conventional melodrama—plots of robbery, arson, and embezzlement. And even that degree of realism was too much to catch the largest audience. By 1965, the principle of all or nothing was completely dominant in the advertisers' minds. The ratings ruled completely. If the rating services found by their samples that a program had fallen a few points below those of the rival networks, the program was dropped as soon as a replacement could be found. Public favor and advertisers' support had veered to less realistic series than the problem dramas, to the more conventionalized suspense drama, to the agent-spy-defender who was more stereotyped than the realistic lawyers, social workers, or doctors, to the simpler kind of battle against mythical international conspirators or old-fashioned bandits and cattle thieves.

Whether modern lawyer, frontier sheriff, or fantasy Batman, the savior figure is like his mythical prototype Lohengrin, mysterious and unattached. Lohengrin, son of Parsifal, Knight of the Holy Grail, comes from over the sea when ordinary mortals need him, but no one can hold him or even know his name. When Elsa becomes too deeply attached to him and violates the

602

taboo about his name, he must sorrowfully leave the world. Superman is in one of his aspects an ordinary mortal concerned about the plotting of wicked people, but in his other aspect he is a supernatural being with unlimited power, constantly thwarting particular plots but never eliminating the plotters. Likewise, the more realistic television champions of the right are nearly all set apart from ordinary mortals. Some of them have been married, but as they appear in the series they have no domestic ties. Mat Dillon in "Gunsmoke," Ben Cartwright in "Bonanza," Dr. Ben Casey, Perry Mason, Danny the Reporter, and Andy Griffith do not have wives, and they stand aloof from the cases in which they are involved. Each of the unattached men in "The Rogues" (1964–65) became interested in a woman, but only momentarily, and Richard Kimball in "The Fugitive" paused often but briefly for a gleam of romance. Even when Mike Hammer of Mickey Spillane's horror series stopped to take one of the beautiful women who offered themselves, he left her immediately, perhaps after killing her. The overriding purpose of such figures, their kinship with the gods of mythology, sets them apart, and, like Lohengrin, they return to their no man's land. The popular series, in spite of Hollywood, seemed to say that in America the Freudian superego, the long-range purpose, is more important than sex and romance, whether that purpose be the devoted idealism of doctor, social worker, or teacher, or the need of the fugitive to clear himself of the accusation of murder.

Most completely mythlike is the Western, with prototype characters and stock situations accumulated from almost a century of popular melodramas about explorers, settlers, cowboys, and Indians; rough but honest heroes, gamblers, and cattle thieves; delicate heroines who learn to be brave and former criminals making a new start. The most romantic aspect of the myth is the thing the camera makes most real: the wide spaces of the West. Although the television Western is usually limited to a few locations—the town street with a hotel, saloon, and gambling room, the mountain shack, the corral, the camping spot by the river—it is bound to have a few shots of men on horseback galloping over a ridge or riding down a dusty trail, bringing to life man's old dream of the romantic outdoors. Audiences all over the world respond to this vision of the opening up of a continent and the working out of basic human relations without the complications of a later society. This type of drama fulfills the function of romance by projecting moral ideals into a distant, large-scale, mythical land where issues are clear, where aggression must be met with force and destroyed without regret or squeamishness, where the men on the side of right are better with fists, knives, and guns than the villains, where they can work out a harmonious relation to land and sky, to horses and cattle, once the few evil men are driven away or killed. The women, too, live their clear-cut roles, as the former sinner making a new start, as the loose woman who plays along with the villain until she feels his sadistic cruelty herself and helps the good people destroy him, or as the delicate girl who develops strength and toughness to bear her share in creating a new home in the West.

The dramatic series, the dominant broadcast type of the 1960s, shows a   *603*

FIGURE *18.6* TV camera technique. The camera creates a sense of being in the midst of the action by shooting through nearby objects to focus on the characters beyond. "The Man from U.N.C.L.E." Photo NBC.

great deal of vitality and considerable variety. By repeating the main characters and the basic pattern of operation, it is effective mass drama, yet each episode offers novelty in a new case and several new characters. Even with stereotyped characters and conventional clichés of plot, the popular comedy series often make a comment on topics of current interest. The young girl that Patty Duke created in the series that bore her name was an ordinary adolescent, but when she thought she had extrasensory perception the show made a comment on the problem ordinary people have in dealing with a controversial topic. The mechanical humor of the "Beverly Hillbillies" became more pointed when a caricature of a beatnik using his specialized hip language was brought into the house. The mock-horror characters of "The Munsters" varied the joke of pride in their abnormality and loyalty to the in-group by involving the family in some topic of public interest, as when one of them planned to take a course in becoming a spy. Even young Beaver gets involved in family budgets, parent-teacher squabbles, and intelligence tests. It is not the function of popular art, or any art, to solve a problem or to make profound philosophical comments, though some artists have been philosophers. It is the artist's job to show the shape and feel of the inner experience as people encounter ideas and problems. A new social problem or a new style or fad may seem theatening since no one knows what changes it may demand. Trivial as these weekly series are, they often do show familiar characters encountering a new problem piece by piece and, if not solving or understanding it, at least learning to live with it. They show it in human terms and relax the fear and confusion in the adjustment of laughter. If one of the most difficult modern problems is to maintain loyalty to a small group while coming into contact with people of quite diver-

604

The Mass Media

gent groups, the comic series, whether about "munsters" or Martians, witches or hillbillies, may be defended as more useful than the Westerns or the international spy melodramas, which usually reject out-group characters in hatred or contempt.

The continued series, by starting each episode at the beginning, accepted an extreme limitation, not daring to risk puzzling those who might miss an episode or might not be attentive enough to follow a continuous development. As the writers of single broadcast plays found, the half-hour or even the hour format is too short for much character development. But in running on through one or several years the series offers the scope of a novel. In fact, the picaresque novel is similar in many ways. Dickens wrote *The Pickwick Papers* in installments for a magazine, and Mr. Pickwick is much like the continuing character in a television series—on a journey, collecting picturesque people, involved in one lively episode after another as though the narrative could go on forever. But before the end Mr. Pickwick has to taste a galling injustice as Mrs. Bardell sues him for breach of promise, and in prison he sees real suffering that is not picturesque. His view of the world and of human nature changes radically; the masquerade of the picturesque is over. Likewise Don Quixote, after many repetitive episodes, comes to a new conclusion about the relation of illusion to reality. His game is over; he has developed. But although some broadcast series have fairly rich details in the incidental characters, there is an unchanging central character. Dickens succeeded in carrying a large popular audience from the repetitive and superficial into an interest in more complex human experiences. It is one thing to develop the suspense of seeing how Perry Mason will solve it this time, another to create a real person facing the complexities of life and being changed by them.

"Peyton Place" is one attempt to create a drama of scope in a program planned as a serial rather than a series. From the popular daytime soap opera it took the sustained suspense and anxiety of people in distress. From the dramas of intimate realism of the 1950s it took the close-up treatment of small rooms and offices, street corners and filling stations, though instead of real local color it gave its scenery and people a standard Hollywood gloss. With the slickness of a woman's magazine, it promised to reveal the sensational reality behind the respectable façade of society, but it revealed only a fairly standard set of weaknesses and mistakes of the past. It attempted depth by using a large number of characters and interweaving many different strands of suspicion, fear, and unresolved tension. It had attractive actors, and it achieved a good deal in human interest. If it was no masterpiece, it did indicate one promising direction a drama series might take.

TECHNIQUES OF TELEVISION

While many people insist that television is only a means of seeing a film and that there are no television techniques distinct from film techniques, television developed not as film but as the addition of the visual element to radio broadcasting. For more than a decade it consisted principally

605

of live broadcasts from studios in close relation with radio and not with Hollywood. Even though the invention of video tape in 1957 caused the virtual disappearance in America of the live broadcast of drama, the programs are still made by TV cameras and not by motion picture photography, and the techniques and habits of the early years continue to influence television programs. It is necessary, therefore, to consider the special techniques that have become familiar to both the producers and the home audience. After that we may be able to see the technical possibilities for television of the future.

The most basic techniques of television are concerned with movement—movement of the actor, movement of the camera, and selecting or editing on the control board. In radio broadcast, as we have seen, a perspective of space is created as the actor moves closer to or farther away from the microphone. In television this perspective is complicated by the addition of a video picture that may correspond to the perspective of the sound track or may be seen in an independent perspective. Whereas the radio play tends to keep everything in one line of attention, putting each new character or action in the center but suggesting, by music or other sound, a vast undefined background, the television screen is more concrete, reducing the imaginary background to a limited, finite world and showing in specific detail the relationships between the characters and the setting.

Early television drama was mostly an art of the close-up. Distant shots, only fair on the movie screen, were much poorer on the television screen, and the early producers accepted the limitations of the close-up and of studio production to create an intimate drama. The Western, of course, needed a few long-distance shots of mountains and plains, but only at the beginning of the picture, to set the mood, or for some momentary situation like the sudden departure of a character from town. The rest of the play could be made with close or medium shots, and the sense of distance would be created not by showing considerable space in one long shot but by cutting back and forth between two characters, as, for instance, enemies shooting at each other as they came from behind trees or rocks or around the corners of houses.

The camera itself creates a perspective, a perspective dear to the realist and standard technique for the candid camera fan. As the camera shoots across people or objects in the foreground to catch those beyond, it creates the illusion of being in the midst of natural action, not action opened to the front for a stage picture or a formal pose. Where the stage setting usually offers a V-shaped arrangement opening toward the audience, the camera controls a V-shaped area or "field" turned the other way, getting wider at a distance from the viewer. The television designer and director often arrange the movement in a zigzag pattern, so that the actors, in coming toward the camera, do not approach directly but toward a person or object to one side of center in the V-area. If the camera is set to look across a table, desk, sideboard, or other center of action, such movement keeps the face of the actor partly toward the camera but still gives the illusion of characters in the midst

The Mass Media

FIGURE *18.7* Three cameras in operation in a large commercial studio. Each mount permits a different range of movement. At the left is a pedestal mount, at the center a crane, and at the right a dolly. Photo NBC.

of action. Actors can be used, even more effectively than objects, to intercept the camera view, framing and giving depth to the over-the-shoulder or under-the-armpit shot. Very strong movement may head straight into the camera, but the zigzag is more casual and natural. Least used is movement straight across the camera; indeed the camera usually covers so limited a space that the actor cannot move far to either side without going out of range of the camera. The camera placed a little above the heads of the actors has an excellent command of the center of action, but if placed very high it tends to make people look small, just as a view from below is deliberately used to make a character seem heavy, threatening, or dominating. By foreground framing, such as shooting through a door or window, between the bars of a bed or chair or the banisters of a staircase, the camera sets the action at a second distance.

Moving the camera, as in the cinema, adds a second dimension of movement. The small modern cameras are easy to "tilt" up or down, "pan" from one side to the other, or put on a rolling "dolly," or platform, to "dolly in" or "dolly out"; both operator and camera can also be put on a flexible crane or boom. Without moving the camera, the operator can shift his turret of lenses from wide angle shot to narrow shot, from distance shot to close-up, or even use a zoom lens to shift from distance to close range as though the camera were flying through the air.

Moving the camera gives a dynamic aspect to a still object—a dagger, a portrait, or a map, for instance—making it come closer and become larger on the screen. By lending a sense of vitality to paintings and sculpture, such movement makes possible effective lectures on art, as the attention is moved through different angles or concentrated on one detail enlarged to fill the screen.

607

Theatre for the Mass Audience

Movement of the camera can be a substitute for movement of the actor or can enhance his movement. Early moviemakers discovered that a camera gets wonderful shots from a truck just ahead of racing men or horses, or a car or train. But camera movement is overdone when it cancels out the movement of an actor or dancer or adds a distracting countermovement. Movement has meaning against solid points of reference—a floor, a setting, a fixed proscenium, or a still audience. Fred Astaire, who made successful dance movies for decades, carefully planned his movement, usually having one or two dancers advance at an angle where a still camera, with very little shift, could pick up a whole dance sequence. The actor's or dancer's movement is strongest with a still camera, and the camera movement is best when the actor does not move. For long, rapid movement, the two must be carefully coordinated.

The third type of movement is created at the control board as the director, seeing on separate monitor screens what all the cameras are covering, chooses which camera image he will send on the air and asks the technical director to "punch up" that camera by pushing the button that makes the connection (FIGURE *18.8*). This is the same kind of process as editing or cutting a film, but in a live studio performance it must be done instantaneously as the show moves along. If the show is recorded on tape, it can be edited further by splicing, though not quite so easily as can film.

The best camera and cutting work keeps a sense of relationship. It can shift the attention easily from a close-up of one person to a wider view of the group as they share in the conversation, then back to one if he is dominant, then to a new center of attention. Or it may follow the movement of a single actor from one point to another, cutting in a close-up of a hand or a small object as it is involved in the action or is needed as a suggestive image. And of course the camera, unlike the radio, can also direct attention to the person who is listening and reacting while the sound track carries the one who is speaking.

The actor is very much aware of his relation to the camera and microphone as he speaks to someone close by in one tone or to someone at a distance in a different tone. In radio drama the microphone is in a set position, but in the television studio it is on a boom that is moved as freely as the camera to help create the perspective of space. The actor knows that he cannot depend on many different takes, as he can in moviemaking, to catch a view that indicates the right reactions, nor can he depend on the separate recording of the dialogue on the sound track. He must constantly be aware of his relation to camera and microphone, knowing that the camera may be on him while the other character is speaking and that he must make some visible response. But the reaction must be small—the lift of an eyebrow or the curl of the lip—since the camera may be using a close-up lens that will make his face fill the screen.

This restriction of acting to the small movement satisfies the directors who think that intimate realism is the best kind of broadcast drama, but it does not please either actors or viewers who enjoy the art of acting. It is as though

FIGURE *18.8* A simple monitor board in a college TV studio. The three lower screens show what the three cameras are picking up. The "line" or "on-the-air" monitor shows what image is being sent on the air. San Francisco State College.

a painter were limited to incomplete sketches in pencil or to one pale tone. There is little chance to create a powerful moment or develop a scene with cumulative force. Such restraint of the actor is not really necessary. By using medium and long shots, directors allow comedians like Jackie Gleason to use broad comic mugging and gestures. Those who enjoy Dick Van Dyke in his song and dance roles such as the flamboyant character created in the film *Mary Poppins* sigh to see his acting confined to the everyday routines of domestic comedy.

Settings for television can add greatly to the perspective of space, with corners and irregular walls or with a series of objects leading zigzag into the not-very-far distance. There are advantages in an indistinct background, and many educational TV productions use it, letting the actor stand out against a dark background, usually with both front and back lighting. The actor's movement varies in effect as he is caught against dark or light, and diminishing the lighting behind him creates an appearance of movement, making him seem to come forward as the background grows darker. But commercial broadcast drama has remained faithful to realistic backgrounds. In the 1950s there were a few experiments on Cameo Playhouse presenting actors in pools of light with no walls and only an occasional door frame or picture frame hanging in blank space. But the sponsors were afraid the viewers would think they were seeing a shoestring type of production that could not afford scenery, and besides, union regulations required that scenery crews be paid whether they were needed or not. So that experiment came to an end. Commercials, like store window displays, often make vivid use of unrealistic backgrounds, free-form sculptural shapes, imaginative drawings, and animated cartoons, reminding us, as many stage settings now do, that the theatre de-

609

FIGURE *18.9* Slightly stylized painted settings for a TV drama about the early flying machines. Photo NBC.

rives not just from a close imitation of everyday reality but from colorful holiday festivals and the processions of important officials and richly decorated pageant wagons past garlanded triumphal arches made bright with fluttering flags and sparkling torches.

Some theorists argue that, since the camera is already one medium for selecting, bounding, and interpreting, there should not be interpretation in another medium, that the material the camera picks up should be real or seem to be real. They argue that although cut-down scenery, with an edge showing, is acceptable on the stage, the camera should not show the edge of the designer's work, only the edge of the picture caught by the camera; that a setting with a strong color, texture, or form of its own would usurp the function of the camera. But some commercials have already showed that design can be a more interesting element in itself if producers of broadcast drama dare to wander from their standard intimate effects, realistic settings, off-center candid-camera composition, and constantly moving camera.

Television drama seems a half-century behind developments in art, fiction, and theatre. The theatre fifty years ago had already felt the impact of Maeterlinck's symbolism, Strindberg's expressionism, and Yeats's formalism, and art was exploring cubism, futurism, abstract expressionism, surrealism, and other imaginative departures from nineteenth-century realism, but television drama has been hidebound, borrowing only a few advanced techniques from radio drama and the movies. So far there has been no one in television as venturesome as Eisenstein, Cocteau, or Bergman in film. In the 1930s Eisenstein broke with the tradition of intimacy and the dynamic camera in

610

The Mass Media

his film *Ivan the Terrible,* giving his groups the formal symmetry and rigid composition of Russian ikons. Orson Welles varied his short scenes in *Citizen Kane* (1941) with a number of distant shots that were held amazing lengths of time. It seemed as if he had nailed the flying camera to the floor, and a powerful effect it was, with the actors moving against solid sculptural forms. When Delbert Mann in 1957 directed Alvin Sapinsley's blank-verse television play *Lee at Gettysburg,* he puzzled the critics by arranging many formally posed scenes and reproducing some of the tonal contrasts of the Mathew Brady photographs of Civil War scenes. The critics missed the restless camera moving them from one informal shot to another in the realistic stress of battle.

Still unexplored are many possible distortions and special effects, some of which can be produced electronically—grain effects, color tonalities, washes moving across the screen in patterned or symbolic shapes. Besides the use of interesting lighting, there are many ways in which the background can be given a more imaginative treatment. The techniques and styles developed in modern drawing, painting, and graphic art have had little use in the studio. In the theatre, settings are often treated as sculptural forms, but rarely in television. It is easy to make the background mobile, with parts of the scenery sliding, rising, flying, floating, turning, twisting, or changing shape, color, and texture. In the active space of a mobile camera the mobile objects are less startling to the audience and easier to combine with the moving actor than they would be on the stage. A rear screen, usually a translucent screen with slides or movies projected from the rear, is often used for realistic scenes to save money. It is very effective for the moving landscape seen at carriage or train windows. Since both the living actor and the projection screen are seen through the TV camera, they can be blended more easily than on the stage. But there is no reason why various surfaces with still or moving pictures could not serve also for drawings, for shadows and indistinct forms, or for fantastic changing shapes. The relation of camera to actor can be varied in many ways besides movement or countermovement. The comedian Ernie Kovacs once produced a remarkable effect in a pantomime by tilting both the stage and the camera. The audience did not see the tilt but saw the actors and objects reacting to a new force of gravity. Marshall McLuhan contends that the image on the television screen is not perceived as a complete picture but as a mosaic created dot by dot, movement by movement, and that the viewer as he sits close enough to touch the screen is far more deeply involved with the action than a spectator is involved with stage or movie screen action. If this is true, then movement, unstable changing forms, and rough texture have more power than the slick, stable, complete walls of the conventional realistic setting. The medium has many technical possibilities that have scarcely been tried.

The most interesting technical characteristic of television, that which makes it different from the movie or any other medium, is the use of multiple cameras that feed into one control board. A movie is usually made with one camera, employing a careful arrangement of setting, lighting, and acting.   *611*

Often days are spent in taking and retaking a single short sequence. If more than one camera is used, each one produces a continuous film. With all the continuous films made by the various cameras during the several retakes, it is easy in cutting to select the best moments and splice them together. The basic method in live television studios is to use several cameras, to keep the action going without interruption, and to do the selecting by the switches of the control board. The director has before him as many monitor screens as there are cameras. He has only to select which image he wants to have go on the air, cutting from one to another by the punch of a button. Or he can divide the screen, showing the picture from one camera on one half and that from another on the other half. He can superimpose one image on another, fade one into another. He has instantaneous control, and his sequence of scenes goes directly on the air or onto a single tape. But the cutting and splicing from several video tapes is not nearly so simple. Whereas the cutter can stop a film and look at each frame to see exactly where to cut, if he stops a tape his image stops. Hence he can only guess approximately where to cut. A special storage monitor that freezes the last image and holds it for several minutes is helpful, but there still remain several advantages in using the multiple-camera pickup and the monitor-board cutting inherited from the days when all drama broadcasting was done live from the studio.

Directors have used the multiple camera and control board set-up principally for convenience in creating camera movement, switching from a close-up camera to a camera ready for a long shot, shifting from one character to another, or cutting in different threads of the story, taking great care that the viewer can adjust comfortably to the changing perspective of space. But the multiple-camera method has many possibilities the realistic dramas do not use. Sudden changes of perspective can be comic. If the director at the control board switches from a camera on one side of a racetrack to a camera on the opposite side, the horses are suddenly seen running in the opposite direction, or, in the same kind of shift, a person facing one way suddenly jumps around facing the opposite way. A sudden change in size, a "jump cut," without a smooth transition of perspective can be startling.

But most intriguing of all multiple-camera possibilities are multiple images, very easy to produce. Superimposition, familiar in both movies and television drama in the soft dissolves of one scene into the next, has had some use, especially to show a dream or the private thought or memory of a character, the face in close-up showing through the scene of the dream, but multiple image has had very little use. The Elizabethan playwrights sometimes set an allegorical character, Death or Vengeance, for instance, on an upper stage balcony to watch the events he was concerned in—an effect easily shown on the television screen by cutting in a small image of the character from one camera into a corner of the screen, the scene of action filling the rest. Or two characters in different scale, one large and one miniature, can talk to each other. A Greek chorus could be created by multiple image. If the main action filled most of the screen, a secondary image could be put along the bottom or all around the edges, duplicating a single actor-dancer in

612

The Mass Media

four, eight, or more multiple images, moving in unison, speaking in multiple voices, creating an emotional effect that would be impersonal and universal. The image could be distorted or made to shimmer or break up, to create various emotional effects. But so far, instead of exploring the electronic possibilities of the camera, broadcasting stations seem bogged down in the habits of intimate, candid-camera realism, varying only to include a few tricks of witches or magicians.

It is clear that television drama, in materials, characterization, and technical means of presentation, falls far short of its potentialities. There is much to look forward to if audiences can be stimulated to demand more and broadcasters to offer more or if a creative artist can be encouraged to use his imagination.

Television as a Public Art

The culture explosion is all around us, with records and paperback books on everyone's shelves, symphony orchestras and theatres in every city, several dozen plays and entertainers on every home screen each week, and comments in the newspapers on the culture consumers. But is it culture that is reaching the masses, or only a packaged commodity? Only a small minority go to hear the symphony orchestras or attend performances in the theatres, and even most college graduates do not read a good book a year. The masses read horror comics and spend endless hours hypnotized and tranquilized before the television set watching one Western, spy story, or situation comedy after another. Chances for improvement seem slight, since broadcasting is paid for and controlled by the advertisers, who want only what is already popular with the mass audience.

When radio broadcasting began, Herbert Hoover, himself a defender of American business, stated positively that the American people would never stand for advertising on the air, that it was inconceivable that they should allow so great a possibility to be drowned in advertising chatter. He approved of a modest announcement by a sponsor. But that announcement is no longer modest. Commercials intrude into every program. Even in the heat of an election the news must be interrupted for commercials, and only in such a grave emergency as the assassination of the President do the networks present an event without interruption. Most Americans have resigned themselves to the presence of commercials, but the more thoughtful are concerned about the effect of commercial control on the programs. Each advertiser wants to sponsor only a show that will draw the largest possible audience and get the highest possible rating. If cheerful, intellectually undemanding entertainment is popular, if violence is popular, these will be found on the screen, for popularity is the criterion for selecting and shaping television shows.

There is ample evidence that advertisers often censor the shows they sponsor on the basis of their own narrow interests or prejudices. It was absurd that a corporation official objected to having a photograph of Franklin D.

Roosevelt in the background of a play about the depression days because, two decades before, he had hated Roosevelt's policies. It was more serious that an official of a sponsoring insurance company would not allow a suicide in a play and that a gas company insisted on deleting all mention of gas chambers from a serious program on the atrocities of Nazi Germany. There is evidence, too, that the men employed in television operation are not always overscrupulous in the methods they use to ensure the popularity of the programs. The scandal of rigged quiz shows, which brought a Congressional investigation in the late fifties, was a warning to the public of the lengths to which men might go in the competition for the largest number of viewers on the air.

Many critics feel very strongly that America should not allow the advertisers to control the programs. In a magazine or newspaper the advertiser controls only his own advertisement; the features are completely in the hands of the editorial staff. In England, when commercial broadcasting was set up to supplement the three public channels, the system was made independent of any direct control by the advertisers.

VIOLENCE IN TELEVISION SHOWS

An immediate problem is the violence in television shows. Westerns and war stories, adventures of private eye or district attorney, and many other action dramas are filled with slugging, torture, and murder. In 1960 volunteer listeners checked the programs for a week in Los Angeles and found the following: 144 murders, 143 attempted murders, 53 "justifiable" killings, 36 robberies, 14 druggings, 13 kidnappings, 12 jail breaks, 12 thefts and burglaries, 11 planned murders, 7 tortures, 6 extortions, 5 blackmailings, 4 attempted lynchings, 1 massacre, 1 mass murder, 1 planned mass murder by arson, 1 mass gun battle, and 3 posse blood baths in which death occurred with such frequency and confusion that the falling bodies eluded tabulation. In 1961 a television series called "The Untouchables" aroused so much protest because of extreme violence that a government investigation was made and the program was cancelled. Harold Mehling in *The Great Time-Killer* offers evidence that, in the competition for the largest number of listeners, advertising executives have insisted on more and ever more violence.

No thoughtful person is happy about the amount of violence on the air, but no one is sure what should be done about it. The connection between violence in art and maladjustment and crime is certainly not direct. While a few cases have been found of a criminal who admitted following the pattern of a crime seen on television, it is not at all certain whether the act seen increased the motivation or only suggested the form. Nobody knows whether, in any given case, the product of someone else's imagination may influence action or may relieve tension and prevent action. Some child psychologists assure us that the young Indian or Lone Ranger in the backyard killing a thousand a day with his "ak-ak-ak" or "Bang-bang, you're dead" is finding a healthy outlet for the normal frustration of childhood. But horror comics and violent movies and television plays cannot be dismissed as unimportant

614

FIGURE *18.10* Violence on the TV screen. The idealist gets rough treatment from a deputy sheriff for probing into the shady activities of a town boss. "The Virginian," a perennial Western of the 1960s. Photo NBC.

outlets for a world jittery about atomic missiles. A grown man in a complex society is not a child letting off steam. Tragedy has constantly dealt with violence, from the rapes, tortures, wars, and hatchet choppings in Aeschylus to the castrations, rapes, and cannibalism in Tennessee Williams. As Eric Bentley says, putting the idea in an extreme form, "Theatrical art is a form of aggression. Like the internal combustion engine, it proceeds by a series of explosions. Since it is in the strictest sense the most shocking of the arts, it has failed most utterly when no shock has been felt and it has failed in a large measure when the shock is mild." But the better dramas have always carried the experience beyond violence, to greater understanding of man's relations to law and order and to his deeper social and philosophical purposes.

It is the simple view of man's nature implied in the violent adventure series that is immature. If we turn off the sadistic anarchy of Mickey Spillane's Mike Hammer, who takes the law into his own hands, we find the childish idealism of Mat Dillon in "Gunsmoke," who must not only expose the evil-doers but destroy them by fist, knife, or bullet. It is no better if we turn to "The Man from U.N.C.L.E.," where foreign agents are bumped off even more casually. Such screen material builds in the viewer callousness to human suffering and an assumption that violence is normal in human relations. If in "Bonanza" one of the Cartwrights must beat up a victim to make him behave, the action is obviously better than killing, but the assumption is that the victim is willing to feel like a naughty child and accept chastisement from a father image. Such drama is a long way from a treatment of adult relationships.

615

Theatre for the Mass Audience

It may be argued that the Western can fit into a vision of maturity in modern life, that in historical perspective the early days of the West are seen as the childhood of America, a time before the establishment of law and order. According to this view, modern life is so obviously different that there is no danger in an imaginative return to the beautiful outdoors and the time of horses and simple emotions. Such indulgence in regression to childhood might be harmless, it is true, if it were balanced with more mature programs, but most of the soap operas and family situation comedies indicate just as little maturity or complexity as the Western. Even when the characters live in cities and wear modern clothes, there is still the oversimplified conflict of good and bad. Stuart Hood, an official of the BBC who buys American programs for English television, explains in *Television Quarterly* why the English reject many American series:

> There is in American programs no original sin. There are bad people and there are good people: there are never, or hardly ever, good people who are bad or bad people who are also good. Apart from the villains who are damned by some awful Calvinist process everyone else is too wholesome to be true. There is wonderful observation and a lot of edge. Sleaziness will be caught; fear, terror, and excitement brought to vivid life; there will be goodness and kindness. But the whole equivocal nature of human life with its delicate balance of good and evil within each of us is not there. So even in the best of series, moral issues will be courageously posed only to be dissolved in emotion, with music and flowers on a grave. It is impossible not to feel let down.

There is irony in the contrast between the actual performance in popular broadcast drama, with fights, knifings, and murder, and the code adopted by the broadcasters themselves, which states that television should be regarded as a guest in the home, welcomed by the entire family. The code rules out profanity, obscenity, vulgarity, suggestive words or gestures, irreverence, illicit sex relations, divorce, and suicide, and it requires that crime and drunkenness be shown only with disapproval. But actually, as long as no vulgar language is used and a conventionally moral ending indicates that wickedness does not triumph, a very large amount of violence is permitted. On the other hand, the television code, like the Hays code for the movies, may be used as an excuse for avoiding the discussion of serious problems.

MASS CULTURE IN THE MODERN WORLD

The level of television broadcasting is only the most recent manifestation of the effect of mass culture in the modern world, a subject that has engaged the attention of many thoughtful writers in the last hundred years. Some writers have been very gloomy in their analyses of mass culture and forecasts for the future. Oswald Spengler in *The Decline of the West* tries to show that Western man is in the downward sweep of a historical cycle, lost in a proliferation of technological gadgets. The Spaniard Ortega y Gasset, in *The Revolt of the Masses,* describes the modern age as a time when the masses are in power, politically and intellectually, destroying minorities and the individual. Lewis Mumford, more optimistic, expresses the belief in *Technics and Civilization* that modern man is emerging from the phase of culture in which he is overwhelmed by factory, big business, and big city and is entering upon a period when the individual will be able to use modern technology without being dominated by the conformity of the masses. Several writers of fiction, notably Aldous Huxley in *Brave New World* and George Orwell in *1984,* have projected into a not-too-distant future vivid pictures of a culture in which men, brainwashed by political leaders, have become mechanized robots without identity.

Recent critics of "masscult" (to use Dwight MacDonald's term) have built up a terrifying picture of a great conspiracy, especially on the part of commercial television broadcasters and advertisers, to brutalize and enslave the masses. A good representation of their ideas is collected in *Mass Culture: The Popular Arts in America,* edited by Bernard Rosenberg and David Manning White in 1956. According to this view, mass entertainment is ground out by teams of cynical hacks in order to make money for businessmen. Whereas folk art grows up among the people, mass art is imposed from above. It is not the product of an artist with something to say or an artisan working in a traditional folk pattern, but a calculated synthetic commodity to satisfy a demand that has been created by advertisement. Everything must be "popularized" or "digested." Music, whether folk song or symphony, must be "arranged" in a standard popular form. News must be reinterpreted by editorial teams in a synthetic style or what George Orwell called "group-speak." A good play or novel has little chance to survive the teams that make adaptations for the movies or television. Any distinctive character must be simplified to fit the stereotypes familiar to the mass audience, anything that might seem offensive to a Victorian must be altered, and the ending must be happy. The standardized diversion is sold with much fanfare, creating the crowd psychology of fashions and fads. The mass audience, according to this view, becomes stupid and passive, wanting only violent sensation or easy distraction, not real artistic experience. It is an uprooted, urban crowd that has been drugged by the incessant din of advertising until it has lost all identity and all sense of purpose except to buy and to demand more entertainment that gives the illusion of reality. Any popular art that pleases this audience is necessarily false and as dangerous as a drug.

Other critics cannot accept such a view of the modern city and the popular arts. In *The Seven Lively Arts,* Gilbert Seldes writes an enthusiastic defense of such popular arts as slapstick movies, blues, jazz, musical comedy, and comic strips. He does not claim that these ephemeral arts have the importance or permanence of the masterpieces of the fine arts but only that their fresh vitality is important and that high levity, as well as high seriousness, has its place. Other critics point out that the attack on the popular arts has been due in part to an overemphasis on literary values. The people who live by the printed word are just the ones, in Marshall McLuhan's view, to be alarmed, because they do not try to understand new ways of thinking and feeling brought in by a new medium of communication, especially one that

617

invokes the senses as directly as television does. The literary critics in most periods have been blind to new forms of theatre.

In the past, popular art has not been the enemy of the fine arts. Aeschylus and Sophocles started from "popular" forms. Shakespeare used materials and methods which, in a comparatively crude form, had delighted the populace in the religious cycles and in street pageants. Molière perfected a form that belonged to street-corner entertainment. In recent times, dramatists like Edmond Rostand converted the material of crude melodrama to poetic romance. The popular musical, as we have seen, is not to be despised as an art form. "Low" farce has its own artistry. In *Lawrence of Arabia,* common materials of spectacle were used in making a superb motion picture. In every instance, genius was the catalyst. Perhaps it is all that is needed to convert the crude or mediocre dramatic forms in our mass media to dramatic classics. If the transformation takes place, literary critics will never know it, for the masterpiece will be popular also—*Hamlet* was—and may be a fine achievement of camera work, acting, song, and dance that does not depend on the written word. The wise student may enjoy whatever he can find of lively art in television entertainment, masterpiece or no masterpiece, and help build better audiences in the hope of better programs.

A BALANCED TELEVISION PROGRAM

No matter what his general view of mass culture, any thoughtful person must see that there is vast room for improvement in television theatre. There are at least two ways in which that improvement may come. Commercial broadcasters may be persuaded to give a greater number of special broadcasts and to improve the average quality of their offerings, and in time more stations and even networks may be made available for broadcasting programs frankly designed for minority tastes.

Although commercial broadcasting officials point out that programing is dependent on public response and that they have to give the public what it wants, they are sensitive to criticism and speak with great pride when they do occasionally offer programs of special worth. For years in the 1940s, NBC supported a major symphony orchestra with Toscanini as conductor, and in 1956 the network paid a half-million dollars to present Laurence Olivier's three-hour movie *Richard III* for an audience of over five million people. In 1961–62 CBS presented six special hour-long broadcasts of the New York Philharmonic Orchestra during prime evening time and commissioned Igor Stravinsky to write music for a new ballet-drama, *Noah and the Flood.* Occasionally a network presents a classic play or even a new play. Even if many viewers turn off the better program, not all do, and some lowbrows are willing to make an occasional excursion into the higher arts.

Potentially more effective than the pressure of free-lance critics is the periodic official survey of the networks. Very early in the development of broadcasting, Congress established a Federal Communications Commission, making clear that the air waves are public property and providing for the licensing of stations in order to serve the public interest, convenience, and necessity. The act specified that licenses were to be reviewed and renewed every three years. Serving the public interest has been taken to mean offering time for public announcements and appeals, for major political addresses, and for a few sustaining educational programs that no advertiser would pay for—a fairly narrow interpretation of responsibility, which might well be widened. Usually the Commission has routinely renewed the license, paying little attention to the difference between what a station promised to do and what its actual programs have shown. But Newton M. Minow, President Kennedy's appointee as chairman of the FCC, took his job seriously and addressed the annual convention of the National Association of Broadcasters on May 9, 1961, with a speech that struck like a bombshell. Urging the broadcasters to sit down and look at their own programs, he continued:

> I assure you that you will observe a vast wasteland. . . . You will see a procession of game shows, violence, audience participation shows, formula comedies about totally unbelievable families, blood and thunder, mayhem, violence, sadism, murder, Western bad men, Western good men, private eyes, gangsters, more violence, and cartoons and, endlessly, commercials. . . . True, you will see a few things you will enjoy. But they will be very, very few. And if you think I exaggerate, try it. . . . If parents, teachers, and ministers conducted their responsibilities by following the ratings, children would have a steady diet of ice cream, school holidays, and no Sunday School. . . . Newspaper publishers take popularity ratings, too. The answers are pretty clear: it is almost always the comics, followed by the advice to the lovelorn columns. But, ladies and gentlemen, the news is still on the front page in all newspapers, the editorials are not replaced by more comics, the newspapers have not become one long collection of advice to the lovelorn. . . . Broadcasting cannot continue to live by the . . . ratings. . . . What I am talking about is balance. . . . You must provide a wider range of choices, more diversity, more alternatives. It is not enough to cater to the notions, whims—you must also serve the nation's needs.

Minow did not follow up his criticism, but the courts have consistently upheld the right and duty of the Commission to review actual program policies in considering renewal of licenses. Several organized listeners' groups have found that they can be heard, especially when it is time for the renewal of licenses and the stations must outline the kind of programs they promise to present.

Listeners who want more than standard entertainment look forward not only to a larger number of special programs but to programing frankly addressed to minority tastes, some paid for by advertisers, some from private donations, and some from public funds. The limitation to twelve channels available in the Very High Frequency range has put a premium on the largest possible audience for each program, but the opening up of Ultra High Frequency channels has made a wider range possible. On the recommendation of the FCC, Congress required that all television sets manufactured after May, 1964, include reception of the UHF bands.

Broadcasting programs for minority taste need not eliminate the advertiser.   619

Many advertisers do not need to appeal to the mass market but only to minorities with means or particular tastes. Book publishers advertise where they can catch the attention of the minority who buy books. Many specialty shops have a sizable clientele though it is naturally smaller than that of the large department stores. And even department stores have special counters, for food delicacies, imported wines, unusual gifts, that do not crowd out their mass sales counters. A large corporation might very well advertise both on a widely popular program and on one designed for a particular minority taste. In its television programs, Hallmark has paid no attention to the ratings, believing that a few unusual dramas of high quality, especially if broadcast before the Christmas, Valentine, and Easter greeting-card holidays, can produce commercial results with a public large enough for their needs.

There are a number of alternatives to a full dependence on advertising. Subscription TV has been tried with partial success in several cities. If the subscribers are in a compact urban area, a cable system or a leased telephone line is practical. In a wider area the programs are broadcast in a scrambled form and only the subscribers have a device for unscrambling. Usually the subscriber pays only for the programs he listens to, agreeing to use a minimum number a month. In spite of the alarm of some commercial broadcasters who have tried to make the public think that a subscription system would be the death of free commercial service, there is no reason to suppose that both commercial and subscription systems could not exist in the same community. The problem is to find the minority audiences for particular tastes. If subscription TV tries to furnish something for everybody, it runs into some of the same dangers as the commercial stations.

The most important alternative to dependence on advertising is government support. The extreme type of government support is the Russian system of government monopoly, with complete control of ideas and taste. Most countries of Western Europe feel that a combination of public and commercial television may avoid the dangers of both the Russian and the American systems. In England that plan has resulted in a much wider range of programing than we have and, as far as drama is concerned, programs of a higher quality. Both the live performance and the separate new play written especially for television had almost disappeared in America by 1959, but the BBC, the corporation under government control, broadcast some 256 plays between April, 1959, and March, 1960, besides many adaptations of novels and stories, and the ITA (Independent Television Authority), supported by advertising, broadcast almost as many. The plays varied from a half-hour to ninety minutes but were not arbitrarily broken up to fit into the American straitjacket of thirty-minute segments sold to the advertisers. A number of American authors write for British broadcast. If they get less pay than for "Bewitched" or "Bonanza," they have more satisfaction in creating an original play than in grinding out another variation on a calculated formula.

Canada likewise has a combination of commercial stations and a government-supported broadcasting system. For a small population, scattered over vast areas, it is expensive to maintain a range of programs, yet Canadians

The Mass Media

insist on the worth of minorities and are willing to pay through taxes for their national system, in order to provide for both mass and minority taste. If 200,000 people in Canada want opera, the minority is considered large enough to justify government support of an opera program.

In this country it has seemed easy to finance both motion pictures and broadcast entertainment since they can be mechanically duplicated for large numbers. Most people have accepted the idea that there must be subsidy for the "handicraft" arts of performance—theatre, dance, and music—since they cannot be duplicated but must be enjoyed directly by limited audiences. It has long been recognized that subsidy is necessary if libraries and art museums are to serve the community well, and it is becoming clearer that subsidy will be necessary to provide a few broadcast programs better than the lowest common denominator of mass taste.

America has already made a start on a noncommercial system with educational television that often combines private, state, and Federal support. Television for use in schools will doubtless be developed far beyond the small beginnings so far. Outside of the schools, educational television has brought hope for an alternative to commercial broadcasting, with better music, drama, and other entertainment for livelier minds. But so far the educational program has leaned heavily on interviews and news reporting, fields already well covered by the commercial networks. Jack Gould, television critic of the *New York Times,* believes that educational TV stations must ask for underwriting from business and offer a discreet mention of the supporting companies without losing control of their programs, just as business companies are listed as patrons of symphony orchestras and dance and opera

FIGURE *18.11* The director at work in a college TV studio. For interviews and some dramatic scenes the director may direct the performers and the camera and sound men from the studio floor. San Francisco State College.

companies. Others believe that Federal, state, and city governments must pay the large cost of providing educational broadcasting to the general public while somehow keeping the system free from the worst dangers of political interference. While the English BBC has kept an admirably independent course, the separate networks of the different states of postwar Germany have seen extremes of government control and then complete avoidance of current problems. The greatest opportunity for public-supported television is to provide better music, art, dance, and drama programs than the limited fare offered in the commercial channels. Central planning and pooling of tapes and a countrywide educational network can bring a wide range of programs to be combined with programs of local origin and interest.

The ideal solution for America would be to offer a wide range of alternatives—more specialized differences among the commercial channels, an active public-supported program, and a third area of privately subsidized programs to provide more controversial and experimental programs than can be expected from either of the other sources. The Ford Foundation helped finance "Omnibus," a weekly hour show that for several years brought superior music, drama, and other features to the air through the regular networks. On both East and West Coasts there are foundations and stations committed to better programs. In New York, Channel 13 is supported by gifts both large and small from listeners.

Technical improvements, as in the other mass media, will be a large factor in determining the future of television. Already radio is so much less expensive than in the past that almost any special interest group or minority language group can afford to broadcast and each member of a family can afford at least a tiny transistor set to select programs to suit his own taste. The conditions of television viewing may change even more. When video tape recording is more advanced, it will be possible for a person to insert a card or small cartridge into a slot in the receiving set and see the program he wants to see. He will be able to buy old programs from a shelf in a store or to subscribe to new series to be delivered by mail. Then he will have a wide choice. He will be able to tune in on a popular program on a commercial or a community station, hook into a community antenna TV service, or take from his shelf an old movie, a recent Hollywood movie, or the latest arrival from some specialized recording and distributing service, say an "Oriental Program-of-the-Month Club."

A discriminating citizen does not have to be a slave to the majority, though he may share some popular tastes. Without being a snob, he insists on his right to some minority activities—the church of his choice, the profession he is devoted to, the entertainments he enjoys, and the arts that please his own taste. The great advantage of a complex urban civilization is that it is easy to belong to a number of different groups with special interests. The liberated individual is able to enjoy the crowd at one moment and to find companions for his more particular interests at others. He does not have to be totally alone.

Minorities are the hope of a democracy that is alive and growing. Some minorities will always be far ahead of the general population, exploring new forms and new ways of living, while other minorities will preserve and cultivate interesting old arts. The whole population need not follow the same path, yet an occasional popular report of separate paths is desirable, just as many people like an explanation of a scientific discovery or an occasional view of prize race horses or dogs. An Olivier in *Henry V* or a Maurice Evans in *Macbeth* can bring Shakespeare to the popular screen occasionally. Commercial television already brings a few glimpses of better things to the wide public. As advertisers recognize that minorities also buy and that it may be profitable to spread their support to programs at several levels of taste, using both the Very High and the Ultra High Frequency bands, even the popular "wasteland" may show more patches of green. As other alternatives to complete commercial control offer oases, the wasteland may blossom. Television has been a fascinating toy, a babysitter for men, women, children, and dogs. In exasperation at all the drivel that comes out, we curse the "moron hours" we spend before the "boob tube," the "idiot box." Marshall McLuhan says that TV is creating a new kind of man. The rest of us would settle for a few good television plays.

EXERCISES

1. INTIMATE REALISM. How much influence of the drama of intimate realism can you find in current television dramatic series or serials? Do you find small settings with rich detail, intimate scenes taken by close-up and medium shots, over-the-shoulder shots, or shots over foreground framing elements? Are there poor- and middle-class homes, the workrooms, shops, and offices of small businesses, with helpless, puzzled, and frustrated characters? Are the little people combined with more heroic or glamorous types?

2. THE COMIC SKIT. Try to formulate the principles of the short dramatic sketches used by the star comedians. To what extent do they break from the strict realism of most serious drama, as, for instance, by having the comedian play to the audience, use soliloquy, show awareness that he is playing, add details not in the script, or give other evidence of spontaneity? Are songs, mime, or dance introduced? Are some backgrounds imaginative and not strictly realistic? Are such techniques appropriate only to broad comedy or could some of them be used in more serious plays?

3. SOCIAL COMMENT IN COMEDY. Examine several situation comedies and fantastic comedies. Are there conflicts between the in-group and the out-group? Is one group right and the other wrong? Does anyone learn more about himself or about other ways of life? Are there compromises and adjustment? To what extent are the conflicts treated as low comedy and to what extent as high comedy, with irony, teasing, and some mutual respect?

623

4. TREATMENT OF VIOLENCE. Analyze and compare two or three Western or spy melodramas for the attitude toward violence. What motivation to violence do the bad men have? What motivation has the hero? Is there immediate provocation? Does the program dwell sadistically on the fighting, on blood, on cruelty? Does the hero regret or deplore violence? Is there any implication that violence is not the normal, civilized way of living? Is any hope for a future time without violence shown?

5. CHARACTER DEVELOPMENT IN THE TV SERIALS. Study some of the serial dramas that continue a single story through a number of episodes. Do the characters grow and change? Does the introduction of new characters show new aspects of some of the old characters? How much exposition of past action is given? Would you be lost if you had not seen the earlier episodes? Are the night serials superior to the daytime soap operas in speed? Sophistication? Complexity of motivation?

6. FILM DRAMA AND BROADCAST DRAMA. Make a comparison of popular television dramas with the standard films. Can you see any ways in which the broadcast dramas are adapted to the intimate home audience in techniques, kind of characters, or human interest?

7. IMAGINATION IN COMMERCIALS. Analyze one or more commercials for the devices used to attract attention and interest. Are the scenes with people treated with complete realism? Are backgrounds treated with freedom and imagination? Are names and words animated? Are objects made to move, change size, shape, or color? Are animated drawings used? Could any techniques of the commercials be used in broadcast drama?

8. REAL AND CONVENTIONAL ART. Examine your own use of a conventional art—say, a daily comic strip or a regular TV series—and your attitude toward it. Is the comic strip or the series addictive like cigarettes or narcotics—that is, habitual, compulsive, and hard to quit? Is it social—that is, do you enjoy sharing it and talking about it with your friends? Is it complex enough for real discussion, analysis, and disagreement? Is it ever memorable, or is it like a newspaper, something to serve a momentary purpose and then be thrown away and forgotten? Is it a soothing escape from the real concerns of your life? Does it sometimes make comments on current interests? Has it moments of unusual achievement? Does it ever surprise you, puzzle you, challenge you, or enlarge your experience?

Have you ever had the experience of a new novel, painting, piece of music, movie, or play that was exciting, puzzling, disturbing, overwhelming, that changed you, enlarged you—an experience you will never forget? Can the theatre do something with both kinds of art?

624

EXERCISES

PLAYS

The two most noteworthy radio plays—both by well-known poets—are Archibald MacLeish, *The Fall of the City* (1937), and Dylan Thomas, *Under Milk Wood* (1954). Some lively poetic plays with patriotic themes and good local color can be read in Norman Corwin, *Thirteen by Corwin* (1942). Several collections of Arch Oboler's radio plays were published, including *Oboler Omnibus* (1945) and *Fourteen Radio Plays* (1946).

Many of the TV plays of intimate realism of the 1950s "Golden Age" were printed, some in small editions that are no longer available: Paddy Chayefsky, *Television Plays** (1955); Horton Foote, *Harrison, Texas* (1956) and *Three Plays* (1962); Tad Mosel, *Other People's Houses* (1956); Reginald Rose, *Six Television Plays** (1956); Rod Serling, *Patterns* (1957); Gore Vidal, *Visit to a Small Planet* (1957); and William Gibson, *The Miracle Worker* (1957). Two collections are useful: Gore Vidal, ed., *Best Television Plays* (1956), and T. and I. Settel, *The Best of Armstrong Circle Theatre* (1959).

CRITICAL WORKS

Radio history can be followed in two lively nostalgic books: Irving Settel, *Pictorial History of Radio* (1960), and Sam J. Slate and Joe Cook, *It Sounds Impossible* (1963). The personalities of past television programs are caught in Jack Alicoate, *Pictorial History of Television* (1959).

Popular types of TV series have had both journalistic comment and serious studies. The Western is analyzed in Robert Warshow, "Movie Chronicle: The Westerner," *Partisan Review*, XXI (March–April, 1954), reprinted in Warshow, *The Immediate Experience** (1962), and in J. W. Evans, "Modern Man and the Cowboy," *Television Quarterly*, I (May, 1962). A heavily scientific analysis is M. C. Topping, Jr., "The Cultural Orientation of Certain 'Western' Characters on Television: A Content Analysis," *Journal of Broadcasting*, IX (Fall, 1965). A survey of heroes in several kinds of series in the early sixties is Joseph Golden, "TV's Womanless Hero," *Television Quarterly*, II (Winter, 1963). Two specific programs were analyzed in *Television Quarterly*, III (Fall, 1964): Richard Averson, "The Fugitive: TV's Rogue-Saint," and "Notes on Peyton Place," by Paul Monash, creator, in an interview by Cecil Smith.

Two journalistic exposés of commercial television give lively accounts of how the programs are put on: Eugene Paul, *The Hungry Eye: An Inside Look at TV, The Shows, The Personalities, The Fabulous Incomes and Fantastic Costs** (1962), tries to be sensational; Stan Opotowsky, *TV: The Big Picture** (1961), gives a more considered account. A satiric novel centering in the production of a popular TV program is Merle Miller and Evan Rhodes, *Only You, Dick Daring!* (1964).

For the serious student an excellent collection of essays covering various aspects of TV is Eugene Burdick and others, *The Eighth Art* (1962). A more systematic overview is Leo Bogart, *The Age of Television* (1958). Good academic introductions are provided in Sidney Head, *Broadcasting in America* (1956), Chester Giraud and Garnet Garrison, *Television and Radio: An Introduction* (1956), and Robert L. Hilliard, *Understanding Television: An Introduc-*

* Available in paperback edition.

tion to Broadcasting (1964). A good practical book is H. Zettl, *Television Production Handbook* (1961), which, in addition, has a good bibliography.

The British picture is presented briefly in Roger Manvell, *The Crowded Air* (1953) and *The Living Screen: What Goes on in Films and Television* (1961). British techniques are presented in Jan Bussell, *The Art of Television* (1952). The point of view of the British audience is presented in H. H. Wilson, *Pressure Groups* (1961), Paula Burton, *British Broadcasting in Transition* (1961), and Gerald Beadle, *Television: A Critical Review* (1963). The Oxford University Press, London, began bringing out an extensive history of broadcasting with Asa Briggs, *The Birth of Broadcasting*, vol. I (1961), vol. II (1964).

Writing for TV is discussed in many books, notably Lola Goelet Yookem, ed., *TV and Screen Writing* (1958), and Eric Barnouw, *The Television Writer* (1962). Speaking for the microphone is treated in Ben Henneke and Edwin Dumit, *Announcer's Handbook* (1959), and Stuart Hyde, *Television and Radio Announcing* (1959). Acting for television is treated in Edwin Duerr, *Radio and Television Acting* (1950), William Hodapp, *The Television Actor's Manual* (1955), and W. K. Kingson and R. Cowgill, *Television Acting and Directing* (1965). On TV directing, besides the books on production, there is William Kaufman, ed., *How to Direct for Television* (1959). Two books deal with visual design: Robert J. Wade, *Designing for TV* (1952), and Richard Levin, *Television by Design* (1961). Dance broadcasting is considered in "Dance on Television," *Television Quarterly,* IV (Summer, 1965), with interviews with four dancers, and William Harpe, "TV Dance in England," in the same issue of *Television Quarterly.* Television critics give their ideas of TV criticism in George Condon, "Critic's Choice," *Television Quarterly,* I (Nov., 1962). Another view is given by Jack Behar, "On TV Criticism," *Television Quarterly,* IV (Summer, 1965).

The broadcast documentary is discussed in A. William Bluem, *The Documentary in American Television* (1964), and George Bluestone, "The Intimate Documentary," *Television Quarterly,* IV (Spring, 1965).

An English official opinion of American programs appears in Stuart Hood, "American Programs and British Audiences," *Television Quarterly,* II (Winter, 1963). An attractive view of Canadian policy is given by Dean Walker, "Canadian TV—The Wasteland and the Pasture," *Television Quarterly,* I (Aug., 1962).

On the question of the influence of violence in the comics, on the TV screen, and in other media, the psychiatrist Frederic Wertham made a sensation with his accusations in *Seduction of the Innocents* (1954). His ideas were refuted by Leslie Fiedler in an article printed in Bernard Rosenberg and David M. White, eds., *Mass Culture* (1957), and were considered in a calmer manner in Robert Warshow, "Paul, the Horror Comics, and Dr. Wertham," *Commentary* (June, 1954), reprinted in Warshow, *The Immediate Experience** (1962). The impact of television on children has been discussed in many books, notably for England, H. Himmelweit, A. Oppenheim, and P. Vince, *Television and the Child* (1958), and for this country, Wilbur Schramm and Lyle T. Parker, *Television in the Lives of Our Children* (1961).

MASS CULTURE AND POPULAR ARTS

The pessimistic view of mass culture is presented in a number of essays in Bernard Rosenberg and David M. White, eds., *Mass Culture: The Popular Arts in*

* Available in paperback edition.

SUGGESTED READING

*America** (1957), in which White's own essay presents a more hopeful point of view. The discussion is carried on in Bernard Berelson, "The Great Debate on Cultural Democracy," in Donald N. Barrett, ed., *Values in America* (1961), and Norman Jacobs, ed., *Culture for the Millions!* (1964).

The wider influences of mass communication are discussed in T. Klapper, *The Effects of Mass Communication* (1960), and Robert C. O'Hara, *Media for the Millions: The Process of Mass Communication* (1961). The most startling theories of the effect of new media is Marshall McLuhan, *Understanding Media: The Extensions of Man** (1964). A general bibliography was compiled by Eleanor Blum, *Reference Books in the Mass Media* (1962).

The classic defense of popular arts is Gilbert Seldes, *The Seven Lively Arts* (1924; reissued with further notes, 1957). In *The Great Audience* (1950), Seldes, too, expressed grave doubts about mass culture. But in *The Public Arts** (1956) he came back to a view with some hope. An English book designed as a guide for school courses, republished in America, is Stuart Hall and Paddy Whannel, *The Popular Arts* (1965). A theory of how the popular performers in vaudeville satisfied needs of their audience is developed in Albert F. McLean, *American Vaudeville as Ritual* (1965).

The problem of the popular arts is also discussed in Louise Bogan, "Some Notes on Popular and Unpopular Art," *Partisan Review*, X (Sept.–Oct., 1943), André Malraux, "Art, Popular Art and the Illusion of the Folk," *Partisan Review*, XVIII (Sept.–Oct., 1951), and Walter Kerr, "Art and the Box Office," *Commonweal*, LXII (Apr. 22, 1955). What can happen to words as well as art in a mass society is studied in Spencer Brown, "Beepage: The Language of Popularization," *Commentary*, XIV (Oct., 1952), and Dorothy B. Jones, *The Language of Our Time* (1960). The class stratification created in a mass society is treated with wry wit in Russell Lynes, "Highbrow, Lowbrow, Middlebrow," *Harper's* (Feb., 1949), reprinted in his *The Taste-Makers* (1954); Robert Warshow, "The Legacy of the 30's: Middle-Class Culture and the Intellectual's Problem," *Commentary*, IV (Dec., 1947), reprinted in his *The Immediate Experience** (1962); and Dwight MacDonald's several essays, gathered in *Against the American Grain** (1962).

Two British works of fiction have presented the fear of an inhuman mass man of the future more vividly than any of the essayists: Aldous Huxley humorously in *Brave New World** (1932) and George Orwell very grimly in *1984** (1949).

The commercial control of TV gets an angry denunciation in Harold Mehling, *The Great Time-Killer* (1962), and a more objective examination in two short books: Marya Mannes, *Who Owns the Air?*, and Robert Lewis Shayon, *Television: The Dream and the Reality*, both published in 1960. There is fuller discussion in Yale Roe, *The Television Dilemma: Search for a Solution* (1962), and Meyer Weinberg, *TV in America: The Morality of Hard Cash* (1962). Commercial censorship is discussed in "Television Censorship: Myth or Menace?" *Television Quarterly*, IV (Summer, 1965). An early study, Charles A. Siepman, *Radio, Television and Society* (1950), considered the social effects of broadcast policy. Both social and legal aspects are discussed in a symposium, John E. Coons, ed., *Freedom and Responsibility in Broadcasting* (1961). A sampling of public opinion is discussed in George A. Steiner, *The People Look at Television: A Study of Audience Attitudes* (1963).

---

* Available in paperback edition.

SUGGESTED READING

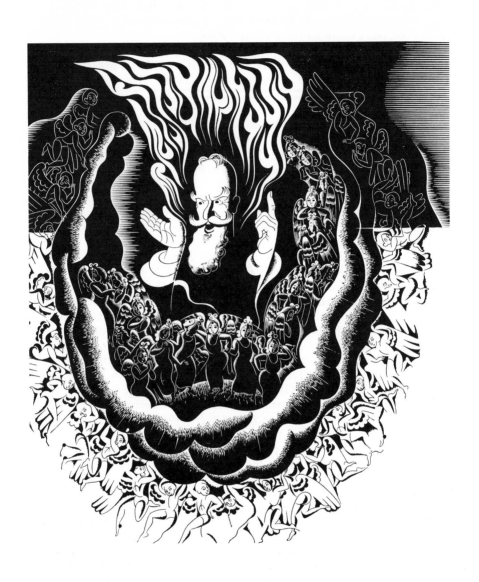

 PART FOUR

EVALUATION

As one of life's most exciting experiences and as one of the oldest
and most universal of the arts, the theatre has occasioned an
enormous amount of writing, some of it extremely good. A number of the best writers of the world, from Aristotle to Goethe,
Lessing, and Schiller and on to Shaw, Camus, and Sartre, have
written about the theatre—theory, history, analyses and descriptions of every sort—exploring it, revealing the secrets of its crafts,
relating it to other social and artistic trends, above all trying to
capture the essence, the intangible atmosphere and color of a
performance before it fades in the memory and is gone. Amidst
the "floating life" in the gay quarters of eighteenth-century Japanese cities, people gathered in the teahouses, vying with one another in writing descriptions of their favorite Kabuki actors and
buying color prints of them, hoping to capture in words and colors
the beauty of the performance they had seen. In the West, theatre
biographies and especially autobiographies are always popular:
theatre personalities are often as adventurous and glamorous offstage as on.

OPPOSITE   Bernard Shaw as Allah, in an illustration from *Poor Shaydullah*,
by Boris Artzybasheff. Shaw's zest for passing judgment on everything
in heaven and earth provoked many such caricatures.
The Macmillan Company, New York, 1931.

Two kinds of professional writers deal directly with the play in performance. One is the literary adviser or staff writer for the company, and the other is the journalistic reviewer for a newspaper or magazine. The one prepares explanatory material before the performance; the other describes and evaluates the play afterwards. They could theoretically be the same person, but in America the staff writer has usually been a publicity agent writing advertisements and propaganda, often making extravagant claims. In reaction, the newspaper critic has usually remained skeptical and sometimes hostile, ready to inform the public if they have been imposed on by an unscrupulous promoter.

Where theatre is not a commercial venture, there is no need for such opposition. The state-supported theatre companies of Germany have a *Dramaturg* or literary adviser on the staff to read new plays, help plan the plays of the season, give lectures, and write program notes and articles for the newspapers and magazines. When the National Theatre was established in London, Kenneth Tynan, who had written brilliant reviews for the *Observer,* was made literary adviser, and he gave up reviewing plays for the newspapers though he continued to write reviews of films. The new resident professional companies in America are realizing that they need a critical writer far different from the old-fashioned press agent. A new profession is opening up.

Dramatic criticism became important early in the nineteenth century when several of the best writers wrote reviews. The theatre of that period was an actor's theatre, and we have brilliant descriptions written by Charles Lamb, Leigh Hunt, and William Hazlitt, who discussed the effects the actor created, without close analysis of the techniques used. To this day good theatre provokes good reviews from knowledgeable critics like John Mason Brown, Eric Bentley, Kenneth Tynan, and dozens of others who discuss all forms of the theatre and all aspects of the performance. At first the movie and television fans were only interested in gossip about their favorite stars. But serious criticism has gradually grown up, and today all the metropolitan newspapers, as well as the weekly periodicals and some television programs, carry reviews of all kinds of dramatic fare and serious discussion of the public responsibilities of the arts. Whether dealing with stage, film, or broadcast drama, the reviewer has essentially the same tasks—to bring the play to life again in his description and to open a discussion with his opinions of its worth.

CHAPTER NINETEEN

THE CRITIC'S ROLE

The performance is not complete without a written review, a permanent record, description, or evaluation to fix the memory and evoke for the future some image of a transitory art. The essence of the theatre is the reaction of the whole audience, but that is unfocused, unclear, and very quick to fade in a general glow. A printed play or a photograph can recall the performance, but only a good review can supplement the playgoer's own analysis, confirm or modify his opinions, stimulate further thinking about the play, and open up new points of view. Yet nothing can cause more distress than a review. The members of the cast and the other people connected with the play wait for it anxiously, praying that it will be favorable, each hoping that he will be mentioned, perhaps praised. Then all too often the critic seems to have missed the point completely or to have set out to make a vicious attack. Percy Hammond, himself a critic, once remarked that "Dramatic criticism is the venom from contented rattlesnakes."

The college review can be a particular source of anguish. Even more than an adult critic, a college writer feels challenged to show that he is not easily taken in. He may declare in flat terms that the production is a failure. After all their hard work and devotion, the theatre workers are furious: "He's unfair . . . he's crazy . . . he's got a grudge . . . who does he think he is? Let him come back stage and try acting himself. . . . He doesn't even mention me. Why doesn't he report that everybody else liked it but him? We don't pretend to be professional—who's he trying to compare us with?" The difficulty is so great that in some places a review in the school paper is not allowed and at others the director warns his workers to pay no attention to the review since the opinion of an inexperienced would-be journalist cannot be an authoritative evaluation.

Yet theatre people, professional or amateur, want the review—a report from the outside and, yes, a verdict, even though it is given by someone who does not know everything. Newspaper editors want a review. As a topic for discussion, a play is of interest to their readers. But the review is not a gossip column or a reporter's account of what happened on stage. It is a description and comment that enables those who have just seen the play to think about it more clearly and those who have not seen it to think about it and have some part in the public discussion.

No playgoer with a mind of his own wants a mere consumer's report— this play is recommended, that play fails. Yet many people do want to be told just that—is it a hit or a flop? The mindless crowd cannot enjoy a thing for its own sake; they want to know that it is the rage, a best seller, on the hit parade, approved by all the fashionable authorities. They are not interested in art, but only in being in the know. They expect the critic to tell them which shows are in fashion and to lead the noisy ballyhoo which will surround the play with the neon-bright shine of success. Yet even the most vapid playgoer is glad of some indication of what kind of play to expect and can enjoy a review that captures the particular quality of some character or scene and enables him to relive the moment of pleasure. He wants some breaking down of the evaluation—at least a score card on which to check his own judgment, with a list of good points on one side against a list of defects on the other. So even the simplest review should provide classification, description, and evaluation.

For the discriminating, the critic is much more than a high-powered salesman, more than a shopper's guide, more than a gossip columnist writing about current fashions in plays. He must be a thoughtful person, with considerable knowledge of what he is talking about, and able to write. The good reader wants him to be an independent person with strong opinions of his own, one who signs his name to his reviews, for only such a person can help the reader clarify his own reactions. Almost worthless is the generalized, predigested "groupspeak" of some of the weekly news magazines and monthly digests. Their approach is born out of the fallacy that it is not necessary to know anything but only to know how to write journalese. Their reports serve to tranquilize the curiosity of those readers who do not want direct experience but only an ersatz product.

The really good critic is expected to write a coherent essay with a live point of view and at the same time to avoid two opposite pitfalls: the temptation to be all enthusiasm and the temptation to be all attack and annihilation. Of course, he must have a devotion to the theatre and can make it quite evident when he approves of a play. Yet, as George Jean Nathan put it, "Art is hot but criticism cold." The sound critic is not a cheerleader but a referee. He is recounting the adventure of intelligence among emotions, not merely

632

wallowing in his own emotions. But neither must the critic be all negative. He may think of himself as a gadfly to sting the performers into keeping up to standards, but he will destroy them rather than improve them unless he shows that he recognizes that they are good enough to be better. It is a temptation to be wittily devastating, to slay with a quick stroke of the pen, as John Mason Brown did when he remarked briefly, "Tallulah Bankhead barged down the Nile as Cleopatra last night—and sank." There is an amusing anecdote of a nineteenth-century critic who remarked that an uneasy actor in *Hamlet* played the King as though he expected someone else to play the ace. Another critic praised an actress for running "the gamut of the emotions from A to B," and James Agee praised Cornel Wilde in the movie *Forever Amber* for using "both his facial expressions frequently." Stark Young once wrote of a bad production of *Macbeth:* "The two murderers . . . seemed to me excellent performers. Their only fault lay in not killing more of the cast."

Devastating comparisons were the specialty of George Jean Nathan, who made his sharp tongue dreaded in New York for four decades. Typical of his method was the remark that an actor "bellowed so loudly as a comic-strip gangster that it was occasionally hard to make out whether he thought he was in a play or a train wreck." It is said that one college newspaper put a production it disapproved of in its place by printing the name of the play as a headline but leaving the column blank. A reviewer sometimes seems like the dentist, who noisily drills on all the bad teeth and ignores the sound ones.

It is much more important, and makes far more interesting reading, for the writer to have some affirmative ideas about the play instead of giving the impression that he would not like it even if it were good. John Mason Brown, who could scold when he wanted to, wrote in a review in 1949,

> It is easier by far to hold the attention while damning than when praising. If this were not true, so many conversationalists would not seem witty whose sole equipment is malice. The bludgeon, the nightstick, the ax, the bazooka, and the flame-thrower are weapons every critic should have in his armory. But the criticism of the arts, which as I see it is bound to be a criticism of life, would be a dull and sorry business were it prepared only to stalk, attack, and extinguish.

At his best the critic may seem an enemy. At the end of nearly four years of writing weekly criticism, Bernard Shaw could speak playfully of the fact that nobody likes a critic. He wrote, ". . . then there are the managers . . . are they grateful? No! They are simply forbearing. Instead of looking up to me as their guide, philosopher, and friend, they regard me merely as the author of a series of weekly outrages on their profession and their privacy." But there is a vast difference between the man who is ardently trying to promote better plays and the man who thinks it smart to disapprove of everything and perhaps in fact has so little confidence in his own opinion that he cannot let himself see good in anything. Molière has his Célimène in *The Misanthrope* hit off such a character among her friends:

The Critic's Role

He scolds at all the latest books and plays,
Thinking that wit must never stoop to praise,
That finding fault's a sign of intellect,
That all appreciation is abject,
And that by damning everything in sight
One shows oneself in a distinguished light.
(Trans. Richard Wilbur)

Even more exasperating than the review that blames without measure is the one that condemns the play for what it never set out to do. This practice has been so frequent that critics need to be reminded of the three rules of evaluation urged long ago by Goethe: first, ask what a work of art set out to do; then ask how it has done it; and, only after those two are explored, ask how much it was worth doing. We expect different things of a farce and a high comedy. It is no use berating a farce for using type characters; we want to know whether the author and the actor have found new types or have given a few fresh touches to the old types. In a short review of an absurdist play, there is no place for a long attack on despair. The critic may incidentally show that he himself does not find life meaningless and even analyze some parts of the play he believes false. But his main job is to help the reader understand this particular view of the absurdity of life and to show the effectiveness of the means used in dramatizing it. For twenty years the *New Yorker* critic Woollcott Gibbs wrote about his dislike for the low-comedy characters in Shakespeare. Instead of such details about his own taste, readers wanted to know what the particular actors made out of the characters. At the most he might have apologized for his blind spot or reported on how the audience took the characters and then have concentrated on other aspects of the play where he did have something to say. If the play is a whodunit, readers want to know how good it is as a whodunit, what particular atmosphere it creates, and how it differs from others. If the critic describes the effects he likes in a whodunit and notes what this one lacks and whether it makes up for those shortcomings by some unexpected qualities, then critic and reader settle into a good confidential relationship, comparing their tastes and checking on how the specimen in question fits the measure. If the reader sees the play after reading the review, he knows a good deal of what to expect. It is infuriating to be led to expect one thing and then feel cheated by finding something else. So evaluation is not enough—we want to know what the play is like, what it has in common with some other plays, and what its own particular qualities are; we want classification and description.

Writing the Review

When it comes down to the actual writing of the review, there are several suggestions to be derived from common practice. It is good journalistic practice to pack the essence of the story into the first few sentences and develop the details later. Then a person who reads no more than the lead sentences will have the most important facts. For the review, the essence is

634

Evaluation

not only the who, when, where, and what of all news stories, but a summary of the judgment. What did the reviewer think of the play as a whole? Sometimes he may start with a particular item and lead into a wider view, but it is easier to get a capsule judgment, a general overall impression, into the first paragraph or so before describing the details. After the opening may come enough of the plot to indicate more definitely what kind of play it is, and enough for those who have not seen it to follow. Next will come comment on the performance, usually starting with the actors and then mentioning other workers—designers, choreographers, and so on—who deserve attention. If a single impression has persisted in the sequence of details, it may be sufficient to end on some detail, but often there is need for a more considered conclusion, a summary judgment, at the end.

To get a statement of a balanced judgment in a few opening sentences is not easy. To find the right details and the right words to suggest the texture and quality of the production and to indicate incidentally the reviewer's own reaction takes careful control and, for most writers, a great deal of rewriting. John Anderson opened a review in the New York *Evening Journal* of January 11, 1929, with this short paragraph:

> Out of the clutter and racket and brownstone complacency of any New York side street Elmer Rice has wrought this new play called *Street Scene,* which William A. Brady, Ltd., presented last night in the Playhouse. It is a play which builds engrossing trivialities into a drama that is rich and compelling and catches in the wide reaches of its curbside panorama the comedy and heartbreak that lie a few steps up from the sidewalks of New York.

The reader feels the grit and sees the comedy and pain spread out on a wide sweep of city sidewalk and knows that Mr. Anderson is impressed with the play.

Let us see how several critics handled their reviews of Arthur Miller's *After the Fall* in January, 1964. This can be done easily because since 1940 the principal daily reviews from the New York city papers have been reproduced together as the *New York Theatre Critics' Reviews.* The opening of the play was important for several reasons. The new company that had been formed to be a kind of national theatre for America was beginning its first season in a new but temporary theatre, while its own theatre was being built in Lincoln Center. The temporary theatre was the first large open-stage theatre built in New York. Further, it had been nine years since Miller had had a new play on Broadway, and it had leaked out that this play treated his own marriage with Marilyn Monroe. There had been a number of preview performances before the official opening, stimulating wide discussion and interest.

The veteran critic Richard Watts, Jr., of the *New York Post* started with a comment on the occasion and said immediately that hopes were partly justified. Under the headline "The New Drama by Arthur Miller" he wrote,

> It has been nine years since we have had a new play from Arthur Miller, and his "After the Fall," with which the Lincoln Center Repertory Theatre

635

The Critic's Role

FIGURE *19.1* A psychological epic played on platforms on an open stage.
Miller's *After the Fall,* with Jason Robards, Jr. and Barbara Loden. New York, 1963.
Photo Inge Morath, Magnum.

inaugurated its career in its large and handsome temporary home near Washington Square last night, has been awaited with virtually unparalleled interest. In considerable part the interest proved justified. Mr. Miller continues to write with power and passion. But his lengthy, undeniably autobiographical drama is also a disappointing and self-indulgent kind of personal apologia, often strong, moving and perceptive, and yet frequently lost in its own waywardness.

John McClain of the *Journal American,* after a petulant remark about the preview showings, went straight to his dislike of the personal element in the play. He wrote, under the headline "Tour de Force by Robards,"

As one of the underprivileged people who had to wait for the official opening to see Arthur Miller's "After the Fall" performed by the spectacular Lincoln Center Repertory Company in their temporary quarters in Washington Square last night, I can only report that I was offended by its lack of taste.

The author is one of our most gifted playwrights, but it seemed regrettable that he chose to consider at such length the tragic frustrations of a character, quite obviously fashioned after Marilyn Monroe, which led to her suicide. I thought the girl might have been permitted to rest in peace.

Quite apart from that the play seemed to me pretentious and intolerably long. Jason Robards, Jr., playing the leading role, gives a magnificent and ceaseless performance—never leaving the stage for an instant during the more than three hours of the proceedings.

But sad to say, I never quite got the message.

Howard Taubman, writing for the *New York Times,* had more room for his enthusiasm for both the company and the play. He took four paragraphs to get past the incidentals and into his image of the play. He began:

Evaluation

Which to celebrate first? The return of Arthur Miller to the theatre with a new play after too long an absence? Or the arrival of the new Repertory Theatre of Lincoln Center with its high promise for a consecration to drama of aspiration and significance?

Celebrate the conjunction of events, for together they may mark a turning point in the American drama. There have been discomfiting years of shrinkage and decline. The new company proclaims a fresh affirmation. The new play, though unsparing in its search for one man's truth, also ends on a note of hope.

In the beginning are the playwright and his vision. "After the Fall," which opened officially last night in the newly built and impressively utilitarian ANTA Washington Square Theatre, is Mr. Miller's distillation of the remembrance of things past.

Autobiographical, as the scuttlebutt has intimated with a wicked leer? Obviously, as even a fool would know. But is that the play's central truth? Unmistakably not. Like all writers who matter and who inevitably write about what they have felt, sensed and learned, Mr. Miller is probing into his own life and those near and dear to him and seeking answers to the eternal riddles that confront human beings on this earth.

Likewise we can compare the way in which three New York film critics move from judgment to description in their reviews of *Morgan!*, an English picture released in 1966. It was directed by Karel Reisz, who had made several films that had pleased both the public and the critics and who was regarded as one of the best directors working in England. The film followed a trend of pictures expressing current unconventional attitudes and using elements of absurd fantasy. And the hero, or antihero, was played by David Warner, a young actor who had played well an unsympathetic role in the popular film *Tom Jones* and who had been selected for the role of Morgan because he was not the glamorous young hero type.

Hollis Alpert, film critic of the *Saturday Review,* who did not like the picture, began his review with a reference to Reisz's previous work:

> One of the leaders of the British rebellion against establishment filmmaking has been Karel Reisz who effectively caught the "anger" of a young working man in *Saturday Night and Sunday Morning,* and then turned from directing to producing for *This Sporting Life.* Now he is back as a director with *Morgan!,* an odd jumble of irreverence, high jinks, black humor, fantasy, and compassion—the latter on behalf of a young, disturbed artist seeking, on the one hand, some sort of truth by which to live, and, on the other, a rapprochement with his pretty, rich wife, who has divorced him. The film, however, tends less to enthrall than to irritate, and one reason for this may be that British anger, ordinarily so dependable a theme for dozens of novels, plays, and films, is beginning to wear thin. Perhaps we are supposed to comprehend automatically Morgan Delt's dissatisfactions with himself, others, and his environment, but the only solid explanation for his unendingly self-indulgent behavior comes at the very end of the film, when we find him in a sanitarium, the victim, presumably, of a nervous breakdown. What has happened before then all at once be-

637

The Critic's Role

comes symptomatic, and if we had begun at the end, instead of the rather incomprehensible beginning, things might have been clearer.

Brendan Gill of *The New Yorker* takes a much more favorable view of the film:

> "Morgan!" is an exceptionally interesting movie, which I had better risk praising too much in order to make sure that I don't praise it too little. Like "Darling," with which it shares an English origin, "Morgan!" amounts to two different movies in one, depending upon the nature of the viewer. To the casual moviegoer, the "Morgan!" that is all glancing surfaces and fashionable camera prankishness should prove continuously entertaining, if a trifle long and overbearing; to the dedicated moviegoer, another and darker "Morgan!" will seem not merely a couple of hours of welcome diversion but an ambitious and unexpectedly successful assault on our received ideas of what is permissible in comedy. As a rowdy, sometimes stumbling march into what James called the enemy country—the famous country of the general lost freshness—it has for its eponymous hero a young artist who seeks with barbaric gusto to smash every last convention and transform our contemporary opulent and unloving wasteland into . . . well, into a paradisal canebrake of inarticulate, shyly affectionate great apes.

Bosley Crowther of the *New York Times* was even more enthusiastic about the picture and expressed his dissatisfaction that the film had not been made in Hollywood:

> Two haunting considerations crystallized in my mind after seeing and vastly enjoying the satiric British farce, elusively titled "Morgan!" which opened at the Sutton the other day. The first was the aptness of it as a flashing illumination of the almost fanatic enthusiasm that mobs of young people have these days for such wild escapist stuff as Batman and the films glorifying James Bond. And the second was the shame that such a picture as this was not made in Hollywood, which used to be a place that was productive of first-class satiric comedies.
>
> The first is the more important, for the idolatry the youngsters have for fantasy creations, and the bent that many older juveniles have for outrageous hairdos and clothing that encase them in their various fantasies, are matters for clear understanding and helpful sympathy. "Morgan!" is a movie that helps us understand.

Sometimes telling the story is the best way of developing the review, after the opening general impression—but never for the sake of the story. Many an inexperienced writer gets lost and puts in too many details. The reviewer should give only enough of the story to make a point, as Kenneth Tynan does in his review of Ionesco's *The Chairs* in the London *Observer* in 1957. He begins by noting that the English more than the French like an attack on logic, and he makes a transition before he tells enough of the plot to show Ionesco's main theme.

That it is virtuoso nonsense nobody denies: Ionesco is a poet of double-talk.

But this is at best a minor gift. It does not explain why *The Chairs* is such an enthralling experience.

It is night on an island. In a round house of many doors sit a nonagenarian couple who will soon fling themselves suicidally into the river. At first, however, all is tranquil. Mad scraps of reminiscence are swapped, the old man bemoans his failure in life, the old woman babies and consoles him. From their moonstruck chatter we gather that he has a message to the world which he has bidden everyone to hear. The guests start to arrive, at first singly, then in pairs, soon in unmanageable droves, until the old-age *pension* resembles Groucho's cabin in *A Night at the Opera*. With this difference: that all the guests are invisible. They are creatures of the old man's dream, and before long he and his wife are plunging in and out of doors with yet more chairs for the unseen multitude, whom they engage, from time to time, in phantom conversation.

The audacity of the idea is breathtaking; here is pure theatre, the stage doing what only the stage can do. As the doorbell rings and the numbers crazily swell, one sees that Ionesco is more than a word-juggler. He is a supreme theatrical conjurer. And what does the trick mean? A hired orator, at the end, speaks the old man's message to the listening throng. Or rather, he would speak it, were he not dumb; and they would listen, if they existed. Moral: truth is a tale told without words to people who cannot hear it. Communication between human beings is impossible.

Since the actor is the heart of the theatre, the reviewer must tell something about the acting. Avoiding technical matters, he makes his comment almost entirely in terms of what the actor does with the character. We have Bernard Shaw's marginal comments on a practice review a young critic sent him, slashing him for trying to talk in technical terms. Beside one sentence Shaw wrote, "Now we are coming to something sensible. You are quite entitled to *describe* her voice: that is quite a different thing to talking about the 'principles of elocution & acting.'" To Shaw the essence of criticism was in description. A little further on he wrote in the margin: "Now here you are saying something definite—you are writing criticism—you are *describing* what you saw. Don't you feel how much better it is than mere pompous and unmeaning phrase slinging . . . ?"

At the least, a few identifying phrases serve to bring back to the playgoer the pleasure of a vivid character—a vivid image, for who remembers the names? In building a picture of the energy and exuberance of *Hello, Dolly!*, Norman Nadel in the *New York World-Telegram and The Sun* gives even the minor characters a quality and life of their own, and then describes in greater detail the performance of the leading character:

Here too are Charles Nelson Reilly and Jerry Dodge as his cowering clerks who break loose for one reckless night in the downstream Babylon, New York City. . . . The caterwauling of Alice Playten as Vandergelder's niece, the dismay of Igors Gavon as her beloved, and the "Deutschland Über Alles" command of David Hartman as a head waiter are some of the other amusing aspects. Which brings me back to Miss Channing. She is spectacular. The eyes roll, the voice modulates from a dry axle to a sunken

FIGURE *19.2* The stripping away of illusions. Melinda Dillon, George Grizzard, Arthur Hill, and Uta Hagen in Albee's *Who's Afraid of Virginia Woolf?* New York, 1962. Photo Friedman-Abeles.

calliope, the body moves like a battle flag, and her energy blinds like sunlight. Where other actresses pretend to eat, she eats, through one of the funniest non-speaking scenes on Broadway. Her Dolly thrives on deceit, and blossoms in the warmth of her open-faced intrigues.

In reviewing *Who's Afraid of Virginia Woolf?* for the London *Observer* of March 31, 1963, Kenneth Tynan mainly discussed the play, but he also gave vivid descriptions of the two leading performances in a very few words. He wrote,

> Mr. Albee's text advances the great American art of insult: it is full of brilliant poetic invective and soaring cadenzas of spite, and it could not be better acted than by Uta Hagen, lecherously booming, and Arthur Hill as her blithely-destructive mate: but it leaves one's heart unbruised and unmoved. It is too funny by half.

Sometimes a character can be described through his assault on our senses. Maurice Richardson, television critic of the London *Observer,* thus described an unpleasant character in a short television drama:

> It may be extremely difficult to create nice characters, but it isn't all that easy to create nasty ones. Dennis Potter deserves some special award—a statuette of Quilp, perhaps—for Mr. Flanders, the little old cockney patient in his *Emergency Ward 9,* for BBC–2's "Thirty-Minute Theatre." He really was a perfect beast, a creeping bag of spite like some monster from allegory, yet convincingly round and quirky, and though too odious to be pathetic, even when wetting his bed, he gave off a whiff of that infantility of the spirit which one likes to think is the ground of malice. Terence de Marney played him brilliantly.

640

Evaluation

For a full description of acting, let us look back to the 1890s, when Bernard Shaw was as brilliant a drama critic as he later was a dramatist. In reviewing Ibsen's *Little Eyolf* in London, amazed at the vitality and range of Janet Achurch in her role as the mother as she disregarded the glamour and charm usually expected of an actress, he wrote:

> . . . As Rita she produced almost every sound that a big human voice can, from a creak like the opening of a rusty canal lock to a melodious tenor note that the most robust Siegfried might have envied. She looked at one moment like a young, well-dressed, very pretty woman: at another she was like a desperate creature just fished dripping out of the river by the Thames Police; yet another moment and she was the incarnation of impetuous, ungovernable strength. Her face was sometimes winsome, sometimes list-lessly wretched, sometimes like the head of a statue of Victory, sometimes suffused, horrible, threatening, like Bellona or Medusa. She would cross from left to right like a queen, and from right to left with, so to speak, her toes turned in, her hair coming down, and her slippers coming off. A more utter recklessness, not only of fashion, but of beauty, could hardly be imagined: beauty to Miss Achurch is only one effect among others to be produced, not a condition of all effects. But then she can do what our beautiful actresses cannot do: attain the force and terror of Sarah Bern-hardt's most vehement explosions without Sarah's violence and abandon-ment, and with every appearance of having reserves of power still held in restraint.

Shaw admitted that he liked the charm and beauty of such an actress as Mrs. Patrick Campbell (a decade later he was madly in love with her), who was playing a smaller role in the same cast, ". . . better than being frightened, harrowed, astonished, conscience-stricken, devastated, and dreadfully de-lighted in general by Miss Achurch's untamed genius."

A good combination of description and evaluation is achieved in Kenneth Tynan's account of Donald Wolfit's *King Lear:*

> He is magnificent in the early scenes, sulking like a beaten dog when Cordelia refuses to play ball with him; and the colloquies with the Fool are horribly moving, with the old man's thoughts storming past his words into the chasm of lunacy. Best of all is the pause that follows his fit of rage at Cornwall's cruelty. "Tell the hot Duke . . ." he begins, and then stops in mid-eruption, veins knotted, fighting hideously to keep his foothold on the tiny edge which stands between him and madness.

A neat evaluation of what was wrong with another Lear appears in Robert Speight's description of Charles Laughton's performance at Stratford-on-Avon in 1962:

> He mortgaged the last scenes of *Lear* up to the hilt by presenting us at the start with a chubby Father Christmas put out by the spoiling of the party. There is no tragedy where there has been no fall, and the cosmic drama was thus reduced to domesticity.

John Mason Brown's description of Lee J. Cobb's performance in *Death of a Salesman* is a brilliant comment on the meaning of the play as well as an evocation of the qualities of the acting.

> Mr. Cobb's Willy Loman is irresistibly touching and wonderfully unsparing. He is a great shaggy bison of a man seen at that moment of defeat when he is deserted by the herd and can no longer run with it. Mr. Cobb makes clear the pathetic extent to which the herd has been Willy's life. He also communicates the fatigue of Willy's mind and body and that boyish hope and buoyancy which his heart still retains. Age, however, is his enemy. He is condemned by it. He can no more escape from it than he can from himself. The confusion, the weakness, the goodness, the stupidity, and the self-sustaining illusions which are Willy—all these are established by Mr. Cobb. Seldom has an average man at the moment of his breaking been characterized with such exceptional skill.

One of the highest functions of a critic is to see the ideal possibilities of a performance and show very specifically how the particular performance falls short. With a new play it is difficult to see what the play promises but does not quite achieve. With a play already known, it is easier. But the critic must be sure that in noting how a performance differs from his own picture he gives full consideration to what the actors actually do. An unconventional performance or a new interpretation may have virtues of its own or reveal an approach to the play that is perfectly valid. Tynan is very convincing in scolding Pamela Brown's approach to *The Way of the World*. We have described this high comedy of Congreve and the famous series of scenes between two proud, independent people who love each other but are determined to keep their independence after marriage. Tynan wrote,

> The scenes between Mirabell and Millamant, which should be the play's delicious crown, do not come off at all. The two lovers remain what Johnson called them, "intellectual gladiators," but the strength is all on one side, and the wrong side at that. Mr. Gielgud, an impeccable Mirabell in plum velvet, has Pamela Brown begging for mercy almost before the battle is joined. That is, of course, a ghastly abdication on her part. Millamant must be the empress of her sex, and her words whether tumbling like a fountain or cascading like Niagara must always flow from a great height. From Miss Brown's mouth they do not flow at all: they leak, half apologetically, in dribs and drabs. Instead of saving up the revelation that she loves Mirabell, she lets us know it from the outset, thereby dethroning the empress and setting an ogling spinster in her place. Miss Brown, to sum up, sees through Millamant, and (what is worse) lets us see through her as well. It is a grave mistake and I will hear no excuse.

But a young critic would seem very arrogant to assume that there is only one way to interpret a play and that the actors and director are stupid not to see it the way he does. He must show very clearly why he thinks a different interpretation would have brought out more important values inherent in the play.

After the actors come the designers, too often crowded out of a notice, though the review would be unbalanced if they got all the attention. When a

642

Evaluation

FIGURE *19.3* Oliver Smith's controversial setting for Michael's *Dylan,* a play of many scenes. The addition of an abstract painting made it a Greenwich Village bar. New York, 1963. Photo Friedman-Abeles.

beautiful college theatre opened in New England with a production that was beautifully designed but poorly acted, Walter Pritchard Eaton wrote, "It is easier to turn on a light than to turn out a Lunt, but not so important." Yet the visual elements can be of great importance and of great interest to the reader.

Oliver Smith's ingenious setting for the play about the poet Dylan Thomas, called *Dylan,* attracted the attention of several of the New York critics. John McClain wrote in the *Journal American:*

> Beyond the towering performance of Mr. Guinness, there is this fantastic contribution of Mr. Smith and his singular set. What he has wrought is something the general shape of a champagne glass, with steps and platforms, which stands in mid-stage and revolves when required.
>
> Don't ask me how it's done, but it can come to represent everything from an airport to a saloon, from a cabin aboard ship to a lady's bed-bath-room, from night-time on a Welsh inlet to the podium at the YM–YWHA Poetry Center.
>
> And in the rare moments when this set is not used, Mr. Smith can drop some hollow frames from above and convince us, as the actors speak through them, that we are all in the Metropolitan Museum.

Taubman in the *New York Times* noted the set but did not like it. He wrote, "Oliver Smith's set, centered on a kind of huge revolving toadstool with a skeletonized superstructure, is an unsatisfactory compromise between illusion and realism."

Lighting, the newest of theatre arts, can also be described and evaluated 643 for the general reader by its effect and by what it adds to the play, without the use of many backstage terms. By the 1930s more and more people were becoming aware that lighting was an important theatre art, and for the first time a lighting designer had his name on the program. Here is Brooks Atkinson's account of Abe Feder's lighting in a review of Orson Welles' *Dr. Faustus* in the *New York Times* for January 31, 1937:

> Modern stagecraft is represented principally in Feder's wizardry of lighting; he isolates the actors in eerie columns of light that are particularly well suited to the diabolical theme of *Dr. Faustus.* . . . The modern switchboard is so incredibly ingenious that stage lighting has become an art in its own right, and apparently Feder is one of the masters. His pools and shapes of light and his crepuscular effects communicate the unearthly atmosphere of Dr. Faustus without diminishing the primary importance of the acting. And when the cup-bearers of Beelzebub climb out of hell the furnace flares of purgatory flood up through a trap door in an awful blaze of light, incidentally giving the actors a sinister majesty. On an unadorned stage Feder's virtuoso lighting gives the production the benefit of the one modern invention that is most valuable to the theatre.

The techniques of moviemaking may be clearly in the mind of the film critic, but he describes them almost completely in terms of the effect the director and cameraman create. Thus Arthur Knight described in the *Saturday Review* the atmosphere of menace created by setting and camera work in Jack Clayton's filming in 1961 of *The Innocents,* based on Henry James's story of ghostly terror, *The Turn of the Screw:*

> Like James he has mastered the art of subtlety. As his camera travels the shadowy stairs and corridors of Bly House, or wanders through the well-tended gardens, menace seems to hover just beyond the edge of the screen. Baroque, twisted statuary impinges on scene after scene, adding what appears to be merely a note of grotesquerie—until, in the final scene of horror, Peter Quint is discovered standing on one of the pedestals. It is a sombre story, and Clayton has staged it against grays and blacks that serve as a constant, half audible reminder of the dark forces at work; while the characters themselves—the innocents—are picked out against these backgrounds with strongly modeled white light. Clayton has discovered and developed a style wholly appropriate to his material.

In reviewing the same movie, Pauline Kael singled out one particularly effective shot:

> And who thought of the marvelous shot of Deborah Kerr with her long hair floating as she kisses the boy, so that as her frightened lips draw back in confusion, we see the hairs hanging below her chin like the sparse beard of an old Chinese?

James Agee describes a telling shot of William Holden as a kept gigolo-writer in *Sunset Boulevard:*

> Yet one of the oddest and most calculated moments in the picture is also one of the best: the lingering, silent, terribly close close-up in which a soft, sleek

Evaluation

clerk whispers to the slightly nauseated kept man: "After all, if the lady is paying. . . ." The intense physical and spiritual malaise of the young man's whole predicament is registered through this brilliantly indirect shot.

While the critic's general impression may be clear from the description and classification, most reviewers try to give some summary evaluation at the very end. It may be put in the form of advice: "If you like surprise and thrills, no matter how far-fetched the plot, get ready for screaming excitement at this one." Or, "Even if the players can only occasionally suggest the desolation of such an experience, they do well with the gentler moments, and make a very human, touching play." Or, "After two acts only occasionally funny, the last act burst out into wild antics that convulsed the house." George Jean Nathan gave a very concise summary of his feeling about Truman Capote's *The Grass Harp,* saying, "The consequence is a play that, while it purports to be fantasy, is too frequently nothing but realism with colored ribbons in its hair." After other critics in the early 1940s had berated William Saroyan for his lack of organization and his overabundance of fantasy and whimsy, Nathan, admitting many weaknesses, wrote an ardent defense, ending with this summary:

> . . . In this William Saroyan, crazy or not crazy, the national theatre, I believe, has discovered its most genuinely gifted new writer. His plays singly and in combination have disclosed and further argue a talent which, as yet undisciplined, vainglorious, cockeyed, and pigheaded, is nevertheless the liveliest and most knowing that has come the way of the local stage in some equinoxes. In that talent, which still resembles a fountain contending against a headwind and helplessly splashing itself all over the place, we engage a whimsical imagination, a lenitive sentiment, a fertile humor, and a human wonder and ache uncommon in our drama and which in sum make his plays, whatever their occasional critical subordinacies, such welcome additions to the file of American playwriting.

A similar strategy was used by Pauline Kael in reviewing *Billy Budd,* a movie made from the short novel of Herman Melville. She wanted to make clear that she liked the film but would not claim too much for it. Throughout the review she emphasized her mixed judgment, praising the film for its "strong story line" and its "core of meaning that charges the story, gives it tension and intellectual excitement," but in her summary statements distinguishing "very good" from "great":

> *Billy Budd* is not a great motion picture, but it is a very good one—a clean, honest work of intelligence and craftsmanship, . . . a good tense movie that doesn't try to tell us too much and so gives us a very great deal. . . . What is missing in the film—the reason it is a very good film but not a great one—is the passion which gives Melville's work its extraordinary beauty and power.

Sometimes the summary evaluation may be enigmatic, indicating that the complexities of the play cannot be pinned down to too exact a statement. In his summary of the impact of *Death of a Salesman,* John Mason Brown used

The Critic's Role

questions, an appropriate method since the play itself suggests that there could be several answers. He wrote,

> Did Willy Loman, so happy with a batch of cement when puttering around the house, or when acquaintances on the road smiled back at him, fail to find out who he was? Did this man, who worked so hard and meant so well, dream the wrong dream? At least he was willing to die by that dream even when it had collapsed for him. He was a breadwinner almost to the end, and a breadwinner even in his death. Did the world walk out on him and his sons see through him? At any rate he could boast one friend who believed in him and thought his had been a good dream. . . . Who knows? Who can say? One thing is certain. No one could have raised the question more movingly or compassionately than Arthur Miller.

A Vision of the Theatre

In making his evaluation, the critic places his own feelings in the wider context of his vision of the theatre and his belief in human values. Even if his primary response to the theatre, as to any real experience in art or life, is subjective, unique, and individual, it is not an isolated experience. No man is completely alone, and no experience exists without relation to memories, hopes, and some ideal concept of what man and his future experiences might be. If a play must be described first of all for what it is in itself, it must be visualized also in comparison with other plays. A complete evaluation may start with the critic's own spontaneous likes and dislikes, but it also involves his ideas of what kind of institution the theatre should be and of how the drama can best serve the spiritual needs and purposes of his day.

The critic must recognize the dangers of his spontaneous likes and dislikes and see them in perspective. It is the mark of an immature critic to find the play either a masterpiece or a disaster. It is not that he should be merely an objective skeptical journalist; he loves the theatre too much to be indifferent. But his love is the source of a difficulty. Either he is blinded with ecstasy or he is torn by the anger of a frustrated idealist. His alternation of love and hate resembles the tempestuous love of a man for a difficult and wayward mistress—the more he loves her, the more he is exasperated when she fails to live up to his ideal. The best moments of the theatre are so wonderful, so full of promise, that the critic may be furious when it fails him. He may have fallen in love with the theatre in his youth, when he discovered that playing a role in a play is a tremendous personal experience, releasing and revealing the deepest emotions, exploring in symbolic form one's own secret identity; when he found that teamwork in rehearsal and performance is more rewarding than almost any other social experience because its fearful anticipation and its surges of work and learning issue in a full completion with the immediate response of the audience. If he was stage-struck—as is likely enough—he may have gone on to discover that while a beginner can do more in the theatre than in any other art, real achievement is as difficult as in

Evaluation

piano playing, surgery, or any other highly complex human activity. Then he may have settled down for a life-long love affair at a safe distance—in the audience.

But even so the course of true love is not smooth. The critic no sooner forms his ideal of what a play should be than the theatre changes, leaving him exasperated and frustrated. The creative artist in the theatre, as in any other art, moves on from one achievement to something different. If his work is really new, it may be so puzzling that it seems a failure. Each of the long features of Charlie Chaplin infuriated some of his critics because it was not exactly like the previous one, yet by the time the next feature was produced, those same critics were ready to denounce the new picture for not being as good as the one they had condemned. It is the critic with neither a wide view of the theatre nor a perspective on his own hopes and fears who is constantly crying that the theatre is dead.

In his wide view of the theatre the critic must recognize that the theatre serves many kinds of human needs and pleasures. Color, movement, and rhythm are immediate pleasures, and part of the critic's job is to describe the texture of a play. As the theatre tells a good story, creates characters, and implies important themes, the critic may describe how this is done and tell us to what extent he agrees or disagrees with the interpretations and the treatment. The theatre can create a documentary sense of reality, and the critic may tell us how convincing he finds the picture and how it corresponds to his view of the facts. But the critic also remembers that not all facts are on the surface and that romantic fantasies may be true to psychological and spiritual facts, just as epic realism may present an abstraction of economic or political facts. The theatre can present well-rounded characters, but the critic remembers that vivid stereotypes and caricatures may also serve to clarify reality. The critic may point out how well the theatre serves the moment, showing the moods and feelings of the day, giving us a journalism of the emotions, reporting the spiritual weather, indicating what thunderstorms and showers to expect. He may also show us how the theatre deals with our long-range yearnings, fears, and ideals, bringing out a particular response for each kind of play. In the theatre we look on the challenge of existence with romantic resolution or realistic compassion, laughing at its earthiness or exulting in its mystery. The critic relates his own likes and dislikes to his wider view of how the play may serve some of the many purposes of the theatre.

Finally the critic must see the drama and his own hopes in terms of the theatre as an institution. Creativity may thrive in solitary moments, but the life of the artist and the public use of the art require organization. Even poetry, which can be written on a scrap of paper, requires some support of the poet and organized distribution of the poem in periodicals and books. Art museums and galleries are institutions for providing a wide range of exhibits of old and new painting to be studied and compared. Symphony orchestras, with the help of large subsidy, are thriving standardized companies, and even opera and ballet have a continuity from one year to the next, offering both performers and patrons a dependable season. Great theatre institutions of the past suggest the possibilities of organization in the theatre. If the Egyptians repeated the same religious drama for several thousand years, the Greeks had new plays every year at the Dionysian festival. Shakespeare's company performed a wide repertory of new plays or new versions of old plays for several decades. As playwright, director, and actor, Molière developed a company that survived his death to be combined in 1680 with the rival companies to form the Comédie Française, an institution that has offered both classics and new plays ever since. Following the example of Paris, other European cities have set up publicly supported institutions.

Broadway is institutionalized, and in spite of its waste and confusion it occasionally gives the artist a chance to do something fine. Even though the film and broadcast industries are organized to turn out rather routine products, they occasionally give the creative artist a chance. But neither Broadway nor Hollywood nor a broadcasting company serves all the needs of the theatre. The great American dream of the twentieth century is a third kind of theatre, decentralized from Broadway—a live theatre based on, supported by, and serving communities all over the country. It was clear from the beginning that this third theatre should be an art theatre rather than a commercial exploitation of talent and that it would therefore need considerable subsidy. As college theatres developed, they were not in harmony with Broadway or Hollywood, and so few of their graduates found jobs in either place that cynics wondered what purpose the colleges had besides teaching teachers to teach teachers. The "little theatres" or community theatres, though they depended on Broadway to try out the new plays, clearly served a very important function, but by using unpaid or low-paid actors they could not achieve as much as a full-time professional company. The resident professional company was the next logical development, and most of the new companies have been established in close relationship with the college and community institutions. In the 1920s the Cleveland Playhouse was converted from a community theatre to a professional theatre with a full-time resident company, and it soon established a teaching relationship with a local college drama department. The big development in resident theatre companies got under way in the early sixties: the opening of the Tyrone Guthrie Theatre in Minneapolis in 1963 and the Ford Foundation's grant to the expansion of the Alley Theatre in Houston were of major importance. Following the example of Princeton and Michigan, a number of universities have aided or sponsored professional companies. At last America is putting real resources behind the dream of local theatres: many kinds of local theatres, with good professional repertory companies at the top of the list.

The critic is very much needed in this time of transition, when America is decentralizing the theatre and building up many local and regional institutions. The mass media of film and broadcast drama have found the largest audience in history, and many viewers are ready to explore live theatre forms. Broadway would be easy for them: it has big publicity and glamorous personalities. But Broadway is expensive and far away for many thousands of

Evaluation

prospective theatregoers. Their hope lies in this third theatre: college and community theatres, the summer theatres which they may visit on vacation trips, and especially the new resident professional companies. But they need critical guidance in order to appreciate these productions so far from the bright lights of Broadway. Not that there is much difficulty in responding to the productions with amateur actors. Like college football teams with professional coaches, college and community theatres have highly trained professional directors and designers and often put on excellent performances. The local theatregoer takes pride in what is accomplished without asking whether Broadway would be impressed. Knowing that the performers are amateurs, he is delighted with their freshness, enthusiasm, and moments of high achievement. In the summer, off in a holiday mood to see shows on the straw-hat circuit or in a reverent mood to see the large productions in the festival theatres, he knows something of what to expect. But he has a different attitude toward the performance of a professional resident company. Dazzled by the national publicity that attends Broadway, Hollywood, and television productions, even the most commonplace ones, he is likely to think that the professionals in the local theatre are not worth seeing and if he sees them he does not know how to assess them. The critic can help here by focusing interest on the actual performance. It is easy to respond to the slick showmanship of a television show as an Ed Sullivan builds up the glamour of each guest personality. But the playgoer who has had his perception sharpened by good criticism will find more real acting in a good performance of a resident professional company than in a dozen presentations of famous personalities. There is no reason for not enjoying both, if he has not been blinded by the overcharged publicity. The critic must show him how to use his eyes in the perspectives of different kinds of theatre.

Early in this century Max Beerbohm described the function of a critic as "to translate, through one's own temperament and intellect, the fine work of another man, to cast new light on its beauties, to reveal things hidden in it, to illustrate and to extend its meaning." This function was described in more chatty terms by John Mason Brown in *Broadway in Review* (1940):

> The dramatic critic is as much a watchdog for beauty as he is a dismisser of cheapness, a scoffer at mediocrity, a hater of incompetence, a seismograph responsive to worthy excitement. His duty is to be rational in the presence of emotion, to think his feelings and to feel his thoughts. His job . . . is to rationalize reactions, interest his readers, suggest quality, recapture mood and atmosphere, comment on the theatre in terms of the theatre no less than of life, be true to what he is personally while being impersonal with those upon whose work he presumes to pass judgment, and to do all three things under pressure of time. While being true to himself, he must be true to such a vision of perfection as may be his and of which every false move in the theatre reminds him by denying it.

Whether we are involved as workers in producing a play or as critics in enjoying and evaluating it, we are participating in the life of our time. The theatre, the most public of the arts, not only provides pleasure and entertainment but serves to show us ourselves, for that is, in Hamlet's words, the true "purpose of playing, whose end both at the first and now, was and is, to hold as 'twere the mirror up to Nature; to show Virtue her own feature, Scorn her own image, and the very age and body of the time, his form and pressure."

EXERCISES

1. WRITING A REVIEW. In writing a review, do not set up a rigid formula but plan an essay with a definite point of view. Can you indicate the point of view and some evaluation in the opening paragraph, with some illustrative detail as proof or example? Can you make sure that as far as they are pertinent you have used all three of the processes: classification, to relate the play to other plays or other experiences; description, to capture the special quality of character, action, or mood; and evaluation, to show how well the play does what it set out to do and what it is worth in a wider perspective of values? Can you explain and use your own emotional responses, both to indicate your immediate pleasure and to show your ultimate admiration and respect?

2. EVALUATING A REVIEW. Write an analysis of a review by a professional critic. Describe how he begins and ends, to what extent he keeps to one impression, and in what way he describes some characters, moments of action, or effects of mood. Does he mention different elements of the production separately or does he make them incidental to his main theme?

To what extent does the critic indicate and explain his own likes and dislikes? To what extent does he take into account other points of view—the audience reaction, for instance, or the contradictions or reservations in his own reactions? To what extent does he reveal his view of the theatre and its purposes and possibilities?

SUGGESTED READING

CRITICISM

There are two kinds of reading for a critic, dramatic theory and practical criticism. Theory has been discussed since Aristotle, and the main documents from ancient Greece to the early twentieth century are gathered in Barrett H. Clark, *European Theories of the Drama* (1921; reissued with a supplement of American writings into the 1940s, 1947, and with further European additions, 1965).

For the last two centuries independent reviews for newspapers and magazines have been written by professional critics, among them many of the best authors. Good anthologies of earlier criticism are James Agate, *The English Dramatic*

* Available in paperback edition.

Critics: An Anthology 1660–1832* (1932); A. C. Ward, ed., *Specimens of English Dramatic Criticism, XVII–XX Centuries* (1945); Montrose J. Moses and John Mason Brown, *The American Theatre as Seen by Its Critics 1752–1934* (1934); and Alan S. Downer, ed., *American Drama and Its Critics* (1965). The dramatic criticism of Charles Lamb, Leigh Hunt, and William Hazlitt may be found in many collections; Hazlitt is available in paperback.

Besides writing many essays and magazine articles over the years, Bernard Shaw was a regular critic for the old London *Saturday Review* from 1895 to 1898. Most of his reviews are gathered in *Dramatic Opinions and Essays* (2 vols., 1907). A complete collection was published in *Our Theatre of the Nineties* (3 vols., 1932). One-volume selections are *Plays and Players* (1952) and *Shaw's Dramatic Criticism, 1895–1898** (1959). Max Beerbohm, an equally brilliant writer, followed Shaw on the *Saturday Review,* and his collected reviews are found in *Around Theatres* (1930) and in several reprints of selections, including a paperback. A selection from James Agate's many volumes of London criticism was edited by Herbert Van Thal, *James Agate: An Anthology** (1961).

A selection from Stark Young's sensitive reviews in the *New Republic* from the 1920s to 1947 is given in *Immortal Shadows** (1948). Brooks Atkinson's long career for the *New York Times* is represented in only one volume, *Broadway Scrapbook* (1947). George Jean Nathan published nearly thirty volumes of criticism, and a selection from many years appeared in *The Magic Mirror* (1960). John Mason Brown can be read in book form in *Upstage* (1930), *Two on the Aisle* (1938), and *Broadway in Review* (1940), and selections from his early books appear with new essays in *Dramatis Personae** (1963). Of recent criticism, Walter Kerr is collected in *The Theatre in Spite of Itself* (1964) and Robert Brustein in *Seasons of Discontent: Dramatic Opinions, 1959–1965* (1965).

Of the work of the two most brilliant younger critics, Kenneth Tynan's *London Observer* reviews are collected in *Curtains* (1961) and Eric Bentley's *New Republic* reviews are collected in *The Dramatic Event** (1954, 1956) and *What Is Theatre?** (1956), but his most original work is to be found in the magazine articles collected in *In Search of Theatre** (1953) and the excellent small volume, *Bernard Shaw* (1947).

Very good suggestions on how to evaluate acting and other aspects of theatre are found in John Mason Brown, *The Art of Playgoing* (1936). A lively discussion of the problems and attitudes of television critics appears in "Critic's Choice," *Television Quarterly,* I (Nov., 1962), and in Jack Behar, "On TV Criticism," *Television Quarterly,* IV (Summer, 1965). An excellent article by Edwin Denby on the problem of writing dance criticism is under the heading "Criticism" in Anatole Chujoy, *The Dance Encyclopedia* (1949). Denby's own "Collected Criticism" was published by *Dance Index,* V, 2 (1946). A delightful anthology of writings from many sources—reviews, biographies, letters, etc.—on many aspects of the theatre is George Oppenheimer, ed., *The Passionate Playgoer: A Personal Scrapbook* (1958).

For some of the best film criticism, the reader might start with James Agee's reviews of the 1940s, republished in *Agee on Film,* vol. I (1958); Robert Warshow, *The Immediate Experience** (1962); and Pauline Kael, *I Lost It at the Movies** (1965).

The problem of nation-wide organization and support for the theatre is discussed in the Rockefeller Panel Report, *The Performing Arts: Problems and*

* Available in paperback edition.

Prospects (1965), and the entire issue of the *Tulane Drama Review* for Fall, 1965 (T29), discusses the public bases for resident, community, and college theatres. An Englishman's survey of the American cultural explosion is Alvin Toffler, *The Culture Consumers: Art and Affluence in America* (1965). The English Theatre situation is described in Ronald E. Sherriff's "Government Support to the Theatre in Great Britain," *Theatre Survey,* VI (Nov., 1965). The American experience of a Federal Theatre project, with its achievements and its political difficulties, is described in Hallie Flanagan, *Arena* (1940). Three early surveys of college and community theatres are Kenneth Magowan, *Footlights Across America: Towards a National Theater* (1929); Albert McCleery and Carl Glick, *Curtains Going Up* (1939); and Norris Houghton, *Advance from Broadway* (1941). An account of the commercial organization of Broadway into the first third of this century is Alfred L. Bernheim, *The Business of the Theatre: An Economic History of the American Theatre, 1750–1932* (1932, 1965).

The reports and discussion on the new repertory companies at a conference in 1964 are published in a bulletin of the New England Theatre Conference: Elliot Norton and Samuel Hirsch, eds., *Repertory Theatre in America: The Problem and the Promise,* New England Theatre Conference, Miss Marie L. Phillips, Secretary, 50 Exchange St., Waltham, Mass., and distributed by the American Educational Theatre Association.

SUGGESTED READING

A general list of books on more than one aspect of theatre

The best histories of drama are John Gassner, *Masters of the Drama* (3rd ed., 1954), and Allardyce Nicoll, *World Drama: From Aeschylus to Anouilh* (1949). The best surveys of theatre forms since the Greeks are Allardyce Nicoll, *The Development of the Theatre* (4th ed., 1958), and the more informal James Laver, *Drama: Its Costume and Decor* (1951). Several books cover both theatre and drama, especially Sheldon Cheney, *The Theatre: Three Thousand Years of Drama, Acting and Stagecraft* (rev. ed., 1952), Kenneth Macgowan and William Melnitz, *The Living Stage* (1955), and Vera M. Roberts, *On Stage* (1962). Quite opposite in purpose and scope are George Freedley and John Reeves, *A History of the Theatre* (rev. ed., 1955), which is an inclusive, encyclopedic source of information, and Richard Southern, *The Seven Ages of the Theatre** (1961), which presents few facts but has comparative sketches of different audience-theatre relationships.

A good library could be made up of anthologies. Besides anthologies of plays and of dramatic criticism, it would include the following seven collections of writings about the theatre: Toby Cole and Helen Krich Chinoy, *Actors on Acting* (1949); Cole and Chinoy, *Directors on Directing** (1963), Cole, *Playwrights on Playwriting: The Meaning and Making of Modern Drama from Ibsen to Ionesco** (1961); Barrett H. Clark, *European Theories of the Drama* (1918; 2d ed., with American theories, 1947; 3d ed., with later European theories, 1965); Barnard Hewitt, *Theatre USA, 1668–1957* (1959); Alois M. Nagler, *Sources of Theatrical History** (1952); John Gassner and Ralph S. Allen, *Theatre and Drama in the Making* (1964).

The three early prophets of the modern theatre—Appia, Craig, and Stanislavsky—are usually met first in the books of their followers and later read by the more serious student of acting and design.

The four key books that had great influence between the two world wars are still very good reading: Kenneth Macgowan and Robert Edmond Jones, *Continental Stagecraft* (1922); Lee Simonson, *The Stage Is Set** (1933); Mordecai Gorelik, *New Theatres for Old** (1940); and Robert Edmond Jones, *The Dramatic Imagination* (1941).

The most stimulating books that have interested theatre students since 1945 would start with Antonin Artaud, *The Theatre and Its Double,** published in Paris in 1938 and in New York in 1958, Francis Fergusson, *The Idea of a Theater** (1949), Eric Bentley, *In Search of Theatre** (1953) and *The Life of the Drama* (1964), Tyrone Guthrie, *A Life in the Theatre** (1959), John Gassner, *Form and Idea in Modern Theatre* (1956), expanded as *Directions in Modern Theatre and Drama* (1965), and Martin Esslin, *The Theatre of the Absurd** (1961).

Of the many accounts of professional productions, four are particularly interesting. Karel Capek, *How the Play Is Produced* (1928), tells of the difficulties in Europe. Joseph Vernon Reed, *The Curtain Falls* (1931), and Moss Hart, *Act One** (1959), were both best-sellers, with highly entertaining accounts of New York production methods a few decades ago. William Gibson, *The See-Saw Log*

* Available in paperback edition.   *653*

(1959), is a much more earnest analysis of the reshaping of his play *Two for the See-Saw* for the New York audience.

There are several good introductions to the theatre, each taking its own point of view. Theodore Hatlen, *Orientation to the Theatre* (1962), has good, brief discussions of kinds of plays and of the problems of the actor, director, and designer. Frank Whiting, *Introduction to the Theatre* (1954; rev. ed., 1961), is especially good on the crafts of building, painting, and lighting scenery. O. G. Brockett, *The Theatre: An Introduction* (1964) is a full, well-balanced treatment, starting with a historical sketch and moving on to consider the professional opportunities in the theatre. For each age or kind of play, he analyzes one play in detail.

Two encyclopedic reference books are very useful: Phyllis Hartnoll, ed., *The Oxford Companion to the Theatre* (2nd ed., 1957), and *Enciclopedia della Spettacola* (9 vols., 1954–62), which has such excellent illustrations and worldwide bibliographies that it is useful even for those who do not read Italian. For America in the twentieth century, a very thorough reference book is Walter Rigdon, ed., *The Biographical Encyclopaedia and Who's Who of the American Theatre* (1966).

FURTHER READING

ACKNOWLEDGMENTS (*continued from p. iv*)

Calder & Boyars Ltd. for material from RHINOCEROS and THE BALD SOPRANO by Eugene Ionesco.

Jonathan Cape Ltd. for material from THE HAIRY APE and THE GREAT GOD BROWN by Eugene O'Neill.

Chatto & Windus Ltd. for material from THE CHERRY ORCHARD by Anton Chekhov (Constance Garnett translation).

Curtis Brown Ltd. for material from PRIVATE LIVES by Noel Coward.

Doubleday & Company, Inc., for material from PRIVATE LIVES by Noel Coward, copyright 1930 by Doubleday & Company, Inc.; and from THE CONSTANT WIFE by W. Somerset Maugham, copyright 1926, 1927 by W. Somerset Maugham.

Faber & Faber Ltd. for material from SWEENEY AGONISTES in COLLECTED POEMS 1909–1962 and MURDER IN THE CATHEDRAL by T. S. Eliot; and from WAITING FOR GODOT by Samuel Beckett.

Samuel French, Inc., for material from THE CHALK CIRCLE (Ethel Van der Veer translation), copyright 1933 by Barrett H. Clark, copyright (in renewal) 1960 by Cecile S. Clark.

David Garnett for material from THE CHERRY ORCHARD by Anton Chekhov (Constance Garnett translation).

Elaine Green Ltd. for material from DEATH OF A SALESMAN and THE CRUCIBLE by Arthur Miller.

Grove Press, Inc., for material from WAITING FOR GODOT by Samuel Beckett (translated from his original French text by the author), copyright © 1954 by Grove Press, Inc.; from RHINOCEROS AND OTHER PLAYS by Eugene Ionesco (Derek Prouse translation), copyright 1960 by John Calder (Publishers) Ltd.; and from THE BALD SOPRANO in FOUR PLAYS by Eugene Ionesco (Donald M. Allen translation), copyright 1958 by Grove Press, Inc.

Harcourt, Brace & World, Inc., for material from SWEENEY AGONISTES in COLLECTED POEMS 1909–1962 by T. S. Eliot; from MURDER IN THE CATHEDRAL by T. S. Eliot, copyright 1935 by Harcourt, Brace & World, Inc., renewed 1963 by T. S. Eliot; and from THE MISANTHROPE by Molière (Richard Wilbur translation).

Harper & Row, Publishers, Inc., for material from OUR TOWN by Thornton Wilder.

William Heinemann Ltd. for material from ON THE ART OF THE THEATRE by Edward Gordon Craig.

Houghton Mifflin Company for material from J. B. and THE FALL OF THE CITY by Archibald MacLeish.

Sidney Kingsley for material from DEAD END.

New Directions Publishing Corporation for material from BLOOD WEDDING in THREE TRAGEDIES OF FEDERICO GARCIA LORCA, copyright 1947 by New Directions Publishing Corporation; from UNDER MILK WOOD by Dylan Thomas, copyright 1954 by Dylan Thomas; and from A STREETCAR NAMED DESIRE by Tennessee Williams, copyright 1947 by Tennessee Williams.

W. W. Norton & Company, Inc., for material from PROMETHEUS BOUND by Aeschylus in THREE GREEK PLAYS (translated with introductions by Edith Hamilton).

Oxford University Press for material from OEDIPUS in SOPHOCLES' THREE TRAGEDIES (H. D. F. Kitto translation); and from SLEEP OF PRISONERS by Christopher Fry.

Random House, Inc., for material from SECOND MAN in FOUR PLAYS BY S. N. BEHRMAN, copyright 1935 and renewed 1962 by S. N. Behrman; from THE CHERRY ORCHARD by Anton Chekhov (Constance Garnett translation); from THE LITTLE FOXES in FOUR PLAYS BY LILLIAN HELLMAN, copyright 1939 by Lillian Hellman; from DEAD END by Sidney Kingsley, copyright 1936 and renewed 1963 by Sidney Kingsley; from ACTORS TALK ABOUT ACTING by Lewis Funke and John E. Booth; from THE GREAT GOD BROWN by Eugene O'Neill, copyright 1926 and renewed 1954 by Arlotta Monterey O'Neill, reprinted from NINE PLAYS BY EUGENE O'NEILL; from THE HAIRY APE by Eugene O'Neill, copyright 1922 and renewed 1949 by Eugene O'Neill, reprinted from NINE PLAYS BY EUGENE O'NEILL; and from RIDERS TO THE SEA by John M. Synge.

Elmer Rice for material from THE ADDING MACHINE in SEVEN PLAYS BY ELMER RICE.

Martin Secker and Warburg Ltd. for material from J. B. by Archibald MacLeish.

655

St. Martin's Press for material from JUNO AND THE PAYCOCK by Sean O'Casey, by permission of Macmillan & Company Ltd. and St. Martin's Press, Inc.

Simon and Schuster for material from THE BACHELOR PARTY in TELEVISION PLAYS by Paddy Chayefsky, copyright © 1955 by Paddy Chayefsky.

The Society of Authors for material from THE APPLE CART by George Bernard Shaw, by permission of the Public Trustee and the Society of Authors.

Thames and Hudson Ltd. for material from ACTORS TALK ABOUT ACTING by Lewis Funke and John E. Booth.

Theatre Arts Books for material from ON THE ART OF THE THEATRE by Edward Gordon Craig. All rights reserved.

Viking Press for material from DEATH OF A SALESMAN by Arthur Miller, copyright © 1949 by Arthur Miller; and from THE CRUCIBLE by Arthur Miller, copyright © 1952, 1953 by Arthur Miller.

A. P. Watt for material from THE CONSTANT WIFE by W. Somerset Maugham, with the permission of the Literary Executor and William Heinemann Ltd.

656

Acknowledgments

INDEX

Index

661

Index

Index

665

Index

667

Index

Index

669

Index

Index

Index

674

Index

675

676

Index

Williams, Tennessee, 10, 19, 140, 157, 213, 223, 237, 322, 338, 388, 573, 594, 615
Wilmington College, 96
Windfall in Athens, 568
wing-and-backdrop, 73, 74, 75, 80–86, 89, 121, 279, 280, 413, 414, 461
Wingless Victory, The, 427
Winter Light, 566
Winterset, 106, 228, 307, 308
Wolfit, Donald, 641
Woman in the Dunes, 570
women: in comedy, 273–74, 277–82
World of Apu, The, 570–71
World of Susie Wong, The, 99
Wouk, Herman, 371
Wozzeck, 105, 116, 123, 310
Wright, Frank Lloyd, 465, 474
Wycherley, William, 277, 279
Wyler, William, 538, 550, 572

Yale University, 30, 228, 235, 294, 344, 359, 462
Yeats, William Butler, 21, 41, 230–31, 232, 293, 610
Yellow Jack, 45, 415
Yellow Jacket, The, 38
Yerma, 231
You Can't Take It with You, 283
Young and the Damned, The, see Los Olvidados
Young, Stark, 24, 25, 633

Zen: influence on dance, 144
Ziegfeld Follies, 88
Zinneman, Fred, 514, 552
Zola, Émile, 7, 8, 10, 55, 293, 402
Zorba the Greek, 533, 568–69
Zorina, Vera, 44
Zukor, Adolph, 489, 492

A 6
B 7
C 8
D 9
E 0
F 1
G 2
H 3
I 4
J 5